DEAD SIMPLE PYTHON

DEAD SIMPLE PYTHON

PYTHON

Idiomatic Python for the Impatient Programmer

Jason C. McDonald

**no starch
press**

San Francisco

Printed in the United States of America

First printing

26 25 24 23 22   1 2 3 4 5

ISBN 13: 978-1-7185-0092-1 (print)
ISBN 13: 978-1-7185-0093-8 (ebook)

Publisher: William Pollock
Production Manager: Rachel Monaghan
Developmental Editor: Frances Saux
Production Editor: Rachel Monaghan
Cover and Interior Design: Octopod Studios
Cover Illustrator: Gina Redman
Technical Reviewers: Steven Bingler with Daniel Foerster, Ryan Palo, Denis Pobedrya, and Simon de Vlieger
Copyeditors: Doug McNair with Anne McDonald
Compositor: Ashley McKevitt, Happenstance Type-O-Rama
Proofreader: James M. Fraleigh
Indexer: JoAnne Burek

For information on distribution, bulk sales, corporate sales, or translations, please contact No Starch Press, Inc. directly at info@nostarch.com or:

No Starch Press, Inc.
245 8th Street, San Francisco, CA 94103
phone: 1.415.863.9900
www.nostarch.com

Library of Congress Cataloging-in-Publication Data

Names: McDonald, Jason C., 1992- author.
Title: Dead simple Python : idiomatic Python for the impatient programmer / Jason C. McDonald.
Description: San Francisco, CA : No Starch Press, Inc., [2023] | Includes index.
Identifiers: LCCN 2022018822 (print) | LCCN 2022018823 (ebook) | ISBN 9781718500921 (print) | ISBN 9781718500938 (ebook)
Subjects: LCSH: Python (Computer program language) | Computer programming.
Classification: LCC QA76.73.P98 M397 2023 (print) | LCC QA76.73.P98 (ebook) | DDC 005.13/3--dc23/eng/20220616
LC record available at https://lccn.loc.gov/2022018822
LC ebook record available at https://lccn.loc.gov/2022018823

In loving memory of Chris "Fox" Frasier.
It'll always be "lern u a snek" to you.

About the Author

Jason C. McDonald is a software developer, speaker, and author of both fiction and nonfiction. By day, he works as a software engineer. By night, he is the founder of MousePaw Media (*https://mousepawmedia.com/*), an open source software company where he trains software development interns. You can usually find him haunting his local coffee shop.

About the Technical Reviewers

Steven Bingler is a software engineer in Boston, Massachusetts, with a master's degree in electrical engineering. He is an experienced technical reviewer who, in his spare time, enjoys cycling, bouldering, and finding new places to eat.

Denis Pobedrya, better known as deniska on the Libera.IRC network, is familiar with some darker corners of Python's data model. He is a self-proclaimed jack-of-all-trades, working in many jobs (including warehouse management). He is currently a Python backend developer for a marketplace service.

Ryan Palo is a mechanical engineer turned software developer writing Python at Flashpoint. He has a master's in computer science (Intelligent Systems). He loves sharing his passion for physics, math, writing, and code, any way he can, primarily through his blog, *https://www.assertnotmagic.com/*. He can usually be found at home with his wife, daughters, cat, dog, various assorted Linux devices, and about eight too many ukuleles.

For **Daniel Foerster**, technical editing for *Dead Simple Python* was a labor of friendship and of passion. He was blessed to encounter Python as a young teen and hasn't met another language that fits his brain so well since. After years of leading development efforts in Python and getting involved with teaching programming in and beyond the workplace, Daniel has turned his vocational emphasis toward pedagogy.

Simon de Vlieger, better known in some circles as supakeen, is a part of the furniture on the Python IRC community. He is a senior programmer with an interest in Python, C, and experimental languages, plus an affinity for software security. He's very much at home on the AVR and other tiny embedded chips. He is employed by Red Hat, where he currently works on building Linux in a sane and repeatable fashion.

3
SYNTAX CRASH COURSE
39

4
PROJECT STRUCTURE AND IMPORTS
73

PART II: ESSENTIAL STRUCTURES   93

5
VARIABLES AND TYPES   95

8
ERRORS AND EXCEPTIONS
183

PART III: DATA AND FLOW
211

9
COLLECTIONS AND ITERATION
213

10
GENERATORS AND COMPREHENSIONS 257

11
TEXT IO AND CONTEXT MANAGERS   289

14
METACLASSES AND ABCs
403

15
INTROSPECTION AND GENERICS
425

16
ASYNCHRONY AND CONCURRENCY   457

17
THREADING AND PARALLELISM   477

PART V: BEYOND THE CODE 511

18
PACKAGING AND DISTRIBUTION 513

19
DEBUGGING AND LOGGING 543

21
THE PARTING OF THE WAYS 619

APPENDIX A
SPECIAL ATTRIBUTES AND METHODS 637

APPENDIX B
PYTHON DEBUGGER (PDB) COMMANDS 647

GLOSSARY 651

INDEX 691

FOREWORD

"Dead simple concurrency? Seriously?"

That was my reaction when I first heard about this book. Python in general is a wonderful language and easier to grok than most, but many (or even most) things in the world of programming are still anything but "dead simple."

But then Jason explained what he had in mind in writing a book with those two words in the title. It's not dead simple in the sense of being a dumbed-down book that presents Python in overly simplistic terms. Rather, it's dead simple in the sense of being a book that people will read and say, "This topic initially seemed hard to understand, but now that you've explained it, it's really obvious to me." Having studied and taught coding in general and Python in particular for 30 years, I'd say that this is absolutely the best goal for any form of teaching: to present the concepts so clearly that the way even the tricky topics work seems inevitable.

But that's not the only area where *Dead Simple Python* is ambitious. The sheer amount of material presented here is equally impressive. This book covers virtually every aspect of Python that someone who wants to write useful code might need. These include everything from the basics of variables, data structures, and loops, to, yes, things like concurrency and parallelism. As I've looked through this book, every single chapter has impressed me with its completeness and wealth of detail.

So, does this book really make concurrency (and everything else) seem dead simple? After years of teaching and writing, I know I can't answer that question for anyone else, but I can say for sure that the examples are engaging and well thought out, the explanations are clear and accessible, and the coverage is outstanding. That's a really tough combination to beat.

Naomi Ceder

ACKNOWLEDGMENTS

You've heard the expression "It takes a village to raise a child." In the same way, it takes a village to write a book. In the case of *Dead Simple Python*, several villages were involved!

The Python community, especially those residing in #python on Libera .Chat IRC, have been been supporting, informing, and challenging me ever since my first "Hello, world" in Python. Most of my knowledge about this language traces back to the lovable nerds in that chatroom. I'm thankful for all the feedback and insight they've provided on *Dead Simple Python*, from its inception through this whole process.

I'm deeply grateful to Forem and the DEV Community (*https://dev.to/*) for their enthusiastic reception of my articles, especially the *Dead Simple Python* article series this book is based on. Special thanks goes to DEV co-founders Ben Halpern and Jess Lee and community manager Michael Tharrington, for encouraging and promoting my writing on that platform. If it hadn't been for the visibility and positive feedback I've been blessed with, I'd never have considered writing this as a book.

Particular thanks to my delightfully pedantic technical editors: Daniel Foerster (pydsigner), Ryan Palo, Denis Pobedrya (deniska), and Simon de Vlieger (supakeen). Andrew Svetlov gave me excellent insight into the ever-changing landscape of asynchrony. Bernát Gábor of the Python Packaging Authority made sure my chapter on packaging was as shiny as a wet platypus. Kyle Altendorf (altendky) taught me the value of src-based project structure and provided feedback on my object-oriented programming chapter. James Gerity (SnoopJ) helped me disambiguate my section on multiple inheritance. Additional technical edits were provided by Gil Gonçalves, grym, and TheAssassin. I can't begin to enumerate all the people involved in the deep technical debates that manifested as recommendations in this book. You know who you are.

A special thank-you to the (herein unnamed) editor whose enthusiasm about my writing first gave me the confidence to pursue writing *Dead Simple Python* in book form in the first place.

Thanks to all my friends in the Python and Ubuntu communities, MousePaw Media, Canonical, and beyond—especially Naomi Ceder, Richard Schneiderman (johnjohn101), James Beecham, Laís Carvalho, Cheuk Ting Ho, Sangarshanan Veera, Raquel Dou, David Bush, John Chittum, Pat Viafore, Éric St-Jean, Chloé Smith, Jess Jang, Scott Taylor, Wilfrantz Dede, Anna Dunster, Tianlin Fu, Gerar Almonte, LinStatSDR, and leaftype. It's always encouraging to be greeted with inquiries about the book's progress!

Last, and certainly most of all, I want to thank those closest to me for their unending support. My mother, Anne McDonald, who contributed valuable editorial and creative feedback, taught me everything I know about writing and has been encouraging my dreams since day one. I'm grateful for the support of my best friend Daniel Harrington, the Tolkien to my Lewis. *Muchas gracias a mi hermanito mayor* Jaime López (Tacoder), the lord of chaos and tacos. Thank you to Bojan Miletić, my unicorn-obsessed brother and co-host on *The Bug Hunters Café*, for his unbounded enthusiasm and support. Deep love and gratitude to my beloved aunt and self-proclaimed biggest fan, Jane McArthur, and my partner-in-troublemaking, Chris "Fox" Frasier—both of whom I miss ferociously.

INTRODUCTION

Python is a unique language. As a software developer, I have come to appreciate it for its particularities. There is a certain artistic beauty about a well-written Python program. I love when I find the most "Pythonic" solution to a problem and then look back and wonder how I thought any other answer would do.

Unfortunately, for years, I was crippled by an instinctual desire to view Python through the lens of the other languages I knew. Although I could read and write in Python, I failed to see the "obviousness" of a particular practice. It was like trying to speak Spanish using only a translation dictionary. I could write Python, but I couldn't really *think* in Python. The essential qualities of the language were lost on me.

Once I started to truly understand Python—to think in it—I found a new delight in the language. Solutions became obvious. Design was a joy, rather than an enigma.

When a brand-new developer cuts their teeth on Python, they have few preconceptions. They have no "native tongue" to hamper their introduction to the language. But for an established developer who picks up Python as a second or third language, the transition is in some ways far rougher. They must not only learn something new, but in many ways, they must *unlearn* something old.

Dead Simple Python is the guidebook for that journey.

Who Is This Book For?

If you are already familiar with another programming language and now wish to learn Python for the first time, without slogging through beginner-oriented courses, this book is for you. I'll be focusing specifically on the "Pythonic" way of doing things, with minimal, targeted explanations of the underlying general programming concepts.

If you're an intermediate-level Python developer, you'll also find this book useful. Although I've been working with Python for many years myself, some of these topics didn't "click" for me until more recently. This book gives the explanations I wish I'd gotten.

If you don't already know programming, despair not. There are hundreds of excellent books and resources for learning Python as a first programming language. I particularly recommend either *Python Crash Course,* 2nd Edition, by Eric Matthes (No Starch Press, 2019) or *Automate the Boring Stuff with Python,* 2nd Edition, by Al Sweigart (No Starch Press, 2019). Afterward, you can return to this book to reinforce and expand upon your newfound knowledge.

What Does "Simple" Mean?

The topics discussed herein may, at first blush, appear anything but simple. You may be wondering how simple a book this thick could actually be!

When I titled this book *Dead Simple Python,* I was describing a retrospective view of the topics, rather than a forward-looking one. One should recognize that any topic worth learning, when first approached, will feel insurmountable. Similarly, any explanation worthy of an existing software developer should possess enough depth to utterly disqualify it from the forward-looking label of "simple."

Instead, I aim to unpack each topic in such a manner that, by the conclusion of the section, the reader cannot help but feel the concept is altogether obvious. Regardless of the topic's initial appearance of complexity, the reader should be ultimately left with an impression that it is actually "dead simple," at which point, they may be assured they are thinking like a native Python developer.

To achieve this level of understanding, I generally start by unpacking the lowest-level, most explicit form of the topic. Once that is established, I add layer upon layer, ultimately reaching the implicit, idiomatic form most commonly used. In this way, I hope to help you, the reader, come away with a solid, comfortable understanding of precisely why and how each feature of the language works.

What's in This Book?

Dead Simple Python is divided into five sections. Unlike many beginner-oriented courses, I'm going to assume you want to start writing production-quality code (rather than just oversimplified tutorial examples) as soon as possible. My approach requires you to do some initial work, but it pays off by ensuring you can apply your new knowledge to live projects more readily.

Part I, "The Python Environment" (Chapters 1–4), firmly establishes you in the world of Python: its philosophy, tools, basic syntax, and project layout. This will provide a solid foundation for writing real, substantial code.

Part II, "Essential Structures" (Chapters 5–8), explores Python's basic structural elements—variables, functions, classes, and exceptions—and teaches you how to use them to their fullest potential.

Part III, "Data and Flow" (Chapters 9–12), covers the many unique ways of controlling execution flow and manipulating data. It discusses data structures, loops, iteration, generators, coroutines, files, and binary data.

Part IV, "Advanced Concepts" (Chapters 13–17), unlocks advanced tactics that can make your code more powerful, including inheritance, introspection, and concurrency. It addresses many of the "scary" topics that are skimmed over by most courses and tutorials.

Part V, "Beyond the Code" (Chapters 18–20), teaches you how to test, debug, and deploy real-life projects.

Finally, Chapter 21 provides an overview of the many directions you can take your Python development journey from here.

What's NOT in This Book

Since this book is intended for existing programmers, I won't be rehashing much general theory. Readers should already know (from a language-agnostic standpoint) what variables and functions are, what the difference is between classes and objects, and so forth. At most, I'll briefly define those concepts that aren't quite ubiquitous in the programming world.

My discussion of topics is far from exhaustive. I'm focusing more on the *why* and *how*, thereby providing a strong foundation. Readers are encouraged to broaden their understanding through additional, independent reading, so I'll leave the comprehensive listing of library functions and the like to the documentation. Many popular features in the standard library, such as random numbers and datetime operations, are afforded little more than incidental explanation when they're used in an example.

To control the scope of this book, I also won't be covering most third-party tools and libraries. I am frequently asked to discuss popular alternatives to the default tools in Python, but as these alternatives fall in and out of favor like the passing of the seasons, I will be sticking largely to the universal defaults. There are scattered exceptions, but only when a third-party tool has become practically ubiquitous in the ecosystem, eclipsing even the standard library.

In general, when a third-party tool or library seems of particular note, I will refer the reader to its official documentation or website.

How to Read This Book

Dead Simple Python is intended more as a guided tour than a desk reference. I recommend starting here, at the beginning, and working your way through the chapters, in order. Whether you're new to the language or have been trying to use it for a while without feeling like you "get it," you'll discover that this approach will fill in many knowledge gaps you never realized you had.

However, if you know of a particular topic you need a better understanding of *right now*, you can skip directly to the chapter that deals with it. Most chapters are written to stand alone, but I will always assume that you have read and understand the material in the preceding chapters.

About the Vocabulary

Nearly any Python book or online article uses vocabulary borrowed from other languages, such as words like *element*, *body*, and *variable*. While this is often assumed to be helpful because it relates Python concepts to readers' existing knowledge, I believe borrowing such vocabulary is ultimately counterproductive. Attempting to understand Python primarily in terms of other languages frustrates many attempts to write clear, idiomatic code. What's more, if one gets in the habit of using the wrong vocabulary, one will find the official documentation profoundly difficult to read.

Therefore, I've decided to adhere doggedly to the official vocabulary, even if a majority of the community considers an approximate synonym acceptable. This may be one of the few books in print that takes this position, but I consider it important. To become a native, you must learn to speak the local dialect!

Theory Recaps

Depending on what languages you already know, there may be some gaps in your theory repertoire. For example, if you are a Haskell developer, you may be unfamiliar with object-oriented programming, or if you are a C++ developer, you may be unfamiliar with pure functional programming.

To bridge these gaps, I provide occasional *Theory Recaps*, brief overviews of the essential theory and best practices related to certain programming paradigms and patterns. That way, if you already know a particular concept, you can skip over the Theory Recap and get right to the Python-specific stuff.

Objective or Opinionated?

It's almost impossible to keep personal opinions out of a technical book, especially one as focused on idiomatic practice as this one, but I like to think I've done my best to remain objective.

Dead Simple Python is not my personal take on Python, but rather it is the distilled collective wisdom of the Python community. I am not the same developer as when I started writing. My own development practices have changed drastically as a result of the two years of research, experimentation, and heated debate that went into this book.

Even so, it's impossible to please everybody all the time. At times, I've made particular note in the text about debates that never reached a satisfactory conclusion. Even matters I consider settled are likely to provoke strong negative reactions from some Python developers; indeed, some of them provoked strong reactions in me until I better understood them.

I recommend you go into this book with an open mind, even if you consider yourself reasonably familiar with programming or even with Python itself. I've made an effort to explain the justifications behind all the recommendations herein, and I would encourage you to expect at least the same degree of reasoning to accompany *any* valid recommendation.

The Examples

I've carefully constructed the majority of my examples in this book to demonstrate realistic (if simplified) use cases for whatever topic I'm discussing. In many situations, I'll deliberately complicate the example to highlight issues and surprises that tutorials often gloss over. I've made an effort to point out all the times my examples get a bit convoluted, but you should know that I may oversimplify or otherwise tiptoe around anything irrelevant to the immediate topic.

This approach also often necessitates longer examples than you may be used to from tutorials, so chapters may appear longer than they effectively are. Don't be discouraged by page counts; take it one section at a time.

All the examples in this book run, or at least fail predictably, except as otherwise noted. I adhere to Python style conventions throughout. I highly recommend retyping each example yourself and experimenting with it.

I've made an effort to label the segments of Python code meant to be saved in files as part of runnable examples. The filename is given, and the sections are numbered :1, :2, and so on. When a section is revised, I tack a letter on after the section, so section :2b would revise section :2a; the revisions themselves are in **bold**.

Nearly all the examples in this book can be found on the book's official GitHub repository: *https://github.com/codemouse92/DeadSimplePython*.

What About a Project?

I've been asked why I don't provide a comprehensive project that we can work through in this book, but the answer is fairly simple: I'm assuming that you're probably here because you already have some project you want to use Python for. Instead of distracting you from that, I'll focus on presenting material in a way that you can apply to your work.

If you *don't* have a project in mind, now may be a great time to start one! Think of a problem you personally wish there were a solution (or a better solution) for, then build that solution. Pick one small part of the problem and start there. There's no magic formula for creating the perfect first project, other than to make it something you'd personally use. Don't worry about making it perfect, or even good, your first time around. There's a truism in this industry: "You always throw the first one away." Don't be afraid to build it wrong at first! This book will give you the tools to go back and make it right.

Of course, if a project is completely impractical to you, you'll do just fine working through this book's examples.

In any case, I do **strongly** recommend creating a personal "firing range" project, for trying out Python in an environment where breaking things won't have significant consequences. I'll introduce running Python code in Chapters 2 and 3, and I'll cover project structure in Chapter 4. I'll revisit project structure when I discuss packaging and distribution in Chapter 18.

Prerequisites

- You should already know the essentials of programming in another language. This book teaches Python, not programming.

- You should have access to a computer capable of running Python 3.7 or later. If you haven't actually installed Python yet, don't worry—we'll be doing that in Chapter 2.

- You should know the basics of using the command line on your computer, especially relative and absolute paths, and navigating the filesystem. If you don't understand all that, go learn it now. (I'll wait.)

- You should have an internet connection, even a slow one, for viewing the documentation and occasionally downloading packages. However, I've tried to maximize the number of examples that work without internet.

Now, go get a cup of your favorite beverage and settle in at your computer with a notebook and pen. Let's get started!

PART I

THE PYTHON ENVIRONMENT

1

THE PYTHON PHILOSOPHY

I believe the best place to start learning Python is not with the language itself, but with the guiding philosophy driving it. To write good Python code, you must first understand what Python is. That's what this chapter will focus on.

What Is Python, Exactly?

Python is a programming language developed in 1991 by Dutch programmer Guido van Rossum. The name refers not to the snake often used as a mascot, but to *Monty Python's Flying Circus* (that fact alone should tell you a lot about the mindset behind the language). What began as a hobby project over Christmas break turned into one of the most perennially popular computer languages today.

From a technical perspective, Python is considered a high-level, general-purpose language, with full support for the procedural, object-oriented, and functional programming paradigms, among others.

Fans of Python are quick to point out its famous readability and simplicity, which lend to an initial feeling that the language is "magic." This has also given rise to a less-than-useful bit of advice for newcomers: "Python is easy; it's just pseudocode!"

That isn't strictly true. Don't let the natural readability fool you: Python is beautifully unique and influenced by many other languages, but it often bears little resemblance to any of them. To truly master it, one must take it by itself, not in strong comparison to other languages. That is exactly what this book will do.

Most importantly, however, Python is an idea. It's the collective creation of a diverse group of nerds, united by nothing more than an audacious desire to build an awesome programming language. When you truly understand Python, it alters your entire perspective. You're a part of something larger; something that has taken on a life of its own.

As Guido van Rossum explained in his famous King's Day speech:

> I believe the most important idea is that Python is developed on the Internet, entirely in the open, by a community of volunteers (but not amateurs!) who feel passion and ownership.

Myths: What Python Isn't

There are a lot of myths about Python, many of which lead to people shunning the language for certain applications, if not altogether.

Myth #1: Python Is Merely a Scripting Language

I consider "scripting language" to be one of the most insidious terms used in discussing programming languages. It implies that the language is somehow unsuited for writing "real" software (see Myth #5).

Python is *turing-complete*, which means that you could implement any programming language in Python and then be able to execute any program written in that language.

To put that another way, anything another programming language can do, Python can do. Whether it's easy, or even advisable, depends on what you're attempting.

Myth #2: Python Is Slow

It's easy to assume that high-level or interpreted languages like Python are naturally slower than compiled or low-level languages like C. In truth, it depends on the implementation of the language and how it's used. In this book, we'll cover several concepts related to improving the performance of Python code.

The default implementation of the Python language interpreter, CPython, is written in C, and it is indeed slower than native machine code. However, there are various libraries and techniques—as well as other implementations of the language, including PyPy—which have much better performance overall (see Chapter 21) and even approach the speed of native machine code.

With all that said, you should understand how performance actually factors into your project. In most situations, Python is plenty fast enough to be a good choice for application development, data analysis, scientific computing, game development, web development, and the list goes on. The performance drawbacks inherent in CPython usually only become problematic when you are dealing with very specific scenarios demanding extraordinarily high performance. Even then, there are ways around the bottlenecks. For the majority of projects, Python's baseline performance is more than sufficient.

Myth #3: Python Cannot Be Compiled

Python is an *interpreted language*, meaning the code is read, interpreted, and executed at runtime by the language's *interpreter*. An end user running a project written in Python will typically have to have the Python interpreter installed.

This contrasts with what I like to call *assembled languages*, like C, C++, or FORTRAN. In these languages, the final result of compilation is machine code, which can be executed directly on any compatible computer without needing an additional program on that machine (or somehow bundled with the code).

PEDANTIC NOTE There's a surprising amount of contention about the term *compiled language*, which is why I like to use the terms *interpreted* and *assembled* to differentiate. This is a rather deep rabbit hole.

Many developers take this to mean that Python cannot be compiled (assembled) to machine code, which seems like the obvious corollary. In fact, it is possible to compile Python to machine code, although this is rarely necessary and seldom done.

If you want to go this route, there are a few options. On UNIX, the built-in *Freeze* tool transpiles to C arrays of Python bytecode, and then it assembles this C code to machine code. This doesn't result in truly assembled Python code, however, because the Python interpreter must still be invoked behind the scenes. Freeze only works on UNIX systems. The *cx_Freeze* tool, as well as *py2exe* on Windows, does much the same thing as Freeze.

To truly compile Python to machine code, you must use an intermediary language. *Nuitka* can be used to transpile Python code C and C++, which can then be assembled to machine code. You can also transpile Python to Java with *VOC*. *Cython* also allows transpiling a specialized form of Python to C, although it's primarily geared toward writing Python extensions in C.

Myth #4: Python Gets Compiled Behind the Scenes

The Python interpreter converts code to *bytecode*, which is then executed. The interpreter includes a *virtual machine*, which executes the Python bytecode similarly to how a CPU executes machine code. Sometimes, the interpreter will do the conversion to bytecode in advance, for performance reasons, generating *.pyc* files containing bytecode. While this is "compiling" in one sense of the term, there is a key difference between compiling to bytecode and compiling to machine code: bytecode is still run through the interpreter, whereas machine code executes directly, without needing an additional program. (Technically, "compiling" to machine code is called *assembling*, although this distinction is often neglected or overlooked.)

In practice, the majority of Python projects ship as source code, or at least Python bytecode, which is run in the Python interpreter installed on the user's machine. There are occasions when a standard executable is preferable, such as for ease of installation on end-user computers or in closed-source projects. For those situations, tools such as *PyInstaller* and *cx_Freeze* exist. These don't compile the code, but rather bundle the Python source code or bytecode with the interpreter so it can be executed by itself (see Chapter 18).

Myth #5: Python Is Unsuitable for Large Projects

I've heard some developers say, "Python is only useful if the whole project fits in one file." This adage is partially based on the misconception that Python projects with multiple files are confusingly structured. This indeed tends to be the trend, but only because so few developers know how to correctly structure a Python project.

In reality, project structure in Python is far simpler than in C++ and Java. Once the developer understands the concepts of packages, modules, and the import system (see Chapter 4), working with multiple code files becomes trivial.

Another reason for this myth has to do with the fact that Python is dynamically typed, rather than statically typed like Java or C++, which some believe makes refactoring harder. This doesn't have to be the case, once the developer knows how to work with Python's type system, instead of against it (see Chapter 5).

Python 2 vs. Python 3

For many years, there existed two major versions of Python. Starting in 2001, *Python 2* was the standard, meaning most books and articles about Python were written for this version. The last release was Python 2.7.

The current version is *Python 3*, known during its development as *Python 3000* or *Py3k*. From its release in 2008 until 2019, we were in a sort of limbo between the two versions; a lot of existing code and packages were written in Python 2, while Python 3 was increasingly recommended for new projects that didn't require legacy support. Many techniques and tools existed for writing code that could run in either version, which eased the transition for many existing projects.

In more recent years, especially since the release of Python 3.5, we've begun moving away from Python 2 altogether. Most major libraries officially supported Python 3, and legacy support became less of a priority.

As of January 1, 2020, Python 2 has been officially retired, and Python 3 is the definitive standard. Since Python 4 is still nothing more than a vague wisp of a rumor at this point, it's safe to say that Python 3 will be with us for years to come.

Unfortunately, many software development teams have been slow (sometimes unavoidably) about porting their code bases from Python 2 to Python 3. This has left a lot of projects in limbo. If you use Python in a professional capacity, there is a good chance you'll have to help transition some code to Python 3. Python's standard library includes a tool called *2to3*, which helps automate this process. Running the code through this tool is a good first step, but you will still need to manually update the code to use some of the newer patterns and tools Python 3 has to offer.

Defining "Pythonic" Code

Among Python developers, you'll hear a lot of talk about *Pythonic* code and what it constitutes, precisely. In a general sense, idiomatic code that makes good use of the language's features is considered Pythonic.

Unfortunately, this is very much open to interpretation. As a result, the topic of best practices in Python is a regular source of heated debate in the community. Don't be alarmed by this. By regularly grappling with our own conventions and standards, we continually improve them and our own understanding along the way.

Our tendency to debate best practices in Python is rooted in our philosophy of *There's Only One Way To Do It (TOOWTDI)*, a phrase coined by PythonLabs in 2000 as a tongue-in-cheek response to the Perl community's own adage of *There's More Than One Way To Do It (TMTOWTDI)*. Despite the historic rivalry between these communities, these philosophies aren't strictly opposing.

Python developers rightly assume there is some single, quantifiably "best" solution to any specific problem. Our task is to figure out what that solution is, but we also know we will often fall far short of the goal. Through continual discussion, debate, and experimentation, we refine our approaches in pursuit of the theoretical Best Solution.

In the same way, the Perl community understands that it is often impossible to definitively arrive at that Best Solution, so they emphasize experimentation instead of compliance with strict standards, in an effort to discover better and better solutions.

In the end, the goal is the same: to ultimately define the best possible solution to a problem. Only the emphasis differs.

In this book, I'll focus a lot on the generally accepted Pythonic ways of writing code. However, I don't claim to be the final authority. My colleagues in the Python community will always have plenty to add to these discussions. I never fail to learn something new from them!

The Zen of Python

In 1999, a discussion started on the official Python mailing list about the need to write down some sort of formal guiding principles for the language. Tim Peters, a prominent member of the community, jokingly laid out a poetic summary of 19 principles to serve as an outline, leaving the 20th spot open for Guido van Rossum to complete (which he never did).

Other community members quickly seized on this summary as a fantastic overview of Python's philosophy, ultimately adopting it wholesale as *The Zen of Python*. The entire text is published by Python as PEP 20.

Beautiful is better than ugly.

Explicit is better than implicit.

Simple is better than complex.

Complex is better than complicated.

Flat is better than nested.

Sparse is better than dense.

Readability counts.

Special cases aren't special enough to break the rules.

Although practicality beats purity.

Errors should never pass silently.

Unless explicitly silenced.

In the face of ambiguity, refuse the temptation to guess.

There should be one—and preferably only one—obvious way to do it.

Although that way may not be obvious at first unless you're Dutch.

Now is better than never.

Although never is often better than *right* now.

If the implementation is hard to explain, it's a bad idea.

If the implementation is easy to explain, it may be a good idea.

Namespaces are one honking great idea—let's do more of those!

This, too, is open to interpretation, and some argue that Tim Peters was kidding when he wrote The Zen of Python. However, if there's one thing

I've learned about Python developers, it's that the line between "kidding" and "serious" is fine as spider silk.

In any case, The Zen of Python is a great place to start when talking about best practices in Python. Many developers, including myself, often refer back to it. I'll refer to it frequently throughout this book.

Documentation, PEPs, and You

Dead Simple Python is intended as a beginning, not an ending, to your learning journey. Once you are well acquainted with the Python language, you can turn to the language's extensive official documentation to learn more about any particular features or tools. These docs are found online at *https://docs.python.org/*.

Any new feature in Python begins its life as a *Python Enhancement Proposal* (PEP). Each is assigned a unique number and published to the official PEP index at *https://python.org/dev/peps/*. Once proposed, a PEP will be considered, discussed, and ultimately accepted or rejected.

Accepted PEPs are effectively extensions of the documentation, as they are the most cohesive and authoritative descriptions of the feature(s) they define. Additionally, there are several Meta-PEPs and Informational PEPs that provide the backbone for the Python community and language.

As such, the official documentation and PEP index should be the first place you go if you have any questions about Python. I'll refer to these frequently throughout this book.

Who Calls the Shots?

To understand how and why the language evolves, it is important to know who's in charge. When a PEP is proposed, who gets to decide if it's accepted or rejected?

Python is an open source project officially owned by the nonprofit Python Software Foundation. Unlike many other popular languages, no formal associations exist between Python and any for-profit organization.

As an open source project, Python is supported by an active and vibrant community. At its heart is the core team, the trusted volunteers who maintain the language and keep the community running smoothly.

Language creator Guido van Rossum served as the Benevolent Dictator for Life (BDFL), making the final decisions on all PEPs and overseeing ongoing development of the language. In 2018, he made the decision to step down from the role.

A few months after his resignation, PEP 13 was created to establish a new system of governance. Now the language is governed by a five-person steering committee, elected by the core team. Every time a new release of the language comes out, a new steering committee is elected.

The Python Community

The Python community is a vast and diverse group of individuals from all over the world, united by their passion for this unique language. Ever since I stumbled upon the community many years ago as an utter novice, I have gained immeasurable help, guidance, and inspiration from it and its people. I've been privileged to offer the same to others in return. This book would not have ever happened without the continual feedback of my Python friends!

The Python community is moderated by the core team and governed by the Python Code of Conduct. In short, it emphasizes open, considerate, and respectful behavior, summarizing itself as follows:

> Overall, we're good to each other. We contribute to this community, not because we have to, but because we want to. If we remember that, these guidelines will come naturally.

I strongly encourage any developer who uses Python to plug into this vibrant community. One of the best ways to participate is through the Libera.Chat IRC #python chatroom. You can find guides to getting onto IRC at *https://python.org/community/*.

If you have any questions about Python, including while you read through this book, I recommend asking for help in the IRC channel. Chances are, you'll find me and most of my technical editors there.

In Chapter 21, I'll discuss the many facets of the Python community.

The Pursuit of the One Obvious Way

The Python mantra "There's Only One Way to Do It" can be quite confusing at first. There are many possible ways to solve any one problem. Are Pythonistas just too enamored with their own ideas?

Thankfully, no. This mantra means something much more encouraging, and it's something every Python developer should understand.

Some insight comes from The Zen of Python, which includes this rather cryptic quip:

> There should be one—and preferably only one—obvious way to do it.

> Although that way may not be obvious at first unless you're Dutch.

Tim Peters was, of course, referring to language creator Guido van Rossum, a Dutch national. As the creator of the language, Guido could usually cut right to the "most obvious way" of solving problems in Python, especially in the early days of the language.

This *obvious way* is Python's term for "the best solution"—a marriage of good practice, clean style, and reasonable efficiency, resulting in elegant code that is comprehensible to even the greenest novice.

The details of the problem being solved will usually inform this "obvious way": one situation may call for a loop, another for recursion, and yet another for a list comprehension. Contrary to the usual implications of the word *obvious*, the solution is often anything but simple to work out. The best solution is only obvious *once you know it*; arriving at it is where things get tricky. Most of us aren't Guido.

However, the *pursuit* of the "one obvious way" is a defining facet of the Python community, and it has had a profound impact on *Dead Simple Python*. A lot of the insights in this book were born out of sometimes intense debate between myself and my fellow Pythonistas. For this reason, I hand-selected my panel of technical editors from those colleagues who are commonly in opposition to me, and often each other, on pedantic technical points.

Anything ultimately adopted as the "right way" to solve a problem is usually accepted as such because of its technical merit, rather than because of some like-minded bias among Python developers, who are among the most exacting folks I've had the privilege of working with. This approach to logic overflows into every other conversation we have (which leads to some rather amazing and enlightening academic debates).

New situations present themselves regularly. There will never come a point in any Python developer's career when coding becomes truly "easy." Situations will arise in every project that demand careful consideration, and often, debate. Developers must attempt to solve problems in the way that seems most obvious to them, then submit the solution to the critique of peers.

The approaches in this book are, in many cases, the most obvious according to my view. Most have been seconded by my colleagues, yet I dare not assert that I am altogether "Dutch" in the Python sense. If you find yourself debating techniques in the Python community, please do not wave this book in anyone's face as evidence that your solution is best! Skill in finding an obvious solution is not something that can be taught; rather it is only learned through practice.

Wrapping Up

Despite the many myths that have been tossed around over the years, Python is a versatile and technically sound language, capable of handling just about any problem you can throw at it. It's a solid choice, whether you are writing automation, crunching massive datasets, building native user applications, implementing machine learning, or crafting web applications and APIs. Most importantly, Python is backed by a vibrant, diverse, and helpful community.

The key to success, then, is writing Python code that makes the most of the strengths and features of the language. The goal is not simply to write code that works, but to write code that both looks and behaves elegantly. The rest of this book will teach you how to do exactly that.

2

YOUR WORKBENCH

Your development environment is a major factor in how productive you'll be in a language. Instead of contenting yourself with a bare-bones default shell, you'll want to assemble a development environment worthy of any production-level project.

A good Python development environment usually consists of the language interpreter, the pip package manager, a *virtual environment*, a Python-oriented code editor, and one or more *static analyzers* to check your code for errors and problems. I'll discuss each of these in this chapter. I'll also introduce the style conventions common in Python and round out the chapter with a guided tour of the most common Python integrated development environments (IDEs).

Installing Python

Before you can do anything, you have to install Python itself, along with a couple of essential tools. As you know from Chapter 1, Python is an interpreted language, so you'll need to install its *interpreter*. You must also install pip, the Python package manager, so you can install additional Python tools and libraries. The exact steps for setup depend on your platform, but I will cover the major platforms here.

In this book, I'm using Python 3.9, the latest version at the time of writing. If you're reading this at a later date, just use the latest stable release of Python 3. All the instructions should work the same. You need only replace the version number in the obvious ways on any commands run in the command line.

This is merely a quick guide to installation. For the complete, official instructions, which cover many more situations and advanced options, see *https://docs.python.org/using/*.

Installing on Windows

On Windows, Python is not generally installed by default, so you'll need to download it yourself from *https://python.org/downloads/windows/* and run that installer. On the first screen of the installer, be sure you check the boxes for **Install the launcher for all users** and **Add Python to PATH**.

Python is also available through the Windows App Store. However, as of the date of my writing, this particular installation method is still officially considered unstable. I recommend downloading the official installer instead.

Installing on macOS

On macOS, you can use either MacPorts or Homebrew to install Python and pip.

Use the following commands to install Python and pip with MacPorts, replacing the 38 with whatever version you want to download (removing the decimal point):

```
sudo port install python38 py38-pip
sudo port select --set python python38
sudo port select --set pip py38-pip
```

Alternatively, here's the command to install both Python and pip in one step with Homebrew:

```
brew install python
```

Use only one of the two methods described above.

Installing on Linux

If you're running a Linux operating system, chances are that Python (python3) is installed by default, although the other tools you need may not be. (I'll show you how to install Python anyway, just to be on the safe side.)

To install Python and pip on Ubuntu, Debian, or related, run this command:

```
sudo apt install python3 python3-pip python3-venv
```

On Fedora, RHEL, or CentOS, you can run this:

```
sudo dnf python3 python3-pip
```

On Arch Linux, run this:

```
sudo pacman -S python python-pip
```

For other distributions, you'll need to search for the Python 3 and pip packages yourself.

Installing from Source

If you're running a UNIX-like system, and if your system either has an outdated version of Python 3 in the system packages or lacks a package manager altogether, you can build Python from source. This is how I usually install the latest Python.

Installing Dependencies

On macOS, there are some relatively complex considerations when it comes to installing Python's build dependencies. You should consult the documentation at *https://devguide.python.org/setup/#macos-and-os-x*.

On most Linux systems, you will need to make sure you have the development files for several libraries that Python relies upon. The best way to install these depends on your system and, more specifically, which package manager you use.

If you're on a Linux distribution that uses the APT package manager—such as Ubuntu, Pop!_OS, Debian, or Linux Mint—then you should either check the box to enable Source Code as a source in your Software Sources or Software & Updates settings or make sure you have it included in your *sources.list* file. (The exact method depends on your system, and that topic is beyond the scope of this book.)

Then, run the following commands:

```
sudo apt-get update
sudo apt-get build-dep python3.9
```

If you get the message `Unable to find a source package for python3.9`, change the 9 to a lower (or higher) number until you find one that works. The dependencies for Python 3 don't really change much between minor versions.

If your Linux distribution uses the DNF package manager, such as if you're on modern Fedora, RHEL, or CentOS, run the following commands:

```
sudo dnf install dnf-plugins-core
sudo dnf builddep python3
```

If you're on an older version of Fedora or RHEL that uses the yum package manager, run the following commands:

```
sudo yum install yum-utils
sudo yum-builddep python3
```

If you're on SUSE Linux, you'll have to install the dependencies, including needed libraries, one by one. Table 2-1 lists these dependencies. If you're on another UNIX-based system, this list will be helpful, although you may need to change the package names or build the dependencies from source.

Table 2-1: Python 3 Build Dependencies According to SUSE Linux

automake	intltool	netcfg
fdupes	libbz2-devel	openssl-devel
gcc	libexpat-devel	pkgconfig
gcc-c++	libffi-devel	readline-devel
gcc-fortran	libnsl-devel	sqlite-devel
gdbm-devel	lzma-devel	xz
gettext-tools	make	zlib-devel
gmp-devel	ncurses-devel	

Downloading and Building Python

You can download the Python source as a Gzipped source tarball, which is a compressed file (*.tgz*), from *https://www.python.org/downloads/source/*. I usually like to move this tarball file into a dedicated directory for Python source tarballs, especially as I tend to have multiple versions of Python at any one time. Within that directory, extract (uncompress) this file with `tar -xzvf Python-3.x.x.tgz`, substituting the name of the tarball you downloaded.

Next, from within the extracted directory, run the following, ensuring that each command succeeds before running the next one:

```
./configure --enable-optimizations
make
make altinstall
```

This should configure Python for normal use, ensure it won't encounter any errors in the current environment, and then install it *alongside* any existing Python installations.

You should always run `make altinstall` if you have any other version of Python already installed. Otherwise, the existing installation may be overwritten or hidden, *breaking* your system! If you are absolutely certain this is the first Python installation on the system, *only then* may you run `make install` instead.

Once the installation is complete, you can use Python right away.

Meet the Interpreter

Now that you've installed that interpreter, you can run Python scripts and projects.

Interactive Session

The interpreter's *interactive session* allows you to enter and run code in real time and see the outcomes. You can start an interactive session on the command line with this command:

```
python3
```

You should be in the habit of specifying `python2` or `python3`, instead of using the `python` command, since the latter may refer to the wrong version (which comes preinstalled on many systems, even today). You can always check the exact version of Python invoked by any of those three commands with the `--version` flag (for example, `python3 --version`).

Although the above should work on Windows, the same as on any other system, the Python documentation recommends the following alternative on Windows instead:

```
py.exe -3
```

Just to keep everything system-agnostic, I'll use `python3` throughout the rest of this book.

When you start the interactive session, you should see something that looks similar to this:

```
Python 3.10.2 (default)
Type "help", "copyright", "credits" or "license" for more information.
>
```

Enter any Python code you want at the prompt >, and the interpreter will run it immediately. You can even enter multiline statements, such as conditional statements, and the interpreter will know more lines are expected before it runs the code. You'll see the three-dot (...) prompt when the interpreter is waiting for more lines. When you're done, press ENTER on a blank line, and the interpreter will run the whole block:

```
> spam = True
> if spam:
...     print("Spam, spam, spam, spam...")
...
Spam, spam, spam, spam...
```

To quit the interactive session, run this command:

```
> exit()
```

The interactive session is useful for testing things out in Python, but not much else. You should know of its existence moving forward, but I won't use it much in this book. Instead, you should be using a proper code editor.

Running Python Files

You write scripts and programs in a text or code editor. I'll introduce several code editors and IDEs at the end of this chapter, but in the meantime, you can use your favorite text editor for writing your code.

Python code is written in *.py* files. To run a Python file (*myfile.py*, for example), you'd use this in the command line (*not* the interpreter):

```
python3 myfile.py
```

Packages and Virtual Environments

A *package* is a collection of code, which is analogous to a library in most other programming languages. Python is rather famous for being "batteries included," since most things "just work" with a simple import statement. But if you need to do something beyond the basics, such as creating a snazzy user interface, you often have to install a package.

Thankfully, installing most third-party libraries is easy. Library authors bundle their libraries into packages, which can be installed using the handy little pip package manager tool that we installed earlier. I'll cover that tool later.

Using multiple third-party packages requires a bit of finesse. Some packages require other packages to be installed first. Certain packages have conflicts with other packages. You can also install specific versions of a package, depending on what exactly you need. Did I mention that some of the applications and operating system components on your computer rely on certain Python packages? This is why virtual environments exist.

A *virtual environment* is a sandbox where you can install only the Python packages you need for a particular project, without the risk of those packages clashing with those for another project (or your system). You create different little sandboxes for each project and install only the packages you want in it. Everything stays neatly organized. You never actually change what Python packages are installed on your system, so you avoid breaking important things that have nothing to do with your project.

You may even create virtual environments that have nothing to do with a particular project. For example, I have a dedicated virtual environment for running random code files in Python 3.10, with a particular set of tools I use for finding problems.

Creating a Virtual Environment

Each virtual environment resides in a dedicated directory. Conventionally, we name this folder *env* or *venv*.

For each project, I typically like to create a dedicated virtual environment inside the project folder. Python provides a tool called *venv* for this.

If you use Git or another *version control system (VCS)* for tracking changes to your code, there's an additional setup step I'll get to in a moment.

To create the virtual environment with the name venv in the current working directory, run the following command in the command line:

```
python3 -m ❶ venv ❷ venv
```

The first venv ❶ is a command that creates a virtual environment, and the second venv ❷ is the desired path to the virtual environment. In this case, venv is just a relative path, creating a *venv/* directory in the current working directory. However, you could also use an absolute path, and you could call it whatever you want. For example, you could create a virtual environment called *myvirtualenv* in the */opt* directory of a UNIX system, like this:

```
python3 -m venv /opt/myvirtualenv
```

Note, I'm specifying python3 here, although I can run this with whatever Python version I want to use, such as python3.9 -m venv venv.

If you use something older than Python 3.3, make sure you install your system's virtualenv package and then use this command:

```
virtualenv -p python3 venv
```

Now if you look at your working directory, you'll notice that the directory *venv/* has been created.

Activating a Virtual Environment

To use your virtual environment, you need to activate it.

On UNIX-like systems, run this command:

```
$ source venv/bin/activate
```

On Windows, run this:

```
> venv\Scripts\activate.bat
```

Alternatively, if you use PowerShell on Windows, run this:

```
> venv\Scripts\activate.ps1
```

Some PowerShell users must first run set-executionpolicy RemoteSigned for virtual environments to work on Windows PowerShell. If you run into trouble, try this.

Like magic, you're now using your virtual environment! You should see (venv) at the start of your command line prompt (not at the end), to indicate that you're using a virtual environment named venv.

GOTCHA ALERT If you have multiple shells (usually terminal windows) open, you should be aware that the virtual environment is only active for the one shell you explicitly activated it in! On shells that support it, look for the (venv) notation to make sure you're using the virtual environment.

While inside your virtual environment, you can still access all the same files on your system that you use outside the virtual environment, but your environment *paths* will be overridden by the virtual environment. Practically speaking, any packages you install in the virtual environment are only usable there, and from the venv, the system-wide packages cannot be accessed unless you explicitly specify otherwise.

If you want the virtual environment to also see the system-wide packages, you can do so with a special flag, which has to be set when you first create the virtual environment. You can't change this after the virtual environment is created.

```
python3 -m venv --system-site-packages venv
```

Leaving a Virtual Environment

To get out of the virtual environment and back to reality . . . er, *ahem*, the system, you need a simple command.

You ready for this, UNIX users? Just run this:

```
$ deactivate
```

That really is it. The same works for Windows PowerShell users.

Things are only slightly more complicated on the Windows command line:

```
> venv\Scripts\deactivate.bat
```

Still pretty painless. Remember, like with activation, if you named your virtual environment something else, you'd have to change the venv in that line accordingly.

Introducing pip

Most of us have great expectations for Python's package system. Python's package manager is *pip*, which usually makes package installation trivial, especially in virtual environments.

System-Wide Packages

Remember, for any Python development work, you should almost always work in virtual environments. This will ensure that you're always using the right packages for your work, without potentially messing up which packages (and versions thereof) are available to other programs on your computer. If you absolutely, positively know you want to install packages in your system-wide Python environment, you may use pip for that as well. First, make sure you are *not* working in a virtual environment, and then use this:

```
python3 -m pip command
```

Replace the *command* with your pip commands, which I'll cover next.

Installing Packages

To install a package, run `pip install` *package*. For example, to install PySide6 within an activated virtual environment, you'd use this:

```
pip install PySide6
```

If you want to install a specific version of something, append two equal signs (==), followed by the desired version number (no spaces):

```
pip install PySide6==6.1.2
```

Bonus: you can even use operators like >=, to mean "at least this version or greater." These are called *requirement specifiers*.

```
pip install PySide6>=6.1.2
```

That line would install the latest version of PySide6 that is at least version 6.1.2. This is really helpful if you want the most recent version of a package but also want to ensure you at least install a *minimum* version of a package (you might not). If it isn't possible to install a version of the package that meets the requirement, pip will display an error message.

If you're on a UNIX-like system, you may need to use `pip install "PySide6>=6.1.2"` instead, since > has another meaning in the shell.

requirements.txt

You can save even more time for yourself and others by writing a *requirements .txt* file for your project. This file lists the packages your project needs. When creating a virtual environment, you and other users can install all the required packages with a single command, using this file.

To create this file, list the name of a pip package, as well as its version (if required), on each line. For example, one of my projects has a *requirements.txt* file like this:

```
PySide2>=5.11.1
appdirs
```

Listing 2-1: requirements.txt

Now anyone can install all those packages in one shot with this command:

```
pip install -r requirements.txt
```

I'll revisit *requirements.txt* in Chapter 18, when I cover packaging and distribution.

Upgrading Packages

You can update an already-installed package with pip as well. For example, to update to the latest version of PySide6, run this:

```
pip install --upgrade PySide6
```

If you have a *requirements.txt* file, you can also upgrade all your required packages at once:

```
pip install --upgrade -r requirements.txt
```

Removing Packages

You can remove packages with this command:

```
pip uninstall package
```

Replace *package* with the package name.

There is one minor wrinkle. Installing one package will also install any other packages it relies upon, which we call its *dependencies*. Uninstalling a package does not remove its dependencies, so you may need to go through and remove them yourself. This can get tricky, since multiple packages may share dependencies and you therefore risk breaking a separate package.

Herein lies one more advantage of virtual environments. Once I'm in that sort of a pickle, I can delete the virtual environment, create a new one, and install only those packages I need.

Finding Packages

Great, so now you can install, upgrade, and remove things. But how do you even know what packages pip has to offer?

There are two ways to find out. The first is to use pip itself to run a search. Say you want a package for web scraping. Run this command:

```
pip search web scraping
```

That will give you a whole ton of results to sift through, but it's helpful at those times when you simply forget the name of a package.

If you want something a lot more browsable and informative, *https://pypi.org/* is the official Python Package Index.

One Warning About pip . . .

Unless you have expertise in the full technical implications, **never** use sudo pip on a UNIX-like system! It can do so many bad things to your system installation—things that your system package manager cannot correct—that if you decide to use it, you will regret it for the remainder of your system's lifetime.

Usually, when someone thinks they need to use sudo pip, they should really use python3 -m pip or pip install --user to install to their local user directory. Most other problems can be solved with virtual environments. Unless you're an expert who fully understands what you're doing and how to reverse it, don't *ever* use sudo pip!

GOTCHA ALERT   Seriously. Never use sudo pip.

Virtual Environments and Git

Working with virtual environments and a VCS, like Git, can be tricky. Within a virtual environment's directory are the *actual packages* you installed with pip. Those would clutter up your VCS repository with big, unnecessary files, and you can't necessarily copy a virtual environment folder from one computer to another and expect it to work anyway.

Thus, you *don't* want to track these files in your VCS. There are two solutions:

1. Only create virtual environments outside of your repository.
2. Untrack the virtual environment directory in the VCS.

There are arguments in favor of both rules, but which one you should use really depends on your project, environment, and particular needs.

If you're using Git, create or edit a file called *.gitignore* in the root directory of your repository. Add this line somewhere in it:

```
venv/
```

Listing 2-2: .gitignore

If you used a different name for your virtual environment, change that line to match. If you're using a different VCS, like Subversion or Mercurial, check the documentation to see how to ignore a directory like *venv*.

Conventionally, every developer who clones your repository will build their own virtual environment, probably using that *requirements.txt* file you provided.

Even if you plan to place your virtual environments outside of the repository, it's good to use your *.gitignore* file, just as a little extra insurance. Best VCS practice is to handpick which files to commit, but mistakes happen. Since *venv* is one of the most conventional names for a virtual environment directory, adding it to the *.gitignore* at least helps prevent some accidental commits. If your team has other standard names for virtual environments, you might consider adding those as well.

The Whole Shebang

Many users and developers who might be running your code will also be using virtual environments. Yet all of this can come apart at the seams very easily if the very first line of your Python file is wrong.

I'm talking about the *shebang*, a special command at the top of a Python file, by which you can make that file directly executable:

```
❶ #!/usr/bin/env python3

print("Hello, world!")
```

Listing 2-3: hello_world.py

The shebang (short for haSH-BANG, or #!) ❶ provides the path to the Python interpreter. While it's optional, I strongly recommend including it in your code, as it means the file can be marked as executable and run directly, like this:

```
./hello_world.py
```

This is helpful, but as I've hinted before, one must be careful with shebangs. A shebang tells the computer where to find the exact Python interpreter to use, so the wrong shebang can break out of the confines of a virtual environment or even point to a version of the interpreter that isn't installed.

You may have seen this kind of shebang in the wild:

```
#!/usr/bin/python
```

Listing 2-4: shebang.py:1a

That line is terribly wrong, because it forces the computer to use a particular system-wide copy of Python. Again, that dismisses the entire purpose of a virtual environment.

PEDANTIC NOTE   You may be wondering how #!/usr/bin/python would even be a valid path on Windows. It does function, thanks to some cleverness outlined in PEP 397. (You still should avoid using it.)

Instead, you should always use this shebang for any Python file that only runs with Python 3:

```
#!/usr/bin/env python3
```

Listing 2-5: shebang.py:1b

If you happen to have a script which runs in *both* Python 2 and Python 3, use this shebang instead:

```
#!/usr/bin/env python
```

Listing 2-6: shebang.py:1c

The rules about shebangs and how they are handled are officially outlined in PEP 394 (for UNIX-like systems) and PEP 397 (for Windows systems). Regardless of which system you develop for, it's good to understand the implications of shebangs in both UNIX and Windows.

File Encoding

Since Python 3.1, all Python files have used the *UTF-8 encoding*, allowing the interpreter to use all of the characters in Unicode. (Prior to that version, the default was to use the old ASCII encoding.)

If you need to use a different encoding system, instead of the default UTF-8, you need to tell the Python interpreter that outright.

For example, to use Latin-1 encoding in a Python file, include this line at the top of your file, right below the shebang. To work, it must be on the first or second line—that's where the interpreter looks for this information:

```
# -*- coding: latin-1 -*-
```

If you want another encoding system, replace latin-1 with whatever you need. If you specify an encoding that Python doesn't recognize, it will throw an error.

Although the preceding is the conventional way to specify encoding, there are two other valid ways to write the above comment. You can use this form, without the hard-to-remember -*-:

```
# coding: latin-1
```

Or you can use this longer but more English-like form:

```
# This Python file uses the following encoding: latin-1
```

Whatever you use, it must be *exactly* as shown above, except for swapping `latin-1` for whatever encoding you want. For this reason, the first or second forms are preferred.

To learn more, read PEP 263, which defined this feature.

Most of the time, you'll be fine using the default UTF-8 encoding anyway; if you need something else, now you know how to inform the interpreter.

A Few Extra Virtual Environment Tricks

As you get used to using virtual environments and pip, you'll pick up additional tricks and tools to make the whole process easier. Here are a few of the more popular ones:

Using a Virtual Environment Without Activating

You can use the binaries that are a part of the virtual environment without activating it. For example, you can execute `venv/bin/python` to run the virtual environment's own Python instance, or `venv/bin/pip` to run its instance of pip. It'll work the same as if you had activated the virtual environment.

For example, assuming my virtual environment is `venv`, I could do this in the terminal:

```
venv/bin/pip install pylint
venv/bin/python

> import pylint
```

It works! Yet, `import pylint` still will not work on the system-wide Python interactive shell (unless, of course, you installed it on the system).

The Alternatives

Throughout this book, I'll be using pip and `venv`, as they're the default tools for modern Python. However, there are a few other solutions out there worth looking into.

Pipenv

A number of Python developers swear by *Pipenv*, which combines both pip and venv into one cohesive tool, with many additional features.

Because the workflow is quite different, I won't cover Pipenv here. If you're interested in it, I recommend reading their superb documentation at *https://docs.pipenv.org/.* You'll find comprehensive setup and usage instructions there, as well as a more detailed explanation of the advantages Pipenv offers.

pip-tools

A number of tasks in pip can be simplified with pip-tools, including automatic updating, aids for writing *requirements.txt*, and more.

If you use pip-tools, you should only install it within a virtual environment. It is designed specifically for that use case.

More information is available at *https://pypi.org/project/pip-tools/.*

poetry

Some Python developers absolutely hate the entire pip workflow. One such developer created *poetry* as an alternative package manager. I don't use it in this book, as it behaves very differently, but I'd be remiss not to point it out.

You can find more information, download directions (the creator does not recommend using pip to install it), and access documentation on their website: *https://python-poetry.org/.*

Introduction to PEP 8

Unlike many languages, where style decisions are left entirely to the discretion of the community at large, Python does have an official style guide, which is published as *PEP 8*. Although the conventions in the guide are intended primarily for standard library code, many Python developers choose to stick to them as a rule.

That doesn't make them mandatory: if you have an objective reason to follow a different style convention in your project, that's fine, although you should apply that style consistently, as much as is reasonable.

PEP 8 itself makes this distinction clear, early on:

> A style guide is about consistency. Consistency with this style guide is important. Consistency within a project is more important. Consistency within one module or function is the most important.

> However, know when to be inconsistent—sometimes, style guide recommendations just aren't applicable. When in doubt, use your best judgment. Look at other examples and decide what looks best. And don't hesitate to ask!

In practice, you'll likely find very little reason to deviate from PEP 8. The style guide is far from all-encompassing. It leaves plenty of breathing room, while making it clear what constitutes a good or bad coding style.

The Line Limit Debate

PEP 8 recommends a line limit of 79 characters, or an 80-character cut-off, though there's a lot of debate on the topic. Some Python developers respect that rule, while others prefer cutoffs of 100 or 120 characters. What to do?

The most common argument for longer limits is that modern monitors are wider and higher resolution. Surely, the 80-character limit is a relic of a bygone era, right? *Definitely not!* There are several reasons to stick to a common line limit. For example:

- Vision-impaired individuals who must work with larger font sizes or zoomed-in interfaces
- Viewing differences in a file between commits in a side-by-side diff
- Split-screen editors, displaying multiple files simultaneously
- Vertical monitors
- Side-by-side windows on a laptop monitor, wherein the editor only has half its usual space
- Individuals with older monitors, who cannot afford to upgrade to the latest 1080p monster
- Viewing code on mobile devices
- Writing coding books for No Starch Press

In all of these scenarios, the reasoning behind the 80-character limit becomes apparent: there simply isn't enough horizontal space for 120 characters or more per line. Soft text wrapping, wherein the remainder of a cut-off line appears on a separate line (without a line number), does solve some of these issues. However, it can be difficult to read, as many people forced to rely on it regularly will attest to.

This doesn't mean that you have to follow this 79-character maximum religiously. There are exceptions. Above all, *readability* and *consistency* are the goals. Many developers embrace the 80/100 rule: an 80-character "soft" cutoff, you try to respect in most cases; and a 100-character "hard" cutoff, you reserve for all those cases where the lower limit would negatively impact readability.

Tabs or Spaces?

Ah yes, the civil war over which many friendships have been strained and many relationships have abruptly ended (okay, maybe just that one?). Most programmers have strong feelings on the topic.

PEP 8 recommends spaces over tabs, but technically, it allows either. The important thing is to *never mix the two*. Use either spaces or tabs, and stick to it throughout your entire project.

If you do use spaces, then there's the debate about how many spaces to use. PEP 8 answers this question, too: *four spaces per indentation level*. Any less can negatively impact code readability, especially for people with visual impairments or some forms of dyslexia.

By the way, most code editors are able to automatically enter four spaces when they press TAB, so there's rarely an excuse to press SPACE repeatedly.

Quality Control: Static Analyzers

One of the most useful tools in any programmer's toolkit is a reliable *static analyzer*, which reads your source code, looking for potential problems or deviations from the standards. If you've never used one before, now is the time to change that. One common type of static analyzer, called a *linter*, checks your source code for common mistakes, potential errors, and style inconsistencies. Two of the most popular linters are *Pylint* and *PyFlakes*.

There are many more kinds of static analyzers available for Python, including static type checkers like *Mypy* and complexity analyzers like *mccabe*.

I'll cover how to install all of these below, and I'll discuss how to use many of them. I recommend you choose only one of these two linters and install the rest of the static analyzers.

Pylint

Pylint is perhaps the most versatile static analyzer in Python. It works decently well by default, and it allows you to customize exactly what you want it to look for and ignore.

You can install the Pylint package with pip, which I recommend doing in a virtual environment. Once installed, you pass Pylint the name of a file you want analyzed, like this:

```
pylint filetocheck.py
```

You can also analyze an entire package or module at once. (I'll define what modules and packages are in Chapter 4.) For example, if you want Pylint to analyze a package called *myawesomeproject* in the current working directory, you'd run this:

```
pylint myawesomeproject
```

Pylint will scan the files and display its warnings and recommendations on the command line. Then, you can edit your file and make the necessary changes.

For example, consider the following Python file:

```
def cooking():
    ham = True
    print(eggs)
    return order
```

Listing 2-7: cooking.py:1a

I'll run the linter on that file with the following in the system command line:

```
pylint cooking.py
```

Pylint provides the following feedback:

```
************* Module cooking
cooking.py:1:0: C0111: Missing module docstring (missing-docstring)
cooking.py:1:0: C0111: Missing function docstring (missing-docstring)
cooking.py:3:10: E0602: Undefined variable 'eggs' (undefined-variable)
cooking.py:4:11: E0602: Undefined variable 'order' (undefined-variable)
cooking.py:2:4: W0612: Unused variable 'ham' (unused-variable)


----------------------------------------------------------------------
Your code has been rated at -22.50/10
```

The linter found five errors in my code: both the module and the function are missing their docstrings (see Chapter 3). I tried to use the variables eggs and order, neither of which exist. I also assigned a value to the variable ham, but I never used that value anywhere.

If Pylint takes umbrage at a particular line of code you feel should be left as is, you can tell the static analyzer to ignore it and move on. You do this with a special comment, either inline on the line in question or at the top of the affected block. For example:

```
# pylint: disable=missing-docstring

def cooking():  # pylint: disable=missing-docstring
    ham = True
    print(eggs)
    return order
```

Listing 2-8: cooking.py:1b

With the first command, I tell Pylint not to alert me about the missing docstring on the module; that affects the entire block of code. The inline comment on the next line will suppress the warning about the missing docstring on the function, and it will only affect that line. If I ran the linter again, I'd only see the other two linter errors:

```
************* Module cooking
cooking.py:5:10: E0602: Undefined variable 'eggs' (undefined-variable)
cooking.py:6:11: E0602: Undefined variable 'order' (undefined-variable)
```

```
cooking.py:4:4: W0612: Unused variable 'ham' (unused-variable)

--------------------------------------------------------------------
Your code has been rated at -17.50/10 (previous run: -22.50/10, +5.00)
```

At this point, I'd edit my code and actually fix the rest of those problems. (Except I won't, for this example.)

You can also control Pylint's project-wide behavior by creating a *pylintrc* file in the root directory of your project. To do this, run the following:

```
pylint --generate-rcfile > pylintrc
```

Find that file; open it; and edit it to turn on and off different warnings, ignore files, and define other settings. The documentation isn't fantastic for this, but you can often work out what different options do from the comments in that *pylintrc* file.

When you run Pylint, it will look for a *pylintrc* (or *.pylintrc*) file in the current working directory. Alternatively, you can specify a different filename for Pylint to read its settings from, such as *myrcfile*, by passing the filename to the --rcfile option when invoking Pylint:

```
pylint --rcfile=myrcfile filetocheck.py
```

Some regular users of Pylint like to create .pylintrc or .config/pylintrc in their home directory (UNIX-like systems only). If Pylint cannot find another configuration file, it will use the one in the home directory.

Although the Pylint documentation is far from comprehensive, it can still be useful. You can find it at *https://pylint.readthedocs.io/*.

Flake8

The *Flake8* tool is actually a combination of three static analyzers:

- *PyFlakes* is a linter, similar in purpose to Pylint. It is designed to work faster and to avoid false positives (both being common complaints about Pylint). It also ignores style rules, which are handled by the next tool.

- *pycodestyle* is a style checker, to help ensure you write PEP 8-compliant code. (This tool used to be called pep8, but it was renamed to avoid confusion with the actual style guide.)

- *mccabe* checks the McCabe (or Cyclomatic) complexity of your code. If you don't know what that is, don't worry—its purpose is essentially just to warn you when your code's structure is getting too complicated.

You can install the Flake8 package with pip, which I typically do within a virtual environment.

To scan a file, module, or package, pass it to flake8 on the command line. For example, to scan my earlier *cooking.py* file (Listing 2-8), I'd use this command:

```
flake8 cooking.py
```

That outputs the following:

```
cooking.py:2:5: F841 local variable 'ham' is assigned to but never used
cooking.py:3:11: F821 undefined name 'eggs'
cooking.py:4:12: F821 undefined name 'order'
```

(You'll notice that Flake8 isn't complaining about the lack of doc-strings; that's disabled by default in this linter.)

By default, only PyFlakes and pycodestyle are run. If you want to analyze the complexity of your code, you also need to pass the argument --max-complexity, followed by a number. Anything higher than 10 is considered too complex, but if you understand McCabe complexity, you can change this to suit your needs. So, for example, to check the complexity of the *cooking.py* file, you'd run this:

```
flake8 --max-complexity 10 cooking.py
```

However you run Flake8, you'll get a comprehensive list of all the errors and warnings in your code.

If you need to tell Flake8 to ignore something it thinks is a problem, you use a # noqa comment, followed by the error code to ignore. This comment should be inline, on the line where the error occurs. If you omit the error code, then # noqa will cause Flake8 to ignore all errors on that line.

In my code, if I wanted to ignore both of the errors I received, it might look like this:

```
def cooking():
    ham = True     # noqa F841
    print(eggs)    # noqa F821, F841
    return order   # noqa
```

Listing 2-9: cooking.py:1c

Here, you see three different scenarios. First, I'm ignoring only warning F841. Second, I'm ignoring two errors (even though one of them isn't actually raised; this is just a silly example). Third, I'm ignoring all possible errors.

Flake8 also supports configuration files. In the project directory, you can create a *.flake8* file. Start a section in that file with the line [flake8], followed by all the Flake8 settings you want to define. (See the documentation.)

Flake8 will also accept project-wide configuration files called *tox.ini* or *setup.cfg*, so long as they have a [flake8] section within them.

For example, if you want to automatically run mccabe each time you invoke Flake8, rather than specify --max-complexity every time, you could define a *.flake8* file that looks like this:

```
[flake8]
max-complexity = 10
```

Listing 2-10: .flake8

Some developers like to define a system-wide configuration file for Flake8, which you can do (only) on a UNIX-like system. In your home folder, create the configuration file as either *.flake8* or *.config/flake8*.

One of the chief advantages of Flake8 over Pylint is the documentation. Flake8 has a complete list of their warnings, errors, options, and the like. You can find the documentation at *https://flake8.readthedocs.io/*.

Mypy

Mypy is an unusual static analyzer because it focuses entirely on *type annotations* (see Chapter 6). Because it involves so many concepts I haven't covered yet, I won't go into much depth here.

Still, now is a good time to get it installed. Like everything else so far, you can install the mypy package from pip.

Once installed, Mypy can be used by passing it the file, package, or module you wish to check:

```
mypy filetocheck.py
```

Mypy will only attempt to check files that have type annotations, and it will ignore the rest.

Style Janitors: Autoformatting Tools

Another tool you may find useful is an *autoformatter*, which can automatically change your Python code—spacing, indentation, and preferred equivalent expressions (such as != instead of <>)—to be PEP 8 compliant. Two options are *autopep8* and *Black*.

autopep8

The autopep8 tool leverages pycodestyle (part of Flake8), even using the same configuration file as that tool to determine what style rules it ultimately follows or ignores.

As always, you can install autopep8 with pip.

By default, autopep8 only fixes whitespace, but if you pass the --aggressive argument to it, it will make additional changes. In fact, if you pass that argument twice, it will do even more. The complete list is beyond the scope of this explanation, so consult the documentation at *https://pypi.org/project/autopep8/* to learn more.

To fix most PEP 8 issues on a Python code file by changing it in place (as opposed to making a copy, which is the default behavior), run this:

```
autopep8 --in-place --aggressive --aggressive filetochange.py
```

Changing the file directly may sound a bit risky, but it really isn't. Style changes are just that: style. They don't affect the actual behavior of the code.

Black

The Black tool is a little more straightforward: it assumes you want to follow PEP 8 in its entirety, and it doesn't overwhelm you with many options as a result.

Like autopep8, you install `black` with pip, although it requires Python 3.6 or later. To format a file with it, pass the filename:

```
black filetochange.py
```

A complete list of Black's few options can be seen via `black --help`.

Testing Frameworks

Testing frameworks form an essential part of any good development workflow, but I won't go into detail about them in this chapter. Python has three major options for testing frameworks: *Pytest*, *nose2*, and *unittest*, in addition to a promising new project called *ward*. All of these can be installed with pip.

More knowledge is essential to cover this topic effectively, so I'll revisit it in Chapter 20.

An Exhibition of Code Editors

You have your Python interpreter, your virtual environments, your static analyzers, and other such tools. Now you are prepared to write code.

You can write Python in any basic text editor, just as you could with practically any other programming language. Yet you'll probably have an easier time writing production-quality code with a proper code editor.

Before I end this chapter, I want to take you on a tour of several of the most popular Python code editors and integrated development environments (*IDEs*) available. This is only a sampling, as there are many more options besides. **If you already know what code editor or IDE you want to use, skip forward to the last section of this chapter.**

IDLE

Python has its own IDE, called *IDLE*, which ships with the standard distribution of Python. It's a fairly bare-bones IDE with two components: an editor and an interface for the interactive shell. You could do worse than IDLE, so if you aren't in the mood to install a different editor right now, start here. However, I recommend exploring your options, as most editors and IDEs have a host of useful features that IDLE lacks.

Emacs and Vim

The purists and old-school hackers among you will be glad to know that Emacs and Vim both have excellent Python support. Setting up either is not for the faint of heart, so I'm not going into any of that here.

If you're already a lover of either (or both?) code editors, you can find excellent tutorials for both at Real Python.

For Emacs, see *https://realpython.com/emacs-the-best-python-editor/*.

For Vim, see *https://realpython.com/vim-and-python-a-match-made-in-heaven/*.

PyCharm

According to "The State of Developer Ecosystem 2021" developer survey by JetBrains, the PyCharm IDE from JetBrains is far and away the most popular option for Python programming. It comes in two flavors: the free *PyCharm Community Edition* and the paid *PyCharm Professional Edition*. (Steps were taken by JetBrains to eliminate bias. See the survey here: *https://www.jetbrains.com/lp/devecosystem-2021/python/*.)

Both versions offer a dedicated Python code editor with autocompletion, refactoring, debugging, and testing tools. It can manage and use virtual environments with ease, and it integrates with your version control software. It even performs static analysis (using its own tool). The professional edition adds tools for data, scientific development, and web development.

If you're familiar with other JetBrains IDEs, like IntelliJ IDEA or CLion, PyCharm would be a great Python IDE to start with. It requires more computer resources than many code editors, but if you have a decently powerful machine, this won't be a problem. If you haven't used JetBrains IDEs before, try the Community Edition before investing in the paid version.

You can find more information and downloads at *https://jetbrains.com/pycharm/*.

Visual Studio Code

Visual Studio Code has excellent Python support. It's the second-most popular Python code editor, according to that 2021 JetBrains survey. It's free and open source, and it runs on virtually every platform. Install the official Python extension from Microsoft, and you're ready to go!

Visual Studio Code supports autocompletion, refactoring, debugging, and virtual environment switching, along with the usual version control integration. It integrates with Pylint, Flake8, and Mypy, among several other popular static analyzers. It even works with the most common Python unit testing tools.

Download it at *https://code.visualstudio.com/*.

Sublime Text

Sublime is another popular multilanguage code editor. It is appreciated for its speed and simplicity, and it is easily customized with extensions and configuration files. Sublime Text is free to try, but if you find you like it and wish to continue using it, you need to purchase it.

The Anaconda plug-in transforms Sublime Text into a Python IDE, with everything: autocompletion, navigation, static analysis, autoformatting, test running, and even a documentation browser. It requires a little more hand-tuned configuration than some of the other options, especially if you want to use virtual environments. However, if Sublime Text is your jam, it's worth it.

Download Sublime Text at *https://sublimetext.com/* and the Anaconda plug-in at *https://damnwidget.github.io/anaconda/.* That second link also provides instructions for installing the plug-in in Sublime Text.

Spyder

If your focus is scientific programming or data analysis, or if you're a fan of MATLAB's interface, you'll be right at home in *Spyder*, a free and open source Python IDE that is also written *in* Python.

In addition to the usual features—a dedicated Python code editor, a debugger, integration with static analyzers, and documentation viewing—Spyder includes integration with many common Python libraries for data analysis and scientific computing. It integrates a full code profiler and variable explorer. Plug-ins exist for supporting unit tests, autoformatting, and editing Jupyter notebooks, among other features.

Download Spyder at *https://spyder-ide.org/.*

Eclipse + PyDev/LiClipse

Eclipse has lost a lot of ground to the newer editors, but it still has a loyal user base. Although it's geared toward languages like Java, C++, PHP, and JavaScript, Eclipse can also become a Python IDE with the *PyDev* plug-in.

If you already have installed Eclipse, which is completely free, then you only need to install the PyDev plug-in from the Eclipse Marketplace. Download Eclipse at *https://eclipse.org/ide/* and look in the marketplace for the plug-in.

Alternatively, you can install *LiClipse,* which bundles Eclipse, PyDev, and other useful tools. The PyDev developers recommend this approach, as it directly supports their development work. You can use LiClipse without a license for 30 days, after which point, you must purchase a license. Download LiClipse from *https://liclipse.com/.*

PyDev offers autocompletion, refactoring, support for type hinting and static analysis, debugging, unit test integration, and many more features. You can find more information about PyDev at *https://pydev.org/.*

The Eric Python IDE

Eric might be the oldest IDE on the list, but it's still as reliable as ever. Named after Eric Idle of *Monty Python's Flying Circus,* Eric is a free and open source IDE written in Python.

It offers everything you could possibly need to write Python: autocompletion, debugging, refactoring, static analysis, testing integration, documentation tools, virtual environment management, and the list goes on.

Find information about Eric and download it at *https://eric-ide.python -projects.org/.*

Wrapping Up

Writing code involves so much more than just code. Having set up your development environment, project, and IDE, you are now prepared to focus exclusively on making your code the best it can be.

By this point, you should have assembled a Python development workbench worthy of any production-level project. At minimum, you should have installed the Python interpreter, pip, venv, one or more static analyzers, and a Python code editor.

Right now, in your code editor or IDE, create a *FiringRange* project for experimenting in while working through this book. For the moment, to be sure everything works, you can make a single Python file in that project with these contents:

```
#!/usr/bin/env python3

print("Hello, world!")
```

Listing 2-11: hello_world.py

Run that like this:

```
python3 hello_world.py
```

You should see the following output:

```
Hello, world!
```

I'll go into the correct structure for Python projects in Chapter 4, but writing and running individual Python files in your firing range project should be sufficient for Chapter 3.

If you're new to the IDE you have selected, take a few minutes now to familiarize yourself with it. You should particularly ensure you know how to navigate and run code, manage files, work with virtual environments, access the interactive console, and use the static analyzers.

3

SYNTAX CRASH COURSE

Python is an unusual mix of common and unique concepts. Before diving into the intricacies of the language, you must first grasp its essential syntax.

In this chapter, you'll learn most of the essential syntactic structures you'll encounter in Python, and you'll also become familiar with the basic mathematical and logical features of the language.

Most Python developers will point newcomers to the official Python tutorial, which is an excellent introduction to the language's structure. While I'll cover all of these concepts in this book in depth, the tutorial is still a good resource worth reading: *https://docs.python.org/3/tutorial/*.

Hello, World!

It won't feel like a proper introduction to the language without the classic Hello World program. In Python, it's written like this:

```
print("Hello, world")
```

Listing 3-1: hello_world.py

There's nothing novel here. You call the print() function to write text to the console, and you pass data in a string, wrapped in quotes as an argument. You can pass whatever sort of data you like, and it will be output on the console.

I can also get input from the console with the input() function:

```
name = input(❶ "What is your name? ")
print("Hello, " + name)
```

Listing 3-2: hello_input.py

I use the input() function and pass my prompt as a string ❶. When I run that code, Python greets me using the name I entered on the console.

Statements and Expression

Each line of code in Python that ends with a line break is a *statement*, sometimes more specifically known as a *simple statement*. Unlike in many C-inspired languages, you don't need to end a line in Python with a special character.

A section of code that evaluates to a single value is called an *expression*. In Python, you can put expressions nearly anywhere a value is expected. The expression is evaluated down to a value, and that value is used in that position in the statement.

For example, in one statement, I can create a variable, and in another statement, I can print its contents to the console:

```
message = "Hello, world!"
print(message)
```

Listing 3-3: hello_statements.py:1a

I assign the expression "Hello, world!" to message, and then I pass the expression message to print().

If you ever need to place multiple statements on the same line, you can separate them with a semicolon (;). To demonstrate this, here are the same two statements as earlier, but packed onto one line, with a semicolon to separate them:

```
message = "Hello, world!"; print(message)
```

Listing 3-4: hello_statements.py:1b

While this is valid code, using this technique is somewhat discouraged. The Python philosophy places a high value on readability, and the placement of multiple statements on the same line often detracts from that.

Stick to placing one statement per line, unless you have a specific reason to do otherwise.

The Importance of Whitespace

When you're looking at a sample of Python source code, the first thing that will probably jump out at you is the use of indentation for nesting. A *compound statement* is made up of one or more *clauses*, each of which consists of a line of code called a *header* and a block of code called a *suite*, which is associated with the header.

For example, this program prints different messages, depending on whether a name is specified:

```
name = "Jason"
❶ if name != "":
    message = "Hello, " + name + "!"
    print(message)
❷ print("I am a computer.")
```

Listing 3-5: hello_conditional.py

I set up a conditional statement with an if header ❶, after which I have a suite made up of two indented lines of code, which "belongs" to the header. These lines of code are executed only if the conditional expression in the header is evaluated to True.

The unindented line ❷ is not part of the suite that belongs to the conditional statement, and it will be run every time.

As I nest deeper, I need to add more indentation:

```
raining = True
hailing = False
if raining:
    if hailing:
        print("NOPE")
    else:
        print("Umbrella time.")
```

Listing 3-6: weather_nested_conditional.py

The first print statement is indented twice, which is how Python knows that it belongs to both preceding conditional statements.

Given the importance of whitespace, the "tabs versus spaces" war is fairly common in Python world. You'll remember from Chapter 2 that the PEP 8 style guide stresses using either four spaces or a single tab per indentation level. **Consistency is key!** Python really doesn't care whether you use tabs, two spaces, four spaces, or even seven spaces (although that's probably a step too far) for each level of indentation. The point is to be consistent within any and every given block of code.

You should use only one indentation style throughout your project, even if your situation provides a technical loophole. Don't mix tabs and spaces. Chances are your IDE has tools to help you with this.

For simplicity's sake, I'll use the PEP 8 convention of four spaces throughout my code examples. While I'd recommend you follow this same convention—you can even configure your editor to insert four spaces each time you hit the TAB key—if you have a strong preference for tabs, you're welcome to use those instead. It really doesn't matter.

Doing Nothing

On occasion, you will need to insert a statement that has absolutely no effect. This is particularly useful when you need to put a syntactically valid placeholder where a suite of code will exist later. For this purpose, Python provides the pass keyword.

For example, I can employ the pass keyword as a placeholder in my if raining conditional, until I'm able to write the final code:

```
raining = True
if raining:
    pass
```

Listing 3-7: raining_pass.py

Just remember, pass does absolutely nothing. That's the only reason it exists.

Comments and Docstrings

To write comments in Python, precede the line with a hash (#). Everything between the hash and the end of the line is a comment and will be ignored by the interpreter.

```
# This is a comment
print("Hello, world!")
print("How are you?") ❶ # This is an inline comment.
# Here's another comment
# And another
# And...you get the idea
```

Listing 3-8: comments.py

If you ran this program, the print statements would both execute. The rest of the second print statement, from the hash onward, is an inline comment ❶ and would be ignored by the interpreter. All the other lines are only comments.

Docstrings

Officially, there is no syntax for "multiline" comments; you just comment each line. There is one special exception: the *docstring*. It looks like this:

```
def make_tea():
    """Will produce a concoction almost,
    but not entirely unlike tea.
    """
    #  ...function logic...
```

Listing 3-9: docstrings.py:1

I define a function that would (theoretically) make tea, and I place the description of the function inside a docstring.

Docstrings exist to provide documentation for functions, classes, and modules, especially public ones. They conventionally begin and end with three quotation marks ("""), allowing the string to automatically span multiple lines. You would typically place docstrings at the top, inside of whatever they're defining, such as in the function above.

PEDANTIC NOTE   You can use any string literal as a docstring, but the standard is to only use triple quotes. See PEP 257.

There are three important distinctions between comments and docstrings:

1. Docstrings are string literals, and they are seen by the interpreter; comments are ignored.
2. Docstrings are used in automatic documentation generation.
3. Docstrings are generally only docstrings when they appear at the top of the module, function, class, or method they define. Comments can live anywhere.

It is perfectly possible to use a triple-quoted string literal to write a sort of "multiline comment," but it's not recommended, since a string literal can easily get left in a place where Python will try to use it as a value.

In short, use docstrings as intended, and stick with comments for everything else. Many Python IDEs have hotkeys for toggling comments on a selection, which can save you a lot of time.

I can access these docstrings later in my code. For instance, given the previous example, I can do this:

```
print(make_tea.__doc__)  # This always works.
help(make_tea)           # Intended for use in the interactive shell.
```

Listing 3-10: docstrings.py:2

Docstrings have their own style conventions, which are outlined in depth in PEP 257.

Declaring Variables

You may have already noticed that Python doesn't have a distinct keyword for declaring a new variable (technically called a *name* in this language; see Chapter 5). Here, I define two variables—name and points:

```
name = "Jason"
points = 4571
print(name)   # displays "Jason"
print(points) # displays 4571
points = 42
print(points) # displays 42
```

Listing 3-11: variables.py

Python is *dynamically typed*, meaning the data type of a value is determined when it is evaluated. This contrasts with statically typed languages, in which you declare the data type initially. (C++ and Java are both statically typed.)

With Python, you can assign a value to a name anytime, by using the assignment operator (=). It infers the data type. If the name is a new variable, Python will create it; if the name already exists, Python will change the value. It's a pretty straightforward system.

In general, there are only two rules to follow with Python variables:

1. Define a variable before you access it; otherwise, you'll get an error.
2. Don't change what kind of data you're storing in the variable, even when replacing a value.

Python is considered a *strongly typed language*, meaning you usually can't magically combine data of different types. For example, it won't allow you to add an integer and a string together. On the other hand, *weakly typed* languages let you do practically anything with different data types, and they try to figure out how to do what you asked for. (JavaScript is weakly typed.) There's an entire spectrum between those last two terms and plenty of debate about what behaviors qualify under which name. While Python is decidedly in the "strongly typed" camp, it still has weaker typing than some languages.

Python is, however, *weakly bound*, so it is possible to assign a value of a different type to an existing variable. While this is technically permissible, it is strongly discouraged, as it can produce confusing code.

What About Constants?

Python doesn't have any formally defined constants. In keeping with PEP 8, you would indicate a variable is intended to be treated as a constant by using all-caps names with underscores. This naming convention is sometimes humorously referred to as *screaming snake case* for the all-caps (screaming) and the underscores (snakes). For example, the name INTEREST_RATE indicates that you don't want the variable redefined or changed in any way. While the interpreter itself won't prevent the variable from being modified, your linter will usually complain if you do.

Mathematics

Python has all the math functionality you would expect from a good programming language; its excellent support for both simple and complicated mathematics is one of the reasons Python is popular for scientific programming, data processing, and statistical analysis.

Meet the Number Types

Before I get into the operations, you should be aware of the three data types used for storing numbers.

Integers (`int`) store whole numbers. In Python, integers are always signed and effectively have no maximum value. Integers use decimal base (base-10) by default, but they can also be specified in binary (`0b101010`), octal (`0o52`), or hexadecimal (`0x2A`).

Floating-point numbers (`float`) store numbers with a decimal part (for example, `3.141592`). You can also use scientific notation (for example, `2.49e4`). Internally, values are stored as double-precision, IEEE 754 floating-point numbers, which are subject to the limits inherent in that format. (For more insight into the limits and gotchas of floating-point arithmetic, read the article "What Every Computer Scientist Should Know About Floating-Point Arithmetic" by David Goldberg: *https://docs.oracle.com/cd/E19957-01/806-3568/ncg_goldberg.html*.)

You can also specify an invalid number with `float("nan")`, a number larger than the largest possible value with `float("inf")`, or a number smaller than the smallest possible value with `float("-inf")`.

Notice that I wrapped the special values in quotes. This is necessary if you want to use these values without *importing* the `math` module (see Chapter 4 for more about importing). If you have imported the `math` module (see "The `math` Module" subsection below), you can use the constants `nan`, `inf`, and so forth, instead of the quoted versions.

Complex numbers (`complex`) can store imaginary numbers by appending `j` to the value, as in `42j`. You can combine a real part with the imaginary part, using addition: `24+42j`.

In case you missed it in math class, an imaginary number has the square root of negative one as one of its factors, even though this value is utterly impossible; there is no value that you can multiply by itself to get negative one! Yet imaginary numbers definitely show up in real-world math. Spooky, no?

Decimal and *Fraction* are two of the additional object types for storing numeric data. `Decimal` stores fixed-point decimal numbers, while `Fraction` does the same for fractions. To use either, you'll need to import them first.

Here's a brief example that uses both types:

```
from decimal import Decimal
from fractions import Fraction

third_fraction = Fraction(1, 3)
third_fixed = Decimal("0.333")
third_float = 1 / 3

print(third_fraction)  # 1/3
print(third_fixed)     # 0.333
print(third_float)     # 0.3333333333333333

third_float = float(third_fraction)
print(third_float)     # 0.3333333333333333

third_float = float(third_fixed)
print(third_float)     # 0.333
```

Listing 3-12: fractions_and_decimals.py

The float() function turns Fraction and Decimal objects into floats.

Operators

Python has the usual operators, with a couple of additions that may not be familiar to some developers.

Here's a bit of code that will demonstrate the math operators. I'll wrap each equation inside a print() statement, so you can run the code and see the results:

```
print(-42)          # negative (unary), evaluates to -42
print(abs(-42))     # absolute value, evaluates to 42
print(40 + 2)       # addition, evaluates to 42
print(44 - 2)       # subtraction, evaluates to 42
print(21 * 2)       # multiplication, evaluates to 42
print(680 / 16)     # division, evaluates to 42.5
print(680 // 16)    # floor division (discard remainder), evaluates to 42
print(1234 % 149)   # modulo, evaluates to 42
print(7 ** 2)       # exponent, evaluates to 49
print((9 + 5) * 3)  # parentheses, evaluates to 42
```

Listing 3-13: math_operators.py

The *unary* (one-operand) negative operator flips the sign of whatever follows it. The abs() function is technically considered a unary operator as well. The rest of the operators here are *binary*, meaning they accept two operands.

There's also a unary + operator, purely so statements like +4 are syntactically valid. It doesn't actually have an effect on any of the built-in types. The statements +-3 and -+3 would both produce the value -3.

In addition to the common arithmetic operators, Python offers *augmented assignment operators*, sometimes informally called *compound assignment operators*. These allow you to perform an operation with the current value of the variable as the left operand.

```
foo = 10
foo += 10    # value is now 20 (10 + 10)
foo -= 5     # value is now 15 (20 - 5)
foo *= 16    # value is now 240 (15 * 16)
foo //= 5    # value is now 48 (240 // 5)
foo /= 4     # value is now 12.0 (48 / 4)
foo **= 2    # value is now 144.0 (12.0 ** 2)
foo %= 51    # value is now 42.0 (144.0 % 15)
```

Listing 3-14: augmented_assignment_operators.py

If you need both floor division (//) and modulo (%) on the same operands, Python provides the divmod() function to efficiently perform the calculation, returning the two results in a tuple. Thus, c = divmod(a, b) is the same as c = (a // b, a % b).

Python also has bitwise operators, which I'll list below for those readers already familiar with bitwise arithmetic. I won't introduce these concepts until Chapter 12:

```
print(9 & 8)     # bitwise AND, evaluates to 8
print(9 | 8)     # bitwise OR, evaluates to 9
print(9 ^ 8)     # bitwise XOR, evaluates to 1
print(~8)        # unary bitwise ones complement (flip), evaluates to -9
print(1 << 3)    # bitwise left shift, evaluates to 8
print(8 >> 3)    # bitwise right shift, evaluates to 1
```

Listing 3-15: bitwise_operators.py

Python also has a binary operator for matrix multiplication, @, although none of the built-in types support it. If you have variables that support this operator, you can use it via x @ y. The related augmented assignment @= also exists.

The math Module

Python provides plenty of additional functions in the math module, along with the five most common math constants: pi, tau, e, inf, and nan.

```
import math

print(math.pi)    # PI
print(math.tau)   # TAU
```

```
print(math.e)     # Euler's number
print(math.inf)   # Infinity
print(math.nan)   # Not-a-Number

infinity_1 = float('inf')
infinity_2 = ❶ math.inf
print(infinity_1 == infinity_2)  # prints True
```

Listing 3-16: math_constants.py

All five constants are floats and can be directly used as such ❶. The official documentation provides a complete list of everything available in the math module.

You might remember a little trick from high school trigonometry, where you could calculate the height of something using your distance to it and the angle from your vantage point to the top of the object. Here's a way to calculate that with Python, using the math module:

```
import math

distance_ft = 65  # the distance to the object
angle_deg = 74    # the angle to the top of the object

# Convert from degrees to radians
angle_rad = ❶ math.radians(angle_deg)
# Calculate the height of the object
height_ft = distance_ft * ❷ math.tan(angle_rad)
# Round to one decimal place
height_ft = ❸ round(height_ft, 1)

print(height_ft)  # outputs 226.7
```

Listing 3-17: surveying_height.py

I use two functions from the math module: math.radians() ❶ and math .tan() ❷. The round() function ❸ is built into the language itself.

GOTCHA ALERT   The round() function can behave in surprising ways with floats, because of how floating-point numbers are stored. You may consider using string formatting instead.

Logic

Python's clean, obvious syntax for logical expressions is one of the attractive elements of the language. Here, I'll cover conditional statements and expressions, as well as the comparison and logic operators.

Conditionals

Conditionals are compound statements composed of if, elif, and else clauses, each made up of a header and a suite. As with most languages, you can have as many elif conditionals in Python as you want, sandwiched between if and (optionally) else. Here's a really simple example:

```python
command = "greet"

if command == "greet":
    print("Hello!")
elif command == "exit":
    print("Goodbye")
else:
    print("I don't understand.")
```

Listing 3-18: conditional_greet.py

This conditional statement is made up of three clauses. The if clause evaluates first, and if the expression in its header evaluates to True, its suite runs, printing "Hello!" Otherwise, it evaluates the expression in the elif header next. If none of the expressions evaluate to True, then the else clause runs.

You'll notice you don't need to wrap the conditional expressions, such as command == "greet", in parentheses, although you may do so anyway if it helps clarify your code. You'll see an example of this shortly.

If you're looking for something similar to the switch statement from your favorite programming language, see the "Structural Pattern Matching" section toward the end of this chapter.

Comparison Operators

Python has all the comparison operators you'd expect. Take a look at these in the context of comparing two integers:

```python
score = 98
high_score = 100

print(score == high_score)  # equals, evaluates to False
print(score != high_score)  # not equals, evaluates to True
print(score < high_score)   # less than, evaluates to True
print(score <= high_score)  # less than or equals, evaluates to True
print(score > high_score)   # greater than, evaluates to False
print(score >= high_score)  # greater than or equals, evaluates to False
```

Listing 3-19: comparison_operators.py

As you can see, Python has operators for equals, not equals, less than, less than or equals, greater than, and greater than or equals.

No surprises there, but what about boolean comparisons? This is where Python takes a different line.

Boolean, None, and Identity Operators

Python offers the values True and False, which are the two values for boolean (type bool) variables. It also has a dedicated None value (type NoneType), which serves in the capacity of a "null" value.

You check for these values in a very different way than with other data types. Instead of the comparison operators, use the special *identity operator* is. (I'll also use the logical operator not below, which I'll discuss separately in a bit.)

Here's an example:

```
spam = True
eggs = False
potatoes = None

if spam is True:          # Evaluates to True
    print("We have spam.")

if spam is not False:     # Evaluates to True
    print("I DON'T LIKE SPAM!")

❶ if spam:                 # Implicitly evaluates to True (preferred)
    print("Spam, spam, spam, spam...")


if eggs is False:         # Evaluates to True
    print("We're all out of eggs.")

if eggs is not True:      # Evaluates to True
    print("No eggs, but we have spam, spam, spam, spam...")

❷ if not eggs:             # Implicitly evaluates to True (preferred)
    print("Would you like spam instead?")


if potatoes is not None:  # Evaluates to False (preferred)
    print("Yum")          # We never reach this...potatoes is None!

if potatoes is None:      # Evaluates to True (preferred)
    print("Yes, we have no potatoes.")


❸ if eggs is spam:         # Evaluates to False (CAUTION!!!)
    print("This won't work.")
```

Listing 3-20: boolean_identity_operators.py

Aside from being a little high in sodium, that code shows the many ways of testing boolean values and checking for None.

You can test if a variable is set to True, False, or None by comparing with the is operator. You can also invert the logic with is not.

Most commonly, when testing against True, you can use the variable as the entire condition ❶. For False, invert that condition test with not ❷.

Take particular note of the last condition, which illustrates an important gotcha with the is operator ❸. It actually compares the identity of the variables, rather than the value. This is particularly troublesome, as the logic looks sound but is a bug waiting for a place to happen. That probably doesn't mean much to you yet, but rest assured, I'll cover this concept in depth in Chapter 5.

For now, you can take this rule for granted: use is *only* for comparing directly to None, and use regular comparison operators for everything else. In practice, we usually say if spam or if not spam, instead of directly comparing to True or False.

Truthiness

Most expressions and values in Python can be evaluated to a True or False value. This is typically done by using the value as an expression by itself, although you can also pass it to the bool() function to convert it explicitly.

```
answer = 42

if answer:
    print("Evaluated to True")   # this runs

print(bool(answer))              # prints True
```

Listing 3-21: truthiness.py

When an expression will evaluate to True, it is considered "truthy." When it will evaluate to False, it is "falsey." The None constant, values representing zero, and empty collections are all considered "falsey," while most other values are "truthy."

Logical Operators

If you're coming from a language where logical operators are a little more difficult to remember, you'll find Python refreshing: it simply uses the keywords and, or, and not!

```
spam = True
eggs = False

if spam and eggs:        # AND operator, evaluates to False
    print("I do not like green eggs and spam.")

if spam or eggs:         # OR operator, evaluates to True
    print("Here's your meal.")
```

```
if (not eggs) and spam:  # NOT (and AND) operators, evaluates to True
    print("But I DON'T LIKE SPAM!")
```

Listing 3-22: logical_operators.py

With the and condition, both expressions must evaluate to True. With the or condition, one or the other (or both) must evaluate to True. The third condition adds not to the picture, requiring that eggs be False and spam be True.

I could have omitted the parentheses on the third condition, as not takes precedence and so is evaluated before and. However, the parentheses help to clarify my intended logic.

In practice, you can use the not keyword to invert any conditional expression, such as in the following:

```
score = 98
high_score = 100
print(score != high_score)      # not equals operator, evaluates to True
print(not score == high_score)  # not operator, evaluates to True
```

Listing 3-23: not_operators.py

Both comparisons do the same thing; the issue becomes readability. In this case, the expression using not is less readable because your eyes might skip over the not keyword, so you might not catch what's happening in the code. The condition employing the != operator is preferred for readability. While you might find situations where not is the best way to invert your conditional logic, remember The Zen of Python: ***Readability counts!***

The Walrus Operator

Python 3.8 introduced *assignment expressions*, which allow you to assign a value to a variable and use that variable in another expression at the same time. This is possible with the so-called *walrus operator* (:=).

```
if (eggs := 7 + 5) == 12:
    print("We have one dozen eggs")

print(eggs)  # prints 12
```

Listing 3-24: walrus.py

With the walrus operator, Python first evaluates the expression on the left (7+5) and then assigns it to the variable eggs. The assignment expression is enclosed in parentheses for readability, although I technically could have omitted them.

The assignment expression is then evaluated to a single value, namely the value of eggs, which is used in the comparison. Since the value is 12, the condition evaluates to True.

What's interesting about the assignment expression is that eggs is now a valid variable in the outer scope, so I can print its value outside of the conditional.

This feature is potentially useful in many scenarios, not only in conditional expressions, as above.

Assignment expressions and the walrus operator were defined in PEP 572, which also contains an in-depth discussion about when and where this feature should be used. Two particularly useful style rules are put forth by this PEP:

- If either assignment statements or assignment expressions can be used, then prefer statements; they are clear declarations of intent.
- If using assignment expressions would lead to ambiguity about execution order, then restructure to use statements instead.

As of the writing of this book, Python assignment expressions are still in their infancy. A lot of debate and controversy still surrounds them. In any case, resist the temptation to abuse the walrus operator to cram as much logic onto one line as possible. You should always aim for readability and clarity in your code, above all else.

Ellipsis

One seldom-used piece of syntax is the *Ellipsis*:

```
...
```

This is sometimes used by various libraries and modules, but seldom consistently. For example, it's used with multidimensional arrays in the NumPy third-party library and when working with type hints from the built-in typing module. When you see it come up, consult the documentation for whatever module you're using.

Strings

There are a few things to know about strings as you move forward. Here, I'll cover the three kinds of strings: string literals, raw strings, and formatted strings.

String Literals

There are multiple ways of defining a *string literal*:

```
danger = "Cuidado, llamas!"
danger = 'Cuidado, llamas!'
danger = '''Cuidado, llamas!'''
danger = """Cuidado, llamas!"""
```

Listing 3-25: string_literals.py

You can wrap a literal in double quotes ("), single quotes ('), or triple quotes (""") of either type. You may remember from earlier that there's something special about triple quotes, but I'll come back to that in a moment.

PEP 8 addresses the use of single and double quotes:

> In Python, single-quoted strings and double-quoted strings are the same. This PEP does not make a recommendation for this. Pick a rule and stick to it. When a string contains single or double quote characters, however, use the other one to avoid backslashes in the string. It improves readability.

The advice about placing quotes inside a string comes in handy when dealing with something like this:

```
quote = "Shout \"Cuidado, llamas!\""
```

Listing 3-26: escaping_quotes.py:1a

This version escapes the double quotes I want to include in the string literal itself. The backslash (\) before the quotes means I want the string to contain that *literal character*, not to have Python treat the double quote as the boundary of a string. The string literal must always be wrapped in matching quotes.

It is possible to avoid backslashes in this scenario, however:

```
quote = 'Shout, "Cuidado, llamas!"'
```

Listing 3-27: escaping_quotes.py:1b

This second version wraps the literal in single quotes, so the double quotes will be automatically interpreted as part of the string literal. That approach is much more readable. By wrapping the string in single quotes, Python will assume the double quotes are characters in the string.

The only time you'd really need to escape either single or double quotes with backslashes would be if you had both types of quotes in the string at once:

```
question = "What do you mean, \"it's fine\"?"
```

Listing 3-28: escaping_quotes.py:2a

Personally, in cases like that, I'd prefer to use (and escape) the double quotes, because they don't evade my attention like an apostrophe would tend to do.

You also have the option to use triple quotes:

```
question = """What do you mean, "it's fine"?"""
```

Listing 3-29: escaping_quotes.py:2b

Remember that triple quotes define *multiline string literals*. In other words, I can use them to do this:

```
❶ parrot = """\
This parrot is no more!
He has ceased to be!
He's expired
    and gone to meet his maker!
He's a stiff!
Bereft of life,
    he rests in peace!"""

print(parrot)
```

Listing 3-30: multiline_string.py

Everything, including newlines and leading whitespace, is literal in triple quotes. If I print("parrot"), it will display exactly like this in the terminal.

The only exception occurs when you use a backslash (\) to escape a particular character, like I did with that newline at the beginning ❶. It is conventional to escape the first newline after the opening triple quotes, just to make the code look cleaner.

The built-in textwrap module has some functions for working with multiline strings, including tools that allow you remove leading indentation (textwrap.dedent).

Alternatively, you can *concatenate* (combine) string literals, simply by writing them next to one another, without any operators between them. For example, spam = "Hello " "world" "!" is valid, resulting in the string Hello world!. If you wrap the assignment expression in parentheses, you can even span multiple lines.

Raw Strings

Raw strings constitute another form of string literal, wherein the backslash (\) is always treated as a literal character. They're preceded with an r, such as in this example:

```
print(r"I love backslashes: \ Aren't they cool?")
```

Listing 3-31: raw_string.py

The backslash is treated like a literal character, which means that nothing can be escaped inside of a raw string. The output of that line of code looks like this:

```
I love backslashes: \ Aren't they cool?
```

This has implications for what type of quotes you use, so beware.

Compare these two lines and their outputs:

```
print("A\nB")
print(r"A\nB")
```

Listing 3-32: raw_or_not.py

The first string is ordinary, so \n is treated as a normal escape sequence: specifically, the newline character. That line break appears in the output, like this:

```
A
B
```

The second string is a raw string, so the backslash (\) is treated as a literal character in its own right. The output would be as follows:

```
A\nB
```

This is particularly useful for regular expression patterns, where you're likely to have plenty of backslashes that you want as part of the *pattern*, not interpreted by Python before it gets there. ***Always use raw strings for regular expression patterns.***

GOTCHA ALERT If the backslash (\) is the last character in your raw string, it'll still act to escape out your closing quote and create a syntax error as a result. That has to do with Python's own language lexing rules, not with strings.

Formatted Strings

A third kind of string literal is a *formatted string* or *f-string*, which is new as of Python 3.6 (defined in PEP 498). It allows you to insert the values of variables into a string in a very elegant manner.

If I wanted to include the value of a variable in a string without an f-string, the code might look like this:

```
in_stock = 0
print("This cheese shop has " + str(in_stock) + " types of cheese.")
```

Listing 3-33: cheese_shop.py:1a

The str() function converts the value passed to it into a string, and then the three strings are *concatenated*, or combined, into one, using the + operator.

Using f-strings, this code becomes more elegant.

```
in_stock = 0
print(f"This cheese shop has {in_stock} types of cheese.")
```

Listing 3-34: cheese_shop.py:1b

You precede the string literal with an f. Inside, you can substitute a variable by wrapping it in curly braces ({ }). The f tells Python to interpret and evaluate as an expression anything in the string that's wrapped in curly braces. This means you're not limited to variables in those curly braces. You can put just about any valid Python code in there, including math, function calls, conditional expressions, or whatever you need.

As of Python 3.8, you can even display both the expression *and* its result by appending a trailing equal sign (=).

```python
print(f"{5+5=}")  # prints "5+5=10"
```

Listing 3-35: expression_fstring.py

There are a couple of gotchas when using f-strings:

First, if you want to wrap an expression in literal curly braces, you must use two curly braces ({{ }}) for every one you want displayed:

```python
answer = 42
print(f"{{answer}}")            # prints "{42}"
print(f"{{{{answer}}}}")        # prints "{{42}}"
print(f"{{{{{{answer}}}}}}")    # prints "{{{42}}}"
```

Listing 3-36: literal_curly_braces.py

If you have an odd number of braces, one pair will be ignored. So, if I used five pairs, the result would be the same as if I only had four: two literal pairs would be printed.

Second, you cannot use backslashes within an expression in an f-string. This makes it difficult to escape quotes inside expressions. For example, this would not work:

```python
print(f"{ord('\"')}")      # SyntaxError
```

To get around this, I'd need to use triple quotes on the outside of the string, to ensure I can employ both single and double quotes inside of the expression.

```python
print(f"""{ord('"')}""")  # prints "34"
```

Backslashes have other roles. The documentation points out the following problematic situation:

```python
print(f"{ord('\n')}")      # SyntaxError
```

There's no direct way around this limitation. Instead, you'd have to evaluate that expression in advance, assign the result to a name, and use it in the f-string.

```python
newline_ord = ord('\n')
print(f"{newline_ord}")    # prints "10"
```

Third, and perhaps least surprising, you cannot put comments inside of f-string expressions; the hash (#) symbol isn't allowed, except as a string literal.

```
print(f"{# a comment}")   # SyntaxError
print(f"{ord('#')}")      # OK, prints "35"
```

Lastly, you can never use f-strings as docstrings.

These small wrinkles aside, f-strings are incredibly straightforward to work with.

Format Specifications

Besides arbitrary expressions, f-strings support *format specifications*, which allow you to control how values are displayed. This is a fairly in-depth topic that could easily become a main section on its own, so I will entrust you to the guidance of the documentation for the bulk of it. I'll breeze over the essentials herein.

Immediately after the expression, you may choose to include one of three special flags: !r, !a, or !s (although that last one is the default behavior, so it can be omitted in most cases). These determine which function is used to fetch the string representation of some value: repr(), ascii(), or str(), respectively (see "String Conversion" below).

Next comes the format specification itself, which always begins with a colon (:), followed by one or more flags. These have to be specified in a particular order to work, although any of them may be omitted if they're not desired:

Align An alignment flag, specifying left (<), right (>), center (^), or (if numeric) split with the sign aligned left but the digits aligned right (=). This is optionally preceded by a character that will be used to fill any blank space in the alignment.

Sign A flag controlling when the sign is displayed on a number. The plus (+) flag displays the sign on both positive and negative numbers, while the minus (-) flag only displays it on negative numbers. A third option is to show a leading space on positive numbers and a sign on negative numbers (SPACE).

Alternative form The hash (#) flag turns on the "alternative form," which has different meanings for different types (see documentation).

Leading zeros The zero (0) flag causes leading zeros to be displayed (unless a fill character is specified for alignment).

Width The width of the output string in characters. This is where the alignment comes into play.

Grouping A flag controlling whether numbers should separate thousands with a comma (,) or an underscore (_). If omitted, no separator is used. If enabled, the underscore separator also appears every four digits in octal, hexadecimal, and binary numbers.

Precision A dot (.), followed by an integer for decimal precision.

Type   A flag controlling how numbers are displayed; common options include binary (b), character (c), decimal (d), hexadecimal (x), exponent notation (e), fixed-point (f), and general (g). There are more (see documentation).

All that is a bit abstract, so here are a few quick examples:

```
spam = 1234.56789
print(f"{spam:=^+15,.2f}")    # prints "===+1,234.57==="

spam = 42
print(f"{spam:#07x}")         # prints "0x0002a"

spam = "Hi!"
print(f"{spam:-^20}")         # prints "--------Hi!---------"
```

Listing 3-37: formatting_strings.py

Complete details about the format specification can be found in the official Python documentation: *https://docs.python.org/3/library/string .html#format-string-syntax.*

Another useful reference is *https://pyformat.info*, although as of this writing, it only shows the format specification in the context of the old format() function. You will need to apply it to f-strings yourself.

Previous String-Formatting Methods

If you're reading older Python code, you may encounter the two previous forms of string formatting: % notation and the newer format(). These have both been superseded by f-strings, which have superior performance. That's because they're parsed and converted to bytecode *before* the code is run.

If you find yourself needing to rewrite a format() call as an f-string, the process is thankfully quite simple.

Here's an example. I'll start out with a couple of variables:

```
a = 42
b = 64
```

Listing 3-38: format_to_fstring.py:1

Before the advent of f-strings, if I wanted to print out a message containing the values of those two variables, I'd have used format():

```
print(❶ "{:#x} and {:#o}".format(❷ a, b))
```

Listing 3-39: format_to_fstring.py:2a

In the old format, a string literal ❶ would contain sets of curly braces, optionally containing the format specifications. The format() function would be called on that string literal (or on a name referencing it). Then, the expressions to be evaluated would be passed to the format() function in order ❷.

That would have the following output:

```
0x2a 0o100
```

Converting this to an f-string is as simple as moving the expressions into the string literal in order and then prepending an f to the literal to make it an f-string:

```
print(f"{a:#x} and {b:#o}")   # prints "0x2a 0o100"
```

Listing 3-40: format_to_fstring.py:2b

The output is the same as before.

Optionally, with `format()`, you could refer to the index of the expression in the argument list:

```
print("{0:d}={0:#x} | {1:d}={1:#x}".format(a, b))
```

Listing 3-41: format_to_fstring.py:3a

That produces this output:

```
42=0x2a | 64=0x40
```

To convert this code to an f-string, you substitute the expressions in place of the indices in the string literal, which you (again) turn into an f-string by prepending an f:

```
f"{a:d}={a:#x} | {b:d}={b:#x}"
```

Listing 3-42: format_to_fstring.py:3b

Converting from % notation is a little less trivial, but most Python 3 code uses `format()` anyway. If you find yourself needing to do this, *https://pyformat .info* does an excellent job of comparing % notation and `format()`.

Template Strings

Template strings constitute one more alternative to f-strings that is worth knowing about, especially as it still fulfills some use cases, including internationalizing user interfaces. Personally, I find template strings a bit more reusable. On the other hand, the drawback is that they're considerably more limited in terms of formatting.

If you know how they work, you'll be equipped to decide for yourself which tool is best for your particular situation.

Here's a template string for greeting a user:

```
from string import Template
```

Listing 3-43: template_string.py:1

To use template strings, I first have to import `Template` from the `string` module.

Then I can create a new `Template` and pass it a string literal:

```
s = Template("$greeting, $user!")
```

Listing 3-44: template_string.py:2

I can name my fields whatever I want, preceding each with a dollar sign ($).

Finally, I call the `substitute()` function on the template I created (s) and pass expressions to each of the fields:

```
print(s.substitute(greeting="Hi", user="Jason"))
```

Listing 3-45: template_string.py:3

The finished string is returned, and in this case, it is passed to `print()` and displayed:

```
Hi, Jason!
```

There are a couple of odd syntax rules with template strings. First, to show a literal dollar sign in the string literal, use two dollar signs ($$). Second, to substitute an expression as part of a word, wrap the name of the field in curly braces ({ }). Both of these rules are demonstrated below:

```
s = Template("A ${thing}ify subscription costs $$$price/mo.")
print(s.substitute(thing="Code", price=19.95))
```

Listing 3-46: template_string.py:4

That outputs the following:

```
A Codeify subscription costs $19.95/mo.
```

There's a handful of additional abilities contained within string templates, but I'll entrust you to the official Python documentation for the rest of that.

String Conversion

I previously mentioned that there are three ways to get the string representation of a value: `str()`, `repr()`, and `ascii()`.

The first function, `str()`, is the one you'll use most often, as it returns the *human-readable* representation of the value.

By contrast, `repr()` returns the *canonical string representation* of the value: that is, (usually) the value as Python sees it. In the case of many basic data types, this will return the same thing as `str()`, but when used on most objects, the output contains additional information useful in debugging.

The `ascii()` function is the same as `repr()`, except that the string literal it returns is completely ASCII-compatible, having escaped any non-ASCII (for example, Unicode) characters.

I'll return to this concept in Chapter 7, when I start defining my own objects.

A Note on String Concatenation

Up to this point, I've been using the addition (+) operator for concatenating strings together. This is acceptable in basic situations.

However, this is seldom the most efficient solution, especially when combining multiple strings. Therefore, it is recommended to prefer the join() method, which is called on a string or string literal instead.

Here's a comparison between the two. I start with a couple of string variables:

```
greeting = "Hello"
name = "Jason"
```

Listing 3-47: concat_strings.py:1

So far, you've seen concatenation with the addition (+) operator, like this:

```
message = greeting + ", " + name + "!"  # value is "Hello, Jason!"
print(message)
```

Listing 3-48: concat_strings.py:2a

Alternatively, I can use the join() method:

```
message = "".join((greeting, ", ", name, "!"))  # value is "Hello, Jason!"
print(message)
```

Listing 3-49: concat_strings.py:2b

I call the join() method on the string that will appear between each piece. In this case, I use an empty string. The join() method accepts a *tuple* of strings—an array-like structure wrapped in parentheses, and therefore, the double set of parentheses in the code. I'll introduce tuples in an upcoming section.

Typical concatenation with + or the join() function has the same result, but the latter function will be *as fast or faster*, especially when you're using other implementations of Python besides CPython. Therefore, whenever you need to concatenate and f-strings aren't right for the job, you should consider using join() instead of the + or += operators. In practice, f-strings are the fastest, but join() is your next-best option.

Functions

Python functions are *first-class citizens*, which means they can be treated like any other object. Even so, you call them as you would in any other programming language.

Here's an example of a very basic function, which prints a selected type of joke to the terminal.

I start with the function header:

```
def tell_joke(joke_type):
```

Listing 3-50: joke_function.py:1

I declared the function with the def keyword, followed by the name of the function. Parameters are named in the parentheses after the function name. The entire header is concluded with a colon (:).

Below the header, indented one level, is the *suite* (or body) of the function:

```
if joke_type == "funny":
    print("How can you tell an elephant is in your fridge?")
    print("There are footprints in the butter!")
elif joke_type == "lethal":
    print("Wenn ist das Nunstück git und Slotermeyer?")
    print("Ja! Beiherhund das Oder die Flipperwaldt gersput!")
else:
    print("Why did the chicken cross the road?")
    print("To get to the other side!")
```

Listing 3-51: joke_function.py:2

You call functions in much the same way as in most languages:

```
tell_joke("funny")
```

Listing 3-52: joke_function.py:3

I'll go into depth on functions and their many cousins in Chapter 6.

Classes and Objects

Python fully supports object-oriented programming. In fact, one of the language's design principles is that "everything is an object," at least behind the scenes.

There's a lot more to classes than meets the eye, but for now, you should just get an absolutely bare-bones familiarity with the syntax.

The following class contains a joke of a selected type and displays it on demand:

```
class Joke:
```

Listing 3-53: joke_class.py:1

I define the class using the class keyword, the name of the class, and a colon (:) at the end of the header.

This is followed by the suite of the class, indented one level:

```
def __init__(self, joke_type):
    if joke_type == "funny":
        self.question = "How can you tell an elephant is in your fridge?"
        self.answer = "There are footprints in the butter!"
    elif joke_type == "lethal":
        self.question = "Wenn ist das Nunstück git und Slotermeyer?"
        self.answer = "Ja! Beiherhund das Oder die Flipperwaldt gersput!"
    else:
        self.question = "Why did the chicken cross the road?"
        self.answer = "To get to the other side!"
```

Listing 3-54: joke_class.py:2

The initializer, which is similar in purpose to the constructor in other OOP languages, is a member function, or *method*, with the name __init__() and at least one parameter, self.

```
def tell(self):
    print(self.question)
    print(self.answer)
```

Listing 3-55: joke_class.py:3

Functions that belong to the class are called methods and are part of the class suite. Methods must accept at least one parameter: self.

You would use this class like so:

```
lethal_joke = Joke("lethal")
lethal_joke.tell()
```

Listing 3-56: joke_class.py:4

You create a new instance of the Joke class by passing the string "lethal" to its *initializer*, the __init__() from earlier. The new object is stored in the variable lethal_joke.

Then, you use the *dot operator* (.) to call the function tell() within the object. Take note that you didn't have to pass any argument for self. That's done automatically when you call the function in this manner.

I'll discuss classes and objects in detail in Chapter 7 and further in Chapter 13.

Error Handling

Python offers error and exception handling functionality through the try compound statement.

For example, if I wanted to get a number from the user, I couldn't reliably predict what they would type in. Trying to convert a string, like "spam", to an integer would cause an error. I can use error handling to take a different action if it isn't possible to convert the user input.

```
num_from_user = input("Enter a number: ")

try:
    num = int(num_from_user)
except ValueError:
    print("You didn't enter a valid number.")
    num = 0

print(f"Your number squared is {num**2}")
```

Listing 3-57: try_except.py

I get a string from the user, and then in the try clause, I attempt to convert it to an integer with the int() function. That would raise a ValueError exception if the string it's trying to convert is not a valid whole number (base 10).

If that exception is raised, I catch it in the except clause and handle the failure.

In any case, the last line would always be run.

There are additional features and subtleties to the try statement, including finally and else clauses, which I'll cover in Chapter 8. For now, it's better to avoid these concepts rather than use them incorrectly.

Tuples and Lists

Two of Python's most common built-in data structures, called *collections*, are tuples and lists.

Lists constitute the most array-like collection in Python. In CPython, they are implemented as variable-length arrays, not as linked lists like the name might suggest.

For example, here is a list of strings with names of cheeses:

```
cheeses = ["Red Leicester", "Tilsit", "Caerphilly", "Bel Paese"]
```

Listing 3-58: cheese_list.py:1

You enclose a list literal in square brackets, separating each item in the list with commas.

You can access or reassign the values of individual items with the same bracket notation used by most programming languages:

```
print(cheeses[1])  # prints "Tilsit"
cheeses[1] = "Cheddar"
print(cheeses[1])  # prints "Cheddar"
```

Listing 3-59: cheese_list.py:2

A *tuple* is somewhat similar to a list, but with a few key differences. First, a tuple cannot have items added, reassigned, or removed after its creation. Attempting to modify the contents of a tuple with bracket notation will result in a TypeError. This is because tuples, unlike lists, are *immutable*, effectively meaning their contents cannot be modified (see Chapter 5 for the full explanation).

Here is an example of a tuple:

```
answers = ("Sir Lancelot", "To seek the holy grail", 0x0000FF)
```

Listing 3-60: knight_tuple.py:1

You enclose tuple literals in parentheses (( )), instead of brackets ([ ]). Nevertheless, you still use bracket notation to access individual items:

```
print(answers[0])  # prints "Sir Lancelot"
```

Listing 3-61: knight_tuple.py:2

As I said, you cannot change the items of a tuple after creation, such as if you tried to reassign the first item:

```
answers[0] = "King Arthur"  # raises TypeError
```

Listing 3-62: knight_tuple.py:3

The guideline is to use tuples for collections of items of different types (*heterogeneous* collections) and to use lists for collections of items of the same type (*homogeneous* collections).

I'll discuss these collections, and many more, in Chapter 9.

Loops

Python has two basic loop types: *while* and *for*.

while Loop

The while loop probably looks familiar from other languages:

```
n = 0

while n < 10:
    n += 1
    print(n)
```

Listing 3-63: while_loop.py

I start the loop with the while keyword, follow it with the condition to test, and finish the header with a colon (:). As long as that condition evaluates to True, the code in the suite of the loop is executed.

When you need to keep running a loop until some condition is met, use while loops. These are particularly useful when you don't know how many iterations of the loop will take place before the condition is met.

Loop Control

You can manually control the loop, using two keywords. The `continue` keyword abandons the current iteration and jumps to the next one. The `break` keyword exits the loop altogether.

One common scenario where you may use these keywords is in an infinite loop used for running a game or a user interface. For example, here's a very simple command prompt:

```
while True:
    command = input("Enter command: ")
    if command == "exit":
        break
    elif command == "sing":
        print("La la LAAA")
        continue

    print("Command unknown.")
```

Listing 3-64: loop_control.py

The loop `while True` is inherently infinite; `True` is always `True`. That's the behavior I actually want here, since I want to keep iterating until the user enters the string `"exit"`, at which point, I manually end the loop with `break`. (By the way, if you've been waiting for a `do-while` loop, this is effectively the way to recreate that behavior.)

The command `"sing"` has a different behavior, after which I'd want to immediately go to the top and prompt the user for another command, skipping the last print statement. The `continue` keyword does exactly that, immediately abandoning the current iteration and jumping back to the top of the loop.

for Loop

Python's `for` loop is a little different from loops in many languages. It's generally used for iterating over a range, list, or other collection.

```
for i in range(1, 11):
    print(i)
```

Listing 3-65: for_loop.py

I start the loop header with the `for` keyword. Technically, this kind of loop is a `for-in` (or "for-each") loop, meaning the loop iterates once for each item in the given range, list, or other collection. This means the loop needs something to iterate over—in this case, a special object called range()— which iterates over a range of values, returning each one in turn. I've specified that I want the range to start with the value 1 and end before 11. The local variable i will refer to the current item for each iteration. Finally, the in keyword precedes the thing I'm iterating over—that is, before range() in this example.

As long as there are items to iterate over, the code belonging to the loop will be executed—in this case, printing out the value of the current item. The loop stops when the last item is iterated over.

Running this code would print the numbers 1 through 10.

This only scratches the surface of loops. See Chapter 9 for more.

Structural Pattern Matching

For many years, developers coming to Python from languages like C, C++, Java, or Javascript would ask if there was a Python equivalent to the switch/case statement (or match/case in Scala, case/when in Ruby, and so on). They'd always be disappointed to hear a resounding "No!" Python only had conditional statements.

At long last, Python 3.10 gained *structural pattern matching* via PEP 634. This provides conditional logic that is at least syntactically similar to switch statements of other languages. In short, you test a single *subject*, such as a variable, against one or more *patterns*. If the subject matches the pattern, the associated suite of code runs.

Literal Patterns and Wildcards

In the most basic use case, you can check a variable against different possible values. These are called *literal patterns*. For example, perhaps I want to display different messages, depending on a user's input lunch order:

```
lunch_order = input("What would you like for lunch? ")

match lunch_order:
    case 'pizza':
        print("Pizza time!")
    case 'sandwich':
        print("Here's your sandwich")
    case 'taco':
        print('Taco, taco, TACO, tacotacotaco!')
    case _:
        print("Yummy.")
```

Listing 3-66: pattern_match.py:1a

The value of lunch_order is compared to each case until it matches one. Once a match is found, the case's suite is run, and the match statement is finished; the value won't be checked against additional patterns once it matches one. So, if the user inputs **"pizza"**, the "Pizza time!" message is displayed. Similarly, if they input **"taco"**, the message "Taco, taco, TACO, tacotacotaco!" is displayed instead.

The underscore (_) in the last case is the *wildcard*, which will match any value. This serves as a fallback case, and it must come last, as it will match anything.

Despite their superficial similarity, match statements are not the same as a C or C++ switch statement. Python's match statements do not have jump tables, and they therefore have none of the potential performance gains of a switch. But don't feel too disappointed, as this also means they're not limited to working with integer types.

Or Patterns

A single case can cover multiple possible values. One way to do this is with an *or pattern*, where possible literal values are separated by the bar character:

```
lunch_order = input("What would you like for lunch? ")

match lunch_order:
    # --snip--
    case 'taco':
        print('Taco, taco, TACO, tacotacotaco!')
    case 'salad' | 'soup':
        print('Eating healthy, eh?')
    case _:
        print("Yummy.")
```

Listing 3-67: pattern_match.py:1b

This pattern will match if the user enters either **"salad"** or **"soup"** at the prompt.

Capture Patterns

One particularly helpful feature of structural pattern matching is the ability to capture part or all of the subject. For example, it isn't very helpful in our example that the fallback case only says "Yummy.". Instead, I'd like to have a default message announcing the user's selection. To do that, I write a *capture pattern* like this:

```
lunch_order = input("What would you like for lunch? ")

match lunch_order:
    # --snip--
    case 'salad' | 'soup':
        print('Eating healthy, eh?')
    case order:
        print(f"Enjoy your {order}.")
```

Listing 3-68: pattern_match.py:1c

This pattern acts like a wildcard, except the value of lunch_order is captured as order. Now, no matter what the user enters, if it doesn't match any of the previous patterns, the value will be captured and displayed in the message here.

Capture patterns don't just have to capture the entire value. For example, I can write a pattern that matches a tuple or list (a *sequence*) and then captures only part of that sequence:

```
lunch_order = input("What would you like for lunch? ")
if ' ' in lunch_order:
    lunch_order = lunch_order.split(maxsplit=1)

match lunch_order:
    case (flavor, 'ice cream'):
        print(f"Here's your very grown-up {flavor}...lunch.")
    # --snip--
```

Listing 3-69: pattern_match.py:1d

In this version, if the lunch order has a space, I split the string into two parts, which are stored in a list. Then, if the second item in the sequence has the value "ice cream", the first part is captured as flavor. Thus, the code can account for Bojan if he decides to break down and have strawberry ice cream for lunch. (And I'm not stopping him!)

The capture pattern feature has one surprising downside: all *unqualified* names in patterns—that is, any bare variable names with no dots—will be used to capture. This means that if you want to use the value assigned to some variable, it must be *qualified*, meaning you must access it within some class or module with the dot operator:

```
class Special:
    TODAY = 'lasagna'

lunch_order = input("What would you like for lunch? ")

match lunch_order:
    case Special.TODAY:
        print("Today's special is awesome!")
    case 'pizza':
        print("Pizza time!")
    # --snip--
```

Listing 3-70: pattern_match.py:1e

Guard Statements

One last trick I'll demonstrate with pattern matching is the *guard statement*, an additional conditional statement that must be satisfied for a pattern to match.

For example, in the current version of my lunch order example, using the logic to split the order by spaces means the code doesn't behave very nicely with other foods with spaces in them. Also, if I enter **"rocky road ice cream"**, it won't match the current ice cream pattern.

Instead of splitting my string by spaces, I can write a pattern with a guard statement that looks for the words *ice cream* in the lunch order.

```
class Special:
    TODAY = 'lasagna'

lunch_order = input("What would you like for lunch? ")

match lunch_order:
    # --snip--
    case 'salad' | 'soup':
        print('Eating healthy, eh?')
    case ice_cream if 'ice cream' in ice_cream:
        flavor = ice_cream.replace('ice cream', '').strip()
        print(f"Here's your very grown-up {flavor}...lunch.")
    case order:
        print(f"Enjoy your {order}.")
```

Listing 3-71: pattern_match_object.py:1f

The pattern here captures the value as ice_cream, but only if the guard statement if 'ice cream' in ice_cream is satisfied. In that case, I use .replace() to remove the words *ice cream* from the captured value, leaving me with only the name of the flavor. I also use .strip() to remove any leading or trailing whitespace from the new string. Finally, I print out my message.

More About Structural Pattern Matching

There are quite a few other tricks and techniques that work with structural pattern matching. They work with objects (see Chapter 7), with dictionaries via mapping patterns (see Chapter 9), and even by support nesting patterns within other patterns.

As with many Python techniques, pattern matching feels like "magic," and there's a strong temptation to use it everywhere possible. Resist this urge! Structural pattern matching is very useful for checking a single subject against multiple possible patterns, but as you can even see from the "ice cream" situation in the lunch order example, it quickly reaches its limits as the possible values of the subject get more elaborate. As a rule, if you're unsure whether you need structural pattern matching in a particular situation, stick with conditional statements.

To learn even more, read PEP 636, which serves as the official tutorial for this topic and demonstrates all of the functionality available with this language feature: *https://peps.python.org/pep-0636/*.

Wrapping Up

You should now have a feeling for Python's syntax and a basic familiarity with its key structures. If you were to stop here, you could probably write Python code that at least works. In fact, many developers new to the language do indeed work with about this much information, implicitly bringing the habits and practices of whatever language they know best.

There is a profound difference between valid code and idiomatic, Pythonic code. Writing the latter is the focus of this book.

4

PROJECT STRUCTURE AND IMPORTS

I've found that structuring a Python project is one of the most often overlooked components of teaching the language. Many developers therefore get their project structure wrong, stumbling through a jumble of common mistakes until they arrive at something that at least works.

Here's the good news: you don't have to be one of them!

In this chapter, I'll introduce import statements, modules, and packages, and I'll show you how to fit everything together without tearing your hair out.

Be aware, I'm skipping over one critical piece of project structure in this chapter: *setup.cfg*, as it relies on concepts we haven't yet covered. Without a *setup.cfg* or *setup.py* file, your project will not be ready to ship to end users. In this chapter, you'll put everything in the right place for development. From there, preparing your project for distribution will be a fairly simple process. I'll cover *setup.cfg*, *setup.py*, and other project structure issues relating to distribution in Chapter 18.

Setting Up the Repository

Before delving into the actual project structure, I want to address how it will fit into your *version control system (VCS)*, which I recommend using. For the rest of this book, I'll assume you're using Git, as that's the most common option.

Once you've created your repository and cloned a local copy to your computer, you can begin to set up your project. At minimum, create the following files:

- *README*, which is a description of your project and its goals
- *LICENSE*, which is your project's license
- *.gitignore*, which is a special file that tells Git what files and directories to ignore
- A directory, which has the name of your project

Your Python code belongs in a separate subdirectory and not in the root of the repository. This is very important, as your repository's root directory will get mighty cluttered with build files, packaging scripts, documentation, virtual environments, and all manner of other things that aren't actually part of the source code.

As an example, in this chapter, I'll use one of my own Python projects: *omission*.

A Python project is composed of modules and packages. In the next section, I'll cover what those are and how to create them.

Modules and Packages

A *module* is any Python (*.py*) file. (Anticlimactic, isn't it?)

A *package*, occasionally called a *regular package*, is one or more modules within a directory. That directory must include a file called *__init__.py* (which can be empty). The *__init__.py* file is important! If it isn't there, Python will not know the directory constitutes a package.

PEDANTIC NOTE   Modules are actually objects, not just files. They can come from places other than the filesystem, including compressed files and network locations. Packages are modules too, just with a __path__ attribute. Chances are, this will never matter for what you're doing, but once you get deep into the import system, this distinction *will* matter.

You can leave the *__init__.py* file empty (it often is), or you can use it to run certain code when the package is first imported. For example, you might use __init__.py to select and rename certain functions, so the end user of the package doesn't need to understand how the modules are laid out. (See the subsection "Controlling Package Imports" later in the chapter.)

If you do forget __init__.py in your package, it becomes an *implicit namespace package*, also just known as a *namespace package*. These behave differently from regular packages. **The two are not interchangeable!** A namespace package allows you to distribute a package in multiple pieces, called *portions*. There are some cool advanced things you can do with namespace packages, but you will seldom need them. As this is a doozy of a rabbit hole, if you need namespace packages, see the documentation at *https://packaging.python.org/guides/packaging-namespace-packages/*. You can also read PEP 420, which officially defined the concept.

GOTCHA ALERT   A number of articles, posts, and Stack Overflow answers claim that since Python 3, you no longer need __init__.py in packages. This is entirely **false**! Namespace packages are for very specific edge cases; they cannot replace "traditional" packages.

In my project structure, *omission* is a package that contains other packages. Thus, *omission* is my *top-level package*, and all the packages underneath it are its *subpackages*. This convention will be important once you start importing stuff.

PEP 8 and Naming

Your packages and modules need clear names to identify them. Consulting with PEP 8 about the naming conventions reveals this:

> Modules should have short, all-lowercase names. Underscores can be used in the module name if it improves readability. Python packages should also have short, all-lowercase names, although the use of underscores is discouraged.

Understand that modules are named by filenames and packages are named by their directory name. Thus, these conventions define how you name your directories and code files.

To reiterate, filenames should be all lowercase, with underscores (_) if that improves readability. Similarly, directory names should be all lowercase, without underscores if at all possible. To put that another way . . .

Do this: *omission/data/data_loader.py*

NOT this: *omission/Data/DataLoader.py*

Project Directory Structure

With that covered, take a look at my project's repository directory structure:

```
omission-git/
├── LICENSE.md
├── omission/
│   ├── __init__.py
│   ├── __main__.py
```

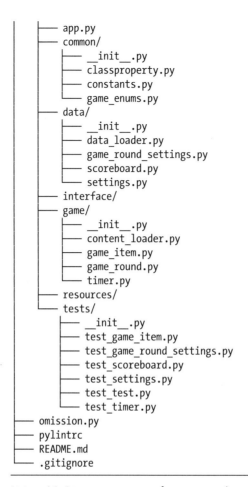

```
        │   ├── app.py
        │   ├── common/
        │   │   ├── __init__.py
        │   │   ├── classproperty.py
        │   │   ├── constants.py
        │   │   └── game_enums.py
        │   ├── data/
        │   │   ├── __init__.py
        │   │   ├── data_loader.py
        │   │   ├── game_round_settings.py
        │   │   ├── scoreboard.py
        │   │   └── settings.py
        │   ├── interface/
        │   ├── game/
        │   │   ├── __init__.py
        │   │   ├── content_loader.py
        │   │   ├── game_item.py
        │   │   ├── game_round.py
        │   │   └── timer.py
        │   ├── resources/
        │   └── tests/
        │       ├── __init__.py
        │       ├── test_game_item.py
        │       ├── test_game_round_settings.py
        │       ├── test_scoreboard.py
        │       ├── test_settings.py
        │       ├── test_test.py
        │       └── test_timer.py
        ├── omission.py
        ├── pylintrc
        ├── README.md
        └── .gitignore
```

Listing 4-1: Directory structure of omission-git/

You'll see that I have one top-level package called *omission*, with four subpackages: *common/, data/, game/,* and *tests/.* Each subpackage contains an *__init__.py* file, which is what designates them as packages. Every file that ends in *.py* is a module.

I also have the directory *resources/,* but that only contains game audio, images, and other sundry files (omitted here for brevity). The *resources/* directory is *not* a regular package, as it doesn't contain an *__init__.py.*

I have another special file in my top-level package: *__main__.py.* This is the file that runs when I execute my top-level package directly, via this command:

```
python3 -m omission
```

I'll come back to *__main__.py* in a bit (see the subsection "Package Entry Points" later in the chapter), as well as explain that lonely little *omission.py* file outside the top-level package.

This is a good project structure to start with, but once tests and packaging get involved, you'll have much better success with a slightly modified structure involving an *src/* directory. I'll cover this in Chapter 18.

How import Works

If you've written any meaningful Python code before, you're almost certainly familiar with the `import` statement for importing modules. For example, to use it to import the module for regex, you'd enter this:

```
import re
```

Once you've imported a module, you can access any variables, functions, or classes defined within it.

When you import the module, you are actually running it, which in turn executes any other `import` statements in the module. If there are any errors or performance costs in those secondarily (and onward) imported modules, they might seem to originate from your otherwise innocent import statement. It also means that Python has to be able to find all those modules.

For example, the module *re.py*, which is part of the Python standard library, has several import statements of its own, which are executed when you `import re`. The contents of those imported modules aren't automatically available to the file you imported re from, but those module files have to exist for `import re` to succeed. If, for some unlikely reason, *enum.py* (another module that is part of the Python standard library) got deleted from your Python environment and you ran `import re`, it would fail with an error:

```
Traceback (most recent call last):
File "weird.py", line 1, in
import re
File "re.py", line 122, in
import enum
ModuleNotFoundError: No module named 'enum'
```

This might seem like a confusing error message. I've seen people erroneously wonder why the outer module (in this example, re) couldn't be found. Others have wondered why the inner module (enum here) is being imported at all, since they didn't ask for it directly in their code.

The problem is that the re module was imported, and that in turn imported the enum module. However, because the enum module is missing, importing re fails with a `ModuleNotFoundError`.

Take note that this scenario is fictional: `import enum` and `import re` will never fail under normal circumstances, because both modules are part of Python's standard library. However, this little example demonstrates the common problem of import statements failing due to missing modules.

Import Dos and Don'ts

There are various ways of importing, but most of them should rarely, if ever, be used.

For the upcoming examples, I'll be using a module called *smart_door.py*, which reads as follows:

```
#!/usr/bin/env python3


def open():
    print("Ahhhhhhhhhhhhhh.")


def close():
    print("Thank you for making a simple door very happy.")
```

Listing 4-2: smart_door.py

Let's say I want to use this module in another Python file, which (in this example) is in the same directory. To run the functions defined in that module, I'd have to first import the module smart_door. The easiest way to do this is as follows:

```
import smart_door
smart_door.open()
smart_door.close()
```

Listing 4-3: use_smart_door.py:1a

The *namespace* of open() and close() is smart_door. A *namespace* is an explicitly defined path to something, such as a function. The function open() has the namespace smart_door, which tells me that open() belongs to that particular module. Remember this from The Zen of Python?

> Namespaces are one honking great idea—let's do more of those!

Python developers really like namespaces because they make it obvious where functions and whatnot are coming from. That comes in handy when you have multiple functions that have similar names or the same name, but that are defined in different modules. Without that bit of namespace, smart_door, you would not know that open() had anything to do with opening the smart door. Appropriately using namespaces can help you avoid massive errors in your code. However, as important as namespaces are, they can get out of hand very quickly if used improperly.

Be advised, in referring to *namespaces*, I'm not necessarily talking about *implicit namespace packages*, which I don't cover in this book.

Here's a look at some good and bad examples of namespaces in action.

Importing Functions from Modules

In my previous `smart_door` function calls, I referenced the namespace on every function call. This is usually best when a function is called only a handful of times, but if you use a function often, it gets tedious to use a namespace for every single function call.

Thankfully, Python provides a way around that. To be able to use the `open()` function without constantly having to precede it with its module name (`smart_door`), I need only know the *qualified name*—that is, the name of the function, class, or variable, preceded by its complete namespace within one of its modules or packages (if any). Within the *smart_door.py* module, the qualified name of the function I want is just open. Thus, I import that function like this, instead:

```
from smart_door import open
open()
```

Listing 4-4: use_smart_door.py:1b

This introduces a new problem. Neither `close()` nor `smart_door.close()` will work in this example, because I didn't import the function outright. The entire `smart_door` module was still run by the import command, but only the `open()` function was actually imported. To use `smart_door.close()`, I'd need to change the code to this:

```
from smart_door import open, close
open()
close()
```

Listing 4-5: use_smart_door.py:1c

This gives me access to both functions, no namespace required.

The Problem of Shadowing

You might have noticed another problem: `open()` is already a built-in Python function! Assume I also need to read a file called *data.txt*, which exists in my current directory. If I try this after importing `open()` from the `smart_door` function (Listing 4-5), my program is going to behave very badly:

```
somefile = open("data.txt", "r")
# ...work with the file...
somefile.close()
```

Listing 4-6: use_smart_door.py:2

When I used `open()` earlier (Listing 4-5), I wanted to use `smart_door` `.open()`. Now, in the same file, I'm trying to call Python's built-in `open()` function to open a text file for reading. Unfortunately, because of the earlier import, the built-in `open()` function has been *shadowed* by `smart_door.open()`, meaning the presence of the latter is making it impossible for Python to even find the former. This code will fail!

```
Traceback (most recent call last):
  File "ch4_import2-bad.py", line 9, in <module>
    somefile = open("data.txt", "r")
TypeError: open() takes no arguments (2 given)
```

I got that error because I'm trying to use the built-in open() function, which accepts two arguments, but I unintentionally called smart_door.open(), which doesn't accept any arguments.

Getting an actual error message is one of the better failure scenarios for this sort of mistake. Imagine if smart_door.open() did accept similar arguments to the built-in open(). Depending on my code, I might wind up with an error elsewhere (perhaps from trying to use a file I hadn't opened), or worse, some form of incorrect but technically valid behavior. This sort of mistake is infamously difficult to debug, so it is wise to avoid.

So how should I fix this? If I were the one who wrote *smart_door.py*, I should just go and change the function name. It's universally considered bad practice to use function names that shadow built-in Python functions anyhow, unless the entire point *is* to shadow. However, assume that I'm not the author of that module and I need another solution. Thankfully, Python offers one in the as keyword, which allows me to create an alias for that function:

```
from smart_door import open as door_open
from smart_door import close

door_open()
close()
```

Listing 4-7: use_smart_door.py:1d

In the import, I use the as keyword to rename smart_door.open() to door _open(), but only in the context of this file. Then, I can refer to door_open() where I wanted smart_door.open().

This leaves Python's built-in open() function unshadowed, so the earlier code for working with the file (Listing 4-6) can function properly.

```
somefile = open("data.txt", "r")
# ...work with the file...
somefile.close()
```

The Trouble with Nested Packages

As you've seen, packages can contain other packages. In my *omission* project, if I wanted to import the module *data_loader.py*, I could use this line (refer back to the *omission* project structure):

```
import omission.data.data_loader
```

The Python interpreter looks for the *omission* package, the *data* package inside that, and the *data_loader* module inside that. The *data_loader* module (and only that module) is imported. This is a good structure, and all's well.

At a certain point, however, nesting packages can become a pain. A function call like `musicapp.player.data.library.song.play()` is just ugly, not to mention, difficult to read. As The Zen of Python muses:

> Flat is better than nested.

Some nesting of packages is certainly okay, but when your project starts looking like an elaborate set of Matryoshka dolls, you've done something wrong. Organize your modules into packages, but keep the structure reasonably simple. Nesting two or three packages deep is okay; deeper is generally not advisable, if it can be avoided.

Although we'd never have overly nested nightmares in an ideal world, real-life projects aren't always that neat. Sometimes, it isn't possible to avoid deep nesting structures. I need another way to keep my import statements sane. Graciously, the import system can handle this:

```
from musicapp.player.data.library.song import play

play()
```

I only have to deal with the deeply nested namespace once, in the actual import statement. After that, I just use the function name, `play()`.

Alternatively, if I want a little bit of namespace, I can have that, too:

```
from musicapp.player.data.library import song

song.do_thing()
```

My import statement has resolved all but that last bit of namespace, `song`, so I still know where the `play()` function is coming from.

The import system is deliciously flexible like that.

Beware of Importing All

Before long, you'll probably find yourself tempted to import all of the hundreds of functions in your module, to save time. This is the point at which many developers go off the rails:

```
from smart_door import *
```

This statement imports nearly everything in the module directly, except for anything preceded by one or more underscores. This import-all pattern is a Very Bad Idea, as you won't know what all is getting imported or what will be shadowed in the process.

The problem gets even worse when you start importing all from multiple modules:

```
from smart_door import *
from gzip import *
open()
```

Doing this, you may be blissfully unaware that open(), smart_door.open(), and gzip.open() all exist and are fighting over the same name in your file! The function gzip.open() will win out in this example, because it's the last version of open() that was imported. The other two functions have been shadowed, which means you effectively can't call them at all.

Since no one is likely to remember every single function, class, and variable in every module that gets imported, one can easily wind up with a whole lot of messes.

The Zen of Python applies to this situation:

> Explicit is better than implicit.
>
> (. . .)
>
> In the face of ambiguity, refuse the temptation to guess.

You should never have to guess where a function or variable is coming from. There should be code somewhere in the file that explicitly tells you where everything comes from, as seen in the preceding examples.

This import * doesn't quite work the same way with packages. By default, a line like from some_package import * will be functionally the same as import some_package, unless the package has been configured to work with import *. I'll come back to this later.

Importing Within Your Project

Now that you know how to structure your project and import from packages and modules, I'll tie everything together.

Recall my *omission* project structure from Listing 4-1. Here's a subsection of that project directory:

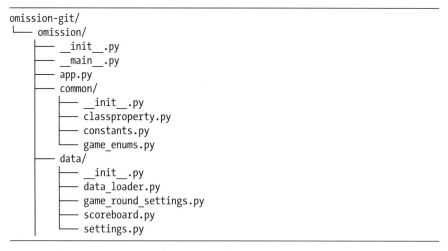

```
omission-git/
└── omission/
    ├── __init__.py
    ├── __main__.py
    ├── app.py
    ├── common/
    │   ├── __init__.py
    │   ├── classproperty.py
    │   ├── constants.py
    │   └── game_enums.py
    ├── data/
    │   ├── __init__.py
    │   ├── data_loader.py
    │   ├── game_round_settings.py
    │   ├── scoreboard.py
    │   └── settings.py
```

Listing 4-8: Directory structure of omission-git/

Any one module in my project may need to be able to import from another module, whether it's within the same package or somewhere else in the project structure. I'll explain how to handle both scenarios.

Absolute Imports

I have a class GameMode defined within the *game_enums.py* module, which lives in the *omission/common* package. I want to use that class within my *game_round_settings.py* module, defined in the *omission/data* package. How do I get to it?

Because I defined *omission* as a top-level package and organized my modules into subpackages, it's pretty straightforward. In *game_round_settings.py*, I'd write the following:

```
from omission.common.game_enums import GameMode
```

Listing 4-9: game_round_settings.py:1a

This line is an *absolute import*. It starts at the top-level package, *omission*, and walks down into the *common* package, where it looks for *game_enums.py*. Inside that module, it finds whatever has the name GameMode and imports that.

Relative Imports

You can also import from a module in the same package or subpackage. This is known as a *relative import* or an *intrapackage reference*. In practice, intra-package references are easy to do wrong. If some developer wanted to import GameMode (which is provided by *omission/common/game_enums.py*) into *omission/data/game_round_settings.py*, they might incorrectly attempt to use something like the following:

```
from common.game_enums import GameMode
```

Listing 4-10: game_round_settings.py:1b

This fails, leaving the developer wondering why it doesn't work. The *data* package (where *game_round_settings.py* lives) has no knowledge of its sibling packages, such as *common*.

A module knows what package it belongs to, and a package knows its parent package (if it has one). Because of this, relative imports can start the search from the current package and move up and down through the project structure.

Within *omission/data/game_round_settings.py*, I can use the following import statement:

```
from ..common.game_enums import GameMode
```

Listing 4-11: game_round_settings.py:1c

The two dots (..) mean "the current package's direct parent package," which, in this case, is *omission*. The import steps up one level, walks down into *common*, and finds *game_enums.py*.

There's some difference of opinion among Python developers about whether to use absolute or relative imports. Personally, I prefer to use absolute imports whenever possible, because I feel it makes the code a lot more readable. You can make up your own mind. The only important factor is that the result should be *obvious*—there should be no mystery about where anything comes from.

Importing from the Same Package

There is one other lurking gotcha here. In *omission/data/settings.py*, I have this statement for importing a class from the module *omission/data/game_round_settings.py*:

```
from omission.data.game_round_settings import GameRoundSettings
```

Listing 4-12: settings.py:1a

You might think that since both *settings.py* and *game_round_settings.py* are in the same package, *data*, I should be able to just use this:

```
from game_round_settings import GameRoundSettings
```

Listing 4-13: settings.py:1b

However, that will not work. It will fail to locate the *game_round_settings.py* module because I am running the top-level package (python3 -m omission), and absolute imports for anything within the package being executed (*omission*) have to start from the top.

I can instead use a relative import, which looks much simpler than the absolute import:

```
from .game_round_settings import GameRoundSettings
```

Listing 4-14: settings.py:1c

In this case, the single dot (.) means "this package."

This probably feels familiar if you're used to the typical UNIX filesystem, although Python takes the concept a bit further:

One dot (.) means the current package.

Two dots (..) takes you back one level, to the parent package.

Three dots (...) takes you back two levels, to the parent of the parent package.

Four dots (....) takes you back three levels.

And so on, and so forth.

Keep in mind that those "levels" aren't just plain directories; they're packages. If you have two distinct packages in a plain directory that isn't a package, you can't use relative imports to jump from one to another. You'll have to work with the Python search path for that. I'll talk more about that later in this chapter.

Entry Points

So far, you've learned how to create modules, packages, and projects, and how to make full use of the import system. The last piece of this puzzle is gaining the ability to control what happens when a package is imported or executed. The parts of the project that are run first when importing or executing are called *entry points*.

Module Entry Points

When you import a Python module or package, it is given a special variable called __name__. This contains the *fully qualified name* of the module or package, which is the name as the import system sees it. For example, the fully qualified name of the module *omission/common/game_enums.py* would be omission.common.game_enums. There is one exception: when a module or package is run directly, its __name__ is set to the value "__main__".

To demonstrate this, assume I have a package called *testpkg*, which contains the module *awesome.py*. It defines a function, greet():

```
def greet():
    print("Hello, world!")
```

Listing 4-15: awesome.py:1

The bottom of that same file also contains a print message:

```
print("Awesome module was run.")
```

Listing 4-16: awesome.py:2a

In another module in the same directory as *testpkg*, I have this module (*example.py*), which I run directly with python3 example.py:

```
from testpkg import awesome

print(__name__)          # prints "__main__"
print(awesome.__name__)  # prints "testpkg.awesome"
```

Listing 4-17: example.py

If I look at the _name_ local variable—which is the __name__ presently assigned to the current module, *example.py*—I'll see the value is "__main__" because I executed *example.py* directly.

The package awesome I imported also has a __name__ variable, which has the value "testpkg.awesome", representing where the package came from in the import system.

If you ran that module, you'd get the following output:

```
Awesome module was run.
__main__
testpkg.awesome
```

That first line is coming from *testpkg/awesome.py*, which is run by the import command. The rest is coming from the two print commands in *example.py*.

But what if I want that first message to appear only if *awesome.py* is executed directly, and *not* when the module is only imported? To accomplish that, I'd check the value of __name__ variable in a conditional statement. I've rewritten my *awesome.py* file to do exactly that:

```
if __name__ == "__main__":
    print("Awesome module was run.")
```

Listing 4-18: awesome.py:2b

If *awesome.py* is executed directly, __name__ will have the value "__main__", so the print statement will run. Otherwise, if *awesome.py* is being imported (or otherwise run indirectly), the conditional will fail.

While you'll frequently see this pattern in Python, some Python experts consider it an anti-pattern, because it can encourage you to both execute and import a module at the same time. While I don't agree that using if __name__ == "__main__" is an anti-pattern, you often don't need it. In any case, be certain you never import your main module from anywhere else in your package.

Package Entry Points

Notice that my *omission* project has a file called __main__ in the top-level package. This file is automatically run when a package is executed directly, but never when importing the package.

So, when executing *omission* via python3 -m omission, Python first runs the *__init__.py* module (as always), followed by its *__main__.py* module. Otherwise, if the package is imported instead, only *__init__.py* is executed.

If you omit *__main__.py* from a package, it cannot be executed directly.

A good *__main__.py* for a top-level package would look something like the following:

```
def main():
    # Code to start/run your package.


if __name__ == "__main__":
    main()
```

Listing 4-19: __main__.py

All the logic for starting the package belongs in the main() function. Then, the if statement checks the _name_ assigned to the __main__.py module. Since this package is being executed directly, the value of _name_ is "__main__", and the code within the if statement, being the call to the main() function, is run. Otherwise, if __main__.py were only being imported, its fully qualified name would include its containing package (for example, omission._main_), the condition would fail, and the code wouldn't run.

Controlling Package Imports

A package's __init__.py file can come in handy when you want to change what is available for import and how it can be used. The most common uses for this file are to simplify imports and to control the behavior of import-all (import *).

Simplifying Imports

Imagine I have a particularly complicated package, rockets, which is made up of dozens of subpackages and hundreds of modules. I can safely assume that many developers using the package won't want to know about most of that functionality. They only want one thing: to define a rocket and then launch it! Instead of expecting all the users of my package to know where those few basic bits of functionality exist in the package structure, I can use __init__.py to expose said functionality directly, making the bits easier to import later:

```
from .smallrocket.rocket import SmallRocket
from .largerocket.rocket import LargeRocket
from .launchpad.pad import Launchpad
```

Listing 4-20: __init__.py:1

This greatly simplifies the usage of the package. I no longer need to remember where things like the SmallRocket and Launchpad classes live in the rockets package structure. I can import them directly from the top-level package and use them:

```
from rockets import SmallRocket, Launchpad

pad = Launchpad(SmallRocket())
pad.launch()
```

Listing 4-21: rocket_usage.py

Beautifully simple, isn't it? Still, nothing is actually *preventing* me from importing things the long-form way (such as from rockets.smallrocket.rocket import SmallRocket) if I need to. The shortcut is there, but it's optional.

Because simplicity is such an essential part of the Python philosophy, it is also an essential component of package design. If you can anticipate the most common ways a user might interact with your package, you can greatly simplify their code by adding a few lines to __init__.py.

Controlling Import-All

By default, import-all doesn't work with a package. You use *__init__.py* to enable and control the behavior of import *, even though such an import statement is generally discouraged. This can be done by assigning a list of strings to _all_, with each string containing something (such as a package or module) to import from the current package.

This works well with the previous trick (Listing 4-20):

```
__all__ = ["SmallRocket", "LargeRocket", "Launchpad"]
```

Listing 4-22: __init__.py:2a

When Python encounters a line like from rockets import *, that list from _all_ (seen as rockets._all_) is unpacked in place of the asterisk (*). This is important in figuring out what you can include in _all_: each item in my list should make sense when substituted for the asterisk in from rockets import *.

In other words, I could change the last line of my *__init__.py* to this, and there would be no error in the code:

```
__all__ = ["smallrocket"]
```

Listing 4-23: __init__.py:2b

This works because, as you already know, the line from rockets import smallrocket is a valid import statement.

On the other hand, this example would *not* work:

```
__all__ = ["smallrocket.rocket"]
```

Listing 4-24: __init__.py:2c

It fails because from rockets import smallrocket.rocket does not make sense. You'll have to consider this principle when defining _all_.

If _all_ is not defined in *__init__.py*, then from rockets import * will behave the same as import rockets.

Program Entry Points

If you've applied all the concepts in this chapter to your project's structure, you can run python3 -m yourproject to start your program.

However, you (or your eventual end user) may want to run the program merely by double-clicking or directly executing some single Python file. With everything else in place, this is trivial to implement.

To make my *omission* project easy to run, I created a single script file *outside the top-level package*, named *omission.py*:

```
from omission.__main__ import main
main()
```

Listing 4-25: omission.py

I import the main() function from *omission/__main__.py* and then exe-cute that function. This is effectively the same as executing that package directly with `python3 -m omission`.

There are better ways to create a program entry point, but I'll cover those in Chapter 18, once I've created the all-important *setup.cfg* file. Again, what you have so far will be enough for development.

The Python Module Search Path

The *module search path*, or *import path*, defines where Python looks for pack-ages and modules and what order it searches in. When you first start the Python interpreter, the module search path is assembled in order, from the directory of the module being executed, the system variable PYTHONPATH, and the default path for the Python instance being used.

You can view the resulting module search path with the following commands:

```
import sys
print(sys.path)
```

Running that code within the context of a virtual environment (in my case, */home/jason/.venvs/venv310*) on my system gives me the following output:

```
[❶ '/home/jason/DeadSimplePython/Code/ch4', ❷ '/usr/lib/python310.zip', ❸ '/
usr/lib/python3.10', ❹ '/usr/lib/python3.10/lib-dynload', ❺ '/home/jason/.
venvs/venv310/lib/python3.10/site-packages']
```

The import system looks through each of the locations in the module search path *in order*. As soon as it finds a match for the module or package being imported, it stops. You can see here that it searches the directory con-taining the module or script I'm running ❶, the standard libraries ❷ ❸ ❹, and then everything installed with pip in the virtual environment ❺.

If you need to add locations to the module search path, the best way is to use a virtual environment and add a file ending in *.pth* to the *lib/python3.x/site-packages* directory. The name of the file doesn't matter, as long as the file extension is *.pth*.

For example, consider the following:

```
/home/jason/bunch_of_code
../../../awesomesauce
```

Listing 4-26: venv/lib/python3.10/site-packages/stuff.pth

Each line must contain exactly one path to be appended. The absolute path */home/jason/bunch_of_code* will be appended to the module search path. The relative path *../../../awesomesauce* is relative to the *.pth* file, so it will point to *venv/awesomesauce*.

Because these are appended to the module search path, this tech-nique cannot be used to replace any packages or modules installed on the system or virtual environment. However, any new modules or packages in my *bunch_of_code/* or *awesomesauce/* directories will be available for import within the virtual environment.

It is possible to modify the variable sys.path or your system's PYTHONPATH variable, but you almost certainly shouldn't be doing this directly! Not only is it an indicator that you're probably handling imports wrong, but it can also break stuff outside of your project. In this regard, sys.path is the worst offender; if someone imports a module where you modify sys.path, it will mangle their module search path!

What Really Happens

Let's look at what really happens under the hood when you import a module. Most of the time, those details won't matter, but every now and then (such as when the wrong module seems to be imported instead of the one you expect), the technical details leak to the surface. It never hurts to know what's going on.

The import statement calls the built-in __import__() function.

If you ever want to manually perform an import, use the importlib module instead of calling __import__().

To import a module, Python uses two special objects: a *finder* and a *loader*. In some cases, it uses an *importer* object, which serves as both a finder and a loader.

The *finder* is responsible for locating the module being imported. There are many places to look for modules—they aren't even necessarily files— and a number of special situations exist that must be handled. Python has several types of finders to handle these different situations, and it gives each one an opportunity to locate a module with a given name.

First, Python uses *meta path finders*, which are stored in the sys.meta_path list. By default, there are three meta path finders:

- The *built-in importer* finds and loads built-in modules.
- The *frozen importer* finds and loads *frozen* modules, meaning modules that have been converted to compiled bytecode (see Chapter 1).
- The *path-based finder* looks in the filesystem for the module.

This search order is the reason why you cannot globally shadow a built-in module; the built-in importer runs before the path-based finder. If you need some additional meta path finder, such as if you were importing a module from a novel location not already supported, you can add it as a *meta hook* by appending it to the sys.meta_path list.

There's some additional complexity to the path-based finder that is worth breaking down. The path-based finder tries each of the *path entry finders* in turn. These path entry finders, also known as *path entry hooks*, are stored in sys.path_hooks. Each one searches every location (known as a *path entry*) listed on the import path, as specified by `sys.path` or the `__path__` attribute of the current package.

If any of the finders locates the module, it returns a *module spec* object with all the information about how to load the module. However, if all the meta path finders return `None`, you'll get a `ModuleNotFoundError`.

Once the module is found, the module spec goes to the *loader*, which is responsible for actually loading the module.

There's a lot of technical detail regarding loading that's beyond the scope of this book, but one thing worth noting is how the loader deals with *cached bytecode*. Ordinarily, once a Python module has been run, a *.pyc* file is generated. The file contains the bytecode, which from then on is *cached*. You'll often see these *.pyc* files hanging out in your project directories. The loader always needs to be sure that the cached bytecode is not out of date before loading it, by using one of two strategies. The first strategy is for the bytecode to also store the timestamp from the last time the source code file was modified. When loading the module, the timestamp of the source code is checked against this cached timestamp. If it doesn't match, the bytecode is out of date, and the source will be recompiled. The second strategy, introduced in Python 3.7, instead stores a *hash*, which is a short and (relatively) unique value algorithmically generated from the source code itself. If the source code changes, the hash will be different from the one stored in the cached bytecode. Python bytecode files that contain this hash are appropriately called *hash-based .pyc* files.

Regardless of how the loader is loading the module, it will add the module object to `sys.modules`—adding it, in fact, just before actually loading, to prevent an import loop if the module being loaded imports itself. Finally, the loader will bind the imported module object to a name in the module importing it, so the imported module can be referenced. (I'll cover name binding in Chapter 5.)

Once the module has been imported, it's cached in `sys.path_importer_cache`, along with the importer object used to import it. This is actually the first place the import system will check for an imported module, even before running through the finders, so importing a module multiple times in a project will still only go through the finding-and-loading process once.

This is a very broad overview of the import system, but most of the time, it's all you'll need to know. To learn all the intricate details, you can read the official documentation at *https://docs.python.org/3/reference/import.html*.

Wrapping Up

The Python import system is often overlooked when learning the language, leading to many headaches for new users. By understanding how to use and import modules and packages, you will greatly reduce the roadblocks between you and a viable project. A little effort now will save you countless hours of confusion and trouble later!

PART II

ESSENTIAL STRUCTURES

5

VARIABLES AND TYPES

Some of the most pernicious misconceptions about Python revolve around its nuances regarding variables and data types. Misunderstandings related to this *one* topic cause countless frustrating bugs, and this is unfortunate. Python's way of handling variables is at the core of its power and versatility. If you understand this, everything else falls into place.

My own understanding of this topic was cemented by "Facts and Myths About Python Names and Values," Ned Batchelder's now-legendary talk at PyCon 2015. I recommend you watch the video of the presentation at *https://youtu.be/_AEJHKGk9ns*, either now or after reading this chapter.

Variables According to Python: Names and Values

Many myths about Python variables stem from people's attempts to describe the language in terms of *other languages*. Perhaps most annoying to Python experts is the misleading aphorism, "Python has no variables," which is really just the product of someone being overly clever about the fact that the Python language uses the terms *name* and *value*, instead of *variable*.

Python developers still use the term *variable* on a regular basis, and it even appears in the documentation, as it is part of understanding the overall system. However, for the sake of clarity, I'll use the official Python terms exclusively throughout the rest of the book.

Python uses the term *name* to refer to what would conventionally be called a variable. A name refers to a value or an object, in the same way that your name refers to you but does not contain you. There may even be multiple names for the same thing, just as you may have a given name and a nickname. A *value* is a particular instance of data in memory. The term *variable* refers to the combination of the two: a name that refers to a value. From now on, I'll only use the term *variable* in relation to this precise definition.

Assignment

Let's look at what happens under the hood when I define a variable per the above definitions like this:

```
answer = 42
```

Listing 5-1: simple_assignment.py:1

The name answer is *bound* to the value 42, meaning the name can now be used to refer to the value in memory. This operation of binding is referred to as an *assignment*.

Look at what happens behind the scenes when I assign the variable answer to a new variable, insight:

```
insight = answer
```

Listing 5-2: simple_assignment.py:2

The name insight doesn't refer to a copy of the value 42, but rather to the same, original value. This is illustrated in Figure 5-1.

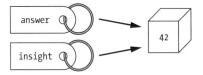

Figure 5-1: Multiple names can be bound to the same value in memory.

In memory, the name insight is bound to the value 42, which was already bound to another name: answer. Both names are still usable as variables. More importantly, insight is not bound to answer, but rather to the same value that answer was already bound to when I assigned insight. A name always points to a value.

Back in Chapter 3, I introduced the is operator, which compares *identity*— the specific location in memory that a name is bound to. This means is doesn't check whether a name points to equivalent values, but rather whether it points to the *same* value in memory.

When you make an assignment, Python makes its own decisions behind the scenes about whether to create a new value in memory or bind to an existing value. The programmer often has very little control over this decision.

To see this, run this example in an interactive session instead of a file:

```
spam = 123456789
maps = spam
eggs = 123456789
```

Listing 5-3: (Interactive session):1

I assign identical values to spam and eggs. I also bind maps to the same value as spam. (In case you didn't catch it, "maps" is "spam" backward. No wonder GPS gets annoying.)

When I compare the names with the comparison operator (==) to check whether the values are equivalent, both expressions return True, as one would expect:

```
print(spam == maps)  # prints True
print(spam == eggs)  # prints True
```

Listing 5-4: (Interactive session):2

However, when I compare the identities of the names with is, something surprising happens:

```
print(spam is maps)  # prints True
print(spam is eggs)  # prints False (probably)
```

Listing 5-5: (Interactive session):3

The names spam and maps are both bound to the same value in memory, but eggs is probably bound to a different but equivalent value. Thus, spam and eggs don't share an identity. This is illustrated in Figure 5-2.

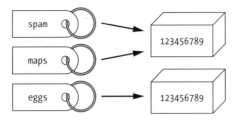

Figure 5-2: spam and maps share an identity;
eggs is bound to an equivalent value, but it
does not share identity.

It just goes to show, spam by any other name is still spam.

Python isn't guaranteed to behave exactly like this, and it may well decide to reuse an existing value. For example:

```
answer = 42
insight = 42
print(answer is insight)  # prints True
```

Listing 5-6: (Interactive session)

When I assign the value 42 to insight, Python decides to bind that name to the existing value. Now, answer and insight happen to be bound to the same value in memory, and thus, they share an identity.

This is why the identity operator (is) can be sneaky. There are many situations in which is appears to work like the comparison operator (==).

GOTCHA ALERT The is operator checks identity. Unless you *really* know what you're doing, only use this to check if something is None.

As a final note, the built-in function id() returns an integer representing the identity of whatever is passed to it. These integers are the values that the is operator compares. If you're curious about how Python handles names and values, try playing with id().

PEDANTIC NOTE In CPython, the value returned from the id() function is derived from the memory address for the value.

Data Types

As you've likely noticed, Python does not require you, the programmer, to declare a type for your variables. Back when I first picked up Python, I joined the #python channel on IRC and jumped right in.

"How do you declare the data type of a variable in Python?" I asked, in all the naivete of a first-year coder.

Within moments, I received a response that I consider to be my first true induction into the bizarre world of programming: "You're a data type."

The room regulars went on to explain that Python is a dynamically typed language, meaning I didn't have to tell the language what sort of information to put in a variable. Instead, Python would decide the type for me. I didn't even have to use a special "variable declaration" keyword. I just had to assign like this:

```
answer = 42
```

Listing 5-7: types.py:1

At that precise moment, Python became my all-time favorite language.

It's important to remember that Python is still a strongly typed language. I touched on this concept, along with dynamic typing, in Chapter 3. Ned Batchelder sums up Python's type system quite brilliantly in his aforementioned PyCon 2015 talk about names and values:

> Names have a scope—they come and go with functions—but they have no type. Values have a type . . . but they have no scope.

Although I haven't touched on scope yet, this should already make sense. Names are bound to values, and those values exist in memory, as long as there is some *reference* to them. You can bind a name to literally any value you want, but you are limited as to what you can do with any particular value.

The type() Function

If you ever need to know a value's data type, you can use the built-in type() function. Recall that everything in Python is an object, so this function will really just return what class the value is an instance of:

```
print(type(answer))  # prints <class 'int'>
```

Listing 5-8: types.py:2

Here, you can see that the value assigned to answer is an integer (int). On rare occasions, you may want to check the data type before you do something with a value. For that, you can pair the type() function with the is operator, like this:

```
if type(answer) is int:
    print("What's the question?")
```

Listing 5-9: types.py:3a

In many cases where this sort of introspection is necessary, it may be better to use isinstance() instead of type(), as it accounts for subclasses and inheritance (see Chapter 13). The function itself returns True or False, so I can use it as the condition in an if statement:

```
if isinstance(answer, int):
    print("What's the question?")
```

Listing 5-10: types.py:3b

Truth be told, there is rarely a need for either. Instead, Python developers prefer a more dynamic approach.

Duck Typing

Python uses what is known (unofficially) as *duck typing*. This isn't a technical term at all; it comes from the old saying:

> If it looks like a duck, walks like a duck, and quacks like a duck,
> then it probably *is* a duck.

Python doesn't care much about what a value's data type is, but rather it cares about the *functionality* of the value's data type. For example, if an object supports all the math operators and functions, and if it accepts floats and integers as operands on the binary operators, then Python considers the object to be a numeric type.

In other words, Python doesn't care if it's actually a robotic duck or a moose in a duck costume. If it has the traits needed, the rest of the details are usually moot.

If you're familiar with object-oriented programming, particularly how quickly inheritance can get out of hand, then this whole concept of duck typing will probably be a breath of fresh air. If your class behaves as it should, it usually won't matter what it inherits from.

Scope and Garbage Collection

Scope is what defines where a variable can be accessed from. It might be available to an entire module or limited to the suite (body) of a function.

As I mentioned already, names have *scope*, whereas values do not. A name can be *global*, meaning it is defined by itself in a module, or it can be *local*, meaning it only exists within a particular function or comprehension.

Local Scope and the Reference-Counting Garbage Collector

Functions (including lambdas) and comprehensions define their own scope; they are the only structures in the language to do so. Modules and classes don't have their own scope in the strictest sense; they only have their own namespace. When a scope reaches its end, all the names defined within it are automatically deleted.

For any particular value, Python keeps a *reference count*, which is simply a count of how many references exist for that value. Every time a value is bound to a name, a reference is created (although there are other ways the language may create references). When there are no more references, the value is deleted. This is the *reference-counting garbage collector*, and it efficiently handles most garbage collection scenarios.

PEDANTIC NOTE Technically, Python's garbage collection behaviors are an implementation detail specific to CPython, the main "flavor" of Python. Other flavors of the language may (or may not) handle this differently, but it probably won't ever matter to you, unless you're doing something insanely advanced and weird.

You can see how this works with a typical function, like this:

```python
def spam():
    message = "Spam"
    word = "spam"
    for _ in range(100):
        separator = ", "
        message += separator + word
    message += separator
    message += "spam!"

    return message
```

Listing 5-11: local_scope.py:1

I create a spam() function, inside of which I define the names message, word, and separator. I can access any of these names inside the function; that is their local scope. It doesn't matter that separator is defined within a for loop, as loops don't have their own scope. I can still access it outside of the loop.

However, I cannot access any of these names outside of the function:

```python
print(message)  # NameError: name 'message' is not defined
```

Listing 5-12: local_scope.py:2

Trying to access message outside the context of the spam() function where it was defined will raise a NameError. In this example, message doesn't exist in the outer scope. What's more, as soon as the function spam() exits, the names message, word, and separator are deleted. Because word and separator each referred to values with a reference count of one (meaning only one name was bound to each), the values are also deleted.

The value of message is not deleted when the function exits, however, because of the return statement at the end of the function (see Listing 5-11) and what I do with that value here:

```python
output = spam()
print(output)
```

Listing 5-13: local_scope.py:3

I bind the value returned by spam() to output in the outer scope, meaning that value still exists in memory and can be accessed outside of the function. Assigning the value to output increases the reference count for that value, so even though the name message is deleted when spam() exits, the value is not.

Interpreter Shutdown

When the Python interpreter is asked to shut down, such as when a Python program terminates, it enters *interpreter shutdown*. During this phase, the interpreter goes through the process of releasing all allocated resources, calling the garbage collector multiple times, and triggering destructors in objects.

You can use the atexit module from the standard library to add functions to this interpreter shutdown process. This may be necessary in some highly technical projects, although in general, you shouldn't need to do this. Functions added via atexit.register() will be called in a last-in, first-out manner. However, be aware that it becomes difficult to work with modules, including the standard library, during interpreter shutdown. It's like trying to work in a building as it's being demolished: the janitor's closet may disappear at any time, without warning.

Global Scope

When a name is defined within a module but outside of any function, class, or comprehension, it is considered to be in *global scope*. Although it's okay to have some global scope names, having too many usually leads to the creation of code that is difficult to debug and maintain. Therefore, you should use global scope names sparingly for variables. There is often a cleaner solution, such as a class (see Chapter 7).

Properly using global scope names in the context of a more local scope, such as a function, requires you to think ahead a little. Consider what I do if I want a function that can modify a global variable storing a high score. First, I define the global variable:

```
high_score = 10
```

Listing 5-14: global_scope.py:1

I'll write this function the wrong way first:

```
def score():
    new_score = 465              # SCORING LOGIC HERE
    if new_score > ❶ high_score: # ERROR: UnboundLocalError
        print("New high score")
    ❷ high_score = new_score


score()
print(high_score)
```

Listing 5-15: global_scope.py:2

When I run this code, Python complains that I'm using a local variable before I've assigned a value to it ❶. The problem is, I'm assigning to the name high_score within the scope of the function score() ❷, and that *shadows*, or hides, the global high_score name behind the new, local high_score name. The fact that I've created a local high_score name *anywhere in the function* makes it impossible for the function to ever "see" the global high_score name.

To make this work, I need to declare that I'm going to use the global name in the local scope, instead of defining a new local name. I can do this with the global keyword:

```python
def score():
    global high_score
    new_score = 465  # SCORING LOGIC HERE
    if new_score > high_score:
        print("New high score")
        high_score = new_score


score()
print(high_score)   # prints 465
```

Listing 5-16: global_scope.py:3

Before I do anything else in my function, I must specify that I'm using the global high_score name. This means that anywhere I assign a value to the name high_score in score(), the function will use the global name, instead of trying to create a new local name. The code now works as expected.

Every time you wish to rebind a global name from within a local scope, you must use the global keyword first. If you're only accessing the current value bound to a global name, you don't need to use the global keyword. It is vital for you to cultivate this habit, because Python won't always raise an error if you handle scope incorrectly. Consider this example:

```python
current_score = 0


def score():
    new_score = 465    # SCORING LOGIC HERE
    current_score = new_score


score()
print(current_score)  # prints 0
```

Listing 5-17: global_scope_gotcha.py:1a

This code runs without raising any errors, but the output is wrong. A new name, current_score, is being created in the local scope of the function score(), and it is bound to the value 465. This shadows the global name current_score. When the function terminates, both the new_score and the local current_score are deleted. In all of this, the global current_score has remained untouched. It is still bound to 0, and that is what is printed out.

Once again, to resolve this problem, I need only use the global keyword:

```python
current_score = 0


def score():
    global current_score
```

```
new_score = 465  # SCORING LOGIC HERE
current_score = new_score
```

```
score()
print(current_score)  # prints 465
```

Listing 5-18: global_scope_gotcha.py:1b

Because I specified that the global current_name is to be used in this function, the code now behaves precisely as expected, printing out the value 465.

The Dangers of Global Scope

There is one more major gotcha to account for with global scope. Modifying any variable at a global level, as in rebinding or mutating on a name outside the context of a function, can lead to confusing behavior and surprising bugs—especially once you start dealing with multiple modules. It's acceptable for you to initially "declare" a name at a global scope, but you should do all further rebinding and mutation of that global name at the local scope level.

By the way, this does *not* apply to classes, which do not actually define their own scope. I'll return to this later in this chapter.

The nonlocal Keyword

Python allows you to write functions within functions. I'll defer discussing the practicality of this until Chapter 6. Here, I mainly want to explore this functionality's impact on scope. Consider the following example:

```
spam = True


def order():
    eggs = 12

    def cook():
      ❶ nonlocal eggs

        if spam:
            print("Spam!")

        if eggs:
            eggs -= 1
            print("...and eggs.")

    cook()


order()
```

Listing 5-19: nonlocal.py

The function order() contains another function: cook(). Each function has its own scope.

Remember, as long as a function only accesses a global name like spam, you don't need to do anything special. However, trying to *assign* to a global name will actually define a new local name that shadows the global one. The same behavior is true of the inner function using names defined in the outer function, which is known as the *nested scope* or *enclosing scope*. To get around this, I specify that eggs is nonlocal, meaning it can be found in the enclosing scope, rather than in the local scope ❶. The inner function cook() has no trouble accessing the global name spam.

The nonlocal keyword starts looking for the indicated name in the innermost nested scope, and if it doesn't find it, it moves to the next enclosing scope above that. It repeats this until it either finds the name or determines that the name does not exist in a nonglobal enclosing scope.

Scope Resolution

Python's rule about which scopes it searches for a name, and in what order, is called the *scope resolution order*. The easiest way to remember the scope resolution order is with the acronym *LEGB*—for which my colleague Ryan gave me the handy mnemonic "Lincoln Eats Grant's Breakfast":

Local

Enclosing-function locals (that is, anything found via nonlocal)

Global

Built-in

Python will look in these scopes, in order, until it finds a match or reaches the end. The nonlocal and global keywords adjust the behavior of this scope resolution order.

The Curious Case of the Class

Classes have their own way of dealing with scope. Technically speaking, classes don't directly factor into the scope resolution order. Every name declared directly within a class is known as an *attribute*, and it is accessed through the dot (.) operator on the class (or object) name.

To demonstrate this, I'll define a class with a single attribute:

```
class Nutrimatic:
    ❶ output = "Something almost, but not quite, entirely unlike tea."

    def request(self, beverage):
        return ❷ self.output


machine = Nutrimatic()
mug = machine.request("Tea")
print(mug)    # prints "Something almost, but not quite, entirely unlike tea."

print(❸ machine.output)
print(❹ Nutrimatic.output)
```

Listing 5-20: class_attributes.py

Those three print statements all output the same thing. Running that code gives me this:

```
Something almost, but not quite, entirely unlike tea.
Something almost, but not quite, entirely unlike tea.
Something almost, but not quite, entirely unlike tea.
```

The name output is a *class attribute* ❶, belonging to the Nutrimatic class. Even within that class, I would not be able to refer to it merely as output. I must access it through self.output ❷, as self refers to the class instance the function (instance method) request() is being called on. I can also access it via machine.output ❸ or Nutrimatic.output ❹ anywhere the object machine or the class Nutrimatic is, respectively, in scope. All of those names point to the exact same attribute: output. Especially in this case, there's no real difference between them.

Generational Garbage Collector

Behind the scenes, Python also has a more robust *generational garbage collector* that handles all of the odd situations a reference-counting garbage collector cannot, such as reference cycles (when two values reference one another). All of these situations, and the ways they're handled by the garbage collector, are far beyond the scope of this book.

Moving forward, the most important takeaway to remember is that the generational garbage collector incurs some performance costs. Thus, it's sometimes worthwhile to avoid reference cycles. One way to do this is with weakref, which creates a reference to a value without increasing that value's reference count. This feature was defined in PEP 205, and the documentation exists at *https://docs.python.org/library/weakref.html*.

The Immutable Truth

Values in Python can be either *immutable* or *mutable*. The difference hinges on whether the values can be *modified in place*, meaning they can be changed right where they are in memory.

Immutable types cannot be modified in place. For example, integers (int), floating-point numbers (float), strings (str), and tuples (tuple) are all immutable. If you attempt to mutate an immutable value, you'll wind up with a completely different value being created:

```
eggs = 12
carton = eggs
print(eggs is carton)   # prints True
eggs += 1
print(eggs is carton)   # prints False
print(eggs)             # prints 13
print(carton)           # prints 12
```

Listing 5-21: immutable_types.py

Initially, eggs and carton are both bound to the same value, and thus, they share an identity. When I modify eggs, it is rebound to a new value, so it no longer shares an identity with carton. You can see that the two names now point to different values.

Mutable types, on the other hand, can be modified in place. Lists constitute one example of a mutable type:

```
temps = [87, 76, 79]
highs = temps
print(temps is highs)  # prints True
❶ temps += [81]
print(temps is highs)  # prints True
print(highs)           # prints [87, 76, 79, 81]
print(temps)           # prints [87, 76, 79, 81]
```

Listing 5-22: mutable_types.py

Because the list is aliased to both temps and highs, any modifications made to the list value ❶ are visible through either name. Both names are bound to the original value, as demonstrated by the is comparisons. This remains the case, even after that value is mutated.

Passing by Assignment

Another frequent question from programmers new to the language is, "Does Python pass by value or by reference?"

The answer is, "Effectively, neither." More accurately, as Ned Batchelder describes it, Python *passes by assignment*.

Neither the values nor the names bound to them are moved. Instead, each value is bound to the parameter via assignment. Consider a simple function:

```
def greet(person):
    print(f"Hello, {person}.")


my_name = "Jason"
greet(my_name)
```

Here, there is one copy of the string value "Jason" in memory, and that is bound to the name my_name. When I pass my_name to the greet() function—specifically, to the person parameter—it's the same as if I had said (person = my_name).

Again, assignment never makes a copy of a value. The name person is now bound to the value "Jason".

This concept of passing by assignment gets tricky when you start working with mutable values, such as lists. To demonstrate this often-unexpected behavior, I've written a function that finds the lowest temperature in a list passed to it:

```
def find_lowest(temperatures):
    temperatures.sort()
    print(temperatures[0])
```

Listing 5-23: lowest_temp.py:1a

At first glance, you may assume that passing a list to the temperatures parameter will make a copy, so it shouldn't matter if you modify the value bound to the parameter. However, lists are mutable, meaning *the value itself* can be modified:

```
temps = [85, 76, 79, 72, 81]
find_lowest(temps)
print(temps)
```

Listing 5-24: lowest_temp.py:2

When I passed temps to the function's temperatures parameter, I only *aliased* the list, so any changes made on temperatures are visible from all the other names bound to that same list value—namely, from temps.

You can see this in action when I run this code and get the following output:

```
72
[72, 76, 79, 81, 85]
```

When find_lowest() sorted the list passed to temperatures, it actually sorted the one mutable list that both temps and temperatures aliased. This is a clear case of a function having *side effects*, which are changes to values that existed before the function call.

An awe-inspiring number of bugs originate from this one type of misunderstanding. In general, functions should not have side effects, meaning that any values passed to the function as arguments should *not* be directly mutated. To avoid mutating the original value, I have to explicitly make a copy of it. Here's how I'd do that in the find_lowest() function:

```
def find_lowest(temperatures):
    sorted_temps = ❶ sorted(temperatures)   # sorted returns a new list
    print(sorted_temps[0])
```

Listing 5-25: lowest_temp.py:1b

The sorted() function has no side effects; it creates a new list using the items in the list passed to it ❶. It then sorts this new list and returns it. I bind this new list to sorted_temps. Thus, the original list (bound to temps and temperatures) is untouched.

If you're coming from C and C++, it may be helpful to remember the potential hang-ups related to pass-by-pointer or pass-by-reference. Although

Python's assignment is scarcely similar from a technical standpoint, the risks of side effects and unintended mutations are the same.

Collections and References

All collections, including lists, employ a clever little semantic detail that can become a royal pain if you don't know to expect it: ***Individual items are references.*** Just as a name is bound to a value, so also are items in collections bound to values, in the same manner. This binding is called a *reference.*

A simple example involves trying to create a tic-tac-toe board. This first version won't work quite how you'd expect.

I'll start by creating the game board:

```
board = [["-"] ❶ * 3] * 3  # Create a board
```

Listing 5-26: tic_tac_toe.py:1a

I'm trying to create a two-dimensional board. You can fill a collection, like a list, with several items, all with the same repeating value, using the multiplication operator ❶, as I've done here. I enclose the repeating value in square brackets and multiply it by the number of repetitions I want. A single row of my board is defined with `["-"] * 3`, which makes a list of three `"-"` strings.

Unfortunately, this won't work the way you'd expect. The problem begins when I attempt to define the second dimension of the array—three copies of the `[["-"] * 3]` list—using multiplication. You can see the problem manifest when I try to make a move:

```
❷ board[1][0] = "X"  # Make a move

# Print board to screen
for row in board:
    print(f"{row[0]} {row[1]} {row[2]}")
```

Listing 5-27: tic_tac_toe.py:2

When I mark a move on the board ❷, I want to see that change in only one spot on the board, like this:

```
- - -
X - -
- - -
```

Instead, I get this nasty surprise:

```
X - -
X - -
X - -
```

Cue the weeping and gnashing of teeth. Somehow, that one change has propagated to *all three rows*. Why?

Initially, I created a list with three "-" values as items ❶. Since strings are immutable and thus cannot be modified in place, this works as expected. Rebinding the first item in the list to "X" does not affect the other two items.

The outer dimension of the list is composed of three list items. Because I defined *one* list and used it *three* times, I now have three *aliases* for one mutable value! By changing that list through one reference (the second row), I'm mutating that one shared value ❷, so all three references see the change.

There are a few ways to fix this, but all of them work by ensuring each row references a separate value, like so:

```
board = [["-"] * 3 for _ in range(3)]
```

Listing 5-28: tic_tac_toe.py:1b

I only needed to change how I defined the game board initially. I now use a *list comprehension* to create the rows. In short, this list comprehension will define a separate list value from ["-"] * 3 three different times. (List comprehensions get complicated; they'll be explained in depth in Chapter 10.) Running the code now results in the expected behavior:

```
- - -
X - -
- - -
```

Long story short, whenever you're working with a collection, remember that an item is no different from any other name. Here is one more example to drive this point home:

```
scores_team_1 = [100, 95, 120]
scores_team_2 = [45, 30, 10]
scores_team_3 = [200, 35, 190]

scores = (scores_team_1, scores_team_2, scores_team_3)
```

Listing 5-29: team_scores.py:1

I create three lists, assigning each to a name. Then, I pack all three into the tuple scores. You may remember from earlier that tuples cannot be modified directly, because they're immutable. That same rule does not necessarily apply to a tuple's items. You can't change the tuple itself, but you can (indirectly) modify the values its items refer to:

```
scores_team_1[0] = 300
print(scores[0])  # prints [300, 95, 120]
```

Listing 5-30: team_scores.py:2

When I mutate the list scores_team_1, that change appears in the first item of the tuple, because that item only aliased a mutable value.

I could also directly mutate a mutable list in the scores tuple through two-dimensional subscription, like this:

```
scores[0][0] = 400
print(scores[0])  # prints [400, 95, 120]
```

Listing 5-31: team_scores.py:3

Tuples don't give you any sort of security about things being modified. Immutability exists mainly for efficiency, not for protecting data. Mutable values are *always* going to be mutable, no matter where they live or how they're referred to.

The problems in the two examples above may seem relatively easy to spot, but things start getting troublesome when the related code is spread out across a large file or multiple files. Mutating on a name in one module may unexpectedly modify an item of a collection in a completely different module, and you might never have expected it.

Shallow Copy

There are many ways to ensure you are binding a name to a *copy* of a mutable value, instead of aliasing the original; the most explicit of these ways is with the copy() function. This is sometimes also known as a *shallow copy*, in contrast to the *deep copy* I'll cover later.

To demonstrate this, I'll create a Taco class (see Chapter 7 for more on classes) that allows you to define the class with various toppings and then add a sauce afterward. This first version has a bug:

```
class Taco:

    def __init__(self, toppings):
        self.ingredients = toppings

    def add_sauce(self, sauce):
        self.ingredients.append(sauce)
```

Listing 5-32: mutable_tacos.py:1a

In the Taco class, the initializer __init__() accepts a list of toppings, which it stores as the ingredients list. The add_sauce() method will add the specified sauce string to the ingredients list.

(Can you anticipate the problem?)

I use the class as follows:

```
default_toppings = ["Lettuce", "Tomato", "Beef"]
mild_taco = Taco(default_toppings)
hot_taco = Taco(default_toppings)
hot_taco.add_sauce("Salsa")
```

Listing 5-33: mutable_tacos.py:2a

I define a list of toppings I want on all my tacos, and then I define two tacos: hot_taco and mild_taco. I pass the default_toppings list to the initializer for each taco. Then I add "Salsa" to the list of toppings to hot_taco, but I don't want any "Salsa" on mild_taco.

To make sure this is working, I print out the list of ingredients for the two tacos, as well as the default_toppings list I started with:

```
print(f"Hot: {hot_taco.ingredients}")
print(f"Mild: {mild_taco.ingredients}")
print(f"Default: {default_toppings}")
```

Listing 5-34: mutable_tacos.py:3

That outputs the following:

```
Hot: ['Lettuce', 'Tomato', 'Beef', 'Salsa']
Mild: ['Lettuce', 'Tomato', 'Beef', 'Salsa']
Default: ['Lettuce', 'Tomato', 'Beef', 'Salsa']
```

Waiter, there's a bug in my taco!

The trouble is, when I created my hot_taco and mild_taco object by passing default_toppings to the Taco initializer, I bound both hot_taco.ingredients and mild_taco.ingredients to the same list value as default_toppings. These are now all aliases of the same value in memory. Then, when I call the function hot_taco.add_sauce(), I mutate that list value. The addition of "Salsa" is visible not only in hot_taco.ingredients, but also (unexpectedly) in mild_taco.ingredients and in the default_toppings list. This is definitely not the desired behavior; adding "Salsa" to one taco should only affect that one taco.

One way to resolve this is to ensure I'm assigning a copy of the mutable value. In the case of my Taco class, I will rewrite the initializer so it assigns a copy of the specified list to self.ingredients, instead of aliasing:

```
import copy


class Taco:

    def __init__(self, toppings):
        self.ingredients = ❶ copy.copy(toppings)

    def add_sauce(self, sauce):
        self.ingredients.append(sauce)
```

Listing 5-35: mutable_tacos.py:1b

I make a copy with the copy.copy() function ❶, which is imported from copy.

I make a copy of the list passed to toppings within Taco.__init__(), assigning that copy to self.ingredients. Any changes made to self.ingredients

don't affect the others; adding "Salsa" to hot_taco does not change mild_taco
.ingredients, nor does it change default_toppings:

```
Hot: ['Lettuce', 'Tomato', 'Beef', 'Salsa']
Mild: ['Lettuce', 'Tomato', 'Beef']
Default: ['Lettuce', 'Tomato', 'Beef']
```

Deep Copy

A shallow copy is all well and good for lists of immutable values, but as previously mentioned, when a mutable value contains other mutable values,
changes to those values can appear to replicate in weird ways.

For example, consider what happens when I try to make a copy of a
Taco object before changing one of the two tacos. My first attempt results
in some undesired behavior. Building on the same Taco class as before (see
Listing 5-35), I'll use the copy of one taco to define another:

```
default_toppings = ["Lettuce", "Tomato", "Beef"]
mild_taco = Taco(default_toppings)
hot_taco = ❶ copy.copy(mild_taco)
hot_taco.add_sauce("Salsa")
```

Listing 5-36: mutable_tacos.py:2b

I want to create a new taco (hot_taco) that is initially identical to mild_taco,
but with added "Salsa". I'm attempting this by binding a copy of mild_taco ❶
to hot_taco.

Running the revised code (including Listing 5-34) produces the
following:

```
Hot: ["Lettuce", "Tomato", "Beef", "Salsa"]
Mild: ["Lettuce", "Tomato", "Beef", "Salsa"]
Default: ["Lettuce", "Tomato", "Beef"]
```

I might not expect any changes made to hot_taco to reflect in mild_taco,
but unexpected changes have clearly happened.

The issue is that, when I make a copy of the Taco object value itself, I am
not making a copy of the self.ingredients list *within* the object. Both Taco
objects contain references to the same list value.

To fix this problem, I can use *deep copy* to ensure that any mutable values inside the object are copied as well. In this case, a deep copy of a Taco
object will create a copy of the Taco value, as well as a copy of any mutable
values that Taco contains references to—namely, the list self.ingredients.
Listing 5-37 shows that same program, using deep copy:

```
default_toppings = ["Lettuce", "Tomato", "Beef"]
mild_taco = Taco(default_toppings)
hot_taco = ❶ copy.deepcopy(mild_taco)
hot_taco.add_sauce("Salsa")
```

Listing 5-37: mutable_tacos.py:2c

The only change is that I'm using `copy.deepcopy()`, instead of `copy.copy()` ❶. Now when I mutate the list inside `hot_taco`, it doesn't affect `mild_taco`:

```
Hot: ["Lettuce", "Tomato", "Cheese", "Beef", "Salsa"]
Mild: ["Lettuce", "Tomato", "Cheese", "Beef"]
Default: ["Lettuce", "Tomato", "Cheese", "Beef"]
```

I don't know about you, but I'm getting hungry for tacos.

Copying is the most generic way to solve the problem of passing around mutable objects. However, depending on what you're doing, there may be an approach better suited to the particular collection you're using. For example, many collections, like lists, have functions that return a copy of the collection with some specific modification. When you're solving these sorts of issues with mutability, you can start by employing copy and deep copy. Then, you can exchange that for a more domain-specific solution later.

Coercion and Conversion

Names do not have types. Therefore, Python has no need of type casting, at least in the typical sense of the term.

Allowing Python to figure out the conversions by itself, such as when adding together an integer (`int`) and a `float`, is called *coercion*. Here are a few examples:

```
print(42.5)    # coerces to a string
x = 5 + 1.5    # coerces to a float (6.5)
y = 5 + True   # coerces to an int (6)...and is also considered a bad idea
```

Listing 5-38: coercion.py

Even so, there are potential situations in which you may need to use one value to create a value of a different type, such as when you are creating a string from an integer. *Conversion* is the process of explicitly casting a value of one type to another type.

Every type in Python is an instance of a class. Therefore, the class of the type you want to create only needs to have an initializer that can handle the data type of the value you're converting from. (This is usually done through duck typing.)

One of the more common scenarios is to convert a string containing a number into a numeric type, such as a `float`:

```
life_universe_everything = "42"

answer = float(life_universe_everything)
```

Listing 5-39: conversion.py:1

Here, I start with a piece of information as a string value, which is bound to the name life_universe_everything. Imagine I want to do some complex mathematical analysis on this data; to do this, I must first convert the data into a floating-point number. The desired type would be an instance of the class float. That particular class has an initializer (__init__()) that accepts a string as an argument, which is something I know from the documentation.

I initialize a float() object, pass life_universe_everything to the initializer, and bind the resulting object to the name answer.

I'll print out the type and value of answer:

```
print(type(answer))
print(answer)
```

Listing 5-40: conversion.py:2

That outputs the following:

```
<class 'float'>
42.0
```

Since there were no errors, you can see that the result is a float with value 42.0, bound to answer.

Every class defines its own initializers. In the case of float(), if the string passed to it cannot be interpreted as a floating-point number, a ValueError will be raised. Always consult the documentation for the object you're initializing.

A Note About Systems Hungarian Notation

If you're coming from a statically typed language like C++ or Java, you're probably used to working with data types. Thus, when picking up a dynamically typed language such as Python, it might be tempting to employ some means of "remembering" what type of value every name is bound to. ***Don't do this!*** You will find the most success using Python if you learn to take full advantage of dynamic typing, weak binding, and duck typing.

I will confess: the first year I used Python, I used *Systems Hungarian notation*—the convention of appending a prefix denoting data type to every variable name—to try to "defeat" the language's dynamic typing system. My code was littered with such debris as intScore, floatAverage, and boolGameOver. I picked up the habit from my time using Visual Basic .NET, and I thought I was brilliant. In fact, I was depriving myself of many opportunities to refactor.

Systems Hungarian notation will quickly render code obtuse. For example:

```
def calculate_age(intBirthYear, intCurrentYear):
    intAge = intCurrentYear - intBirthYear
    return intAge
```

```
def calculate_third_age_year(intCurrentAge, intCurrentYear):
    floatThirdAge = intCurrentAge / 3
    floatCurrentYear = float(intCurrentYear)
    floatThirdAgeYear = floatCurrentYear - floatThirdAge
    intThirdAgeYear = int(floatThirdAgeYear)
    return intThirdAgeYear


strBirthYear = "1985"    # get from user, assume data validation
intBirthYear = int(strBirthYear)

strCurrentYear = "2010"  # get from system
intCurrentYear = int(strCurrentYear)

intCurrentAge = calculate_age(intBirthYear, intCurrentYear)
intThirdAgeYear = calculate_third_age_year(intCurrentAge, intCurrentYear)
print(intThirdAgeYear)
```

Listing 5-41: evils_of_systems_hungarian.py

Needless to say, this code is quite painful to read. On the other hand, if you make full use of Python's typing system (and resist the urge to store every intermediate step), the code will be decidedly more compact:

```
def calculate_age(birth_year, current_year):
    return (current_year - birth_year)


def calculate_third_age_year(current_age, current_year):
    return int(current_year - (current_age / 3))


birth_year = "1985"    # get from user, assume data validation
birth_year = int(birth_year)

current_year = "2010"  # get from system
current_year = int(current_year)

current_age = calculate_age(birth_year, current_year)
third_age_year = calculate_third_age_year(current_age, current_year)
print(third_age_year)
```

Listing 5-42: duck_typing_feels_better.py

My code became far cleaner once I stopped treating Python like a statically typed language. Python's typing system is a big part of what makes it such a readable and compact language.

Terminology Review

I've introduced a lot of important new words in this section. Since I'll be using this vocabulary frequently throughout the rest of the book, doing a quick recap here is prudent.

alias (v.) To bind a mutable value to more than one name. Mutations performed on a value bound to one name will be visible on all names bound to that mutable value.

assignment (n.) The act of binding a value to a name. Assignment never copies data.

bind (v.) To create a reference between a name and a value.

coercion (n.) The act of implicitly casting a value from one type to another.

conversion (n.) The act of explicitly casting a value from one type to another.

copy (v.) To create a new value in memory from the same data as another value.

data (n.) Information stored in a value. You may have copies of any given data stored in other values.

deep copy (v.) To both copy an object to a new value *and* copy all the data from values referenced within that object to new values.

identity (n.) The specific location in memory that a name is bound to. When two names share an identity, they are bound to the same value in memory.

immutable (adj.) Of or relating to a value that *cannot* be modified in place.

mutable (adj.) Of or relating to a value that *can* be modified in place.

mutate (v.) To change a value in place.

name (n.) A reference to a value in memory, commonly thought of as a "variable" in Python. A name must always be bound to a value. *Names have scope, but not type.*

rebind (v.) To bind an existing name to a different value.

reference (n.) The association between a name and a value.

scope (n.) A property that defines what section of the code a name is accessible from, such as from within a function or within a module.

shallow copy (v.) To copy an object to a new value but *not* copy the data from values referenced within that object to new values.

type (n.) A property that defines how a raw value is interpreted, for example, as an integer or a boolean.

value (n.) A unique copy of data in memory. There must be a reference to a value, or else the value is deleted. *Values have type, but not scope.*

variable (n.) A combination of a name and the value the name refers to.

weakref (n.) A reference that does not increase the reference count on the value.

To help keep us grounded in these concepts, we usually use the term *name* instead of *variable*. Instead of *changing* something, we *(re)bind a name* or *mutate a value.* Assignment never copies—it literally always binds a name to a value. Passing to a function is just assignment.

By the way, if you ever have trouble wrapping your head around these concepts and how they play out in your code, try the visualizer at *http://pythontutor.com/.*

Wrapping Up

It's easy to take something like variables for granted, but by understanding Python's unique approach, you can better avail yourself of the power that is available through dynamic typing. I must admit, Python has somewhat spoiled me. When I work in statically typed languages, I find myself pining for the expressiveness of duck typing.

Still, working with Python-style dynamic typing can take getting used to if you have a background in other languages. It's like learning how to speak a new human language: only with time and practice will you begin to think in the new tongue.

If all this is making your head swim, let me reiterate the single most important principles. Names have scope, but no type. Values have type, but no scope. A name can be bound to any value, and a value can be bound to any number of names. It really is that dead simple! If you remember that much, you'll go a long way.

6

FUNCTIONS AND LAMBDAS

Functions are one of the most elementary concepts in programming, yet Python packs a surprising amount of versatility into them. You'll recall from Chapter 3 that functions are first-class objects, so they are treated no differently from any other object. This fact, combined with the power of dynamic typing, opens up so many possibilities.

Python has full support for *functional programming*, a distinct paradigm from which we get those "lambdas," or anonymous functions, you keep reading about online. If you're used to languages like Haskell or Scala, a lot of the concepts in this chapter are going to seem familiar to you. However, if you're more used to object-oriented programming, such as in Java or C++, this may be the first time you've encountered many of these concepts.

When learning Python, it makes sense to dive into functional programming early on. It is perfectly possible to write idiomatic Python code without ever creating a single class (see Chapter 7). By contrast, functions and functional programming concepts underpin much of the language's most powerful features.

THEORY RECAP: FUNCTIONAL PROGRAMMING

Before digging into Python functions, you need to understand the functional programming paradigm.

If you're coming from a pure functional language like Haskell, Scala, Clojure, or Elm, this section won't give you any useful new information. Skip ahead to "Python Function Essentials."

Otherwise, even if you think you've used functional programming principles before, stick with me. A lot of developers don't realize all that's involved in this paradigm.

WHAT DO WE MEAN BY "FUNCTIONAL"?

To understand what functional programming is, you must understand what it is not. Chances are, you've been using either *procedural programming* or *object-oriented programming* up to this point. Both of those paradigms are *imperative*; you describe precisely how to accomplish a goal through specific, concrete processes.

Procedural programming organizes around *control blocks* and focuses heavily on *control flow*. Object-oriented programming organizes around classes and objects, and it focuses on *state*—specifically, the attributes (member variables) of those objects (see Chapter 7).

Functional programming is organized around *functions*. This paradigm is considered *declarative*, meaning problems are broken down into abstract steps. The programming logic is mathematically consistent and basically unchanged from one language to the next.

In functional programming, you write a function for each step. Each function accepts an input and produces an output, is self-contained, and does exactly one thing; it does not care about the rest of the program. Functions also lack *state*, meaning they do not store information between calls. Once a function exits, all of its local names go out of scope. Every time the function is called on the same input, it generates the same output.

Perhaps most importantly, functions should have no *side effects*, meaning they shouldn't mutate anything. If you pass a list to a pure function, the function should never change that list. Instead, it should output a brand-new list (or whatever value is expected).

The chief beauty of functional programming is that you can change the implementation of any one function without affecting anything else. As long as the input and output are consistent, it doesn't matter how the task is accomplished. This sort of code is much easier to debug and refactor than more *tightly coupled* code, in which each function relies on the implementation of the others.

Pure or Not?

It's easy to think that one is "doing functional programming" just because functions and lambdas are involved, but again, the paradigm organizes around *pure functions*, which have no side effects or state and only perform a single task per function.

Python's functional programming behavior is generally considered "impure," largely due to the existence of mutable data types. Extra effort is necessary to ensure functions have no side effects, as you saw in Chapter 5.

Given proper care, you can write pure functional code in Python. However, most Pythonistas choose to borrow specific ideas and concepts from functional programming, and to combine them with other paradigms.

In practice, you will find the most success if you follow the rules of functional programming *until you have a specific, well-reasoned motive to break them*. Those rules, in order from strictest to least strict, are as follows:

1. Every function should do one specific thing.

2. A function's implementation should never affect the behavior of the rest of the program.

3. Avoid side effects! The one exception to this should occur when a function belongs to an object. In that case, the function should only be able to mutate that object's members (see Chapter 7).

4. In general, functions shouldn't have (or be affected by) state. Providing the same input should always yield the same output.

Rule 4 is the most likely to have exceptions, especially where objects and classes are concerned.

In short, you'll often find that writing an entire, large Python project to be pure functional is a tad impractical. Instead, incorporate the principles and concepts of the paradigm into your style.

Functional Programming Myths

One common misconception about functional programming is that it avoids loops. In fact, because iteration is fundamental to the paradigm (as you'll see shortly), loops are essential. The idea is to avoid fussing with control flow, so *recursion* (a function calling itself) is often preferred to manual loops. However, you can't always avoid loops. If a few show up in your code, don't be alarmed. Your main focus should be to write pure functions.

Understand, functional programming is not a magic bullet. It offers many advantages and is especially well-suited to a number of situations, but it is not without its downsides. Some important algorithms and collections, such as union-find and hash tables, cannot be implemented efficiently, if at all, in pure functional programming. There are a number of situations where this paradigm has worse performance and higher memory usage than the alternatives. Concurrency is notoriously difficult to achieve in pure functional code.

(continued)

These topics get technical very quickly. For most developers, it's sufficient to understand that these issues exist with pure functional programming. If you find yourself needing to know more, there are many white papers on and discussions about these problems.

Functional programming is an excellent addition to your arsenal of knowledge, but be prepared to use it in conjunction with other paradigms and approaches. There are no magic bullets in programming.

Python Function Essentials

I briefly touched on functions in Chapter 3. Building on that knowledge, I'll gradually construct a more complex example in this chapter.

I'll start by creating a function that rolls a single die with a specified number of sides:

```
import random


def roll_dice(sides):
    return random.randint(1, sides)
```

Listing 6-1: dice_roll.py:1a

I define a function named roll_dice(), which accepts a single parameter, sides. This function is considered pure, because it has no side effects; it accepts a value as an input and returns a new value as an output. I return a value from the function using the return keyword.

The random module has a number of functions for producing random values. Here, I use its random.randint() function to generate a pseudorandom number in Python. I generate a random number between 1 and 20 (the value of sides in this example) inclusively, with random.randint(1, 20).

Here's my usage for the function:

```
print("Roll for initiative...")
player1 = ❶ roll_dice(20)
player2 = roll_dice(20)
if player1 >= player2:
    print(f"Player 1 goes first (rolled {player1}).")
else:
    print(f"Player 2 goes first (rolled {player2}).")
```

Listing 6-2: dice_roll.py:2a

Later, I call the function and pass the value 20 as an argument ❶, so the function call is effectively the same as rolling a 20-sided die. The value that the first function call returns is bound to player1; the second call's return is bound to player2.

PEDANTIC NOTE   The terms *parameter* and *argument* are commonly confused. A *parameter* is a "slot" in the function definition that accepts some data, while an *argument* is the data that is passed to the parameter in the function call. The definitions of those two words come from general computer programming, not just Python.

Because I defined roll_dice() as a function, I can use it as many times as I want. If I want to change its behavior, I only need to modify the function in the one place where it is defined, and every usage of that function will be affected.

Say I wanted to roll multiple dice at once and return the results in a tuple. I can rewrite the roll_dice() function to do that:

```
import random


def roll_dice(sides, dice):
    return tuple(random.randint(1, sides) for _ in range(dice))
```

Listing 6-3: dice_roll.py:1b

To allow rolling multiple dice, the function accepts a second parameter, dice, which represents the number of dice being rolled. The first parameter, sides, still represents the number of sides on any one of the dice.

The scary-looking line of code at the top of the function is a *generator expression*, which I'll cover in Chapter 10. For now, you can take it for granted that I'm generating one random number for each die being rolled and packing the results in a tuple.

Since my function now has a second parameter in the function call, I pass two arguments:

```
print("Roll for initiative...")
player1, player2 = roll_dice(20, 2)
if player1 >= player2:
    print(f"Player 1 goes first (rolled {player1}).")
else:
    print(f"Player 2 goes first (rolled {player2}).")
```

Listing 6-4: dice_roll.py:2b

The returned tuple can be *unpacked*, meaning each item in the tuple is bound to a name I can use to access the value. The number of names listed on the left (separated by commas) and the number of values in the tuple *must* match for this to work, or else Python will raise an error. (See Chapter 9 for more on unpacking and tuples.)

Recursion

Recursion occurs when a function calls itself. This can be helpful when you need to repeat the entire logic of a function but a loop is unsuitable or feels too cluttered, as in the upcoming example.

For example, returning to my dice-rolling function, I can accomplish the exact same result using recursion, instead of that generator expression I was using earlier (although in practice, the generator expression is usually considered more Pythonic).

```
import random


def roll_dice(sides, dice):
    if dice < 1:
        return ()
    roll = random.randint(1, sides)
    return (roll, ) + roll_dice(sides, dice-1)
```

Listing 6-5: dice_roll_recursive.py:1a

I store the resulting roll for this function call in roll. Then, in the recursive call, I pass my sides parameter as is, while reducing the number of dice to roll by one, to account for the die I just rolled. Finally, I combine the tuple that is returned from that recursive function call with the result of the roll on this function call, and I return the resulting longer tuple.

The usage is essentially the same as before:

```
dice_cup = roll_dice(6, 5)
print(dice_cup)
```

Listing 6-6: dice_roll_recursive.py:2a

If you were to print out each value being returned, in order from deepest recursive call to outermost, here's what you would see:

```
()
(2,)
(3, 2)
(6, 3, 2)
(4, 6, 3, 2)
(4, 4, 6, 3, 2)
```

Listing 6-7: Returns from recursive calls to roll_dice(6, 5)

When the number of dice left is zero or negative, I return an empty tuple instead of recursively calling it again. If I don't do that, the recursion will try to run forever. Thankfully, Python will pull the plug at some point and just crash the program, instead of letting it consume all your computer's memory (as some other programming languages are apt to do). The *recursion depth* is how many recursive function calls have not returned yet, and Python caps it at approximately one thousand.

 Typically, the effective maximum recursion depth is 997 in CPython, even though it should be 1000 according to the source code. Go figure.

If the recursion depth goes any deeper than the limit, the entire program stops and raises an error:

```
RecursionError: maximum recursion depth exceeded while calling a Python object
```

This is why it's so important that you build some means of stopping when you use recursion. In the roll_dice function, this stopping mechanism is at the very top of the function:

```
if dice < 1:
    return ()
```

Since dice is getting decremented every time the function calls itself, sooner or later, it will reach zero. When it does, it returns an empty tuple, instead of producing another recursive call. Then, the rest of the recursive calls can finish running and return.

There may be cases in which a recursion depth of a thousand is not enough. If you need more, you can override the maximum:

```
import sys
sys.setrecursionlimit(2000)
```

The sys.setrecursionlimit() function allows you to set a new maximum recursion depth. In this case, my new limit is 2000. The benefit of this approach is that once you no longer need your limit, you can set it back to the default so it can keep *other* recursive calls from getting out of hand.

GOTCHA ALERT It is still possible to have more serious problems if you raise the recursion limit too far. These problems might include stack overflows or segmentation faults, which are particularly difficult to debug. Recursion can also affect program performance. *Be careful with recursion!* How much is "too much" depends on your system.

Default Argument Values

You might imagine that I would need to roll a single die far more often than any other option. As it stands right now, I would have to manually specify that I only want to roll one 20-sided die:

```
result, = roll_dice(20, 1)
```

I have to manually pass a 1 as the second argument of roll_dice to specify that I'm rolling a single die.

By the way, that trailing comma after result is how I unpack a single value from a single-item tuple, meaning the actual value of the only item in the tuple is now bound to result. (See Chapter 9 for more on unpacking.)

Since rolling a single die is likely the most common action I want to take with this function, I want to make it more convenient to use. I can use *default argument values* to accomplish this:

```python
import random


def roll_dice(sides, dice=1):
    return tuple(random.randint(1, sides) for _ in range(dice))
```

Listing 6-8: dice_roll.py:1c

The dice parameter now has a default argument value of 1. Thus, any-time I don't specify the second argument, dice will use its default argument value. This makes it possible to use a simplified function call to roll a single six-sided die:

```python
result, = roll_dice(6)
```

If I do want to roll multiple dice, I can still pass that second argument:

```python
player1, player2 = roll_dice(20, 2)
```

When you specify a default argument value for a parameter, you are defining an *optional parameter*. Conversely, a parameter with no default argument value is a *required parameter*. You can have as many of each as you like, but you must list all required parameters *before* your optional parameters. Otherwise, the code won't run.

When using optional parameters, there is one significant trap lurking in the dark: default argument values are only evaluated once, when the function is defined. One place where this gets treacherous is when you're using any mutable data type, such as a list. Consider this code for generating values in a Fibonacci sequence, which doesn't quite work as expected:

```python
def fibonacci_next(series ❶ =[1, 1]):
  ❷ series.append(series[-1] + series[-2])
    return series
```

Listing 6-9: fibonacci.py:1a

This is going to have a problem because the default argument value [1, 1] ❶ is evaluated when Python first processes the function definition, creating a single mutable list with the value [1, 1] in memory. That gets mutated on the first function call ❷ and then returned.

This usage of the function shows the problem:

```
fib1 = fibonacci_next()
print(fib1)  # prints [1, 1, 2]
fib1 = fibonacci_next(fib1)
print(fib1)  # prints [1, 1, 2, 3]

fib2 = fibonacci_next()
print(fib2)  # should be [1, 1, 2] riiiiight?
```

Listing 6-10: fibonacci.py:2

Everything looks okay in the code, but it isn't. fib1 is now bound to the same mutable value as series, so any changes to fib1 are reflected in the default argument value *for every function call.* The second function call mutates this list further.

When I call fibonacci_next() a third time, I'm probably expecting to start with a clean slate, [1, 1, 2], which would be the result of a single mutation on the original default argument value. Instead, I'm getting the value of that single mutable value I've been messing with this whole time: fib2 is now a third alias to the list. Oops!

This becomes apparent when I examine the output. This is what I'd be expecting:

```
[1, 1, 2]
[1, 1, 2, 3]
[1, 1, 2]
```

But this is what I actually get:

```
[1, 1, 2]
[1, 1, 2, 3]
[1, 1, 2, 3, 5]
```

In short, *never use mutable values for default argument values.* Instead, use None as a default value, as shown in the following:

```
def fibonacci_next(series=None):
    if series is None:
        series = [1, 1]
    series.append(series[-1] + series[-2])
    return series
```

Listing 6-11: fibonacci.py:1b

The proper way is to use None as the default argument value, and then to create a new mutable value if that default is being used.

Running that same usage code as before (Listing 6-9) now produces the expected output:

```
[1, 1, 2]
[1, 1, 2, 3]
[1, 1, 2]
```

Keyword Arguments

Readability matters. Unfortunately, function calls with multiple parameters aren't always the most readable bits of code. *Keyword arguments* help resolve this by attaching labels to arguments in function calls.

Arguments that are mapped to their parameters by the order you pass them in, like in all the prior examples, are called *positional arguments*.

If you knew nothing about the roll_dice() function from earlier and you encountered this line of code, what would you think it did?

```
dice_cup = roll_dice(6, 5)
```

Listing 6-12: dice_roll.py:3a

You would probably guess that this is rolling multiple dice, and perhaps that it is specifying how many sides those dice have—but which is which? Is it rolling six five-sided dice or five six-sided dice? You can imagine how confusing this would be with even more arguments. This is the shortcoming of positional arguments.

As The Zen of Python says:

> In the face of ambiguity, refuse the temptation to guess.

It can't be good, then, to force the reader to guess. I can eliminate the ambiguity by using *keyword arguments*. I don't need to change the function definition at all to be able to use keyword arguments. I only need to change my function call:

```
dice_cup = roll_dice(sides=6, dice=5)
```

Listing 6-13: dice_roll.py:3b

Each of those names comes from the earlier function definition of roll_dice, where I specified it had two parameters: sides and dice. In my function call, I can assign values directly to those parameters by name. Now, there is no question about what each argument does. Specify the name of the parameter, matching what is in the function definition, and then assign the desired value directly to it. That's all.

When using keyword arguments, you don't even have to list them in order, just as long as all the required parameters receive values:

```
dice_cups = roll_dice(dice=5, sides=6)
```

Listing 6-14: dice_roll.py:3c

This can be even more helpful when you have multiple optional parameters on the function. Consider if I rewrote roll_dice() so that the dice being rolled were six sided, by default:

```
import random


def roll_dice(sides=6, dice=1):
    return tuple(random.randint(1, sides) for _ in range(dice))
```

Listing 6-15: dice_roll.py:1d

Keyword arguments allow you to simplify your function calls even further:

```
dice_cups = roll_dice(dice=5)
```

Listing 6-16: dice_roll.py:3d

You're only passing a value to one of the optional arguments, dice. For the other one, sides, the default value is used. It no longer needs to matter whether sides or dice appears first in the function's parameter list; you can just use the ones you want and leave the rest alone.

It is even possible to mix and match positional arguments and keyword arguments:

```
dice_cups = roll_dice(6, dice=5)
```

Listing 6-17: dice_roll.py:3e

Here, 6 is passed as a positional argument to the first parameter in the function definition, sides. Then, I pass 5 as a keyword argument to the parameter dice.

This can come in handy, particularly when you don't want to bother with naming the positional arguments but you still want to use one of many possible optional parameters. The only rule here is that your keyword arguments must come after your positional arguments in the function call. (See also the section "Keyword-Only Parameters" later in the chapter.)

On Overloaded Functions

If you're coming from a strictly typed language such as Java or C++, you're probably used to writing *overloaded functions*, wherein you can write multiple functions with the same name but different parameters. Typically, overloaded functions in languages that support them provide a consistent interface (function name), while supporting arguments of different types.

Python usually doesn't need overloaded functions. Using dynamic typing, duck typing, and optional parameters, you can write single functions that handle all the input scenarios you need to throw at Python.

If you really, really need overloaded functions—and you probably don't—you actually can create them with *single-dispatch functions*. I'll cover this in Chapter 15.

Variadic Arguments

With the skills discussed so far, even while using optional parameters, you still have to anticipate how many arguments can potentially get passed to your function. This is fine in most cases, but sometimes, you'll have no idea how many to expect.

To solve this, your first instinct might be to pack all the arguments into a single tuple or a list. That works in some situations, but other times, it can become an extra inconvenience when calling the function.

A better solution is to use *arbitrary arguments lists*, also called *variadic arguments*, which automatically pack multiple arguments into a single *variadic parameter* or *variadic positional parameter*. In the dice-rolling function, I want to allow the rolling of multiple dice, where each die may have a different number of sides:

```
import random


def roll_dice(*dice):
    return tuple(random.randint(1, d) for d in dice)
```

Listing 6-18: dice_roll_variadic.py:1a

I turn the parameter dice into a variadic parameter by preceding it with a single asterisk (*). All the arguments passed to roll_dice will now be packed into a tuple, bound to the name dice.

Within the function, I can use this tuple in the usual manner. In this case, I'm using a generator expression (see Chapter 10) to roll each die specified in dice.

The placement of the variadic parameter is important: it must come *after* any positional parameters in the function definition. Any parameters I list after it will only be usable as keyword arguments, because the variadic parameter consumes all the remaining positional arguments.

Here's my usage:

```
dice_cup = roll_dice(6, 6, 6, 6, 6)
print(dice_cup)

bunch_o_dice = roll_dice(20, 6, 8, 4)
print(bunch_o_dice)
```

Listing 6-19: dice_roll_variadic.py:2

In both function calls, I'm listing the dice I want to roll, with the number representing the number of sides of each die. In the first call, I'm rolling five six-sided dice. In the second call, I'm rolling four dice: a 20-sided die, a 6-sided die, an 8-sided die, and a 4-sided die.

If I wanted to use the recursive approach, I'd populate the argument list by automatically unpacking that tuple into the function call:

```
def roll_dice(*dice):
    if dice:
        roll = random.randint(1, dice[0])
        return (roll,) + roll_dice(❶ *dice ❷ [1:])
    return ()
```

Listing 6-20: dice_roll_variadic.py:1b

Most of this code is going to look similar to the earlier recursive version. The most significant change is in what I'm passing to the recursive function call. The asterisk (*) in front of the name unpacks the tuple dice into the argument list ❶. I already processed the first item in the list, so I use the slice notation [1:] to remove that first item ❷ (see Chapter 9), to ensure it isn't processed again.

PEDANTIC NOTE   If you want to use recursion, be prepared for a doozy of a debate in justifying it. Many Pythonistas consider recursion to be an anti-pattern, particularly when you can just use a loop.

Keyword Variadic Arguments

To capture an unknown number of *keyword arguments*, precede the parameter name with *two* asterisks (**), making the parameter a *keyword variadic parameter*. The keyword arguments passed to the function are packed into a single dictionary object, so as to preserve the association between keyword and value. They are similarly unpacked by being preceded with two asterisks.

This doesn't show up very often in the wild. After all, if you didn't know what the arguments were named, it would be hard to use them.

One case where keyword variadic arguments are commonly useful is in blindly relaying arguments to another function call:

```
def call_something_else(func, *args, **kwargs):
    return func(*args, **kwargs)
```

Listing 6-21: variadic_relay.py:1

The call_something_else() function has one positional argument, func, where I'll pass a *callable* object, such as another function. The second parameter, args, is a variadic parameter for capturing all the remaining positional arguments. Last is the keyword variadic parameter, kwargs, for capturing any keyword arguments; sometimes, the name kw is used instead. Remember, either of these can be empty and this code will still work.

You can check whether an object is callable by passing it to the *callable()* function.

The names args and kwargs are conventionally used for positional variadic and keyword variadic parameters, respectively. However, if you can think of names that better fit your particular situation, that's certainly acceptable!

When the function calls the callable object func, it first unpacks all the positional arguments that were captured, and then it unpacks all the keyword arguments. The function code doesn't need any knowledge of the callable object's parameter list; instead, any and every argument passed to call_something_else() after that first positional argument will get blindly passed on.

You can see this in action here:

```
def say_hi(name):
    print(f"Hello, {name}!")


call_something_else(say_hi, name="Bob")
```

Listing 6-22: variadic_relay.py:2

When I run that code, the call_something_else() function will call say_hi(), passing the argument name="Bob" to it. That produces the following output:

```
Hello, Bob!
```

This bit of magic will come back into play shortly in writing *decorators* (see the section "Decorators" later in this chapter).

Keyword-Only Parameters

You can use variadic parameters to turn some of your keyword parameters into *keyword-only parameters*, which were introduced in PEP 3102. These parameters cannot have values passed in as positional arguments, but rather only as keyword arguments. This can be especially useful in ensuring that particularly long or perilous parameter lists are used in the proper manner, instead of as nigh-on unreadable chains of positional arguments.

To demonstrate this, I'll rewrite my roll_dice() function to have two keyword-only parameters:

```
import random


def roll_dice(*, sides=6, dice=1):
    return tuple(random.randint(1, sides) for _ in range(dice))
```

Listing 6-23: dice_roll_keyword_only.py:1

I use the unnamed variadic parameter *, which ensures every parameter that follows it in the list can only be accessed by name. If the caller passes in too many positional arguments (or in this case, *any* positional arguments), a TypeError is raised.

This affects the usage, such that I can only use keyword arguments now:

```
dice_cup = roll_dice(sides=6, dice=5)
print(dice_cup)
```

Listing 6-24: dice_roll_keyword_only.py:2

Attempting to use positional arguments raises an error:

```
dice_cup = roll_dice(6, 5)  # raises TypeError
print(dice_cup)
```

Listing 6-25: dice_roll_keyword_only.py:3

Positional-Only Parameters

As of Python 3.8 (via PEP 570), it is also possible to define *positional-only parameters*. This is useful when the parameter name is either unhelpful or likely to be changed down the road, meaning any code using it as a keyword parameter would be likely to break in the future.

You'll recall that positional parameters must always come first in the parameter list. Placing a forward slash (/) in the list designates all preceding parameters as positional-only:

```
import random


def roll_dice(dice=1, /, sides=6):
    return tuple(random.randint(1, sides) for _ in range(dice))
```

Listing 6-26: dice_roll_positional_only.py:1

In this example, the parameter dice still has a default value of 1, but it is now positional-only. On the other hand, sides can be used as either a positional or a keyword parameter. Here's that behavior in action:

```
roll_dice(4, 20)            # OK; dice=4, sides=20
roll_dice(4)               # OK; dice=4, sides=6
roll_dice(sides=20)        # OK; dice=1, sides=20
roll_dice(4, sides=20)     # OK; dice=4, sides=20

roll_dice(dice=4)          # TypeError
roll_dice(dice=4, sides=20) # TypeError
```

Listing 6-27: dice_roll_positional_only.py:2

The first four examples all work, because the positional-only argument dice is either included as the first argument or omitted altogether. Any attempt to access dice by keyword fails with a TypeError.

Argument Types: All Together Now!

To ensure everything is clear regarding positional parameters and keyword parameters, I'll take a moment to review with this (admittedly contrived) example:

```
def func(pos_only=None, /, pos_kw=None, *, kw_only=None):
```

The parameter pos_only is positional-only, as it comes before the forward-slash (/) marker. If I have any positional-only parameters, they must appear first in the list. Because this parameter has a default value, it is optional. However, if I wanted to pass an argument to it, it would need to be the first positional argument passed to the function; otherwise, a TypeError would be raised.

Next is the pos_kw parameter, which can be either positional or keyword. It comes after any positional-only parameters and after the forward-slash (/) marker, if there is one.

Finally, after the asterisk (*) marker, I have kw_only, which is a keyword-only parameter. In this example, if my function receives more than two positional arguments, a TypeError will be raised.

Nested Functions

From time to time, you may want to reuse a piece of logic *within* a function but not clutter up your code by making yet another function. In this situation, you can nest functions within other functions.

I can use this to improve the recursive version of roll_dice(), making the logic for rolling a single die into something more reusable in the function:

```
import random


def roll_dice(sides=6, dice=1):
    def roll():
        return random.randint(1, sides)

    if dice < 1:
        return ()
    return (roll(), ) + roll_dice(sides, dice-1)
```

Listing 6-28: dice_roll_recursive.py:1b

In this example, I moved the logic for rolling a single die into a nested function roll(), which I can call from anywhere in the function roll_dice().

The direct benefit of abstracting out this logic is that it can be maintained more easily, without disrupting the rest of the code.

Here's the usage:

```
dice_cup = roll_dice(sides=6, dice=5)
print(dice_cup)
```

Listing 6-29: dice_roll_recursive.py:2b

That produces the usual random output.

In production, I'd rarely use a nested function for something that trivial. Normally, I'd employ a nested function for more complex logic that sees frequent reuse, especially if it is used in multiple places in the outer function.

You'll recall from Chapter 5 that the nested function can access the names of its enclosing scope. However, if I wanted to rebind or mutate any of those names from within the nested function, I'd need to use the nonlocal keyword.

Closures

You can create a function that builds and returns a kind of function called a *closure*, which encloses one or more nonlocal names. This pattern acts as a sort of "function factory."

Building on the dice example, I'll write a function that returns a *closure* for rolling a particular set of dice:

```
import random


def make_dice_cup(sides=6, dice=1):
    def roll():
        return tuple(random.randint(1, sides) for _ in range(dice))

  ❶ return roll
```

Listing 6-30: dice_cup_closure.py:1

I create the function make_dice_cup(), which accepts the arguments for sides and dice. Inside make_dice_cup(), I define a nested function roll(), which uses sides and dice. When that nested function is returned by the outer function (no parentheses!) ❶, it becomes a closure, because it encloses sides and dice.

```
roll_for_damage = make_dice_cup(sides=8, dice=5)
damage = roll_for_damage()
print(damage)
```

Listing 6-31: dice_cup_closure.py:2

I bind the closure returned by make_dice_cup() to the name roll_for _damage, which I can now call as a function without any arguments. The closure continues to use sides and dice with the values I specified earlier to roll dice and return values; it is now a function in its own right.

Caution is necessary when using closures, as you can easily violate the rules of functional programming with them. If a closure has the ability to mutate the values it encloses, it becomes a sort of de facto object, and a difficult one to debug at that!

Recursion with Closures

The previous closure example didn't use the recursive form of the dice-rolling code because, while it's possible to implement such closure correctly, it's even easier to do it wrong.

Here's the most apparently obvious, yet wrong, way to make that closure recursive:

```
import random


def make_dice_cup(sides=6, dice=1):
    def roll():
        nonlocal dice
        if dice < 1:
            return ()
        die = random.randint(1, sides)
        dice -= 1
        return (die, ) + roll()

    return roll
```

Listing 6-32: dice_cup_closure_recursive.py:1a

Using what you know about names and scope so far, can you anticipate what's wrong with the above?

The giveaway that something is wrong with the closure is the keyword nonlocal, as it indicates I'm mutating or rebinding a nonlocal name: dice.

Attempting to use this closure will reveal the problem:

```
roll_for_damage = make_dice_cup(sides=8, dice=5)
damage = roll_for_damage()
print(damage)

damage = roll_for_damage()
print(damage)
```

Listing 6-33: dice_cup_closure_recursive.py:2

That code produces the following output (for example):

```
(1, 3, 4, 3, 7)
()
```

The first time the closure roll_for_damage() is used, everything is fine. However, dice isn't reset when the function exits, so all subsequent calls to the closure find that dice == 0. Thus, they only return ().

To write a recursive closure, you need to use an optional parameter on the closure:

```
import random


def make_dice_cup(sides=6, dice=1):
    def roll(dice=dice):
        if dice < 1:
            return ()
        die = random.randint(1, sides)
        return (die, ) + roll(dice - 1)

    return roll
```

Listing 6-34: dice_cup_closure_recursive.py:1b

In this version, I use the nonlocal name dice as the default value of the new, local parameter dice. (Recall, this will only work with immutable types.) This behaves precisely as expected, as it still closes over sides and the nonlocal dice, but it rebinds neither.

Stateful Closures

While it is generally best to write closures as pure functions, it is occasionally useful to create a *stateful closure*—that is, a closure that retains a little bit of state between calls that it can use. In general, you should avoid using stateful closures unless no other solution presents itself.

Just to demonstrate this, I'll create a stateful closure that limits how many times a player can reroll a group of dice:

```
import random


def start_turn(limit, dice=5, sides=6):
    def roll():
        nonlocal limit
        if limit < 1:
            return None
        limit -= 1
        return tuple(random.randint(1, sides) for _ in range(dice))

    return roll
```

Listing 6-35: dice_roll_turns.py:1

I write the closure roll() so that it only allows the caller to reroll the dice a maximum number of times, specified by limit, before the function starts returning None. By this design, after the limit is reached, a new closure must be created. The logic of tracking how many times a player can roll the dice has been abstracted out into the closure.

This closure is very limited and predictable in how it mutates and uses its state. It's important to limit your closures in this way, since debugging a stateful closure can be difficult. There is no way to see the current value of `limit` from outside the closure; it's simply not possible.

You can see this predictable behavior at work in the usage:

```
turn1 = start_turn(limit=3)
while toss := turn1():
    print(toss)

turn2 = start_turn(limit=3)
while toss := turn2():
    print(toss)
```

Listing 6-36: dice_roll_turns.py:2

Running that code produces the following randomized output, wherein each turn gets three tosses of the dice; each toss is represented by a tuple:

```
(4, 1, 2, 1, 1)
(4, 2, 3, 1, 5)
(1, 6, 3, 4, 2)
(1, 6, 4, 5, 5)
(2, 1, 4, 5, 3)
(2, 4, 1, 6, 1)
```

A stateful closure can be useful in situations where writing an entire class (see Chapter 7) brings in too much boilerplate. Since I only have one piece of state, `limit`, and I am using it predictably, this approach is acceptable. Anything more complicated, and debugging becomes impractically difficult.

As I pointed out earlier, anytime you see `nonlocal` in a closure, you should be extra cautious, as it indicates the presence of state. This can be acceptable on occasion, but there is usually a better approach. Stateful closures are not pure functional programming!

Lambdas

A *lambda* is an anonymous (nameless) function made up of a single expression. The structure is as follows:

```
lambda x, y: x + y
```

On the left side of the colon is the parameter list, which may be omitted if you don't want to accept any arguments. On the right is the return expression, which is evaluated when the lambda is called and the result is implicitly returned. To use a lambda, you must bind it to a name, whether by assignment or by passing it as an argument to another function.

For example, here's a lambda that adds two numbers:

```
add = lambda x, y: x + y
answer = add(20, 22)
print(answer)  # outputs "42"
```

Listing 6-37: addition_lambda.py

I bind the `lambda` to the name `add` and then call it as a function. This particular lambda accepts two arguments and then returns their sum.

Why Lambdas Are Useful

Many programmers can't imagine ever needing nameless functions. It would seem to make reuse completely impractical. After all, if you're just going to bind a lambda to a name, shouldn't you have just written a function?

To understand how lambdas can be useful, let's take a look at an example *without* lambdas first. This code represents a player character in a basic text adventure game:

```
import random

health = 10
xp = 10
```

Listing 6-38: text_adventure_v1.py:1

I'm keeping track of my character's stats in a couple of global names at the top, `health` and `xp`, which I'll use throughout my program:

```
def attempt(action, min_roll, ❶ outcome):
    global health, xp
    roll = random.randint(1, 20)
    if roll >= min_roll:
        print(f"{action} SUCCEEDED.")
        result = True
    else:
        print(f"{action} FAILED.")
        result = False

    scores = ❷ outcome(result)
    health = health + scores[0]
    print(f"Health is now {health}")
    xp = xp + scores[1]
    print(f"Experience is now {xp}")

    return result
```

Listing 6-39: text_adventure_v1.py:2

My `attempt()` function handles rolling the dice, using the outcome to decide whether the player's action succeeded or failed, and then modifying the values of the global `health` and `xp` variables accordingly. It determines how those values should be changed, based on the value returned from calling the function passed to outcome.

The part to focus on is the parameter outcome ❶—which, by its usage in attempt() ❷, should be a function that accepts a boolean value and returns a tuple of two integers representing the desired changes to health and xp, respectively.

Expanding on that example, I'll use what I've built so far:

```
def eat_bread(success):
    if success:
        return (1, 0)
    return (-1, 0)


def fight_ice_weasel(success):
    if success:
        return (0, 10)
    return (-10, 10)


❶ attempt("Eating bread", 5, eat_bread)
  attempt("Fighting ice weasel", 15, fight_ice_weasel)
```

Listing 6-40: text_adventure_v1.py:3a

There's no real pattern to the outcomes of each possible action, so I have to write functions for each one: in this example, eat_bread() and fight_ice_weasel(). Even this example is a bit oversimplified, as the code determining the outcome might involve a bunch of mathematics and randomization. Regardless, since I need a separate outcome function for each action, this code is going to grow rapidly, leading to a maintainability nightmare.

(Be advised, the if statement above is not the most Pythonic way to write that code; I deliberately chose that structure to illustrate the logic.)

When I attempt an action ❶, I pass the string representing the action, the minimum dice roll necessary to succeed, and the function determining the outcome. When passing a function, remember not to include the trailing parentheses. Here, I want to pass the function itself, not the value it returns.

This sort of usage is where lambdas come in. I can replace the eat_bread() and fight_ice_weasel() functions, plus the two calls to attempt(), with just the following:

```
attempt("Eating bread", 5,
        lambda success: (1, 0) if success else (-1, 0))

attempt("Fighting ice weasel", 15,
        lambda success: (0, 10) if success else (-10, 10))
```

Listing 6-41: text_adventure_v1.py:3b

The third argument of each is a lambda, which accepts a single parameter named success and returns a value depending on the value of success. Let's isolate just that first lambda:

```
lambda success: (1, 0) if success else (-1, 0))
```

When the lambda is called, if the value of success is True, then (1, 0) will be returned. Otherwise, (-1, 0) is returned.

That lambda is being passed to (and thus bound to) the outcome parameter of the attempt() function, and it is subsequently called with a single boolean argument.

By using lambdas in this manner, I can create many different possible outcomes in my code with only one line of code.

Remember that *a lambda may only consist of a single return expression*! This makes lambdas suitable for short, clear fragments of logic, especially when the code is made more readable by keeping that logic close to its usage within another function call. If you want anything more complex, you'll need to write a proper function.

Lambdas as Sorting Keys

One of the most common situations where a lambda comes in handy is when specifying a *key function*, which is a callable that returns the part of a collection or object that should be used for sorting. A key function is typically passed to another function that is responsible for sorting data in some manner.

For example, here I have a list of tuples containing first and last names, and I want to sort the list by last name:

```
people = [
    ("Jason", "McDonald"),
    ("Denis", "Pobedrya"),
    ("Daniel", "Foerster"),
    ("Jaime", "López"),
    ("James", "Beecham")
]

by_last_name = sorted(people, ❶ key=lambda x: x[1])
print(by_last_name)
```

Listing 6-42: sort_names.py

The sorted() function uses the key argument ❶, which is always a function or other callable, by passing each item to it and then using the value returned from that callable to determine the sorting order. Since I want the tuples sorted by last name, which is the second item of each tuple, I have the lambda return that item, which is x[1].

The end result is that by_last_name contains the list, sorted by last name.

Decorators

Decorators allow you to modify the behavior of a function (or even multiple functions) by wrapping it in an additional layer of logic. This changes the function's behavior without you having to rewrite the function itself.

To demonstrate this, here's another example with my text adventure game hero. I want to define multiple game events that affect the player character's statistics in different ways, and I want those changes displayed as they happen. I'll start with an implementation that doesn't use decorators. This code only uses concepts I've already covered so far in this book, so I'll mainly draw your attention to some inefficiencies.

I'll start by defining my global variables:

```
import random

character = "Sir Bob"
health = 15
xp = 0
```

Listing 6-43: text_adventure_v2.py:1a

Next, I'll define functions for each action the player can take:

```
def eat_food(food):
    global health
 ❶ if health <= 0:
        print(f"{character} is too weak.")
        return

    print(f"{character} ate {food}.")
    health += 1
 ❷ print(f"   Health: {health} | XP: {xp}")


def fight_monster(monster, strength):
    global health, xp
 ❸ if health <= 0:
        print(f"{character} is too weak.")
        return

    if random.randint(1, 20) >= strength:
        print(f"{character} defeated {monster}.")
        xp += 10
    else:
        print(f"{character} flees from {monster}.")
        health -= 10
        xp += 5
 ❹ print(f"   Health: {health} | XP: {xp}")
```

Listing 6-44: text_adventure_v2.py:2a

Each function represents an action the player can take, and some common code is shared between these functions. First, each function checks the character's health to determine if the character is even able to perform the action ❶ ❸. If the character's health is sufficient, the player performs the action, which alters the character's statistics. When the action is completed (or if the character's health is too low to take an action), the current stats are displayed ❷ ❹.

And then, of course, I have the usage:

```
eat_food("bread")
fight_monster("Imp", 15)
fight_monster("Direwolf", 15)
fight_monster("Minotaur", 19)
```

Listing 6-45: text_adventure_v2.py:3

That works, but as I said, the repeated code in Listing 6-44 is not very Pythonic. Your first instinct might be to move the common code—the code that checks the health and displays the statistics—out into their own functions. However, you would still need to remember to call each one within *every character action function*, and they're easy to overlook. Furthermore, each function would still need that conditional statement at the top to ensure the code isn't run when health is too low.

This situation, where I want to run the same code before and after every function, can be perfectly solved with decorators.

Here, I'll create a decorator toward the top of the text adventure game code:

```
❶ import functools
import random

character = "Sir Bob"
health = 15
xp = 0


def character_action(func):
❷     @functools.wraps(func)
❸     def wrapper(*args, **kwargs):
        if health <= 0:
            print(f"{character} is too weak.")
            return

        result = func(*args, **kwargs)
        print(f"    Health: {health} | XP: {xp}")
        return result

❹     return wrapper
```

Listing 6-46: text_adventure_v2.py:1b

A decorator is most often implemented as a closure, which closes over a function (or any other callable object) being modified. The decorator itself, character_action(), accepts a func parameter, which is the callable being modified.

Within the decorator definition is the *wrapper*, which is the callable where the decorator's logic lives ❸. As I said, most commonly, the closure pattern is used for this. However, the wrapper can be implemented with any callable, including a class. (Technically, I could even implement the wrapper as a noncallable, but this is seldom, if ever, useful.)

Because I don't know how many arguments will be passed to any function I'll apply the decorator to, I set up the wrapper to accept variadic arguments.

The @functools.wraps(func) line ❷ prevents the callable being wrapped from having its identity concealed from the rest of the program. Without that line, wrapping the callable would mess up external access of such important function attributes as __doc__ (the docstring) and __name__. This line is itself a decorator that ensures all the important attributes of the callable are retained by the now-wrapped function, thus making them accessible outside the function in all the usual ways. (To use that special decorator, I must import functools first ❶.)

Inside the wrapper, I put all that logic I want to run before and after each function. After checking health, I call the function that is bound to func, unpacking all the variadic arguments into the call. I also bind the return value to result, so I can ensure that gets returned from the decorator after I print the stats.

As with any closure, it is supremely important that the outer function return the inner function ❹.

Now, I can use the decorator I wrote and refactor my other functions:

```
@character_action
def eat_food(food):
    global health
    print(f"{character} ate {food}.")
    health += 1


@character_action
def fight_monster(monster, strength):
    global health, xp
    if random.randint(1, 20) >= strength:
        print(f"{character} defeated {monster}.")
        xp += 10
    else:
        print(f"{character} flees from {monster}.")
        health -= 10
        xp += 5
```

Listing 6-47: text_adventure_v2.py:2b

To apply decorators to a function, I list each decorator I want to apply directly above the function definition, one decorator per line. I precede each decorator name with an @ symbol. In my example, I only apply a single decorator to each function, but you can use as many as you like. They will be applied in order, with each decorator wrapping whatever is immediately below it.

Since I moved all the repetitive logic about checking health and displaying stats out of the individual functions and into the decorator, my code is cleaner and easier to maintain. If you run the code, it works the same as before.

Type Hints and Function Annotations

Python 3.5 onward allows you to specify *type hints*, which are exactly that: *hints* about what data type should be passed in or returned. These are not strictly necessary, given Python's robust dynamic type system, but they may have a few benefits.

First, type hinting aids in documentation. The function definition now shows what type of information it wants, which is especially helpful when your IDE auto-magically shows hints as you type arguments in.

Second, type hints help you catch potential bugs sooner. Static type checkers like *Mypy* are the primary tools for this (see Chapter 2). Some IDEs, like PyCharm, may warn you if you're doing something weird, like passing a string to something type-hinted as an integer.

If you're familiar with statically typed languages like Java and C++, this might make you a little excited.

However, understand that using type hints does not trade Python's dynamic typing for static typing!

Python will not raise an error if you pass the wrong type.

Python will not try to convert data to the specified type.

Python will actually ignore these hints altogether!

GOTCHA ALERT   Lambdas do not support type hinting.

Type hints are specified with *annotations*, which are extra pieces of information that are permitted by the Python language but are not actually processed by the interpreter itself. There are two kinds of annotations.

Variable annotations specify the expected type on a name, like this:

```
answer: int = 42
```

Function annotations specify type hints on parameters and function returns. Here, I apply function annotations to the roll_dice() function from earlier:

```
import random
import typing


def roll_dice(sides: int = 6, dice: int = 1) -> typing.Tuple[int, ...]:
    # --snip--
```

Listing 6-48: dice_roll.py:1e

This notation allows me to denote what types I expect for the parameters and return. In this case, both parameters should receive an integer, so I follow each name with a colon and then int as the expected data type. If there's a default value of the expected type, it is included after the type hint.

GOTCHA ALERT If a parameter has a default value of None, instead of a default value of the expected type, use the type hint typing.Optional[int], where the expected type (int, in this case) appears in the brackets.

I denote the return type with an arrow (->) and the expected type. Collections like tuples and lists are a little trickier to specify with type hints. From the typing module, I can use the notation Tuple[ ], which is a *generic type*. Every value of this particular tuple should be an int, but since I don't really know how many will be returned, I specify a ... to say, "There may be more." Now, the function will be expected to return one or more integers, but no other types.

By the way, if you don't know what or how many types will be returned in a tuple, you can use the notation typing.Tuple[typing.Any, ...]

That return type hint in the preceding code example is pretty long. I could shorten it by defining a *type alias*, like this:

```
import random
import typing


TupleInts = typing.Tuple[int, ...]


def roll_dice(sides: int = 6, dice: int = 1) -> TupleInts:
    # --snip--
```

Listing 6-49: dice_roll.py:1f

I define TupleInts as a type alias for Tuple[int, ...], and I can use it the same way throughout my code.

Again, Python itself won't act on these type hints; it will only recognize the notation system as valid and store it in the __annotations__ attribute of the function, nothing more.

I can now run this code through Mypy:

```
mypy dice_roll.py
```

If there are any mismatches between the type hints and the actual usage, Mypy will list these in detail, so they can be fixed.

Duck Typing and Type Hints

You might think that type hinting is incompatible with duck typing, but thanks to the typing module, the two generally play very well with one another.

For example, if you wanted a function that could accept a single parameter of any type that could be iterated over (see Chapter 9), such as a tuple or a list, you could use `typing.Iterable[]`, with the contained type in the brackets. For this example, I'll presume that the iterable may contain any type.

```
def search(within: typing.Iterable[typing.Any]):
```

The parameter `within` is type-hinted to be an iterable with `typing.Iterable[ ]`. The hint `typing.Any` within the square brackets indicates that the `Iterable` can contain items of any data type.

The typing module contains many different such types, enough to fill up a separate chapter altogether. The best way to learn more about type hinting is to read the documentation: *https://docs.python.org/library/typing.html*. I also recommend taking a look at PEP 484, which defined type hinting, and PEP 3107, which defined function annotations.

Should You Use Type Hinting?

Type hinting is entirely optional, and there are cases for it and against it. Some argue that it clutters up the code, impairing the natural readability that Python attained through dynamic typing. Others see it as a much-needed tool for mitigating the bugs made possible through the lack of static typing.

In practice, you don't need to make a wholesale "use or don't use" decision. Because type hinting is optional, you can use it in cases where it improves the readability and stability of the code and skip it in cases where it doesn't. Even within a function, you can define a type hint for one parameter and omit it for the next.

Ultimately, the decision is up to you and your team alone. Only you know if and when type hints will be helpful. In short, *know thine own project*.

Since this book focuses on idiomatic Python above all else, and since type hinting is entirely optional, I won't use it in any future examples.

Wrapping Up

I hope you come away from this chapter with a newfound appreciation for functional programming in the Python language. Even when the paradigm is not embraced wholesale, its concepts and guidelines inform Pythonic code.

I'll still apply functional concepts as I move into object-oriented programming in the next chapter. I've found that, when combined correctly, these paradigms interact in surprisingly positive ways.

7

OBJECTS AND CLASSES

Objects are the bread and butter of many a programmer. Python makes full use of objects, even to the point of inspiring the mantra, "Everything is an object." However, if you've worked with classes and objects in any other language, Python's take may surprise you.

Object-oriented programming (or *OOP*) is a paradigm in which data and its corresponding logic is organized into objects. If you're familiar with such languages as Java, C++, Ruby, and C#, you're well acquainted with these concepts.

Yet, object-oriented programming in Python is not mutually exclusive with functional programming; in fact, the two paradigms work very well together.

In this chapter, I'll cover the essentials of object-oriented programming in Python: creating classes with attributes, modules, and properties. I'll demonstrate adding various behaviors via special methods, and I'll wrap up with a summary of the situations in which classes are the most useful.

THEORY RECAP: OBJECT-ORIENTED PROGRAMMING

Python uses class-based, object-oriented programming, so that's what I discuss herein. If you're coming from a class-based, object-oriented language like Java or C++, this section won't give you any useful insights. You can skip right to the "Declaring a Class" section.

Otherwise, even if you've used objects and classes in passing, I strongly recommend you hang in there with me. There's a deep canyon of difference between "coding with objects" and object-oriented programming.

In object-oriented programming, code is organized into classes, from which you create objects. A *class* is a sort of blueprint for creating one or more objects, which are known as *instances* in Python. Imagine you have a blueprint for a house; although you create one blueprint, it can be used to build many separate houses. Each of those houses is structurally identical, but with different contents.

Objects are composed of *member variables* and *member functions*, which are known respectively as *attributes* and *methods* in Python. More broadly, an instance has data in the form of attributes, and it has methods that work on that data.

The purpose of a class is *encapsulation*, which means two things:

1. The data and the functions that manipulate said data are bound together into one cohesive unit.

2. The implementation of a class's behavior is kept out of the way of the rest of the program. (This is sometimes referred to as a *black box*.)

For example, a basic social media comment could be implemented as a class. It has specific attributes (data): the text of the comment and the number of likes the comment received. It also has specific methods that work on the attributes: editing and liking. The code that uses this class shouldn't care about how the behavior is implemented, while the class's methods allow the desired behavior to be invoked.

A method that exists purely to access an attribute is called a *getter*, while a method that modifies an attribute is called a *setter*. Particularly in Python, the existence of these methods should be justified by some form of data modification or data validation that the methods perform in conjunction with accessing or modifying the attribute. If a method does none of that and merely returns from or assigns to the attribute, it is known as a *bare* getter or setter, which is considered an anti-pattern, especially in Python.

With this Comment class, one particular comment ("My pet llama is a brilliant coder!!!") is an instance of the class. You can have multiple instances of the same class, and each of those objects will contain distinct data; modifying the contents of one object will not affect any other instance of the same class.

There are two important relationships in object-oriented programming. The first is *composition*, wherein an object contains other objects. For example, you might create a Like class to store the username of the person liking the comment. A particular Comment instance might have a list of Like instances. This is also called a *has-a* relationship: a Comment *has a* Like.

The second type of relationship is *inheritance*, wherein a class inherits and builds on another existing class. For example, I might create an AuthorComment class that has the same attributes and methods as a Comment, along with some additional attributes or methods. This is called an *is-a* relationship: an AuthorComment *is a* Comment. Inheritance is a big topic, so I'll cover it in depth in Chapter 13.

Declaring a Class

Creating a new class is simple. I'll create a class named SecretAgent:

```
class SecretAgent:
```

Listing 7-1: Initializing a class

Below this, in the accompanying suite of the class declaration, I'd add any methods I want to include in the object. An object is known as an *instance* of a class in Python. I'll cover this in detail shortly.

In Python, everything is an object, in that everything inherits from the object class. In Python 3, this inheritance from object is implicit, as seen in Listing 7-1. In Python 2, you had to explicitly inherit from object, or from another class that inherits from object. (I cover inheritance in Chapter 13. You can take it for granted here.)

Here's the SecretAgent class declaration again, this time explicitly inheriting from object, as Python 2 would have required:

```
class SecretAgent(object):
```

Listing 7-2: Initializing a class with explicit inheritance

Listings 7-1 and 7-2 are functionally identical. Python developers really hate *boilerplate code*, which is code that is widely reused, with little or no modification. That is why Python 3 added the shorter technique seen in Listing 7-1. Unless you need to support Python 2, the shorter technique is preferred. You'll encounter both ways often enough, so it's important to know that they do the exact same thing in Python 3.

The Initializer

A class often has an *initializer* method for defining the initial values of *instance attributes*, which are the member variables that exist in each instance. If your instance will have no instance attributes, you don't need to define __init__().

I want each instance of SecretAgent to have a code name and a list of secrets. Here's the initializer for my SecretAgent class, which has two instance attributes:

```
class SecretAgent:

    def __init__(self, codename):
        self.codename = codename
        self._secrets = []
```

Listing 7-3: secret_agent.py:1a

The initializer must have the name __init__ to be recognized as an initializer, and it must accept at least one argument, conventionally called self. This self argument references the instance the method is acting on.

In this case, I also accept a second argument, codename, which I use as the initial value of one of my instance attributes. This self.codename attribute will be the code name of the secret agent.

Instance attributes are part of the class instance itself, so I must access them through the dot (.) operator on self. All instance attributes should be declared in the initializer method, rather than on the fly in other instance methods. Therefore, I'm also defining self._secrets as an empty list. This will be a list of secrets the particular secret agent (instance) is keeping.

Lastly, an initializer must never return a value via the return keyword; if it does, calling the initializer will raise a TypeError. However, you may use return by itself to explicitly exit the method, if you ever need to.

Whenever I create a new class instance, the initializer is automatically called. Here, I create three SecretAgent instances and provide arguments for the codename parameter of the initializer:

```
from secret_agent import SecretAgent
mouse = SecretAgent("Mouse")
armadillo = SecretAgent("Armadillo")
fox = SecretAgent("Fox")
```

Listing 7-4: secret_agent_usage.py:1

In this module, I import my SecretAgent class and create three new instances. You'll notice that I didn't need to pass anything to the first parameter, self. That's taken care of behind the scenes. Instead, my first argument, "Mouse", is passed to the second parameter of the initializer, codename. Each instance also has its own empty _secrets list.

The Constructor

If you're coming from C++, Java, or some similar language, you may expect to write a *constructor*—a function that constructs an instance of a class—or you may think that the initializer does the same thing as a constructor. In fact, Python 3 splits the duties of a typical constructor between the initializer __init__() and the constructor __new__().

In Python, the constructor __new__() takes care of actually creating the instance in memory. When you create a new instance, the constructor is automatically called first, followed by a call to the initializer. The constructor is the only method in the class to be called automatically before the object is created!

You don't normally need to define a constructor; one is provided automatically. The only time you would create a constructor would be if you needed additional control over the process. However, to familiarize you with the syntax, I'll write a very basic (and effectively pointless) constructor, which could go in a class definition:

```
def __new__(cls, *args, **kwargs):
    return super().__new__(cls, *args, **kwargs)
```

The constructor always has the name __new__, and it implicitly accepts a class as its first parameter, cls (in contrast to the initializer, which accepts a class instance on self). Since the initializer accepts parameters, I also need to prepare the constructor to accept these on the constructor, so I use variadic arguments to capture these arguments and pass them on to the initializer parameters.

The constructor must return the class instance that gets created. Technically, I could return whatever I wanted here, but the expected behavior would almost certainly be to return an instance that has been instantiated from the SecretAgent class. To do that, I call the __new__ function on the parent class, which you may recall (from Listing 7-2) is object. (I'll return to super() in Chapter 13. Don't worry about understanding it now.)

In practice, if this is all your constructor needs to do, just omit it! Python automatically handles the constructor behavior if you don't write any code for it. Only write a constructor when you need to control the behavior around instantiating the class instance itself. In any event, that scenario is rare; it is perfectly plausible that you will never write a constructor in your entire Python programming career.

The Finalizer

The *finalizer* is called when a class instance finally reaches the end of its lifespan and is cleaned up by the garbage collector. It exists solely to handle any technically complex cleanup that your particular class may require. As with the constructor, you will seldom, if ever, need to write this function yourself. If you do, it's important to understand: the finalizer is only called if the class instance (value) itself is cleaned up by the garbage collector!

If any references to the class instance still exist, the finalizer won't be called; furthermore, depending on the implementation of Python you're using, the garbage collector might not always clean up the class instance when you'd expect, if at all.

Therefore, only use the finalizer for code directly relating to garbage-collecting the class instance. It should never contain code that needs to be run as part of any other circumstance.

Here's a rather useless finalizer that prints a message when the garbage collector cleans up a SecretAgent class instance:

```
def __del__(self):
    print(f"Agent {self.codename} has been disavowed!")
```

Listing 7-5: secret_agent.py:2

A finalizer always has the name __del__ and accepts a single parameter, self. It must not return anything.

To demonstrate this finalizer, I'll create and manually delete an instance. It is possible to delete a name, thereby unbinding it from its value, by using the del keyword. Given the SecretAgent class with that finalizer method, I can create and then delete a name referring to a class instance:

```
from secret_agent import SecretAgent
weasel = SecretAgent("Weasel")
del weasel
```

Listing 7-6: secret_agent_disavow.py

I create a new instance from the SecretAgent class and bind it to the name weasel. Then, I immediately delete the name by using the del operator. The name weasel is now undefined again. Coincidentally, because no references remain to the SecretAgent instance the name was bound to, that instance is cleaned up by the garbage collector, which first calls the finalizer.

PEDANTIC NOTE This garbage collector behavior is implementation-specific to CPython. Other implementations of Python may behave differently.

Thus, running that code displays this output:

```
Agent Weasel has been disavowed!
```

Note that del only deletes the name, not the value! If you have multiple names bound to the same value, and if you del one of those names, then the other names and their values will be unaffected. In other words, del will not force the garbage collector to delete the objects.

Attributes

All variables belonging to a class or instance are called *attributes*. Attributes belonging to the instance itself are called *instance attributes*, which are also sometimes referred to as *member variables*. Attributes belonging to the class itself are *class attributes*, which are also sometimes called *class variables*.

Many intermediate-level Python programmers don't realize there is a significant difference between the two. I must admit, I spent the first few years of my Python development career using them utterly incorrectly!

Instance Attributes

An *instance attribute* exists on the instance itself; its value is unique to the instance and is not available to other instances. All instance attributes should be declared in the class's initializer.

Revisiting the __init__() method from Listing 7-3, you'll see I have two instance attributes:

```
class SecretAgent:
    def __init__(self, codename):
        self.codename = codename
        self._secrets = []
```

Class Attributes

A *class attribute* exists on the class, instead of on an individual instance. In practice, this means that all related class instances effectively "share" a class attribute, although it would exist even without any instances.

Class attributes are declared at the top of the class, outside of any methods. Here, I add one class attribute directly into the suite of the class:

```
class SecretAgent:

    _codeword = ""

    def __init__(self, codename):
        self.codename = codename
        self._secrets = []
```

Listing 7-7: secret_agent.py:1b

The attribute _codeword belongs to the SecretAgent class. Typically, all class attributes are declared before any methods to make them easier to find, although this is just convention. The important part is that they are defined outside of any methods.

The class attribute can be accessed like this:

```
❶ SecretAgent._codeword = "Parmesan"
  print(armadillo._codeword)  # prints "Parmesan"
  print(mouse._codeword)      # prints "Parmesan"

❷ mouse._codeword = "Cheese"
  print(mouse._codeword)      # prints "Cheese"
  print(armadillo._codeword)  # prints "Parmesan"
```

Listing 7-8: secret_agent_usage.py:2a

I can access the class attribute _codeword directly through the class, or through any instances instantiated from the class. If the class attribute is rebound or mutated on the class itself ❶, the changes will appear in all cases. However, if a value is assigned to the name on an instance, it will create an instance attribute with the same name ❷, which shadows the class attribute on that instance, without affecting other instances.

Class attributes are particularly useful for constant values that the class's methods use. I also find them more practical and maintainable than global variables in many cases, especially in GUI programming. For example, I often employ class attributes when I need to maintain a shared instance of a widget, like a window.

Scope-Naming Conventions

If you're coming from a language that has class scope, you may wonder why I haven't mentioned it yet. Isn't data hiding an important part of encapsulation? In fact, Python has no formal concept of data hiding. Instead, PEP 8 outlines a naming convention that indicates whether an attribute is safe to modify externally (public) or not (nonpublic).

While I talk a lot about attributes in this section, these naming conventions apply to methods as well.

Nonpublic

By preceding a name with an underscore, I declare that the attribute _secrets is intended to be *nonpublic*, meaning it shouldn't be modified (or, ideally, accessed) outside of the class. This is more of a social contract via style convention; I'm not actually hiding anything.

This may seem dangerous to many developers coming from languages with explicit scope, like Java, but it works out pretty well. As my pal "grym" likes to put it, "If you know why you shouldn't stick a fork in a toaster, you are therefore qualified to stick a fork in a toaster." In other words, if the client is going to disregard the underscore warning label, they probably know what they're doing. (On the off-chance they don't, they're fully responsible for the consequences.) That little underscore hanging out after the dot operator is advertising "You really shouldn't mess with me!"

Public

The attribute codename, which does not start with an underscore, is intended to be *public*. It is okay for this attribute to be accessed or modified externally, as it won't really affect the behavior of the class. Public attributes are preferable to writing a plain getter/setter pair of methods; the behavior is the same, but the result is cleaner, with less boilerplate.

If an attribute needs a custom getter or setter, one approach is to define the attribute as nonpublic and create a public *property*, which I'll come back to shortly.

Name Mangling

Python does offer *name mangling*, which rewrites an attribute or method name to prevent it from being shadowed by derived (inheriting) classes.

This provides a sort of weak form of data hiding. It can also be useful for an added level of forewarning: "No, *really*, if you mess with this attribute, terrible things will happen!"

To mark an attribute (or method) for name mangling, precede the name with two underscores (__), like this:

```
class Message:

    def __init__(self):
        self.__format = "UTF-8"
```

Listing 7-9: message.py:1

The __format attribute will be name mangled, so accessing it externally in the ordinary manner will not work:

```
msg = Message()
print(msg.__format)  # AttributeError
```

Listing 7-10: message.py:2

This will raise an `AttributeError` because the `msg` instance does not have an attribute named __format; the name of that attribute was mangled. Be aware that name mangling is *not* a true form of data hiding! It is still perfectly possible to access a name-mangled attribute:

```
print(msg._Message__format)
```

Listing 7-11: message.py:3

The name-mangling pattern is predictable: an underscore, the name of the class, and then the name of the attribute, with its two leading underscores.

Public, Nonpublic, or Name Mangled?

When deciding whether to make an attribute public or nonpublic, I ask myself one question: could changing this attribute externally cause unexpected or negative behavior in the class? If the answer is yes, I make the attribute nonpublic by preceding it with an underscore. If the answer is no, I leave the attribute public. It is up to the coder using the class to respect the rules or suffer the consequences.

As to name mangling, in practice, I very rarely employ this pattern. I reserve it only for those cases where (a) I need to avoid a naming conflict in the context of inheritance or (b) external access of the attribute will have exceptionally horrific effects on the behavior of the class, and thus, an extra degree of warning is justified.

Always remember that Python does not have private class scope. Truly secret data should be properly encrypted, not just concealed from your API. There are also no optimization benefits to private class scope, unlike in languages like Java, since all attribute lookups occur at runtime.

 There are a few hacker-y ways to achieve a form of true data hiding, but they're too complex or impractical for regular usage.

Methods

A class is nothing without its methods, which make encapsulation possible. There are three distinct types of methods: instance methods, class methods, and static methods.

Instance Methods

Instance methods are your run-of-the-mill methods, which exist on the instance itself. The first parameter, conventionally named self, provides access to the instance attributes of the instance.

Here, I add an instance method to my SecretAgent class:

```
def remember(self, secret):
    self._secrets.append(secret)
```

Listing 7-12: secret_agent.py:3

Besides the required first parameter, the instance method accepts a second parameter, secret, which is appended to the list bound to the instance attribute _secrets.

I call this method on the instance, using the dot operator:

```
mouse.remember(("42.864025, -72.568511"))
```

Listing 7-13: secret_agent_usage.py:2b

The dot operator implicitly passes mouse to the self parameter, so my first argument, the tuple of coordinates (notice the extra set of parentheses), is passed to the second parameter, secret, on the remember() method.

Class Methods

Like class attributes, *class methods* belong to the class, instead of to the instances instantiated from the class. These are useful for working with class attributes.

Back in Listing 7-7, I defined _codeword as a class attribute so all SecretAgent instances would be aware of the code word; it's something all agents should have in common. I need a way to inform all the agents at once of the new code word, so I'll add a class method, inform(), which will modify the _codeword class attribute:

```
@classmethod
def inform(cls, codeword):
    cls._codeword = codeword
```

Listing 7-14: secret_agent.py:4

I precede a class method with the built-in @classmethod decorator. A class method receives the class as its first argument, so the first parameter is named cls. Class attributes like _codeword are accessed on the class passed to cls.

One of the benefits of this approach is that I don't have to worry about whether I'm calling inform() on the class or on an instance. Because the method is a class instance, it will always access the class attribute on the class (cls), instead of the instance (self), and thus avoid accidentally shadowing _codeword on a single instance (see Listing 7-8).

I don't plan to include a getter for this attribute. After all, secret agents have to keep secrets!

To use this method, I would call something like this:

```
SecretAgent.inform("The goose honks at midnight.")
print(mouse._codeword)  # prints "The goose honks at midnight."

fox.inform("The duck quacks at midnight.")
print(mouse._codeword)  # prints "The duck quacks at midnight."
```

Listing 7-15: secret_agent_usage.py:3

I can call the inform() class method directly on the SecretAgent class, or on any SecretAgent instance, such as fox. The changes that inform() makes to the class attribute _codeword appear on the class itself and all its instances.

When calling the class method with the dot operator, the class is implicitly passed to the cls parameter. That parameter name is still just a convention; the @classmethod decorator is what ensures that the first argument is always the class, never the instance.

One awesome use of class methods is to provide alternative means of initializing instances. For example, the built-in integer class offers int.from _bytes(), which initializes a new int class instance, using a bytes value.

Static Methods

A *static method* is a regular function defined within a class, which accesses neither the instance attributes nor the class attributes. The only difference between a static method and a function is that a static method belongs to the class for namespace reasons.

The main reason to write a static method comes up when your class offers some functionality that doesn't need to access any of the class or instance attributes or methods. For example, you may write a static method for handling some particularly complicated algorithm that is critical to your class's implementation. By including the static method in the class, you are indicating that the algorithm is part of the class's self-contained implementation logic, even though it does not access any attributes or methods.

I'll add a static method to the SecretAgent class, which handles one thing all the agents would do the same, regardless of their data—answer questions:

```
@staticmethod
def inquire(question):
    print("I know nothing.")
```

Listing 7-16: secret_agent.py:5

I precede the static method with the @staticmethod decorator. You'll notice that I don't need to worry about a special first parameter, since the method doesn't need access to any attributes. When this method is called on a class or on an instance, it only prints out the message, "I know nothing."

Properties

Properties constitute a special variety of instance method that allows you to write getters and setters that behave so it appears that you were directly accessing an instance attribute. Properties allow you to write a consistent interface, where you use the object directly through what appear to be its attributes.

It is preferable to use properties, instead of making the user remember whether to call a method or use an attribute. Using properties is also much more Pythonic than cluttering your class with bare getters and setters that don't augment attribute access or modification.

PEDANTIC NOTE The above assertion set off a heated debate among my colleagues, some of whom really hate properties. I've tried to address the counterpoints toward the end of this section, but I firmly believe my position above stands.

Setting Up the Scenario

To demonstrate properties in action, I'll expand on my SecretAgent class. Here's the class so far. First, to set up, I'll move it to a new file:

```
class SecretAgent:

    _codeword = None

    def __init__(self, codename):
        self.codename = codename
        self._secrets = []

    def __del__(self):
        print(f"Agent {self.codename} has been disavowed!")

    def remember(self, secret):
        self._secrets.append(secret)
```

```
@classmethod
def inform(cls, codeword):
    cls._codeword = codeword

@staticmethod
def inquire(question):
    print("I know nothing.")
```

Listing 7-17: secret_agent_property.py:1

Next, I will add one more class method to encrypt whatever message is passed to it, using an encryption system of my own devising. This method has nothing to do with properties per se, but I include it to make the example complete:

```
@classmethod
def _encrypt(cls, message, *, decrypt=False):
    code = sum(ord(c) for c in cls._codeword)
    if decrypt:
        code = -code
    return ''.join(chr(ord(m) + code) for m in message)
```

Listing 7-18: Using a property with no getter

The _encrypt() class method uses the _codeword class attribute to perform a basic substitution cipher encoding on a string message. I use sum() to find the sum of the Unicode code points (as integers) for each character in _codeword. I pass a character (string) to the ord() function, which returns the Unicode code point as an integer. This sum of code points is bound to code. (The odd-looking loop here is actually a generator expression, which I'll cover in Chapter 10. You can take it for granted here that it calls ord() on each character in the string bound to cls._codeword.)

I use code to offset the Unicode code point of each character in the message. The chr() function returns the character associated with the given code point. I pass to it the sum of the current code point and code, for each character in the message. (Once again, I'm employing a generator expression here.)

GOTCHA ALERT

Writing my own encrypt function is fine for the context of a silly example or toy program, where security doesn't matter. If you have any data you truly need to keep secret, *NEVER* write your own encryption functions! An unbelievable amount of academic research, experimentation, and testing goes into engineering encryption algorithms. Stick with well-established, industry-accepted algorithms and tools.

Defining a Property

A *property* behaves like an attribute, but it is made up of three instance methods: a *getter*, a *setter*, and a *deleter*. Remember that a property appears to be an ordinary attribute to the user of the class. Accessing the property calls the getter, assigning a value to it calls the setter, and deleting the property with the del keyword calls the deleter.

Like an ordinary getter or setter method, a property might access or modify a nonpublic attribute, multiple attributes, or even no attributes at all. It all depends on what behavior you want.

Here, I'll define a property called secret for my SecretAgent class, which will serve as the getter, setter, and deleter for my _secrets instance attribute. This approach will allow me to add logic, such as having the setter encrypt the assigned data before storing it in the _secrets attribute.

Before defining the property itself, I need to define the three functions that will make up the property. Technically, I can call them whatever I like, but the convention is to name them getx, setx, or delx, where x is the name of the property. I'm also making these nonpublic methods, since I want the client to use the property directly.

First, the getter:

```
def _getsecret(self):
    return self._secrets[-1] if self._secrets else None
```

Listing 7-19: secret_agent_property.py:3

The getter, _getsecret(), accepts no parameters and should return the value of the property. In this example, I want the getter to return the last item stored in the list bound to the instance attribute self._secrets, or if the list is empty, to return None.

Next, the setter:

```
def _setsecret(self, value):
    self._secrets.append(self._encrypt(value))
```

Listing 7-20: secret_agent_property.py:4

The setter, _setsecret(), accepts a single parameter, which receives the value being assigned to the property in the call (see Listing 7-23). In this case, I assume this is some sort of string, which I run through the static method _encode() I defined earlier and then store in the list self._secrets.

Finally, here's the deleter:

```
def _delsecret(self):
    self._secrets = []
```

Listing 7-21: secret_agent_property.py:5

The *deleter*, _delsecret(), accepts no parameters and returns no value. This method is called when the property is deleted, either in the background, by the garbage collector, or explicitly, with del secret. In this example, when the property is deleted, I want the entire list of secrets to be cleared.

You actually don't need to define a deleter if you have no need for special behavior when the decorator is deleted. Consider what you want to happen if del is called on your decorator, such as when you are deleting an associated attribute that the property controls; if you can't think of anything, skip writing the deleter.

Finally, I define the property itself:

```
secret = property(fget=_getsecret, fset=_setsecret, fdel=_delsecret)
```

Listing 7-22: secret_agent_property.py:6a

This is defined on the class itself, outside of the __init__() method and after the functions that make it up. I pass the three methods to the fget, fset, and fdel keyword arguments, respectively (although you can also pass them as positional arguments, in that same order). I bind the property to the name secret, which becomes the property name.

The property can now be used as if it were an instance attribute:

```
mouse = SecretAgent("Mouse")
mouse.inform("Parmesano")

print(mouse.secret)       # prints "None"
mouse.secret = "12345 Main Street"
print(mouse.secret)       # prints "χϘϘϚϚφjÏЦДφCКИҍҍK"
mouse.secret = "555-1234"
print(mouse.secret)       # prints "ϚϚϚϒχϘϘϚ"

print(mouse._secrets)     # prints two values
del mouse.secret
print(mouse._secrets)     # prints empty list
```

Listing 7-23: secret_agent_property.py:7a

Every time I try to retrieve the value of the property, the getter is called. Meanwhile, assigning a value to the property calls the setter. There's no need to remember and explicitly call dedicated getter or setter methods; I treat the property like an attribute.

You'll recall that the deleter for secrets clears the contents of the _secrets list. Just before deleting the property, the list contains two secrets. After deleting, the list is empty.

It is not necessary to define all three parts of the property. For example, I don't want the secret property to even have a getter, so I can remove _getsecret() from my class code. Secret agents shouldn't share their secrets, after all.

```
    def _setsecret(self, value):
        self._secrets.append(self._encrypt(value))

    def _delsecret(self):
        self._secrets = []

    secret = property(❶ fset=_setsecret, fdel=_delsecret)
```

Listing 7-24: A secret property with no getter

Because I don't pass an argument to fget, the default value of None is used instead ❶. This property has a setter and a deleter, but no getter.

As a result, I can assign to secret, but I can't access the value:

```
mouse = SecretAgent("Mouse")
mouse.inform("Parmesano")

mouse.secret = "12345 Main Street"
mouse.secret = "555-1234"

print(mouse.secret)  # AttributeError
```

Listing 7-25: Using a property with no getter

Assigning values to mouse.secret works as before, since that calls the setter.

However, attempting to access the value throws an AttributeError. I could instead have written a getter for secrets that always returned None, but the client would have to remember that it returned this useless value. Recall The Zen of Python:

> Errors should never pass silently.
>
> Unless explicitly silenced.

If a particular usage is not desired, especially when it comes to designing a class or interface, the usage should *explicitly fail*.

Property with Decorators

Creating a property is easy enough, but the approach to implementing it that I've shown thus far doesn't really feel very Pythonic, because I have to rely on my method names to remind me that they're part of a property. Thankfully, there's another way.

Python offers a cleaner approach to defining properties: with decorators. There are two approaches to this technique.

Approach 1: property() and Decorators

The first approach is to still employ the property() function but use decorators to denote the associated methods. The chief benefit of this approach is the added readability, and it is mainly used when the getter will be omitted. I can use the name of the property as the method name and rely on the decorator to clarify its role.

Here's my rewritten code for the secret property, using this approach:

```
secret = property()
```

Listing 7-26: secret_agent_property.py:3b

In this approach, I define secret as a property before writing its methods. I pass no arguments to property(), so all three functions default to None. Next, I add the getter:

```
@secret.getter
def secret(self):
    return self._secrets[-1] if self._secrets else None
```

Listing 7-27: secret_agent_property.py:4b

My getter method now must have the same name as the property, secret. If it doesn't, it will fail with an AttributeError when the getter is first called, rather than when the class is created. The method is preceded by the decorator @secret.getter. This designates it as the getter for the property, just as if I had passed it to property(fget=).

Here's the setter:

```
@secret.setter
def secret(self, value):
    self._secrets.append(self._encrypt(value))
```

Listing 7-28: secret_agent_property.py:5b

Similarly, the setter method must share its name with the property it relates to, and it is preceded by the decorator @secret.setter.

Finally, the deleter:

```
@secret.deleter
def secret(self):
    self._secrets = []
```

Listing 7-29: secret_agent_property.py:6b

Similar to the getter and setter, the deleter is preceded by the decorator @secret.deleter.

This version works as is, but there is an even better technique.

Approach 2: Decorators Without property()

The second approach to declaring a property with decorators is even shorter, and it is the most commonly used. This approach is preferred when defining a property that has a getter.

If you have defined a getter, you don't have to explicitly create and assign a property(). Instead, the decorator @property can be applied to the getter:

```
@property
def secret(self):
    return self._secrets[-1] if self._secrets else None

@secret.setter
def secret(self, value):
    self._secrets.append(self._encrypt(value))
```

```
@secret.deleter
def secret(self):
    self._secrets = []
```

I precede the getter function with the decorator @property, instead of @secret.getter, which creates a property with the same name as the method. Since this defines the property secret, I don't need secret = property() anywhere in my code.

Bear in mind, this shortcut only works with the getter method. The setter and deleter must be defined in the same manner as before.

As before, I can omit any of the three methods if their behavior is not desired. For example, if I don't want secret to be readable, I omit the getter, so my full property code looks like this:

```
❶ secret = property()

@secret.setter
def secret(self, value):
    self._secrets.append(self._encrypt(value))

@secret.deleter
def secret(self):
    self._secrets = []
```

Because I don't have a getter, I must explicitly declare my property up front ❶. In this version, assignment and deletion of secret works as before, but accessing the value raises an AttributeError.

When Not to Use Properties

There's some debate about when to use properties, versus traditional getter and setter methods. One of the chief drawbacks of properties is that they conceal that some calculation or processing is being performed upon assignment, which the client might not expect. This especially becomes a problem if this processing is particularly long or complicated, such that a client may need to run it concurrently with async or threads (see Chapters 16 and 17); you cannot run an assignment concurrently with the same ease as running a method concurrently.

You must also consider the expected behavior of an assignment. When a value is directly assigned to an attribute, you would typically expect the same value to be retrievable *from* that attribute. In reality, depending on how you wrote your properties, the value might be transformed when assigned or accessed. You'll need to take this client expectation into consideration when designing your class.

Some camps believe properties should only be used as a way of deprecating attributes that used to be public or that have been removed entirely. Others, like myself, find properties useful as replacements for otherwise relatively simplistic getters and setters that still involve more logic than plain assignment and access.

In any case, properties are some of those cool features of Python that are all too easy to misuse or misapply. Carefully consider the implications of properties, public attributes, or methods in your specific case. Take the occasion to consult the advice of other experienced Python developers, such as in the Libera.Chat IRC #python channel. (If you want to debate the most Pythonic general position on properties, though, bring a helmet.)

Special Methods

Special methods are my favorite part of Python object-oriented programming. I'm trembling a little with excitement right now (or maybe I had too much coffee). *Special methods*, sometimes called *magic methods*, allow you to add support to your classes for virtually any Python operator or built-in command!

Special methods are also colloquially known as *dunder methods*—which is short for "*d*ouble *under*score"—because they begin and end with two underscore characters (__). You've already seen three examples of special methods: __init__(), __new__(), and __del__(). The Python language defines about a hundred special methods, most of which are documented at *https://docs.python.org/3/reference/datamodel.html*. I'll cover a number of the most common ones here. In future chapters, I'll discuss other special methods as they become relevant. I also list all the special methods in Python in Appendix A.

Scenario Setup

For the examples in this section, I'll use a new class, GlobalCoordinates, which will store a global coordinate as latitude and longitude. This class is defined as follows:

```python
import math
class GlobalCoordinates:

    def __init__(self, *, latitude, longitude):

        self._lat_deg = latitude[0]
        self._lat_min = latitude[1]
        self._lat_sec = latitude[2]
        self._lat_dir = latitude[3]

        self._lon_deg = longitude[0]
        self._lon_min = longitude[1]
        self._lon_sec = longitude[2]
        self._lon_dir = longitude[3]

    @staticmethod
    def degrees_from_decimal(dec, *, lat):
        if lat:
            direction = "S" if dec < 0 else "N"
        else:
            direction = "W" if dec < 0 else "E"
        dec = abs(dec)
        degrees = int(dec)
```

```
        dec -= degrees
        minutes = int(dec * 60)
        dec -= minutes / 60
        seconds = round(dec * 3600, 1)
        return (degrees, minutes, seconds, direction)

    @staticmethod
    def decimal_from_degrees(degrees, minutes, seconds, direction):
        dec = degrees + minutes/60 + seconds/3600
        if direction == "S" or direction == "W":
            dec = -dec
        return round(dec, 6)

    @property
    def latitude(self):
        return self.decimal_from_degrees(
            self._lat_deg, self._lat_min, self._lat_sec, self._lat_dir
        )

    @property
    def longitude(self):
        return self.decimal_from_degrees(
            self._lon_deg, self._lon_min, self._lon_sec, self._lon_dir
        )
```

Listing 7-30: global_coordinates.py:1

You can probably work out what's going on here, based on the knowledge you have so far. The class `GlobalCoordinates` converts and stores a latitude and longitude as tuples of degrees, minutes, seconds, and a string literal representing a cardinal direction.

I chose to create this particular class because its data lends itself well to a healthy subset of the special methods I'll cover.

Conversion Methods

There are many ways to represent the same data, and most clients will expect to be able to convert an object containing data to any Python primitive type that makes sense. For example, global coordinates could be expressed as strings or hashes. You should carefully consider what data types your class should support conversion to. Here, I cover some special methods for data conversions.

Canonical String Representation: __repr__()

When writing a class, it is considered good practice to define, at minimum, the __repr__() instance method, which returns the *canonical string representation* of the object. This string representation should ideally contain all the data necessary to create another class instance with the same contents.

If I don't define a __repr__() instance method for GlobalCoordinates, Python falls back on its default version for objects, which is pretty uselessly underwhelming. I'll create an instance of GlobalCoordinates and print this default representation via repr():

```
from global_coordinates import GlobalCoordinates
nsp = GlobalCoordinates(latitude=(37, 46, 32.6, "N"),
                        longitude=(122, 24, 39.4, "W"))
print(repr(nsp))
```

Listing 7-31: global_coordinates_usage.py:1

Running that prints out the following canonical string representation:

```
<__main__.GlobalCoordinates object at 0x7f61b0c4c7b8>
```

Not good for much, is it? Instead, I'll define my own __repr__() instance method for the class:

```
def __repr__(self):
    return (
        f"<GlobalCoordinates "
        f"lat={self._lat_deg}°{self._lat_min}'"
        f"{self._lat_sec}\"{self._lat_dir}   "
        f"lon={self._lon_deg}°{self._lon_min}'"
        f"{self._lon_sec}\"{self._lon_dir}>"
    )
```

Listing 7-32: global_coordinates.py:2

I return a string containing all the information needed to recreate the instance: the class name, the latitude, and the longitude.

Rerunning the code in Listing 7-31 now produces more useful information:

```
<GlobalCoordinates lat=37°46'32.6"N  lon=122°24'39.4"W>
```

Human-Readable String Representation: __str__()

The __str__() special method has a similar purpose to __repr__(), except that it's meant to be human-readable, as opposed to the more technically inclined canonical representation, which is more useful for debugging.

If you don't define __str__(), the __repr__() function will be used instead, but that wouldn't be desirable in this example. The user should only see the pretty coordinates!

Here's my __str__() instance method for GlobalCoordinates:

```
def __str__(self):
    return (
        f"{self._lat_deg}°{self._lat_min}'"
        f"{self._lat_sec}\"{self._lat_dir} "
```

```
        f"{self._lon_deg}°{self._lon_min}'"
        f"{self._lon_sec}\"{self._lon_dir}"
    )
```

Listing 7-33: global_coordinates.py:3

Unlike with __repr__(), I omit all that boring technical information and focus on composing and returning a string representation a user might want to see.

This method is called when an instance of the class is passed to str(), although passing the instance directly to print() or as an expression in a formatted string will also invoke __str__(). For example:

```
print(f"No Starch Press's offices are at {nsp}")
```

Listing 7-34: global_coordinates_usage.py:2

That outputs the following:

```
No Starch Press's offices are at 37°46'32.6"N 122°24'39.4"W
```

Lovely and readable!

Unique Identifier (Hash): __hash__()

The __hash__() method typically returns a *hash value*, which is an integer that is unique to the data within the class instance. This allows you to use instances of the class in certain collections, such as keys in a dictionary or values in a set (see Chapter 9). It's often helpful to write this method yourself, as the default behavior results in every class instance having a unique hash value, even if two instances contain the exact same data.

The __hash__() method should only depend on values that won't change for the life of the instance! Several collections rely on these hash values *never changing*, but the value of a mutable object might change.

Here's my __hash__() function for GlobalCoordinates:

```
def __hash__(self):
    return hash((
        self._lat_deg, self._lat_min, self._lat_sec, self._lat_dir,
        self._lon_deg, self._lon_min, self._lon_sec, self._lon_dir
    ))
```

Listing 7-35: global_coordinates.py:4

I've taken the most common approach, which is to create a tuple containing all the important instance attributes and then to call hash() on the tuple, which returns the hash value of whatever is passed to it. I then return that hash value.

GOTCHA ALERT   According to the documentation, if you define __hash__(), you should also define __eq__() (see the "Comparison Methods" subsection).

Additional Conversion Special Methods

Python has special methods for converting the data in the instance to other forms. It is up to you to decide which of these you will define on your class:

- __bool__() should return True or False. If this isn't defined, the automatic conversion to a boolean value will check whether __len__() returns a nonzero value (see Chapter 9); otherwise, True will always be used.

- __bytes__() should return a bytes object (see Chapter 12).

- __ceil__() should return an int numeric value, usually resulting from rounding up a float value to the nearest integer.

- __complex__() should return a complex numeric value.

- __float__() should return a float numeric value.

- __floor__() should return an int numeric value, usually resulting from rounding down a float numeric value to the nearest integer.

- __format__() should accept a string representing the format specification (see Chapter 3) and return a string representation of the instance, with the specification applied. How exactly you apply the specification is up to you.

- __index__() should return the same value as __int__(), which must also be defined if you write this method. The presence of this method indicates that the class should be considered a type of integer; you don't have to throw away any data to get the integer value (lossless conversion).

- __int__() should return an int numeric value. You may simply have this function call __ceil__(), __floor__(), __round__(), or __trunc__().

- __round__() should return an int numeric value, usually resulting from rounding a float numeric value up or down.

- __trunc__() should return an int numeric value, usually resulting from dropping the non-whole (decimal) part of a float numeric value.

You only need to define the special methods that make sense for your class. In my case, *none* of these additional conversion methods are particularly suitable for a pair of global coordinates.

Comparison Methods

Python has six comparison special methods that correspond to the six comparison operators in Python: ==, !=, <, >, <=, and >=. Each one conventionally returns a boolean value.

If one of these special methods is called, but the method isn't defined, the class instance will return the special value NotImplemented to alert Python that the comparison didn't happen. This allows the language to decide the best response. In the case of comparisons with built-in types, NotImplemented will be coerced to the boolean value False, so as to not break algorithms that rely on those functions. In most other situations, a TypeError will be raised.

Equals: __eq__()

The __eq__() special method is called by the equals (==) operator. I'll define this method for my GlobalCoordinates class:

```
def __eq__(self, other):
    if not ❶ isinstance(other, GlobalCoordinates):
        return ❷ NotImplemented

    return (
        self._lat_deg == other._lat_deg
        and self._lat_min == other._lat_min
        and self._lat_sec == other._lat_sec
        and self._lat_dir == other._lat_dir
        and self._lon_deg == other._lon_deg
        and self._lon_min == other._lon_min
        and self._lon_sec == other._lon_sec
        and self._lon_dir == other._lon_dir
    )
```

Listing 7-36: global_coordinates.py:5

All comparison special methods accept two parameters: self and other. These represent the operands on the left and right of the operator, so a == b would call a.__eq__(b).

In the ongoing example, it would only make sense to compare two GlobalCoordinates class instances to one another. Comparing a GlobalCoordinates instance directly to an integer or a float wouldn't be logical. Thus, this is one of those rare scenarios where type matters. I use isinstance() to ensure other is an instance of the GlobalCoordinates class (or a subclass thereof) ❶. If it is, I compare the instance attributes that constitute the latitude and longitude of one GlobalCoordinates instance to the same attributes of the other instance. I return True if they all match.

However, if other is of a different type, the comparison doesn't happen, so I return the special value NotImplemented ❶.

Not Equals: __ne__()

The __ne__() special method corresponds to the not-equals (!=) operator. If undefined, a call to __ne__() *delegates* to __eq__(), just returning the opposite value that __eq__() does. If this is what you're expecting, there's no need to define __ne__().

However, if there's more complex logic to your not-equals comparison, it might make sense to define it.

Less Than and Greater Than: __lt__() and __gt__()

The special methods __lt__() and __gt__() correspond to the less-than (<) and greater-than (>) operators, respectively. These two special methods are *reflections* of one another, meaning one operator in the pair can be substituted for the other. The expression a < b calls a.__lt__(b), but if that returns

NotImplemented, Python automatically flips the logic and calls b.__gt__(a). Thus, if you're only comparing instances of the same class, you can often get away with defining just one of the two special methods: usually, __lt__(). The same is true of __le__() and __ge__(), which correspond to less-than-or-equal-to (<=) and greater-than-or-equal-to (>=).

Be careful with this reflection, however! If you want to support comparing objects of different types, you should define both special methods in the pair.

In my particular example, there's no clear logic for less than or greater than on two GlobalCoordinates, so I'm not defining any of those four special methods. Since I don't define them, calls to any of them will return NotImplemented.

Binary Operator Support

Special methods will also let you add support for *binary operators*—operators with two operands—to your class. If any of the methods are undefined, they will default to returning NotImplemented, which, in the context of an expression, will usually cause an error to be raised.

With GlobalCoordinates, I'll only implement the subtraction operator (-) via the __sub__() method:

```
def __sub__(self, other):
    if not isinstance(other, GlobalCoordinates):
        return NotImplemented

    lat_diff = self.latitude - other.latitude
    lon_diff = self.longitude - other.longitude
    return (lat_diff, lon_diff)
```

Listing 7-37: global_coordinates.py:6

As with comparison special methods, binary-operator special methods require two parameters: self and other. In my case, it's logical for these operands to be GlobalCoordinates class instances; if other is of a different type, I return NotImplemented. Otherwise, I perform the math and return a tuple representing the difference between latitudes and longitudes in decimal degrees.

Because I'm only supporting subtraction of two GlobalCoordinates instances, I'm done. However, if I were supporting subtracting some other type, I'd have to also implement __rsub__(), which is the reflection of __sub__(). The expression a - b calls a.__sub__(b), but if that returns NotImplemented, then Python tries to call b.__rsub__(a) behind the scenes. Because a - b is not the same as b - a, I must define those two methods separately; b.__rsub__(a) should return the value of a - b.

A third method, __isub__(), corresponds to the subtraction-augmented assignment operator (-=). If this method is undefined, that operator will fall back on the __sub__() and __rsub__() functions (a -= b becomes a = a - b), so you'd only need to define __isub__() if you needed some special behavior.

All 13 binary operators, as well as `divmod()`, rely on the same three sorts of special methods, although there is no augmented assignment for `divmod()`. For your reference, Table 7-1 outlines them all.

Table 7-1: Operator Special Methods

Operator	Method	Reflected method	Augmented method
Addition (+)	__add__()	__radd__()	__iadd__()
Subtraction (-)	__sub__()	__rsub__()	__isub__()
Multiplication (*)	__mul__()	__rmul__()	__imul__()
Matrix multiplication (@)	__matmul__()	__rmatmul__()	__imatmul__()
Division (/)	__truediv__()	__rtruediv__()	__itruediv__()
Floor division (//)	__floordiv__()	__rfloordiv__()	__ifloordiv__()
Modulo (%)	__mod__()	__rmod__()	__imod__()
divmod()	__divmod__()	__rdivmod__()	N/A
Power/exponent (**)	__pow__()	__rpow__()	__ipow__()
Left shift (<<)	__lshift__()	__rlshift__()	__ilshift__()
Right shift (>>)	__rshift__()	__rrshift__()	__irshift__()
Logical AND (and)	__and__()	__rand__()	__iand__()
Logical OR (or)	__or__()	__ror__()	__ior__()
Logical XOR (xor)	__xor__()	__rxor__()	__ixor__()

Unary Operator Support

You can also add support for unary operators—those with only one operand. Unary-operator special methods accept one parameter: `self`. As before, all three default to returning `NotImplemented` if undefined.

In the case of my `GlobalCoordinates`, I'd like to override the invert operator (~) to return a `GlobalCoordinates` instance that is the opposite position on the globe, in terms of both latitude and longitude:

```
def __invert__(self):
    return GlobalCoordinates(
        latitude=self.degrees_from_decimal(-self.latitude, lat=True),
        longitude=self.degrees_from_decimal(-self.longitude, lat=False)
    )
```

Listing 7-38: global_coordinates.py:7

Not much new there; I'm creating and returning a new instance of `GlobalCoordinates` from the negated current latitude and longitude.

The unary operators and their special methods are as follows:

__abs__() handles the absolute value `abs()` operation function.

__invert__() handles the invert/binary flip ~ operator.

__neg__() handles the negative-sign operator -.

__pos__() handles the positive-sign operator +.

Making Callable

The last of the special methods I'll cover in this chapter concerns making an instance *callable*, meaning the instance can be treated like a function. This special method, __call__(), can accept any number of arguments and return anything.

To wrap up my example, I'll write a __call__() method that, when passed another GlobalCoordinate instance, will return the distance between the two in degrees, minutes, and seconds. This is a rather contrived example without obvious usage, however, and I wouldn't have made GlobalCoordinates callable in real life. This merely completes my example:

```
def __call__(self, ❶ other):
    EARTH_RADIUS_KM = 6371

    distance_lat = math.radians(other.latitude - self.latitude)
    distance_lon = math.radians(other.longitude - self.longitude)
    lat = math.radians(self.latitude)
    lon = math.radians(self.longitude)
    a = (
        math.sin(distance_lat / 2)
        * math.sin(distance_lat / 2)
        + math.sin(distance_lon)
        * math.sin(distance_lon / 2)
        * math.cos(lat)
        * math.cos(lon)
    )
    c = 2 * math.atan2(math.sqrt(a), math.sqrt(1-a))

❷   return c * EARTH_RADIUS_KM
```

Listing 7-39: global_coordinates.py:8

Remember, __call__() can be written to accept any parameters you want. In my case, I accept another GlobalCoordinate class instance on other ❶. Then, I calculate the distance between the two points in kilometers and return that result as a float ❷.

Now, I can use any class instance of GlobalCoordinate in the same manner as a function:

```
nostarch = GlobalCoordinates(latitude=(37, 46, 32.6, "N"),
                             longitude=(122, 24, 39.4, "W"))

psf = GlobalCoordinates(latitude=(45, 27, 7.7, "N"),
                        longitude=(122, 47, 30.2 "W"))

distance = nostarch(psf)
print(distance)  # 852.6857266443297
```

Listing 7-40: global_coordinates_usage.py:3

I define two instances of GlobalCoordinate, and then I calculate the distance between them by passing one instance to the other and storing the result. Indeed, the distance from No Starch Press's offices to those of the Python Software Foundation is about 852 kilometers (529 miles).

More Special Methods: Looking Ahead

There are several more special methods, but I'll cover those in chapters where their functionality is relevant. Be on the lookout for special methods relating to *iterables* (Chapter 9), *context managers* (Chapter 11), and *async* (Chapter 16). You can also refer to Appendix A for a complete list of special methods.

Class Decorators

Classes support *decorators*, much like functions do. Class decorators wrap the instantiation of the class, allowing you to intervene in any number of ways: adding attributes, initializing another class containing an instance of the one being decorated, or performing some behavior immediately on the new object.

To demonstrate this, I need to set up for a decently believable example. I'll create a class for CoffeeRecipe that contains the recipe for a particular coffee shop menu item. I'll also create a separate class for a CoffeeOrder, which is a single person's coffee order:

```python
class CoffeeOrder:

    def __init__(self, recipe, to_go=False):
        self.recipe = recipe
        self.to_go = to_go

    def brew(self):
        vessel = "in a paper cup" if self.to_go else "in a mug"
        print("Brewing", *self.recipe.parts, vessel)


class CoffeeRecipe:

    def __init__(self, parts):
        self.parts = parts



special = CoffeeRecipe(["double-shot", "grande", "no-whip", "mocha"])
order = CoffeeOrder(special, to_go=False)
order.brew()  # prints "Brewing double-shot grande no-whip mocha in a mug"
```

Listing 7-41: coffee_order_decorator.py:1

By this point, you can probably figure out what's going on here.

Next, I'm opening a drive-thru coffee shack that only does to-go orders, so I don't want to have to specify each order as to go manually.

Instead of writing a whole new `CoffeeOrder` class, I can define a class decorator that allows me to specify that all orders are to go (or not) up front:

```
import functools
❶ def auto_order(to_go):
    def decorator(cls):
        @functools.wraps(cls)
        def wrapper(*args, **kwargs):
            ❷ recipe = cls(*args, **kwargs)
            ❸ return (CoffeeOrder(recipe, to_go), recipe)
        return wrapper
    ❹ return decorator
```

Listing 7-42: coffee_order_decorator.py:2

This decorator accepts the additional argument to_go, so I have to wrap the decorator itself in another function, creating a double closure ❶. The decorator is returned from the outermost function ❹, but the decorator's effective name will always come from the outermost function name. This pattern works with all decorators, not just class decorators.

The decorator, itself, will look pretty familiar, if you recall Chapter 6. After initializing an instance of the wrapped class ❷, I immediately use that instance to initialize a `CoffeeOrder` instance, which I return in a tuple with the `CoffeeShackRecipe` instance ❸.

I can now create a new `CoffeeShackRecipe` that inherits from `CoffeeRecipe` and adds nothing new, and then I can apply the decorator to make it always make orders to go:

```
@auto_order(to_go=True)
class CoffeeShackRecipe(CoffeeRecipe):
    pass


order, recipe = CoffeeShackRecipe(["tall", "decaf", "cappuccino"])
order.brew()  # prints "Brewing tall decaf cappuccino in a paper cup"
```

Listing 7-43: coffee_order_decorator.py:3

The only reason I created this new class is to extend it with the @auto _order decorator, without losing the ability to create `CoffeeRecipe` instances when I want them.

In the usage, you see that I can now specify a `CoffeeShackRecipe` as I would a `CoffeeRecipe`, but the `CoffeeShackRecipe` instance will return both a `CoffeeOrder` instance and a `CoffeeShackRecipe` instance. I call brew() on the `CoffeeOrder`. Neat trick, no?

Structural Pattern Matching with Objects

Structural pattern matching, which was added in Python 3.10, supports matching objects in patterns by their attributes.

For example, I might have a class that represents a pizza, and I might want to perform structural pattern matching based on attributes in a given Pizza object:

```
class Pizza:

    def __init__(self, topping, second_topping=None):
        self.first = topping
        self.second = second_topping

order = Pizza("pepperoni", "mushrooms")

match order:
    case Pizza(first='pepperoni', second='mushroom'):
        print("ANSI standard pizza")
    case Pizza(first='pineapple'):
        print("Is this even pizza?")
```

Listing 7-44: pattern_match_object.py:1a

In each pattern, I specify the object that I'm expecting the subject order to be—in this case, Pizza—and then I list the attributes of that object and the expected values thereof. For example, if order.first is "pepperoni" and order.second is "mushroom", then I print "ANSI standard pizza".

In the second case, you'll see I don't even need to specify an expected value for each attribute. If order.first is "pineapple", then the message "Is this even pizza?" will be displayed, regardless of the second value. (However, I like pineapple on pizza! Sorry, not sorry.)

Capture patterns can come into play here, too. If the second topping is "cheese", but the first is something else, I want to capture the first topping as first, so I can use the value in the case suite:

```
# --snip--

match order:
  # --snip--
    case Pizza(first='pineapple'):
        print("Is this even pizza?")
    case Pizza(first=first, second='cheese'):
        print(f"Very cheesy pizza with {first}.")
```

Listing 7-45: pattern_match_object.py:1b

Here, if the value of order.second is "cheese", then the value of order .first is captured as first, which I use in the message.

I'll also use capture patterns to create a fallback case here:

```
# --snip--

match order:
  # --snip--
    case Pizza(first=first, second='cheese'):
        print(f"Very cheesy pizza with {first}.")
```

```
        case Pizza(first=first, second=second):
            print(f"Pizza with {first} and {second}.")
```

Listing 7-46: pattern_match_object.py:1c

Here, if none of the preceding patterns match, then I capture both
`order.first` and `order.second` and use them to compose a generic message
about the pizza.

This works well if you don't mind typing out the names of the attributes. However, there are times when this feels redundant. For example, if
you have a `Point` class that represents a point in three-dimensional space, it
would feel a bit tedious to spell out *x*, *y*, and *z* every time:

```
class Point:
    def __init__(self, x, y, z):
        self.x_pos = x
        self.y_pos = y
        self.z_pos = z


point = Point(0, 100, 0)

match point:
    case Point(x_pos=0, y_pos=0, z_pos=0):
        print("You are here.")
    case Point(x_pos=0, y_pos=_, z_pos=0):
        print("Look up!")
```

Listing 7-47: point.py:1a

That pattern feels pretty long for something, especially when most
people would expect to specify a point in 3D space as *x*, *y*, *z*.

Instead of writing out the attributes every time, I can define the special
`__match_args__` class attribute, which specifies how a pattern's values map
positionally to the object's attributes:

```
class Point:
    __match_args__ = ('x_pos', 'y_pos', 'z_pos')

    def __init__(self, x, y, z):
        self.x_pos = x
        self.y_pos = y
        self.z_pos = z


point = Point(0, 123, 0)

match point:
    case Point(0, 0, 0):
        print("You are here.")
    case Point(0, _, 0):
        print("Look up!")
```

Listing 7-48: point.py:1b

I define __match_args__ as a tuple of strings representing the attributes I want to map to positional values in pattern matching on the object. That is, the first positional value in the pattern maps to x_pos, the second maps to y_pos, and so on. Now, I can shorten my patterns by omitting the names of the attributes.

PEDANTIC NOTE   The __match_args__ class attribute is automatically defined on dataclasses (not discussed).

Functional Meets Object Oriented

As I've mentioned, functional and object-oriented programming can fit together very well. Here are the functional programming rules for methods (adapted slightly from the function rules in Chapter 6):

1. Every method should do one specific thing.
2. A method's implementation should never affect other methods, nor should it affect the behavior of the rest of the program.
3. Avoid side effects! A method should only directly mutate attributes belonging to its class, and only when that behavior is an expected part of the method's purpose.
4. In general, methods shouldn't have (or be affected by) state, other than the attributes belonging to its class. Providing the same input should always yield the same output, unless the method's expected behavior dictates otherwise.

To summarize all that in another way, the only state that methods should have is the attributes of their class or instance, and only when relying on that state is essential to the purpose of the method.

Don't hesitate to use functional patterns in the context of object-oriented programming. Treat an instance like you would any other variable. Attributes should only be modified by their instance's or class's methods, called via the dot operator:

```
thing.action()  # this can mutate attributes in thing
```

When an object is passed to a function, it should not be mutated (no side effects):

```
action(thing)  # should not modify thing; returns new value or object
```

If you combine the rules of functional and object-oriented programming, your code will be much easier to maintain.

When to Use Classes

Unlike with class-centric languages such as Java and C#, it is not always necessary to write classes in Python. An important part of object-oriented programming in Python is to know when to use classes and when *not* to.

Classes Aren't Modules

You shouldn't use a class where a module will be sufficient. Python modules already allow you to organize variables and functions by purpose or category, so you don't need to use classes in the same manner.

The purpose of a class is to bundle data with the methods responsible for accessing and modifying that data. Thus, your decision on whether to make a class should be based on the data. Do the attributes make sense as a cohesive object? Let the word *attribute* be the hint: is the data descriptive of the thing your object is attempting to represent?

Also, you should ensure that any methods included in the class directly relate to the attributes. In other words, think of methods as things the object can *do*. Any method that doesn't fit this criteria doesn't belong in the class.

Similarly, beware of how you structure classes. A House has a kitchen sink, but the attributes and methods relating to the kitchen sink belong in their own KitchenSink class, and an *instance* of said class belongs in the house. (This is a compositional relationship between the two classes.)

Single Responsibility

One of the essential rules in object-oriented programming is the *single-responsibility principle.* Just like a function, a class should have a single, well-defined responsibility. A function *does* something, while a class *is* something.

Avoid writing *god classes*, which try to do many different things in one class. Not only are these bug prone and difficult to maintain, but they also make for a very confusing code structure.

Sharing State

Class attributes and class methods allow you to write *static classes*, which provide one of the preferred ways to share state across multiple modules in your program. Static classes are cleaner and more predictable than global variables, and they are easier to write, maintain, and debug than the singleton design pattern. (And if you've never heard of singletons, all the better for you.)

The single-responsibility principle still applies here. For example, a static class containing current user preferences might make sense, but the current user profile shouldn't be thrown into that same class.

Are Objects Right for You?

Just because you *can* write your entire program with classes and objects doesn't mean you *should*.

Instead, you should reserve classes and objects for what they're best at: *encapsulation*. Remember:

Modules organize things by purpose and category.

Functions perform tasks with provided data (arguments) and return values.

Collections store cohesive sets of data, which are accessed predictably (see Chapter 9).

Classes define objects, which contain attributes and related behaviors (methods).

Take the time to select the right tools for the job. When you do this, you'll find that classes and objects complement modules, functions (and functional programming), and collections.

Wrapping Up

Depending on the language you come from, classes and objects are probably either your bread and butter or things you seldom use, if at all. In Python, you can't get away from objects—everything is one, after all—but you do get to decide what role classes will play in your code.

In any case, whether you follow more traditional object-oriented programming techniques or favor a functional approach, Python classes provide a reliable way of organizing data. Properties make it possible to write getters and setters that look the same as accessing an ordinary attribute. Special methods even make it possible to create whole new data types that work with all of Python's language features.

Objectively speaking, Python is one classy language.

8

ERRORS AND EXCEPTIONS

In many languages, exceptions are regarded
as the archnemeses of programmers and
the hallmarks of some degree of failure.
Something, somewhere was used improperly!
Python developers, on the other hand, recognize
exceptions as friends that help write better code.

Python offers many familiar error-handling tools, but the way we use
them may look different from what you're used to. These tools can help
you do more than clean up messes. You might even say, error handling in
Python is "exceptional."

I'll start by demonstrating what exceptions look like in Python and how
to read their accompanying messages. I'll cover catching exceptions, handling them, and raising them. Then, I'll show you how to leverage errors to
control the flow of your program. Finally, I'll give you a tour of the common
exception types.

Exceptions in Python

If case *exceptions*, which are sometimes called *errors* in Python, are unfamiliar to you, here's the general definition:

> exception: (computing) An interruption in normal processing, typically caused by an error condition, that can be handled by another part of the program. (Wiktionary)

Let's start with a seemingly innocuous program: a number-guessing game. I'm only using concepts introduced in previous chapters, so see if you can spot the bug before I point it out.

First, I create a function that selects a random number, which the player will have to try to guess:

```
import random


def generate_puzzle(low=1, high=100):
    print(f"I'm thinking of a number between {low} and {high}...")
    return random.randint(low, high)
```

Listing 8-1: number_guess.py:1

Next, I create a function that gets a guess from the user and outputs whether the number guessed was too high, too low, or correct:

```
def make_guess(target):
    guess = int(input("Guess: "))

    if guess == target:
        return True

    if guess < target:
        print("Too low.")
    elif guess > target:
        print("Too high.")
    return False
```

Listing 8-2: number_guess.py:2a

I return a boolean value to indicate whether the guess is correct or not.

The following function is responsible for running the game and tracking how many guesses the player has left:

```
def play(tries=8):
    target = generate_puzzle()
    while tries > 0:
        if make_guess(target):
            print("You win!")
            return
```

```
        tries -= 1
        print(f"{tries} tries left.")

    print(f"Game over! The answer was {target}.")
```

Listing 8-3: number_guess.py:3

I call the play() function when the module is executed directly, thereby starting the game:

```
if __name__ == '__main__':
    play()
```

Listing 8-4: number_guess.py:4

If I test this game by playing it the normal way, everything seems to work as expected. Here's my first playthrough:

```
I'm thinking of a number between 1 and 100...
Guess: 50
Too low.
7 tries left.
Guess: 75
Too low.
6 tries left.
Guess: 90
Too high.
5 tries left.
Guess: 87
You win!
```

Our first instinct as programmers is to test things politely. We have a subconscious sense about what will cause the code to break, and we inherently tiptoe around those possible errors. However, if you've done any meaningful testing, you know the value of "doing horrible things to your code," as Stack Overflow cofounder Jeff Atwood says.

Or, as programmer Bill Sempf puts it:

> QA Engineer walks into a bar. Orders a beer. Orders 0 beers.
> Orders 999999999 beers. Orders a lizard. Orders −1 beers.
> Orders a sfdeljknesv.

So, proper testing of this code involves throwing input to it that it doesn't expect or understand, like so:

```
I'm thinking of a number between 1 and 100...
Guess: Fifty
Traceback (most recent call last):
  File "./number_guess.py", line 35, in <module>
    play()
  File "./number_guess.py", line 25, in play
    if make_guess(target):
```

```
File "./number_guess.py", line 10, in make_guess
    guess = int(input("Guess: "))
ValueError: invalid literal for int() with base 10: 'Fifty'
```

Listing 8-5: Traceback from running number_guess.py

Eww, a bug! My program can't handle numbers spelled out as words. Clearly, I need to do something about this.

Reading Tracebacks

That block of output you receive when an error occurs is called the *traceback*, and it tells you what went wrong and where. It includes the details of the error that occurred, the line where it happened, and the entire *call stack*—which contains the function calls leading directly from the main function to the error. The entire call stack will always be displayed; it is up to you to determine the location of the coding mistake.

I recommend reading tracebacks from the bottom up. Let's take apart that traceback I received in Listing 8-5, piece by piece, starting from the final line:

```
ValueError: invalid literal for int() with base 10: 'Fifty'
```

This tells you what went wrong. Specifically, a ValueError was raised because the value 'Fifty' was passed to the int() function. The with base 10 part has to do with the default value of the base parameter. In other words, Python can't convert the string 'Fifty' to an integer using the int() function.

This last line of the traceback is the single-most important. Always read and completely understand it before moving forward with fixing the bug!

The two lines above the error tell you precisely where the error occurred: in file ./number_guess.py, on line 10, in the make_guess() function:

```
File "./number_guess.py", line 10, in make_guess
    guess = int(input("Guess: "))
```

Python even gives you the offending line in question, and sure enough, you can see the int() function wrapped around input().

Sometimes, you can stop there and go fix the problem. In this case, the problem is right here. In other situations, the error may occur because of a mistake in the code further up in the call stack, such as passing bad data to a parameter. Even though I know that's not the problem here, I'll go up another step:

```
File "./number_guess.py", line 25, in play
    if make_guess(target):
```

You already know that the error is occurring in the make_guess() function, and that is being called from within ./number_guess.py, on line 25, in the play() function. No problem here; the argument target had nothing to do with the error. Likewise, this part of the code can't possibly have caused the error:

```
File "./number_guess.py", line 35, in <module>
    play()
```

Now I'm at the top of the traceback. The play() function is being called on line 35 of ./number_guess.py, and the call isn't occurring inside of any function; rather it's coming from the module scope, as indicated by <module>.

That first line is always the same, but it's a useful reminder if you ever forget how to read a traceback properly:

```
Traceback (most recent call last):
```

The most recently executed code is always listed last! Thus, as I've said before, always read tracebacks from the bottom up.

Catching Exceptions: LBYL vs. EAFP

In many languages, the common practice is to test the input before trying to convert it to an integer. This is known as the *Look Before You Leap (LBYL)* philosophy.

Python has a different approach, officially known as *Easier to Ask Forgiveness than Permission (EAFP)*. Instead of preventing errors, we embrace them, using try statements to handle exceptional situations.

I'll rewrite my make_guess() function to use error handling:

```
def make_guess(target):
    guess = None
    while guess is None:
        try:
            guess = int(input("Guess: "))
        except ValueError:
            print("Enter an integer.")

    if guess == target:
        return True

    if guess < target:
        print("Too low.")
    elif guess > target:
        print("Too high.")
    return False
```

Listing 8-6: number_guess.py:2b

I initially set the value of guess to None, so that as long as I don't have something usable assigned to guess, I keep prompting the user for input. I use None instead of 0, since 0 is still technically a valid integer.

On each iteration of the loop, in the context of try, I attempt to get the user input and convert it to an int(). If that conversion fails, int() will raise a ValueError, as you saw earlier.

If ValueError is raised, it can only mean that the user entered some non-numeric input, such as 'Fifty' or an empty string. I catch that error and handle the situation by printing an error message. Because guess is still None, the entire loop repeats to prompt for input again.

If int() is successful, no further action is taken in this section of code, and I move on to the rest of the function. The so-called *happy path*, the one with no errors, is efficient.

To understand why the EAFP approach is the preferred error-handling philosophy, compare it to the LBYL strategy. Here's the LBYL approach to confirming that the string only contains digits:

```python
def make_guess(target):
    guess = None
    while guess is None:
        guess = input()
        if guess.isdigit():
            guess = int(guess)
        else:
            print("Enter an integer.")
            guess = None

    if guess == target:
        return True

    if guess < target:
        print("Too low.")
    elif guess > target:
        print("Too high.")
    return False
```

Listing 8-7: number_guess.py:2c

While this code is perfectly valid, it's not very efficient. I run isdigit() on *every single guess*, whether it's erroneous or not, and then I run the int() conversion if it passes the test. Thus, I process the string in guess *twice* on the happy path, and once in the case of an error. Contrast this with the EAFP strategy with the try statement from earlier, where I only ever process the string once.

Some will complain, "Yes, but, error handling is expensive!" True, but only on the exceptions. A successful try typically has very little overhead in Python. The extra code for handling special cases is run when an error occurs. If you've designed your code right, the happy path should be far more common than the exceptional path, such as in the example above.

The EAFP approach is also easier to think about. Instead of coming up with tests to anticipate every possible erroneous input—an arduous task in more complex, real-world scenarios—you only need to anticipate the likely exceptions, catch them, and handle them accordingly. That said, it can sometimes take some real effort to figure out what errors to expect. Be prepared to invest time here, either way.

Multiple Exceptions

The try statement is not limited to a single error type. I can handle multiple scenarios in one compound statement.

To demonstrate this, I'll create a simple, callable AverageCalculator class that will accept a list of inputs and use them to recalculate a stored running average:

```
class AverageCalculator:

    def __init__(self):
        self.total = 0
        self.count = 0

    def __call__(self, *values):
        if values:
            for value in values:
                self.total += float(value)
                self.count += 1
        return self.total / self.count
```

Listing 8-8: average_calculator.py:1

There are a few possible errors that can occur while using this AverageCalculator class, but I'd prefer to let the user interface code handle those, so they can be used for displaying error messages.

Here's a basic command line interface for the calculator:

```
average = AverageCalculator()
values = input("Enter scores, separated by spaces:\n    ").split()
try:
    print(f"Average is {average(*values)}")
except ❶ ZeroDivisionError:
    print("ERROR: No values provided.")
except (❷ ValueError, ❸ UnicodeError):
    print(f"ERROR: All inputs should be numeric.")
```

Listing 8-9: average_calculator.py:2

There are three errors that can occur when calling average():

The user might pass no values, meaning total (the divisor of the division in `__call__()`) might be zero and thus raise a ZeroDivisionError ❶.

One or more of the inputs might not be convertible by float(), thus raising a ValueError ❷.

There might be a problem encoding or decoding Unicode, which will raise a `UnicodeError` ❸. (Actually, that last one is entirely redundant with `ValueError` in this case; I'm only including it to demonstrate the concept.)

I handle all three exceptional cases by calling `average()` within the try clause's suite and then catching the errors in the except clauses.

When a `ZeroDivisionError` is caught ❶, I print that no values were provided by the user.

I handle the `ValueError` ❷ and the (redundant) `UnicodeError` ❸ in the same way; either error would occur if the user tried inputting something non-numeric. By specifying both in a tuple after except, I catch either error and handle both the same way—in this case, by printing a message that some inputs weren't numeric.

To demonstrate this in a reasonably contained example, I've written slightly convoluted code here. In the real world, I'd place the try statement within the `__call__()` method itself. While this example code departs from idiomatic Python, it demonstrates a more complex try statement, albeit without any truly useful error-handling behavior (which I'll get to shortly).

Beware the Diaper Anti-pattern

Sooner or later, every Python developer will discover that a bare except clause will work:

```
try:
    some_scary_function()
except:
    print("An error occurred. Moving on!")
```

Listing 8-10: diaper_antipattern.py

Here, a bare except allows you to catch all exceptions in one. This is one of the most insidious anti-patterns in Python. It catches and silences literally every conceivable exception, whether you expect it to or not.

The entire point of an exception is to alert you that your program is now in an *exceptional state*, meaning it can no longer proceed along the ordinary, intended happy path without unexpected or even disastrous results. By silencing every error, you have created a situation where you have no idea what those exceptional states are or what is causing them. You've thrown away your precious traceback and forced the program to continue as if nothing had happened.

In his book *How to Make Mistakes in Python*, Mike Pirnat calls this the *diaper pattern*:

> [A]ll the precious context for the actual error is being trapped in the diaper, never to see the light of day or the inside of your issue tracker. When the "blowout" exception occurs later on, the stack trace points to the location where the secondary error happened, not to the actual failure inside the try block.

Worse yet, if your program never raises another exception but keeps attempting to work in its invalid state, weird behavior will often abound.

Instead, always explicitly catch a particular exception type! Any error that you cannot foresee is probably related to some bug that needs to be resolved.

As usual, The Zen of Python has something to say about this:

> Errors should never pass silently.
>
> Unless explicitly silenced.

There's another diabolical side effect of this anti-pattern, which I can demonstrate with this simple program for greeting someone by name:

```
def greet():
    name = input("What's your name? ")
    print(f"Hello, {name}.")


while True:
    try:
        greet()
        break
    except:
        print("Error caught")
```

Listing 8-11: no_escape.py:1a

If I were running this program in the Linux terminal and decided I wanted to quit, I'd press CTRL-C. Look what happens when I do exactly that:

```
What's your name? ^CError caught
What's your name? ^CError caught
What's your name? ^CError caught
What's your name?
```

Ack! I'm trapped! The trouble is, the KeyboardInterrupt, which is produced by pressing CTRL-C on a UNIX terminal, uses the except system. It's getting caught, "handled," and utterly ignored. There's no escape from this program, except to kill my terminal altogether and manually kill the Python process. (Thankfully in this example, you can still quit by typing a name.)

The KeyboardInterrupt exception does not itself inherit from the Exception class, like errors do. Thus, some (overly) clever developer might try this:

```
def greet():
    name = input("What's your name? ")
    print(f"Hello, {name}.")


while True:
    try:
        greet()
        break
```

```
    except Exception:
        print("Error caught")
```

Listing 8-12: no_escape.py:1b

I'm no longer catching KeyboardInterrupt, which is good, so I can now escape with CTRL-C. Unfortunately, this is still a form of the *diaper anti-pattern*, for the reasons I mentioned earlier: it catches every conceivable error! The one time this might be acceptable would be in conjunction with logging, which I'll address later in this chapter.

Raising Exceptions

You can also *raise* exceptions to indicate the occurrence of a problem that your code cannot recover from automatically, such as when someone calling a function you wrote passes an unusable argument. There are several dozen common exceptions available for you to raise as needed (see "A Gallery of Exceptions" near the end of this chapter).

To demonstrate this, here's a function that accepts a string containing numbers (separated by spaces) and calculates the average. Here, I'm catching the most common error scenario and providing a more useful and relevant error:

```
def average(number_string):
    total = 0
    skip = 0
    values = 0
    for n in number_string.split():
        values += 1
❶     try:
            total += float(n)
❷     except ValueError:
            skip += 1
```

Listing 8-13: average.py:1

I split the provided string into the individual space-separated parts, looping through each part. Within a try clause ❶, I attempt to convert each part to a floating-point number and add it to the total accumulator. If any of the values cannot be converted to a number, thereby raising a ValueError ❷, I mark that I've skipped an item, and I move on.

I continue with that function:

```
❸ if skip == values:
        raise ValueError("No valid numbers provided.")
    elif skip:
        print(f"<!> Skipped {skip} invalid values.")

    return total / values
```

Listing 8-14: average.py:2

Once I've processed the string, I check whether I've skipped all the values ❸. If I have, I'll raise another ValueError, passing my error message to the constructor of the exception. Otherwise, if only some of the values have been skipped, I'll print a helpful message and move on.

Raising an exception breaks out of the function *immediately*, in the same manner as a return statement. Thus, I don't need to worry about the final return statement being run if I have no values (such as if the user passed in an empty string).

The usage of that function is as follows:

```
while True:
    line = input("Enter numbers (space delimited):\n    ")
    avg = average(line)
    print(avg)
```

Listing 8-15: average.py:3a

I'll run that code and try some inputs:

```
Enter numbers (space delimited):
    4 5 6 7
5.5
```

The first input works just fine, returning the average of the four numbers I specified.

```
Enter numbers (space delimited):
    four five 6 7
<!> Skipped 2 invalid values.
3.25
```

The second input works as well, skipping my two invalid values and returning the average of the other two.

```
Enter numbers (space delimited):
    four five six seven
Traceback (most recent call last):
  File "./raiseexception.py", line 25, in <module>
    avg = average(line)
  File "./raiseexception.py", line 16, in average
    raise ValueError("No valid numbers provided.")
ValueError: No valid numbers provided.
```

The third input contains no valid numbers, so it crashes the program, which is exactly what I wanted. Reading the traceback, you can see the exception I raised earlier and where I raised it from.

I wouldn't ship a program like this, so I can, in turn, catch the exception I raised. I'll rewrite my infinite loop at the bottom of the program, like so:

```
while True:
    try:
        line = input("Enter numbers (space delimited):\n    ")
        avg = average(line)
```

```
        print(avg)
    except ValueError:
        print("No valid numbers provided.")
```

Listing 8-16: average.py:3b

I wrap the user input/output logic in a try clause, and then I catch the ValueError and print a nice message instead. Let's try out this new version:

```
Enter numbers (space delimited):
    four five six
No valid numbers provided.
Enter numbers (space delimited):
    4 5 6
5.0
```

Perfect! When the input is bad, the exception I raised inside the average() function is caught here, and the appropriate message is printed. (I can press CTRL-C to quit.)

Using Exceptions

Like everything else in Python, exceptions are objects that you can both use directly and extract information from.

You can, for example, use exceptions to handle the logic of accessing values from a dictionary, without knowing in advance whether the key you specified is valid. (There's some debate about whether and when to use this approach, which I'll revisit in Chapter 9.)

As an example of using exceptions with dictionaries, here's a program that allows a user to look up an email address by a person's name.

I start by defining a dictionary containing names and email addresses:

```
friend_emails = {
    "Anne": "anne@example.com",
    "Brent": "brent@example.com",
    "Dan": "dan@example.com",
    "David": "david@example.com",
    "Fox": "fox@example.com",
    "Jane": "jane@example.com",
    "Kevin": "kevin@example.com",
    "Robert": "robert@example.com"
}
```

Listing 8-17: address_book.py:1

Here is my lookup function:

```
def lookup_email(name):
    try:
        return friend_emails[name]
```

```
    except KeyError ❶ as e:
        print(f"<No entry for friend {e}>")
```

Listing 8-18: address_book.py:2

I start by trying to use the name argument as a key on my dictionary, within the context of a try clause. If the key is not in the dictionary, a KeyError will be raised, which I'll catch. I capture said exception with as e ❶, allowing me to use the exception object later. In the case of a KeyError, str(e) will return the value that I just tried to use as a key in the dictionary.

Finally, here's the code using that function:

```
name = input("Enter name to look up: ")
email = lookup_email(name)
print(f"Email: {email}")
```

Listing 8-19: address_book.py:3

If I run this code and pass a name that isn't in my dictionary, I see the result of the error handling:

```
Enter name to look up: Jason
<No entry for friend 'Jason'>
Email: None
```

Exceptions and Logging

An unusual aspect of KeyError is that its message consists purely of the erroneous key. Most exceptions contain their complete error message, one use of which is *logging*, wherein errors, warnings, and other informational messages are printed to the terminal or saved to a file for inspection by the end user, in case of bugs. Users expect programs to behave well and not crash, but errors aren't always avoidable. It's common for software to log errors to a file or the terminal, to aid in debugging crashes and bugs.

To demonstrate this, I'll write a very basic calculator program, which is intended to demonstrate the concept without getting too deep into the logging tools and practices themselves. I'll cover logging more thoroughly in Chapter 19.

Logging Configuration

My calculator program will need a few imports that may be unfamiliar to you:

```
import logging
from operator import add, sub, mul, truediv
import sys
```

Listing 8-20: calculator.py:1

The `logging` module contains Python's built-in logging tools, which I'll use in a moment. The `operator` module contains optimized functions for performing mathematical operations on arbitrary values, which I'll use in my calculator function. Third, `sys` provides tools for interacting with the interpreter itself; in my case, I'll use one of its functions later on to tell my program to exit.

The `logging.basicConfig()` function allows me to configure my logging level, as well as specify things like which file to write the log to:

```
logging.basicConfig(filename='log.txt', level=logging.INFO)
```

Listing 8-21: calculator.py:2

There are five increasing severity levels of logging: `DEBUG`, `INFO`, `WARNING`, `ERROR`, and `CRITICAL`. By passing `level=logging.INFO`, I'm telling the logging module to log all messages of that level, as well as the three severity levels above it (`WARNING`, `ERROR`, and `CRITICAL`). That means only log messages marked as `DEBUG` are ignored on this setting.

With the argument `filename=log.txt`, I also specify that the log should be written to a file called *log.txt*. I could also leave this blank if I wanted to print the log to the console instead.

GOTCHA ALERT   In practice, `logging.basicConfig()` should usually only appear in the `if __name__ == "__main__":` section of your program, as this will change the *global* behavior of the logging module. (See Chapter 19.)

Here is my actual `calculator()` function:

```
def calculator(a, b, op):
    a = float(a)
    b = float(b)
    if op == '+':
        return ❶ add(a, b)
    elif op == '-':
        return sub(a, b)
    elif op == '*':
        return mul(a, b)
    elif op == '/':
        return truediv(a, b)
    else:
        ❷ raise NotImplementedError(f"No operator {op}")
```

Listing 8-22: calculator.py:3

The math operator functions, such as `add()` ❶, are coming from the operator module I imported earlier.

The `calculator()` function doesn't perform error checking by design, according to the *single-responsibility principle* from Chapter 7. Code that uses the `calculator()` function should provide the right arguments to the function, anticipate and handle the errors itself, or crash with an explicit unhandled error (thereby indicating the code is erroneous).

There is one exception (no pun intended). If the user specifies an operator in the op parameter that I don't support in my calculator() function, I raise NotImplementedError ❷. This exception should be raised anytime functionality that doesn't exist is requested.

GOTCHA ALERT Don't confuse NotImplementedError with NotImplemented. Any special (dunder) method that is not implemented should return NotImplemented, so code relying on such a special method is informed without failing. Any custom method or function (or, in this case, functionality) that hasn't been implemented yet (or never will be) should return NotImplementedError, so any attempted usage will fail with an error.

Logging Errors

The following is my usage of the calculator() function, along with all the error handling and logging code. I'll break this down into several pieces and discuss each separately:

```
print("""CALCULATOR
Use postfix notation.
Ctrl+C or Ctrl+D to quit.
""")

❶ while True:
    ❷ try:
        equation = input(" ").split()
        result = calculator(*equation)
        print(result)
```

Listing 8-23: calculator.py:4

First, I print the program name and some user instructions. Then, in my program loop ❶, within a try ❷, I attempt to collect the input from the user and pass it to the calculator() function. If that works, I print the result, and the loop starts over. However, there are a number of errors that can occur, and I handle them in my except clauses:

```
except NotImplementedError as e:
    print("<!> Invalid operator.")
    logging.info(e)
```

Listing 8-24: calculator.py:5

If I encounter the NotImplementedError, which I capture as a usable object with as e, it means an invalid operator was specified in the op= argument passed to calculator(). After printing some information for the user, I log this (as level INFO) by passing the error, e, to the logging.info() function. That logs the error message (which you'll see in a moment), but it throws away the traceback, which I do not need to show to the program's user, since the problem was their input.

```
except ValueError as e:
    print("<!> Expected format: <A> <B> <OP>")
    logging.info(e)
```

Listing 8-25: calculator.py:6

The `ValueError` is raised if `float()` was not able to convert the arguments a or b to floating-point numbers. That might mean that the user entered non-numeric characters for one of the operands, or that the operator was specified in the wrong order. Remember, I ask the user for *postfix notation*, meaning the operator comes after the two operands. In either case, I remind the user of the format they need to use, and once again, I log the error to level `INFO`:

```
except TypeError as e:
    print("<!> Wrong number of arguments. Use: <A> <B> <OP>")
    logging.info(e)
```

Listing 8-26: calculator.py:7

The `TypeError` shows up if the user passes either too many or too few arguments to the `calculator()` function. Once again, I log this as level `INFO`, print a reminder for the user about the proper format of input, and move on:

```
except ZeroDivisionError as e:
    print("<!> Cannot divide by zero.")
    logging.info(e)
```

Listing 8-27: calculator.py:8

If the user tries to divide by zero, it raises the error `ZeroDivisionError`. Handling that error is, again, a matter of logging to `INFO` and notifying the user:

```
except (KeyboardInterrupt, EOFError):
    print("\nGoodbye.")
    sys.exit(0)
```

Listing 8-28: calculator.py:9

Lastly, I use `KeyboardInterrupt` and `EOFError` to catch the UNIX terminal keystrokes CTRL-C (abort) and CTRL-D (end of file), respectively. In either case, I print a friendly farewell message and then use `sys.exit(0)` to properly quit the program. Technically, I could have left both of these uncaught, but that would have resulted in an ugly error message appearing upon quitting the program. That might scare some users into thinking there's a bug in the program.

I'll run this program now and try things out:

```
CALCULATOR
Use postfix notation.
Ctrl+C or Ctrl+D to quit.
```

```
 11 31 +
42.0
 11 + 31
<!> Expected format: <A> <B> <OP>
 11 + 31 + 10
<!> Wrong number of arguments. Use: <A> <B> <OP>
 11 +
<!> Wrong number of arguments. Use: <A> <B> <OP>
 10 0 /
<!> Cannot divide by zero.
 10 40 @
<!> Invalid operator.
 ^C
Goodbye.
```

All in all, this is a clean user experience. All the errors I've anticipated are being caught and handled appropriately, and I can quit nicely.

Reviewing the Logs and Cleaning Up

Take a look at the *log.txt* file that's been created:

```
INFO:root:could not convert string to float: '+'
INFO:root:calculator() takes 3 positional arguments but 5 were given
INFO:root:calculator() missing 1 required positional argument: 'op'
INFO:root:float division by zero
INFO:root:No operator @
```

Listing 8-29: log.txt

Here are all five of the error messages that were logged while I used the program.

Practically speaking, in production software, I'd never write any of the expected errors to a file, because it would result in a huge and unwieldy file! Thus, I might change all my logging commands to `logging.debug()`, to log the error messages at the DEBUG level. That way, if I were to need to peruse the errors during debugging, I'd only need to change my logging configuration to `logging.basicConfig(filename='log.txt', level=logging.DEBUG)`. I'd ship with a logging level of INFO, thereby suppressing the DEBUG messages. That way, the end user wouldn't see a bloated log.

Bubbling Up

There's one nonoptimal part of the logging scheme I've created: any unexpected errors won't get logged. Ideally, any exception I haven't anticipated should be logged at level ERROR but still be allowed to crash the program, so the code doesn't try to carry on in an unhandled exceptional state.

Thankfully, any error you catch can be re-raised, or *bubbled up* in Python terminology. Since the error isn't caught again after being re-raised, the program will crash.

I'm leaving the rest of the earlier try statement the same (Listings 8-23 through 8-28), but I'm adding one more except to the end:

```
except Exception as e:
    logging.exception(e)
  ❶ raise
```

Listing 8-30: calculator.py:10

The except clauses are evaluated in order, which is why this new clause has to appear at the end of the current try statement. I don't want this "catch-all" to gobble up the exceptions I specifically want to handle separately.

This may seem dangerously close to the diaper anti-pattern, except here, I don't hide the error, and I'm only catching *actual errors*—that is, any object that inherits from Exception. Non-error "exceptions" like StopIteration and KeyboardInterrupt, which don't inherit from Exception, won't get caught by this except clause.

I log the error message, *along with the traceback*, at ERROR level, using the special method logging.exception(e). When the user sends me the log file with his bug report, I, the developer, will need this traceback to find and fix the bug.

Then, I bubble up the error with a bare raise statement, which raises the *last-caught* exception ❶. (I could also have done raise e, but the bare raise is preferred in this context for brevity in my code and traceback.) It is *absolutely essential* that I bubble up the error here, lest this become a case of the diaper anti-pattern.

Exception Chaining

When you catch one exception and then raise another, you're at risk of losing the context of the original error. To avoid this situation, Python offers *exception chaining*, whereby you can raise a new exception without throwing away all the helpful information already provided. This feature was added in Python 3.0 (via PEP 3134).

I'll apply this concept to a program for looking up the city and state of famous landmarks. I start by defining the dictionaries for the program:

```
cities = {
    "SEATTLE": "WASHINGTON, USA",
    "PORTLAND": "OREGON, USA",
    "BOSTON": "MASSACHUSETTS, USA",
}

landmarks = {
    "SPACE NEEDLE": "SEATTLE",
    "LIBERTY SHIP MEMORIAL": "PORTLAND",
    "ALAMO": "SAN ANTONIO",
}
```

Listing 8-31: landmarks.py:1

Here is the function for looking up landmarks and their corresponding cities in the dictionaries:

```
def lookup_landmark(landmark):
    landmark = landmark.upper()
    try:
        city = landmarks[landmark]
        state = cities[city]
❶ except KeyError as e:
        ❷ raise KeyError("Landmark not found.") from e
    print(f"{landmark} is in {city}, {state}")
```

Listing 8-32: landmarks.py:2

In this function, I try to find the landmark in the landmarks dictionary. If it's not there, a KeyError is raised, which I catch ❶ and then re-raise with more useful information in the error message ❷. When I raise the new exception, I use from e to specify that it was caused by the exception (e) I caught. This ensures that the traceback shows what led to the error: either the city or the landmark not being found.

Here's an example usage of this function:

```
lookup_landmark("space needle")
lookup_landmark("alamo")
lookup_landmark("golden gate bridge")
```

Listing 8-33: landmarks.py:3

I test the lookup_landmark() function by looking up three landmarks, two of which ("alamo" and "golden gate bridge") are going to throw an exception, but for different reasons. In the case of the Alamo, although the landmark is in the landmarks dictionary, the corresponding city of "SAN ANTONIO" is missing from the cities dictionary. In the case of the Golden Gate Bridge, the landmark isn't even in the landmarks dictionary. (Sorry, San Francisco!)

PEDANTIC NOTE This implementation is more than a bit silly, but that is a necessary evil for this technical example. The better design here would be to split the two dictionary lookups between two try statements; the best design would be to use some collection better suited to this situation, since a dictionary really isn't.

The code as written won't get to the last line, because the second-to-last line will throw an exception, as you'll see in the output:

```
SPACE NEEDLE is in SEATTLE, WASHINGTON, USA
Traceback (most recent call last):
  File "./chaining.py", line 18, in lookup_landmark
    state = cities[city]
❶ KeyError: 'SAN ANTONIO'

❷ The above exception was the direct cause of the following exception:

Traceback (most recent call last):
```

```
      File "./chaining.py", line 25, in <module>
        lookup_landmark("alamo")
      File "./chaining.py", line 20, in lookup_landmark
        raise KeyError("Landmark not found.") from e
❸ KeyError: 'Landmark not found.'
```

The first call to lookup_landmark() works, as you can see from the output. Remembering that you read traceback from the bottom up, you see that the second call fails, raising the "Landmark not found" error ❸.

Above that traceback is a notification that the exception was caused by a different exception ❷.

Sure enough, in the traceback above that, you find the problem; Python couldn't find the city of "SAN ANTONIO" in the cities dictionary ❶.

Even if I hadn't taken the time to add raise KeyError from e earlier, Python would ordinarily have included the context, although the two tracebacks would have been separated with a message I consider far more cryptic and less helpful:

```
During handling of the above exception, another exception occurred:
```

So, even though you might be able to get away without explicit exception chaining, it's just a good habit to take on.

You can explicitly disable chaining with raise e from None.

Else and Finally

Up to this point, all my error handling examples have relied on try and except, which leaves the rest of the code to run the same in any case, whatever happens, unless I call return or take advantage of the breaking behavior of a raise statement to bail out of a function.

There are two more optional clauses for try statements: else runs if there is no exception, and finally runs in any situation, but in a surprising way.

Else: "If All Goes Well"

You would use the else clause for any section of code that should only run if none of the except clauses caught anything.

To demonstrate this, I'll revise my program for finding the average of a list of numbers. This time, I want it to always output a valid float value. The average of an empty string should be the constant math.inf (the result of division by zero), and the presence of any non-numeric values should produce the constant math.nan.

```
import math


def average_string(number_string):
    try:
        numbers = [float(n) for n in number_string.split()]
```

```
except ValueError:
    total = math.nan
    values = 1
```

Listing 8-34: average_string.py:1

Every time the average_string() function is called, it first tries to create a list of float values. If any part of the string is non-numeric, a ValueError is raised. I catch that exception, assign the value math.nan to total, and ensure there is a 1 in values, which I will use as the divisor in the upcoming division.

If no exception was raised by that first try clause, the else clause is run:

```
else:
    total = sum(numbers)
    values = len(numbers)
```

Listing 8-35: average_string.py:2

The total and values are calculated based on the now-valid assumption that numbers is a list of float values. *The else clause only runs if the try raises no exceptions.*

So, why not just return math.nan in the except ValueError clause? That would certainly be a bit more efficient, but there are two reasons I chose not to do that:

1. This approach better accommodates later refactoring; the rest of the math is always executed, and it always produces a valid result (except for the division-by-zero scenario I handle separately in the next part of the code).

2. If I need to add a finally clause anywhere, the code will still behave as expected (see next section).

Here's the rest of the program. Notice that I have a separate try statement to handle attempted division by zero:

```
    try:
        average = total / values
    except ZeroDivisionError:
        average = math.inf

    return average


while True:
    number_string = input("Enter space-delimited list of numbers:\n    ")
    print(average_string(number_string))
```

Listing 8-36: average_string.py:3

I've handled all of the exceptional paths that could be reasonably anticipated in the code. Testing this out, everything behaves as expected, with
no unhandled exceptions.

```
    4 5 6 7
5.5

inf
    four five six
nan
```

Finally: "After Everything"

The finally clause is always executed, no matter what! There aren't any
exceptions to this: even raise or return will not prevent the finally clause
from being executed. This is what sets finally apart from plain code after
the try statement.

Because of this, finally is especially well-suited for any cleanup code
you need to run, *no matter what.*

Here's a function that reads numbers from a file, one number per line,
and finds the average. In this case, I want exceptions to be raised if the file
contains non-numeric data or if the file cannot be found.

For this example, I'll use manual opening and closing of a file—
although in production, I'd use a *context manager* for this instead (see
Chapter 11).

```
def average_file(path):
    file = open(path, 'r')

    try:
      ❶ numbers = [float(n) for n in file.readlines()]
```

Listing 8-37: average_file.py:1

When the average_file() function is called, it attempts to open the file
indicated by the argument path. If this file doesn't exist, file.open() will
raise a FileNotFoundError exception, which I'm allowing as is, in this case.

Once the file is opened, I try to iterate over it, converting it into a list of
numbers ❶. (You're welcome to take this particular line of code for granted
for now. See Chapters 10 and 11.)

```
    except ValueError as e:
        raise ValueError("File contains non-numeric values.") from e
```

Listing 8-38: average_file.py:2

If any of the values are non-numeric, I catch the ValueError. In this
clause, I raise a chained exception with more specific information describing what was wrong with the file.

Otherwise, if no errors were raised by the try clause, the else clause runs:

```
else:
    try:
        return sum(numbers) / len(numbers)
    except ZeroDivisionError as e:
        raise ValueError("Empty file.") from e
```

Listing 8-39: average_file.py:3

This clause's suite attempts to calculate and return the average, but it also contains a nested try statement to handle an empty file.

After either the except or the else clause has run, the finally clause is always executed, *even after a* raise *or* return! This is important, because no matter the outcome, the file needs to be closed:

```
finally:
    print("Closing file.")
    file.close()
```

Listing 8-40: average_file.py:4

I'll test the program with four files, three of which I've created: a file containing integers called *numbers_good.txt*, a file containing words called *numbers_bad.txt*, an empty file called *numbers_empty.txt*, and a nonexistent file called *nonexistent.txt*.

Let's examine the output of these four scenarios one by one. These have to be run separately, because the program execution ceases when an exception is raised:

```
print(average_file('numbers_good.txt'))
```

Listing 8-41: average_file.py:5a

The file *numbers_good.txt* contains 12 integers, each on a separate line. Running that scenario, I get the following output:

```
Closing file.
42.0
```

The function works correctly; it opens the file and calculates the average of the values. Notice when the finally clause runs, as evidenced by the printed message "Closing file." Although it is running *after* the return statement in the average_file() function from earlier, it appears *before* the function returns. This is a good thing, because the finally clause in this function is responsible for closing the file, which absolutely *must* happen.

Now for the second scenario:

```
print(average_file('numbers_bad.txt'))
```

Listing 8-42: average_file_usage.py:5b

The *numbers_bad.txt* file contains words, not numbers. This output is a lot longer because of the exception:

```
❶ Closing file.
  Traceback (most recent call last):
    File "tryfinally.py", line 5, in average_file
      numbers = [float(n) for n in file.readlines()]
    File "tryfinally.py", line 5, in <listcomp>
      numbers = [float(n) for n in file.readlines()]
  ValueError: could not convert string to float: 'thirty-three\n'

  The above exception was the direct cause of the following exception:

  Traceback (most recent call last):
    File "tryfinally.py", line 20, in <module>
      print(average_file('numbers_bad.txt'))  # ValueError
    File "tryfinally.py", line 7, in average_file
      raise ValueError("File contains non-numeric values.") from e
  ValueError: File contains non-numeric values.
```

In this case, a ValueError is raised. Yet, once again, the finally clause is run ❶ before the exception is raised, even though the raise statement seems to come first in the function's source code.

Here's the third scenario:

```
print(average_file('numbers_empty.txt'))
```

Listing 8-43: average_file_usage.py:5c

The file *numbers_empty.txt* is, as its name suggests, an empty file. The output is as follows:

```
❶ Closing file.
  Traceback (most recent call last):
    File "tryfinally.py", line 10, in average_file
      return sum(numbers) / len(numbers)
  ZeroDivisionError: division by zero

  The above exception was the direct cause of the following exception:

  Traceback (most recent call last):
    File "tryfinally.py", line 21, in <module>
      print(average_file('numbers_empty.txt'))  # ValueError
    File "tryfinally.py", line 12, in average_file
      raise ValueError("Empty file.") from e
❷ ValueError: Empty file.
```

You can see that the error message about the empty file is working as well ❷. Also, as before, it is evident the finally clause is running ❶ before the exception is raised.

Now for the last scenario:

```
print(average_file('nonexistent.txt'))
```

Listing 8-44: average_file_usage.py:5d

This is attempting to read from a file that *doesn't exist.* Here's the output of that scenario:

```
Traceback (most recent call last):
  File "tryfinally.py", line 22, in <module>
    print(average_file('nonexistent.txt'))  # FileNotFoundError
  File "tryfinally.py", line 2, in average_file
    file = open(path, 'r')
FileNotFoundError: [Errno 2] No such file or directory: 'nonexistent.txt'
```

This exception comes from the file.open() call, which, if you refer back to the source code for average_file(), you'll notice occurs *before* the try statement. The finally clause only runs if its connected try clause is executed; since control flow never reached the try, the finally never gets called. Just as well, since there's no point in trying to close a file that was never opened.

Creating Exceptions

Python has quite the menagerie of exceptions, and their uses are very well documented. Sometimes, however, you need something a bit more customized.

All error-type exception classes inherit from the Exception class, which in turn inherits from the BaseException class. This dual hierarchy exists to let you catch all error exceptions, as I did earlier, without also reacting to the special, non-error exceptions like KeyboardInterrupt, which inherit from BaseException and not Exception.

When making a custom exception class, you can inherit from any exception class you like. However, avoid inheriting from BaseException, as that class is not designed to be directly inherited from by custom classes. Sometimes, it's best to inherit from the exception class that is closest in purpose to the one you're making (see the next section). However, if you're at a loss, you can inherit from Exception.

Before going through all the effort to write a custom exception, consider why you *want* to. My recommendation is to ensure your use case fits at least two of these three criteria:

1. No existing exception effectively describes the error, even if you provide a custom message.

2. You will raise or catch the exception more than once.

3. You need to be able to catch this specific exception, without catching any of the similar built-in exceptions.

If your use case cannot satisfy at least two of these criteria, you *probably* don't need a custom exception and can instead use one of the existing exceptions.

Most of the time, the need for custom exceptions arises in more complicated projects, so it's very difficult to create a practical example for this. For demonstration purposes, here's the code for a uselessly simple and rather silly custom exception and its usage:

```
class ❶ SillyWalkException(❷ RuntimeError):
    def __init__(self, ❸ message="Someone walked silly."):
        super().__init__(message)


def walking():
    ❹ raise SillyWalkException("My walk has gotten rather silly.")


try:
    walking()
❺ except SillyWalkException as e:
    print(e)
```

Listing 8-45: silly_walk_exception.py

I define a new class with the name of the exception ❶, and I inherit from the most *specific* exception class that makes sense ❷. In this case, I'm inheriting from RuntimeError because my exception doesn't fit into the description of any of the other built-in exceptions.

There's some debate about whether it's necessary to write an initializer for custom exceptions. I prefer to, because it provides an opportunity to specify a default error message ❸. Writing your own initializer also allows you to accept and store multiple parameters for various bits of information, not just the message attribute that all Exception classes must have (although I don't do that here).

If you accept a string for a message and don't want to provide a default, you can get away with this version to define the custom exception class with nothing more than a header and a docstring:

```
class SillyWalkException(RuntimeError):
    """Exception for walking silly."""
```

Either way, the custom exception can be raised ❹ and caught ❺ in the same way as any other exception.

A Gallery of Exceptions

The Python documentation provides an exhaustive list of all the built-in exceptions and their uses. You can find this list at *https://docs.python.org/library/exceptions.html*.

However, since that documentation can feel like an information dump, I'll briefly cover the most common exception classes. There are four base classes from which all the other exceptions are inherited; when you need to catch an entire category of exceptions, you can often use these:

BaseException is the base class for all exceptions. Remember not to inherit directly from this; it's not designed to be used as such.

Exception is the base class for all error-type exceptions.

ArithmeticError is the base class for arithmetic-related errors.

LookupError is the base class for any error related to finding values in collections.

PEDANTIC NOTE   There's also BufferError, which relates to memory errors behind the Python language. No other exceptions inherit from this one, and you shouldn't either.

Next, after the base exception classes, come the *concrete exceptions*, each of which describes a particular type of error. As of this writing, there are 35 concrete exceptions in the Python language, although I'm only covering some of the most common of these (see the documentation for the rest). A few others will be introduced in later chapters. All of these inherit directly from Exception, except as noted:

AttributeError is raised when accessing or assigning to a class attribute that doesn't exist.

ImportError is raised when an import statement isn't able to find a package, module, or a name within the module. You may also encounter the subclass exception ModuleNotFoundError.

IndexError is raised when an index (subscript) is out of range for a sequential collection, such as a list or tuple. This inherits from LookupError.

KeyError is raised when a key is not found in a dictionary. This inherits from LookupError.

KeyboardInterrupt is raised when the user presses a KEY-KEY combination to interrupt the running program, such as with CTRL-C on UNIX-like systems. This inherits from BaseException, not Exception.

MemoryError is raised when Python runs out of memory. However, there are still steps you can take to (probably) fix the problem, usually by deleting stuff.

NameError is raised when a name is not found in the local or global scope. This isn't used in relation to class attributes (see AttributeError) or imports (see ImportError).

OSError is both a concrete error and a base class for many exceptions relating to the operating system, including FileNotFoundError (which is raised when a file cannot be opened). I'll explore some of these in later chapters.

OverflowError is raised when an arithmetic operation would produce a result that is too large to be represented or stored. This mainly occurs with floating-point numbers. Integers never raise OverflowError, because they have no official size limits in Python; they will raise a BufferError if a similar situation occurs. This inherits from ArithmeticError.

RecursionError is raised when a function calls itself too many times (see Chapter 6), whether directly or indirectly. This inherits from RuntimeError.

RuntimeError is a sort of catch-all for any error that doesn't fit into the other categories.

SyntaxError is raised if there are any syntax errors in the Python code. These often come up when you run your program, but you may encounter them at any point during runtime when using arbitrary execution (see Chapter 15). This also includes the subclasses IndentationError and TabError.

SystemError is raised when the interpreter has an internal error. There's not much you can do about these errors; report them to the developers of the Python implementation you use.

SystemExit is raised when sys.exit() is called. Be careful about catching this, as you can prevent your program from quitting normally! This inherits from BaseException.

TypeError is raised when an operation or function tries to act on an object of the wrong type. This is the best exception to raise if your function is not intended to work on a particular value type received as an argument.

UnboundLocalError, a subclass of NameError, is raised when you try to access a local name that has no value yet assigned to it. This inherits from NameError.

ValueError is raised when an operation or function tries to act on an argument that is the right *type*, but the wrong *value*.

ZeroDivisionError is raised when trying to divide by zero, whether through the true division (/), floor division (//), modulo (%), or divmod() operators. This inherits from ArithmeticError.

Wrapping Up

I've spent a lot of time discussing how and when to use exceptions and error handling. This is a vast topic, yet the syntax itself boils down to the structure of try, except, else, finally, and the raise keyword.

PART III

DATA AND FLOW

9

COLLECTIONS AND ITERATION

Looping through an array is one of the most elementary algorithms in programming. Often, it's one of the first things a new developer does after "Hello, world!" The very principle of starting indices at zero was probably the first paradigm shift you encountered while learning to code. Yet, this is Python; loops and containers here operate on a whole different level.

In this chapter, I'll cover Python loops and then explore the various collections Python offers for storing and organizing data. Next, I'll define the concepts of iterables and iterators and start putting them to work in the context of loops. Then, I'll provide an overview of several iteration tools. Finally, I'll implement my own iterable class.

Grab a mug of your favorite beverage, and let's go!

Loops

Python has two types of loops: `while` and `for`. As you'll see in this chapter, they are not meant to be interchangeable. Rather each has unique purposes.

while Loops

The `while` loop is the most traditional of the loops. As long as the expression in its header evaluates to `True`, the suite of the loop is executed. For example, the following loop keeps prompting the user to enter a valid number until they do so:

```
number = None
while number is None:
    try:
        number = int(input("Enter a number: "))
    except ValueError:
        print("You must enter a number.")

print(f"You entered {number}")
```

Listing 9-1: get_number.py:1a

As long as the value of `number` is `None`, the suite of the `while` loop keeps repeating. I request input from the user with `input()` and attempt to convert it to an integer with `int()`. However, if the user has typed in anything other than a valid integer, a `ValueError` will be raised, and no new value will be assigned to `number`. Thus, the loop will repeat.

As soon as the user enters a valid integer, the loop exits and the number is printed to the screen.

Here's an example output of this program:

```
Enter a number: forty
You must enter a number.
Enter a number:
You must enter a number.
Enter a number: 40
You entered 40
```

If I want to provide a mechanism for quitting instead of entering a number, I could use the break keyword to exit the loop manually. Here, I allow the user to quit by entering a *q* instead of a number:

```
number = None
while number is None:
    try:
        raw = input("Enter a number ('q' to quit): ")
        if raw == 'q':
            break
        number = int(raw)
    except ValueError:
```

```
        print("You must enter a number.")

print(f"You entered {number}")
```

Listing 9-2: get_number.py:1b

I get the raw input first and check for the string value `'q'`. If I find it, I escape the loop manually with **break**. Otherwise, I attempt to convert the input to an integer as before.

There's one problem with this approach, as seen in the output:

```
Enter a number ('q' to quit): foo
You must enter a number.
Enter a number ('q' to quit): q
You entered None
```

The last line of output isn't right. I want the program to quit right away instead.

To fix this, I use a little-known feature of loops in Python: the else clause. When a Python loop finishes normally, the else suite is run; however, it is *not* run if the loop is aborted with a break, return, or raised exception.

By moving my final print statement to the else clause of the loop, I ensure it only runs if a valid number is entered:

```
number = None
while number is None:
    try:
        raw = input("Enter a number ('q' to quit): ")
        if raw == 'q':
            break
        number = int(raw)
    except ValueError:
        print("You must enter a number.")
else:
    print(f"You entered {number}")
```

Listing 9-3: get_number.py:1c

Running this code demonstrates the new behavior:

```
Enter a number ('q' to quit): q
```

Upon encountering a *q*, the loop exits immediately, without executing the last print() statement.

for Loops

For the majority of this chapter, I'll focus on the mechanics of the for loop. For now, it will suffice for you to understand that the purpose of a for loop is to traverse through, or *iterate over*, a collection of values.

Like while, the for loop has an else clause that is only executed when the loop finishes normally, and not when it is manually aborted with break, return, or a raised exception.

A simplistic example will be enough for now:

```
numbers = ["One", "Two", "Three"]

for number in numbers:
    print(number)
else:
    print("We're done!")
```

Listing 9-4: print_list.py

I define a list of strings, which I assign to numbers. Then, I loop through each value in numbers and print each out to the terminal. When I'm done, I announce that fact with another message.

Here's the output:

```
One
Two
Three
We're done!
```

For the rest of this chapter, I'll unpack everything happening behind the scenes here, which is surprisingly vast. You will learn how to utilize iteration to its fullest potential in your code.

Collections

A *collection* is a container object containing one or more *items* organized in some fashion. Each item is bound to a value; the values themselves are not contained within the collection object. There are five fundamental types of collections in Python, each with multiple variations: tuple, list, deque, set, and dict (dictionary).

Once you understand how each collection behaves, using collections effectively is simply a matter of memorizing their methods; in lieu of that, most Python developers rely on the documentation. In a pinch, you can also run help(*collection*) in a Python interactive shell, where *collection* is the collection you want more information about.

Tuples

As you know from Chapter 3 and the usages since, a *tuple* is a *sequence* (an array-like collection) that is *immutable*, meaning that once it is created, its items cannot be added, removed, or reordered.

Conventionally, tuples are used for heterogeneously typed, sequentially ordered data, such as when you need to keep different but associated values together. For example, here's a tuple containing a customer name, a coffee order, and an order size, in ounces:

```
order = ("Jason", "pumpkin spice latte", 12)
```

Listing 9-5: order_tuple.py:1

You define a tuple as a comma-separated sequence of values, enclosed in parentheses.

In many cases, the parentheses around a tuple are technically optional. They are only used to disambiguate the tuple from its surroundings, such as when passing a tuple to an argument. It's good practice to always include them.

Because the contents of a tuple are *ordered*, you can access individual items by index, or *subscript*, specified in square brackets:

```
print(order[1])  # prints "pumpkin spice latte"
```

Listing 9-6: order_tuple.py:2

If you need a tuple with a single item, leave a trailing comma after the item, like so:

```
orders = ("pumpkin spice latte",)
```

This is primarily useful when one of your functions is expected to return a tuple, but you don't know in advance how many elements you'll need to return in that tuple.

Since tuples are immutable, they don't offer any built-in methods for adding, changing, or removing items. You define a tuple once, in its entirety, up front, and then you access the items it contains.

Named Tuples

The collections module provides a strange little variant of the tuple called the *named tuple*, which allows you to define a tuple-like collection with named fields. Like a normal tuple, a named tuple is an immutable collection. Its primary use is adding keys to the values, while still retaining its subscript-able behavior:

```
from collections import namedtuple

CoffeeOrder = namedtuple(❶ "CoffeeOrder", ❷('item', 'addons', 'to_go'))

order = CoffeeOrder('pumpkin spice latte', ('whipped cream',), True)
print(❸ order.item)  # prints 'pumpkin spice latte'
print(❹ order[2])    # prints 'True'
```

Listing 9-7: coffeeorder_namedtuple.py

I define a new namedtuple with the type name CoffeeOrder ❶, which I also bind to the name CoffeeOrder. I name three fields in that named tuple: item, addons, and to_go ❷.

Next, I create a new instance of the named tuple by passing the values to the CoffeeOrder initializer, and I bind the instance to order. I can access the values within order by field name ❸ or by subscript ❹.

In practice, most Pythonistas prefer dictionaries or classes to named tuples, but all three have their place.

Lists

Lists are sequence collections that are *mutable*, meaning items can be added, removed, and reordered. Conventionally, lists are used for homogeneously typed, sequentially ordered data, such as this list of specials at the fictional Uncomment Café:

```
specials = ["pumpkin spice latte", "caramel macchiato", "mocha cappuccino"]
```

Listing 9-8: specials_list.py:1

You define a list as a comma-separated sequence, enclosed in square brackets. As with tuples, you can access individual items via their index, specified in square brackets:

```
print(specials[1])      # prints "caramel macchiato"
```

Listing 9-9: specials_list.py:2

You can use lists as arrays, stacks, or queues. Here are a few of the most commonly used methods on list:

```
drink = specials.pop()  # return and remove last item
print(drink)            # prints "mocha cappuccino"
print(specials)         # prints ['pumpkin spice latte', 'caramel macchiato']
```

Listing 9-10: specials_list.py:3

I use pop() to return and remove items from the list. If I don't pass an index to pop(), the last item is removed by default.

If I pass an index as an argument to pop(), the indicated item is removed instead:

```
drink = specials.pop(1)  # return and remove item [1]
print(drink)             # prints "caramel macchiato"
print(specials)          # prints ['pumpkin spice latte']
```

Listing 9-11: specials_list.py:4

I can also add new items to the end of the list, using append():

```
specials.append("cold brew")  # inserts item at end
print(specials)               # prints ['pumpkin spice latte', 'cold brew']
```

Listing 9-12: specials_list.py:5

The new item, "cold brew", is passed to append(), and it is added at the end of the list.

If I want to add an item somewhere else in the list, I can use insert():

```
specials.insert(1, "americano")   # inserts as item [1]
print(specials)                   # prints ['pumpkin spice latte', 'americano', 'cold brew']
```

Listing 9-13: specials_list.py:6

The first argument is a target index, 1, and the new item, "americano", is the second argument.

These are the three most common methods for modifying lists. Python has more, many of which are quite interesting. As I've mentioned, the official documentation is your best resource for learning all the available methods.

PEDANTIC NOTE If you want a traditional dynamically sized array, which compactly stores exactly one data type, check out the array module: *https://docs.python.org/3/ library/array.html*. In practice, this is seldom needed.

Deques

The collections module provides another sequence, *deque* (pronounced "deck"), which is optimized for accessing the first and last items. This makes it a good option to use as a stack or queue when performance especially matters.

In this example, I'll use deque to track the people waiting in line at the Uncomment Café:

```
from collections import deque
customers = deque(['Daniel', 'Denis'])
```

Listing 9-14: customers_deque.py:1

After I import deque from collections, I create a new deque, which I bind to customers. I pass a list of two customers as the list's initial value, although I could have omitted this and started with an empty deque instead.

Simon enters the café and gets in line, so I add him to the end of the deque with append():

```
customers.append('Simon')
print(customers)  # prints deque(['Daniel', 'Denis', 'Simon'])
```

Listing 9-15: customers_deque.py:2

Then, the barista helps the next person in line, so I return and remove the first customer, Daniel, from the front ("left") of the line, using popleft():

```
customer = customers.popleft()
print(customer)   # prints 'Daniel'
print(customers)  # prints deque(['Denis', 'Simon'])
```

Listing 9-16: customers_deque.py:3

There are once again two people in line. James slips in front of everyone else (how rude!), so I append him to the "left" of the deque with appendleft():

```
customers.appendleft('James')
print(customers)  # prints deque(['James', 'Denis', 'Simon'])
```

Listing 9-17: customers_deque.py:4

But that's okay by Simon, because the last person in line wins a free drink. I return and remove the last item from the deque:

```
last_in_line = customers.pop()
print(last_in_line)  # prints 'Simon'
```

Listing 9-18: customers_deque.py:5

After all this, the deque only has James and Denis:

```
print(customers)  # prints deque(['James', 'Denis'])
```

Listing 9-19: customers_deque.py:6

Sets

A *set* is a built-in, mutable, *unordered* collection, in which all items are guaranteed to be unique. If you try to add an item that already exists in the set, the new duplicate will be discarded. You'll primarily use a set for fast inclusion checks and various operations relating to set theory (math), especially in large data sets.

Every value stored in a set must be *hashable*, which the Python documentation defines as having "a hash value that never changes during its lifetime." Hashable objects implement the special method __hash__(). All the built-in immutable types are hashable, since they never change value throughout their lifetime. However, many mutable types are not hashable.

I'll use a set to run a raffle at the Uncomment Café, where each customer can only enter once:

```
raffle = {'James', 'Denis', 'Simon'}
```

Listing 9-20: raffle_set.py:1

I first define the set as a comma-separated sequence of values, surrounded by curly braces ({}). In this case, I provide three initial values.

As customers come in, I add their names to the set with add(). If their name is already in the set, such as in the case of Denis, it won't be added another time if I try to add it:

```
raffle.add('Daniel')
raffle.add('Denis')
print(raffle)  # prints {'Daniel', 'Denis', 'Simon', 'James'}
```

Listing 9-21: raffle_set.py:2

The print statement shows the current items in the set. Just remember that sets are *unordered*, so there is no guarantee of the order in which the items will appear.

I can remove items from the set using discard(). Since Simon won something earlier, I'll remove his name:

```
raffle.discard('Simon')
print(raffle)  # prints {'Daniel', 'Denis', 'James'}
```

Listing 9-22: raffle_set.py:3

I could have also used remove() to remove a value, but that raises a KeyError if the specified value is not in the set; discard() never raises an error.

Finally, I return and remove an arbitrary item from the set with pop():

```
winner = raffle.pop()
print(winner)  # prints arbitrary item of set, e.g. 'Denis'
```

Listing 9-23: raffle_set.py:4

Be aware, *arbitrary* does not mean *random*! The pop() method always returns and removes whichever item happens to be in the first position in the set. Because set is unordered and Python makes no guarantees about the internal sequence of the items, you cannot trust set for reliable randomness.

GOTCHA ALERT To specify an empty set, you would use set(), as an empty pair of curly braces ({ }) specifies an empty dictionary instead.

frozenset

The immutable twin to set is frozenset, which works in much the same manner. They differ in the same way that list and tuple do: once created, a frozenset cannot have items added or removed.

To demonstrate this, I'll create a frozenset for storing all previous prize-winners and use that as part of the next raffle:

```
raffle = {'Kyle', 'Denis', 'Jason'}
prev_winners = frozenset({'Denis', 'Simon'})
```

Listing 9-24: raffle_frozenset.py:1

A frozenset is specified by passing a set literal (shown here), an existing set, or another linear collection to the frozenset() initializer. After I initially define prev_winners, I cannot change the contents of the frozenset—it's immutable. The regular set, raffle, can still be modified.

One of the most exciting features of set and frozenset is that they both support *set mathematics*. You can use math and logic operators for finding the union (|), intersection (&), difference (-), and symmetric difference (^). It's also useful for testing if one set is a subset (< or <=) or superset (> or >=)

of the other. The documentation also outlines several other functions for combining and comparing sets of either type.

In my example, I'll remove all the previous winners (prev_winners) from the raffle set using the -= operator:

```
raffle -= prev_winners  # remove previous winners
print(raffle)           # prints {'Jason', 'Kyle'}
```

Listing 9-25: raffle_frozenset.py:2

Then I can pop() an arbitrary item off of raffle to find my winner:

```
winner = raffle.pop()
print(winner)  # prints arbitrary item of set, e.g. 'Kyle'
```

Listing 9-26: raffle_frozenset.py:3

Yay for Kyle! He wins a three-day, one-night trip to Antarctica, courtesy of Frozen Set Airlines. (Bundle up, buddy.)

Dictionaries

A *dictionary* (type dict) is a mutable collection that stores data in *key-value* pairs, instead of in linear fashion. This associative manner of storage is known as *mapping*. Keys can be virtually any type, as long as that type is hashable. It's easiest to remember that hashable types are virtually always immutable.

The value in the pair can be anything. Looking up a value by key is particularly fast, regardless of the amount of data in the dictionary. (In other languages, this type of collection is referred to as a *hashmap*; in CPython, the dictionary is implemented as a hash table.)

I'll use a dictionary to store the menu at the Uncomment Café:

```
menu = {"drip": 1.95, "cappuccino": 2.95}
```

Listing 9-27: menu_dict.py:1

I create the dictionary as a sequence of comma-separated key-value pairs, wrapped in curly braces, with a colon (:) separating the key and value in each pair. In this case, the key is a string that is the name of the drink, and the value is a floating-point number representing the price.

I access individual items by key, specified in square brackets ([ ]):

```
print(menu["drip"])  # prints 1.95
```

Listing 9-28: menu_dict.py:2

If the key being accessed is not in the dictionary, a KeyError is raised.

I can add or modify items by assigning a value to a key specified in square brackets. Here, I'll add the "americano" key to the menu, with a price value of 2.49:

```
menu["americano"] = 2.49
print(menu)  # prints {'drip': 1.95, 'cappuccino': 2.95, 'americano': 2.49}
```

Listing 9-29: menu_dict.py:3

For whatever reason, the Americano isn't terribly popular at the café, so I wind up removing it from the dictionary, using the del operator on the key:

```
del menu["americano"]   # removes "americano" from dictionary
print(menu)             # prints {'drip': 1.95, 'cappuccino': 2.95}
```

Listing 9-30: menu_dict.py:4

Once again, if the key specified in the square brackets were not in the dictionary, a KeyError would be raised.

Check or Except?

There's a bit of debate about whether one should check for a key in a dictionary directly with the in operator or use a try statement with a KeyError instead.

Here's the EAFP ("Easier to Ask Forgiveness than Permission") approach, using try:

```
menu = {'drip': 1.95, 'cappuccino': 2.95, 'americano': 2.49}


def checkout(order):
    try:
        print(f"Your total is {❶ menu[order]}")
    except KeyError:
        print("That item is not on the menu.")


checkout("drip")  # prints "Your total is 1.95"
checkout("tea")   # prints "That item is not on the menu."
```

Listing 9-31: checkout_dict_eafp.py

Within a try statement, I try to access the value in the dictionary menu associated with the key order ❶. If the key is invalid, a KeyError will be raised and I will catch it in the except clause. I can then take the appropriate action.

This approach is better suited to instances where invalid keys are an *exceptional* situation (thus, "exceptions"). Typically, an except clause is a more expensive operation in terms of performance, but it's an expense that is completely justified for handling errors and other exceptional situations.

Here's the LBYL ("Look Before You Leap") approach, using the `in` operator:

```python
menu = {'drip': 1.95, 'cappuccino': 2.95, 'americano': 2.49}


def checkout(order):
 ❶ if order in menu:
        print(f"Your total is {❷ menu[order]}")
    else:
        print("That item is not on the menu.")


checkout("drip")  # prints "Your total is 1.95"
checkout("tea")   # prints "That item is not on the menu."
```

Listing 9-32: checkout_dict_lbyl.py

In this approach, I check whether `order` is a key in the `menu` dictionary before I do anything ❶. If it's there, I can safely access the value associated with the key ❷. This approach may be preferable if you expect to frequently check for invalid keys, since either outcome is reasonably likely. Failure is more the *rule* than the *exception*, so it's better for both scenarios to have roughly the same performance.

The LBYL approach is generally frowned upon when an invalid key is an exceptional situation, because it has to look in the dictionary for a valid key twice: once when checking and once when accessing. By contrast, the EAFP approach only has to access a valid key once, since it handles the possible `KeyError`.

As with all issues of performance, you can't know for sure until you profile the code. You can rely on the assumptions herein, unless you specifically need the logic structure of one approach or the other. However, if performance is critical, profile the code (see Chapter 19).

Dictionary Variants

Python has a `collections` module that offers a few variations on the built-in `dict`. Here are the three most common variations, along with their unique behavior:

> `defaultdict` allows you to specify a callable that produces a default value. If you attempt to access the value on an undefined key, a new key-value pair will be defined, using this default value.
>
> `OrderedDict` has extra functionality for tracking and managing the order of key-value pairs. Since Python 3.7, the built-in `dict` also officially preserves insertion order, but `OrderedDict` is specifically *optimized* for reordering and has additional behaviors for it.
>
> `Counter` is designed specifically for counting hashable objects; the object is the key, and the count is an integer value. Other languages call this type of collection a *multiset*.

You should only use one of these specialized dictionary types if you actually need its behavior, so I won't go into more detail here. Each is optimized for a specific use case and is not likely to have optimal performance in other scenarios. The official documentation is your best bet if you need further details: *https://docs.python.org/3/library/collections.html*.

Unpacking Collections

All collections can be *unpacked* into multiple variables, meaning each item is assigned to its own name. For example, I can unpack a deque of three customers into three separate variables. I first create the deque of customers:

```
from collections import deque

customers = deque(['Kyle', 'Simon', 'James'])
```

Listing 9-33: unpack_customers.py:1a

Next, to unpack the deque. I place a comma-separated list of names to unpack into, in order, on the left side of an assignment operator:

```
first, second, third = customers
print(first)    # prints 'Kyle'
print(second)   # prints 'Simon'
print(third)    # prints 'James'
```

Listing 9-34: unpack_customers.py:2a

Sometimes, you'll see this left-hand part wrapped in parentheses, but using parentheses isn't required when unpacking a linear collection like this. (I'll demonstrate where parentheses fit into unpacking a dictionary in the next section.) I place the collection I'm unpacking on the right side of the assignment operator.

There's one major limitation to unpacking: you have to know how many values you're unpacking! To demonstrate this, I'll go back and add one more customer to the deque with the append() method:

```
from collections import deque

customers = deque(['Kyle', 'Simon', 'James'])
customers.append('Daniel')
```

Listing 9-35: unpack_customers.py:1b

If I were to specify too many or too few names on the left, a ValueError would be raised. Since my deque contains four values, trying to unpack into three names fails:

```
first, second, third = customers   # raises ValueError
print(first)                       # never reached
```

```
print(second)                    # never reached
print(third)                     # never reached
```

Listing 9-36: unpack_customers.py:2b

To fix this, I could specify a fourth name on the left. However, for this example, I want to ignore the fourth value. I can ignore any item by unpacking it into an underscore:

```
first, second, third, _ = customers
print(first)     # prints 'Kyle'
print(second)    # prints 'Simon'
print(third)     # prints 'James'
```

Listing 9-37: unpack_customers.py:2c

The underscore (_), when used as a name, conventionally indicates that the value should be ignored. I can use the underscore as many times as I need, such as if I want to ignore the last two values in the collection:

```
first, second, _, _ = customers
print(first)    # prints 'Kyle'
print(second)   # prints 'Simon'
```

Listing 9-38: unpack_customers.py:2d

Only the first two values in customers will be unpacked, and the second two will be effectively ignored.

By the way, if you ever need to unpack a collection that only contains one value, leave a trailing comma after the name you're unpacking into:

```
baristas = ('Jason',)
barista, = baristas
print(barista)  # prints 'Jason'
```

Starred Expressions

If you have no idea how many additional values there are in the collection, you can capture multiple unpacked values using a *starred expression*:

```
first, second, *rest = customers
print(first)     # prints 'Kyle'
print(second)    # prints 'Simon'
print(rest)      # prints ['James', 'Daniel']
```

Listing 9-39: unpack_customers.py:2e

The first two values are unpacked into first and second, and the remainder (if any) are packed into a list assigned to rest. As long as the collection being unpacked has at least two values, one for each of the nonstarred names on the left, this will work. If there are only two values in the collection, rest will be an empty list.

You can use starred expressions anywhere in the unpacking list, including the beginning. Here's an example where I unpack the first and last values individually and pack all the rest into a list named middle:

```
first, *middle, last = customers
print(first)     # prints 'Kyle'
print(middle)    # prints ['Simon', 'James']
print(last)      # prints 'Daniel'
```

Listing 9-40: unpack_customers.py:3

You can even use starred expressions to ignore multiple values:

```
*_, second_to_last, last = customers
print(second_to_last)  # prints 'James'
print(last)            # prints 'Daniel'
```

Listing 9-41: unpack_customers.py:4

By preceding the underscore with an asterisk, I capture multiple values but ignore them, instead of packing them into a list. In this scenario, I unpack the last two values in the collection.

You can only have one starred expression per unpacking statement, because starred expressions are *greedy*—consuming as many values as they're allowed. Python unpacks values into all the other names before evaluating the starred expression. Using multiple starred expressions in the same statement makes no sense, since it's impossible to tell where one stops and another starts.

Unpacking Dictionaries

Dictionaries can be unpacked like any other built-in type of collection. By default, only the keys are unpacked, as seen when I unpack the dictionary representing the café menu.

I start by defining my dictionary:

```
menu = {'drip': 1.95, 'cappuccino': 2.95, 'americano': 2.49}
```

Listing 9-42: unpack_menu.py:1

Then, I unpack the dictionary:

```
a, b, c = menu
print(a)  # prints 'drip'
print(b)  # prints 'cappuccino'
print(c)  # prints 'americano'
```

Listing 9-43: unpack_menu.py:2a

If I want the values instead, I must unpack using a *dictionary view*, which provides access to the keys and/or values in a dictionary. In this case, I use the values() dictionary view:

```
a, b, c = menu.values()
print(a)  # prints 1.95
print(b)  # prints 2.95
print(c)  # prints 2.49
```

Listing 9-44: unpack_menu.py:2b

I can unpack the keys and values together by unpacking from the items() dictionary view. This returns each key-value pair as a tuple:

```
a, b, c = menu.items()
print(a)  # prints ('drip', 1.95)
print(b)  # prints ('cappuccino', 2.95)
print(c)  # prints ('americano', 2.49)
```

Listing 9-45: unpack_menu.py:2c

I can also unpack each of the key-value tuples in the same statement by using parentheses around a pair of names a tuple will be unpacked into:

```
(a_name, a_price), (b_name, b_price), *_ = menu.items()
print(a_name)    # prints 'drip'
print(a_price)   # prints 1.95
print(b_name)    # prints 'cappuccino'
print(b_price)   # prints 2.95
```

Listing 9-46: unpack_menu.py:3

For brevity, I chose to only unpack the first two items in the menu dictionary and ignore the rest. I unpack the first tuple from menu.items() into the pair (a_name, a_price), so the first item of the tuple is stored in a_name and the second item is stored in a_price. The same thing happens with the second key-value pair in the dictionary.

You can use this unpacking strategy with parentheses to unpack two-dimensional collections, such as a list of tuples or a tuple of sets.

Structural Pattern Matching on Collections

Starting from Python 3.10, it is possible to perform structural pattern matching on tuples, lists, and dictionaries.

In patterns, tuples and lists are interchangeable. They are both matched against sequence patterns. *Sequence patterns* use the same syntax as unpacking, including the ability to use starred expressions. For example, I could match on the first and last elements of a sequence and ignore everything in the middle:

```
order = ['venti', 'no whip', 'mocha latte', 'for here']

match order:
    case ('tall', *drink, 'for here'):
        drink = ' '.join(drink)
        print(f"Filling ceramic mug with {drink}.")
    case ['grande', *drink, 'to go']:
        drink = ' '.join(drink)
        print(f"Filling large paper cup with {drink}.")
    case ('venti', *drink, 'for here'):
        drink = ' '.join(drink)
        print(f"Filling extra large tumbler with {drink}.")
```

Listing 9-47: match_coffee_sequence.py

Sequence patterns are the same, whether enclosed in parentheses or square brackets. The list order is compared against each pattern. For each, the first and last items are checked, and the rest of the items are captured via wildcard as drink. Within each case, I join together the elements in drink to determine what to fill the chosen vessel with.

I could also pattern match against specific values in a dictionary, using a *mapping pattern*. Here's almost the same example, reworked to used a dictionary instead:

```
order = {
    'size': 'venti',
    'notes': 'no whip',
    'drink': 'mocha latte',
    'serve': 'for here'
}

match order:
    case {'size': 'tall', 'serve': 'for here', 'drink': drink}:
        print(f"Filling ceramic mug with {drink}.")
    case {'size': 'grande', 'serve': 'to go', 'drink': drink}:
        print(f"Filling large paper cup with {drink}.")
    case {'size': 'venti', 'serve': 'for here', 'drink': drink}:
        print(f"Filling extra large tumbler with {drink}.")
```

Listing 9-48: match_coffee_dictionary.py:1a

Mapping patterns are wrapped in curly braces. Only the keys I specify in the pattern are checked, while any other keys are ignored. In this version, I check the 'size' and 'serve' keys, as well as the value associated with the key 'drink', which I capture as drink.

If you run this version of the code, versus the previous one, you'll notice that I'm leaving the 'notes' off (for example, 'no whip'). To fix that, I could capture all remaining keys via wildcard instead, like this:

```
order = {
    'size': 'venti',
    'notes': 'no whip',
    'drink': 'mocha latte',
    'serve': 'for here'
}

match order:
    case {'size': 'tall', 'serve': 'for here', **rest}:
        drink = f"{rest['notes']} {rest['drink']}"
        print(f"Filling ceramic mug with {drink}.")
    case {'size': 'grande', 'serve': 'to go', **rest}:
        drink = f"{rest['notes']} {rest['drink']}"
        print(f"Filling large paper cup with {drink}.")
    case {'size': 'venti', 'serve': 'for here', **rest}:
        drink = f"{rest['notes']} {rest['drink']}"
        print(f"Filling extra large tumbler with {drink}.")
```

Listing 9-49: match_coffee_dictionary.py:1b

PEDANTIC NOTE   Because any keys not explicitly listed in the mapping pattern are ignored anyway, the wildcard for ignoring all remaining keys without capturing them, two asterisks and an underscore (**_), is not legal in mapping patterns.

Although I chose to demonstrate capturing with a wildcard in a mapping pattern, it is worth noting that I can still directly access the subject, order, from within any of the cases. In this particular example, I could have just as easily written the code like this:

```
match order:
    case {'size': 'tall', 'serve': 'for here'}:
        drink = f"{order['notes']} {order['drink']}"
        print(f"Filling ceramic mug with {drink}.")
    case {'size': 'grande', 'serve': 'to go'}:
        drink = f"{order['notes']} {order['drink']}"
        print(f"Filling large paper cup with {drink}.")
    case {'size': 'venti', 'serve': 'for here'}:
        drink = f"{order['notes']} {order['drink']}"
        print(f"Filling extra large tumbler with {drink}.")
```

Listing 9-50: match_coffee_dictionary.py:1c

As before, any keys omitted from each mapping pattern are ignored for purposes of pattern matching.

Accessing by Index or Key

Many collections are *subscriptable*, meaning individual items can be accessed via an index specified in square brackets. You've already seen this with lists:

```
specials = ["pumpkin spice latte", "caramel macchiato", "mocha cappuccino"]
print(specials[1])  # prints "caramel macchiato"
specials[1] = "drip"
print(specials[1])  # prints "drip"
```

Listing 9-51: subscript_specials.py:1a

Subscriptable collection classes implement the special methods __getitem__(), __setitem__(), and __delitem__(), where each accepts a single-integer argument. You can see this in action by using the special methods directly, instead of the square-bracket notation from a moment ago. This code is functionally identical to the above:

```
specials = ["pumpkin spice latte", "caramel macchiato", "mocha cappuccino"]
print(specials.__getitem__(1))  # prints "caramel macchiato"
specials.__setitem__(1, "drip")
print(specials.__getitem__(1))  # prints "drip"
```

Listing 9-52: subscript_specials.py:1b

These same special methods are implemented by the dict class, except that they accept a *key* as the sole argument. Because dictionaries don't have a formal "index," they are not considered subscriptable collections.

Slice Notation

Slice notation allows you to access specific items or ranges of items in a list or tuple. Of the five fundamental types of collections, only tuple and list can be sliced. Neither set nor dict is subscriptable, so slice notation won't work on them. While deque is subscriptable, it cannot be sliced using slice notation, because of how it is implemented.

To take a *slice* of a list or tuple, you use square brackets around the slice notation, which generally consists of three parts, separated by colons:

```
[start:stop:step]
```

The *inclusive* index of the first item you want to include in the slice is *start*. The *exclusive* index, *stop*, is *just past* where the slice stops. The *step* part allows you to skip over items and even reverse the order.

You aren't required to specify all three arguments, but be mindful of the colons. If you want a slice, as opposed to a single element accessed by index, you must *always* include the colon separating *start* and *stop*, even if you don't specify one or the other: ([*start: stop*], [*start:*], [*:stop*]).

Similarly, if you define *step*, you must precede it with its own colon: ([*:stop: step*], [*::step*], [*start::step*]).

Slice notation never returns an IndexError! If the notation is invalid for the list or tuple in question, or if it is otherwise ill-formed, it will return an empty list [ ]. You should always test your slice notation before relying on it.

That's rather theoretical, so here are some practical examples, using a list of coffee orders:

```
orders = [
    "caramel macchiato",
    "drip",
    "pumpkin spice latte",
    "drip",
    "cappuccino",
    "americano",
    "mocha latte",
]
```

Listing 9-53: slice_orders.py:1

Start and Stop

By specifying the start and stop for a slice, I can specify a range:

```
three_four_five = orders[3:6]
print(three_four_five)  # prints ['drip', 'cappuccino', 'americano']
```

Listing 9-54: slice_orders.py:2

The slice starts at index 3 and ends just before 6, so it includes the items at indices 3, 4, and 5.

One important rule: *start* must always refer to an item that comes before *stop*. By default, lists are traversed first to last, so the *start* must be less than *stop*.

A slice doesn't require all three arguments. If you leave out *start*, the slice begins at the first element. If you leave off *stop*, the slice finishes with the final element.

If I wanted all the items in the list except the first four, I'd use this:

```
after_third = orders[4:]
print(after_third)  # print ['cappuccino', 'americano', 'mocha latte']
```

Listing 9-55: slice_orders.py:3

I start at index 4. Then, since I didn't specify a *stop* after the required colon, the slice includes the rest of the items up to the very end of the list.

I can access the first two items in the list this way:

```
next_two = orders[:2]
print(next_two)  # prints ['caramel macchiato', 'drip']
```

Listing 9-56: slice_orders.py:4

I didn't specify a start before the colon, so it defaults to the beginning of the list. The end, which is *exclusive*, is 2, so the slice includes all items before index 2. This gives me the first two items in the list.

Negative Indices

I can also use negative numbers as indices, which enable me to count backward from the end of the list or tuple. For example, an index of -1 refers to the last item in the list:

```
print(orders[-1])  # prints 'mocha latte'
```

Listing 9-57: slice_orders.py:5

Negative indices work with slicing, too. For example, if I wanted to get the three orders at the end of the list, I could use this:

```
last_three = orders[-3:]
print(last_three)  # prints ['cappuccino', 'americano', 'mocha latte']
```

Listing 9-58: slice_orders.py:6

The slice starts at the third index from the end (-3) and goes to the end. When determining negative indices, remember that -1 is the last item—that is, it's one index before the "end," which *has* no index.

If I wanted the third-from-last and second-from-last orders, but not the last order, I could define both *start* and *stop* as negative indices:

```
last_two_but_one = orders[-3:-1]
print(last_two_but_one)  # prints ['cappuccino', 'americano']
```

Listing 9-59: slice_orders.py:7

Remember, the *start* index must always come before the *stop*, and lists are traversed from left to right, by default. Thus, the *start* must be -3, or third-from-end, and the *stop* must be -1; so the last included index is -2, or second-from-end.

Steps

By default, lists are traversed first to last, from the lowest index to the highest, one by one. The third part of the slice notation, *step*, lets you change that behavior so you can better control which values are included in the slice, and in what order.

For example, I could create a slice containing every other coffee order, starting from the second order, by setting the *step* part to 2:

```
every_other = orders[1::2]
print(every_other)  # prints ['drip', 'drip', 'americano']
```

Listing 9-60: slice_orders.py:8

I *start* the slice at index 1. Since I haven't specified a *stop* index, the slice goes to the end of the list. The *step* argument of 2 tells Python to grab every second item. With the orders list, that means the slice will consist of the items at indices 1, 3, and 5.

A negative *step* argument reverses the direction the list or tuple is read in. For example, a *step* of -1, with no *start* or *stop*, will return a reversed version of the entire orders list:

```
reverse = orders[::-1]
```

Listing 9-61: slice_orders.py:9

You'll notice I had to precede the -1 with two colons, to delineate that no values had been specified for *start* or *stop*. Otherwise, Python would have no way to know that the -1 was for the third argument.

I can even get a reversed version of the data sliced in Listing 9-60, although there's a bit of a trick to it. Here's the code:

```
every_other_reverse = orders[-2::-2]
print(every_other_reverse)  # prints ['americano', 'drip', 'drip']
```

Listing 9-62: slice_orders.py:10

The *step* of -2 means the slice grabs every other value in reverse order. The list is traversed from right to left. That changes the behavior of *start* and *stop*. I *start* at the second-to-last item (-2), but because I omitted a value for *stop*, it defaults to the beginning of the list, instead of the end. If I left off both *start* and *stop*, I'd get every other value in reverse, starting from the last item.

This reversed behavior radically affects what values are used for *start* and *stop*, and this misunderstanding can easily result in bugs. For example, if I want the third, fourth, and fifth items in reverse order, my first attempt might look like the following, which would *not* work:

```
three_to_five_reverse = orders[3:6:-1]   # WRONG! Returns empty list.
print(three_to_five_reverse)             # prints []
```

Listing 9-63: slice_orders.py:11a

The negative *step* value means I'm traversing the list in reverse order. Remember that *start* must always be traversed before *stop*.

If I traverse the list from ending to beginning, then I have to reverse the *start* and *stop* values, like so:

```
three_to_five_reverse = orders[5:2:-1]
print(three_to_five_reverse)  # prints ['americano', 'cappuccino', 'drip']
```

Listing 9-64: slice_orders.py:11b

Moving backward through the list, the slice starts at index 5 and stops at index 2, which is not included.

Copy with Slice

One more thing to know about slices is that they always return a new list or tuple with the selected items; the original list or tuple still exists as it was. This code creates a perfect shallow copy of the list:

```
order_copy = orders[:]
```

Listing 9-65: slice_orders.py:12

Since neither *start* nor *stop* is specified, the slice includes all items.

Slice Objects

You can also directly create a slice object for reuse by using the slice() initializer method.

```
my_slice = slice(3, 5, 2)  # same as [3:5:2]
print(my_slice)
```

The *start*, *stop*, and (optionally) *step* values are passed as positional arguments. In practice, this approach is more limited than regular slice notation, since it is not possible to omit the *stop* value.

In any case, I can now use my_slice in place of slice notation, such as in the print() statement above.

Slicing on Custom Objects

If you want to implement slicing in your own objects, you'll only need to accept a slice object as an argument on the same special methods needed to make the object subscriptable: __getitem__(self, sliced), __setitem__(self, sliced), and __delitem__(self, sliced). Then, you can get the three parts of the slice object with sliced.start, sliced.stop, and sliced.step.

A decent example for this would be pretty involved, so I'll leave this explanation here.

Using islice

You can still slice a deque or any collection that isn't subscriptable by using itertools.islice(), which behaves the same as slice notation, except that it doesn't support negative values for any of the parameters.

The arguments that islice() accepts are ordered, so you have to remember the order:

```
islice(collection, start, stop, step)
```

For example, islice() can take a slice from a dictionary, which cannot be sliced by ordinary slice notation because it isn't subscriptable. Here, I get every other item from the dictionary:

```
from itertools import islice

menu = {'drip': 1.95, 'cappuccino': 2.95, 'americano': 2.49}

menu = dict(islice(❶ menu.items(), 0, 3, 2))  # same as [0:3:2]
print(menu)
```

Listing 9-66: islice_orders.py

I pass the dictionary as a list of tuples to the islice ❶, followed by the *start*, *stop*, and *step* values necessary to take every other item. Then, I create a new dictionary from the islice and bind it to menu. Running that code produces the following output:

```
{'drip': 1.95, 'americano': 2.49}
```

The in Operator

You can use the in operator to quickly check whether a particular value is contained in any collection.

As before, I'll start with a list of orders:

```
orders = [
    "caramel macchiato",
    "drip",
    "pumpkin spice latte",
    "drip",
    "cappuccino",
    "americano",
    "mocha cappuccino",
]
```

Listing 9-67: in_orders.py:1

For example, I might need to see if anyone wants a mocha cappuccino in my orders list before I open the new bottle of chocolate syrup:

```
if "mocha cappuccino" in orders:
    print("open chocolate syrup bottle")
```

Listing 9-68: in_orders.py:2

I place the value I'm looking for to the left of the in operator and the collection I'm searching to the right. The operator returns True if at least one instance of the value is found in the collection; otherwise, it returns False.

You can also check whether a list omits a specific item. For example, I might decide to shut off the coffee maker if no one wants any drip coffee right now. I can check if there are any orders for "drip" with this code:

```
if "drip" not in orders:
    print("shut off percolator")
```

Listing 9-69: in_orders.py:3

The addition of not inverts the in condition, so the expression evaluates to True if the value is *not* found in the collection.

You can add support for the in operator to your custom classes by implementing the special method __contains__().

Checking Collection Length

To find out how many items a collection contains, use the len() function. That's all there is to it. For example, if I have a list of waiting customers, I can find out how many customers are standing in line:

```
customers = ['Glen', 'Todd', 'Newman']
print(len(customers))  # prints 3
```

Listing 9-70: len_customers.py

The len() function returns the number of items in customers as an integer. Since there are three items in customers, the value 3 is returned. In the case of a dictionary, len() would return the number of key-value pairs.

You'll use len() less than you might expect when you employ iteration, which changes the way you traverse through collections such that you seldom need to know the length.

You don't even need len() when testing whether a collection is empty. If a collection contains content, it is "truthy," meaning it can be evaluated directly to True. Otherwise, if the collection is empty, it is "falsey," meaning it evaluates directly to False. I'll use this to see if there are any customers in the café right now.

```
customers = []

if ❶ customers:  # if not empty...
    print("There are customers.")
else:
    print("Quiet day.")

print(bool(customers))
```

Listing 9-71: no_customers.py

Because customers is empty, it is "falsey," meaning it evaluates to False in a boolean context, such as when used as an expression ❶. Therefore, when the above program is run, the following is displayed:

```
Quiet day.
False
```

Sure enough, if I directly cast customers to a boolean value, it prints False.

Usually, the only time you'll use len() is when you need the length of a collection as a piece of data in its own right, such as when calculating the average number of orders per day for the week:

```
orders_per_day = [56, 41, 49, 22, 71, 43, 18]
average_orders = sum(orders_per_day) // len(orders_per_day)
print(average_orders)
```

Listing 9-72: average_orders.py

The average_orders is printed to the screen:

```
42
```

Iteration

All collections in Python are designed to work with *iteration*, by which you can directly access items on demand, one by one. Iteration patterns aren't even limited to collections. You can leverage this concept to generate or process data *iteratively*: "on demand," instead of all up front. You'll see this in depth in Chapter 10.

Before you can start using iteration effectively, you must understand how it actually works. Then, you can use it to access, sort, and process items in collections.

Iterables and Iterators

One of the most compelling features of Python is its approach to iteration, by way of two fairly straightforward concepts: *iterables* and *iterators*.

An *iterable* is any object whose items or values can be accessed one at a time, on demand. For example, a list is an iterable; you can iterate over each item in the list, one by one. For an object to be iterable, it must have an associated iterator, which is returned from the object's instance method __iter__().

An *iterator* is the object that performs the actual iteration, providing ready access to the next item in the iterable it is traversing. To be an iterable, an object needs to implement the special method __next__(), which accepts no parameters and returns a value. This method advances to the next item in the iterable it traverses and returns that value.

Iterators must also implement the method __iter__(), which returns the iterator object itself (usually self). This convention is necessary so that code that accepts an iterable can also accept an iterator without any difficulty, as you'll see shortly.

That's really all there is to it! All collections are iterables, and each has at least one dedicated companion iterator class.

I'll implement a custom iterator class later in this chapter.

Manually Using Iterators

Before introducing automatic iteration, it's helpful to understand what is going on behind the scenes when using an iterator.

To demonstrate this, I'll traverse the values in a list, using an iterator I manually access and control. I'll go through this example twice: once, directly calling the special methods; and another time, allowing Python to call them implicitly.

I'll start by defining a list, which is an iterable:

```
specials = ["pumpkin spice latte", "caramel macchiato", "mocha cappuccino"]
```

Listing 9-73: specials_iteration.py:1

To iterate over the collection, I first acquire an iterator:

```
first_iterator = specials.__iter__()
second_iterator = specials.__iter__()
print(type(first_iterator))
```

Listing 9-74: specials_iteration.py:2

A list, like all iterables, implements the special method __iter__(), which returns an iterator object for this list. I acquire two separate iterators here, each of which can operate independently of the other.

When I check the data type of first_iterator, I see it's an instance of the class list_iterator, as seen in the output:

```
<class 'list_iterator'>
```

I use the iterator object to access the items in the list specials:

```
item = first_iterator.__next__()
print(item)
```

Listing 9-75: specials_iteration.py:3

The first call to the iterator's __next__() method advances to the first item in the list and returns its value, which I bind to item and print to the screen, outputting the following:

```
pumpkin spice latte
```

A subsequent call advances to and returns the second item:

```
item = first_iterator.__next__()
print(item)
```

Listing 9-76: specials_iteration.py:4

That outputs the following:

```
caramel macchiato
```

Each iterator tracks its position in the iterable separately. If I call the __next__() method on second_iterator, it advances to and returns the first item in the list:

```
item = second_iterator.__next__()
print(item)
```

Listing 9-77: manual_iteration.py:5

Printing item shows the first item in the list:

```
pumpkin spice latte
```

Yet first_iterator still remembers its own position and can be advanced to the third item in the list:

```
item = first_iterator.__next__()
print(item)
```

Listing 9-78: specials_iteration.py:6

That prints the value of the third item:

```
mocha cappuccino
```

Once an iterator has run through all the items in the iterable being traversed, calling __next__() again raises the special exception StopIteration:

```
item = first_iterator.__next__()  # raises StopIteration
```

Listing 9-79: specials_iteration.py:7

Thankfully, I don't need to call __iter__() and __next__() manually, in any case. Instead, I can use Python's built-in functions iter() and next() and pass in the iterable or iterator, respectively. The special methods will be invoked behind the scenes.

Here's that same example again, but now using those built-in functions:

```
first_iterator = iter(specials)
second_iterator = iter(specials)
print(type(first_iterator))  # prints <class 'list_iterator'>
```

```
item = next(first_iterator)
print(item)                        # prints "pumpkin spice latte"

item = next(first_iterator)
print(item)                        # prints "caramel macchiato"

item = next(second_iterator)
print(item)                        # prints "pumpkin spice latte"

item = next(first_iterator)
print(item)                        # prints "mocha cappuccino"

item = next(first_iterator)  # raises StopIteration
```

Listing 9-80: specials_iteration.py:2b-7b

As you can see, there's a lot of repetition in this manual approach, which suggests that I could use a loop to handle iteration. In fact, using a for loop is the standard way to work with iteration, as it calls iter() and next() implicitly, so I don't have to. However, to drive the underlying mechanics home first, I'll wrap this same manual iteration logic in a while loop:

```
  specials = ["pumpkin spice latte", "caramel macchiato", "mocha cappuccino"]
❶ iterator = iter(specials)

  while True:
      try:
          item = ❷ next(iterator)
    ❸ except StopIteration:
          break
      else:
          print(item)
```

Listing 9-81: specials_iteration_v2.py

I first acquire an iterator for the specials list ❶. Then, in an infinite while loop, I try to access the next value in the iterable by passing the iterator to next() ❷. If this raises the StopIteration exception ❸, I know I've traversed all the items in the specials list, and I break out of the loop with the break keyword. Otherwise, I print out the item I receive from the iterator.

Although it's helpful to understand how to manually handle iterators, you will seldom need to! A for loop would almost always handle the example in Listing 9-81:

```
specials = ["pumpkin spice latte", "caramel macchiato", "mocha cappuccino"]

for item in specials:
    print(item)
```

Listing 9-82: specials_iteration_v3.py

This eliminates the need to directly acquire an iterator. I'll cover this approach next.

Iterating with for Loops

One very helpful rule for loops and iteration in Python is that *you never need a counter variable for loop control.* In other words, virtually none of the traditional loop algorithms you're used to apply here! Python always has a better way, mainly because iterables can directly control for loops.

Take another look at that queue of people at the Uncomment Café. For each person in line, the barista would take an order, make it, and deliver it. Here's how I would do that. (For expediency of example, this code merely announces that each order is ready.)

```
customers = ['Newman', 'Daniel', 'Simon', 'James', 'William',
             'Kyle', 'Jason', 'Devin', 'Todd', 'Glen', 'Denis']

for customer in customers:
    # Take order
    # Make drink
    print(f"Order for {❶ customer}!")
```

Listing 9-83: iterate_orders_list.py

I loop through the `customers` list, which is an iterable. On each iteration, I bind each current item to `customer` so it works in the suite of the loop like any other variable ❶.

For each item in the list, I print a string announcing the order for the customer for that iteration. Here's the output of that code (truncated):

```
Order for Newman!
Order for Daniel!
Order for Simon!
# --snip--
```

A linear collection is pretty straightforward (no pun intended). Iterables with multiple values in any given item, such as from the `items()` dictionary view or from a two-dimensional list, must be treated differently.

To demonstrate this, I'll rewrite `customers` as a list of tuples, with each tuple containing a name and a coffee order. Then, I'll loop through them to announce their order:

```
customers = [
    ('Newman', 'tea'),
    ('Daniel', 'lemongrass tea'),
    ('Simon', 'chai latte'),
    ('James', 'medium roast drip, milk, 2 sugar substitutes'),
    ('William', 'french press'),
    ('Kyle', 'mocha cappuccino'),
    ('Jason', 'pumpkin spice latte'),
    ('Devin', 'double-shot espresso'),
    ('Todd', 'dark roast drip'),
    ('Glen', 'americano, no sugar, heavy cream'),
    ('Denis', 'cold brew')
]
```

```
for ❶ customer, drink in customers:
    print(f"Making {drink}...")
    print(f"Order for {customer}!")
```

Listing 9-84: iterate_orders_dict.py:1

In the for loop, I iterate over the list customers. On the left, I unpack each tuple item on the list into two names: customer and drink ❶.

Here's the resulting output:

```
Making tea...
Order for Newman!
Making lemongrass tea...
Order for Daniel!
Making chai latte...
Order for Simon!
# --snip--
```

Sorting Collections in Loops

Loops also allow you to do more advanced processing of this data. For example, let's say everyone could submit their orders through an app. (We are programmers, after all.)

I might want to sort the list of orders alphabetically, so I can search through them more easily. However, I still want to follow a first-come, first-served rule. Therefore, I don't want to modify the original customers list, since its sequence still matters:

```
for _, drink in ❶ sorted(customers, ❷ key=lambda x: ❸ x[1]):
    print(f"{drink}")
```

Listing 9-85: iterate_orders_dict.py:2

The sorted() ❶ function returns a list of the sorted items from whatever collection is passed to it. By default, it will sort by the first value in an item, in ascending order. In this case, the first item is the customer name, but I want to sort by the name of the drink ordered instead. I change this behavior by passing a callable *key function* to the key= named argument ❷. This callable, a lambda in this case, must accept an item as an argument and return the value I want to sort that item by. In this case, I want to sort by the second item in each tuple, which I return via x[1] ❸. Through all of this, customers remains unchanged.

You'll also notice that I use the underscore in the unpacking list to ignore the first value in each tuple, the customer name, because I don't need it in this loop. This is usually the best way to pick and choose items from a small tuple in a for loop. On the other hand, if each item were a collection with many subitems, it might work better to bind the entire item to one name and access what I need from it in the suite of the loop.

Running that code, I get this output for this part:

```
americano, no sugar, heavy cream
chai latte
cold brew
# --snip--
```

Enumerating Loops

You never need a counter variable for loop control. This will come as a major paradigm shift to many developers, who are used to C-style loop control. You may wonder what to do if you need the index itself.

Python offers enumerate() for such situations. The added benefit of using this function instead of manual indices is that it works with all iterables, even those that aren't subscriptable.

I'll use enumerate() to see the order of each person in line, along with their order:

```
for number, ❶ (customer, drink) in enumerate(customers, start=1):
    print(f"#{number}. {customer}: {drink}")
```

Listing 9-86: iterate_orders_dict.py:3

Here, enumerate() returns a tuple with the count (which is sometimes, coincidentally, the index) as an integer in the first position and the item from the collection in the second. By default, the count would start at 0, but I want the first person in line to be displayed as "#1"—so I override this default by passing 1 to start=.

Since my collection consists of tuples, I have to use compound unpacking with parentheses to get each item from within the tuple item ❶. Once I have the number, the customer name, and the drink, I compose those pieces together into a single print statement.

The output of this part of the code looks like this:

```
#1. Newman: tea
#2. Daniel: lemongrass tea
#3. Simon: chai latte
# --snip--
```

Mutation in Loops

You'll notice that I've been using a list for my queue of customers, whereas before, I used a deque and removed customers from the queue after serving them. This is preferable, so I'll start by defining the customers deque:

```
from collections import deque

customers = deque([
```

```
    ('Newman', 'tea'),
    ('Daniel', 'lemongrass tea'),
    ('Simon', 'chai latte'),
    ('James', 'medium roast drip, milk, 2 sugar substitutes'),
    ('William', 'french press'),
    ('Kyle', 'mocha cappuccino'),
    ('Jason', 'pumpkin spice latte'),
    ('Devin', 'double-shot espresso'),
    ('Todd', 'dark roast drip'),
    ('Glen', 'americano, no sugar, heavy cream'),
    ('Denis', 'cold brew')
])
```

Listing 9-87: process_orders.py:1

Combining the knowledge so far, you might think, "Aha! I only need to use a deque and popleft() after each customer." Yet, if I try to follow that approach, it won't run:

```
for customer, drink in customers:
    print(f"Making {drink}...")
    print(f"Order for {customer}!")
    customers.popleft()  # RuntimeError
```

Listing 9-88: process_orders.py:2a

The issue here is that I'm mutating the collection while I'm iterating over it! This can confuse the iterator, potentially causing all sorts of undefined behavior, so Python tries not to allow it. Attempting to mutate a collection while iterating over it, whether you're adding, removing, or reordering items, usually raises a RuntimeError.

There are two ways to fix this problem. The first is to make a copy of the collection before iterating over it:

```
for customer, drink in ❶ customers.copy():
    print(f"Making {drink}...")
    print(f"Order for {customer}!")
  ❷ customers.popleft()

print(customers)  # prints deque([])
```

Listing 9-89: process_orders.py:2b

I had to use the copy() method, since deques don't support the slice notation that would have allowed the snazzier colon in square brackets ([:]). Because the loop is iterating over a copy of the collection ❶, I am free to mutate the original however I like ❷, although this is seldom considered the ideal solution.

Since I want to remove items until the collection is emptied, I can use a while loop instead of a for loop:

```
while customers:
  ❶ customer, drink = ❷ customers.popleft()
```

```
    print(f"Making {drink}...")
    print(f"Order for {customer}!")
```

Listing 9-90: process_orders.py:2c

The while loop iterates until the collection customers indicates it is empty by evaluating to False. On each iteration, I use popleft() to access the next item, since that both returns and removes the item from the collection ❷. Unpacking is done in the suite of the loop ❶.

On the other hand, if I wanted to expand or reorder the contents of a collection while iterating over it, I'd need to create a new collection.

To demonstrate this, here is a rather convoluted example. For every drink ordered, I want to create a second serving of the same drink later. (I'll leave the purpose behind this to your imagination.) In my first attempt at this, I'll do this the wrong way, which won't work.

As usual, I start by defining my list:

```
orders = ["pumpkin spice latte", "caramel macchiato", "mocha cappuccino"]
```

Here, I'm attempting to add the same drink to the end of the list I'm iterating over:

```
for order in orders:
    # ... do whatever ...
    orders.append(order)  # creates infinite loop!

print(orders)
```

Listing 9-91: double_orders.py:2a

This example is particularly evil because, unlike the prior example, a RuntimeError is not raised when I attempt to mutate orders from within the suite of the loop. Instead, because there's always a new item at the end of the list orders, the loop keeps running until the program runs out of memory and dies. Yuck.

To correct this, I need to create a new list for appending to:

```
new_orders = orders[:]
for order in orders:
    # ... do whatever ...
    new_orders.append(order)
orders = new_orders

print(orders)
```

Listing 9-92: double_orders.py:2b

I define new_orders as a copy of orders, using slice notation to create the exact copy. Then, I iterate over orders, but I append to new_orders. Finally, when I'm done, I rebind orders to the new list, throwing the old list away.

Loop Nesting and Alternatives

As you might expect, you can nest loops. One situation where I might use this would be when running a coffee-tasting event where I wanted each guest to taste each type of coffee. Here's a program to tell me who to give what sample to.

I start by defining two lists: one of samples and the other of guests:

```
samples = ['Costa Rica', 'Kenya', 'Vietnam', 'Brazil']
guests = ['Denis', 'William', 'Todd', 'Daniel', 'Glen']
```

Listing 9-93: tasting_lists.py:1

Now I iterate over both lists at once:

```
for sample in samples:
    for guest in guests:
        print(f"Give sample of {sample} coffee to {guest}.")
```

Listing 9-94: tasting_lists.py:2a

The outer loop iterates over the list samples. For each item in samples, the inner loop iterates over the list of guests, giving each one a sample.

Running that code produces the following output (truncated for brevity):

```
Give sample of Costa Rica coffee to Denis.
Give sample of Costa Rica coffee to William.
Give sample of Costa Rica coffee to Todd.
Give sample of Costa Rica coffee to Daniel.
Give sample of Costa Rica coffee to Glen.
Give sample of Kenya coffee to Denis.
Give sample of Kenya coffee to William.
# --snip--
```

Using nested loops is seldom considered the best solution in Python, for a couple of reasons. First, nesting itself is something Python developers like to avoid, as suggested by The Zen of Python:

> Flat is better than nested.

Nested structures are less readable and more *brittle*, meaning they are easily mistyped, due to their reliance on multiple levels of indentation. Python developers conventionally like to avoid any unnecessary nesting. A readable solution that is *flatter* (with less nesting) will almost invariably be preferred.

Second, *it's impossible to break out of nested loops*. The continue and break keywords can only control the loop they're directly in, not any outer or inner loops thereof. There are some "clever" ways around this, like putting the nested loop in a function and breaking out of the function by using a return statement. However, these hacks add complexity, nesting layers, or both, and they are thus discouraged.

Instead, anytime you're thinking of using a nested loop, consider whether there are any viable alternatives. In the case of my example, I can achieve the same result as before in a single loop by using the product() function from the incredibly versatile itertools module (which I'll introduce properly later):

```
from itertools import product  # Put this line at top of module

for ❶ sample, guest in ❷ product(samples, guests):
    print(f"Give sample of {sample} coffee to {guest}.")
```

Listing 9-95: tasting_lists.py:2b

The itertools.product() function combines two or more iterables into a single iterable that contains tuples with every possible combination of items ❷. I unpack each of these tuples into names I can use to access the individual values in the suite of the loop ❶.

The output is the exact same as before.

Between the built-in iteration functions and the itertools module, Python has functions to cover most common situations where nested loops might ordinarily be used. If nothing already exists to do what you want, you can always write your own iterable function (called a *generator*; see Chapter 10) or an iterable class (see later in this chapter).

It may be impossible to avoid nested loops in most cases, but you'll often find there is a cleaner, flatter solution.

Iteration Tools

Python has a whole bevy of handy tools for iterating over containers. For most of these, the official documentation is your friend. I'll skim through some of the most common and useful tools here.

Basic Built-in Tools

A number of iteration tools are built into the language itself. Each of these requires you to pass at least a single iterable.

- all() returns True if every item in the iterable evaluates to True.
- any() returns True if any item in the iterable evaluates to True.
- enumerate() (seen earlier) is an iterable that returns a tuple for each item in the iterable you pass to it. The first value in the tuple is the item's "index," and the second is the item value itself. This even works with iterables that aren't subscriptable. This tool optionally accepts a start= argument, which defines the integer value to use as the first index.
- max() returns the largest item in the iterable. It optionally accepts a key= argument, which is usually a callable specifying what part of a collection item to sort on.
- min() is the same as max(), except that it returns the smallest item in the iterable.

- range() is an iterable that returns a sequence of integers from an optional starting value (default 0) to one less than an ending value. An optional third argument can define the step. The range(3) iterable produces the values (0,1,2), while range(2,5) produces the values (2,3,4), and range(1,6,2) produces the values (1,3,5).

- reversed() returns an iterator that iterates through the iterable, backward.

- sorted() returns a list containing all the items of the iterable, sorted. It optionally accepts a key= argument, which is used in the same way as on max().

- sum() returns the sum of all the items in the iterable, so long as all the items are numeric values. It optionally accepts a start= argument, which is the initial value of the sum.

The last three built-in iterables I'll cover are more complicated, so I'll detail each in the following subsections.

Filter

The filter iterable allows you to search for values in an iterable that fit a particular criterion. Say I have a list of orders and I want to find out how many of them call for drip coffee:

```
orders = ['cold brew', 'lemongrass tea', 'chai latte', 'medium drip',
          'french press', 'mocha cappuccino', 'pumpkin spice latte',
          'double-shot espresso', 'dark roast drip', 'americano']

drip_orders = ❶ list(❷ filter(❸ lambda s: 'drip' in s, ❹ orders))

print(f'There are {❺ len(drip_orders)} orders for drip coffee.')
```

Listing 9-96: orders_filter.py

To create the filter instance, I call its initializer ❷ and pass two arguments: the callable to use for filtering ❸ and the iterable being filtered ❹. I convert this filter iterable to a list ❶ before assigning that list to drip_orders.

Remember, the callable you use for filtering can be a function, a lambda, or anything else that can be treated as a function. Whatever the callable is, it should return a value that can be evaluated to a boolean, indicating whether the value passed to it should be included in the end result. In this case, that filtering callable will be a lambda, which returns True if the string 'drip' is anywhere in the value passed to it ❸. Because the logic is simple, the lambda makes sense, but if I had wanted more complicated test logic, I would have written a proper function instead. The filter iterable will contain those items that pass the test specified by the lambda.

Finally, I print out the number of items in drip_orders ❺, which is the number of items that filter extracted from orders.

It just goes to show, you can even make a coffee filter with Python!

Map

The map iterable will pass every item in an iterable to a callable as an argument. Then, it will pass the returned value back as its own current iterative value.

In my café, I can define a function for brewing and then use map() to apply that function to each of the pending orders.

I'll start by defining my orders list:

```
orders = ['cold brew', 'lemongrass tea', 'chai latte', 'medium drip',
          'french press', 'mocha cappuccino', 'pumpkin spice latte',
          'double-shot espresso', 'dark roast drip', 'americano']
```

Listing 9-97: brew_map.py:1

I'll also define a function to handle brewing:

```
def brew(order):
    print(f"Making {order}...")
    return order
```

Listing 9-98: brew_map.py:2

This function accepts an order as its sole argument, and then it returns that same order after it has been "made."

I want to call brew() for each item in orders, passing each current order as an argument. For that, I'll use map():

```
for order in map(brew, orders):
    print(f"One {order} is ready!")
```

Listing 9-99: brew_map.py:3

In my for loop, I create an instance of the map iterable, passing the brew() function and the orders collection to the map initializer.

For each item in orders, the brew() function is called, and the item is passed as the argument. The value returned by brew() is then passed back by the map to the loop, which binds it to order, so it can be used in the suite of the loop. This process repeats until every item in orders has been iterated over.

You can also use map() with multiple iterables, with the current item of each being used as one of the arguments to the callable. Once one of the iterators has run out of values, map is done. Here's how I would use it to add the cost and tip for multiple orders:

```
from operator import add

cost = [5.95, 4.95, 5.45, 3.45, 2.95]
tip = [0.25, 1.00, 2.00, 0.15, 0.00]

for total in map(add, cost, tip):
    print(f'{total:.02f}')
```

Listing 9-100: grand_total_map.py

I have two lists: cost contains the price of each order, and tip contains the tip given for each order. In the loop, I create a map that calls the operator.add() function, passing the current item from cost as the first argument and the current item from tip as the second argument. The sum of the two values is returned and bound to total. I print that total value out, formatting it to display values to two decimal places.

Running that code outputs this:

```
6.20
5.95
7.45
3.60
2.95
```

Zip

The zip iterable combines multiple iterables together. On each iteration, it takes the next value for each iterable in turn and packs them all together into a tuple. Once one of the iterables has been exhausted, zip stops.

This is particularly useful if you want to create a dictionary from multiple lists, although you could populate any collection using zip.

Here, I start with two lists. One list represents the regular customers, and one represents their usual orders. I want to turn this into a dictionary, so I can look up "the usual" by customer name:

```
regulars = ['William', 'Devin', 'Kyle', 'Simon', 'Newman']
usuals = ['french press', 'double-shot espresso', 'mocha cappuccino',
          'chai latte', 'tea', 'drip']

usual_orders = ❶ dict(❷ zip(❸ regulars, ❹ usuals))
```

Listing 9-101: usuals_zip.py

I create a zip iterable ❷ whose items are tuples derived from the items in the regulars ❸ and usuals ❹ iterables: ('William', 'french press'), ('Devin', 'double-shot espresso'), and so forth. Then, I pass this iterable to the dict() initializer ❶, creating a dictionary (usual_orders) with the first item of each tuple as the key and the second item of each tuple as the value.

I'll demonstrate that this works by looking up and printing Devin's usual order:

```
print(usual_orders['Devin'])  # prints 'double-shot espresso'
```

Listing 9-102: usuals_zip.py

The dictionary contains five items, since the shortest iterable, regulars, had five items. As a result, the excess item in usuals (namely, 'drip') is ignored by zip.

Itertools

The itertools module contains many useful classes for working with iteration. Very few Python developers memorize all of these. They instead refer to the documentation via the website or the help() command, whenever the topic comes up.

Here are a few highlights. Understand that I'll skip most of the optional arguments, for the sake of brevity:

accumulate repeatedly performs a two-argument function and uses the result of each call as the first argument for the next call. The current item in the iterable is the second argument. On each iteration, the current result is returned. By default, this uses the operator.add() function.

chain produces a list containing each item from each iterable passed to it, in order. chain([1,2,3], [4,5,6]) would produce 1, 2, 3, 4, 5, and 6.

combinations produces every possible subsequence of items in the provided iterable, with the specified number of items in each combination. combinations([1,2,3], 2) would produce (1, 2), (1, 3), and (2, 3).

dropwhile drops (skips) items in an iterable as long as some expression evaluates to True, and then it returns every item after that. So dropwhile(lambda n:n!=42, [5,6,42,7,53]) would produce 42, 7, and 53, since the predicate lambda returns True until it encounters the value 42.

filterfalse is the same as filter, except that it works in exactly the opposite manner: the callable must return False to include the item.

islice performs slices on nonsubscriptable iterables. It is identical in behavior to slicing, except that it doesn't support negative values for the *start*, *stop*, or *step*.

permutations produces every possible permutation of the items in the provided iterable, with the specified number of items in each permutation. permutations([1,2,3], 2) would produce (1, 2), (1, 3), (2, 1), (2, 3), (3, 1), and (3, 2).

product produces the Cartesian product of the provided iterables. product([1,2], [3,4]) would produce (1, 3), (1, 4), (2, 3), and (2, 4).

starmap behaves like map, except that it passes each item in the provided iterator as a starred argument. starmap(func, [(1,2), (3,4)] would call func(1,2) and then func(3,4).

takewhile behaves in exactly the opposite way as does dropwhile. It takes items from the provided iterator, as long as the provided predicate evaluates to True. As soon as the predicate evaluates to False, it ignores the rest of the items.

There are a few more classes in itertools besides these. Read the documentation for more information!

Custom Iterable Classes

Though Python offers plenty of collections and other iterables, there may arise a situation when you need to write your *own* iterable class. Thankfully, this is not difficult.

Often, you'll write two classes: an *iterable* and a corresponding *iterator*. This is a matter of separation of concerns: the iterable is responsible for storing or generating values, while the iterator is responsible for tracking the current position in that iterable. This allows you to make multiple independent iterator instances for the same iterable.

There are situations where it is beneficial for a single class to be both an iterable and an iterator. One such situation occurs when the iterable object's data is nonreproducible, such as with data streamed over a network. Another case is infinite iterators, which I'll revisit in Chapter 10.

For now, I'll stick with the typical two-class approach. Here's a simple iterable class that I can use for tracking café patrons and the details of their orders. (In the real world, I probably wouldn't solve the problem with a custom iterable class like this, but it works as an example.)

I'll start by defining the iterable class for tracking customers:

```
class CafeQueue:

    def __init__(self):
        self._queue = []
        self._orders = {}
        self._togo = {}
```

Listing 9-103: cafequeue.py:1

The class will have three instance attributes: _queue, a list containing customer names; _orders, a dictionary storing customer orders; and _togo, a dictionary storing whether the customer wants their order to go or not.

To make the class iterable, I define the __iter__() special method:

```
    def __iter__(self):
        return CafeQueueIterator(self)
```

Listing 9-104: cafequeue.py:2

The __iter__() method must return an instance of the corresponding iterator class. (I'll define this class in a moment.)

To make this iterable class useful, I'd like to do some other things with it, besides iterate over its data. The add_customer() instance method will allow me to add a new customer:

```
    def add_customer(self, customer, *orders, to_go=True):
        self._queue.append(customer)
        self._orders[customer] = tuple(orders)
        self._togo[customer] = to_go
```

Listing 9-105: cafequeue.py:3

I will want to check how many customers are in line by using the len()
built-in function, so I must define the __len__() special instance method:

```
def __len__(self):
    return len(self._queue)
```

Listing 9-106: cafequeue.py:4

Remember, len() is only for when I actually need to work with the
length of the queue itself. For example, if I wanted an LCD display in the
cafe to show how many customers are in line, the code for that display could
use len() on a CafeQueue object to get that data. Even so, I never use len()
directly in the loop header as part of iteration.

Finally, I'd like to check whether a particular customer is in the queue,
so I define the __contains__() special method:

```
def __contains__(self, customer):
    return (customer in self._queue)
```

Listing 9-107: cafequeue.py:5

Now that I have the CafeQueue class, I can define the corresponding iterator class, which I'm calling CafeQueueIterator. Ordinarily, these two classes
would be defined in the same module, as I've done here.

I'll start with the iterator's initializer:

```
class CafeQueueIterator:

    def __init__(self, ❶ cafe_queue):
        self._cafe = cafe_queue
        self._position = 0
```

Listing 9-108: cafequeue.py:6

This iterator class is responsible for keeping track of its own position in
the iterable. The initializer receives a single argument: the iterable instance
associated with the iterator instance ❶.

This is why, in the iterable's __iter__() method, I can use the line return
CafeQueueIterator(self) (see Listing 9-108). I pass the iterable instance to the
iterator initializer, where it is stored as the instance attribute _cafe.

An iterator class must define the special method __next__(), which
returns the next item in the iterable:

```
def __next__(self):
    try:
        customer = self._cafe._queue[self._position]
    ❶ except IndexError:
        ❷ raise StopIteration

    orders = self._cafe._orders[customer]
    togo = self._cafe._togo[customer]
```

```
❸ self._position += 1

❹ return (customer, orders, togo)
```

Listing 9-109: cafequeue.py:7

The __next__() method is responsible for keeping track of the iterator's position in the iterable. Iterables can be infinite (something I'll cover in depth in Chapter 10), so there is no built-in means of stopping iteration. In __next__(), if I've iterated over all the items in the iterable ❶, I raise StopIteration ❷. Otherwise, after retrieving the current item from the iterable, I must update the iterator's position ❸ before finally returning the item ❹.

Each item contains multiple elements, so I pack the data for an item into a tuple: (customer, orders, to_go). This can be unpacked in a for loop during iteration. If you look at the CafeQueue class again (Listing 9-103), you'll notice that orders will be a tuple of varying length, containing each order for the customer.

The special method __iter__() must also be defined in an iterator class. This method is always expected to return an iterator, but since this instance *is* an iterator, __iter__() only needs to return self.

```
    def __iter__(self):
        return self
```

Listing 9-110: cafequeue.py:8

Now that I have both my iterable (CafeQueue) and iterator (CafeQueueIterator) classes written, I can use them like any other collection. I create a new CafeQueue and populate it with data:

```
queue = CafeQueue()
queue.add_customer('Newman', 'tea', 'tea', 'tea', 'tea', to_go=False)
queue.add_customer('James', 'medium roast drip, milk, 2 sugar substitutes')
queue.add_customer('Glen', 'americano, no sugar, heavy cream')
queue.add_customer('Jason', 'pumpkin spice latte', to_go=False)
```

Listing 9-111: cafequeue.py:9

Before I iterate over the collection, I'll test using len() and in:

```
print(len(queue))        # prints 4
print('Glen' in queue)   # prints True
print('Kyle' in queue)   # prints False
```

Listing 9-112: cafequeue.py:10

I can see how many customers are in the queue with len() and check for individual customers using in. All's well, so far!

I want to use this new iterable to automate making and delivering orders to the customers. Remember that each item in the iterable will be a tuple (customers, orders, to_go) and that orders is itself a tuple of unknown length. Although it's simple in this example, you can imagine that brewing an order could theoretically be quite involved, so I'll use the stand-alone brew() function from Listing 9-98 to handle each order:

```python
def brew(order):
    print(f"(Making {order}...)")
    return order
```

Listing 9-113: cafequeue.py:11

Nothing remarkable there.

So then, here's the loop for working with the CafeQueue instance queue:

```python
for customer, orders, to_go in queue:
  ❶ for order in orders: brew(order)
    if to_go:
        print(f"Order for {customer}!")
    else:
        print(f"(Takes order to {customer})")
```

Listing 9-114: cafequeue.py:12

The for loop iterates over queue, unpacking each item tuple into three names: customer, orders, and to_go.

I use a nested loop to pass each item in the orders tuple to the brew() function ❶. This particular for loop is pretty simple, so I can write it as a flat statement.

GOTCHA ALERT I didn't use map(brew, orders) because it wouldn't actually print anything by itself. Rather map() creates a generator that would have to be iterated over anyway, so the for loop is the better technique in this case.

Finally, I use to_go to determine whether to announce the order is ready or to take it out to the customer's table.

Wrapping Up

Iteration simplifies how one works with loops and collections. Practically any class can be an iterable if it defines an __iter__() method, which returns a corresponding iterator object. An iterator class keeps track of its position in traversing its corresponding iterable, and it must have a __next__() method for returning the next item in the iterable. All Python collections are iterables, and the language offers a number of useful iterator classes, including many in the itertools module.

Python's for loop is designed specifically for working with iterables and iterators; it handles the calls to __iter__() and __next__() behind the scenes, allowing you to focus on what you want to do with each item instead.

Now's a good time to get a coffee refill before we dive into the next chapter, wherein I'll introduce the related concepts of *infinite iterators*, *generators*, and *generator expressions*. (Bring me back a pumpkin spice latte while you're up there, hey?)

10

GENERATORS AND COMPREHENSIONS

In the previous chapter, we escaped all the headaches of traditional index-based loops. However, we haven't yet completely escaped the nested loop.

The solution is to employ *generator expressions*, which allow you to rewrite the entire logic of a loop in a single statement. You can even create lists in this manner, with the much-loved *list comprehensions*. Before I get there, I'll introduce *generators*, which provide a more compact alternative to custom iterable classes in many situations. You'll also encounter the oft-overshadowed cousin of the generator, the humble *simple coroutine*, which provides an iterative solution for inputs.

Lazy Evaluation and Eager Iterables

The features I cover in this chapter all build on the principles of iterators, and many utilize the concept of *lazy evaluation*, which describes a process in which an iterator does not provide the next value until it is requested.

This behavior, paired with the fact that iterators do not care how many items are possible in their iterable, provides the power behind generator objects.

While *iterators* are lazy, the definition of an iterable is not! Understanding this distinction is important when you're writing code that works with large amounts of data. Incorrectly defining an iterable can lock your program in an infinite loop. In some cases, you can even chew through all available system memory and raise a `MemoryError` or even crash your machine. (I crashed my system twice while writing this chapter.)

For example, collection literals are incredibly *eager*, in that they evaluate all of their items upon creation. Programmer Kyle Keen demonstrates this phenomenon with the following example, which I've restructured slightly for clarity:

```
import time
sleepy = ['no pause', time.sleep(1), time.sleep(2)]
# ...three second pause...
print(sleepy[0])  # prints 'no pause'
```

Listing 10-1: sleepy.py:1a

Python eagerly evaluates each of the expressions in the list literal before assigning it to `sleepy`, which means it calls the two `time.sleep()` functions.

This behavior can mean that collections have the potential to become a performance bottleneck when working with a lot of data or particularly complex expressions.

Thus, you must choose your approaches carefully! One of the best ways to handle large amounts of data is to use either generators or *generator expressions*, which I'll cover shortly.

Infinite Iterators

Lazy evaluation makes it possible to have *infinite iterators*, which provide values on demand without ever being exhausted. This behavior is very important to some features I cover in this chapter.

The `itertools` module offers three infinite iterators:

- `count()` counts from the given numeric value, `start`, adding the optional step value each time. So, `count(5, 2)` would produce the values 5, 7, 9, 11, and so on, forever.

- `cycle()` cycles through each item in the given iterable, infinitely. Therefore, `cycle([1,2,3])` would produce 1, 2, 3, 1, 2, 3, on and on, forever.

- `repeat()` repeats the given value, either endlessly or up to an optionally specified number of times. Therefore, `repeat(42)` would produce the value 42 forever, while `repeat(42, 10)` would produce the value 42 up to 10 times.

However, as I mentioned earlier, the very behavior that makes infinite iterators useful also makes them dangerous: they have no brakes! When passed to a for loop that has no break statement, the loop becomes infinite. When unpacked with a starred expression or used to create a collection, the Python interpreter locks up or even crashes the system. Use infinite iterators with caution!

Generators

A powerful alternative to the iterator class is the *generator function*, which looks like an ordinary function, except for its use of a special yield keyword. When a generator function is called directly, it returns a *generator iterator* (also known as a *generator object*) that encapsulates the logic from the suite of the generator function.

On each iteration, the generator iterator will run up to (and including) a yield statement, and then it will wait for another call to the special method __next__(), which Python implicitly creates behind the scenes. You will recall from Chapter 9 that __next__() is the special method responsible for providing the next value in an iterator; it is called anytime an iterator object is passed to the next() function or used in a for loop. Once a generator iterator receives the call to __next__(), it will continue running until it hits another yield.

For example, I can use a generator to generate license plate numbers:

```
from itertools import product
from string import ascii_uppercase as alphabet


def gen_license_plates():
    for letters in ❶ product(alphabet, repeat=3):
        letters = ❷ "".join(letters)
        if letters == 'GOV':
            continue

        ❸ for numbers in range(1000):
            yield f'{letters} {numbers:03}'
```

Listing 10-2: license_generator.py:1

I declare the gen_license_plates() generator function like any other function.

To generate all the possible combinations of letters, I use the itertool .product iterable. The predefined string string.ascii_uppercase, which I'm locally renaming to alphabet, will provide the values for each letter within an iterable collection (a string).

I iterate over all the possible combinations of three letters by initializing a product iterator ❶ that iterates over the alphabet string three times, concatenated. I join the three letters into a single string ❷.

Before I iterate over the numbers, I ensure that letters is not equal to the string 'GOV'. If it is, the generator will skip that iteration of letter combinations, as I imagine in this scenario that `'GOV'` is reserved for government vehicles only.

Finally, I iterate over all possible numbers, 000 to 999 ❸.

The line that makes this function a generator is the `yield` statement. Every time this line is reached in the program execution, the value is returned, and then the generator waits for another call to __next__(). When __next__() is called again, the generator resumes exactly where it left off, thereby producing and yielding the next value.

I must call my generator function to create the generator iterator I want to use, which I'll bind to a name:

```
license_plates = gen_license_plates()
```

Listing 10-3: license_generator.py:2

The name `license_plates` is now bound to the generator iterator created by `gen_license_plates()`. This is the object with the __next__() method.

I can treat `license_plates` the same as any iterator. For example, I'll loop through all possible license plates, although this will take a long time to execute:

```
for plate in license_plates:
    print(plate)
```

Listing 10-4: license_generator.py:3a

That outputs the following (redacted):

```
AAA 000
AAA 001
AAA 002
# --snip--
ZZZ 997
ZZZ 998
ZZZ 999
```

Most real-world scenarios wouldn't want all the possible numbers at once. Here's a more practical usage:

```
registrations = {}


def new_registration(owner):
    if owner not in registrations:
        plate = ❶ next(license_plates)
        registrations[owner] = plate
        return plate
    return None
```

Listing 10-5: license_generator.py:3b

I define a function, `new_registration()`, which handles all of the logic for a new license plate registration. If the name is not already in the system, it retrieves the next plate from the iterator `license_plates` ❶ and stores it in the registrations dictionary, with the given owner as the key. Then, it returns the plate number for convenience. If the name is already in the system, it will return None.

To make the example a little more interesting, I'm manually fast-forwarding through a few thousand license plates:

```
# Fast-forward through several results for testing purposes.
for _ in range(4441888):
    next(license_plates)
```

Listing 10-6: license_generator.py:4

Now, I'll put the new_registration() function to use:

```
name = "Jason C. McDonald"
my_plate = new_registration(name)
print(my_plate)
print(registrations[name])
```

Listing 10-7: license_plates.py:5

I use the new_registration() function to register myself at this fictional DMV, and then I store the returned license plate number in my_plate, which I print out. I also directly check the registrations dictionary, to see what license plate was registered to me.

The output of this program is as follows:

```
GOW 888
GOW 888
```

Generators vs. Iterator Classes

Recall that a __next__() method in an iterator class will raise the StopIteration exception to announce that there are no more items to iterate over. Generators don't require that exception to be explicitly raised; what's more, since Python 3.5, they don't even allow it. When the generator function terminates, either by reaching its end or explicitly with a return statement, StopIteration is raised automatically, behind the scenes.

As an Iterator Class

To demonstrate this, I'll write an iterator class that randomly generates traffic on a freeway. Once it's working, I'll rewrite it as a generator function.

I'll start by defining a couple of lists of possibilities:

```
from random import choice

colors = ['red', 'green', 'blue', 'silver', 'white', 'black']
vehicles = ['car', 'truck', 'semi', 'motorcycle', None]
```

Listing 10-8: traffic_generator_class.py:1

Next, I create a `Traffic` class for my iterator:

```
class Traffic:
    def __iter__(self):
        return self
```

Listing 10-9: traffic_generator_class.py:3

I don't need an initializer, since I have no instance attributes. I make this class an iterable by defining the `__iter__()` special method, which returns `self`.

I also need to define `__next__()` for this class to be an iterator:

```
    def __next__(self):
        vehicle = choice(vehicles)

        if vehicle is None:
            raise StopIteration

        color = choice(colors)

        return f"{color} {vehicle}"
```

Listing 10-10: traffic_generator_class.py:4

In the `__next__()` special method, I randomly select a vehicle from the global `vehicles` list, using `random.choice()`. If I select the item `None` from that list, I raise the `StopIteration` exception to indicate an end (gap) in the stream of traffic. Otherwise, I select a random color from the global `colors` list, and then I return a formatted string containing the vehicle and color.

I can use my `Traffic` iterator as follows:

```
# merge into traffic
count = 0
for count, vehicle in enumerate(Traffic(), start=1):
    print(f"Wait for {vehicle}...")

print(f"Merged after {count} vehicles!")
```

Listing 10-11: traffic_generator_class.py:5

I iterate over each vehicle, print out its description, and keep count of how many vehicles have passed. Once `StopIteration` is raised by `Traffic()`, the loop ends and the final `print()` statement is run. One example output of this code is as follows:

```
Wait for green car...
Wait for red truck...
Wait for silver car...
Merged after 3 vehicles!
```

That works fine, but the iterator class has a lot of extra boilerplate. Instead, I can write the iterator as a generator function, which I'll do next.

As a Generator Function

As before, I'll reuse the lists from the previous example to define a couple of lists containing possibilities:

```
from random import choice

colors = ['red', 'green', 'blue', 'silver', 'white', 'black']
vehicles = ['car', 'truck', 'semi', 'motorcycle', None]
```

Listing 10-12: traffic_generator.py:1

Now, I'll define the traffic() generator function:

```
def traffic():
    while True:
        vehicle = choice(vehicles)

        if vehicle is None:
            return

        color = choice(colors)
        yield f"{color} {vehicle}"
```

Listing 10-13: traffic_generator.py:2

I declare this generator function like any other function, although I must structure it to run continuously, the same as if I were going to print() each item. I accomplish this with an infinite loop. As soon as the function returns, either implicitly by reaching its end (which is not possible in this case) or via a return statement, the iterator will raise StopIteration behind the scenes.

Since I don't know how much traffic is going to be randomly generated, I want this generator function to run indefinitely, until it selects a None value from vehicles. Then, instead of raising StopIteration, I exit the function with return to indicate that iteration is finished. Since Python 3.5, raising StopIteration within a generator function will raise a RuntimeError instead.

The usage is the same as before, except that I'm now iterating over the generator, not the iterator class:

```
# merge into traffic
count = 0
for count, vehicle in enumerate(traffic(), start=1):
    print(f"Wait for {vehicle}...")

print(f"Merged after {count} vehicles!")
```

Listing 10-14: traffic_generator.py:3

The output is effectively the same as before (although remember, it's random):

```
Wait for white truck...
Wait for silver semi...
Merged after 2 vehicles!
```

Closing Generators

Generators, like any iterators, can be infinite. However, when you're done with an iterator, you should close it, since leaving it sitting idle in memory for the rest of your program would be a waste of resources.

To demonstrate this, here's my traffic generator, rewritten to be infinite. I start by using the lists I wrote for the earlier example:

```
from random import choice

colors = ['red', 'green', 'blue', 'silver', 'white', 'black']
vehicles = ['car', 'truck', 'semi', 'motorcycle', None]
```

Listing 10-15: traffic_infinite_generator.py:1

Here's my rewritten traffic generator function, which is the same as Listing 10-13, except that I've dropped the return logic:

```
def traffic():
    while True:
        vehicle = choice(vehicles)
        color = choice(colors)
        yield f"{color} {vehicle}"
```

Listing 10-16: traffic_infinite_generator.py:2a

Since the function can never reach its end and has no return statement, the generator is an infinite iterator.

I can use this generator in whatever way I want. For example, I could write a function for a car wash that uses the generator but limits how many vehicles can be washed:

```
def car_wash(traffic, limit):
    count = 0
    for vehicle in traffic:
        print(f"Washing {vehicle}.")
        count += 1
        if count >= limit:
            traffic.close()
```

Listing 10-17: traffic_infinite_generator.py:3

I would pass a traffic iterator to the car_wash() function, along with an integer value bound to limit representing how many vehicles can be washed. The function iterates over traffic, washing each car, and keeping count.

Once the limit has been reached (or surpassed), I don't want to keep the traffic iterable around anymore, especially as it may have been instantiated right in the argument list, so I close it. This causes GeneratorExit to be raised within the generator, which in turn causes StopIteration to be raised—ending the loop, and thus, the function.

Now that I've written the generator and the function using it, here's how I put the two together:

```
car_wash(traffic(), 10)
```

Listing 10-18: traffic_infinite_generator.py:4a

A new iterator is created from the `traffic()` generator function and passed right to the `car_wash()` function. When the function is finished, it also closes the iterator. It can now be cleaned up by the garbage collector.

A new iterator can still be created from the `traffic()` generator function, but the old iterator is exhausted.

I can create a generator iterator instead and use it in `car_wash()`, which ultimately closes it:

```
queue = traffic()
car_wash(queue, 10)
```

Listing 10-19: traffic_infinite_generator.py:4b

Since the `car_wash()` function closes the iterator queue, I can no longer pass it to `next()` to get a result, as you can see if I add this erroneous line:

```
next(queue)  # raises StopIteration, since car_wash called close()
```

Leaving out the error, running that code produces something like the following redacted output:

```
Washing red motorcycle.
Washing red semi.
# --snip--
Washing green semi.
Washing red truck.
```

Behavior on Close

Rather than exiting quietly, I can have the generator do something else when it is closed explicitly. I accomplish this by catching the `GeneratorExit` exception:

```
def traffic():
    while True:
        vehicle = choice(vehicles)
        color = choice(colors)
        try:
            yield f"{color} {vehicle}"
        except GeneratorExit:
            print("No more vehicles.")
            raise
```

Listing 10-20: traffic_infinite_generator.py:2b

I wrap my yield statement in a try clause. When `traffic.close()` is called, `GeneratorExit` is raised at the yield statement the generator is waiting at. I can catch this exception and do whatever I like, such as print out a message. Most important is that I must re-raise the `GeneratorExit` exception, or else the generator will never actually close!

Without making any changes to the usage of this generator (Listings 10-17 and 10-19), running the code shows this new behavior at work:

```
Washing green semi.
Washing black truck.
# --snip--
Washing blue motorcycle.
Washing silver semi.
No more vehicles.
```

Throwing Exceptions

One seldom-used feature of generators is the `throw()` method, which can be used to put the generator into some sort of exceptional state, especially when that requires some special behavior beyond the run-of-the-mill `close()`.

For example, if you're using a generator to retrieve values from a thermometer device over a network connection, and if the connection is lost, a default value (say, 0) is returned from the query instead. You don't want to log that default value, since it's wrong! Instead, you'll want the generator to return the constant `NaN` for that iteration.

You could write a different function that detects that the network connection is lost, which would retrieve from trying to query the disconnected device. Then, you can cause the generator to raise an exception at the yield statement it's idling at by using the `throw()` method. Your generator can catch that exception and yield `NaN`.

This is similar to how `close()` will raise `GeneratorExit`; in fact, `close()` is functionally identical to `throw(GeneratorExit)`.

As amazingly useful as that sounds, there aren't as many real-world use cases for `throw()`. The thermometer example is one of the few valid such scenarios, but even that would likely be solved better by having the generator call the function for checking the network connection.

I've had to write a fairly contrived example using my `traffic()` generator to demonstrate this behavior. I'm catching `ValueError` to allow skipping a vehicle; that is the exception that I will raise at the yield statement with the `throw()` method in the usage later.

```
from random import choice
colors = ['red', 'green', 'blue', 'silver', 'white', 'black']
vehicles = ['car', 'truck', 'semi', 'motorcycle', None]


def traffic():
    while True:
        vehicle = choice(vehicles)
        color = choice(colors)
```

```
        try:
            yield f"{color} {vehicle}"
    ❶ except ValueError:
        ❷ print(f"Skipping {color} {vehicle}...")
        ❸ continue
        except GeneratorExit:
            print("No more vehicles.")
            raise
```

Listing 10-21: traffic_generator_throw.py:1

When the `ValueError` exception is raised at the `yield` statement, it will be caught ❶ and the generator will announce that the current vehicle is being skipped ❷, before moving to the next iteration of its infinite loop ❸.

This would really only be conceivably useful if I abstracted out the logic of washing a car into its own function. That function can raise exceptions:

```
def wash_vehicle(vehicle):
    if 'semi' in vehicle:
        raise ValueError("Cannot wash vehicle.")
    print(f"Washing {vehicle}.")
```

Listing 10-22: traffic_generator_throw.py:2

The `wash_vehicle()` function checks that it's not being asked to wash a semi. If it is, a `ValueError` is raised.

I'll write a function, `car_wash()`, which will handle passing each vehicle from `traffic()` to `wash_vehicle()`:

```
def car_wash(traffic, limit):
    count = 0
    for vehicle in traffic:
        try:
            wash_vehicle(vehicle)
        except Exception as e:
            ❶ traffic.throw(e)
        else:
            count += 1
        if count >= limit:
            traffic.close()
```

Listing 10-23: traffic_generator_throw.py:3

In the context of the `car_wash()` function, I catch all exceptions thrown from my call to `wash_vehicle()`. This catch-all is completely acceptable because I'm re-raising the caught exception within the generator, using `traffic.throw()` ❶. That way, the logic of which exceptions can be raised and how they are handled is handled solely by the `wash_vehicle()` function and the traffic generator. If any exception is passed to `traffic.throw()` that is not explicitly handled by the generator, that exception will be raised and left uncaught at the `yield` statement, so there is no implicit error silencing.

If there's no exception from calling `car_wash()`, I increment my count of vehicles washed. If an exception was caught, I don't want to increment, since I don't want to count the skipped semis in the number of vehicles washed.

Finally, I create a `traffic()` generator and pass it to the `car_wash()` function:

```
queue = traffic()
car_wash(queue, 10)
```

Listing 10-24: traffic_generator_throw.py:4

Running that code produces something like the following:

```
Washing white car.
Washing red motorcycle.
Skipping green semi...
Washing red truck.
Washing green car.
Washing blue truck.
Washing blue truck.
Skipping white semi...
Washing green truck.
Washing green motorcycle.
Washing black motorcycle.
Washing red truck.
No more vehicles.
```

You can see that 10 vehicles are washed and all the semis are skipped. It works exactly as designed.

As I said, this was a contrived example. There's probably little reason to have the *generator* handle the `ValueError` exception, when I could have handled it in the `car_wash()` function instead. While I cannot guarantee that there is never a use for `throw()`, if you think you need it, you're often overlooking a simpler way of handling the problem.

PEDANTIC NOTE   There is no `__throw__()` special method. To implement this behavior in a custom class, you would define `throw()` as an ordinary member function.

yield from

When using a generator, you are not limited to yielding data from the current generator iterator. You can temporarily hand off control to other iterables, generators, or coroutines, by using `yield from`.

In my traffic generator, I want to add a small chance of a biker gang being generated. I start by writing a generator specifically for a biker gang. As with prior examples, I'm reusing those same lists:

```
from random import choice, randint

colors = ['red', 'green', 'blue', 'silver', 'white', 'black']
vehicles = ['car', 'truck', 'semi', 'motorcycle', None]
```

Listing 10-25: traffic_bikers_generator.py:1

Here's my new `biker_gang()` generator function:

```
def biker_gang():
    for _ in range(randint(2, 10)):
        color = ❶ choice(colors)
        ❷ yield f"{color} motorcycle"
```

Listing 10-26: traffic_bikers_generator.py:2

The `biker_gang()` generator will use the `random.randint()` function to select a random number between 2 and 10 and generate a biker gang of that size. For each bike in the gang, a random color is selected ❶ and a motorcycle of the selected color is yielded ❷.

To use it, I add three lines to my original infinite `traffic()` generator from Listing 10-16:

```
def traffic():
    while True:
        if randint(1, 50) == 50:
            ❶ yield from biker_gang()
            ❷ continue

        vehicle = choice(vehicles)
        color = choice(colors)
        yield f"{color} {vehicle}"
```

Listing 10-27: traffic_bikers_generator.py:3

I use `random.randint()` to determine whether to generate a biker gang, at a 1-in-50 probability. To generate the biker gang, I use `yield from` to hand off execution flow to the `biker_gang()` generator ❶. The `traffic()` generator will stay paused at this position until the `biker_gang()` generator is finished, at which point, control is passed back to this generator and it resumes.

Once `biker_gang()` is done, I skip to the next iteration of the infinite loop with `continue` to generate another vehicle ❷.

The usage of the `traffic()` generator is pretty much the same as before:

```
count = 0
for count, vehicle in enumerate(traffic()):
    print(f"{vehicle}")
    if count == 100:
        break
```

Listing 10-28: traffic_bikers_generator.py:4

Running this code will (probably) show the new biker gang–generation logic at work. Here's an example output (redacted):

```
black motorcycle
green truck
# --snip--
red car
black motorcycle
black motorcycle
```

```
blue motorcycle
white motorcycle
green motorcycle
blue motorcycle
white motorcycle
silver semi
# --snip--
blue truck
silver truck
```

You are not limited to passing off control to other generators. You can use yield from to iterate over any iterable object, whether it be a collection, an iterator class, or a generator object. Once the iterable is exhausted, control reverts back to the calling generator.

Generator Expressions

A *generator expression* is an iterator that wraps the entire logic of a generator into a single expression. Generator expressions are lazy, so you can use them to work with large amounts of data without locking up your program.

To demonstrate how to create and use generator expressions, I'll rebuild my earlier license plate generator. I'll write a generator function containing a single for loop. Later, I'll transform this into a generator expression.

This loop generates all the possible license plate numbers consisting of the letters *ABC* and three following digits:

```
def license_plates():
    for num in range(1000):
        yield f'ABC {num:03}'
```

Listing 10-29: license_plates.py:1a

The iterable range(1000) produces all the integers from 0 to 999. The loop iterates through those values, assigning the current value of each iteration to num. Within the loop, I create the license plate number with f-strings, using string formatting to pad num with leading 0s as necessary, to ensure there are always three digits.

I want to print the values to test. Since this is also an iterator object, it is best to print the values it produces from its usage, instead of from within the iterator itself. I print from the generator like this:

```
for plate in license_plates():
    print(plate)
```

Listing 10-30: license_plates.py:2a

Running this code prints the following (redacted):

```
ABC 000
ABC 001
```

```
ABC 002
# --snip--
ABC 997
ABC 998
ABC 999
```

Because this generator function is so simple, containing only one loop, it is an ideal case for a generator expression. I'll rewrite as follows:

```
license_plates = (
    f'ABC {number:03}'
    for number in range(1000)
)
```

Listing 10-31: license_plates.py:1b

The generator expression is enclosed in the outer parentheses and is bound to the name `license_plates`. The generator expression itself is essentially an inversion of the loop syntax.

Within the generator expression, the logic from the suite of the loop earlier (Listing 10-30) is declared first, where I define an expression that will be evaluated on each iteration. I create a string composed of the letters *ABC* and the number from the current iteration, left-padded with zeroes to three digits. Similar to a return in a lambda, the `yield` in the generator expression is implied.

Next, I declare the loop itself. As before, I iterate over a `range()` iterable, using the name `number` for the value on each iteration.

The revised usage here prints out all the possible license plates:

```
for plate in license_plates:
    print(plate)
```

Listing 10-32: license_plates.py:2b

Generator Objects Are Lazy

Remember, all generator objects are lazy, whether they were produced by generator functions or generator expressions. This means generator objects produce values on demand, and not a moment sooner.

Recall the modified version of Kyle Keen's eager-evaluation demonstration from Listing 10-1. I can replicate that same essential logic in a generator expression, and you can see this lazy evaluation at work:

```
import time
sleepy = (time.sleep(t) for t in range(0, 3))
```

Listing 10-33: sleepy.py:1b

Unlike the list—whose very *definition* caused the program to sleep for three seconds before continuing, because every item was being evaluated at definition—this code runs instantly, because it defers evaluation of its values until they're needed. Defining the generator expression itself does not execute `time.sleep()`.

Even when I manually iterate over the first value in `sleepy`, there is no delay:

```
print("Calling...")
next(sleepy)
print("Done!")
```

Listing 10-34: sleepy.py:2

Because `time.sleep(0)` is called on the first iteration of the generator expression, `next(sleepy)` returns instantly. Subsequent calls to `next(sleepy)` would cause the program to sleep, but that won't happen until I request it.

There's one critical exception to the lazy evaluation of generator expressions: the expression in the leftmost `for` statement is evaluated immediately. For example, consider what would happen if you were to write this:

```
import time
sleepy = (time.sleep(t) for t in [1, 2, 3, 4, 5])
```

Listing 10-35: sleepy.py:1c

That version of the generator expression has none of the desired lazy evaluation behavior, as the list `[1, 2, 3, 4, 5]` in the for loop is evaluated immediately when the generator expression is first encountered. This is by design, so any errors in the loop's expression will be raised with a traceback to the generator expression's declaration, rather than the first *usage* of the generator expression. However, because the list here evaluates instantly, we don't actually see a delay.

Generator Expressions with Multiple Loops

Generator expressions can support more than one loop at a time, replicating the logic of a nested loop. You list the loops in order, from outermost to innermost.

I'll rewrite my license plate generator expression to generate all possible combinations of letters and numbers, starting with AAA 000 and ending with ZZZ 999. There are 17,576,000 possible results for this, so this is fast only because generator expressions are lazy; the values are not created until they're requested.

```
from itertools import product
from string import ascii_uppercase as alphabet

license_plates = (
    f'❶ "".join(letters)} {number:03}'
    for letters in ❷ product(alphabet, repeat=3)
  ❸ for number in range(1000)
)
```

Listing 10-36: license_plates.py:1c

The generator expression, which is wrapped in parentheses and bound to license_plates, spans three lines here for readability. I could have written it as a single line, but once a generator expression starts involving multiple loops, it's usually best to split it over multiple lines.

In my generator expression, I'm employing two loops. For the first (and outermost) loop, I iterate over all the possible combinations of three letters via itertools.product ❷, as I did in Listing 10-2. The product iterator produces a tuple of values on each iteration, which I must concatenate together into a string using "".join() ❶ when creating the formatted string.

For the second (or inner) loop, I iterate over all possible numbers between 000 and 999, as before ❸.

On each iteration, I use an f-string to generate the license plate.

The result is an iterator bound to license_plates that can lazily generate all the possible license plate numbers. The next license plate is not created until it's requested.

I can use the license_plates generator expression the same as I would a generator object. Its usage is no different from what you saw in Listing 10-5 through Listing 10-7:

```
registrations = {}


def new_registration(owner):
    if owner not in registrations:
        plate = next(license_plates)
        registrations[owner] = plate
        return True
    return False


# Fast-forward through several results for testing purposes.
for _ in range(4441888):
    next(license_plates)

name = "Jason C. McDonald"
my_plate = new_registration(name)
print(registrations[name])
```

Listing 10-37: license_plates.py:2c

The output of this program is as follows:

```
GOV 888
```

Conditionals in Generator Expressions

As you may notice, this produced license plates starting with the letters *GOV.* I need to integrate that conditional from Listing 10-2 to check for that reserved combination of letters, which I'll do next.

I can add a conditional to my generator expression from Listing 10-36, to incorporate this limitation:

```
from itertools import product
from string import ascii_uppercase as alphabet

license_plates = (
    f'{"".join(letters)} {numbers:03}'
    for letters in product(alphabet, repeat=3)
    if letters != ('G', 'O', 'V')
    for numbers in range(1000)
)
```

Listing 10-38: license_plates.py:1d

I've added the conditional: if the value of the tuple letters is *not* ('G', 'O', 'V'), the value will be used. Otherwise, the iteration will be skipped (an implicit continue).

Order matters here! The loops and conditionals are evaluated from top to bottom, as if they were nested. If I'd checked for ('G', 'O', 'V') further down, continue would be implicitly called on a thousand separate iterations, but since it *precedes* the second loop, the numbers are never iterated over on ('G', 'O', 'V') at all; the generator expression continues on the first loop.

This syntax can be a bit pesky to keep straight at first. I like to think of it as a nested loop, where the yield line at the end has been yanked out and stuck on the front. The equivalent generator function, written with a single nested loop, would look like this:

```
def license_plate_generator():
    for letters in product(alphabet, repeat=3):
        if letters != ('G', 'O', 'V'):
            for numbers in range(1000):
                yield f'{"".join(letters)} {numbers:03}'
```

The last line moves to the front, and you drop the yield keyword, since that's implied in generator expressions. You also drop the colons from the end of each of the other lines. This way of writing generator expressions is helpful for making sure your logic is sound.

Running the code again produces the following:

```
GOW 888
```

As you can see, the conditional is working. Instead of GOV 888, the result is now GOW 888.

You can also use if-else in the context of a generator expression, but there is one catch: the placement is different from with just an if! This subtlety catches a lot of Python developers unawares, even the experienced ones.

Let me show you what I mean. Here's a generator expression with an if, which produces all the integers less than 100 that are divisible by 3:

```
divis_by_three = (n for n in range(100) if n % 3 == 0)
```

Listing 10-39: divis_by_three.py:1a

That works, but now, I want to print out "redacted" for every number that *isn't* divisible by 3. You might logically try the following (as I did while writing this chapter, and it failed):

```
divis_by_three = (n for n in range(100) if n % 3 == 0 else "redacted")
```

Listing 10-40: divis_by_three.py:1b

Running that produces this:

```
SyntaxError: invalid syntax
```

Eep! The reason for this error becomes clear if you convert the generator expression to a generator function, using the technique I described earlier in this chapter:

```
def divis_by_three():
    for n in range(100):
        if n % 3 == 0:
        else:  # SyntaxError!
            "redacted"
            yield n
```

That syntax is outright nonsense. The generator expression itself does not support the else clause—in fact, every compound statement may only have one clause in a generator expression. However, the generator expression does support a *ternary expression*, which is a compact conditional expression:

```
def divis_by_three():
    for n in range(100):
        yield n if n % 3 == 0 else "redacted"
```

Ternary expressions follow the form *a* if *expression* else *b*. The ternary expression evaluates to value *a* if *expression* evaluates to True—or to *b*, otherwise. These sorts of expressions can show up anywhere, from assignment to return statements. However, their use is discouraged in most situations, as they are hard to read. Ternary expressions are mainly only used in lambdas and generator expressions, where full-size conditional statements are out of the question.

I can convert that generator function logic back into a generator expression:

```
divis_by_three = (n if n % 3 == 0 else "redacted" for n in range(100))
```

Listing 10-41: divis_by_three.py:1c

That version evaluates correctly. Hooray! However, if I were to revert to using an if and dropping the else statement, I'd be back to having problems:

```
divis_by_three = (n if n % 3 == 0 for n in range(100))
```

Listing 10-42: divis_by_three.py:1d

Running that gives me this:

```
SyntaxError: invalid syntax
```

If I convert that back to generator function logic, the problem becomes evident again:

```
def divis_by_three():
    for n in range(100):
        yield n if n % 3 == 0  # syntax error
```

Without an else, that's not a ternary expression, so I have to go back to the normal if statement:

```
def divis_by_three():
    for n in range(100):
        if n % 3 == 0:
            yield n
```

That can be converted back to a generator expression that works:

```
divis_by_three = (n for n in range(100) if n % 3 == 0)
```

Listing 10-43: divis_by_three.py:1e (same as 1a)

This can be a bit infuriating to remember offhand. I recommend you write your logic as a generator function first and then convert it to a generator expression.

Nested Generator Expressions

One inefficiency in my use of the current version of the license plate generator expression is that I'm joining the string together on every iteration. My generator expression in Listing 10-38 joined each combination of letters once, instead of once for every combination of letters *and* numbers. What's more, in my conditional, the code would look cleaner and be more maintainable if I had a nice, clean string to work with, instead of the tuple being produced by product().

Unlike generator functions, generator expressions are limited to nested single-clause compound statements, and thus, a single top-level loop. I can overcome this by *nesting* one generator expression inside the other. This is effectively the same as writing two separate generator expressions and having one use the other.

Here's how I'd use this technique in my license plate generator code:

```
from itertools import product
from string import ascii_uppercase as alphabet

license_plates = (
    f'❶ {letters} {numbers:03}'
    for letters in (
        "".join(chars)
        for chars in product(alphabet, repeat=3)
    )
    if letters != 'GOV'
    for numbers in range(1000)
)
```

Listing 10-44: license_plates.py:1e

The inner nested generator expression handles iterating over the results of product(), joining the three letters into a single string. In the outer generator expression, I iterate over the inner expression to get the string containing the next combination of letters. Then, before I iterate over the numbers, I ensure that letters is not equal to the string 'GOV'. If it is, the generator expression will skip that iteration of letter combinations.

This approach improves the readability of my code. Instead of having to add cruft to the f-string by calling join() inside of it, I can directly include {letters} ❶.

While this is the cleanest approach to license plate generation I've used *so far*, I wouldn't use the above code in production, because I've arguably reached the practical limit of readability for generator expressions. When things get this complicated, you should just reach for ordinary generator functions. The generator function in Listing 10-2 is much more readable and maintainable than the equivalent generator expression in Listing 10-44.

List Comprehensions

If you wrap a generator expression in square brackets ([ ]) instead of parentheses, you create a *list comprehension*, which uses the enclosed generator expression to populate the list. This is the most common and perhaps the most popular usage of generator expressions.

However, since I'm declaring an *iterable*, I'm losing the lazy evaluation inherent in the generator expression. List comprehensions are eager because list definitions are eager. For that reason, I'd likely never write the license plate generator expression as a list comprehension; it would take several seconds to finish, and that doesn't make for a pleasant user experience. Make sure you only use a list comprehension when you actually need a list object: that is, when you need to store the values in a collection for later processing or use. Otherwise, use a generator expression.

List comprehensions are preferable to filter() for purposes of readability, as they're easier to write and debug, and they look cleaner. I can rewrite the coffee filter() example from Chapter 9 (Listing 9-96) as a list comprehension:

```
orders = ['cold brew', 'lemongrass tea', 'chai latte', 'medium drip',
          'french press', 'mocha cappuccino', 'pumpkin spice latte',
          'double-shot espresso', 'dark roast drip', 'americano']

drip_orders = [❶ order ❷ for order in orders ❸ if 'drip' in order]

print(f'There are {len(drip_orders)} orders for drip coffee.')
```

Listing 10-45: orders_comprehension.py

Remember, a list comprehension is just a type of generator expression. I iterate over every item order in the iterable orders ❷. If the string 'drip' can be found in the current order, then I'll add that item to drip_orders ❸. I don't need to do anything with order besides adding it to the list, so I lead the generator expression with a bare order ❶.

Functionally, this code is the same as before, but this version with the list comprehension is *much* cleaner! filter() has its uses, but most of the time, you'll find that generator expressions or list comprehensions will serve your purposes better.

Set Comprehensions

Just as you can create a list comprehension by enclosing a generator expression in square brackets, so also can you create a *set comprehension* by enclosing in curly braces ({ }). This will use the generator expression to populate a *set*.

There aren't any surprises here, so I'll keep the example very basic. This set comprehension will find all the possible remainders from dividing 100 by an odd number less than 100. Sets will exclude any duplicates, making the results easier to comprehend:

```
odd_remainders = {100 % divisor for divisor in range(1, 100, 2)}
print(odd_remainders)
```

Listing 10-46: odd_remainders.py

For every other integer divisor between 1 and 99 inclusive, I find the remainder of dividing 100 by the divisor, using the modulo operator. The result is added to the set.

Running that code gives me this:

```
{0, 1, 2, 3, 5, 6, 7, 8, 9, 10, 11, 13, 14, 15, 16, 17, 18, 19, 21,
22, 23, 25, 26, 27, 29, 30, 31, 33, 35, 37, 39, 41, 43, 45, 47, 49}
```

Set comprehensions really do work the same as list comprehensions, except for which collection is created. Sets are unordered and contain no duplicates.

Dictionary Comprehensions

A dictionary comprehension follows almost the same structure as a set comprehension, but it requires colons. Both a set comprehension and a dictionary comprehension are enclosed in curly braces ({ }), like their respective collection literals. A dictionary comprehension additionally uses a colon (:) to separate key-value pairs, and this is what distinguishes it from a set comprehension.

For example, if I wanted a dictionary comprehension that uses an integer between 1 and 100 as the key and the square of that number as the value, I would write this:

```python
squares = {n : n ** 2 for n in range(1,101)}
print(squares[2])
print(squares[7])
print(squares[11])
```

Listing 10-47: squares_dictionary_comprehension.py

The key expression, on the left side of the colon, is evaluated before the value expression, on the right. I use the same loop for creating both key and value.

Be aware, like with list and set comprehensions, dictionary comprehensions are eager. The program will evaluate the dictionary comprehension until the range() iterable I'm using is exhausted.

Here's the output:

```
4
49
121
```

That's all there is to it! Again, besides the colon, everything is the same as in any other generator expression.

Hazards of Generator Expressions

Generator expressions, along with the different types of comprehension, can be addictive, partly because one feels really smart when crafting them. There's something about powerful one-liners that gets programmers very excited. We really like being clever with our code.

However, I must caution against going too crazy with generator expressions. As The Zen of Python reminds us:

> Beautiful is better than ugly.
>
> …
>
> Simple is better than complex.
>
> Complex is better than complicated.
>
> …

Sparse is better than dense.

Readability counts.

Generator expressions can be beautiful—but they can also become dense, unreadable messes when used unwisely. List comprehensions are especially vulnerable to abuse. I'll lay out some examples of where list comprehensions and generator expressions aren't suitable.

They Quickly Become Unreadable

The following example appeared in a survey by Open edX. In the original, each list comprehension was on a single line. For the sake of reproducing it legibly, without giving my typesetter fits, I've taken the liberty of splitting each of the three list comprehensions across multiple lines. Unfortunately, it really doesn't do much to improve things:

```
primary = [
    c
    for m in status['members']
    if m['stateStr'] == 'PRIMARY'
    for c in rs_config['members']
    if m['name'] == c['host']
    ]

secondary = [
    c
    for m in status['members']
    if m['stateStr'] == 'SECONDARY'
    for c in rs_config['members']
    if m['name'] == c['host']
    ]

hidden = [
    m
    for m in rs_config['members']
    if m['hidden']
    ]
```

Can you tell what's going on? You probably could if you read it for a while, but why would you want to? The code is as clear as mud, and sure enough, it was rated as the most unreadable example in the survey.

List comprehensions and generator expressions are powerful, but it doesn't take much for them to become unreadable like this. Since generator expressions essentially "flip" the order of statements, so the loop comes after the statement that relates to it, it is harder to comprehend the logic in this format. The above would be better written in the context of a traditional loop.

My colleague "grym" from Libera.Chat IRC shared an even more abhorrent example of how easily abused list comprehensions are:

```
cropids = [self.roidb[inds[i]]['chip_order'][
    self.crop_idx[inds[i]] % len(self.roidb[inds[i]]['chip_order'])]
```

```
    for i in range(cur_from, cur_to)
]
```

Don't ask me what it does. None of us wanted to figure it out. My soul burns just reading it.

They Don't Replace Loops

Since generator expressions and comprehensions are so neat and compact, it might be tempting to write clever one-liners in place of garden variety for loops. Resist this temptation! Generator expressions are suited for creating lazy iterators, while list comprehensions should only be employed when you actually need to create a list.

The reason for this is best understood by studying an example. Imagine you were reading through someone else's code and you encountered this:

```
some_list = getTheDataFromWhereever()
[API.download().process(foo) for foo in some_list]
```

The first thing that stands out is that, although a list comprehension is meant to create a list value, that value is not being stored anywhere. Anytime a value is implicitly discarded like this, it should be a warning that the pattern is being abused.

Second, you can't tell at a glance whether the data in some_list is being mutated directly. This is a case of a list comprehension being used inappropriately, in place of a loop. It's somewhat unreadable, as it obfuscates the behavior of the code, and it also makes debugging difficult.

This is one case where the author should have stuck with loops, which would have looked like this:

```
some_list = getTheDataFromWhereever()
for foo in some_list:
    API.download().process(foo)
```

In this form, it's not so unexpected that the values in some_list are being mutated, although it's still bad practice for a function to have side effects like this. Most importantly, debugging is easier.

They Can Be Hard to Debug

The nature of a generator expression or comprehension is that you're packing everything into one gigantic statement. The benefit of this is that you eliminate a bunch of intermediate steps. The drawback is . . . you eliminate a bunch of intermediate steps.

Think about debugging in a typical loop. You can step through it, one iteration at a time, using your debugger to observe the state of each variable as you go. You can also use error handling to deal with unusual edge cases.

None of that can help you in a generator expression, where either everything works or nothing works. You can try to parse through the errors and output to figure out what you did wrong, but I assure you, it's a confusing experience.

You can avoid some of this madness by avoiding generator expressions or list comprehensions on your first version of the code. Write the logic the obvious way, using traditional loops, iterator tools, or normal generators (coming up). Once you know it's working, *then and only then* should you collapse the logic into a generator expression, and *only* if you can do so without eschewing all your error handling (try statements).

This may sound like a lot of extra work, but I follow this exact pattern in competitive code golfing, especially when I'm up against the clock. My understanding of generator expressions is usually my main advantage against less-experienced competitors, but I *always* write the standard loop or generator first; I cannot afford to waste time debugging bad logic in a generator expression.

When to Use Generator Expressions

It's difficult to set a hard-and-fast rule on when generator expressions should be used. As always, the important factor is readability. Most of my preceding examples split the generator expression across multiple lines, but they're primarily intended to be written on one line. If doing so results in code that is difficult to visually parse, think twice about using generator expressions at all.

In a way, a generator expression is to an iterator as a lambda is to a function, in that it's particularly useful for defining a one-off iterator right where you'll use it. You can even omit the extra parentheses around a generator expression when it's the sole argument. A generator expression, like a lambda, is best suited for simple, one-off logic that would benefit from being declared right where it's used.

When the purpose of this one-off iterator is to populate a list, a list comprehension would be used. The same is true of set comprehensions and dictionary comprehensions for their respective collections.

Generators are preferred over generator expressions whenever you're working with more complicated logic. Because a generator expression follows the same syntactic structure as an ordinary function, it isn't prone to becoming unreadable in the same way generator expressions are.

Simple Coroutines

The *coroutine* is a type of generator that *consumes* data on demand, instead of producing data, and it waits patiently until it receives it. For example, you could write a coroutine to maintain a running average temperature; you can periodically send a new temperature to the coroutine, and it will immediately recalculate the average with each new value.

There are two kinds of coroutines. What I'm covering here is the *simple coroutine*. Later, when I cover concurrency, I'll introduce the *native coroutine* (also known as the *asynchronous coroutine*), which employs and further builds on these concepts.

For the rest of this chapter, when I refer to *coroutines*, assume I'm talking about simple coroutines.

Because coroutines are generators, you can use close() and throw() with them. Control can be handed off to another coroutine, using yield from. Only next() will not work here, since you are sending values, rather than retrieving them; instead, you use send().

For example, I want to count the number of vehicles (from the earlier traffic() generator) of a particular color in an iterative fashion. Here's a coroutine that does that:

```
from random import choice


def color_counter(color):
    matches = 0
    while True:
      ❶ vehicle = yield
        if color in vehicle:
            matches += 1
        print(f"{matches} so far.")
```

Listing 10-48: traffic_colors_coroutine.py:1a

The color_counter() coroutine function accepts a single argument: a string for the color of the vehicle being counted. This argument will be passed when the generator iterator is created.

I want this coroutine to receive data until I explicitly close it, so I use an infinite loop. The key difference between a generator and a coroutine is the location where the yield statement appears. Here, the yield expression is being *assigned* to something—specifically, to the name vehicle ❶. The data sent to the coroutine is assigned to vehicle, which I can then process by checking whether the color matches and incrementing the count of vehicles that match. Finally, I print out the current count.

As I mentioned, I'll reuse the infinite traffic generator from earlier to create the data:

```
colors = ['red', 'green', 'blue', 'silver', 'white', 'black']
vehicles = ['car', 'truck', 'semi', 'motorcycle']


def traffic():
    while True:
        vehicle = choice(vehicles)
        color = choice(colors)
        yield f"{color} {vehicle}"
```

Listing 10-49: traffic_colors_coroutine.py:2

The usage of my color_counter() coroutine is not too different from that of a generator, but there are a few key differences:

```
counter = color_counter('red')
```

Listing 10-50: traffic_colors_coroutine.py:3

Before I can use the coroutine, I have to create a coroutine object (actually, a generator iterator) from the coroutine function. I bind this object to counter.

I send data to a coroutine by using its send() method. However, before a coroutine can receive data, it must be *primed* by passing None to send():

```
counter.send(None)  # prime the coroutine
```

Listing 10-51: traffic_colors_coroutine.py:4a

Priming causes the coroutine to run up to its first yield statement. Without priming, whatever value is first sent is lost, as it's the yield statement that receives the value sent in.

Alternatively, I could prime like this:

```
next(counter)  # prime the coroutine
```

Listing 10-52: traffic_colors_coroutine.py:4b

It doesn't matter which you use. I prefer the technique in Listing 10-51, because it makes it clear I'm priming a coroutine, rather than working with any old generator.

After priming, I can use the coroutine:

```
for count, vehicle in enumerate(traffic(), start=1):
    if count < 100:
        counter.send(vehicle)
    else:
        counter.close()
        break
```

Listing 10-53: traffic_colors_coroutine.py:5a

I iterate over the traffic() generator, sending each value to the coroutine counter by using the send() method. The coroutine processes the data and prints out the current count of red vehicles.

In the context of my loop, once I've iterated through a hundred vehicles, I manually close the coroutine and break out of the loop.

Running this code produces the following redacted output:

```
0 so far.
0 so far.
1 so far.
# --snip--
19 so far.
```

```
19 so far.
19 so far.
```

There is no __send__() special method. To implement coroutine-like behavior in a custom class, you would define send() as an ordinary member function.

Returning Values from a Coroutine

In real projects, one very rarely wants to print the results and be done. For most coroutines to be useful, you need some way to retrieve the data being produced.

To do this with my color counter, I'll change one line in my coroutine and drop the print() statement I no longer want, like this:

```
def color_counter(color):
    matches = 0
    while True:
        vehicle = yield matches
        if color in vehicle:
            matches += 1
```

Listing 10-54: traffic_colors_coroutine.py:1b

I place the name matches after the yield keyword to indicate that I want to yield the value bound to that variable. Because a coroutine instance is really a special kind of generator iterator, it can both accept and return values with the yield statement. In this case, on each iteration, a new value is accepted and assigned to vehicle, and then the current value of matches is yielded.

The usage is very similar; it requires just a simple change:

```
matches = 0
for count, vehicle in enumerate(traffic(), start=1):
    if count < 100:
        matches = counter.send(vehicle)
    else:
        counter.close()
        break

print(f"There were {matches} matches.")
```

Listing 10-55: traffic_colors_coroutine.py:5b

Every time a value is sent via counter.send(), a value is also returned and assigned to matches. I print out this value after the loop is done, instead of seeing a running count.

The new output is now one line, such as this:

```
There were 18 matches.
```

Sequence of Behavior

The order in which things happen in coroutines can be a little difficult to anticipate. To understand this, here is an oversimplified coroutine that only outputs its input:

```
def coroutine():
    ret = None
    while True:
        print("...")
      ❶ recv = ❷ yield ret
      ❸ print(f"recv: {recv}")
      ❹ ret = recv


co = coroutine()
current = ❺ co.send(None)
❻ print(f"current (ret): {current}")

for i in range(10):
  ❼ current = ❽ co.send(i)
  ❾ print(f"current (ret): {current}")

co.close()
```

Listing 10-56: coroutine_sequence.py

Here's the sequence of behavior when using a generator as both a generator and a coroutine like this:

1. The coroutine is primed with `co.send(None)` ❺, advancing it to the first yield statement ❷ and yielding the initial value of ret (None). This value is printed out external to the coroutine ❻.
2. The first input to the coroutine (0) is accepted from `co.send()` ❽ and stored in recv ❶.
3. The value of recv (0) is printed out ❸ and then stored in ret ❹.
4. The coroutine advances to the next yield ❷.
5. The current value of ret (0) is yielded ❷, stored in current ❼, and printed in the for loop ❾. The for loop advances.
6. The next input (1) is accepted from `co.send()` ❽ and stored in recv ❶.
7. The new value of recv (1) is printed out ❷ and then stored in ret.
8. The coroutine advances to the next yield.
9. The current value of ret (1) is yielded ❷, stored in current ❼, and printed in the for loop ❾. The for loop advances.
10. And so on and so forth.

In simpler terms, the coroutine will always yield a value before it accepts a new value from send(). This is because the right side of the assignment expression is evaluated before the left side. The behavior is consistent with the rest of Python, even though it may feel a bit surprising in this context before you're used to it.

What About Async?

Some Python developers insist that simple coroutines have no place in modern Python code, that they've been entirely replaced by *native coroutines*—also known as *async coroutines*. This may be the case, but the difference in usage is nontrivial. Native coroutines have a number of advantages, but they have to be called differently. (I'll cover asyncio and native coroutines in Chapter 16.)

Wrapping Up

In this chapter, I've covered the various forms of generator objects—generator expressions, comprehensions, and simple coroutines—and introduced infinite iterators.

Generators and coroutines make it possible to utilize lazy evaluation in your iterative code, wherein values are only evaluated on demand. When these features are utilized correctly, your code can process large amounts of data without hanging or crashing.

I'll build on many of these features in Chapter 16, when I introduce asynchrony.

11

TEXT IO AND CONTEXT MANAGERS

I find that a project doesn't feel *real* until I start working with files. Text-based files, the most common way to store data, are the key to retaining state between program runs.

While it's perfectly simple to open a text file in Python, there are many silent subtleties that are often overlooked until they bite you in the rear. Many developers make do with some idiosyncratic combination of techniques that appear to work but are far removed from the beauty and simplicity of idiomatic Python.

In this chapter, I'll break down the two central components involved in working with text files: *streams* and *path-like objects*. I'll cover the myriad ways of opening, reading from, and writing to files, discuss how to work with the filesystem, and wrap up with a whirlwind tour of some common file formats.

Standard Input and Output

So far, we've taken functions like print() and input() for granted. They're practically always the first functions a developer learns in a language, but they're also an essential starting point for a true understanding of text input and output. Let's take a deeper look.

Revisiting print()

As you've seen throughout this book, the print() function takes a string argument and prints it on the screen. That is simple enough, but the functionality of print() does not end there. You can use print() to quickly and flexibly output multiple values in a number of ways, and as you'll see in a later section, you can even use it to write to files.

Standard Streams

To fully understand the potential of print(), you must understand streams. When you use print(), you send the string to the *standard output stream*, a special communication channel provided by your operating system. The standard output stream behaves like a queue: you push data, usually strings, to the stream, and these strings can be picked up in order by other programs or processes, notably the terminal. Your system sends all strings provided to print() to the standard output stream, by default.

Your system also has a *standard error stream* to display error messages. Normal output is sent to the standard output stream, and error-related output is sent to the standard error stream.

So far in this book, when I've wanted to print an error message, I've used an ordinary print() call, the same as for a normal message:

```
print("Normal message")
print("Scary error occurred")
```

Listing 11-1: print_error.py:1a

This is fine as long as the user only needs the error output to appear in the terminal. However, say the user wants to use the terminal to pipe all program output into files, so that normal output goes into one file and error output goes into the other. Here's an example in bash:

```
$ python3 print_error.py > output.txt 2> error.txt
$ cat output.txt
A normal message.
A scary error occurred.
$ cat error.txt
$
```

The user would expect *output.txt* to contain Normal message and *error.txt* to contain Scary error occurred. However, because print() sends messages to the standard output stream by default, both messages got exported to *output.txt*. Meanwhile, *error.txt* is completely empty.

To send the error text to the standard error stream instead, I have to specify it by using the file= keyword argument on print():

```
import sys
print("Normal message")
print("Scary error occurred", file=sys.stderr)
```

Listing 11-2: print_error.py:1b

I first import the sys module, which gives me access to sys.stderr, a handle to the standard error stream. I send the error message to the standard error stream by specifying the argument file=sys.stderr in my second print() call. The normal message still goes to standard output, as the default argument is file=sys.stdout.

Revising the shell session from before, the usage is the same, but you can see the outputs are now sent where they're expected to be:

```
$ python3 print_error.py > output.txt 2> error.txt
$ cat output.txt
A normal message.
$ cat error.txt
A scary error occurred.
```

The ordinary message has been piped to the file *output.txt*, and the error message has been piped to the file *error.txt*. This is the standard expected behavior for output from command-line programs being used in this manner.

As the parameter name file= suggests, the print() function is not limited to the standard streams. In fact, as you'll see in a moment, it is quite well suited to writing text to files.

Flush

One important fact to know is that standard streams are implemented as *buffers*: data can be pushed to a buffer, which behaves like a queue. That data will wait there until it is picked up by the terminal, or whatever process or program is intended to display it. In the case of standard output and standard error, text is pushed to the stream buffer, and then the buffer is *flushed* when its contents are all printed to the terminal. Flushing doesn't always happen when you expect, for a plethora of reasons (all beyond the scope of this book). On occasion, you will send a message with print() and then wonder why it hasn't printed to the terminal yet.

Usually, it's best to let the system decide when to flush the standard streams, instead of forcing it yourself. However, in some cases, you may want to force it. For example, you may want to add something to the end of a line already displayed on the terminal.

Here's a simple progress indicator that does exactly that. I'll use time .sleep() to indicate that some time-consuming process is happening, like a download. I want to ensure the user knows the program hasn't crashed, so

I display a "Downloading . . . " message, adding another dot every tenth of a second:

```
import time

print("Downloading", end='')
for n in range(20):
    print('.', end='', flush=True)
    time.sleep(0.1)
print("\nDownload completed!")
```

Listing 11-3: progress_indicator.py

The `end=` keyword argument on `print()` prevents a new line from being printed. I'll come back to this later. The important piece for the example is the `flush=` keyword argument. If I'd omitted that, the user wouldn't have seen anything until the loop had finished, because the buffer would have waited for the newline character before writing out to the terminal. However, by forcing the buffer to flush, the line on the terminal updates on each loop iteration.

If you need all your `print()` calls to flush every time by default, you can run Python in *unbuffered mode*, by passing the -u flag to the Python interpreter when you invoke your program, as in python3 -u -m mypackage.

Printing Multiple Values

The `print()` function can accept any number of ordered arguments, and each will be converted into strings using each value's `__str__()` special method. This is a sort of quick and dirty alternative to formatting with f-strings.

For example, I might want to store an address in multiple pieces and then be able to print out the whole thing. I'll initialize the individual values:

```
number = 245
street = "8th Street"
city = "San Francisco"
state = "CA"
zip_code = 94103
```

Listing 11-4: address_print.py:1

I could use formatted strings to put the address together:

```
print(f"{number} {street} {city} {state} {zip_code}")
```

Listing 11-5: address_print.py:2a

While this works, I can do the same thing without the f-string, resulting in a simpler `print()` statement:

```
print(number, street, city, state, zip_code)
```

Listing 11-6: address_print.py:2b

The `print()` statement converts each argument to a string and then concatenates the pieces together, with a space between each piece (by default). In either case, the output is the same:

```
245 8th Street San Francisco CA 94103
```

The benefits of this `print()` statement without f-strings are readability and efficiency. Since the final output is nothing more than all the pieces concatenated together with spaces, and since I have no need to store the whole string in a single value in memory, the f-string is overkill.

Here's another example of the `print()` function's innate concatenating abilities. I can quickly generate a table of property values from a dictionary. First, here's that dictionary:

```
nearby_properties = {
    "N. Anywhere Ave.":
    {
        123: 156_852,
        124: 157_923,
        126: 163_812,
        127: 144_121,
        128: 166_356,
    },
    "N. Everywhere St.":
    {
        4567: 175_753,
        4568: 166_212,
        4569: 185_123,
    }
}
```

Listing 11-7: market_table_print.py:1

I want to print out a table, with the street, number, and formatted property value, separating each column with a tab character (\t). I'll use an f-string first, just so you can see why I wouldn't use that approach:

```
for street, properties in nearby_properties.items():
    for address, value in properties.items():
        print(f"{street}\t{address}\t${value:,}")
```

Listing 11-8: market_table_print.py:2a

While this produces the desired output (which I'll show in a moment), the f-string adds an unnecessary layer of complexity. Since I'm separating each column with a tab character, I can once again make better use of `print()` instead:

```
for street, properties in nearby_properties.items():
    for address, value in properties.items():
        print(street, address, f"${value:,}", sep='\t')
```

Listing 11-9: market_table_print.py:2b

The sep= argument allows me to define what string should be used between each of the values. This sep string is a space by default, as in Listing 11-6, but here, I'm using a tab character (\t) as a separator instead.

I prefer this solution because it's much more readable. I still use an f-string to format value to display the desired comma separator, lest I get uglier output like $144121. The values bound to street and address do not need any special treatment.

Here's the output, which is the same for either version of the code:

```
# --snip--
N. Anywhere Ave.        127     $144,121
N. Anywhere Ave.        128     $166,356
N. Everywhere St.       4567    $175,753
# --snip--
```

Another advantage of this approach is that if I decide I want to separate columns with spaces and a vertical bar character, I only need to change the sep= argument:

```
for street, properties in nearby_properties.items():
    for address, value in properties.items():
        print(street, address, f"${value:,}", sep=' | ')
```

Listing 11-10: market_table_print.py:2c

If I had used f-strings, I would have needed to change the character I was using for each separation.

Here's the new output:

```
# --snip--
N. Anywhere Ave.  |  127  |  $144,121
N. Anywhere Ave.  |  128  |  $166,356
N. Everywhere St. |  4567 |  $175,753
# --snip--
```

The print() function also has an end= parameter, to determine what to append to the end of the output. By default, this is a newline character (\n), but you can change this in the same manner as sep=.

One common use is to set end=\r, which will cause the next printed line to overwrite the previous line. This is especially useful in status updates, such as progress messages.

Revisiting input()

The input() function allows you to receive user input from the terminal, that is, from the *standard input stream*. Unlike with print(), the input() function has no extra features here, but it is useful to have a formal familiarity with input() moving forward.

The sole argument accepted by input() is prompt, an optional string that is printed to standard output without adding a trailing newline character. The value passed to prompt= is usually a message that informs the user what they're supposed to input. This argument can be any value that can be converted to a string via its __str__() method, the same as in the ordered arguments passed to print().

Here's a basic prompt for an MLS number, perhaps intended as part of a property search program:

```
mls = input("Search: MLS#")
print(f"Searching for property with MLS#{mls}...")
```

Listing 11-11: search_input.py

Running this prompts the user for an MLS number and then reports that it's searching for a property with that number:

```
Search: MLS#2092412
Searching for property with MLS#2092412...
```

There is absolutely nothing more to using input().

PEDANTIC NOTE   When reading code or tutorials written in Python 2, you'll probably encounter the use of a raw_input() function. This was needed in Python 2 because the input() function at the time was generally impractical and terribly unsafe—it implicitly evaluated user input as an expression—and thus, Pythonistas avoided it like the plague. In Python 3, the old, dangerous input() was removed, and raw_input() was renamed to input(), so there's no longer cause for concern.

Streams

To work with any data file, you need to obtain a *stream*, also called a *file object* or *file-like object*, which offers methods for reading from and writing to that particular file in memory. There are two kinds of streams. *Binary streams*, which form the foundation of all streams, work with data in binary (1s and 0s). *Text streams* handle the encoding and decoding of text from binary.

Streams can work with more than just traditional files, such as your run-of-the-mill *.txt* files, Word documents, or what have you. The objects for the standard output (sys.stdout), standard error (sys.stderr), and standard input (sys.stdin) that you've already been using are, in fact, streams. Everything you know about the standard streams is the same on any stream.

For this chapter, I'll focus exclusively on text streams. I'll dig into binary data and binary streams in Chapter 12.

You can create a stream that works with a file by using the built-in open() function. There is a *lot* to using this function, but I'll start with the most simplistic usage.

The code in this entire section will assume every file is in the same directory as the Python module opening it. If the file is somewhere else on the machine, you'll need a path, which is a separate topic I'll explore later in this chapter.

To read a file named *213AnywhereAve.txt* (the contents of which are identical to the output coming up), I'll create a stream to work with it. Python beautifully handles creating the stream to the file in the background, so I only need to use the open() function:

```
house = open("213AnywhereAve.txt")
print(house.read())
house.close()
```

Listing 11-12: read_house_open.py:1a

The open() function returns a stream object—specifically, a TextIOWrapper object—that works with the contents of the *213AnywhereAve.txt* file. I bind this stream object to house.

Next, I read the entire contents of the file by calling the read() method on house and passing the string it returns directly to print().

Once I'm done working with the file, I *must* close it, and I do that on the last line. It's important not to leave file closing to the garbage collector, as that is neither guaranteed to work nor portable across all Python implementations. What's more, when writing to a file, Python is not guaranteed to finish making changes to the file until close() is called. This means that if you forget to close before your program ends, your changes may be lost in part or in whole.

Assuming the *213AnywhereAve.txt* file exists in the same directory as this Python module, this code will output the entire contents of the file to the screen:

```
Beautiful 3 bed, 2.5 bath on 2 acres.
Finished basement, covered porch.
Kitchen features granite countertops and new appliances.
Large fenced yard with mature trees and garden space.
$856,752
```

You can only read from this particular stream. Writing to a file requires me to open it differently, which I'll return to shortly.

Context Manager Basics

A *context manager* is a type of object that automatically handles its own cleanup tasks when program execution leaves a certain section of code, or *context*. This context is provided by a Python with statement. (This is the last of Python's compound statements, alongside familiar friends such as if, try, and def, to name a few.) To really understand how this works, I'll unpack the underlying logic and build up to the use of context managers.

There's one remaining problem in Listing 11-12. As it stands, the example is pretty safe, as house.read() isn't going to fail unless I'm unable to open the file. In reality, though, I'd do more after opening than just printing out the contents of the file. I may process the data in any number of ways, store it in a collection, or search it for something in particular. There's lots of room for errors and exceptions. With this approach, if I successfully open the file but experience any sort of exception while reading from or working with that file—say, a KeyError if I tried to read it into a dictionary—the close() method would never get called.

To get around this, I can wrap the close() call in the finally clause of a try statement:

```
house = open("213AnywhereAve.txt")
try:
    print(house.read())
finally:
    house.close()
```

Listing 11-13: read_house_open.py:1b

If the file *213AnywhereAve.txt* does not exist, it will raise a FileNotFoundError exception. If I'm able to open it successfully, I can try to read() from the house stream. I'm not catching any exceptions, so they'll automatically bubble up from this try statement. Because the close() call is in the finally clause, it will be called whether there's an error or not.

In practice, though, always remembering to call close() is utterly impractical, not to mention a royal pain. If you forget, or if the program terminates before you can call close(), all sorts of pesky bugs can result.

Thankfully, all stream objects are context managers, so they can clean up after themselves with a with statement, encapsulating that entire try-finally logic (Listing 11-13) into a single statement:

```
with open("213AnywhereAve.txt") as house:
    print(house.read())
```

Listing 11-14: read_house_open.py:1c

This opens the *213AnywhereAve.txt* file, binds the stream to house, and then runs the line of code for reading and printing from that file. There's no need for a manual call to house.close(), because the with statement handles that automatically in the background.

I'll dig into the mechanics of with more later on, but as it is the canonical way of working with (most) streams, I'll use it exclusively from here on out.

GOTCHA ALERT   Don't ever use with on the standard streams (sys.stdout, sys.stderr, and sys.stdin). Using with on standard streams will call close() on them, at which point, *you can't use them* without restarting your Python instance! There are (convoluted) ways of reopening the standard streams, but honestly, it's best not to close them to begin with.

File Modes

The open() function optionally accepts a second argument: *mode=*, which should be a string dictating how the file should be opened, which in turn defines what operations may be performed on the stream object—reading, writing, and so on. If you don't pass a mode= argument, Python uses mode='r', which opens the file for reading only.

There are eight different file modes for text-based files (see Table 11-1), and the behavior of each is a little different. The base modes are as follows:

- r opens the file for *reading*.
- w opens the file for *writing*; it truncates (erases) the file contents first.
- a opens the file for *append* writing (that is, writing to the end of the existing file).
- x *creates* a new file and opens it for writing; the file must not already exist.

Adding the addition (+) flag adds either reading or writing, whichever is missing from the mode. The most important usage is the mode r+, which allows you to both read from and write to the file *without* the contents being erased first.

The behavior of each mode can feel a bit unexpected at times. Table 11-1, which is based in part on a Stack Overflow answer by industryworker3595112 (see *https://stackoverflow.com/a/30931305/472647/*), breaks down the functionalities of the modes.

Table 11-1: File Modes

Functionalities	Modes							
	r	r+	w	w+	a	a+	x	x+
Allow read	✓	✓		✓		✓		✓
Allow write		✓	✓	✓	✓	✓	✓	✓
Can create new file			✓	✓	✓	✓	✓	✓
Can open existing file	✓	✓	✓	✓	✓	✓		
Erase file contents first			✓	✓				
Allow seek	✓	✓	✓	✓		✓*	✓	✓
Initial position at start	✓	✓	✓	✓			✓	✓
Initial position at end					✓	✓		

*Only allows seek on read

In a stream, the *position* dictates where you read to and write from within the file. The seek() method allows you to change this position, if the mode supports it. By default, the position will be at either the start or the end of the file. I'll cover this in depth in a later section.

You can also use the mode= parameter to switch between *text mode* (t), which is the default, and *binary mode* (b). In Chapter 12, I'll work exclusively in binary mode. For now, at least be aware of which mode you're opening a file in. For example, the argument mode='r+t' opens the file in read-write text mode, and it is the same as mode='r+'. By contrast, mode='r+b' opens the file in read-write binary mode. For this entire chapter, I'll only use the default text mode.

When you're opening a file in read mode (r or r+), the file *must* already exist. If it doesn't, the open() function will raise FileNotFoundError.

Create mode (x or x+) expects precisely the opposite: the file *must not* already exist. If it does, the open() function will raise FileExistsError.

Write mode (w or w+) and append mode (a or a+) have neither of these problems. If the file exists, it will be opened; if it doesn't, it will be created.

If you attempt to write to a stream opened only for reading (r) or read from a stream opened only for writing (w, a, or x), that read or write operation will raise the io.UnsupportedOperation error.

If you want to check in advance which operations a stream supports, use the readable(), writable(), or seekable() methods on the stream. For example:

```
with open("213AnywhereAve.txt", 'r') as file:
    print(file.readable())  # prints 'True'
    print(file.writable())  # prints 'False'
    print(file.seekable())  # prints 'True'
```

Listing 11-15: check_stream_capabilities.py

Reading Files

To read from a file, you first acquire a stream, opening it in one of the readable modes ('r', 'r+', 'w+', 'a+', or 'x+'). From there, you can read in one of four ways: read(), readline(), readlines(), or iteration.

For all of the examples in this section, I'll read from the following text file:

```
78 Somewhere Road, Anytown PA
Tiny 2-bed, 1-bath bungalow. Needs repairs.
Built in 1981; original kitchen and appliances.
Small backyard with old storage shed.
Built on ancient burial ground.
$431,998
```

Listing 11-16: 78SomewhereRd.txt

The read() Method

I can use the read() method to read the complete contents of the 78SomewhereRd.txt file like this:

```
with open('78SomewhereRd.txt', 'r') as house:
    contents = house.read()
    print(type(contents))  # prints <class 'str'>
    print(contents)
```

Listing 11-17: read_house.py:1a

After acquiring the stream house, which I opened in read mode, I call the read() method to read the entire file in as a single string, which I bind to contents. Each of the lines in the *78SomewhereRd.txt* file ends with a newline character (\n), and those are retained in the string. If I print contents as a raw string via repr(), you can see the literal newline characters:

```
print(repr(contents))
```

This line of code outputs the following (redacted for brevity):

```
'78 Somewhere Road, Anytown PA\nTiny 2 bed, 1 bath # --snip--'
```

(Remember, those literal \n characters are only there because I printed the raw string. A normal print of contents would recognize the newline characters and create new lines accordingly.)

By default, read() will read characters until the end of the file is encountered. You can alter this behavior with the size= argument, which takes a maximum number of characters to read. For example, to read a maximum of 20 characters from the file (and less if the end of the file is encountered first), I would do the following:

```
with open('78SomewhereRd.txt', 'r') as house:
    print(house.read(20))
```

Listing 11-18: read_house.py:1b

This would output the following:

```
78 Somewhere Road, A
```

The readline() Method

The readline() method behaves exactly like read(), except that it reads only up to and including a newline (\n), instead of just the end of the file. I can use this to read the first two lines of the file. As before, I'm using repr() to show the raw strings, as I want to actually *see* the newline characters for the sake of the example:

```
with open('78SomewhereRd.txt', 'r') as house:
    line1 = house.readline()
    line2 = house.readline()
    print(repr(line1))
    print(repr(line2))
```

Listing 11-19: readline_house.py

The house stream remembers my position in the file, so after each call to readline(), the stream position is set to the beginning of the next line.

Running this code outputs the first two lines, which I print as raw strings so I can see the literal newline characters:

```
'78 Somewhere Road, Anytown PA\n'
'Tiny 2 bed, 1 bath bungalow.\n'
```

The readline() method also has a size= positional argument, which works like read(size=), except that it will stop at the first newline it encounters if the size is greater than the line's length.

The readlines() Method

I can read all the lines in the file at once as a list of strings, using readlines():

```python
with open('78SomewhereRd.txt', 'r') as house:
    lines = house.readlines()
    for line in lines:
        print(line.strip())
```

Listing 11-20: readlines_house.py

Each individual line is stored in a string, and all the strings are stored in the list lines. Once I've read all of the lines, I'll print each one out, removing the trailing newline character from each string by using the strip() method on the string object. This removes any leading and trailing whitespace characters, including newlines.

Running that code outputs this:

```
78 Somewhere Road, Anytown PA
Tiny 2-bed, 1-bath bungalow. Needs repairs.
Built in 1981; original kitchen and appliances.
Small backyard with old storage shed.
Built on ancient burial ground.
$431,998
```

The readlines() method has a hint= parameter, which is similar to the size= parameter on read(). The critical difference is that readlines() *always* reads entire lines. If the number of characters specified in hint= is short of the next newline, readlines() will still read up to (and including) that next newline.

Reading with Iteration

Streams themselves are iterators—they implement the __iter__() and __next__() special methods. This means I can iterate over a stream directly!

```python
with open('78SomewhereRd.txt', 'r') as house:
    for line in house:
        print(line.strip())
```

Listing 11-21: iterate_house.py

The output is the same as in the last example, but this iterative approach doesn't have the overhead of creating a list I'll only throw away after printing.

If you're only reading a file once, direct iteration over the stream is usually going to be the cleaner and (probably) more efficient solution.

On the other hand, if you need to access the contents of a file more than once in your program's execution, you'll almost always want to read the data into memory—that is, to read it from the stream and store it in a typical Python collection or other value. It's always faster to read from a value in memory than from a file!

Stream Position

After every read and write operation, your position in the stream will change. You can use the tell() and seek() methods to work with the stream position.

The tell() method returns your current stream position as a positive integer, representing the number of characters from the start of the file.

The seek() method allows you to move back and forth within a stream, character by character. When working with text streams, it accepts one argument: a positive integer representing a new position to move to, represented by the number of characters from the beginning. This method works on any stream, as long as it isn't opened in append mode ('a' or 'a+').

The most common use is to jump to the beginning of the file with seek(0). To demonstrate that, I'll print out the first line of the *78SomewhereRd.txt* file three times:

```
with open('78SomewhereRd.txt', 'r') as house:
    for _ in range(3):
        print(house.readline().strip())
        house.seek(0)
```

Listing 11-22: iterate_house.py

After opening the file, I loop three times. On each iteration of the loop, I print out the current line, with the newline removed with strip(). Then, I reposition the stream at the beginning of the file, before the next loop iteration.

The output is as follows:

```
78 Somewhere Road, Anytown PA
78 Somewhere Road, Anytown PA
78 Somewhere Road, Anytown PA
```

Additionally, you can skip to the end of the stream with seek(0, 2), meaning you're moving 0 positions away from the end of the file (a whence of 2). When doing this, you must provide 0 as the first argument and 2 as the second argument; nothing else works for this.

The seek() method can also be used to skip to other stream positions, not just the start or the end. A trivial demonstration of this would be to skip one character each time I read the opening line:

```
with open('78SomewhereRd.txt', 'r') as house:
    for n in range(10):
        house.seek(n)
        print(house.readline().strip())
```

Listing 11-23: iterate_house_mangle.py

Instead of passing 0 to seek(), I'm passing n, the iteration count from the loop, before reading the line. On each iteration, the first line is printed again, but with one less character at the beginning:

```
78 Somewhere Road, Anytown PA
8 Somewhere Road, Anytown PA
Somewhere Road, Anytown PA
Somewhere Road, Anytown PA
omewhere Road, Anytown PA
mewhere Road, Anytown PA
ewhere Road, Anytown PA
where Road, Anytown PA
here Road, Anytown PA
ere Road, Anytown PA
```

That's an interesting example, though it's not very useful. Don't worry—I'll employ seek() in a more practical fashion in some upcoming examples.

Writing Files

The first thing to remember about writing to a stream is that you're always *overwriting*, never *inserting*! This doesn't matter when you're appending to the end of a file, but in all other cases, it can cause confusion and undesired results.

When modifying a file, read the contents into memory, modify the file there, and then write it out again, to reduce the chances of obliterating data because of a bug. You can write out the new data either in place or to a temporary file that you move into place. I'll introduce the latter technique later on in this chapter, when I discuss the pathlib module. For now, I'll just overwrite files in place. Either technique will prevent a lot of annoying and destructive bugs.

There are three ways to write to a stream: the write() method, the writelines() method, and the print() function. Before using any of these, you must be certain your stream is open in a writable file mode (anything except 'r') and know your current stream position! All file modes but one have an initial stream position at the beginning of the file. The exception is the append mode ('a' and 'a+'), which has an initial position at the end of the file. As you read from and write to the stream, that position will change.

The write() Method

The `write()` method writes the given string to the file, starting at the current stream position, and it returns an integer representing how many characters it wrote to the file. Remember, though, it overwrites any data that's in the way, from the stream position until the end of the new data. To prevent accidental data loss, read the file into memory, modify the data there, and then write it back out to the same file.

That property description in *78SomewhereRd.txt* isn't very appealing. I'll write a program to improve the description and write the updated real estate listing to the file:

```
with open('78SomewhereRd.txt', 'r+') as real_estate_listing:
    contents = real_estate_listing.read()
```

Listing 11-24: improve_real_estate_listing.py:1a

First, I open the file in read-write mode. Instead of directly modifying the file contents via the stream, I'll read the file's data into memory as a string, binding it to contents. I'll revise the description by working on this string, rather than with the stream itself:

```
    contents = contents.replace('Tiny', 'Cozy')
    contents = contents.replace('Needs repairs', 'Full of potential')
    contents = contents.replace('Small', 'Compact')
    contents = contents.replace('old storage shed', 'detached workshop')
    contents = contents.replace('Built on ancient burial ground.',
                                'Unique atmosphere.')
```

Listing 11-25: improve_real_estate_listing.py:2a

I use the `replace()` string method to replace the unappealing words and phrases with more attractive ones.

Once I'm happy with the new version of my string, I can write it out to the file:

```
    real_estate_listing.seek(0)
    real_estate_listing.write(contents)
```

Listing 11-26: improve_real_estate_listing.py:3a

I position myself at the start of the file, since I want to overwrite everything there, using `real_estate_listing.seek(0)`. Then, I write the new contents of the file. Any of the old contents that are in the way are overwritten.

The last remaining trouble is that the new contents are shorter than the old contents, so some old data will be left hanging out at the end of the file. After `write()`, the stream position is at the end of the new data I just wrote, so I can clean up the leftovers from the old data with this:

```
    real_estate_listing.truncate()
```

Listing 11-27: improve_real_estate_listing.py:4

By default, the truncate() method erases everything from the current stream position through to the end of the file. It does this by truncating (or shortening) the file to a given number of bytes, which can be passed as an argument. If no explicit size is passed in, truncate() uses the value provided by the tell() method, which corresponds to the current stream position.

Once the flow leaves the with statement, the stream is flushed and closed, ensuring the changes to the file are written.

That program doesn't output anything on the command line. If I open the *78SomewhereRd.txt* file, I can see the new description:

```
78 Somewhere Road, Anytown PA
Cozy 2-bed, 1-bath bungalow. Full of potential.
Built in 1981; original kitchen and appliances.
Compact backyard with detached workshop.
Unique atmosphere.
$431,998
```

The writelines() Method

Just as readlines() stores the contents of the file as a list of strings, writelines() writes out a list of strings to a file. That is all it does. The writelines() method doesn't insert newline characters at the end of each string in the list provided to it. The sole difference between write() and writelines() is that the latter accepts a list of strings, instead of just a single string, and returns nothing.

I can modify the file using writelines(). For this example, I restored the *78SomewhereRd.txt* file to what it was in Listing 11-16.

```
with open('78SomewhereRd.txt', 'r+') as real_estate_listing:
    contents = real_estate_listing.readlines()
```

Listing 11-28: improve_real_estate_listing.py:1b

I open the file *78SomewhereRd.txt* as before, but this time, I read the contents in with real_estate_listing.readlines(), which returns a list of strings I bind to the name contents.

Next, I make my changes to the description by modifying that list of strings. Once again, I'm not working with the stream here at all, but rather with the list of strings containing the data I read from the stream.

```
new_contents = []
for line in contents:
    line = line.replace('Tiny', 'Cozy')
    line = line.replace('Needs repairs', 'Full of potential')
    line = line.replace('Small', 'Compact')
    line = line.replace('old storage shed', 'detached workshop')
    line = line.replace('Built on ancient burial ground',
                        'Unique atmosphere')
    new_contents.append(line)
```

Listing 11-29: improve_real_estate_listing.py:2b

I iterate over each line in contents, make the necessary substitutions, and store the modified lines in a new list, new_contents. I'll be the first to admit that this implementation is much less efficient than the version using write(), but this technique becomes useful when you're working with many lines that need to be individually processed.

Finally, I can write out the new file contents using writelines():

```
real_estate_listing.seek(0)
real_estate_listing.writelines(new_contents)
real_estate_listing.truncate()
```

Listing 11-30: improve_real_estate_listing.py:3b-4

I pass the list of strings to writelines(). Because the newline character was retained at the end of each line as it was read in by readlines(), those same newline characters are being written out. If I had removed them, however, I would have had to add them back in manually before calling writelines().

The output is the same for the example in the previous section.

Writing Files with print()

You know that print() outputs data using the sys.stdout stream by default, but you can override this by passing a stream to the file= argument. One particular use for this is to conditionally output either to the terminal or to a file. The simple formatting features on print() make it an excellent alternative to write(), in some cases.

The rules of usage are identical to write() and writelines(): you must have a stream that is writable, and you must be mindful of the stream position.

To demonstrate this, I'll rewrite the real estate listings table produced by Listing 11-14 to output to a file, instead of the standard output. I'll reuse the nearby_properties dictionary from Listing 11-7:

```
nearby_properties = {
    "N. Anywhere Ave.":
    {
        123: 156_852,
        124: 157_923,
        126: 163_812,
        127: 144_121,
        128: 166_356
    },
    "N. Everywhere St.":
    {
        4567: 175_753,
        4568: 166_212,
        4569: 185_123
    }
}
```

Listing 11-31: print_file_real_estate_listing.py:1

Here's my revised code for generating the real estate listings table:

```python
with open('listings.txt', 'w') as real_estate_listings:
    for street, properties in nearby_properties.items():
        for address, value in properties.items():
            print(street, address, f"${value:,}",
                  sep=' | ',
                  file=real_estate_listings)
```

Listing 11-32: print_file_real_estate_listings.py:2

I open the file *listings.txt* in write mode, since I want to either create or completely replace that file when this code runs. The loop iterating over nearby_properties and the call to print() are both essentially unchanged from before. The difference here is that I pass the real_estate_listings stream to the file= parameter of print().

The output is the same as before, but it is written to the *listings.txt* file instead of being printed to the terminal:

```
# --snip--
N. Anywhere Ave.   |  127  | $144,121
N. Anywhere Ave.   |  128  | $166,356
N. Everywhere St.  |  4567 | $175,753
# --snip--
```

Line Separators

If you have any experience with writing portable code, you may remember that in Windows operating systems, lines are separated with both the carriage return and the newline (\r\n), while only the newline (\n) is used in UNIX systems. This difference can be a royal pain when working with files in many languages.

On the other hand, Python streams abstract this difference out behind the scenes. When writing to a stream in text mode using print(), write(), or writelines(), you only ever use the *universal newline*—which is the newline character (\n)—as your line separator. Python will always substitute the system-appropriate line separator.

In the same way, when reading from files using read(), readline(), or readlines(), you only need to work with the newline character as the line separator.

Context Manager Details

So far in this chapter, I've used a context manager via the with statement every time I've opened a file, to idiomatically ensure streams are closed as soon as they're no longer needed.

Like many of Python's compound statements, with statements utilize certain special methods to work with objects. This means with is not limited to streams: it can be made to handle virtually any situation that calls for try-finally logic. To demonstrate this, I'll unpack precisely how the with statement interfaces with streams, and then I'll apply that knowledge to a custom class.

How Context Managers Work

For an object to be a context manager, it must implement two special methods: __enter__() and __exit__().

Streams implement both of these methods. The __exit__() method closes the stream, eliminating the need to remember to manually close the stream.

The __enter__() method is responsible for any setup before the context manager is used. This method doesn't do anything interesting in the case of a stream, although some context manager classes make more use of __enter__(), as you'll see in the custom context manager example later.

According to PEP 343, which defined context managers, the with compound statement is roughly equivalent to this:

```
VAR = EXPR
VAR.__enter__()
try:
    BLOCK
finally:
    VAR.__exit__()
```

The expression passed to the with statement is used to initialize an object. The __enter__() method is called on that object to perform whatever tasks should be completed before the object is used. (Again, in the case of streams, this method does nothing.) Next, the suite of the with statement is called within the context of a try clause. Whether it succeeds or fails, the __exit__() method will be called, usually to perform any necessary cleanup tasks on the object.

Recalling the example from Listing 11-17, if Python didn't have with statements, I'd need to use the following code to ensure a file was closed, whether there was an error or not:

```
real_estate_listing = open("213AnywhereAve.txt")
try:
    print(real_estate_listing.read())
finally:
    real_estate_listing.close()
```

Listing 11-33: read_real_estate_listing_file.py:1a

Because streams like real_estate_listing are context managers, I can instead represent that same logic as follows:

```
real_estate_listing = open("213AnywhereAve.txt")
real_estate_listing.__enter__()
try:
    print(real_estate_listing.read())
```

```
finally:
    real_estate_listing.__exit__()
```

Listing 11-34: read_real_estate_listing_file.py:1b

Once again, __enter__() does nothing, but it is called as a matter of convention on context managers. The __exit__() method closes the stream when I'm done. This version feels more verbose, but as it uses the special methods of the context manager, the logic can be handled entirely in a single with statement:

```
with open("213AnywhereAve.txt") as real_estate_listing:
    print(real_estate_listing.read())
```

Listing 11-35: read_real_estate_listing_file.py:1c

This is much easier to remember and type. It's all made possible by context managers.

Using Multiple Context Managers

You can use multiple context managers in a with statement, which can open up all sorts of possibilities. For example, say I want to be able to read from two files at once, perhaps to combine them into one or to look for differences between them. (In the interest of expediency, I won't actually do anything with these files in this example; I'll just open them.)

To open multiple streams in a single with statement, I separate the open() expressions in the header with a comma, like this:

```
with open('213AnywhereAve.txt', 'r') as left, open('18SomewhereLn.txt', 'r') as right:
    # work with the streams left and right however you want
```

Listing 11-36: multiple_streams.py

I can use the streams left and right in the usual manner. When the with statement ends, both streams are closed automatically.

Implementing the Context Management Protocol

The *context management protocol* is the fancy, official term for the __enter__() and __exit__() special methods. Any object that implements these two special methods can be managed by the with statement. They're not limited to working with streams; you can use them to automate doing anything that needs to be done before or after usage of an object.

Remember that these methods need only be implemented. If you don't need one or the other to actually do anything, don't write any functionality into the unneeded method.

To demonstrate this, I'll work with the example of a house showing. Before you can show a prospective buyer a home, you have to unlock the front door. When you leave, you lock the door again. This sort of pattern is precisely what a context manager is for.

First, I define the entire House class:

```python
class House:
    def __init__(self, address, house_key, **rooms):
        self.address = address
        self.__house_key = house_key
        self.__locked = True
        self._rooms = dict()
        for room, desc in rooms.items():
            self._rooms[room.replace("_", " ").lower()] = desc

    def unlock_house(self, house_key):
        if self.__house_key == house_key:
            self.__locked = False
            print("House unlocked.")
        else:
            raise RuntimeError("Wrong key! Could not unlock house.")

    def explore(self, room):
        if self.__locked:
            raise RuntimeError("Cannot explore a locked house.")

        try:
            return f"The {room.lower()} is {self._rooms[room.lower()]}."
        except KeyError as e:
            raise KeyError(f"No room {room}") from e

    def lock_house(self):
        self.__locked = True
        print("House locked!")
```

Listing 11-37: house_showing.py:1

This class relies entirely on concepts from prior chapters, so I won't detail implementation here. In short, a House object is initialized with an address, a value to use as the house key, and a keyword argument describing each room. You'll notice that my initializer converts underscores in the keyword argument names to spaces before storing the room name in the self._rooms dictionary. It changes both the room name and the description to lowercase. This will make the usage of the class feel more obvious and less error-prone.

The important part of this example is the HouseShowing class, which I'll ultimately write as a context manager by defining the __enter__() and __exit__() special methods in the upcoming Listing 11-39 and Listing 11-41, respectively. First, I'll define the class and its initializer:

```python
class HouseShowing:

    def __init__(self, house, house_key):
        self.house = house
        self.house_key = house_key
```

Listing 11-38: house_showing.py:2

In the initializer, I accept two arguments: a House instance and the key value with which to unlock the house. In the next two sections, I'll add the __enter__() and __exit__() special instance methods, to make HouseShowing a context manager.

The __enter__() Method

Before I can show any room in the House, I must always unlock the house first. If the key is wrong, I can't get in, so there's no point in continuing with the showing. Since this behavior should always occur before any other use of a House instance, it is handled by the __enter__() special instance method:

```
def __enter__(self):
    self.house.unlock_house(self.house_key)
    return self
```

Listing 11-39: house_showing.py:3

I attempt to unlock the house using the key with which I initialized HouseShowing. Notice that I don't perform any error handling here. Always allow errors originating from the usage of your class to bubble up through this method, so the developer using your class can fix their code.

Importantly, I *must* return the instance from __enter__() for the with statement to be able to work with it!

The user should be able to work with this object directly, instead of having to drill down into an attribute. The main purpose of a house showing is to see the different rooms, so I write a method for that:

```
def show(self, room):
    print(self.house.explore(room))
```

Listing 11-40: house_showing.py:4

Once again, you'll notice that I don't handle any of the possible exceptions from house.explore() here, as they all relate to the usage of the class. If the error stems from how the class is used, the exception should be handled in the usage as well.

The __exit__() Method

When I leave the house, either because the tour is over or I couldn't find a sunroom, I always want to lock up. That behavior is handled by the special instance method __exit__():

```
    def __exit__(self, exc_type, exc_val, exc_tb):
  ❶ if exc_type:
        print("Sorry about that.")
  ❷ self.house.lock_house()
```

Listing 11-41: house_showing.py:5

This method must accept three arguments besides self. If an exception is raised anywhere in the suite of the with statement, these three parameters will describe the exception's type (exc_type), message (exc_val), and traceback (exc_tb). If there is no exception, all three of these parameters will have the value None. The parameter names I'm using here are conventional. You can call them whatever you like, but I recommend sticking with these names unless you have a good reason to change them.

Although __exit__() must accept these arguments, you're not required to do anything with them. They're useful if you need to take different close or cleanup actions when certain exceptions occur. In my case, if there was any exception ❶, I apologize to the client while locking up the house ❷. In my particular code, I make no use of the message (exc_val) and traceback (exc_tb) arguments. If there was no exception, I only lock the house.

Importantly, __exit__() *does not have any role in raising or handling the error*! It acts as a listener, eavesdropping on any exceptions that occur in the with suite. Within __exit__(), I use conditional statements to work with the exceptions passed as arguments. I cannot use try for this, because any exceptions never bubble up through __exit__() directly, as you'll notice in Listing 11-34. I should never re-raise the exceptions passed in either, because any exception that occurs in the suite of the with will be raised by the responsible statement and should be handled by the caller. Once again: __exit__() has no role in handling these exceptions. The only exceptions that an __exit__() method should ever handle are those its own suite directly caused.

Using the Custom Class

Now that my class is a context manager, I can write my usage. I start by creating a House object:

```
house = House("123 Anywhere Street", house_key=1803,
              living_room="spacious",
              office="bright",
              bedroom="cozy",
              bathroom="small",
              kitchen="modern")
```

Listing 11-42: house_showing.py:6

In creating the House instance, I'm defining a house_key value of 1803, which is the value I'll have to provide later when defining the HouseShowing.

I create a new HouseShowing in the context of a with statement, passing the House instance I created (house) to it. For the sake of example, I'm using the wrong house_key value (9999), so I should get an exception:

```
with HouseShowing(house, house_key=9999) as showing:
    showing.show("Living Room")
    showing.show("bedroom")
    showing.show("porch")
```

Listing 11-43: house_showing.py:7a

In the header, I create a new instance of HouseShowing. Its __enter__() method is called by the with statement. The value returned from __enter__() is bound to showing. If I had forgotten to return anything from __enter__() in Listing 11-39, showing would have been bound to None, and this code wouldn't have worked.

Since house_key is wrong and I cannot unlock the house, here's the output from running the program as it is right now:

```
Traceback (most recent call last):
  File "context_class.py", line 57, in <module>
    with HouseShowing(house, 9999) as showing:
  File "context_class.py", line 38, in __enter__
    self.house.unlock_house(self.house_key)
  File "context_class.py", line 15, in unlock_house
    raise RuntimeError("Wrong key! Could not unlock house.")
RuntimeError: Wrong key! Could not unlock house.
```

Because the house_key value was wrong, showing.__enter__() encountered an exception, which I allowed to remain unhandled. This is important, because my code in Listing 11-43 is wrong. I need to pass the correct value for house_key. The with statement didn't even try to run its suite. It encountered an exception and gave up.

I'll correct the value I'm passing to house_key:

```
with HouseShowing(house, house_key=1803) as showing:
    showing.show("Living Room")
    showing.show("bedroom")
    showing.show("porch")
```

Listing 11-44: house_showing.py:7b

Now, I'll be able to unlock the house. In the suite of the with statement, I make three calls to the show() method. The first two will work, because the House instance bound to house has those rooms defined (see Listing 11-42), but the third will fail with an exception. Take a look at the output:

```
House unlocked.
The living room is spacious.
The bedroom is cozy.
Sorry about that.
House locked!
Traceback (most recent call last):
  File "context_class.py", line 22, in explore
    return f"The {room.lower()} is {self._rooms[room.lower()]}."
KeyError: 'porch'

The above exception was the direct cause of the following exception:

Traceback (most recent call last):
  File "context_class.py", line 60, in <module>
    showing.show("porch")
  File "context_class.py", line 42, in show
    print(self.house.explore(room))
```

```
File "context_class.py", line 24, in explore
    raise KeyError(f"No room {room}") from e
KeyError: 'No room porch'
```

The with statement calls showing.__enter__() on HouseShowing, which in turn calls house.unlock_house(), as indicated by the message House unlocked. Then, with each call to showing.show() in the suite of the with statement, a description of the requested room is printed out.

The third call to showing.show() in Listing 11-44, requesting to see the porch, fails with an exception because the house doesn't have a porch. Instead, showing.__exit__() is called, and the exception is passed to it. The apology is printed, and then house.lock_house() is called.

After all this, the traceback of the exception is printed.

To fix the problem with the code, I'd need to drop the request to see the porch and replace it with a room that does exist. Perhaps I'll look at the kitchen instead.

```
with HouseShowing(house, 1803) as showing:
    showing.show("Living Room")
    showing.show("bedroom")
    showing.show("kitchen")
```

Listing 11-45: house_showing.py:7c

Running this version outputs the following:

```
House unlocked.
The living room is spacious.
The bedroom is cozy.
The kitchen is modern.
House locked!
```

No errors here. The house is unlocked, the requested rooms are shown, and then the house is locked again. Because there were no exceptions raised in the suite, house.__exit__() does not print the apology from before.

Paths

So far, I've used files located in the same directory as the module opening them. In real programs, a file may be anywhere on the system. This is far from trivial, which is probably why most tutorials skim over this topic. I'll dive deep into file paths here.

First, file paths are not the same on all operating systems. UNIX-style systems, such as macOS and Linux, use the POSIX file path conventions, while Windows uses an entirely different scheme. Second, you can't always be sure what directory your code is being run in, so relative paths only get you so far. Third, you can't make assumptions about the name or location of important directories, such as the user's home directory. In short, file paths are tricky to generalize.

To get around all of these issues, Python offers two modules: os and pathlib. Up until Python 3.6, using the os package and its submodule (os.path) was the standard way of working with file paths. Even now, this remains a common approach. The os package allows you to work portably with whatever operating system your code is running on, yet the package as a whole is plagued with complexity, verbosity, and some pretty snarly legacy code. It's also considered something of a "junk drawer," since it contains all the functions and classes designed for working with the operating system. Thus, it can be hard to know what to use from the os module or even how to use it.

The pathlib module was introduced in Python 3.4 and became fully supported by open() in Python 3.6. It offers a cleaner, better organized, and more predictable way of handling paths. More importantly, it replaces most of os.path and cleanly incorporates much of the filesystem functionality offered by os and another useful module: glob, which allows you to find multiple paths fitting a particular pattern, following UNIX rules.

I recommend preferring pathlib for the sake of maintainability, readability, and performance, so that's what I'll focus on here. If you find yourself working with legacy code, or if you need a few of the advanced functions in os.path, refer to the official documentation for the os.path module: *https://docs.python.org/3/library/os.path.html*.

Path Objects

The pathlib module provides several related classes that represent filesystem paths. These are called *path-like* classes—as of Python 3.6, they all inherit from the os.Pathlike abstract class—and they are immutable representations of a filesystem path. Importantly, path-like objects are *not* based on strings; they're unique objects with their own behaviors, based on the parts of a path and how those parts fit together, so they abstract out a lot of the logic.

One of the nice things about pathlib path objects is that they handle all the different filesystem conventions quietly, behind the scenes, as appropriate to the system: current directory (.), parent directory (..), slashes (/ or \), and so forth.

There are two types of path-like objects: *pure paths* and *concrete paths*.

Pure Paths

A *pure path* represents a path and allows you to work with it, without accessing the underlying filesystem. Instantiating an object from the PurePath class will automatically create a PurePosixPath or PureWindowsPath object behind the scenes, depending on the operating system. You can usually entrust this to Python to figure out, although you can instantiate the specific type of path if you need it for your code.

```
from pathlib import PurePath
path = PurePath('../some_file.txt')
```

```
with open(path, 'r') as file:
    print(file.read())  # this is okay (assuming file exists)

# create empty file if none exists
path.touch()            # fails on Pure paths!
```

Listing 11-46: relative_path.py:1a

I can pass the PurePath object to the open() function to open *../some_file.txt.* However, I cannot interact with the filesystem through the path object itself, as I attempt to do with path.touch(), which fails.

If you only intend to use the path in a call to open(), or if you otherwise don't plan to interact with the system directly through the path object's methods, then you should use a pure path, which will help prevent you from accidentally modifying the filesystem.

Concrete Paths

A *concrete path* provides methods for interacting with the filesystem. Instantiating an object from the Path class will create either a PosixPath or a WindowsPath object:

```
from pathlib import Path
path = Path('../some_file.txt')

with open(path, 'r') as file:
    print(file.read())  # this is okay (assuming file exists)

# create empty file if none exists
path.touch()            # okay on Path!
```

Listing 11-47: relative_path.py:1b

This code is exactly the same as in Listing 11-46, except that I'm defining a Path object instead of a PurePath. As a result, I can still open the path, but I can also use methods on the path object to interact directly with the filesystem. For example, I can use path.touch() to create an empty file at *../some_file.txt,* if that file doesn't already exist.

If you are explicitly coupling your implementation to a particular operating system, use either the Windows or the Posix form of the class; otherwise, use the PurePath or Path class.

Parts of a Path

A path-like object is made up of parts that the path class joins together behind the scenes, based on the operating system. There are two ways of writing a path: *absolute* and *relative.* Both ways of writing paths work in all the PurePath and Path objects.

An *absolute* path is one that starts from the root of the filesystem. The absolute path to a file always starts with an *anchor* and ends with the *name*—the full filename. The name consists of a *stem* (that is, the filename) before the first nonleading dot and, typically, one or more *suffixes* after the dot. For example, consider the following fictional path:

```
/path/to/file.txt
```

The anchor here is the leading forward slash (/). The name is `file.txt`, with a stem of `file` and a suffix of `.txt`. I'll break down a couple of more complex examples shortly.

These parts can be retrieved from the path-like object. You can use the `PurePath.parts()` method, which returns a tuple of parts. Otherwise, you can access specific components as properties.

Here's a function that prints out each part of a path passed to it. I'll discuss the function, then employ it in the next couple of sections to dissect a Windows path and a POSIX path, respectively.

```python
import pathlib


def path_parts(path):
    print(f"{path}\n")

    print(f"Drive: {path.drive}")
    print(f"Root: {path.root}")
    print(f"Anchor: {path.anchor}\n")

    print(f"Parent: {path.parent}\n")
    for i, parent in enumerate(path.parents):
        print(f"Parents [{i}]: {parent}")

    print(f"Name: {path.name}")
    print(f"Suffix: {path.suffix}")
    for i, suffix in enumerate(path.suffixes):
        print(f"Suffixes [{i}]: {suffix}")
    print(f"Stem: {path.stem}\n")

    print("------------------\n")
```

Listing 11-48: path_parts.py:1

The `path.parents` property is an iterable collection. The first item, `parents[0]`, is the immediate parent and is the same as `path.parent`. The next item, `parents[1]`, is the parent of `parents[0]`, and so on.

The `path.suffixes` property is a list of the suffixes, as some files can have more than one, especially on POSIX. These will be listed left to right, so `path.suffixes[-1]` is always the last suffix.

Now that I have this function, I can run a couple of paths through it to see the parts, which I'll do in Listings 11-49 and 11-50.

Parts of a Windows Path

I'll start by breaking down an absolute path on Windows. (It doesn't matter here whether you're working with a pure path or a concrete path; the paths *themselves* are structured the same in both.)

I break down the parts of an example path on Windows in Figure 11-1.

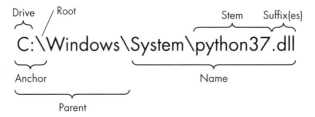

Figure 11-1: Parts of a Windows absolute path

In a Windows path, the anchor consists of the *drive*, which is C: in Figure 11-1, and a *root*, which is \. The *parent* is the path to the containing directory—in this case, C:\Windows\System\. That can be further broken down into three subparents: C:\ (also the anchor), Windows\, and System\.

The *name* consists of the *stem*, which is usually the filename (python37) before the first nonleading dot; and the *suffix* or *suffixes*, which is the file extension (.dll) after the dot.

I'll break that down again, using my function from Listing 11-48:

```
path_parts(pathlib.PureWindowsPath('C:/Windows/System/python37.dll'))
```

Listing 11-49: path_parts.py:2a

You'll notice that I used forward slashes as the directory separator, which are not typically employed in Windows paths. The pathlib module allows me to use either forward slashes (/) or escaped backslashes (\\) for paths on any system, and it handles the switch behind the scenes. (Remember that single backslashes are escape characters in Python.) Forward slashes are less prone to typos, and using them eliminates the risk of accidentally omitting one of the pair of backslashes. I therefore recommend sticking with forward slashes when you can.

Running that code outputs all the parts of the path:

```
C:\Windows\System\python37.dll

Drive: C:
Root: \
Anchor: C:\

Parent: C:\Windows\System

Parents [0]: C:\Windows\System
Parents [1]: C:\Windows
Parents [2]: C:\
Name: python37.dll
```

```
Suffix: .dll
Suffixes [0]: .dll
Stem: python37
```

This is consistent with the parts I outlined in Figure 11-1. I have the absolute path to each parent in ascending order, starting from the immediate parent of the file, C:\Windows\System.

The name is python37.dll, which is broken into the stem (python37) and one suffix (.dll).

Parts of a POSIX Path

Filesystem paths on UNIX-like systems, like Linux or macOS, are a little different. They follow the path conventions laid out by the POSIX standard.

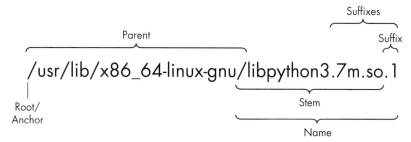

Figure 11-2: Parts of a POSIX absolute path

In a POSIX absolute path, the *root* only contains the *anchor* (/). The *drive* part is always empty on POSIX paths, but the property itself exists for compatibility. The *name* part at the end consists of a *stem* (which again is generally the filename) before the first nonleading dot, plus one or more *suffixes* (which usually make up the file extension).

Passing that path to my path_parts() function from Listing 11-48 shows all these parts:

```
path_parts(pathlib.PurePosixPath('/usr/lib/x86_64-linux-gnu/libpython3.7m.so.1'))
```

Listing 11-50: path_parts.py:2b

The output is as follows:

```
/usr/lib/x86_64-linux-gnu/libpython3.7m.so.1

Drive:
Root: /
Anchor: /

Parent: /usr/lib/x86_64-linux-gnu

Parents [0]: /usr/lib/x86_64-linux-gnu
Parents [1]: /usr/lib
Parents [2]: /usr
Parents [3]: /
```

```
Name: libpython3.7m.so.1
Suffix: .1
Suffixes [0]: .7m
Suffixes [1]: .so
Suffixes [2]: .1
Stem: libpython3.7m.so
```

This example demonstrates a unique issue you may encounter with file extensions. While there are valid file extensions that consist of multiple suffixes, such as *.tar.gz* (for a GZ-compressed tarball), not every suffix is part of the file extension. This is a perfect example: the intended filename is libpython3.7m, but pathlib incorrectly interprets the .7m as one of the suffixes because of its leading dot. Meanwhile, because the intended file extension (.so.1) is actually composed of two suffixes, the stem is incorrectly detected as libpython3.7m.so and the suffix as just .1. You'll need to keep this in mind when looking for the file extension on a path. There's no simple or obvious way to resolve this; you have to take it case by case, as needed for your code. In short, don't rely too much on pathlib's ability to discern the stem and suffix; it can fail you in quite annoying ways.

Creating a Path

You can define a path using the desired class initializer, such as PureWindowsPath or PosixPath, by passing the path as a string. From there, you can use the path with open() or any other file operation. For example, on my own UNIX system, I can access my bash history like this:

```
from pathlib import PosixPath

path = PosixPath('/home/jason/.bash_history')
```

Listing 11-51: read_from_path.py:1a

Because I'm specifying a POSIX-format path and I plan to access the underlying filesystem using the methods on my path object, I use PosixPath class. If I wanted this to work on Windows as well, I'd use Path, but since .bash_history isn't necessarily a file that appears on Windows, I'll stick with PosixPath here.

After initializing the path-like object and binding it to path, I can open it. There are two ways to do this; either pass it to open() or use the functionally identical open() method on the Path object (not available on PurePath). I'll use the latter:

```
with path.open('r') as file:
    for line in file:
        continue
    print(line.strip())
```

Listing 11-52: read_from_path.py:2

In this example, I only want the last line of the file, so I have to iterate over the whole thing. By time the loop finishes, the name line will have been bound to the string of the last line read. There's no easier way to seek the end of a text file for reading.

Finally, I print out this line, stripping off the trailing line break by using the strip() method.

Running that code shows me the last line I ran in my shell:

```
w3m nostarch.com
```

This works well on my machine, but it certainly won't work on yours, unless your username is *also* jason. It also won't work if your system structures home directories differently than mine. I need a more portable approach, and this is where pathlib really shines.

```
from pathlib import PosixPath

path = PosixPath.joinpath(PosixPath.home(), '.bash_history')
```

Listing 11-53: read_from_path.py:1b

The joinpath() method combines two or more paths together and is available on all six pathlib classes. PosixPath.home() returns the absolute path to the current user's home directory. (The same method exists on WindowsPath and refers to the user directory.)

I join .bash_history to this home directory path.

GOTCHA ALERT It's important not to include the anchor (the leading slash /) on any but the first argument passed to joinpath(). Such a path is considered absolute, and it will cause all the preceding arguments to be thrown away. (However, if you need to define an absolute path, you *will* need it on the first argument.)

I can use this new path in the exact same way as in Listing 11-51. Running the revised code produces the same output:

```
w3m nostarch.com
```

Yet, there's an even shorter way: pathlib classes implement the forward-slash operator (/) to make it easier to join path-like objects to each other, or even to strings:

```
from pathlib import PosixPath

path = PosixPath.home() / '.bash_history'
```

Listing 11-54: read_from_path.py:1c

I'll leave it to you to decide whether that reads cleaner than PosixPath. joinpath(), but I certainly prefer it. They're functionally identical, so use whichever one feels more readable in your particular situation.

There's one other shortcut I can use in this code. On UNIX-like systems, the tilde character (~) refers to the user's home folder, so I could just write my entire path using this convention and then have `pathlib` expand to the full absolute path:

```
from pathlib import PosixPath

path = PosixPath('~/.bash_history').expanduser()
```

Listing 11-55: read_from_path.py:1d

This is the most readable approach by far, and it behaves the same as before.

Relative Paths

A *relative* path is one that starts from the current position, instead of the root of the filesystem. Path-like objects can handle relative paths just as easily as absolute ones. Relative paths are based on the *current working directory*, which is the directory the user (or system) is currently running commands from.

This is useful, for example, if I have a Python program, `magic_program`, that I invoke from the command line and to which I can pass a path. The path will be received by the program as a string and will be interpreted as a `Path` object. If my current working directory were something long or difficult to type, it would be quite inconvenient to have to type an absolute path to a file contained in (or below) that directory, like this:

```
$ magic_program /home/jason/My_Nextcloud/DeadSimplePython/Status.txt
```

This invocation is painful! If I'm already in that *DeadSimplePython/* directory, I should be able to pass a relative path:

```
$ magic_program DeadSimplePython/Status.txt
```

Whew! That's much easier to use. Because of relative paths, it would be possible to write this program.

You can get the current working directory with the `Path.cwd()` command, like this:

```
from pathlib import Path
print(Path.cwd())
```

That code would print out the absolute path to the current working directory, in the appropriate path format for your system.

Any path that does not lead with an anchor (typically /) is considered a relative path. Additionally, a single dot (.) represents the current directory, and a double dot (..) represents the previous, or parent, directory. In this way, you can construct a relative path in the same manner as an absolute path. For example, if I wanted to look for a `settings.ini` file in the parent of the current working directory, I could do so with the following:

```
from pathlib import Path
path = Path('../settings.ini')
```

This path can be converted to an absolute path using the `Path.resolve()` method. It resolves the dot operators (. and ..) in paths and any symbolic links. Other redundant path elements, such as extra slashes or unnecessary dot operators (such as ./dir1/../dir1///dir2), are cleaned up.

Although I could resolve the path in a subsequent line of code, I prefer to modify that line to resolve the path right on the spot.

```
from pathlib import Path
path = Path('../settings.ini').resolve()
```

path is now an absolute path to *settings.ini*.

Paths Relative to Package

Sooner or later, you'll want to package noncode resources (like images or sounds) alongside your Python project and then access them from your code. You won't know for certain where the user has placed your Python project directory on his or her filesystem; even if you knew where it *should* be, the user or system might have moved it. You need a way to create the absolute path to the noncode resources you shipped with your package. "Aha!" you may think. "This is a perfect situation for a relative path!" You would be wrong.

A common trap to fall into is to assume that the current working directory is the location of the current or main Python module. *That is not necessarily the case!* When you set up your project correctly, as I described in Chapter 4, you can run a Python module from anywhere on the system. Your current location is the current working directory, and all paths will be relative to that location. You need a way to find the resources that does *not* depend on the current working directory; in other words, relative paths are out.

I'll use my *omission* project from Chapter 4 as an example. Here's the project structure:

```
omission-git/
├── LICENSE.md
├── omission/
│   ├── __init__.py
│   ├── __main__.py
│   ├── app.py
│   ├── common/
│   ├── data/
│   ├── interface/
│   ├── game/
│   │   ├── __init__.py
│   │   └── content_loader.py
│   ├── resources/
│   │   ├── audio/
│   │   ├── content/
│   │   │   └── content.txt
│   │   ├── font/
│   │   └── icons/
│   └── tests/
├── omission.py
```

```
├── pylintrc
├── README.md
└── .gitignore
```

Listing 11-56: File structure for omission *project*

With my module *omission/game/contentloader.py*, I want to load the text file containing the game content, which is stored at *omission/resources/content/content.txt*.

In my initial attempt, I incorrectly assumed the current working directory would be the location of *content_loader.py*. Thus, I tried to open the *content.txt* file with a relative path something like this:

```python
from pathlib import Path

path = Path('../resources/content/content.txt')

with path.open() as file:
    data = file.read()
```

Listing 11-57: content_loader.py:1a

Because I was starting my *omission* program by running *omission.py* from the root of my repository, *omission-git* was incidentally my working directory, so this code appeared to work.

Temporarily sticking the following line of code into my *content_loader.py* module confirmed that, by printing out the absolute path to that directory:

```python
print(Path.cwd())  # prints '/home/jason/Code/omission-git'
```

"That's easy," I thought to myself. "I just write all my paths relative to omission-git." (This is where things went really wrong!) I changed my code to use paths relative to that *omission-git/* directory like this:

```python
from pathlib import Path

path = Path('omission/resources/content/content.txt')

with path.open() as file:
    data = file.read()
```

Listing 11-58: content_loader.py:1b

The program appeared to work now—I could pass path to open() and read the contents without any problems. All my tests passed, and I happily moved on. It wasn't until I started packaging that I discovered something was still wrong. If I executed the *omission.py* module from any directory other than the one it was stored in, the program would crash with a FileNotFoundError.

After checking the current working directory again, as before, I realized what I mentioned earlier: the current working directory is wherever the module is invoked *from*, not where it lives, and all paths are relative to that current working directory.

The solution was to base my relative paths off of the special __file__ attribute of modules, which contains the absolute path to the module on the current system. I utilize that special attribute like this:

```
from pathlib import Path

path = Path(__file__).resolve()
path = path.parents[1] / Path('resources/content/content.txt')

with path.open() as file:
    data = file.read()
```

Listing 11-59: content_loader.py:1c

I convert the __file__ attribute to a Path object. Since this attribute may return a relative path, I use resolve() to convert it to an absolute path, so I don't have to bother with the current working directory. path is now an absolute path to the current module. I need to work with an absolute path for the rest of this code to work.

Next, now that I have an absolute path to this *content_loader.py* module, I can craft a path to the file I want *relative to this module*. Knowing my project's directory structure, I need to start from the top-level package, omission, instead of in the game subpackage this module is in. I get this part of the path with path.parents[1], for the parent path, one level removed.

Finally, I combine the absolute path of the omission package with the relative path to the file I want. The result is an absolute path to my *content.txt* file that will work, no matter where the omission package lives on the filesystem or where it's executed from.

This approach works for most practical cases, but beware that __file__ is an *optional* attribute. It's not defined for built-in modules, C modules that are statically linked to the interpreter, and anything run in the REPL. To get around these problems, you can use the rather robust pkg_resources module to achieve the same end as you would with __file__. You can learn more about this from *https://setuptools.readthedocs.io/en/latest/pkg_resources.html.*

Unfortunately, both __file__ and libraries like pkg_resources are incompatible with some packaging tools. This is really more of problem with the tools than with the pattern, since no one has any alternatives! There's no more elegant solution here. Just be aware of this limitation when selecting packaging tools.

Path Operations

The pathlib concrete path objects provide methods of performing many common file operations in a platform-agnostic fashion. Two of the most convenient of these methods are Path.read_text() and Path.write_text(), which provide a quick way to read and write entire text files without having to define a separate stream object or with statement. In this usage, the stream object is created and managed internally, within the Path object. The former reads in and returns the entire contents of the file as a string; the latter writes a string out as a file, overwriting the existing file if there is one.

Table 11-2 outlines several more of the file operation methods on Path. Each of these would be run directly on a Path, WindowsPath, or PosixPath object, referred to as path below.

Table 11-2: Filesystem Operations on Path

File operation methods	Functionalities
path.mkdir()	Creates a directory at path. If the optional parents= argument is True, it will create any missing parent directories.
path.rename(*name*)	Renames the item (file or directory) at path to *name*. On Unix, if the file *name* exists at the path and the user has the correct permissions, it will be replaced.
path.replace(*name*)	Renames the item (file or directory) at path to *name*, replacing any existing file by that name. Unlike rename, this will *always* replace any existing file by the same name, assuming the correct file permissions.
path.rmdir()	Removes the directory at path. It must be empty; otherwise, an OSError will be raised.
path.unlink()	Removes the file or symbolic link (filesystem shortcut) at path. Cannot be used to remove directories. In Python 3.8 and later, if the optional missing_ok= argument is True, attempting to remove a file that does not exist will *not* raise FileNotFoundError.
path.glob()	Returns a generator of path-like objects for all items at path that match the specified *pattern*, according to the syntax of a Unix-style glob search.
path.iterdir()	Returns a generator of path-like objects for all items at path.
path.touch()	Creates an empty file at path. Normally, nothing happens if it already exists. If the optional exist_ok= argument is False and the file exists, a FileExistsError is raised.
path.symlink_to(*target*)	Creates a symbolic link at path to *target*.
path.link_to(*target*)	Creates a hard link at path to *target* (Python 3.8 and later only).

In addition, you get information about the file or directory a Path object points to, as shown in Table 11-3.

Table 11-3: File Information Methods on Path

File information methods	Functionalities
path.exists()	Returns True if path points to an existing file or symbolic link.
path.is_file()	Returns True if path points to a file or symbolic link to a file.
path.is_dir()	Returns True if path points to a directory or symbolic link to a directory.
path.is_symlink()	Returns True if path points to a symbolic link.
path.is_absolute()	Returns True if path is absolute.

I've only covered a portion of `pathlib`'s functionality. I strongly recommend you browse through the official module documentation, which has a complete list of methods and their usages: *https://docs.python.org/3/library/pathlib.html*.

Out-of-Place File Writes

As I mentioned earlier in the chapter, `path.replace()` is particularly useful as part of a technique for preventing file corruption if there's a computer or program crash during writing. Instead of directly modifying a file in place, you can write to a new file and then replace the old file with the new version.

To demonstrate this, I'll rewrite one of my earlier examples (Listings 11-37 through 11-39) to employ `pathlib` and use this technique:

```python
from pathlib import Path

path = Path('78SomewhereRd.txt')

with path.open('r') as real_estate_listing:
    contents = real_estate_listing.read()
    contents = contents.replace('Tiny', 'Cozy')
    contents = contents.replace('Needs repairs', 'Full of potential')
    contents = contents.replace('Small', 'Compact')
    contents = contents.replace('old storage shed', 'detached workshop')
    contents = contents.replace('Built on ancient burial ground.',
                                'Unique atmosphere.')
```

Listing 11-60: rewrite_using_tmp.py:1

I read in the file from *78SomewhereRd.txt* as before, except that this time, I only open the file in read mode, instead of read-write. Once I've finished with it, I can safely close the file. My revised data is waiting in the string `contents`.

Now, I create a new temporary file path and write my data out to that new file:

```python
tmp_path = path.with_name(path.name + '.tmp')

with tmp_path.open('w') as file:
    file.write(contents)
```

Listing 11-61: rewrite_using_tmp.py:2

I use `path.with_name()` to create a new `Path`, with the name provided as an argument. In this case, the new name is the same as the old name, but with `.tmp` appended to the end. I open that new path in write mode and write the string `contents` out to it.

At this point, my original *78SomewhereRd.txt* and my new *78SomewhereRd.txt.tmp* files exist side by side. I conclude by moving the temporary file into the place of the original, overwriting it.

```python
tmp_path.replace(path)   # move the new file into place of the old one
```

Listing 11-62: rewrite_using_tmp.py:3

That `replace()` method has the operating system perform the replacement, instead of doing it itself. This is a virtually instantaneous operation, in contrast to writing to the file, which may take a bit of time, depending on the size. Now, I only have the revised *78SomewhereRd.txt*, and the temporary file is gone.

The benefit of this technique is that, had my computer crashed while I was writing to the file, the worst outcome would be that I'd have a corrupt *78SomewhereRd.txt.tmp* file. My original *78SomewhereRd.txt* would be unchanged and unharmed.

The os Module

Python's os module allows you to interface with the operating system in a relatively platform-agnostic fashion. Most code written before Python 3.6, and even a lot of modern code, still uses the `os.path` and os modules for handling paths. As I've mentioned, `pathlib` is going to be the better tool for working with the filesystem in most cases, but os still has many uses. For some longtime Python developers, using os is also just a habit.

As of Python 3.8, `os.path` has 12 functions, with no existing equivalent in `pathlib`. One example is `os.path.getsize(`*pathlike*`)`, which returns the size of the item at *pathlike* in bytes. Meanwhile, os itself has dozens of functions for interacting with the filesystem in a much more low-level, technical fashion than `pathlib`.

Thankfully, since Python 3.6, `pathlib` and os play well together. I recommend using `pathlib` as much as you can—it will fully satisfy the majority of use cases—and bring in the os or `os.path` modules anytime you need one of their unique functionalities. The documentation will be helpful if you want to learn more about these modules: *https://docs.python.org/3/library/os.html*.

The os module is not limited to working with the filesystem, so it will come up again in later chapters.

File Formats

Up to this point, I've worked entirely with plaintext files. This works for storing plain strings, but it's not usually sufficient for more structured data. Here, I'll discuss working with other file formats.

In many cases, you'll get more reliable results by using an existing standard file format. However, it's always possible to design your own format and write custom parser logic for it, so long as you're willing to put the effort into designing, testing, and maintaining it.

Python offers tools for a few of the most common formats in the standard library, and many other formats are supported through third-party libraries. Here, I'll cover usage of the popular JSON format and then give an overview of a few other common formats.

The process of converting Python data to a format for storage is called *serialization*, and the reverse is *deserialization*.

JSON

JSON, or *JavaScript Object Notation*, is one of the most popular text-based file formats among Python developers. JSON data can be structured in a variety of ways, the most common being storing the contents of a Python dictionary in a file.

The built-in json module allows you to easily convert data between JSON data and many built-in Python data types and collections. In the case of JSON, serialization and deserialization are not perfect inverses of one another, as seen in Table 11-4.

Table 11-4: JSON Serialization and Deserialization Types

Python (to serialize)	JSON (serialized)	Python (deserialized)
dict	object (All keys are strings!)	dict
list tuple	array	list
bool	boolean	bool
str	string	str
int int-derived enums	number (int)	int
float float-derived enums	number (real)	float
None	null	None

Anything directly derived from these Python types can also be JSON-serialized, but all other objects *cannot* be serialized to JSON on their own and must be converted to a type that can be.

To make a custom class JSON-serializable, you would need to define a new object that subclasses json.JSONEncoder and overrides its default() method. See the documentation for more information about this: *https://docs.python.org/3/library/json.html#json.JSONEncoder*.

Writing to JSON

Writing to JSON is refreshingly simple, in comparison to working with many other file formats. You use the json.dump() function to convert data to JSON format and write it to a file. Alternatively, you use json.dumps() to create and write JSON code to a string if you want to wait and write it to a stream later. I'll demonstrate the former technique in this example.

I'll work with my nearby_properties nested dictionary from Listing 11-7, which I want to write out to a file I'll call *nearby.json*:

```python
import json

nearby_properties = {
    "N. Anywhere Ave.":
```

```
{
    123: 156_852,
    124: 157_923,
    126: 163_812,
    127: 144_121,
    128: 166_356
},
"N. Everywhere St.":
{
    4567: 175_753,
    4568: 166_212,
    4569: 185_123
}
}
```

Listing 11-63: write_house_json.py:1

The only change from the prior example (Listing 11-7) is that I'm now importing the json module.

I'm converting a dictionary containing only serializable types (see Table 11-4) directly to a stream using json.dump():

```
with open('nearby.json', 'w') as jsonfile:
    json.dump(nearby_properties, jsonfile)
```

Listing 11-64: write_house_json.py:2

First, I use open() to create a writable stream for the *nearby.json* file. The json.dump() function requires two arguments. The first is the object being written out, which can be *any* serializable object. In this case, I'm writing out the dictionary nearby_properties.

The second argument is the stream I want to write to, which must be a writable text-based stream. Here, I pass jsonfile, which is the text-based stream opened in write mode in the with statement.

That's all it takes to write a Python dictionary to a JSON file!

The json.dumps() function works in exactly the same manner, except that it returns a Python string containing the JSON code, rather than requiring you to pass a stream to it.

After running my code, I can open up the newly created *nearby.json* and see the contents, which are in JSON format:

```
{
    "N. Anywhere Ave.": {
        "123": 156852,
        "124": 157923,
        "126": 163812,
        "127": 144121,
        "128": 166356
    },
    "N. Everywhere St.": {
        "4567": 175753,
        "4568": 166212,
```

```
        "4569": 185123
    }
}
```

Listing 11-65: nearby.json

Reading from JSON

You can directly deserialize a JSON file into the corresponding Python
object using the json.load() function, which accepts the source stream
object as an argument. If I have JSON code in a Python string, I can
also deserialize it directly with json.loads(), passing the string as an
argument.

    I'll use json.load() to deserialize my nested dictionary from my *nearby
.json* file:

```
import json

with open('nearby.json', 'r') as jsonfile:
    nearby_from_file = json.load(jsonfile)
```

Listing 11-66: read_house_json.py:1

    I open the JSON file in read mode, and then I pass the stream to
json.load(). That will return the deserialized object, which in this case
is a dictionary I bind to nearby_from_file.

    There is one important difference between this dictionary and the one
I started with in Listing 11-65. I'll demonstrate this difference by printing
out the literal representation of each key and value:

```
for k1, v1 in nearby_from_file.items():
    print(repr(k1))
    for k2, v2 in v1.items():
        print(f'{k2!r}: {v2!r}')
```

Listing 11-67: read_house_json.py:2

    The f-string here embeds the values of k2 and v2 in the string, and the
!r formats them as if they had been run through repr().

    Can you spot the difference with this dictionary in the output?

```
'N. Anywhere Ave.'
'123': 156852
'124': 157923
'126': 163812
'127': 144121
'128': 166356
'N. Everywhere St.'
'4567': 175753
'4568': 166212
'4569': 185123
```

The key values for the inner dictionaries are strings now—instead of integers, as in the original dictionary (Listing 11-63)—because the key in a JSON object is always a string. This is a perfect example of serialization and deseralization not being inverse operations. If I wanted to get back to using integers for my keys, I'd need to rewrite this code to handle that conversion iteratively. That's beyond the scope of this chapter, so I'll leave this example as is.

Other Formats

I could devote an entire book just to working with file formats in Python (although I don't think my editor would go for it). Instead, I'll breeze through several of the most common formats. For each of these, you can pair the concepts from this chapter with the documentation for the particular modules or libraries you're using.

CSV

One of the most common structured text formats is *CSV*, which stands for *comma-separated values*. As its name suggests, it separates individual values with commas. Sets of values are separated by newline characters (\n).

CSV format is used by nearly all spreadsheets and databases, although seldom in a standardized manner. A CSV file exported by Excel may not be the same as one exported by a UNIX program. These subtle differences, known as *dialects*, ordinarily make working with CSV a bit tricky.

Python's standard library includes a csv module that not only handles serializing to and deserializing from CSV files, but also abstracts out the differences between CSV dialects.

To learn more about the csv module, see the Python documentation: *https://docs.python.org/3/library/csv.html#module-csv*.

INI

The *INI* format is excellent for storing configuration files, especially settings. It's an informal standard that is designed to be human-readable and easy to parse. You'll find INI files on Windows and Unix systems alike. You've almost certainly encountered files like *php.ini* and *Desktop.ini*—and perhaps, you've even encountered *tox.ini*, which is used by many Python tools, including flake8 and pytest. It's also common to find *.conf*, *.cfg*, and even *.txt* files that use this INI format.

Python's standard library includes the configparser module for working with INI-style files, although this module invented its own format for multiline strings. This makes the module's output potentially incompatible with anything other than Python's configparser, and it has no support for nested sections. It also can't work with the value-type prefixes used by Windows Registry-style INI files.

See the official documentation for configparser to learn how to use it: *https://docs.python.org/3/library/configparser.html#module-configparser*.

Alternatively, the third-party library *configobj* supports nested sections and the standard multiline strings, along with many other features lacking in configparser. Files created by this module are compatible with other INI parsers, especially those in other languages. The official documentation for this library is available at *https://configobj.readthedocs.io/en/latest/*.

XML

XML is a structured markup language based upon the idea of tags, elements, and attributes. Many other file formats use the XML syntax, including *XHTML*, *SVG*, *RSS*, and most office document formats (*DOCX* and *ODT*). You can use XML to devise your own text-based file formats.

Python developers often shun XML in favor of JSON, for two reasons: *simplicity of usage* and *security*. The same structures can be represented in both JSON and XML, but working with XML in Python involves eight different modules. These are all covered in detail at *https://docs.python.org/3/library/xml.html*. Given a choice between XML and JSON, you'll always find it easier to work with the latter.

XML also has a number of security vulnerabilities, which must be taken into account whenever you're deserializing untrusted or unauthenticated data. The built-in Python modules specifically are vulnerable to some of these attacks, so when security is a factor, the documentation advises use of the *defusedxml* and *defusedexpat* third-party libraries.

Alternatively, you can use the third-party library *lxml*, which addresses many of these issues. More information about this library is available at *https://lxml.de/*.

HTML

I doubt I need to tell you what *HTML* is, since it is ubiquitous on the internet. Python allows you to work with HTML files via the built-in html module and its two submodules: html.parser and html.entities. This is a very deep rabbit hole (unsurprisingly), so I'll leave you to explore it on your own if you're interested. The documentation is a good place to start: *https://docs.python.org/3/library/html.html*.

There are also some excellent third-party libraries for working with HTML, including *lxml.html* (part of *lxml*) and *beautifulsoup4*. You can learn more about the latter at *https://www.crummy.com/software/BeautifulSoup/*.

YAML

YAML is a popular alternative to markup languages like XML; its name is a recursive acronym for *YAML Ain't Markup Language*. YAML covers many of the same use cases as XML, but with a simpler syntax.

The latest version of this language—YAML 1.2—implements all the features of JSON, in addition to its own syntax. This means all JSON is also valid YAML 1.2. Besides this, all JSON output by Python using default settings is compatible with YAML 1.0 and 1.1. Thus, at least in Python, YAML is always a superset of JSON. One particular advantage of YAML over JSON is its support for comments.

The third-party *PyYAML* library is listed on the Python wiki as being the only YAML parser that has attempted compliance with the YAML standard. More information about this library can be found at *https://pyyaml.org/*.

YAML does have potential security concerns—namely, it can be used to execute arbitrary Python code. The PyYAML library has a `yaml.safe_load()` function that mitigates this risk, so that should be used instead of `yaml.load()`.

TOML

Another option for configuration files is *TOML*, an acronym for *Tom's Obvious, Minimal Language*. It's an open format created by Tom Preston-Werner. It draws inspiration from INI, but it implements a formal specification.

The most popular third-party library for working with TOML is appropriately called *toml*. You can learn more about it at *https://github.com/uiri/toml/*.

ODF

The *Open Document Format* (ODF) is an XML-based document format developed and maintained by the Organization for the Advancement of Structured Information Standards (OASIS). It is being widely adopted and is increasingly becoming a ubiquitous document standard. It is used by nearly all modern word processors, including LibreOffice, Microsoft Word, and Google Docs.

The primary use for ODF is when working with data ordinarily handled by an office suite. Perhaps you're writing a grammar checker, a spreadsheet validator, a word processor, or a slide deck organizer.

One of the most popular Python libraries for working with the Open Document Format is *odfpy*, which is developed and maintained by the European Environmental Agency. More information and documentation for this library is available at *https://github.com/eea/odfpy/wiki/*.

RTF

The *Rich Text Format* (RTF) is a popular document format that supports basic text formatting. Although it's a proprietary format originally developed by Microsoft for Word, it's relatively common for basic documents because of its simplicity and portability. Although the format is no longer in active development and has lost ground to the Open Document Format, it is still just as usable as ever.

There are a few third-party packages for working with Rich Text Format. The most popular library for Python 2 was *PyRTF*. Two forks of that library exist for Python 3: *PyRTF3* and *rtfx*. (As of this writing, the *PyRTF3* library is unmaintained, although it is still available in pip.) *RTFMaker* is a newer alternative, presently under active development. Unfortunately, documentation for all four libraries is sparse, so plan on sailing into uncharted waters if you use any of these libraries.

Alternatively, if none of these libraries do what you need or you don't want to work without documentation, the Rich Text Format is simple enough that you can write your own basic parser with a little research. It's a closed specification, so it can be hard to find the official documents, but version 1.5 of the Rich Text Format Specification is archived here: *http://www.biblioscape.com/rtf15_spec.htm*.

Wrapping Up

Who would have guessed how much was involved in working with text files in Python? I've only scratched the surface of this topic, the complexity of which is belied by the existence of so many five-minute beginner's tutorials.

Opening a file is easy enough, using a `with` statement and the `open()` function. The `pathlib` module handles paths in a platform-agnostic fashion, so you can stop worrying about which way your slash is supposed to lean. Dozens of modules (from the standard library and third-party developers) exist for handling the countless text-based file formats out there, often via a few method calls. When you put all these pieces together, you ultimately get delightfully simple, yet robust, patterns for handling text files.

In the next chapter, I'll introduce the techniques necessary to work with binary data in Python, especially in the context of reading and writing binary files.

It feels good to move beyond the boundaries of the program execution and create real files on the user's computer, doesn't it?

12

BINARY AND SERIALIZATION

01100010 01101001 01101110 01100001 01110010 01111001. This is the language of computers, the delight of hackers, and the subject of that one computer science joke you have memorized. If a programming language wants a chance to gain the admiration of elite developers, it must allow working with *binary*.

For the programmers who haven't encountered binary yet, I'll start by breaking down the fundamentals, particularly as Python sees them, and the different ways of expressing binary data and performing bitwise operations. With that foundation in place, I'll cover how to read and write files in binary, and I'll wrap up with a whirlwind tour of some of the most common binary file formats.

Binary Notation and Bitwise

For those who are new to the fine art of bit twiddling, I'll breeze through it now. Even if you already know how to do bitwise manipulation, I recommend hanging in there for the next few pages for a review—and perhaps some little surprises.

Number Systems Refresher

Binary is a number system with only two digits—0 and 1—which correspond to the open and closed position (respectively) of gates on circuit boards. This is the foundation of all computer programming. Typically, this binary is abstracted out for better human comprehension through CPU instructions and data types, and then further toward human language through various programming constructs. Although you won't usually need to think much about binary, there are times when manipulating it directly is the most effective way to solve a problem.

In Python, when writing a numeric literal in binary, you prefix it with 0b to differentiate it from run-of-the-mill decimal (base-10) numbers. For example, while 11 is the decimal value "eleven," 0b11 is the binary value for "three."

A binary *bit* is a single digit. A *byte* is usually made up of eight bits, although uncommonly, this can vary. Within a byte, place values typically ascend from right to left, as with decimal numbers. You can compose any number by switching on (1) or off (0) the bits at different positions. In a byte, the rightmost place has a value of 1, and each subsequent place has double the preceding value. The value of each place is demonstrated in Table 12-1.

Table 12-1: Place Values of Bits

128	64	32	16	8	4	2	1

So, the byte 0b01011010 would be equivalent to 64 + 16 + 8 + 2, or 90. The computer interprets particular bytes differently, depending on the data type—something determined by the code, rather than stored in the binary data. From a low-level perspective, the same sequence of bits could represent the integer 90, the ASCII character 'Z', a part of a floating-point number, a bytecode instruction . . . the possibilities are endless. Thankfully, you don't need to worry about how the computer handles this interpretation. Trust the language for that.

Hexadecimal

You can also represent numeric literals in the *hexadecimal*, or base-16 number system, which is so named because there are 16 unique digits for the decimal values 0 through 15. The first 10 use the ordinary digits 0 through 9 and the letters A through F as digits for values 10 through 15, respectively. The decimal value 16 cannot be represented with a single digit in hexadecimal; it is instead represented by 10 in this system. In Python, as in most programming languages, you prefix hexadecimal literals with 0x to differentiate them from decimal numbers. 0x15 would represent decimal value 21, because 0x10 (16) + 0x05 (5) = 0x15 (21).

When manually composing larger numbers in any number system, mentally or on paper, it's useful to think of each *place value* as the base value raised to the place number (starting from zero). For example, the decimal number 4972 could be thought of as 2 + 70 + 900 + 4000, which can further be broken down as $(2 * 10^0) + (7 * 10^1) + (9 * 10^2) + (4 * 10^3)$.

Table 12-2 demonstrates this with base 10 (decimal), base 2 (binary), and base 16 (hexadecimal).

Table 12-2: Place Values in Various Number Systems

Number system	Place values				
	$10000\ (n^4)$	$1000\ (n^3)$	$100\ (n^2)$	$10\ (n^1)$	$1\ (n^0)$
Decimal	$10^4\ (10000)$	$10^3\ (1000)$	$10^2\ (100)$	$10^1\ (10)$	$10^0\ (1)$
Binary	$2^4\ (16)$	$2^3\ (8)$	$2^2\ (4)$	$2^1\ (2)$	$2^0\ (1)$
Hexadecimal	$16^4\ (65536)$	$16^3\ (4096)$	$16^2\ (256)$	$16^1\ (16)$	$16^0\ (1)$

You can use this principle to convert a decimal value to another system, such as hexadecimal. For example, if I wanted to convert the decimal value 2630, I'd first determine the highest place value needed with the formula $\lfloor \log_{16} 2630 \rfloor$, which gives me 2. Then, I'd perform the conversion as shown in Table 12-3.

Table 12-3: Converting Decimal to Hexadecimal

Value to convert	2630	70	6
Place value	$\lfloor 2630/16^2 \rfloor$ = 0xA (10)	$\lfloor 70/16^1 \rfloor$ = 0x4	$\lfloor 6/16^0 \rfloor$ = 0x6
Current hexadecimal value	0xA00	0xA40	0xA46
Calculate remaining value	$2630\ \%\ 16^2$ = **70**	$70\ \%\ 16^1$ = **6**	$6\ \%\ 16^0$ = 0

The decimal value 2630 has the hexadecimal value 0xA46.

Hexadecimal is useful in the context of binary because you can exactly express each possible value of a byte (eight bits) in two digits, from 0x00 (0) to 0xFF (255). Hexadecimal is a more succinct way of representing binary: 0b10101010 can be written as 0xAA.

Hexadecimal Humor

Hexadecimal employs the first six letters of the Latin alphabet as digits, and among developers, this has led to a traditional brand of puns known as *hexspeak*. Hexadecimal numbers such as 0xDEADBEEF and 0xC0FFEE have valid numeric values and are visually recognizable; the former has traditionally been used on some ancient IBM systems for uninitialized memory, because it was easy to spot amidst the wall of hexadecimal that was a core dump.

In the same way, you can sometimes mark special data in your binary. This can make your binary files a little easier to read and debug manually, and besides, it's fun! Just be mindful that normal data may coincidentally show up in hexspeak, too—for example, a normal integer value that happens to read as 0xDEADBEEF—so use it with caution.

Octal

The third most common number system for representing binary data is *octal*, or base-8. Octal literals are prefixed with 0o (zero, followed by a lowercase letter *o*). Octal uses digits for decimal values 0 through 7, but it writes 8 as 0o10. Thus, decimal values 9 and 10 would be 0o11 and 0o12, respectively.

Table 12-4 shows that place value table again, this time including octal.

Table 12-4: Place Values in Various Number Systems

Number systems	Place values				
	10000 (n^4)	1000 (n^3)	100 (n^2)	10 (n^1)	1 (n^0)
Decimal	10^4 (10000)	10^3 (1000)	10^2 (100)	10^1 (10)	10^0 (1)
Binary	2^4 (16)	2^3 (8)	2^2 (4)	2^1 (2)	2^0 (1)
Octal	8^4 (4096)	8^3 (512)	8^2 (64)	8^1 (8)	8^0 (1)
Hexadecimal	16^4 (65536)	16^3 (4096)	16^2 (256)	16^1 (16)	16^0 (1)

Every 8-bit byte can be represented by three octal digits, with the highest value (0xFF) being 0o377. Although octal doesn't map to bytes as cleanly or obviously as hexadecimal, it is still useful in some scenarios because it's more compact than binary but doesn't require six extra digits like hexadecimal. Octal is used for UNIX file permissions, and it simplifies specifying individual parts of some UTF-8 characters and some assembly op codes. If you have trouble picturing these use cases, you probably don't need octal. You could go through your entire career without needing it! Regardless, it is helpful to know about it for the rare cases when you might need it.

Number Systems on Integers

It's important to remember that binary, octal, decimal, and hexadecimal are all *number systems*; that is, they're different ways of representing the same *whole number*, or *integer*. The decimal number 12 can be represented as 0b1100, 0xc, or 0o14, but binding any of these literals to a name in Python will still store an integer with the decimal value 12.

Consider the following:

```
chapter = 0xc
print(chapter)  # prints '12'
```

Listing 12-1: print_integer.py:1a

By default, printing an integer always shows the value in decimal. I can instead show the value in another number system by using one of the built-in functions for that purpose: bin(), oct(), or hex():

```
chapter = 0xc
print(bin(chapter))  # prints '0b1100'
print(hex(chapter))  # prints '0xc'
print(oct(chapter))  # prints '0o14'
```

Listing 12-2: print_integer.py:1b

Regardless of how you display it, the actual value bound to chapter is unchanged.

Two's Complement

In binary on most computers, negative numbers are represented as the *two's complement* of the positive number. This technique is preferred over simply using a single bit to indicate positive or negative, as it allows you to store one additional value in the byte.

For example, the positive number 42 would be 0b00101010 in binary. To get -42, I'd find the two's complement by inverting each of the bits (giving me 0b11010101) and then adding 0b1, ultimately producing 0b11010110 (you carry the 1: 0b01 + 0b01 = 0b10).

To convert a negative number back to a positive, you only need to repeat the process. Starting with -42, or 0b11010110, I invert each of the bits, giving me 0b00101001. Then, I add 0b1, producing 0b00101010, which is positive 42.

Python *almost* uses two's complement—it actually does something more complex, as you'll see in a later section—so it instead shows negative binary numbers by placing a negative sign on the binary representation of the positive form of the number, as seen below:

```
print(bin(42))   # prints  '0b101010'
print(bin(-42))  # prints '-0b101010'
```

Listing 12-3: negative_binary.py:1

As a bit wrangler myself, this may be the only thing I dislike about Python, although I understand its purpose.

Thankfully, it is possible to see the (approximate) two's complement notation by using a *bitmask*, a binary value that uses strategically placed 1s to keep certain bits in a value and throw away the rest. In this case, I want the first eight bits of the value (one byte), so I take the bitwise AND the value with a bitmask of eight 1s:

```
print(bin(-42 & 0b11111111))  # prints '0b11010110'
```

Listing 12-4: negative_binary.py:2

That shows exactly what I'd expect: the eight-bit-long two's complement representation of -42.

Byte Order

In this section, I'm not referring to Python at all, but rather to the computer memory *underneath* everything. We're all the way down to silicon right now.

Most data is made up of multiple bytes, but the sequence the bytes appear in depends on the *byte order* used by your platform: either *big-endian* or *little-endian*.

Byte order has everything to do with how the computer stores data in memory. Each one-byte-wide slot in memory has a numeric address, typically represented in hexadecimal. Memory addresses are consecutive. Let's consider a value, say 0xAABBCCDD (2,864,434,397 in decimal), that is composed of four bytes: 0xAA, 0xBB, 0xCC, and 0xDD. This value can be stored in a four-byte-wide chunk of memory, with each byte having an address. For example, the computer might decide to store that data in the memory at addresses 0xABCDEF01, 0xABCDEF02, 0xABCDEF03, and 0xABCDEF04, as shown in Table 12-5.

Table 12-5: An Empty Four-Byte Chunk of Memory with Addresses

Address	0xABCDEF01	0xABCDEF02	0xABCDEF03	0xABCDEF04
Value				

Now here's the challenge: in what order do we store those bytes? Your first instinct might be to store them as you'd write them on paper, like in Table 12-6.

Table 12-6: Data Stored in Memory in Big-Endian Byte Order

Address	0xABCDEF01	0xABCDEF02	0xABCDEF03	0xABCDEF04	Whole value
Hex value	0xAA	0xBB	0xCC	0xDD	= 0xAABBCCDD
Equivalent	2852126720	+ 12255232	+ 52224	+ 221	= 2864434397

We call this byte order *big-endian*, because the value representing the largest part of the value is stored in the lowest, or leftmost, address. The big-endian byte order is often the easiest to reason about, because it orders bytes from left to right, just like how you'd write it on paper.

In contrast, on little-endian systems, the bytes are reversed, as shown in Table 12-7.

Table 12-7: Data Stored in Memory in Little-Endian Byte Order

Address	0xABCDEF01	0xABCDEF02	0xABCDEF03	0xABCDEF04	Whole value
Hex value	0xDD	0xCC	0xBB	0xAA	= 0xDDCCBBAA
Equivalent	221	+ 52224	+ 12255232	+ 2852126720	= 2864434397

As the name *little-endian* suggests, the byte representing the smallest part of the number is stored in the lowest memory address.

Endianness only affects primitive data types, like integers and floating-point numbers. It will not affect collections, such as strings, which are just arrays of individual characters.

Although little-endian byte order sounds confusing, it makes a few little technical optimizations possible on the hardware. Most modern computers, including all Intel and AMD processors, use little-endian.

In most programming languages, we conventionally write binary numbers in big-endian. It's the byte order used when you display an integer in binary in Python with bin().

Often, the only time you need to be concerned about byte order is when your binary data is going to leave your program, such as when writing it to a file or sending it over a network.

Python Integers and Binary

Like in most programming languages, binary and hexadecimal literals are integers in Python. However, one implementation detail behind Python integers bleeds into the binary logic of the language: *integers are effectively infinite.*

In Python 2, the int type had a fixed size of 32 bits, or four bytes. Python 2 also had the long type, which had an unlimited size. In Python 3, the long type was adopted as the new int, so all integers now have a theoretically infinite size.

This behavior has one critical consequence for binary: two's complement notation must effectively lead with an infinite number of 1 bits. This is why Python uses the rather unconventional negative binary notation. There's no rational way to express an infinite number of 1s! It also means you can't directly type a binary literal for a negative integer. Instead, you have to use the negation operator (-) before the binary literal of the *positive* integer and trust Python to figure things out.

Since Python uses that negative binary notation, the negative binary form of a number reads the same as the positive binary form. The two's complement notation would only be accurate if you could see the infinite leading 1 bits. This has a weird consequence elsewhere, as you'll see shortly.

Bitwise Operations

You can work directly with binary data using the *bitwise operators*, which perform operations on individual bits. There are six bitwise operators, and Python offers all of them, although a couple behave a bit differently than you'd ordinarily expect.

The *Bitwise And* operator (&) produces a new binary value, where each bit is 1 if the corresponding bits in the left and right operands are both 1.

For example, 0b1101 & 0b1010 produces 0b1000, because only the leftmost bit is 1 in both operands:

```
  0b1101
& 0b1010
= 0b1000
```

The *Bitwise Or* operator (|) produces a value where each bit is 1 if either the left or the right operand is 1 (or if both are). For example, 0b1101 | 0b1010 produces 0b1111, because each of the four bits is on in at least one of the operands.

```
  0b1101
| 0b1010
= 0b1111
```

The *Bitwise Exclusive Or* operator (^), also known as a *Bitwise XOR*, sets a bit to 1 if it is on in either operand, but not in both. For example, 0b1101 ^ 0b1010 produces 0b0111; the first bit is on in both operands, so it is off here, but the other three bits are on in only one operand, so they're included.

```
  0b1101
^ 0b1010
= 0b0111
```

The *Bitwise Inversion* operator (~), also known as the *Bitwise Not*, flips each bit in the operand given, such that 0b0101 would become (approximately) 0b1010.

```
~ 0b0101
= 0b1010
```

However, since in Python, integers are infinite, the new value would have infinite leading 1 bits. Therefore, the real result of ~0b0101 is actually 0b111...1010.

```
~ 0b000...0101
= 0b111...1010
```

Since infinite 1s are hard to print, Python shows the result in negative binary notation—placing a negative sign at the front and subtracting 1 to get around the two's complement. Remember, this convention is what allows Python to display a negative number as the negative binary form of the positive number. Unfortunately, it makes it a bit harder to read the results of normal bit twiddling.

Whenever this gets in your way, you can print the bitmasked form:

```
print(bin(~0b0101))            # prints '-0b110' (that is, -0b0101 - 0b1)
print(bin(~0b0101 & 0b1111))   # prints '0b1010' (much better)
```

Listing 12-5: bitwise_inversion.py

Remember that the first value is *internally* correct, as it has the infinite leading 1s that make it a negative Python integer. The second only *looks* correct, but it lacks those leading 1s, so it's actually wrong.

The last two bitwise operators are the *Left Shift* (<<) and *Right Shift* (>>) operators. In binary arithmetic, there are two types of shifts, of which a programming language can only use one on its shift operators. The *logical shift* allows bits to "drop off" the end of the number, shifting in zeros at the other end to replace discarded bits. The *arithmetic shift* does the same as the logical shift, but it will also shift in the *sign bit* (1 in negative numbers) where necessary to preserve the sign.

Every language must decide which form of bitwise shift its operators should use, and Python uses the *arithmetic shift*. In addition, because of the infinite nature of integers, you cannot discard bits with a left shift; the integer will keep growing to accommodate them, as you can see here:

```
print(bin(0b1100 << 4))    # prints '0b11000000'
```

Listing 12-6: bitwise_shift.py:1

That probably won't have any profound effect on your code, but it may change how you implement some binary algorithms that rely on discarding bits with a left shift.

A right shift will preserve the sign, so it will shift in 0s on the left for positive integers and 1s for negative integers:

```
print(bin(0b1100 >> 4))    # prints  '0b0' (0b0...0000)
print(bin(-0b1100 >> 4))   # prints '-0b1' (0b1...1111)
```

Listing 12-7: bitwise_shift.py:2

In summary, Table 12-8 shows those bitwise operators again, as well as their corresponding special methods.

Table 12-8: Bitwise Operators

Operator	Use	Binary (not Python) example	Special method
&	Bitwise And	1100 & 1011 ⇒ 1000	__and__(*a*, *b*)
|	Bitwise Or	1100 | 1011 ⇒ 1111	__or__(*a*, *b*)
^	Bitwise Exclusive Or (Bitwise XOR)	1100 ^ 1011 ⇒ 0111	__xor__(*a*, *b*)
~	Bitwise Inversion (Bitwise Not)	~1100 ⇒ 0011	__inv__(*a*) __invert__(*a*)
<<	Left (arithmetic) Shift	0111 << 2 ⇒ 11100	__lshift__(*a*, *b*)
>>	Right (arithmetic) Shift	0111 >> 2 ⇒ 0001 1..1010 2 ⇒ 1..1110	__rshift__(*a*, *b*)

These operators also work on boolean values, which are internally based on integers (much to the consistent annoyance of one of my colleagues!). They won't work like this on other types—only on booleans and integers.

Be cautious when using bitwise with existing custom classes! Because they're uncommonly used compared to many other operators, some classes choose to repurpose the bitwise operators for altogether unrelated purposes. Thus, performing bitwise operations on anything except an integer or boolean can result in wildly unpredictable behavior. Be sure to read the documentation on any class you want to use before you rely on the bitwise operators with it!

You can make your own objects work with the bitwise operators themselves by implementing the corresponding special methods from Table 12-8.

Bytes Literals

Another way to represent binary in Python is with a *bytes literal*, which looks like a string literal prepended with b, such as b"HELLO" or b"\xAB\x42". These are not strings, but rather sequences of bytes, with each byte represented by either an ASCII character (such as "H" for 0x48) or a hexadecimal escape sequence (such as "\x42" for 0x42). Unlike integer objects, bytes literals have the explicit size and implied byte order you give them.

Here's that example bytes literal, which contains the binary equivalent of the string "HELLO":

```
bits = b"HELLO"
```

Listing 12-8: bytes_literal.py:1a

Although a bytes literal isn't exactly a string, most of the rules of string literals still apply here, with two major exceptions. First, a bytes literal can only contain ASCII characters (values 0x00 to 0xFF), partly because each item in a bytes literal must be exactly one byte in size, and partly for backward compatibility with Python 2 and other languages that use ASCII text encoding. Second, unlike strings, bytes literals cannot be formatted via f-strings.

PEDANTIC NOTE   As of Python 3.5, you can format bytes literals with old-fashioned string formatting, known as *%-interpolation*. If you find yourself needing string formatting or substitution on bytes literals, see PEP 461.

In all Python strings, you can use the escape sequence '\xhh' to represent a character with the hexadecimal value *hh*. Unlike in some languages, the escape sequence must always contain a two-digit hexadecimal number. It does not matter whether the digits A through F are uppercase or lowercase: '\xAB' and '\xab' are treated the same, although Python always outputs the latter.

For example, if I knew the hexadecimal codes I needed for "HELLO", I could use them in place of some (or all) the ASCII character literals:

```
bits = b"\x48\x45\x4C\x4C\x4F"
```

Listing 12-9: bytes_literal.py:1b

These hexadecimal literals are also needed when the desired value cannot be represented by a visible character, such as '\x07', which in ASCII is the nonprinting control code BEL, which sounds the system bell. (And yes, print('\x07') will indeed play a sound, assuming you haven't turned off your system bell in your terminal or system settings.)

You can also create raw bytes literals, wherein the backslash character (\) is always treated as a literal character. Because of this, raw bytes literals cannot interpret escape sequences, which limits their usefulness. However, if you don't need escape sequences and do want literal backslashes, then raw bytes literals can occasionally come in handy. To define a raw bytes literal, precede the string with either rb or br. I demonstrate this below:

```
bits_escaped = b"\\A\\B\\C\\D\\E"
bits_raw = br"\A\B\C\D\E"
print(bits_raw)                   # prints b'\\A\\B\\C\\D\\E'
print(bits_escaped == bits_raw)   # prints 'True'
```

Listing 12-10: bytes_literal.py:2

Both bits_escaped and bits_raw have exactly the same value, as demonstrated by the comparison in the print() statement, but the value assigned to bits_raw was easier to type.

Bytes-Like Objects

If you need to store binary data, Python offers *bytes-like objects*. Unlike integers, these objects have a fixed size and an *implied* byte order. This means they have the byte order you followed when you provided the bytes to the bytes-like object; it also means you are responsible for explicitly defining the byte order of the data you provide. This can be helpful when the infinite nature of integers gets underfoot. Bytes-like objects also provide a number of utility functions, unlike bytes literals.

There's one drawback: the bitwise operators don't work with bytes-like objects. That may sound strange, and even annoying, and the exact reasons for this are largely unknown. There are two very plausible reasons, however.

First, it's essential to avoid unexpected behavior relating to byte order. If you tried to perform a bitwise operation on a big-endian and a little-endian object greater than one byte, the result's byte order would be unclear. You'd run the risk of getting garbage output, which would be quite difficult to debug.

Second, it's difficult to predict how to handle bitwise operations on bytes-like objects of different lengths. You could pad them to be the same length, but you'd again need to know the byte order to do that correctly.

Instead of making the language guess how to implicitly resolve these difficult patches of logic, bytes-like objects just don't support bitwise operators. There are a couple of ways to perform bitwise manipulations on bytes-like objects, but they're a little more involved. I'll come back to that shortly.

There are two primary bytes-like objects: bytes, which is immutable, and bytearray, which is mutable. Both objects are identical in all other regards: they provide the same functionality as any other Python sequence and offer the same methods and behaviors. The two objects are even interoperable.

The decision of whether to use bytes or bytearray comes down solely to whether you want a mutable or an immutable object. For simplicity, I'll mainly use the bytes object in this section; the code would be the same for bytearray.

Creating a bytes Object

There are six ways to create a bytes-like object—not counting the default and copy initializers, which create an empty object or copy the value of another bytes-like object, respectively.

The trouble is, passing a binary literal to the initializer unexpectedly results in an empty bytes object. This occurs because a binary literal is really an integer, and passing an integer *n* to the bytes() constructor creates an empty bytes object with a size of *n* bytes:

```
bits = bytes(0b110)
print(bits)  # prints '\x00\x00\x00\x00\x00\x00'
```

Listing 12-11: init_bytes.py:1a

The bits object is exactly six (0b110) bytes long, and each of those bits is set to zero. Although this may feel like surprising behavior, remember that any binary data passed to bytes must have an explicit byte order, something that isn't inherent to Python integers.

You can create a bytes object from binary literals in a couple of ways. One way is to pass an iterable of integers to the bytes initializer. However, each of the integers provided by the iterable must be positive and representable in a single byte—that is, it must be between the values of 0 and 255, inclusive—or a ValueError will be raised.

The fastest way to do that here is to pack my binary literal into a tuple by itself:

```
bits = bytes((0b110,))
print(bits)  # prints "b'\x06'"
```

Listing 12-12: init_bytes.py:1b

Recall that I must provide a trailing comma (,) in a single-element tuple, or else it will be interpreted as a literal integer instead.

Another way to accomplish this same goal would be to wrap the binary literal in square brackets ([ ]) to define a list. Because each integer in the iterable fits in a single byte, the order in which the items are provided by the iterable effectively defines the byte order.

Yet another way to initialize a bytes object is to assign a bytes literal:

```
bits = b'\x06'
print(bits)  # prints "b'\x06'"
```

Listing 12-13: init_bytes.py:2a

In the case of bytearray, you'd pass that literal to the initializer:

```
bits = bytearray(b'\x06')
print(bits)  # prints "b'\x06'"
```

Listing 12-14: init_bytes.py:2b

No surprises there.

Finally, I can create a bytes object from any string, although I must explicitly state the text encoding being used:

```
bits = bytes('☺', encoding='utf-8')
print(bits)  # prints "b'\xe2\x98\xba'"
```

Listing 12-15: init_bytes.py:3

The smiley face emoji (☺) is a Unicode character with a UTF-8 encoding that spans three bytes: 0xE298BA. If you're familiar with Unicode, you'll notice what is not happening here: bytes is *not* using the formal Unicode code point for the smiley face emoji (U+263A), but rather, it is using the internal binary representation that UTF-8 uses.

I could have left the keyword off the encoding= argument, and many Python programmers will, but I prefer to spell it out explicitly. Just know that bytes('☺', 'utf-8') is equivalent.

PEDANTIC NOTE   UTF-8 string literals don't actually have a byte order; they read as if they were big-endian, but that's only coincidental. Some other systems, like UTF-16 and UTF-32, offer variants for the different byte orders.

Using int.to_bytes()

Perhaps the easiest way to convert between an integer and a bytes-like object is with the int.to_bytes() method.

As mentioned, when working with bytes, you must specify the byte order. The byte order required is often determined by your situation, such as what particular file format you're working with. Networks always use big-endian byte order.

Beyond that, the choice is somewhat arbitrary. If the data is only being used by my application, I'll usually stick to big-endian, which is my preference; if the data will be handled by system processes, I'll employ the system's byte order, which I determine with the following:

```
import sys

print(sys.byteorder)  # prints 'little'
```

Listing 12-16: int_to_bytes.py:1

The sys.byteorder attribute provides the byte order of the current system as a string. On my machine, as on most modern computers, the value is the string 'little', for little-endian.

Now, I can create my bytes object:

```
answer = 42
bits = answer.to_bytes(❶ 4, byteorder=sys.byteorder)
print(bits.hex(❷ sep=' '))  # prints '2a 00 00 00'
```

Listing 12-17: int_to_bytes.py:2a

I start by binding an integer value to the name answer. All int objects have a to_bytes() method for converting the value to a bytes-like object. I call that method on answer, passing the desired size in bytes (arbitrary for this example) of the resulting bytes-like object ❶ and the byte order to use. I bind the bytes object to the name bits.

Finally, to make the output more readable, I print out the value of bits in hexadecimal, instead of the default bytestring, separating the individual byte values with spaces ❷. The value 42 is representable with only one byte, and this byte (2a) appears on the left, since I'm using little-endian byte order.

When I try this with negative numbers, things get a little trickier. The same method as above would not work for the value -42:

```
answer = -42
bits = answer.to_bytes(4, byteorder=sys.byteorder)
print(bits.hex(sep=' '))
```

Listing 12-18: int_to_bytes.py:3a

This code fails on the answer.to_bytes() method call with the following:

```
Traceback (most recent call last):
  File "tofrombytes.py", line 10, in <module>
    bits = answer.to_bytes(4, byteorder=sys.byteorder)
OverflowError: can't convert negative int to unsigned
```

To get around this, I must explicitly specify that the integer is *signed*, meaning two's complement is being used to represent negative numbers:

```
answer = -42
bits = answer.to_bytes(4, byteorder=sys.byteorder, signed=True)
print(bits.hex(sep=' '))  # prints 'd6 ff ff ff'
```

Listing 12-19: int_to_bytes.py:3b

This version works as expected, as you can see from the output of the print statement.

By default, the signed parameter is False to avoid surprises, many originating from the fact that Python only *pretends* to use two's complement but is really doing its own thing. In any case, you should get into the habit of setting it to True when converting anything that *might* be a negative number to an integer. If the integer value is positive, setting signed to True won't have any effect:

```
answer = 42
bits = answer.to_bytes(4, byteorder=sys.byteorder, signed=True)
print(bits.hex(sep=' '))  # prints '2a 00 00 00'
```

Listing 12-20: int_to_bytes.py:2b

Sequence Operations

Nearly all operations you can perform on a sequence like a tuple or a list, you can do with bytes-like objects. For example, to see if there's a particular sequence of bytes in a larger bytes object, you can use the in operator:

```
bits = b'\xaa\xbb\xcc\xdd\xee\xff'
print(b'\xcc\xdd' in bits)  # prints 'True'
```

Listing 12-21: bytes_in.py

The in operator here is acting like it would with a string.

I won't go into any more depth on these operations here, as they behave precisely like they would in tuple (for bytes) or list (for bytearray).

Converting bytes to int

You can create an integer from a bytes object using int.from_bytes(). I'll start by defining a bytes object to convert from:

```
import sys

bits = ❶ (-42).to_bytes(4, byteorder=sys.byteorder, signed=True)
```

Listing 12-22: bytes_to_int.py:1

In the same way I called to_bytes() on a name bound to an integer value, I call the same method on an integer literal wrapped in parentheses here ❶. This code defines a new bytes object, bound to the name bits, with the same value as in Listing 12-19.

To convert the value from bits into an integer value, I use the int.from _bytes() method, which I'm calling on the int class:

```
answer = int.from_bytes(bits, byteorder=sys.byteorder, signed=True)
print(answer)  # prints '-42'
```

Listing 12-23: bytes_to_int.py:2

I pass bits to the method and indicate the byteorder and the bytes object used. I also indicate via signed=True that the bytes object is using two's complement to represent negative values. The byte order and signed values are not remembered by the bytes object; you'll need to know these whenever converting from bytes objects to integers.

The value of answer is -42, which was obtained from the bytes object.

struct

The deeper you get into Python's inner workings, the more you discover the C language peeking through. This is largely owing to the fact that CPython, the primary implementation of Python, is written in C. Interoperability with C remains a factor in how the language is implemented. One example of this is the struct module. It was originally created to allow data to be moved between Python values and C structs. It soon proved to be a handy way to convert values to packed binary data, specifically *contiguous* binary data, which is stored one item after the next in memory.

The modern struct module uses bytes for storing this binary data, providing the sixth way of creating bytes-like objects. Unlike int.to_bytes(), which is limited to integers, the struct.pack() method can also convert floating-point numbers and strings (character arrays) to binary, using whichever byte order you request. However, remember that strings themselves are unaffected by byte order. You can also use struct.pack() to pack multiple values into the same bytes object and later unpack those individual values into separate variables.

By default, struct will align all values to the exact sizes expected by the C compiler on your system, padding (or truncating padding) where necessary, although you can change this alignment behavior to use standard sizes instead.

struct Format String and Packing

The byte order, alignment behavior, and data types for struct are determined by the *format string*, which must be passed to any of the module's functions, or else to the initializer of the struct.Struct object, which lets you reuse the format string more efficiently.

Often, the first character of the format string defines the byte order and alignment behavior, as in Table 12-9.

Table 12-9: struct Format String Byte Order Flags

Character	Behavior
@	Use native byte order and alignment (default).
=	Use native byte order, but no alignment.
<	Little-endian, no alignment.
>	Big-endian, no alignment.
!	Network standard: big-endian, no alignment (same as >).

If you omit this initial character, struct will use the native byte order and alignment (same as if you start with @), padding the data as necessary to make sense to the C compiler. The rest of the string indicates the data types and order of the values being packed into the struct. Each of the basic C data types is represented by a character, as shown in Table 12-10.

Table 12-10: struct Format Characters

Character	C type	Python type	Standard size
?	_Bool (C99)	bool	1
c	char	bytes(1)	1
b	signed char	int	1
B	unsigned char	int	1
h	short	int	2
H	unsigned short	int	2
i	int	int	4
I	unsigned int	int	4
l	long	int	4
L	unsigned long	int	4
q	long long	int	8
Q	unsigned long long	int	8
e	(IEEE 754 binary16 "half precision")	float	2
f	float	float	4
d	double	float	8
s	char[]	bytes	
p	char[] (Pascal string)	bytes	
x	(pad byte)	effectively bytes(1)	

Most of these types are self-explanatory, especially if you know C (or C++, for that matter). When using native alignment, the size of each type will depend on the system; otherwise, struct uses the standard size.

If I wanted to pack two integers and a boolean, in that order, using big-endian notation (and standard sizes), I'd use the following format string:

```
import struct

bits = struct.pack('>ii?', 4, 2, True)
print(bits)  # prints '\x00\x00\x00\x04\x00\x00\x00\x02\x01'
```

Listing 12-24: struct_multiple_values.py:1a

Here, I use the struct.pack() function, to which I pass the format string and all the values I want to pack, in order. This creates a bytes object.

Alternatively, I can precede the type character with the desired number of values of that type. Here, I specify two adjacent integer values with 2i, instead of ii. The outcome is the same as before:

```
import struct

bits = struct.pack('>2i?', 4, 2, True)
print(bits)  # prints '\x00\x00\x00\x04\x00\x00\x00\x02\x01'
```

Listing 12-25: struct_multiple_values.py:1b

The format character 'e' refers to the *half-precision* floating-point number introduced in the 2008 revision of the IEEE 754, which is the document that defines the floating-point standard used by all modern computers.

The pad byte, 'x', is exactly one empty byte (\x00). Use 'x' to manually pad your data. For example, to pack two integers with exactly three empty bytes between them, I'd use the following:

```
import struct

bits = struct.pack('>i3xi', -4, -2)
print(bits)  # prints '\xff\xff\xff\xfc\x00\x00\x00\xff\xff\xff\xfe'
```

Listing 12-26: struct_ints_padded.py:1

There are two ways to represent strings in struct. Typically, you must *null-terminate* traditional strings ('s'), meaning the last character is always \x00, to mark the end. The number preceding the format character is the length of the string in characters; '10s' would be a 10-character string (that is, 9 characters and the null terminator byte). I can pack the string "Hi!" like this:

```
import struct

bits = struct.pack('>4s', b"Hi!")
print(bits)  # prints 'Hi!\x00'
```

Listing 12-27: struct_string.py:1

You'll notice that I wrote my string as a bytes literal by prepending it with b. The struct.pack() method cannot work directly with strings, but rather must have a bytes literal where the format calls for a string. (A little later, I have an example where I convert a typical UTF-8 string to a bytes literal.)

As long as you know the size of your string and the data will only ever be read by your code, you don't have to include the null terminator byte here. However, it's good to be in the habit if you'll be sending your data out of Python. If a C program tried to work with a string that lacked a null terminator, some pretty strange behavior could result.

Alternatively, you can use a Pascal string ('p'), which begins with a single byte representing the size as an integer. This string format doesn't require a null termination character, because its size is explicitly stored in the first byte. However, it also effectively limits the maximum size of the string to 255 bytes.

```
bits = struct.pack('>4p', b"Hi!")
print(bits)  # prints '\x03Hi!'
```

Listing 12-28: struct_string.py:2

Another consideration is that you may need to pad your struct to the *word size*, which is the smallest addressable chunk of memory, on your system. This is especially relevant when packing data to be handed off to C.

For example, a C struct of two longs and one short has a length of 24 bytes, but the format string '@llh' only produces an 18-byte chunk of binary. To correct this, append the format string with a zero, followed by the largest type in your struct; in this case, that format string would be '@llh0l':

```
struct.calcsize('@llh')    # prints '18' (wrong)
struct.calcsize('@llh0l')  # prints '24' (correct, what C expects)
```

There is never any danger in padding this way. If it's not needed, the size will be unaffected. This is only applicable when using native byte order and alignment (@), which is necessary for exchanging data with C. If you're specifying byte order manually or using network standard (no alignment), this won't matter and will have no effect.

There are also three types I've deliberately omitted from Table 12-10: ssize_t (n), size_t (N), and void* (P). These are only available if you're using native byte ordering and alignment (@), but you won't need those unless you're moving data between C and Python. See the documentation if you need to know about them: *https://docs.python.org/3/library/struct.html# format-characters.*

Unpacking with struct

To unpack data from a struct back into Python values, I must first determine the appropriate format string for the binary data.

Consider an integer packed into bytes using native byte order and alignment:

```
import struct

answer = -360
bits = struct.pack('i', answer)
```

Listing 12-29: struct_int.py:1

As long as I know that bits uses native ordering and contains a single integer, I can retrieve that integer with struct.unpack():

```
new_answer, = struct.unpack('i', bits)
print(new_answer)  # prints '-360'
```

Listing 12-30: struct_int.py:2

Notice that I included a trailing comma (,) after new_answer in the assignment statement. The struct.unpack() function always returns a tuple, which I must unpack. Since that tuple contains only one value, the trailing comma forces it to unpack; otherwise, new_answer would be bound to the tuple itself.

As one more example, I'll unpack the two integers from the bytes-like object from Listing 12-26:

```
first, second = struct.unpack('>i3xi', bits)
print(first, second)  # prints '-4 -2'
```

Listing 12-31: struct_ints_padded.py:2

The three pad bytes ('3x') are discarded, and the two integers are unpacked into the names first and second.

When working with struct, it is absolutely imperative that you know the format string that was used to pack the struct in the first place. Observe what would happen if I changed the format string in a few ways:

```
wrong = struct.unpack('<i3xi', bits)   # wrong byte order
print(*wrong)                          # prints '-50331649 -16777217'

wrong = struct.unpack('>f3xf', bits)   # wrong types
print(*wrong)                          # prints 'nan nan'

wrong = struct.unpack('>hh3xhh', bits) # wrong integer type
print(*wrong)                          # prints '-1 -4 -1 -2'

wrong = struct.unpack('>q3xq', bits)   # data sizes too large
print(*wrong)                          # throws struct.error
```

Listing 12-32: struct_ints_padded.py:3

All but the last example *seem* to work, but all the values I've unpacked are wrong. The moral is simple: know your layout so you can use the correct format strings.

struct objects

If you need to use the same format string repeatedly, the most efficient approach is to initialize a struct.Struct object, which provides methods analogous to the struct functions. For example, here I want to repeatedly pack two integers and a floating-point number into bytes objects, so I'll create a Struct object.

```
import struct

packer = struct.Struct('iif')
```

Listing 12-33: struct_object.py:1

I create a Struct object with the format string 'iif', and I bind it to the name packer. The Struct object remembers this format string and uses it for any pack() or unpack() calls on the object.

Next, I'll write a generator that produces some strange numeric data and packs it into bytes-like objects:

```
def number_grinder(n):
    for right in range(1, 100):
        left = right % n
        result = left / right
        yield packer.pack(left, right, result)
```

Listing 12-34: struct_object.py:2

In this example, I'm iterating over integers 1 through 99 as the right operand of division, and then I'm taking as the left operand the modulo of the right value and whatever number was passed to the function as n. Then, I perform the division with left and right, binding the result to result. (There's no particular reason for this math; it's just for fun.)

Next, I use packer.pack() and pass it the operands and the result of the division. The packer object uses the format string I passed to its initializer earlier.

In the next part of my code, I retrieve the packed struct data from the generator and, for the sake of the example, unpack the data again, using the packer object:

```
for bits in number_grinder(5):
    print(*packer.unpack(bits))
```

Listing 12-35: struct_object.py:3

If you run that code, you'll see the left, right, and result values that had been packed into the bytes objects yielded by the generator. This is a silly example, of course; in the real world, I would have done something useful with this binary data, such as storing it in a file, instead of merely unpacking it again.

Bitwise on Bytes-Like Objects

As I mentioned earlier, bytes-like objects, including bytes and bytearray, do not directly support bitwise operators. Annoying as this may seem, it makes sense when you consider that bytes-like objects don't know their own byte order. If you performed a bitwise operation between a big-endian and a little-endian value, it would be impossible to determine the byte order of the result. If there's one thing that Python developers hate, it's unclear behavior.

It is possible to perform bitwise operations on bytes-like objects, but you must use one of two workarounds.

Bitwise Operations via Integers

The first option is to convert the bytes-like objects to integers first, which resolves the byte order. Integers in Python are technically infinite, so this approach can be leveraged for handling binary data of differing lengths.

Here, I write a function to handle a bitwise operation between two bytes-like objects:

```
def bitwise_and(left, right, *, byteorder):
    size = max(len(left), len(right))
```

Listing 12-36: bitwise_via_int.py:1

My `bitwise_and()` function accepts three arguments: the two bytes-like objects (`left` and `right`) as operands for the bitwise operation, plus the byteorder. You will recall that the `*` in the parameter list forces all parameters after it, namely `byteorder`, to be keyword-only arguments. I don't offer a default argument for `byteorder`, for the same reason bytes objects don't have bitwise operators. If the user is unable to provide this argument explicitly, the function should fail, rather than potentially producing garbage output.

To convert the result back to bytes in the last step, I must know the size of the result (which should be size of the largest bytes object passed to it) so I don't chop off leading or trailing zeros—or actual data, if this were for another bitwise operation!

Because bytes is a sequence, it implements the `__len__()` special method. In my function, I take the `max()` of the lengths of the two bytes arguments, and I use that value as the size of the output. Here's the next piece of the function I started in Listing 12-36:

```
    left = int.from_bytes(left, byteorder=byteorder)
    right = int.from_bytes(right, byteorder=byteorder)
```

Listing 12-37: bitwise_via_int.py:2

I convert the `left` and `right` bytes-like objects to integers by using the `int.from_bytes()` method, employing the byte order passed to my function. Meanwhile, in writing my code, I must assume the arguments from Listing 12-36 are mutable, lest `bitwise_and()` have a risk of side effects.

Please note, *I am not using* `signed=True` *here*! This is utterly vital for the bitwise operation to turn out right. Otherwise, my function will interpret any bytes-like object with a `1` in the most significant bit as indicative of a negative integer. This would thereby pad the significant end of the integer with infinite `1`s. The effective result of `0xCCCCCC & 0xAAAA` according to this function would then be `0xCC8888`, rather than the correct value of `0x008888`.

Now that I have integer forms of these arguments, I can use the normal bitwise operator on them. Here's the last piece of the function, continued from Listing 12-37:

```
    result = left & right
    return result.to_bytes(size, byteorder, signed=True)
```

Listing 12-38: bitwise_via_int.py:3

I bind the result of the bitwise operation to result. Finally, I convert result back to a bytes object, using the size I determined earlier, the byteorder passed to my function, and signed=True to handle conversion of any possible negative integer values. I return the resulting bytes-like object.

I'll use my bitwise_and() function to perform a bitwise operation with any two bytes-like objects:

```
bits = b'\xcc\xcc\xcc'    # 0b110011001100110011001100
bitfilter = b'\xaa\xaa'   # 0b1010101010101010

result = bitwise_and(bits, bitfilter, byteorder='big')
print(result)             # prints "b'\x00\x88\x88'"
```

Listing 12-39: bitwise_via_int.py:4

The result is exactly right! It doesn't matter what bytes-like objects I pass to this function; it will work as expected.

Bitwise Operations via Iteration

The bitwise-via-integers approach is the most flexible, but it can be impractical when you're working with a lot of data, since you're duplicating the contents of the two bytes objects in int. For the algorithmic efficiency crowd, the integer approach has a space complexity of $\Theta(n)$. Another option is to use iteration, instead of using integers as intermediary objects. Interestingly, both options have roughly the same time complexity. In fact, the iterative approach is slightly *slower*! Its strength is a lower space complexity, which lets it avoid excessive memory consumption when processing a large amount of data.

When you have a lot of binary data on which to perform bitwise operations, it's sometimes better to leverage the iterable nature of bytes-like objects. Here, I'll write another function for performing a bitwise operation on two bytes-like objects, this time with iteration:

```
def bitwise_and(left, right):
    return bytes(l & r for l, r in zip(left, right))
```

Listing 12-40: bitwise_via_iter.py:1a

Within my bitwise_and() function, I employ a generator expression to create a new bytes object, which I ultimately return. Iterating over bytes-like objects yields positive integer values equivalent to each byte. The zip() function allows me to iterate over both the left and right bytes objects at the same time, and then I take the bitwise and (&) of the pair of integers produced on each iteration.

I use this function in much the same manner as with the integer version, except that I don't need to bother with the byte order. The implicit byte order of the operands is used. (As mentioned earlier, it's your responsibility to ensure the byte orders are the same!)

Here's the usage of my function from Listing 12-40:

```
bits = b'\xcc\xcc\xcc'    # 0b110011001100110011001100
bitfilter = b'\xaa\xaa'   # 0b1010101010101010

result = bitwise_and(bits, bitfilter)
print(result)             # prints "b'\x88\x88'"
```

Listing 12-41: bitwise_via_iter.py:2

This present approach has one significant limitation: I can only reliably perform bitwise operations if the operands are the same length. Otherwise, the result will only be as long as the shortest operand object.

It is possible to work with operands of different sizes, but for that, I must know the byte order again, so I know which side to pad. It took me and my colleague Daniel Foerster a fair bit of back-and-forth to work out a reliable and Pythonic solution to this particular problem.

Here's an expanded form of the iterative `bitwise_and()` function from Listing 12-40, which now handles bytes-like objects of different sizes:

```
import itertools


def bitwise_and(left, right, *, byteorder):
    pad_left = itertools.repeat(0, max(len(right) - len(left), 0))
    pad_right = itertools.repeat(0, max(len(left) - len(right), 0))

    if byteorder == 'big':
        left_iter = itertools.chain(pad_left, left)
        right_iter = itertools.chain(pad_right, right)
    elif byteorder == 'little':
        left_iter = itertools.chain(left, pad_left)
        right_iter = itertools.chain(right, pad_right)
    else:
        raise ValueError("byteorder must be either 'little' or 'big'")

    return bytes(l & r for l, r in zip(left_iter, right_iter))
```

Listing 12-42: bitwise_via_iter.py:1b

I create `pad_left` and `pad_right`, which are iterables for the padding on the left or right operands, respectively. Each of these uses `itertools .repeat()` to produce the value 0 on each iteration, up to a particular number of iterations. That limit is calculated as how many more bytes the other operand has than one I'm padding, or zero if this operand is the larger of the two.

Next, I create two more iterables that combine the padding and the operand for each side of the bitwise operation. The byte order determines the order in which I combine the padding and operand iterables, as the padding must be applied to the higher-value end.

If anything other than `'big'` or `'little'` is passed to the `byteorder` parameter, I raise a `ValueError`. (The exception and its message I raise there are the same as what `int.from_bytes()` would raise with a nonsense `byteorder` argument.)

Finally, with the `left_iter` and `right_iter` iterables, which will produce the same number of bytes, I perform the iterative bitwise in a generator expression, as before.

The usage and return of this version of my `bitwise_and()` function is identical to that of the integer-based version:

```
bits = b'\xcc\xcc\xcc'    # 0b110011001100110011001100
bitfilter = b'\xaa\xaa'   # 0b1010101010101010

result = bitwise_and(bits, bitfilter, byteorder='big')
print(result)             # prints "b'\x00\x88\x88'"
```

Listing 12-43: bitwise_via_iter.py:2b

Again, the advantage of the iterative approach is that it is optimized for space complexity. In terms of time complexity, it is slower than the integer-based approach from earlier, so it should be reserved for working with particularly large bytes-like objects. Otherwise, stick with `int.from_bytes()` and `int.to_bytes()` for bitwise operations on bytes-like objects.

memoryview

When you're slicing a bytes object, a copy of the data being sliced is created. Ordinarily, this has no negative effects, especially when you're going to assign the data anyway. However, when you're working with particularly large slices, especially repeatedly, all that copying can create some serious performance slowdowns.

The `memoryview` class helps alleviate that, by accessing the raw memory data of any object that implements the *buffer protocol*, a set of methods that provide and govern access to an underlying memory array. Bytes-like objects fit this qualification, and you'll most often use `memoryview` with bytes and bytearray. You won't often encounter the buffer protocol in any types other than binary-oriented objects, although `array.array` is a notable exception. (In fact, the buffer protocol is defined and implemented at the C level, rather than in Python itself, so implementing it in your own classes is decidedly nontrivial.)

Since `memoryview` is designed to provide very low-level access to memory, it has a lot of particularly advanced methods and concepts, which I won't get into here. I will show you its most basic usage: slicing, or accessing a part of, a bytes-like object by reading in place, rather than by making a copy of the sliced data. Although this is only called for when dealing with particularly large buffers, I'll demonstrate with a small bytes object for brevity.

In this example, I want to employ slicing to confirm that a bit of binary data fits a particular format—perhaps that two `0xFF` bytes appear after every three bytes. (Why I'd do this in the real world is beyond me; I just needed an example.) Effectively, I want to slice the fourth and fifth bytes from every five bytes, as the first three of each set of five can be anything.

I'll start with the version without memoryview first, for reference:

```
def verify(bits):
    for i in range(3, len(bits), 5):
        if bits[i:i+2] != b'\xff\xff':
            return False
    return True
```

Listing 12-44: slicing_with_memoryview.py:1a

With this function, I iterate based on the fourth byte (the first in the pair), via the for loop. As soon as I reach the end of bits, I know I've processed everything. (If this ever slices out only the last byte, the code runs just fine and returns False, as it should.)

Within each iteration of my loop, I slice out the two bytes I care about with bits[i:i+2] and compare that to the b'\xff\xff' I'm checking for. If it doesn't match, I immediately return False. However, if the code makes it through the loop without that condition failing, then the function returns True.

Here's the usage:

```
good = b'\x11\x22\x33\xff\xff\x44\x55\x66\xff\xff\x77\x88'
print(verify(good))  # prints 'True'

nope = b'\x11\x22\x33\xff\x44\x55\x66\x77\xff\x88\x99\xAA'
print(verify(nope))  # prints 'False'
```

Listing 12-45: slicing_with_memoryview.py:2

As I mentioned, this code is perfectly fine in most cases. When I slice, I make a copy of those two bytes. But if that slice is something on the order of two *kilobytes* in length, with hundreds of slices being made, I may run into some serious performance issues with all that copying.

This is where memoryview comes in handy. I'll update my example to use that instead.

```
def verify(bits):
    is_good = True
    view = memoryview(bits)
    for i in range(3, len(view), 5):
        if view[i:i+2] != b'\xff\xff':
            is_good = False
            break
    view.release()
    return is_good
```

Listing 12-46: slicing_with_memoryview.py:1b

The code is functionally the same as before, except that this time, I create a memoryview object, which I bind to the name view, to give me direct access to the underlying memory of bits.

I can use memoryview in essentially the same way as I would bytes, except that slicing on a memoryview only views the data in place, rather than creating a copy of the data.

It is *vital* that I release the memoryview as soon as I'm done with it, by calling the release() method on my memoryview object. Objects that support the buffer protocol know when they're being watched by a memoryview, and they will change their behavior in various ways to prevent memory errors. For example, a bytearray object will not resize as long as there's a memoryview of it. It is always safe to call the release() method; at worst, it will do nothing at all. Once I release a memoryview, I cannot use it further. Attempting to do so would raise a ValueError.

Unfortunately, my code is still rather un-Pythonic, what with having to assign a value to is_good and return with that name at the function end. I'd like to polish that up.

Hmm . . . I have to remember to close something when I'm finished with it. Surely, that means memoryview is also a context manager that I can use in a with statement. Sure enough, that works! I can incorporate that technique to make my function more concise and Pythonic:

```
def verify(bits):
    with memoryview(bits) as view:
        for i in range(3, len(view), 5):
            if view[i:i+2] != b'\xff\xff':
                return False
    return True
```

Listing 12-47: slicing_with_memoryview.py:1c

That's more like it. This code still behaves the same as the preceding two versions, but it reads cleaner and doesn't make copies of the data it's slicing out. The usage and outcome are the same as in Listing 12-45.

Reading and Writing Binary Files

Just as you can write strings out to a file using a stream, you can use a stream to write binary data to a file. Binary file formats, as you'll see later, have a few advantages over text-based file formats, especially in terms of compact file sizes and faster processing. The techniques are almost identical to those in Chapter 11, with one critical difference: the stream must be opened in *binary mode*, instead of the default text mode. This returns a BufferedReader, BufferedWriter, or BufferedRandom object, depending on the mode you open with (see Table 11-1 from Chapter 11).

There are a number of existing file formats for storing data in binary, which I'll discuss later, but for this example, I'll create my own format using struct. This may be called for sometimes in your own projects, when you need to store very specific data in a particular manner. Designing your own binary file format can require considerable thought and planning, but when done right, a custom file format can be made to fit your data like a glove. As you'll see, struct is particularly suitable for this, because of its format strings.

Organizing the Data

In this section, I'll create a basic class structure for keeping track of a personal bookshelf. Ultimately, I'll be able to write this bookshelf data to a binary stream (including a binary file) and create a bookshelf from a binary stream.

I'll break my code down into three files: *book.py*, *bookshelf.py*, and *__main__.py*, all in the same package. That package will also need to contain an *__init__.py* file, which will be empty in this case. All of these files will go into a directory, *rw_binary_example/*, which will become the package. Here's my file structure for the example:

```
rw_binary_example/
├── book.py
├── bookshelf.py
├── __init__.py
├── __main__.py
```

Listing 12-48: File structure of rw_binary_example/ *package*

The Book class

The basic unit of data in my code is a Book, which I'll write as its own class:

```
import struct


class Book:

    packer = ❶ struct.Struct(">64sx64sx2h")

    def __init__(self, title="", author="", pages=0, pages_read=0):
        self.title = title
        self.author = author
        self.pages = pages
        self.pages_read = pages_read

    def update_progress(self, pages_read):
        self.pages_read = min(pages_read, self.pages)
```

Listing 12-49: book.py:1

Most of this will look familiar by now. A book has a title, an author, a page count (pages), and an instance attribute for tracking how many pages have been read (pages_read). I also provide an update_progress() method to update the number of pages the user has read so far.

The line of particular interest here is the one where I define the class attribute packer. I bind this name to a Struct object, wherein I define the binary format for my object in a format string ❶. Here, I use the Struct object instead of the pack() function directly from the struct module. I do this for two reasons: (1) so there's a single canonical source for the binary format I'm using and (2) because it means the format string is *precompiled* into a Python bytecode object, making for more efficient reuse.

I'm using big-endian byte order, not only because it's familiar, but also because it's what I'd use if I wanted to send this data over the internet (although I'm not doing so here). If I have to make a somewhat arbitrary decision, like choosing a byte order, I might as well maximize the possibilities of what I can do with the data!

I'll also set a limit on the size of my string. I need a predictable format so I can read from the binary data later, and working with data that varies in size can be forbiddingly difficult. For my program, I set a size limit of 64 bytes, which should be sufficient for encoding most book titles and authors. I use 64s in my format string to denote the struct fields for title and author. I also follow each of these fields with a padding byte (x), which will guarantee that these fields can always be interpreted as C-style null-terminated strings, even if all 64 characters are used. That makes for one less potential bug if my data needs to be interpreted by code in another programming language.

I also specify two 2-byte (short) integers (2h) for storing the page count and pages read. This should be sufficient space for both, since a book with more than 32,767 pages is rather an absurd idea. (I could also make this number unsigned, but I don't really need the slightly higher maximum value. Perhaps I'll find a clever use for negative values in a later version of my code.) If I try to pack too large a value into a struct field, a struct.error exception will be raised.

Now that I have my class and its format string, I can write an instance method for converting to binary the book data from the Book class I started in Listing 12-49:

```
def serialize(self):
    return self.packer.pack(
        self.title.encode(),
        self.author.encode(),
        self.pages,
        self.pages_read
    )
```

Listing 12-50: book.py:2

To use the precompiled format string from earlier, I call the pack() method on the self.packer instance attribute, instead of using struct.pack(). I only need to pass the data I'm packing into binary.

I must call the encode() method on each of my strings to convert them from UTF-8 to bytes literal strings. I could also have used self.title .encode(encoding='utf-8') to explicitly specify the encoding. I might specify the encoding if I were using some string encoding other than the default UTF-8.

The integer values, self.pages and self.pages_read, can be passed as is.

The self.packer.pack() method returns a bytes object, which I then return from the serialize method.

The Bookshelf class

My program will store a collection of Book objects in a Bookshelf, which will be little more than a thin wrapper around a list:

```
import struct
from .book import Book

class Bookshelf:
    fileinfo = ❶ struct.Struct('>h')
    version = 1

    def __init__(self, *books):
        self.shelf = [*books]

    def __iter__(self):
        return iter(self.shelf)

    def add_books(self, *books):
        self.shelf.extend(books)
```

Listing 12-51: bookshelf.py:1

I'm importing the Book class from the book module that lives in the same package as this module, so I use a relative import, as seen on the first line.

The Bookshelf class initializes the list, self.shelf, which will store any book objects passed as arguments to the initializer. Users can also add more books to the shelf with the add_books() method.

I allow iterating over the books directly by returning the iterator for the list from __iter__(), as there's no need to reinvent the wheel here.

I could add some other features, such as removing or looking up specific books, but I want to keep this simple, to focus on converting this data to binary.

Most important to this example is the additional Struct that I've created and bound to fileinfo. I'll use it to store the file format ❶. Along with that, I have a version class attribute for tracking the file format version number. This way, if I later change my *.shlf* file format, I can tell my future code how to read both the old and the new files.

I define a method for writing this data to a binary stream. You'll recall from Chapter 11 that files are opened as streams. I can also apply these same techniques to send the data to another process or over a network to another machine.

```
def write_to_stream(self, stream):
    stream.write(self.fileinfo.pack(self.version))
    for book in self.shelf:
        stream.write(book.serialize())
```

Listing 12-52: bookshelf.py:2

The write_to_stream() method accepts a stream object as an argument. I write the *.shlf* file format version, version, to the binary stream first. My code can later check this first value and ensure the *.shlf* file being read follows the expected format.

Next, I iterate over the `Book` objects in the `self.shelf` list, call the `serialize()` method on each book, and write the returned bytes object to the stream using `stream.write()`. Since the stream automatically moves its position to the end of the last data I wrote to the binary file, I don't need to call `stream.seek()` at any point.

Writing to a File

Now, I can put my `Book` and `Bookshelf` classes to work to store some data:

```
from .bookshelf import Bookshelf
from .book import Book


def write_demo_file():
    # Write to file

    cheuk_ting_bookshelf = Bookshelf(
        Book("Automate the Boring Stuff with Python", "Al Sweigart", 592, 592),
        Book("Doing Math with Python", "Amit Saha", 264, 100),
        Book("Black Hat Python", "Justin Seitz", 192, 0),
        Book("Serious Python", "Julien Danjou", 240, 200),
        Book("Real-World Python", "Lee Vaughan", 370, 370),
    )
```

Listing 12-53: __main__.py:1

I import my `Book` and `Bookshelf` classes at the top of the module. In my `write_demo_file()` function, I create the new `Bookshelf` object `cheuk_ting_bookshelf` and fill it with some data. Cheuk Ting sure has good taste in books!

Next, within that same `write_file()` method, I add the following to open a file in binary write mode:

```
    with open('mybookshelf.shlf', 'bw') as file:
        cheuk_ting_bookshelf.write_to_stream(file)
```

Listing 12-54: __main__.py:2

You'll recall from Chapter 11 that including b in the mode string on `open()` will open the stream in *binary mode*, instead of the default text mode. I want to write out the file, overwriting its contents if the file already exists, so I use w mode.

To aid you in following this example, I'll create a stub function for my `read_demo_file()` function now and fill it in later:

```
def read_demo_file():
    """TODO: Write me."""
```

Listing 12-55: __main__.py:3a

After opening my file, I pass it to the `write_to_stream()` method of my `cheuk_ting_bookshelf` object.

At the bottom of *__main__.py*, I must include the usual boilerplate for executing my `main()` function:

```
if __name__ == "__main__":
    write_demo_file()
```

Listing 12-56: __main__.py:4a

That's it! Running the package (via `python3 -m rw_binary_example`) creates a new file in my current working directory entitled *mybookshelf.shlf*. If you open that file in a text editor capable of displaying binary files, such as Visual Studio Code, you'll likely see the titles and authors of the books displayed amidst a bunch of strange symbols.

I've created a binary file containing my data! (I'll admit, I did some serious chuckling to myself after I got this example working.)

Reading from a Binary File

The *.shlf* file I created is merely a blob of binary data, with no information on how to read it. For my *.shlf* format to be of any use, I need to expand my program to be able to read in the data from *.shlf* files, converting that binary data back into strings and integers.

In the `Book` class again, I add a method for creating a new object from the binary data I would read from a *.shlf* file:

```
@classmethod
def deserialize(cls, bits):
    title, author, pages, pages_read = cls.packer.unpack(bits)
    title = title.decode()
    author = author.decode()
```

Listing 12-57: book.py:3

I've chosen to make this a class method, rather than an instance method, to prevent the undesired side effect of overwriting another book. The method accepts a bytes object, and I use the `Book.packer` class attribute (see Listing 12-49) to unpack the binary data into four names.

I use `decode()` to convert the strings from bytes to UTF-8. As before, if I were decoding into anything other than UTF-8, I'd need to specify the encoding via the `encoding=` parameter of `decode()`.

The `unpack()` method automatically converts the integer values to `int`.

Finally, within this same `deserialize()` class method, I create and return a new `Book` object from the values I unpacked:

```
    return cls(title, author, pages, pages_read)
```

Listing 12-58: book.py:4

I'll put this new class method to work in my `Bookshelf` class.

Next, I'll add a `from_stream()` class method for creating a new Bookshelf from a binary stream:

```
@classmethod
def from_stream(cls, stream):
    size = cls.fileinfo.size
    version, = cls.fileinfo.unpack(stream.read(size))
    if version != 1:
        raise ValueError(f"Cannot open .shlf v{version}; expect v1.")
```

Listing 12-59: bookshelf.py:3

My `from_stream()` class method receives a stream object as an argument, `stream`.

Before I do any processing, I need to check the format version of a *.shlf* file, in case some user in the future tries to open a (theoretical, for now) version-2 file with this package. To do that, I first determine how many bytes to read off the beginning of my file, where I stored the version data. Struct objects like `cls.fileinfo` (see Listing 12-51) have a size attribute, which returns an integer representing the exact number of bytes needed to represent data packed into that Struct.

I read the number of bytes indicated by size from the binary stream using `stream.read(size)`, and I pass the returned bytes literal to `cls.fileinfo.unpack()`. That returns a tuple of values, but as the tuple has only one value in this case, I must be careful to unpack that value into `version`, rather than binding the tuple itself to that name.

I check the returned file format version before proceeding, raising a `ValueError` if the format version is wrong for this code. A future expanded version of this code might allow me to switch which Struct object I use in the Book module, based on the format version of the file being read.

Now, I prepare to read the data for the individual books:

```
    size = Book.packer.size
    shelf = Bookshelf()
```

Listing 12-60: bookshelf.py:4

I get the size in bytes of the Struct object the Book class uses, and I store that in `size`. I instantiate a new Bookshelf object, which I bind to `shelf`. I'm now ready to read the rest of the data in the binary stream:

```
    while bits := stream.read(size):
        shelf.add_books(Book.deserialize(bits))

    return shelf
```

Listing 12-61: bookshelf.py:5

Within the header of a loop, I use `stream.read(size)` to read the next segment of data from the binary stream, which I bind to `bits`. I'm using an *assignment expression*, via the *walrus operator*, in this context, so I can also check the value of bits right here in the loop header. Then, I implicitly check that *bits* is not an empty bytes literal (bytes())—the value of bits will be "falsey," or implicitly evaluate to False in the conditional, only if it is actually empty—which would indicate that I've reached the end of the stream. Any other value of bits, even b'\x00', would cause this expression to evaluate to True.

Within the suite of this loop, I create a new Book from the binary data in bits, using the Book.deserialize() class method. Then, I add that Book object to the Bookshelf object bound to shelf, which I build here.

Finally, after the loop completes, I return shelf.

Because of how I've structured the Bookshelf and Book classes, the code for reading a *.shlf* file is quite elegant. I'll fill in my read_demo_file() function in the *__main__.py* module now.

Laís received some book recommendations from her friend Cheuk Ting in a *.shlf* file, so she needs to open that file. Here is the code that allows her to do so with the Bookshelf class:

```
def read_demo_file():
    with open('mybookshelf.shlf', 'br') as file:
        lais_bookshelf = Bookshelf.from_stream(file)

    for book in lais_bookshelf:
        print(book.title)
```

Listing 12-62: __main__.py:3b

I open the *mybookshelf.shlf* file in *binary read* mode (br). I pass the file stream object to Bookshelf.from_stream(), and then I bind the resulting Bookshelf object to lais_bookshelf.

Finally, to verify everything has worked, I iterate over each book in lais_bookshelf and print the titles.

I must be certain to call read_demo_file():

```
if __name__ == "__main__":
    write_demo_file()
    read_demo_file()
```

Listing 12-63: __main__.py:4b

Running that code outputs the following:

```
Automate the Boring Stuff with Python
Doing Math with Python
Black Hat Python
Serious Python
Real-World Python
```

Laís's bookshelf is now identical to Cheuk Ting's!

I hope Cheuk Ting remembers to recommend *Dead Simple Python* to Laís, too, after she gets done with it.

Seek with Binary Stream

When working with streams, you can change stream position if you only want to read or modify part of a stream, rather than traversing or processing the whole thing. Recall from Chapter 11 that you can work with the stream position on a text stream using the tell() and seek() methods. You can use these same methods with binary stream objects, namely BufferedReader, BufferedWriter, and BufferedRandom, but with some additional functionality on seek().

The seek() method accepts two arguments. The first is offset, which is the number of bytes to move in the stream. Positive offset values move forward, and negative offset values move backward.

The second argument is whence, which provides the starting position that offset moves from. With text streams, the offset must be zero. That limitation doesn't exist on binary streams!

With binary streams, there are three possible values for whence: 0 for start, 1 for current position, and 2 for end. If I wanted to seek to six bytes from the end of a stream, I'd do something like this:

```
from pathlib import Path
Path('binarybits.dat').write_bytes(b'ABCDEFGHIJKLMNOPQRSTUVWXYZ')


with open('binarybits.dat', 'br') as file:
    file.seek(-6, 2)
```

Listing 12-64: seek_binary_stream.py:1

Providing a whence of 2 means I start seeking from the end of the stream, and the offset argument of -6 moves back six bytes from there.

Similarly, if I then wanted to move forward two bytes from the current stream position, I'd use the following:

```
    file.seek(2, 1)
```

Listing 12-65: seek_binary_stream.py:2

The whence argument of 1 starts the seek from the current position, and the offset argument of 2 moves forward two bytes from there.

One word of caution when using seek(): only use positive offsets when starting at the beginning of your file (a whence of 0, the default), or the statement will raise an OSError. Similarly, be careful not to rewind past the start of the stream when using a negative offset and a whence of 1.

Always use negative offsets when starting at the end of your file (a whence of 2). Positive offsets won't raise an error, but seeking past the end of the buffer is rather pointless, if benign. Seeking past the end and then writing data to the buffer from that position will actually drop said data into a black hole; it won't be written to the stream. If you want to append to a stream, position yourself at the end with file.seek(0, 2).

BufferedRWPair

One of the fun things about writing a book like *Dead Simple Python* is discovering unfamiliar techniques. While perusing the Python documentation for this section, I learned about another type of binary stream called a BufferedRWPair, which accepts two stream objects: one to read from and another to write from. (These *must* be different stream objects!)

The primary use of BufferedRWPair is in working with a socket or a two-way pipe, wherein your code communicates with another process on the system through two separate buffers: one for receiving data from the other process and another for sending data.

Another use would be to simplify the process of reading data from one source, possibly process it, and then send it somewhere else. For example, I could use this to read data from a device's serial port and write it directly out to a file.

I won't write a full example for this here, as it would be fairly involved and likely use topics I haven't covered. (I prefer to stay reasonably relevant.) The usage of BufferedRWPair is about the same as any other byte stream, except that you'd explicitly initialize it by passing two streams: one to read and one to write.

For a simple example, I'll first create a binary file containing some data using the normal means:

```
from pathlib import Path
Path('readfrom.dat').write_bytes(b'\xaa\xbb\xcc')
```

Listing 12-66: creating_bufferedrwpair.py:1

This code only creates the file *readfrom.dat*, so I have something to read from in the important part of the example.

I create a BufferedRWPair by passing it a stream to read and a stream to write. I'll use the open() method on Path to create the streams:

```
from io import BufferedRWPair
with BufferedRWPair(Path('readfrom.dat').open('rb'), Path('writeto.dat').open('wb')) as buffer:
    data = buffer.read()
    print(data)  # prints "b'\xaa\xbb\xcc'"
    buffer.write(data)
```

Listing 12-67: creating_bufferedrwpair.py:2

To verify this works, I'll open *writeto.dat* directly in read mode to see its contents:

```
Path('writeto.dat').read_bytes()  # prints "b'\xaa\xbb\xcc'"
```

Listing 12-68: creating_bufferedrwpair.py:3

That's clearly an oversimplified example, but you get the essential idea. There are many uses for BufferedRWPair in advanced situations. Chances are, you'll know when you need it.

Serialization Techniques

As mentioned in Chapter 11, *serialization* is the process of converting data to a format that can be stored. This data can be written to a file, transmitted over a network, or even shared between processes. The inverse operation is *deserialization*, which converts the serialized data back into its original form, or at least a close equivalent.

I also touched on a number of formats used for serialization, especially JSON and CSV. All of these formats were text based and intended to be human readable, which makes them excellent candidates for files that the user should be able to modify by hand. Human-readable formats are also *futureproof*, meaning in this case that the deserialization process can be reverse engineered if the presently used technology or format specification ever ceases to exist. (And that happens more often than you might think!)

There are a few disadvantages of using human-readable, text-based serialization formats, rather than *binary* serialization formats. The first is size: it will virtually always take more memory to represent non-string data as a string than to use its original, binary form. Text-based formats are also often slower to deserialize, in contrast to binary formats. This is one reason why binary formats are better suited to the *virtual machine* design pattern, wherein different bytes correspond to different behaviors. Most interpreted languages, including Python itself, use some form of this design pattern internally.

The third disadvantage of text-based serialization formats is the same as one of its advantages: the file can be easily modified. You may want to discourage users from directly editing particularly complex or fragile data, as minor errors can corrupt the file. Using binary serialization formats is an effective way of discouraging file tampering.

A good example of this is *Minecraft's .dat* file format, which contains serialized game world data in a binary format. (The fact that *Minecraft* is written in Java is beside the point; principles of serialization are language agnostic.) It's important to note that obfuscation is not an effective security technique. *Minecraft .dat* files are still editable by the end user, as evidenced by third-party programs like MCEdit.

If you want to protect your serialized data, *encryption* is your only answer. How you apply encryption depends on your situation.

For example, the space simulator game *Oolite* uses XML to serialize player data so the file can still be read and edited by the user, but it includes a hash string of the data in the file so the game can detect cheating and make minor adjustments to gameplay.

In an application where security really matters, the serialized data will often be fully encrypted. Many applications will store saved passwords in this manner, encrypted behind a master password or key, to prevent the data from being intercepted. The passwords must be serialized and stored to disk for the program to retain them, but the encryption ensures that no one else can deserialize the data.

Obscuring a user's own data with nonstandard binary serialization formats and encrypting it when security is not a factor are widespread anti-patterns. Locking in your users by limiting their access to their data in this manner is generally considered unethical. Use these tools wisely and strongly consider making your serialization format specifications public.

In short, your decision on whether to use text-based or binary serialization depends entirely on your situation. Binary serialization can offer smaller file sizes, faster deserialization, and the added benefit of discouraging tampering by end users. However, binary-based formats are not as futureproof as text-based formats, and they can also give users an uneasy feeling of opacity about the data. These are the reasons why they're seldom used for serializing settings.

Forbidden Tools: pickle, marshal, and shelve

Pickle is a common built-in serialization tool. It stores Python objects in a binary format that can be saved to a file and then later deserialized, or *unpickled*, into a Python object again. Sounds perfect, right?

There's a big red box at the top of the documentation that screams about security concerns with pickle, and it may be tempting to overlook that. "This is merely a calculator app," a developer might say. "Security doesn't matter here."

Except the security here has nothing to do with the data itself. Pickled data can be tampered with to execute arbitrary code, meaning if you use pickle for serialization, your Python program can be made to do *literally anything*. If someone modifies pickled data on a user's machine, which isn't difficult to do, your harmless Python program will become malware as soon as it unpickles that file.

It's possible to guard against file tampering by signing data with a message authentication module called hmac, but at that point, it would be more straightforward to use the other techniques from this chapter to serialize data in a secure fashion. Pickled data isn't intended to make sense outside of Python anyway, whereas a custom serialization approach *could* be made portable.

What's more, pickle is painfully slow and produces some pretty bloated files. It's practically the most inefficient way to serialize anything to a file, even before I consider security.

There are two related built-in tools in Python: marshal and shelve. The former, marshal, is really only intended to be used internally by Python, as its deliberately undocumented specification can change between Python versions. It also has the same issues related to security and performance as does pickle, so it shouldn't be considered an alternative. Even if it were perfect, it would still not be intended for your use.

The shelve module is built on pickle, and it should be dismissed for the same reasons as pickle.

Frankly, pickle, marshal, and shelve offer no advantages over other serialization-to-file techniques. They're like sudo pip: they *appear* to work until they completely kick the pooch, at which point, you discover in the most painful way possible how much evil they conceal.

Ignore the myriad tutorials and misguided Stack Overflow answers on this one. Unless you're transferring data directly between processes, please forget that these modules exist at all, except to warn other Python developers away from them. Leave the `pickle` in the fridge.

You may wonder why these modules are even included in the standard library in the first place. There are a few factors.

First, `pickle` does have one valid use: transferring data between running processes. This is safe because the data is never written to a file. Speed and size are still problems here, but there are efforts to mitigate these issues, as it's believed to be easier to redeem `pickle` than to invent a whole new protocol. Python 3.8 saw a new version of the `pickle` protocol, which is meant to improve handling of large data (see PEP 574). I'll revisit `pickle` in Chapter 17, when I cover multiprocessing.

Second, plenty of Python code exists that relies on these modules. At one time, `pickle` was considered the "one obvious way" of serializing data, although it has long since fallen out of favor as its flaws have become apparent. There's already a move to deprecate and remove many so-called "dead batteries" (a reference to Python's "batteries included" nature) from the standard library, but `pickle` isn't on that list because of its use in multiprocessing.

That leaves only one solution: accept that `pickle`, `marshal`, and `shelve` have their uses, but that serialization-to-file is not among them.

Serialization Formats

So if `pickle` and friends are out, what options remain? Thankfully, quite a few! I've compiled a short list of some of the most common and popular binary serialization formats, but it is far from exhaustive. If you are interested in any of these file formats, peruse the official documentation for the associated module or library.

Property List

The *property list*, or *.plist* file, is a serialization format that was created for the NeXTSTEP operating system in the 1980s and was further developed for its descendants: macOS and GNUstep. Although it is primarily used with these platforms, you can certainly employ property lists in your own project. This is one of the best ways to perform binary serialization without `pickle`.

There are two major flavors of property list: binary and the human-readable, XML-based form. Both can be serialized and deserialized with the built-in `plistlib` module.

One of the advantages of property lists in Python is that they can directly serialize most basic types, including dictionaries, which are frequently used as the top-level objects (like with JSON).

To learn more, read the official documentation at *https://docs.python.org/3/library/plistlib.html*.

MessagePack

One of the leading formats for binary serialization is *MessagePack*, which is designed to produce simple, compact serialized output. It is based on JSON, and for the most part, it can represent the same sort of data.

The official third-party package, *msgpack*, can be installed via pip. More information and official documentation can be found on the MessagePack website: *https://msgpack.org/*.

BSON

Another binary serialization format based on JSON is called *BSON* (for "binary JSON"). Being a binary format, BSON is much faster to deserialize than JSON. It also usually produces files that are smaller, though still larger than those produced by MessagePack. In certain situations, BSON files can even be larger than the equivalent JSON file. BSON also provides some additional types over MessagePack.

As MongoDB makes significant use of the BSON format, the MongoDB package for Python, *pymongo*, provides a *bson* package. A fork of this package is also available simply as *bson*, if you don't want the whole *pymongo* package. You can also learn more about BSON from the specification's official website: *http://bsonspec.org/*.

CBOR

The *Concise Binary Object Representation*, or *CBOR*, is a binary serialization format that focuses on concise encoding. Like BSON and MessagePack, it is also based on the JSON data model. Unlike its cousins, CBOR is officially defined as an internet standard by the Internet Engineering Task Force in RFC 8949, and it is employed in the Internet of Things.

There are a few packages available through pip for working with CBOR, the most up-to-date of which is *cbor2*. More information about the format is available from the official website: *https://cbor.io/*.

NetCDF

The *Network Common Data Form*, or *NetCDF*, is a binary serialization format designed primarily for working with array-oriented scientific data. It was created in 1989, based on NASA's Common Data Format, although the two formats are no longer compatible. NetCDF is still maintained by the *University Corporation for Atmospheric Research* (*UCAR*).

The *netCDF4* package from pip provides modules for working with the NetCDF format. You can also learn more about the format at *https://www.unidata.ucar.edu/software/netcdf/*.

Hierarchial Data Format

The *Hierarchial Data Format*, or *HDF*, is a binary serialization format designed for storing large amounts of data. It is developed and maintained by the not-for-profit HDF Group, and it is used heavily in science, engineering, finance, data analysis, and even creative projects. It has had a central role in some major NASA projects, and it was employed in producing movies such as *The Lord of the Rings* and *Spider-Man 3*.

HDF5 is the latest version of the format and is the current recommended standard. The HDF Group still supports and maintains HDF4.

A number of third-party modules exist for working with HDF. Two of the leading options are *h5py* and *tables*. More information about the format is available from The HDF Group's website: *https://www.hdfgroup.org/*.

Protocol Buffers

Google's *Protocol Buffers* is an increasingly popular binary serialization format, but I'm addressing it last because it operates in a very different manner from the others.

Unlike in most formats, which have existing standard specifications, you define a tailor-made specification for your file in a special *.proto* schema file. This schema is then compiled into your favorite language, using Google's proto compiler; in the case of Python, it produces a Python module. You would then use this generated module for serialization and deserialization, according to the specification you created.

If you're interested in this, refer to Google's official documentation: *https://developers.google.com/protocol-buffers/docs/pythontutorial*.

A Few More

There are also a number of binary serialization formats designed for specific purposes, such as *GRIB* in meteorology and *FITS* in astronomy. Often, the best way to find a serialization format that fits your purpose is to think about your data first, how it should be stored, and in what situations it needs to be deserialized. Once you find a format that fits your particular need, find (or write) a module to work with it in Python.

PEDANTIC NOTE   You may notice that I've omitted the built-in *xdrlib* module for working with the older XDR serialization format. It's deprecated as of Python 3.8, and PEP 594 has it slated for removal in Python 3.10, so it's best to not start using it.

Wrapping Up

Binary is the language of computers. It is one of the most reliable ways for your program to share data outside of itself, whether through files (as you've seen here) or across processes or networks. Binary serialization formats generally offer smaller file sizes and faster deserialization than text-based formats, at the cost of less human readability. Whether you should use text or binary for any particular task partly depends on your audience: *text is for humans, binary is for computers*. Besides this, consider the available tooling for any given format and its suitability for the data you want to encode. For example, even if a user will never need to interact with a settings file, *.json* remains a popular format, if for no other reason than the ease of debugging it!

The goal of a programmer is ultimately to serve as the translator between humans and computers. It takes time to master thinking in bits and bytes, binary and hexadecimal, but it's a skill well worth cultivating. No matter how high up the tower of abstractions a programmer climbs, they can never really escape the fundamental computer language upon which everything is built. An expert programmer is one who is fluent in both human language and computer logic; the more you know of both, the better you can utilize the tools Python or any other language offers you.

PART IV

ADVANCED CONCEPTS

13

INHERITANCE AND MIXINS

Knowing when to use inheritance is even more important than knowing how. The technique is extraordinarily useful for some situations but fantastically ill-suited for most others, making it one of the more controversial topics in object-oriented programming. Syntactically, inheritance is simple to implement. Logistically, the issues surrounding it are so intricate and nuanced that it deserves a chapter of its own.

THEORY RECAP: INHERITANCE

Inheritance allows you to write classes that share common code, and often, a common interface. To understand how it works, recall my blueprint (class) analogy for building houses (objects) from Chapter 7. Say you've now designed a three-bedroom variant, instead of the original two-bedroom form. Everything remains the same, but you've added a room to the side.

Now, if you improve the original blueprint to upgrade the wiring in the kitchen, you'll want to see those changes in both the two-bedroom and the three-bedroom blueprints. However, you don't want that third bedroom to appear on the blueprint for the two-bedroom house.

This is where inheritance comes into play. You can write a class called House3B that inherits from House. The *derived* class, House3B, is initially identical to the *base* class, House, but you can extend the derived class to contain additional methods and attributes, or even to *override* (replace) some of the methods of the base class. This is called an *is-a* relationship, because a House3B is a House.

THE SOLID PRINCIPLES

Good object-oriented design follows five rules, represented by the acronym *SOLID*. These five principles are at the core of deciding when and how to use inheritance.

It's critical to note, however, that you must apply your own common sense to these principles. It is absolutely possible to follow SOLID to the letter and still write horrendous, unmaintainable code! This doesn't mean there's anything wrong with the rules, only that you must apply your own common sense to all design decisions.

Let's take a look at each of the SOLID principles, individually:

S: Single-Responsibility Principle

Just like a function, a class should have a single, well-defined responsibility. The difference between the two is that a function *does* something, while a class *is* something. My own aphorism here is, "A class is defined by its constituent data."

The essential point is to avoid writing *god classes*, which are classes that try to do many different things. God classes invite bugs, complicate maintenance, and obfuscate code structure.

O: Open-Closed Principle

Once a class is being used in the source code at large, you should avoid changing it in ways that could affect its usage. The client code using your class shouldn't need to change much, if at all, when you update the class.

Once your code has shipped, changing an object's *interface*—the set of public methods and attributes that are used to interact with the class or object—should be avoided whenever possible. You must also be cautious about changing methods and attributes that derived classes directly rely upon. Instead, it is better to use inheritance to extend the class.

L: Liskov Substitution Principle

When using inheritance, you must be able to substitute the derived class for the base class in usage, without changing the desired behavior of the program. This helps prevent surprises and logic errors. If there are significant changes in behavior between the base class and the derived class, you probably shouldn't use inheritance; the derived class should be an altogether distinct base class, instead.

This does not imply that either the *interfaces* or the *implementations* have to be identical, especially in Python. A derived class may need to accept different arguments on methods than the base class does, but the same usage on both the base class and the derived class should produce similar observable behaviors or at least fail explicitly. It's a bad surprise if a call to a method on a base class returns an integer and an identical call on a derived class returns a string.

I: Interface Segregation Principle

In designing the interface of your class, think about the needs of the *client*, the end developer using your class, even if that client is future-you. Do not force the client to know about or work around parts of the interface that they won't use.

For example, it would be a violation of the interface segregation principle to require every class defining a job for a printer to inherit from a complex PrintScanFaxJob base class. It would be better to write separate PrintJob, ScanJob, and FaxJob base classes, each with an interface fit for the single responsibility of that class.

D: Dependency Inversion Principle

In object-oriented programming, you'll have classes that depend on other classes, and this can sometimes result in a lot of repeated code. If you later discover that you need to swap out one of those classes or change implementation details, you'll have to make the changes in each instance of the repeated code. This makes refactoring painful.

Instead, you can use *loose coupling*, which is the technique of ensuring that changes to one thing don't break other areas of your code. For example, rather than class A depending directly on a specific class B, you can write a class that offers a single, abstract interface to serve as a bridge to B, as well as to the related classes C and D (if needed).

This SOLID principle is called the *Dependency Inversion Principle* because it is the reverse of how many people first think about object-oriented programming. Instead of a derived class inheriting behavior from a base class, both the base class and the derived class rely on an abstract interface.

(continued)

One way to achieve loose coupling is through *polymorphism*, wherein multiple classes with different behaviors and features offer a common interface. In this way, you can write simpler client code, such as a single function that works the same when working with different classes.

Polymorphism is often achieved with inheritance. For example, say you have a Driver class that interacts with a Car class. If you wanted Driver to also work with other vehicles, you could instead write a Vehicle class, from which Car, Motorcycle, Boat, and Starship all inherit. This way, since Driver interacts with Vehicle, it can automatically use any of those vehicle classes. (This approach works because of the Liskov Substitution Principle.)

Another approach to achieving loose coupling is through composition. When designing a user interface (UI), it's common to have *controller* classes that provide an abstract interface to trigger common functionality, like displaying dialog boxes or updating the status bar. You don't want to repeat the UI-controlling code throughout your project because of trivial differences, like different buttons on a dialog box. A controller class abstracts these implementation details out of the rest of your program, making them easier to use, maintain, and refactor. Changes to the implementation for a common functionality only need to occur in one place.

When to Use Inheritance

Inheritance can quickly get out of hand, primarily because it feels clever. You must know when *not* to use it.

While many languages use inheritance and polymorphism to allow working with many different types of data, Python seldom has such a need. Instead, the language uses duck typing, accepting an argument on the sole merit of its interface. For example, Python does not force you to inherit from a particular base class to make your object an iterator; instead, it recognizes any object with the methods __iter__() and __next__() as an iterator.

Since a class is defined by its constituent data, inheritance should extend this definition. If two or more classes need to contain the same sort of data and provide the same interface, inheritance is likely justified.

For example, the built-in BaseException class contains several common attributes describing all exceptions. Other exceptions, such as ValueError and RuntimeError, contain the same data, justifying their inheriting from BaseException. The base class defines a common interface for interacting with this data. Derived classes extend the interface and attributes to serve their needs as necessary.

If you're tempted to use inheritance purely to require the implementation of a particular interface in a derived class, or to allow extending a fairly complex interface, consider using *abstract base classes* instead. I'll come back to that topic in Chapter 14.

Crimes of Inheritance

Remember: *decisions about object-oriented design must be based on the data being encapsulated.* Bearing that rule in mind will help you steer clear of many atrocities commonly seen in object-oriented code. There are many misuses of inheritance, and I'll cover a few of the most egregious here.

One major inheritance anti-pattern is the *god class*, which lacks a single clear responsibility and instead stores or provides access to a large set of shared resources. A god class quickly becomes bloated and unmaintainable. It's better to use class attributes to store anything that needs to be shared mutably between objects. Even a global variable is less of an anti-pattern than a god class.

Another inheritance anti-pattern is the *stub class*, which is a class that contains little to no data. Stub classes usually show up because the developer's motivations for inheritance were based on minimizing repeated code, rather than a consideration of the encapsulated data. This creates a plethora of fairly useless objects with unclear purposes. Better ways exist to prevent repeated code, such as using ordinary functions from a module, instead of writing methods or employing composition. Methods, and thus common code, can be shared between classes with techniques like mixins and abstract base classes (Chapter 14).

Mixins, which I'll introduce later in this chapter, are really a form of composition that just happens to leverage Python's inheritance mechanisms. They aren't an exception to the rules.

The third reason for atrocious inheritance schemes is the devilish old desire to produce "clever" code. Inheritance is a nifty-looking hammer, but don't use it to pound in screws. You get better architecture and fewer bugs with composition.

Basic Inheritance in Python

Before I dive into the deeper mechanics of inheritance, I want to properly cover the basics.

I'll use the popular personal task management technique of bullet journaling as an example. In real life, a *bullet journal* is a physical book made up of one or more *collections*, which are titled sets of items—bulleted tasks, events, and notes. There are different kinds of collections for different purposes. For an example of inheritance in Python, I'll write some classes that emulate a bullet journal.

First, I will write a pared-down Collection class, which I'll inherit from shortly. Remember, a class should be crafted around its data, not its behavior. To keep the example small, I'll mainly write stub functions, with little to no actual behavior.

```
class Collection:

    def __init__(self, title, page_start, length=1):
        self.title = title
        self.page_start = page_start
```

```
        self.page_end = page_start + length - 1
        self.items = []

    def __str__(self):
        return self.title

    def expand(self, by):
        self.page_end += by

    def add_item(self, bullet, note, signifier=None):
        """Adds an item to the monthly log."""
```

Listing 13-1: bullet_journal.py:1

By itself, a Collection in a bullet journal only needs three things: a title (self.title), its page numbers (self.page_start and self.page_end), and its items (self.items).

I add a __str__() special instance method for displaying the title when the collection is converted to a string. Implementing this method means I can directly print() a Collection object. I also offer two instance methods: expand(), for adding another page to the collection; and add_item(), for adding an entry to the collection. (I skipped writing the logic for this method for brevity.)

Next, I'll write a class for the MonthlyLog, which is a specialized type of Collection for tracking events and items in the context of an entire month. It still has to have a title, page numbers, and a set of items. In addition, it needs to store events. Because it *extends* the data stored, inheritance is a good fit for this situation.

```
class MonthlyLog(Collection):

    def __init__(self, month, year, page_start, length=2):
      ❶ super().__init__(❷ f"{month} {year}", page_start, length)
        self.events = []

    def __str__(self):
        return f"{❸ self.title} (Monthly Log)"

    def add_event(self, event, date=None):
        """Logs an event for the given date (today by default)."""
```

Listing 13-2: bullet_journal.py:2

You will recall from Chapter 7 that, when instantiating a derived class, one must explicitly call the initializer of the base class. I do that here with super().__init__() ❶. I create the title from month and year ❷, and I also pass the page_start and length arguments directly. The base class initializer creates these instance attributes, which will be accessible to the MonthlyLog object because it inherits from Collection ❸.

I override the __str__() special instance method, this time appending "(Monthly Log)" to the collection title.

I also define the instance method add_event() specifically for MonthlyLog, for logging events on the calendar view I would store in self.events. I won't implement this calendar behavior here because it's pretty involved and also irrelevant to the example.

Here's one more derived class, FutureLog, which is a collection belonging to one of the next six months:

```
class FutureLog(Collection):

    def __init__(self, start_month, page_start):
        super().__init__("Future Log", page_start, 4)
        self.start = start_month
        self.months = [start_month]  # TODO: Add other five months.

    def add_item(self, bullet, note, signifier=None, month=None):
        """Adds an item to the future log for the given month."""
```

Listing 13-3: bullet_journal.py:3

The FutureLog class also inherits from Collection, with the added attribute self.months, which is a list of months. The class also has a predefined title and length, which I pass to the Collection initializer via super.__init__(), as I did in MonthlyLog.

I also override the instance method add_item() so it now accepts month in addition to the other arguments and so would store the bullet, note, and signifier in the appropriate month in FutureLog. The month parameter is optional, so I don't violate the Liskov Substitution Principle. As before, I've skipped the implementation here to keep things moving along.

I want to briefly mention that, much like how I can check if an object is an instance of a class with isinstance(), I can check if a *class* is derived from another class with issubclass():

```
print(issubclass(FutureLog, Collection))  # prints True
```

Here's a very basic usage of my classes, in which I create a FutureLog, a MonthlyLog, and a Collection, adding some items to each:

```
log = FutureLog('May 2023', 5)
log.add_item('June 2023', '.', 'Clean mechanical keyboard')
print(log)       # prints "Future Log"

monthly = MonthlyLog('April', '2023', 9)
monthly.add_event('Finally learned Python inheritance!')
monthly.add_item('.', 'Email Ben re: coffee meeting')
print(monthly)  # prints "April 2023 (Monthly Log)"

to_read = Collection("Books to Read", 17)
to_read.add_item('.', 'Anne of Avonlea')
print(to_read)  # prints "Books to Read"
```

Listing 13-4: bullet_journal.py:4

Because I wrote so many stub functions, this won't do much, but the fact that it doesn't fail at least proves what's working. (Famous last words, I know.) A derived class has the same attributes and methods as its base class, but it can override any of those and add more.

PEDANTIC NOTE On rare occasions, you may encounter technical writings that refer to "new-style classes." *Classes*, as they're known today, were introduced in Python 2.2 and were originally called *new-style classes*. The far more limited "old" flavor of classes remained available until their removal in Python 3.

Multiple Inheritance

When a class inherits from multiple base classes, it gains all of the attributes and methods of those base classes. This is known as *multiple inheritance.*

In languages that permit it, multiple inheritance can be a powerful tool, but one that presents many thorny challenges. I'll therefore discuss how Python gets around many of these obstacles and what issues remain. As with normal inheritance, your decision about whether to use multiple inheritance should be based primarily on the data, rather than just on the desired functionality.

Method Resolution Order

One potential issue with multiple inheritance occurs if more than one base class has a method of the same name. Suppose you have a class Calzone, which inherits from both Pizza and Sandwich, and both base classes provide a method __str__(). If I call __str__() on an instance of Calzone, Python must *resolve* which method to call, meaning it must decide which class's __str__() method to execute. The rule the language uses to perform this resolution is called the *method resolution order.*

In this section, I'll explain how Python determines the method resolution order. To check the method resolution order on a particular class, consult that class's __mro__ attribute.

Here are the classes for my Calzone multiple-inheritance scenario:

```
class Food:
    def __str__(self):
        return "Yum, what is it?"


class Pizza(Food):
    def __str__(self):
        return "Piiiizzaaaaaa"


class Sandwich(Food):
    def __str__(self):
        return "Mmm, sammich."
```

```
class Calzone(Pizza, Sandwich):
    pass
```

Listing 13-5: calzone.py:1

The classes Pizza and Sandwich are both derived from the Food class. A Calzone is considered both a type of Pizza and a type of Sandwich, so it inherits from both of those classes. The question is, what will be printed when this code runs?

```
calzone = Calzone()
print(calzone)  # What gets printed??
```

Listing 13-6: calzone.py:2

Which version of the __str__() special instance method is Calzone inheriting? Because both Pizza and Sandwich derive from Food and both override the special instance method __str__(), Python must resolve the ambiguity about which class's implementation of __str__() to use when Calzone.__str__() is called.

The situation above is known in software development as the *diamond inheritance problem*, or sometimes more ominously as the "Deadly Diamond of Death" (cue scary thunder). It's one of the nastier method resolution problems that arise with multiple inheritance.

Python solves the diamond inheritance problem with a straightforward approach: a technique known as the *C3 Method Resolution Order (C3 MRO)*, or more formally, the *C3 superclass linearization*. (Try saying that 10 times fast.) Python does this automatically, behind the scenes. You need only know how it functions so you can use it to your advantage.

In short, the C3 MRO involves generating a *superclass linearization*—a list of base classes each class inherits from—following a simple set of rules. The superclass linearization is the order in which classes are searched for the method being called.

To demonstrate this, here's the linearization list of the first class, Food. In the (non-Python) notation here, L[Food] is the linearization of class Food.

```
L[Food] = Food, object
```

Like all classes in Python, Food inherits from the ubiquitous object, so the linearization is Food, object. In this linearization, Food is considered the *head*, meaning it's the first item in the linearization list and thus the next class to be considered. The rest of the list is considered the *tail*. In this case, the tail is just one item: object.

The Pizza class inherits from Food. To do this, Python must look at the linearization of each class Pizza directly inherits from and consider each item in the linearization in turn.

In the following non-Python notation, I'm using merge() to indicate the linearizations from base classes I have yet to consider. By the time I'm done, merge() should be empty. Each linearization is wrapped in curly braces ({ }).

The class being considered in each step is in *italics*, and a class that has just been added to the linearization on that step is in **bold**.

Using this notation, I can illustrate the linearization process for Pizza. The C3 MRO here will traverse the heads from left to right. In creating the superclass linearization for Pizza, the C3 MRO doesn't care what methods each class has; it only cares where a class appears in the linearizations it is merging:

```
L[Pizza] = merge(Pizza, {Food, object})
```

Python first considers whether to add the leftmost head—the current class, Pizza—to the linearization:

```
L[Pizza] = merge(Pizza, {Food, object})
```

If a head class is not in any tail for any linearization being merged, it is added to the new linearization and removed from any other positions. Since Pizza doesn't appear in any tail, it is added to the linearization.

Next, Python examines the new leftmost head, which is the head of the linearization that needs to be merged:

```
L[Pizza] = Pizza + merge({Food, object})
```

The Food class doesn't appear in any tail, so it is added to the Pizza linearization and removed from the linearization being merged:

```
L[Pizza] = Pizza + Food + merge({object})
```

That means object is the new head of the linearization being merged. Python now considers this new head. Since object doesn't appear in any tail—obviously, since the only linearization being merged no longer has a tail—it can be added to the new linearization:

```
L[Pizza] = Pizza + Food + object
```

There is nothing left to merge. The linearization for Pizza is Pizza, Food, and object. The Sandwich class evaluates to nearly the same linearization:

```
L[Sandwich]: Sandwich + Food + object
```

This gets a little more complicated with multiple inheritance, so let's consider the Calzone class. I will need to merge the linearizations of Pizza and Sandwich, in that particular order, matching the order of the classes in Calzone's inheritance list (Listing 13-5).

```
L[Calzone] = merge(
    Calzone,
    {Pizza, Food, object},
    {Sandwich, Food, object}
)
```

The C3 MRO first inspects the leftmost head, Calzone:

```
L[Calzone] = merge(
    Calzone,
    {Pizza, Food, object},
    {Sandwich, Food, object}
)
```

Since Calzone doesn't appear in any tail, it's added to the new linearization:

```
L[Calzone] = Calzone + merge(
    {Pizza, Food, object},
    {Sandwich, Food, object}
)
```

The new leftmost head to be considered is Pizza. It, too, doesn't appear in any tail, so it is also added to the new linearization.

```
L[Calzone] = Calzone + Pizza + merge(
    {Food, object},
    {Sandwich, Food, object}
)
```

When Pizza is removed from the linearizations being merged, Food becomes the new head of that first linearization. As it's the new leftmost head, it's considered next. However, Food also appears in the tail of the linearization headed by Sandwich, so it cannot be added to the linearization yet.

The next head is considered instead:

```
L[Calzone] = Calzone + Pizza + merge(
    {Food, object},
    {Sandwich, Food, object}
)
```

Sandwich doesn't appear in any tails, so it can be added to the new linearization and removed from the linearizations being merged. The C3 MRO goes back to considering the leftmost head, which is Food:

```
L[Calzone] = Calzone + Pizza + Sandwich + merge(
    {Food, object},
    {Food, object}
)
```

The Food class appears as the head of both linearizations being merged, but not in any tails, so it can be added. It is also removed from all linearizations to be merged.

```
L[Calzone] = Calzone + Pizza + Sandwich + Food + merge(
    {object},
    {object}
)
```

This leaves only object as the head in each linearization to merge. Since it appears only as a head, not as a tail, it can be added.

```
L[Calzone] = Calzone + Pizza + Sandwich + Food + object
```

There's the finished superclass linearization for Calzone.

To think of that another way, the linearization process will always look for the next-nearest ancestor of the class being considered, as long as that ancestor is not being inherited by any ancestor not yet considered. For Calzone, the next-nearest ancestor is Pizza, which isn't inherited by either Sandwich or Food. The Sandwich class is next, and only once both Pizza and Sandwich are accounted for can their common ancestor, Food, be added.

Bearing this in mind and revisiting that question of ambiguity from Listing 13-6, repeated below, which version of __str__() gets called here?

```
calzone = Calzone()
print(calzone)  # What gets printed??
```

In order to determine which base class is providing the __str__() method being called, the superclass linearization for Calzone is consulted. According to the method resolution order, Python would first check Calzone for a __str__() method. Failing to find that, it checks Pizza next and finds the desired method. Sure enough, running this code, the output is as follows:

```
Piiiizzaaaaaa
```

Ensuring Consistent Method Resolution Order

When using multiple inheritance, the order in which you specify base classes matters. Here, I'll create a PizzaSandwich class, representing a sandwich where you use slices of pizza instead of bread:

```
class PizzaSandwich(Sandwich, Pizza):
    pass


class CalzonePizzaSandwich(Calzone, PizzaSandwich):
    pass
```

Listing 13-7: calzone.py:3a

The PizzaSandwich class derives from (Sandwich, Pizza). Recall that Calzone inherits from (Pizza, Sandwich). Both PizzaSandwich and Calzone have the same base classes, but they inherit from them in different orders. That means that PizzaSandwich has a slightly different linearization than Calzone:

```
L[PizzaSandwich] = PizzaSandwich + Sandwich + Pizza + Food + object
```

If I went overboard and put a calzone between two slices of pizza, I'd get a CalzonePizzaSandwich, which inherits from (Calzone, PizzaSandwich).

Since Calzone and PizzaSandwich inherit from the same base classes in different orders, what will happen when I try to resolve the __str__() method on CalzonePizzaSandwich? Here's how the C3 MRO tries to solve that.

```
L[CalzonePizzaSandwich] = merge(
    CalzonePizzaSandwich,
    {Calzone, Pizza, Sandwich, Food, object},
    {PizzaSandwich, Sandwich, Pizza, Food, object}
)
```

The leftmost head, **CalzonePizzaSandwich**, is considered and added first, since it doesn't appear in any tails:

```
L[CalzonePizzaSandwich] = CalzonePizzaSandwich + merge(
    {Calzone, Pizza, Sandwich, Food, object},
    {PizzaSandwich, Sandwich, Pizza, Food, object}
)
```

The new leftmost head, Calzone, is checked next and added.

```
L[CalzonePizzaSandwich] = CalzonePizzaSandwich + Calzone + merge(
    {Pizza, Sandwich, Food, object},
    {PizzaSandwich, Sandwich, Pizza, Food, object}
)
```

Next, the C3 MRO looks at Pizza, the new leftmost head. It skips this class for now, since Pizza appears in the tail of one of the lists.

Next, it considers the next head, PizzaSandwich:

```
L[CalzonePizzaSandwich] = CalzonePizzaSandwich + Calzone + merge(
    {Pizza, Sandwich, Food, object},
    {PizzaSandwich, Sandwich, Pizza, Food, object}
)
```

That class can be added, since it's only a head. After adding PizzaSandwich to the new linearization and removing it from the linearizations to merge, the C3 MRO reconsiders the leftmost head:

```
L[CalzonePizzaSandwich] = CalzonePizzaSandwich + Calzone + PizzaSandwich + merge(
    {Pizza, Sandwich, Food, object},
    {Sandwich, Pizza, Food, object}
)
```

Pizza is still not eligible to be added, since it's still in the tail of the second linearization. The head of the next list, Sandwich, is considered next:

```
L[CalzonePizzaSandwich] = CalzonePizzaSandwich + Calzone + PizzaSandwich + merge(
    {Pizza, Sandwich, Food, object},
    {Sandwich, Pizza, Food, object}
)
```

No dice! Sandwich appears in the tail of the first linearization being merged. Python cannot determine the method resolution order here because both heads in the last step, Pizza and Sandwich, are also in the tail of the other linearization. The CalzonePizzaSandwich class would cause Python to raise the following:

```
TypeError: Cannot create a consistent method resolution
```

The fix for this particular situation is trivial: I'd need to switch the order of base classes on PizzaSandwich, like this:

```
class PizzaSandwich(Pizza, Sandwich):
    pass


class CalzonePizzaSandwich(Calzone, PizzaSandwich):
    pass
```

Listing 13-8: calzone.py:3b

Now, the linearization of CalzonePizzaSandwich works:

```
L[CalzonePizzaSandwich] = merge(
    CalzonePizzaSandwich,
    {Calzone, Pizza, Sandwich, Food, object},
    {PizzaSandwich, Pizza, Sandwich, Food, object}
)

L[CalzonePizzaSandwich] = CalzonePizzaSandwich + merge(
    {Calzone, Pizza, Sandwich, Food, object},
    {PizzaSandwich, Pizza, Sandwich, Food, object}
)

L[CalzonePizzaSandwich] = CalzonePizzaSandwich + Calzone + merge(
    {Pizza, Sandwich, Food, object},
    {PizzaSandwich, Pizza, Sandwich, Food, object}
)

L[CalzonePizzaSandwich] = CalzonePizzaSandwich + Calzone + merge(
    {Pizza, Sandwich, Food, object},
    {PizzaSandwich, Pizza, Sandwich, Food, object}
)

L[CalzonePizzaSandwich] = CalzonePizzaSandwich + Calzone + PizzaSandwich + merge(
    {Pizza, Sandwich, Food, object},
    {Pizza, Sandwich, Food, object}
)

L[CalzonePizzaSandwich] = CalzonePizzaSandwich + Calzone + PizzaSandwich + Pizza + merge(
    {Sandwich, Food, object},
    {Sandwich, Food, object}
)
```

```
L[CalzonePizzaSandwich] = CalzonePizzaSandwich + Calzone + PizzaSandwich + Pizza + Sandwich +
merge(
    {Food, object},
    {Food, object}
)

L[CalzonePizzaSandwich] = CalzonePizzaSandwich + Calzone + PizzaSandwich + Pizza + Sandwich +
Food + merge(
    {object},
    {object}
)

L[CalzonePizzaSandwich] = CalzonePizzaSandwich + Calzone + PizzaSandwich + Pizza + Sandwich +
Food + object
```

When using multiple inheritance, pay close attention to the order in which you specify base classes.

Be aware that the fixes aren't always trivial, like in my example here. As you can imagine, the problem is made worse when inheriting with three or more classes. I won't go into these here, but know that understanding the C3 MRO is a major part of the solution. Raymond Hettinger outlines some other techniques and considerations in his article "Python's super() considered super!" which you can read here: *https://rhettinger.wordpress.com/2011/05/26/super-considered-super/*.

To learn more about the C3 MRO, I recommend the article that accompanied the addition of this MRO to Python 2.3: *https://www.python.org/download/releases/2.3/mro/*.

Interestingly, aside from Python, only a handful of relatively obscure languages use the C3 MRO by default; Perl 5 and onward offers it optionally. It's one of the relatively unique advantages of Python.

Explicit Resolution Order

While you must always work out the correct inheritance order for your code to run, you can also explicitly call methods on the base classes you want:

```
class PizzaSandwich(Pizza, Sandwich):
    pass


class CalzonePizzaSandwich(Calzone, PizzaSandwich):
    def __str__(self):
        return Calzone.__str__(self)
```

Listing 13-9: calzone.py:3c

This will ensure that CalzonePizzaSandwich.__str__() calls Calzone.__str__(), regardless of the method resolution order. You will notice that I have to pass self explicitly, since I'm calling the __str__() instance method on the Calzone class and not on an instance.

Resolving Base Class in Multiple Inheritance

Another challenge with multiple inheritance is ensuring the initializers for all the base classes are called, with the right arguments passed to each. By default, if a class doesn't declare its own initializer, Python will use the method resolution order to find one. Otherwise, if an initializer is declared by a derived class, it won't implicitly call the base class initializers; that must be done explicitly.

Your first thought might be to use super() for this. Indeed, that can work, but only if you have planned it out in advance! The super() function looks at the next class (not the current class) in the superclass linearization for the instance. If you're not expecting this, it can lead to some freaky and unexpected behavior or errors.

To demonstrate how this should be handled, I'll add initializers on my first three classes:

```
class Food:
    def __init__(self, ❶ name):
        self.name = name


class Pizza(Food):
    def __init__(self, toppings):
        super().__init__("Pizza")
        self.toppings = toppings


class Sandwich(Food):
    def __init__(self, bread, fillings):
        super().__init__("Sandwich")
        self.bread = bread
        self.fillings = fillings
```

Listing 13-10: make_calzone.py:1a

Because Pizza and Sandwich both inherit from Food, they need to call the initializer on Food via super().__init__() and pass the required argument, name ❶. All is working as expected.

But Calzone is trickier, since it needs to call __init__() on both Pizza *and* Sandwich. Calling super() only provides access to the first base class in the method resolution order, so this would still only call the initializer on Pizza:

```
class Calzone(Pizza, Sandwich):
    def __init__(self, toppings):
        super().__init__(toppings)
        # what about Sandwich.__init__??


# The usage...
pizza = Pizza(toppings="pepperoni")
sandwich = Sandwich(bread="rye", fillings="swiss")
```

```
calzone = Calzone("sausage")  # TypeError: __init__() missing 1 required positional argument:
'fillings'
```

Listing 13-11: make_calzone.py:2a

The method resolution order on `Calzone` means that `super().__init__()` calls the initializer on `Pizza`. However, the call to `super().__init__()` in `Pizza.__init__()` (Listing 13-10) will now try to call `__init__()` on the next class in the linearization for the `Calzone` instance. That is, `Pizza`'s initializer will now call `Sandwich.__init__()`. Unfortunately, it will pass the wrong arguments, and the code will throw a rather confusing `TypeError`, complaining about a missing argument.

The easiest way to handle initializers with multiple inheritance might seem to be to call the `Pizza` and `Sandwich` initializers directly and explicitly, like this:

```
class Calzone(Pizza, Sandwich):
    def __init__(self, toppings):
        Pizza.__init__(self, toppings)
        Sandwich.__init__(self, 'pizza crust', toppings)

# The usage...
pizza = Pizza(toppings="pepperoni")
sandwich = Sandwich(bread="rye", fillings="swiss")
calzone = Calzone("sausage")
```

Listing 13-12: make_calzone.py:2b

This doesn't solve the problem because my use of `super()` in the base classes still doesn't play well with the multiple inheritance. Also, if I were to change the base classes, or even just their names, I would also have to rewrite the `Calzone` initializer.

The preferred method is to still use `super()` and write the base classes of `Sandwich` and `Pizza` to be used *cooperatively*. This means their initializers, or any other instance methods meant to be used with `super()`, can work either alone or in the context of multiple inheritance.

For the initializers to work cooperatively, they must not make assumptions about what class will be called with `super()`. If I initialize `Pizza` by itself, then `super()` will refer to `Food`, but when `Pizza.__init__()` is accessed via `super()` from an instance of `Calzone`, it will refer to `Sandwich` instead. It all depends on the method resolution order on the instance (rather than the class).

Here, I'll rewrite `Pizza` and `Sandwich` so their initializers are cooperative:

```
class Food:
    def __init__(self, name):
        self.name = name


class Pizza(Food):
    def __init__(self, toppings, name="Pizza", **kwargs):
```

```
    super().__init__(name=name, **kwargs)
    self.toppings = toppings


class Sandwich(Food):
    def __init__(self, bread, fillings, name="Sandwich", **kwargs):
        super().__init__(name=name, **kwargs)
        self.bread = bread
        self.fillings = fillings
```

Listing 13-13: make_calzone.py:1b

Both initializers will accept keyword arguments and must also accept any other unknown keyword arguments in the variadic parameter, **kwargs. This is important, as it will be impossible to know in advance all the arguments that may be passed up via super().__init__().

Each initializer explicitly accepts the arguments it needs, and then it sends the rest up the method resolution order via super().__init__(). In both cases, however, I provide a default value for name for when Pizza or Sandwich is instantiated directly. I pass name up to the next initializer, along with all the leftover arguments (if any) in **kwargs.

To use these cooperative initializers, the new Calzone class looks like this:

```
class Calzone(Pizza, Sandwich):
    def __init__(self, toppings):
        super().__init__(
            toppings=toppings,
            bread='pizza crust',
            fillings=toppings,
            name='Calzone'
        )


# The usage...
pizza = Pizza(toppings="pepperoni")
sandwich = Sandwich(bread="rye", fillings="swiss")
calzone = Calzone("sausage")
```

Listing 13-14: make_calzone.py:2c

I only need one call to super().__init__(), which will point to Pizza .__init__(), due to the method resolution order. However, I pass all the arguments for all the initializers in the superclass linearization. I only use keyword arguments, each with a unique name, to ensure that every initializer can pick up what it needs, regardless of the method resolution order.

Pizza.__init__() uses the toppings keyword argument and then passes the rest on. Sandwich.__init__() is next in the method resolution order, and it picks up bread and fillings before passing name up to the next class, Food. More importantly, this code will still work, even if I swap the order of Pizza and Sandwich in the inheritance list for Calzone.

As you can see from just that simple example, designing cooperative base classes requires some careful planning.

Mixins

One particular upside of multiple inheritance is that you can work with mixins. A *mixin* is a special type of incomplete (and even invalid) class that contains functionality you might want to add to multiple other classes.

Typically, mixins are used to share common methods for logging, database connections, networking, authentication, and much more. Whenever you need to reuse the same methods (not just functions) across multiple classes, mixins are one of the best ways to accomplish that.

Mixins do use inheritance, but they are the exception to the rule that inheritance decisions should be based on data. Mixins essentially rely on a form of *composition* that happens to leverage the inheritance mechanism. A mixin seldom has its own attributes; instead, it often relies its on expectations about the attributes and methods of the classes that use it.

In case that's making your brain hurt a bit, here's an example.

Say I'm creating an application that relies on a *live* settings file that can be updated at any time. I'll write multiple classes that need to grab information from this settings file. (In reality, I'm only writing one such class for the example. You can imagine the rest.)

First, I create the file *livesettings.ini*, which I'll store in the same directory as the module I'm about to write. Here are contents of that *.ini* file:

```
[MAGIC]
UserName = Jason
MagicNumber = 42
```

Listing 13-15: livesettings.ini

Next is my mixin, which contains only the functionality for working with this settings file:

```
import configparser
from pathlib import Path


class SettingsFileMixin:

    settings_path = Path('livesettings.ini')
    config = configparser.ConfigParser()

    def read_setting(self, key):
        self.config.read(self.settings_path)
        try:
            return self.config[self.settings_section][key]
        except KeyError:
            raise KeyError("Invalid section in settings file.")
```

Listing 13-16: mixins.py:1

The class SettingsFileMixin is not a complete class by itself. It lacks an initializer and even refers to an instance attribute it doesn't have, self.settings_section. This is okay, as mixins are never intended to be used by themselves. That missing attribute will need to be provided by any class that uses the mixin.

The mixin does have a couple of class attributes, settings_path and config. Most importantly, it has a read_setting() method, which reads a setting from the *.ini* file. This method uses the configparser module to read and return a setting specified by key from a particular section: self.settings_section, in the *.ini* file that the class attribute settings_path points to. If the section, the key, or even the file does not exist, the method will raise a KeyError.

Here's a class that prints a greeting to the user. I want this class to acquire the username from the *livesetting.ini* file. To do that, I'll have this new class use the mixin SettingsFileMixin by inheriting from it:

```python
class Greeter(SettingsFileMixin):

    def __init__(self, greeting):
        self.settings_section = 'MAGIC'
        self.greeting = greeting

    def __str__(self):
        try:
            name = self.read_setting('UserName')
        except KeyError:
            name = "user"
        return f"{self.greeting} {name}!"
```

Listing 13-17: mixins.py:2

The Greeter class is initialized with a string to use as the greeting. In the initializer, I define that self.settings_section instance attribute upon which the SettingsFileMixin relies. (In a production-quality mixin, you'd document the necessity for this attribute.)

The __str__() instance method uses the self.read_setting() method from the mixin, as if it had been defined as part of this class.

The usefulness of this becomes obvious if I add another class, such as one that works with the MagicNumber value from *livesetting.ini*:

```python
class MagicNumberPrinter(SettingsFileMixin):

    def __init__(self, greeting):
        self.settings_section = 'MAGIC'

    def __str__(self):
        try:
            magic_number = self.read_setting('MagicNumber')
        except KeyError:
            magic_number = "unknown"
        return f"The magic number is {magic_number}!"
```

Listing 13-18: mixins.py:3

I can have as many classes as I want read from *livesetting.ini* by having them inherit SettingsFileMixin. That mixin provides the single canonical source of that functionality in my project, so any improvements or bug fixes I make to the mixin will be picked up by all the classes that use it.

Here's an example usage of my Greeter class:

```
greeter = Greeter("Salutations,")
for i in range(100000):
    print(greeter)
```

Listing 13-19: mixins.py:4

I run the print() statement in a loop to demonstrate the effects of changing the livesettings.ini file live.

If you're trying this out along with the book, open the *.ini* file before starting the module and change UserName to yours, *but do not save the changes yet.* Now run the *mixins.py* module. Once it starts, save the changes to *livesettings.ini* and observe the change:

```
# --snip--
Salutations, Jason!
Salutations, Jason!
Salutations, Jason!
Salutations, Bob!
Salutations, Bob!
Salutations, Bob!
# --snip--
```

Wrapping Up

Inheritance isn't quite the dirty word in Python that it sometimes is in other languages. It provides the mechanism for extending classes and enforcing interfaces, resulting in clean and well-structured code in situations that would otherwise lead to spaghetti.

Multiple inheritance works well in Python, thanks to the C3 linearization method resolution order, which sidesteps most of the problems usually presented by the diamond inheritance problem. This, in turn, makes it possible to use mixins to add methods to classes.

With all these shiny, clever-looking tools, it is important to remember that inheritance in its many forms can also easily get out of hand. Before employing any of the tactics in this chapter, you should fully determine what problem you're trying to solve. At the end of the day, your goal is to create readable, maintainable code. Although inheritance can detract from this when used wrong, if employed judiciously, these techniques can make your code significantly easier to read and maintain.

14

METACLASSES AND ABCS

Python developers are well familiar with the mantra, "Everything is an object." When looking at the class system in Python, however, this becomes a paradox: If everything is an object, then what is a class? The seemingly arcane answer to that question unlocks another powerful tool in the Python toolbox: abstract base classes, which are one way of outlining expected behaviors of a type when using duck typing.

In this chapter, I'll be digging into metaclasses, abstract base classes, and how you can use them to write more maintainable classes.

Metaclasses

Classes are instances of *metaclasses*, in the same way that objects are instances of classes. More precisely, every class is an instance of type, and type is a metaclass. Metaclasses allow you to override how a class is created.

To build on the analogy from Chapter 13, just as a house can be constructed from a blueprint, the blueprint can be made from a template. A metaclass is that template. One template can be used to produce many different blueprints, and many different houses can be built from any one of those blueprints.

Before I go any further, a disclaimer is appropriate: you may reasonably go through your entire career without even once using metaclasses directly. By themselves, they're almost certainly not the solution to whatever problem you're thinking about using them for. Tim Peters summarizes this warning exceptionally well:

> [Metaclasses] are deeper magic than 99% of users should ever worry about. If you wonder whether you need them, you don't (the people who actually need them know with certainty that they need them, and don't need an explanation about why).

However, understanding metaclasses *does* help with comprehending other Python features, including abstract base classes. Django, a Python web framework, also makes frequent use of metaclasses internally. Rather than trying to contrive a somewhat believable usage for metaclasses, I'll stick to the bare minimum to demonstrate how they work.

Creating Classes with type

You might have used the type() callable in the past to return the type of a value or object, like this:

```
print(type("Hello"))    # prints "<class 'str'>"
print(type(123))        # prints "<class 'int'>"

class Thing: pass
print(type(Thing))      # prints "<class 'type'>"

something = Thing()
print(type(something))  # prints "<class '__main__.Thing'>"

print(type(type))       # prints "<class 'type'>"
```

Listing 14-1: types.py

The type() callable is actually a metaclass, rather than a function, meaning it can be used to create classes the same way in which a class is used to create instances. Here's an example of creating a class from type():

```
Food = type('Food', (), {})
```

Listing 14-2: classes_from_type.py:1

First, I create a class Food. It inherits from nothing and has no methods or attributes. I'm literally instantiating the metaclass. This is an effective equivalent to the code below:

```
class Food: pass
```

(In production code, I'd never define an empty base class, but doing so here is helpful for demonstration purposes.) Next, I'll instantiate the type metaclass again to create another class, Pizza, which derives from Food:

```
def __init__(obj, toppings):
    obj.toppings = toppings

Pizza = type(❶ 'Pizza', ❷ (Food,), ❸ {'name':'pizza', '__init__':__init__})
```

Listing 14-3: classes_from_type.py:2

I define the function __init__(), which will be the initializer of the upcoming Pizza class. I named the first parameter obj, since this isn't *actually* a member of a class yet.

Next, I create the Pizza class by calling type() and passing the name for the class ❶, a tuple of base classes ❷, and a dictionary of methods and class attributes ❸. This is where I pass the __init__ function I wrote.

Here is the functional equivalent of the preceding:

```
class Pizza(Food):
    name = pizza

    def __init__(self):
        self.toppings = toppings
```

As you can see, the normal syntax for creating a class is a lot more readable and practical. The benefit of the type metaclass is that you can create classes somewhat dynamically during runtime, although there is seldom a practical reason to do so.

The familiar approach of creating a class with the class keyword is really just syntactic sugar for instantiating the type metaclass. Either way, the end result is the same, as this usage indicates:

```
print(Pizza.name)                        # 'name' is a class attribute
pizza = Pizza(['sausage', 'garlic'])     # instantiate like normal
print(pizza.toppings)                    # prints "['sausage', 'garlic']"
```

Listing 14-4: classes_from_type.py:2

Custom Metaclasses

You can create a custom metaclass to use as a blueprint for classes. In this way, metaclasses are really only useful for modifying the deep internal behavior of how the language instantiates and works with the class.

A metaclass will often override the __new__() method, as this is the constructor method that governs the creation of the class. Here's an example of this, via an admittedly pointless metaclass, Gadget:

```
class Gadget(type):

    def __new__(self, name, bases, namespace):
        print(f"Creating a {name} gadget!")
        return super().__new__(self, name, bases, namespace)
```

Listing 14-5: metaclass.py:1

The special method __new__() is what is called behind the scenes when you invoke type() or any other metaclass, such as you saw in Listing 14-2. The __new__() method here prints a message that the class is being created, and it then invokes the __new__() method from the type base metaclass. This method is expected by the language to accept four arguments.

The first parameter here is self. The __new__() method is written as an instance method on the metaclass, because it is supposed to be a class method on any instance of this metaclass. If you're feeling lost, read that a few times and let it sink in, remembering that a class is an instance of a metaclass.

Another special method often implemented by metaclasses is __prepare__(). Its purpose is to create the dictionary that stores all the methods and class attributes for the class being created (see Chapter 15). Here's one for my Gadget metaclass:

```
    @classmethod
    def __prepare__(cls, name, bases):
        return {'color': 'white'}
```

Listing 14-6: metaclass.py:2

The @classmethod decorator indicates that this method belongs to the metaclass itself, not to a class instantiated from this metaclass. (If your brain starts to overheat at this point, I highly recommend eating a scoop of ice cream.) The __prepare__() method also must accept two more parameters, conventionally named name and bases.

The __prepare__() special method returns the dictionary that stores all the attributes and methods on the class. In this case, I'm returning a dictionary that already has a value, so all classes created from the Gadget metaclass will have a color class attribute, with the value 'white'.

Otherwise, I would just return an empty dictionary that each class can fill. In fact, I can omit the __prepare__() method in that case; the type metaclass already provides this method via inheritance, and the Python interpreter is smart about handling a lack of a __prepare__ method anyway.

That's it for the Gadget metaclass!

Now, I'll create an ordinary class using the Gadget metaclass:

```
class Thingamajig(metaclass=Gadget):
    def __init__(self, widget):
        self.widget = widget

    def frob(self):
        print(f"Frobbing {self.widget}.")
```

Listing 14-7: metaclass.py:3

The interesting feature here is that I've specified the metaclass in the inheritance list using metaclass=Gadget.

The added behavior from the Gadget metaclass is present, as you can see from this example usage:

```
thing = Thingamajig("button")   # also prints "Creating Thingamajig gadget!"
thing.frob()                    # prints "Frobbing button."

print(Thingamajig.color)        # prints "white"
print(thing.__class__)          # prints "<class '__main__.Thingamajig'>"
```

Listing 14-8: metaclass.py:4

The Thingamajig class is instantiated, and I can use it in the same way as any other class, except for certain key differences: instantiating the class prints a message, and Thingamajig has a color class attribute with the default value "white".

GOTCHA ALERT   Multiple inheritance gets tricky when metaclasses are involved. If class C inherits from classes A and B, the metaclass of C must be either the same as or a subclass of the metaclasses of A and B.

Those are the basic principles of creating and using metaclasses. If you are still tracking with me, congratulate yourself, as this is a difficult topic.

You may have observed that I could have implemented those same behaviors with Gadget and Thingamajig via ordinary inheritance, instead of mucking about with a custom metaclass, and you are absolutely right! The trouble is, it's nearly impossible to think of good uses for metaclasses, so we always wind up contriving some awful example like the above, just to demonstrate *how* they work. As Tim Peters said, "The people who actually need them know with certainty that they need them, and don't need an explanation about why."

In my own work, I once used a metaclass to implement __getattr__() (discussed in Chapter 15), which provides fallback behavior when a class attribute is not defined. A metaclass was undeniably the right solution to the problem. (Then my co-worker Patrick Viafore pointed out that I was also solving the wrong problem. Go figure.)

Metaclasses are also the best way to implement the singleton design pattern in Python, wherein you only ever have one instance of an object in existence. However, the singleton is almost never useful in Python, as you can accomplish the same thing with static methods.

There's a reason Python developers have struggled to come up with viable examples for metaclasses for decades. Metaclasses are something you will seldom, if ever, use directly, except in that rare instance when you instinctively *know* it's the right tool for the job.

Type Expectations with Duck Typing

Metaclasses do enable the powerful concept of abstract base classes in Python. These allow you to codify expectations for a type in terms of their behaviors. Before I can explain abstract base classes, however, I need to unpack some important principles of duck typing in Python.

In Chapter 13, I asserted that in Python, you do not need to use inheritance in order to write a function that accepts objects of different types as arguments. Python employs duck typing, meaning that instead of caring about an object's *type*, it only expects an object to provide the needed interface. When working with duck typing, there are three ways of ensuring a particular argument has the necessary functionality: catching exceptions, testing for attributes, or checking for a particular interface.

EAFP: Catching Exceptions

Back in Chapter 8, I introduced the philosophy of *Easier to Ask Forgiveness than Permission (EAFP)*, which advocates raising an exception if an argument is missing functionality. This is ideal in situations where you're providing the arguments yourself in your code, since unhandled exceptions will alert you to the places where the code needs to be improved.

However, it is unwise to use this technique anywhere an unhandled exception might evade detection until a user attempts to use the program in an unexpected or untested way. This consideration is known as *fail-fast*: a program in an erroneous state should fail as early in the call stack as possible, to reduce the chances of bugs evading detection.

LBYL: Checking for Attributes

For more complex or brittle code, it may be better to adhere to the philosophy of *Look Before You Leap (LBYL)*, in which you check for the functionality you need on an argument or value before proceeding. There are two ways to do this. For situations where you rely on one or two methods on an object, you can use the hasattr() function to check for the methods, or even attributes, that you need.

However, using hasattr() isn't necessarily as simple or clear as one might hope. Here's an example of a function that multiplies every third element in the collection passed to it:

```
def product_of_thirds(sequence):
    if not ❶ hasattr(sequence, '__iter__'):
        raise ValueError("Argument must be iterable.")
```

```
    r = sequence[0]
    for i in sequence[1::3]:
        r *= i
    return r


print(product_of_thirds(range(1, 50)))   # prints '262134882788466688000'
print(product_of_thirds(False))          # raises TypeError
```

Listing 14-9: product_of_thirds.py:1a

Right at the top of my product_of_thirds function, I use the hasattr()
function to check that the argument sequence has an attribute named
__iter__ ❶. This works because all methods are technically attributes. If
the argument doesn't have an attribute by that name, I raise an error.

However, this technique can be subtly wrong. For one thing, not
everything that is iterable is necessarily subscriptable, and the code
in Listing 14-9 is erroneously assuming that it is. Meanwhile, consider
what would happen if I passed an instance of the following class to
product_of_thirds():

```
class Nonsense:
    def __init__(self):
        self.__iter__ = self
```

While this example is contrived, there is nothing stopping a developer
from hackishly repurposing a name that is assumed to mean something
else—yes, nasty things like this show up in real code. The result would
cause the hasattr() test to pass anyway. The hasattr() function only checks
that the object has *some* attribute with that name; it doesn't concern itself
with the attribute's type or interface.

Second, one must be careful about making assumptions regarding what
any single function will actually do. Building on my example in Listing 14-9,
I might add the following logic to try to check that my sequence contained
values that could be multiplied by one another:

```
def product_of_thirds(sequence):
    if (
        not hasattr(sequence, '__iter__')
        or not hasattr(sequence, '__getitem__'
    ):
        raise TypeError("Argument must be iterable.")
    elif not hasattr(sequence[0], '__mul__'):
        raise TypeError("Sequence elements must support multiplication.")

    r = sequence[0]
    for i in sequence[1::3]:
        r *= i
    return r

# --snip--
```

```
print(product_of_thirds(range(1, 50)))   # prints '262134882788466688000'
print(product_of_thirds("Foobarbaz"))    # raises WRONG TypeError
```

Listing 14-10: product_of_thirds.py:1b

By checking for __getitem__() along with __iter__(), I know the object has to be subscriptable.

Still another problem is that a string object does implement __mul__() but doesn't use it as expected. Trying to run this version of the code raises a TypeError when passing a string to product_of_thirds(), but with the wrong message:

```
TypeError: can't multiply sequence by non-int of type 'str'
```

Hmm, that's not the message I specified. The problem is that the test failed to identify that the function logic—namely, multiplication between collection items—makes no sense on a string.

Third, sometimes inheritance itself can create situations where a hasattr() test result can be subtly wrong. For example, if you wanted to ensure that an object implemented the special method __ge__ (for the >= operator), you might expect this to work:

```
if not hasattr(some_obj, '__ge__'):
    raise TypeError
```

Unfortunately for this test, __ge__ is implemented on the base class object, from which all classes inherit, so this test will *virtually never fail*, even when you expect it should.

All this is to say that while hasattr() is appropriate for extremely simple scenarios, as soon as your expectations about an argument's type get complicated, you need a better way to look before leaping with duck typing.

Abstract Classes

An *abstract base class (ABC)* allows you to specify particular interfaces that must be implemented by any class that inherits from the ABC. If the derived class does not provide the expected interface, the class instantiation will fail. This provides a more robust means of checking whether an object has particular traits, such as being iterable or subscriptable. In one sense, you can consider an ABC to be a sort of interface contract: the class agrees to implement the methods specified by the ABC.

ABCs cannot be directly instantiated; they can only be inherited by another class. Typically, an ABC only defines what methods are expected, and it leaves the actual implementation of those methods to the derived class. Under some circumstances, an ABC may provide the implementations of some methods.

You can use ABCs to check that your object actually implements an interface. This technique avoids the subtly wrong situation of a method being defined on some distant base class. If an ABC mandates that __str__()

be implemented, any class that inherits from that ABC will be expected to implement __str__() itself, or else I won't be able to instantiate the class; it will not matter that object.__str__() is valid.

A word of caution: Python's concept of abstract base classes should not be compared to virtual and abstract inheritance in C++, Java, or other object-oriented languages. Despite some similarities, they work in fundamentally different ways. Treat them as separate concepts.

Built-in ABCs

Python provides an ABC for iterators and a few other common interfaces, but it doesn't *require* you to inherit from a particular base class to make your object an iterator. The distinction between an ABC and ordinary inheritance is that an ABC seldom provides the actual functionality—instead, inheriting from the ABC means the class is required to implement the expected methods.

The collections.abc and numbers modules contain nearly all of the built-in abstract classes, with a few others floating around contextlib (for with statements), selectors, and asyncio.

To demonstrate how ABCs fit into an LBYL strategy, I'll rewrite the example I started in Listing 14-10. I will use two ABCs to ensure the argument sequence has the interface my product_of_thirds() function expects:

```
from collections.abc import Sequence
from numbers import Complex


def product_of_thirds(sequence):
    if not isinstance(sequence, Sequence):
        raise TypeError("Argument must be a sequence.")
    if not isinstance(sequence[0], Complex):
        raise TypeError("Sequence elements must support multiplication.")

    r = sequence[0]
    for i in sequence[1::3]:
        r *= i
    return r


print(product_of_thirds(range(1, 50)))   # prints '262134882788466688000'
print(product_of_thirds("Foobarbaz"))    # raises TypeError
```

Listing 14-11: product_of_thirds.py:1c

The implementation of the product_of_thirds() function expects the argument sequence to be a sequence, and thus an iterable—or else it wouldn't work with the for loop—and its elements to support multiplication.

I check for an expected interface using isinstance() to find out if the given object is an instance of a class or an instance of a subclass thereof. I ensure that sequence itself is derived from collections.abc.Sequence, meaning it implements the __iter__() instance method.

I also check the first element of the sequence to ensure it is derived from numeric.Complex, which implies (among other things) that it supports basic numeric operations, including multiplication. Although a string implements the special method _mul_(), it does *not* derive from numeric .Complex. It couldn't reasonably do so, since it doesn't support the rest of the expected mathematical operators and methods. Thus, it fails the test here, as it should.

Deriving from ABCs

ABCs are useful for identifying which classes implement a particular interface, so it's beneficial to consider which ABCs your own classes should inherit from, especially when you are writing a library for other Python developers to use.

To demonstrate this, I'll rewrite my example from the end of Chapter 9 with custom iterable and iterator classes to use ABCs, thereby allowing the interface checking with isinstance().

First, I need to import a few ABCs from the collections.abc module. I'll explain why I'm importing these ABCs shortly, when I actually use them.

```
from collections.abc import Container, Sized, Iterable, Iterator
```

Listing 14-12: cafe_queue_abc.py:1a

Then, I'll modify my CafeQueue class from the Chapter 9 example to use three abstract base classes that promise important components of the class's functionality:

```
class CafeQueue(Container, Sized, Iterable):

    def __init__(self):
        self._queue = []
        self._orders = {}
        self._togo = {}

    def __iter__(self):
        return CafeQueueIterator(self)

    def __len__(self):
        return len(self._queue)

    def __contains__(self, customer):
        return (customer in self._queue)

    def add_customer(self, customer, *orders, to_go=True):
        self._queue.append(customer)
        self._orders[customer] = tuple(orders)
        self._togo[customer] = to_go
```

Listing 14-13: cafe_queue_abc.py:2a

I've made no changes to the implementation of this class, but I am now inheriting from three different ABCs, all of which come from the collections.abc module. I selected these particular ABCs based on the methods I'm implementing on the class. The CafeQueue class implements __iter__() to work with iteration, so I inherit from the ABC Iterable. The Container ABC requires __contains__(), which allows CafeQueue to work with the in operator. The Sized ABC requires __len__(), which means CafeQueue objects work with len(). The functionality is the same as it was in Chapter 9, but now, there is a reliable way of testing that this class supports iteration, in, and len().

Because ABCs use metaclasses under the hood, they have the same problems with multiple inheritance that metaclasses do. I don't have issues here because type(Container), type(Sized), and type(Iterable) are all instances of the abc.ABCMeta metaclass, but I wouldn't be able to simultaneously inherit from an ABC or class that uses an altogether different metaclass.

I can achieve the same effect in a cleaner and simpler way by using the Collection ABC, which itself inherits from Container, Sized, and Iterable. This shortens the import line:

```python
from collections.abc import Collection, Iterator
```

Listing 14-14: cafe_queue_abc.py:1b

More importantly, it cleans up the inheritance list on the CafeQueue class:

```python
class CafeQueue(Collection):

    def __init__(self):
        self._queue = []
        self._orders = {}
        self._togo = {}

    def __iter__(self):
        return CafeQueueIterator(self)

    def __len__(self):
        return len(self._queue)

    def __contains__(self, customer):
        return (customer in self._queue)

    def add_customer(self, customer, *orders, to_go=True):
        self._queue.append(customer)
        self._orders[customer] = tuple(orders)
        self._togo[customer] = to_go
```

Listing 14-15: cafe_queue_abc.py:2b

This version is effectively identical to the previous one in Listing 14-13.

Next, I adjust my CafeQueueIterator class from Chapter 9 to use the Iterator ABC:

```python
class CafeQueueIterator(Iterator):

    def __init__(self, iterable):
```

```
            self._iterable = iterable
            self._position = 0

        def __next__(self):
            if self._position >= len(self._iterable):
                raise StopIteration

            customer = self._iterable._queue[self._position]
            orders = self._iterable._orders[customer]
            togo = self._iterable._togo[customer]

            self._position += 1

            return (customer, orders, togo)

        def __iter__(self):
            return self
```

Listing 14-16: cafe_queue_abc.py:3

Once again, I haven't changed the implementation from the version in Chapter 9, except to inherit from Iterator. That ABC requires the __next__() method and inherits from Iterable, thereby also requiring __iter__().

Here's a revised usage of my CafeQueue class, to demonstrate ABCs at work:

```
def serve_customers(queue):
 ❶ if not isinstance(queue, Collection):
        raise TypeError("serve_next() requires a collection.")

    if not len(queue):
        print("Queue is empty.")
        return

    def brew(order):
        print(f"(Making {order}...)")

    for customer, orders, to_go in queue:
        for order in orders: brew(order)
        if to_go:
            print(f"Order for {customer}!")
        else:
            print(f"(Takes order to {customer})")


queue = CafeQueue()
queue.add_customer('Raquel', 'double macchiato', to_go=False)
queue.add_customer('Naomi', 'large mocha, skim')
queue.add_customer('Anmol', 'mango lassi')

serve_customers(queue)
```

Listing 14-17: cafe_queue_abc.py:4a

In the serve_customers() function, I check that the queue argument is an instance of a class inheriting from the Collection ABC before proceeding ❶, as the function logic is relying on both len() and iteration.

Running this code produces what you'd expect:

```
(Making double macchiato...)
(Takes order to Raquel)
(Making large mocha, skim...)
Order for Naomi!
(Making mango lassi...)
Order for Anmol!
```

Although there are no functional changes to the example, ABCs contribute two advantages. First, anyone using my classes can check their functionality through the standard library ABCs. Second, and perhaps more important, it's an insurance policy against one of these special methods the code relies on being accidentally removed from a class.

Implementing Custom ABCs

There often isn't a preexisting abstract base class for everything you need, so you'll need to write your own. You can make a class an ABC by having it inherit from abc.ABC or another ABC *and* giving it at least one method marked with the @abstractmethod decorator.

For my CafeQueue example, I'll create a custom ABC to define a queue of customers. The rest of my code will expect a queue of customers to have certain methods and behaviors, so I'll use the ABC to codify those expectations up front:

```
from collections.abc import Collection, Iterator
from abc import abstractmethod


class CustomerQueue(Collection):

    @abstractmethod
    def add_customer(self, customer): pass

    @property
    @abstractmethod
    def first(self): pass
```

Listing 14-18: cafe_queue_abc.py:1c

I make the CustomerQueue class inherit from Collection so its own derived classes must implement __iter__(), __len__(), and __contains__(), and so CustomerQueue indirectly inherits from ABC via Collection. Then, I add two additional abstract methods—add_customer() and the property first()—each marked with the @abstractmethod decorator, which I imported from abc. Any class that inherits from CustomerQueue must implement that property and those methods.

Before Python 3.3, if you wanted to require some types of methods in an abstract class, you had to use special decorators like @abstractproperty, @abstractclassmethod, and @abstractstaticmethod. You'll still see code like that, but thankfully, that's no longer necessary; instead, as long as @abstractmethod is the innermost decorator, you can use the usual method decorators, like @property.

While I can add abstract methods to require derived classes to have particular instance methods, class methods, static methods, and even properties, I *cannot* require derived classes to have particular instance attributes. ABCs are intended to specify *interfaces*, not data.

None of my abstract methods need implementations here, although I could write default implementations to be explicitly called via super().

I can now update my CafeQueue class to inherit from this new CustomerQueue ABC:

```python
class CafeQueue(CustomerQueue):

    def __init__(self):
        self._queue = []
        self._orders = {}
        self._togo = {}

    def __iter__(self):
        return CafeQueueIterator(self)

    def __len__(self):
        return len(self._queue)

    def __contains__(self, customer):
        return (customer in self._queue)

    def add_customer(self, customer, *orders, to_go=True):
        self._queue.append(customer)
        self._orders[customer] = tuple(orders)
        self._togo[customer] = to_go

    @property
    def first(self):
        return self._queue[0]
```

Listing 14-19: cafe_queue_abc.py:2c

I need to add the required property, first(), which, in my case, I use to peek at the name of the first person in line. If I don't add this property, running the code would produce an error like this:

```
TypeError: Can't instantiate abstract class CafeQueue with abstract method first
```

Since I have implemented first(), I don't need to worry about that error occurring.

I'll also update the serve_customers() function to require a CustomerQueue, rather than a Collection. I can do this here because CustomerQueue inherits from Collection, so any class that inherits from CustomerQueue will also satisfy the interface of Collection.

```
def serve_customers(queue):
    if not isinstance(queue, CustomerQueue):
        raise TypeError("serve_next() requires a customer queue.")

    if not len(queue):
        print("Queue is empty.")
        return

    def brew(order):
        print(f"(Making {order}...)")

    for customer, orders, to_go in queue:
        for order in orders: brew(order)
        if to_go:
            print(f"Order for {customer}!")
        else:
            print(f"(Takes order to {customer})")


queue = CafeQueue()
queue.add_customer('Raquel', 'double macchiato', to_go=False)
queue.add_customer('Naomi', 'large mocha, skim')
queue.add_customer('Anmol', 'mango lassi')

print(f"The first person in line is {queue.first}.")
serve_customers(queue)
```

Listing 14-20: cafe_queue_abc.py:4b

In addition to testing whether queue is an instance of a class that inherits from CustomerQueue, I use the queue.first property toward the end, to test it out.

Running that code still produces the expected output:

```
The first person in line is Raquel.
(Making double macchiato...)
(Takes order to Raquel)
(Making large mocha, skim...)
Order for Naomi!
(Making mango lassi...)
Order for Anmol!
```

Aside from being able to check who is first in line, the functionality here hasn't changed from prior versions of this example. As before, using ABCs here ensures that CafeQueue implements all the functionality the rest of my code depends on. If part of the expected interface is missing, the code will fail right away, instead of mid-execution.

Virtual Subclasses

As you start relying on custom abstract classes, you may reach a conundrum: you might require an argument to be an instance of a class derived from your custom ABC, and yet, you may want to somehow allow instances of certain preexisting classes to be used as well. For example, you cannot modify the built-in list class just to report that it satisfies some interface you specified in a custom ABC.

Virtual subclassing allows you to cause an ABC to report certain classes as being derived, even if they aren't. This allows you to indicate particular built-in and third-party classes as fulfilling the interface outlined by one of your custom ABCs.

This works because calling isinstance(Derived, Base) or issubclass(Derived, Base) first checks for and calls the method Base.__instancecheck__(Derived) or Base.__subclasscheck__(Derived), respectively. Otherwise, Derived.__isinstance__(Base) or Derived.__issubclass__(Base) is called.

A critical limitation of virtual subclassing is that you're bypassing the interface enforcement and instead reporting that *you* have verified that a particular class satisfies the interface. You can make any class a virtual subclass of ABC, but it's entirely your own responsibility to ensure it has the expected interface.

Setting Up the Example

I'll first create an example of a custom ABC that doesn't use virtual subclassing, but where virtual subclassing can be helpful. Say that I'm creating a library of super-useful functions all related to palindromes, and I want to ensure I'm working with objects that implement certain methods: specifically, __reversed__(), __iter__(), and __str__(). I don't want to require any further methods, since I'll write a custom class for working with a sentence palindrome, which is more complex than a word palindrome. Unfortunately, there isn't a built-in ABC that supports all those methods and *only* those.

There are different forms of palindromes, and I want to be able to interact with them all in the same way. This is why I create the custom Palindromable ABC:

```
from abc import ABC, abstractmethod


class Palindromable(ABC):

    @abstractmethod
    def __reversed__(self): pass

    @abstractmethod
    def __iter__(self): pass

    @abstractmethod
    def __str__(self): pass
```

Listing 14-21: palindrome_check.py:1

The `Palindromable` ABC class doesn't expand on any other ABC, so I only inherit from `abc.ABC`. With this ABC, I require the three methods I mentioned.

I now build a special `LetterPalindrome` class that interprets a string as a letter-based palindrome or sentence palindrome. This class inherits from the ABC `Palindromable`:

```
class LetterPalindrome(Palindromable):

    def __init__(self, string):
        self._raw = string
        self._stripped = ''.join(filter(str.isalpha, string.lower()))

    def __str__(self):
        return self._raw

    def __iter__(self):
        return self._stripped.__iter__()

    def __reversed__(self):
        return reversed(self._stripped)
```

Listing 14-22: palindrome_check.py:2

The initializer of `LetterPalindrome` accepts a string, strips out any non-letters, and converts it to all lowercase, thereby allowing it to check whether it's a palindrome by reversing it and comparing it to the original.

Although I'm omitting it for reasons of space, I could also create a `WordPalindrome` class, which similarly accepts a string but reverses it word by word, instead of letter by letter.

I also implement all three required methods. Remember that, because the ABC mandates a `__str__()` method, I *must* implement it here. It doesn't matter that one of the base classes—namely, `object`—has implemented `__str__()`; the ABC overwrote it as an abstract method, forcing me to reimplement it.

GOTCHA ALERT This gets tricky as soon as multiple inheritance gets involved, so be mindful of the method resolution order. If class `X(ABC)` has an abstract method `foo()` and class `Y` provides method `foo()`, then while class `Z(X, Y)` will need to reimplement `foo()`, class `Z(Y, X)` will *not!*

Below is my function for checking whether something is a palindrome. This function doesn't care about the form of the palindrome; it just returns True as long as comparing the iterable to its reverse matches, item for item:

```
def check_palindrome(sequence):

    if not isinstance(sequence, Palindromable):
        raise TypeError("Cannot check for palindrome on that type.")

    for c, r in zip(sequence, reversed(sequence)):
        if c != r:
```

```
        print(f"NON-PALINDROME: {sequence}")
        return False
    print(f"PALINDROME: {sequence}")
    return True
```

Listing 14-23: palindrome_check.py:3

Before doing anything, I check that sequence is an instance of a class derived from `Palindromable`. If it is, I iteratively compare the items on sequence and its reversed form, indirectly relying on sequence.__iter__() and sequence.__reversed__(). In addition, I print a result onto the screen, indirectly using sequence.__str__().

If I passed this function an instance of any class that lacked those three methods, this code wouldn't make sense, and I would fail-fast with an exception. The particular strength of abstract base classes is that they aid in safely and effectively utilizing a form of duck typing. As long as a class can be used in a certain manner, it satisfies the ABC and nothing else matters.

I'll try out my palindrome checker so far by instantiating a couple of LetterPalindrome instances and passing them to check_palindrome():

```
canal = LetterPalindrome("A man, a plan, a canal - Panama!")
print(check_palindrome(canal))    # prints 'True'

bolton = LetterPalindrome("Bolton")
print(check_palindrome(bolton))   # prints 'False'
```

Listing 14-24: palindrome_check.py:4

Running that code outputs what I expect:

```
PALINDROME: A man, a plan, a canal - Panama!
True
NON-PALINDROME: Bolton
False
```

Using Virtual Subclassing

Because my check_palindrome() function expects a class that inherits from my `Palindromable` ABC, that function would fail to work with some built-in classes, like lists, which could be palindromic in their own right. Instead, trying to pass a list to check_palindrome() fails with a TypeError:

```
print(check_palindrome([1, 2, 3, 2, 1]))  # raises TypeError
```

Listing 14-25: palindrome_check.py:5a

The code fails because list isn't derived from `Palindromable`. I can't reasonably go back and edit Python's list class (nor should I try). Instead, I can make list a virtual subclass of `Palindromable`.

There are two ways of accomplishing this. The easiest is to register any class with an ABC by using the `register()` method, like this:

```
Palindromable.register(list)
print(check_palindrome([1, 2, 3, 2, 1]))  # prints 'True'
```

Listing 14-26: palindrome_check.py:5b

That revised version works now because list is a virtual subclass of Palindromable. Instead of changing the list class to actually inherit from the Palindromable ABC, I have the ABC claim that list is among its derived classes.

However, this only applies to list so far. If I tried to pass a tuple to check_palindrome(), which should also work, it similarly fails. Sure, I could register tuple the same as I did with list, but it would be a pain to have to register every imaginable compatible class as a virtual subclass of Palindromable.

Anything could be considered a valid virtual subclass of Palindromable, as long as it implements the required methods and was *ordered* (so that the elements can be reversed reliably) and *finite*. Thinking it through, any class that is ordered would probably also be subscriptable via __getitem__(), and if it were finite, it would have a __len__() method as well. The built-in ABC collections.abc.Sequence mandates both of these methods, in addition to __iter__() and __reversed__().

I can make Sequence a virtual subclass of Palindromable, thereby making any class that inherits from Sequence also a virtual subclass of Palindromable. I do that like this:

```
from collections.abc import Sequence  # This should be at the top of the file

# --snip--

Palindromable.register(Sequence)
print(check_palindrome([1, 2, 3, 2, 1]))  # prints 'True'
```

Listing 14-27: palindrome_check.py:5c

Now I can use list, tuple, and any other class that inherits from collections.abc.Sequence with check_palindrome().

If my rules for what qualifies as a Palindromable get any more complicated, as they often will in real life, I'll need to either add more calls to Palindromable.register() or find another technique altogether. To deal with these potential complications, I can implement a special class method on the ABC called __subclasshook__(), which is called by __subclasscheck__() and augments the subclass checking behavior.

```
from abc import ABC, abstractmethod
from collections.abc import Sequence

class Palindromable(ABC):

    @abstractmethod
```

```
def __reversed__(self): pass

@abstractmethod
def __iter__(self): pass

@abstractmethod
def __str__(self): pass

@classmethod
def __subclasshook__(cls, C):
    if issubclass(C, Sequence):
        return True
    return NotImplemented
```

Listing 14-28: palindrome_check.py:1d

The logic for the __subclasshook__() class method can be as simple or complex as I need it to be, and in this case, it's extraordinarily simple. In any case, __subclasshook__() must return True if C should be considered a subclass of the Palindromable ABC, False if it definitely shouldn't, and NotImplemented otherwise. This last part is important! When __subclasshook__() returns NotImplemented, it causes __subclasscheck__() to then check if C is an actual subclass, rather than a virtual one. If I returned False at the end of the method, it would cause my LetterPalindrome class to no longer be considered a subclass of Palindromable.

Unlike with most special methods, Python doesn't require me to implement __subclasscheck__() directly, because that would mean I had to reimplement all the complicated subclass checking logic.

With this change made, I no longer need to register list and Sequence as virtual subclasses:

```
print(check_palindrome([1, 2, 3, 2, 1]))                    # prints 'True'
print(check_palindrome((1, 2, 3, 2, 1)))                    # prints 'True'

print(check_palindrome('racecar'))                          # prints 'True'
print(check_palindrome('race car'))                         # prints 'False'
print(check_palindrome(LetterPalindrome('race car')))       # prints 'True'

print(check_palindrome({1, 2, 3, 2, 1}))                    # raises TypeError
```

Listing 14-29: palindrome_check.py:5d

As you can see, check_palindrome() now works with list, tuple, and str, in addition to LetterPalindrome.

Meanwhile, passing a set to check_palindrome() fails, which makes sense, because a set is unordered and cannot be reliably reversed.

Such is the beauty of duck typing with ABCs! I am able to write fail-fast code using a LBYL strategy, but I don't have to specify every conceivable class that would work with that code. Instead, by creating a Palindromable abstract base class and adding collections.abc.Sequence as a virtual subclass, I've made my function work with practically any class that implements the needed interface.

Wrapping Up

Metaclasses are the mysterious "blueprints" from which classes are instantiated, in the same way classes are the blueprints for objects. Although seldom used by themselves, metaclasses allow you to override or extend how a class is created.

You can use abstract base classes, or ABCs, to mandate and then check for a specific interface on a class.

None of this means you shouldn't use the type hints I mentioned back in Chapter 6. When it comes to enforcing a particular interface from a user perspective, annotations are going to be quite useful in clarifying how your code should be used. The purpose of ABCs and subclass checks is to make code that fails fast in situations where it cannot hope to succeed, especially when it may fail in subtle or unpredictable ways. Duck typing, inheritance, and type hints are complementary concepts. How they intersect in your code depends on you.

15

INTROSPECTION AND GENERICS

Introspection is the ability of code to access information about itself at runtime and respond accordingly. As an interpreted language, Python excels at introspection. By understanding how Python inspects objects, you can uncover a number of patterns for improving and optimizing your code.

In this chapter, I'll cover special attributes, which make this introspection possible. By making use of these special attributes, I'll cover generic functions, descriptors, and slots, and I'll even build an (effectively) immutable class. Then, while on the topic of code running itself, I'll touch on the dangers of arbitrary execution.

Special Attributes

Python achieves introspection primarily by storing important information in *special attributes* on the different objects in use. These special attributes give Python runtime knowledge about names, project structure, relationships between objects, and more.

Like special methods, all special attributes start and end with a double underscore (_).

You've already seen several of these special attributes in preceding chapters, like the special attribute __name__, which contains the name of the module being executed, except on the entry point module, where it has the value "__main__":

```
if __name__ == "__main__":
    main()
```

There is also the special attribute __file__, which contains the absolute path to the current module and can be used to find files in a package:

```
from pathlib import Path

path = Path(__file__) / Path("../resources/about.txt")
with path.open() as file:
    about = file.read()
```

In both cases, Python is able to access information about the structure of the project at runtime. That's introspection at work.

I'll introduce the various special attributes as I need them in this chapter. As a handy reference, I've listed all the special attributes in Python in Appendix A.

Inside Object Attribute Access: The __dict__ Special Attribute

To write introspective code, you must understand how Python stores the names and values of attributes. Every class and every object has an instance of the special attribute __dict__, which is a dictionary that stores attributes and methods. Much of the behavior relating to object attribute access depends on which dictionary—the one on the class or the one on the instance—contains a particular attribute or method. This is actually more complicated than you might expect.

Consider the following simple class structure defining a Llama as a Quadruped:

```
class Quadruped:
    leg_count = 4

    def __init__(self, species):
        self.species = species
```

```
class Llama(Quadruped):
    """A quadruped that lives in large rivers."""
    dangerous = True

    def __init__(self):
        self.swimming = False
        super().__init__("llama")

    def warn(self):
        if self.swimming:
            print("Cuidado, llamas!")

    @classmethod
    def feed(cls):
        print("Eats honey with beak.")
```

Listing 15-1: llama.py:1

The Quadruped and Llama classes here are designed specifically to demonstrate attribute access, so please overlook the violations of good object design here.

Let's inspect the __dict__ special attributes for the instance and two classes we created, to learn where Python stores everything:

```
llama = Llama()

from pprint import pprint

print("Instance __dict__:")
pprint(llama.__dict__)

print("\nLlama class __dict__:")
pprint(Llama.__dict__)

print("\nQuadruped class __dict__")
pprint(Quadruped.__dict__)
```

Listing 15-2: llama.py:2a

I'm using the pprint module and function to *pretty-print* the dictionaries, meaning I see each key-value pair in the dictionary on its own line. Pretty printing is useful for displaying complex collections in a more readable way. The output for this code shows the contents of the __dict__ special attributes:

```
Instance __dict__:
{ ❶ 'species': 'llama', 'swimming': False}

Llama class __dict__:
mappingproxy({'__doc__': 'A quadruped that lives in large rivers.',
              '__init__': <function Llama.__init__ at 0x7f191b6170d0>,
              '__module__': '__main__',
              'dangerous': True,
              'feed': <classmethod object at 0x7f191b619d60>,
```

❷ 'warn': <function Llama.warn at 0x7f191b617160>})

```
Quadruped class __dict__
mappingproxy({'__dict__': <attribute '__dict__' of 'Quadruped' objects>,
              '__doc__': None,
              '__init__': <function Quadruped.__init__ at 0x7f191b617040>,
              '__module__': '__main__',
              '__weakref__': <attribute '__weakref__' of 'Quadruped' objects>,
            ❸ 'leg_count': 4})
```

You might be surprised at where some things are located. The instance attributes of species and swimming are found on the instance itself ❶, but all the instance methods are stored on the class (rather than the instance) ❷, along with the class attributes and custom class methods. Quadruped.__dict__ stores the Quadruped class attribute leg_count ❸.

PEDANTIC NOTE   Nearly all the inherited special methods are stored in the __dict__ attribute of the universal base class, object, but the output of that is so impractically long that I've chosen to omit it here. You can look yourself if you're curious, via pprint(object.__dict__).

Another oddity is that the class __dict__ attribute is actually of type mappingproxy, a special class defined in types.MappingProxyType. Technical details aside, it's effectively a read-only view of a dictionary. The class's __dict__ attribute is this MappingProxyType, but the instance's __dict__ attribute is just an ordinary dictionary. Because of this, however, you cannot directly modify a class __dict__ special attribute.

Lastly, although it's impractical to depict here, all the special attributes and methods of the class itself are defined in the *metaclass's* __dict__ attribute. In most cases, including here, you can see that with pprint(type.__dict__).

You can see there are some complex rules regarding where any given attribute or method is stored. Although I can directly access any class or instance attribute or method through the right __dict__ special attribute, actually performing that lookup correctly is non-trivial. Python provides a better way.

Listing Attributes

There are two functions built for the purpose of inspecting the __dict__ attribute of any class or instance: vars() and dir().

The vars() function prints the __dict__ attribute for the given object or class, like this:

```
llama = Llama()

from pprint import pprint

print("Instance __dict__:")
pprint(vars(llama))

print("\nLlama class __dict__:")
```

```
pprint(vars(Llama))

print("\nQuadruped class __dict__")
pprint(vars(Quadruped))
```

Listing 15-3: llama.py:2b

The output of this code should be identical to that for Listing 15-2.

Running vars() without any argument inside a class, object, or function prints out the __dict__ for the current scope. Outside the scope of any objects, functions, and classes, it prints a dictionary representing the local symbol table. If you want the local or global symbol table as a dictionary, you can also run locals() or globals(), respectively. Be warned that you should never attempt to modify local or global values using the dictionaries returned from these functions.

The dir() built-in function returns a list of all names (but not values) in the current scope or the scope of the given object or class. By default, dir() compiles that list using the __dict__ attributes, and it will also include names from the base classes. You can override this behavior by writing your own __dir__() method, which you might do if you've modified your class in other ways, to handle names that aren't actually attributes.

In practice, these four functions—vars(), locals(), globals(), and dir()—are usually only useful when you're working in the interactive prompt, or else during debugging.

Getting an Attribute

To access an attribute, say leg_count or swimming, I'd ordinarily use the dot operator (.), like this:

```
print(llama.swimming)    # prints 'False'
print(Llama.leg_count)   # prints '4'
```

Listing 15-4: llama.py:3a

The dot operator on a class or object is syntactic sugar for the built-in function getattr(). Here are the equivalent function calls:

```
print(getattr(llama, 'swimming'))    # prints 'False'
print(getattr(Llama, 'leg_count'))   # prints '4'
```

Listing 15-5: llama.py:3b

In both cases, I pass two arguments to getattr(): the object I'm searching on, followed by the name I'm searching for as a string.

Behind the scenes, the getattr() function employs two special methods: __getattribute__(), which handles the complex lookup logic, and __getattr__(), which the user can optionally implement to further extend the behavior of the getattr() function on a class.

Ultimately, either object.__getattribute__() or type.__getattribute__() is involved in searching on an instance or class, respectively. Even if this special method is reimplemented by a derived class or metaclass, that reimplementation will have to explicitly call object.__getattribute__() or type.__getattribute__() to avoid infinite recursion. This is just as well, as it would be no small matter to correctly reimplement all the behavior of __getattribute__().

The __getattribute__() special method works by searching through the __dict__ objects on the instances and classes, following the method resolution order. If it doesn't find the attribute it's searching for, it raises an AttributeError. From there, getattr() will check whether the special method __getattr__() has been defined—that's the special user-defined method used as a fallback for attribute lookup when __getattribute__() fails. If __getattr__() has been defined, it is called by getattr() as a last step.

Here, I'll use __getattribute__() directly:

```
print(object.__getattribute__(llama, 'swimming'))   # prints 'False'
print(type.__getattribute__(Llama, 'leg_count'))    # prints '4'
```

Listing 15-6: llama.py:3c

Objects and metaclasses both have a __dict__ special attribute, which is used to store all other attributes by name. This is why you can add attributes to an object or class arbitrarily, even from outside the class definition. (There's an alternative means of storing attributes, which I'll return to later.)

Here is a rough reimplementation of the getattr() function, demonstrating how __getattribute__() and __gettattr__() are actually used in attribute lookups:

```
llama = Llama()

try:
    print(object.__getattribute__(llama, 'swimming'))
except AttributeError as e:
    try:
        __getattr__ = object.__getattribute__(llama, '__getattr__')
    except AttributeError:
        raise e
    else:
        print(__getattr__(llama, 'swimming'))

try:
    print(type.__getattribute__(Llama, 'leg_count'))
except AttributeError as e:
    try:
        __getattr__ = type.__getattribute__(Llama, '__getattr__')
    except AttributeError:
        raise e
    print(__getattr__(Llama, 'leg_count'))
```

Listing 15-7: llama.py:3d

While this is not identical to what's really happening in getattr(), it's close enough to understand what's going on. In the first block, I'm accessing llama.swimming, and in the second, Llama.leg_count. In both cases, I start by calling the appropriate __getattribute__() special method in a try clause. If an AttributeError is raised, I next check if __getattr__() has been implemented; this, too, is done with __getattribute__(). If __getattr__() does exist, it's called to perform a fallback attribute check, but if it doesn't, the original AttributeError is raised again.

Whew! That's a lot of work. Thankfully, Python hides all this complexity from us. To access an attribute or method, use the dot operator if you know the name of what you're looking for in advance, or use getattr() to perform lookups at runtime, using a string for the name:

```
# Either of these works!
print(llama.swimming)               # prints 'False'
print(getattr(Llama, 'leg_count')   # prints '4'
```

Listing 15-8: llama.py:3e

As for overriding the normal behavior, __getattr__() is usually the only one of the two special methods involved that you should ever implement. One common use of __getattr__() is to provide a default value for attributes that don't exist. As a rule, you should leave __getattribute__() alone.

Checking for an Attribute

To check for the existence of an attribute, use the hasattr() function, like this:

```
if hasattr(llama, 'larger_than_frogs'):
    print("¡Las llamas son más grandes que las ranas!")
```

Listing 15-9: llama.py:4a

Behind the scenes, hasattr() calls getattr() in a try statement, similar to if I had done this:

```
try:
    getattr(llama, 'larger_than_frogs')
except AttributeError:
    pass
else:
    print("¡Las llamas son más grandes que las ranas!")
```

Listing 15-10: llama.py:4b

Setting an Attribute

Setting an attribute isn't quite as involved as accessing one. The setattr() function relies on the __setattr__() special method. By default, setting an attribute to a value should always work. Here, I set the instance attribute larger_than_frogs on llama to True:

```
setattr(llama, 'larger_than_frogs', True)
print(llama.larger_than_frogs)  # prints 'True'
```

```
setattr(Llama, 'leg_count', 3)
print(Llama.leg_count)            # prints '3'
```

Listing 15-11: llama.py:5a

I pass three arguments to setattr(): the object or class to change the attribute on, the attribute name as a string, and the new value. The setattr() method completely ignores inheritance and the method resolution order; it is only concerned with modifying the __dict__ on the specified object or class. If the attribute exists on that __dict__, the method alters it; otherwise, the method creates a new attribute on the __dict__.

Behind the scenes, setattr() relies on the special method __setattr__(), and the code in Listing 15-11 is effectively doing the following:

```
object.__setattr__(llama, 'larger_than_frogs', True)
print(llama.larger_than_frogs)    # prints 'True'

type.__setattr__(Llama, 'leg_count', 3)
print(Llama.leg_count)            # prints '3'
```

Listing 15-12: llama.py:5b

That, in turn, modifies llama.__dict__ and Llama.__dict__, respectively. There's one funny detail here: while I could have modified llama.__dict__ manually, Llama.__dict__ is a mappingproxy, meaning it is read-only for everyone and everything *except* type.__setattr__(), which alone knows the secret to modifying the data represented in a mappingproxy. (Seriously, it's not even documented.)

GOTCHA ALERT   Accessing an attribute follows the method resolution order. Setting an attribute does *not*. Misunderstanding this behavior can lead to many bugs.

When setting an attribute, either via setattr() or the dot operator, pay careful attention to whether you are modifying an existing class attribute or merely shadowing it with an instance attribute. Accidental shadowing creates all sorts of bad surprises, as we've seen before. Here's what I mean:

```
setattr(llama, 'dangerous', False)  # uh oh, shadowing!
print(llama.dangerous)              # prints 'False', looks OK?
print(Llama.dangerous)              # prints 'True', still dangerous!!
```

Listing 15-13: llama.py:6a

In my call to setattr() here, I'm adding the key 'dangerous' to the instance's special attribute llama.__dict__, ignoring altogether the existence of the same key on the class's special attribute, Llama.__dict__. The print statements demonstrate the resulting shadowing.

Unexpected shadowing is not a problem particular to setattr() but exists with any assignment to an attribute:

```
llama.dangerous = False   # same problem
print(llama.dangerous)    # prints 'False', looks OK?
print(Llama.dangerous)    # prints 'True', still dangerous!!
```

Listing 15-14: llama.py:6b

To ensure I don't shadow class attributes with instance attributes, I must be careful to only modify class attributes on the class, never on an instance thereof:

```
Llama.dangerous = False   # this is better
print(llama.dangerous)    # prints 'False', looks OK?
print(Llama.dangerous)    # prints 'False', we are safe now
```

Listing 15-15: llama.py:6c

To control how an object handles assignment to its attributes, you can reimplement the __setattr__() special method yourself. Use caution here, too. Your implementation of __setattr__() can actually *prevent* attributes from working altogether if it never modifies the __dict__ special attribute and never calls object.__setattr__() (or type.__setattr__(), when working with class attributes).

Deleting an Attribute

The delattr() method deletes attributes. It relies on the __delattr__() special method and works in the same manner as setattr(), except that it returns an AttributeError if the requested attribute doesn't exist.

Normally, you would use the del operator for this purpose, like this:

```
print(llama.larger_than_frogs)  # prints 'True'
del llama.larger_than_frogs
print(llama.larger_than_frogs)  # raises AttributeError
```

Listing 15-16: llama.py:7a

This is the same as calling delattr() directly, like so:

```
print(llama.larger_than_frogs)  # prints 'True'
delattr(llama, 'larger_than_frogs')
print(llama.larger_than_frogs)  # raises AttributeError
```

Listing 15-17: llama.py:7b

The delattr() function invokes __delattr__() the same way that setattr() invokes __setattr__(). If you want to control the deletion of attributes, you can reimplement __delattr__(), although you should use the same caution when altering this special method as with __setattr__().

Function Attributes

If all objects can have attributes, and if functions are objects, then surely, functions can have attributes. This is indeed the case, but they don't work in the way you might think.

In practice, you will rarely need to use function attributes directly. They're mainly useful for enabling other patterns and techniques to work. These tasks border "deep magic" territory, whence we find metaclasses (Chapter 14).

Interestingly, function attributes were originally added to Python purely because they looked like they *should* exist. Libraries could already abuse __docstring__ to hack in an approximation of function attribute behavior anyway. Meanwhile, other developers were trying to approximate function attributes by creating classes that consisted purely of class attributes and a __call__() method, a technique that has a fair bit of performance overhead compared to a normal function with attributes.

Thus, the Python developers reasoned, "Well, if they're going to do it anyway, we might as well provide a formal and obvious mechanism for it."

The Wrong Way to Use Function Attributes

To demonstrate function attributes and their pitfalls, consider the following example, in which I initially use function attributes incorrectly. This code defines a multiplier function that stores one of its operands in a function attribute. I'll get to why this entire technique is a bad idea in a moment.

In this example, multiplier() multiplies the argument n by the value factor and prints the result:

```
def multiplier(n):
    factor = 0
    print(n * factor)
```

```
❶ multiplier.factor = 3
❷ multiplier(2)            # prints 0
  print(multiplier.factor) # prints 3
```

Listing 15-18: function_attribute.py:1a

In the usage, I incorrectly attempt to change the value of factor to 3 by assigning the value to a function attribute ❶. As you can see, the output of the function call is 0, proving this did not work as expected ❷, as the local-scope variable is still 0. Yet, if I inspect multiplier.factor, this function attribute's value is indeed 3. What happened?

The problem is that function attributes are not the same thing as local-scope variables, but rather exist inside the multiplier object's __dict__ attribute. If I print this __dict__ attribute, you can see that it includes the multiplier.factor attribute:

```
def multiplier(n):
    factor = 0
    print(n * factor)
```

```
print(multiplier.__dict__) # prints {}
```

```
multiplier.factor = 3
print(multiplier.__dict__)  # prints {'factor': 3}
```

Listing 15-19: function_attribute.py:1b

What's more, I cannot access function attributes within the function by name only, as I tried to do with the print call in the multiplier() function. The only way to access the function attributes is through getattr(), either directly or via the dot operator, like this:

```
def multiplier(n):
    print(n * multiplier.factor)


print(multiplier.__dict__)  # prints {}
multiplier.factor = 3
print(multiplier.__dict__)  # prints {'factor': 3}
multiplier(2)               # prints 6
```

Listing 15-20: function_attribute.py:1c

As you can see, the multiplication operation now succeeds.

There's still another technical problem with this code: if I fail to assign an initial value to multiplier.factor, the call to multiplier() in Listing 15-20 will fail. I can correct this problem by having the multiplier() function define a default value for that function attribute, if it is undefined.

Here's the final working version:

```
def multiplier(n):
    if not hasattr(multiplier, 'factor'):
        multiplier.factor = 0
    print(n * multiplier.factor)


multiplier(2)                     # prints 0
print(multiplier.__dict__)  # prints {'factor': 0}
❶ multiplier.factor = 3
print(multiplier.__dict__)  # prints {'factor': 3}
multiplier(2)                     # prints 6
```

Listing 15-21: function_attribute.py:1d

At the top of multiplier(), I check whether the factor function attribute has been defined. If it hasn't, I set it to a default value of 0. Then, by changing the function attribute externally ❶, I can change the behavior of the function.

As I've said from the start, though, this is only a simple example to demonstrate how function attributes work. My usage is not even remotely Pythonic!

Mutability and Function Attributes

You'll recall from Chapter 6 that functions should be *stateless*. Given what the function is designed to do, one may reasonably expect that `multiplier(2)` will return the same value every time. That premise has been violated because `multiplier()` stores state in its function attributes. Changing `multiplier.factor` will change the value returned by `multiplier(2)`.

In other words, *function attributes are attributes on a mutable object*. This is a logic error waiting to bite you! Consider the following simplistic example, where I try to change a function attribute on one function and it changes elsewhere, too:

```
def skit():
    print(skit.actor)

skit.actor = "John Cleese"
skit()    # prints "John Cleese"

sketch = skit
sketch()  # prints "John Cleese"
sketch.actor = "Eric Idle"
sketch()  # prints "Eric Idle"

skit()    # prints "Eric Idle"...yikes!
```

Listing 15-22: bad_function_attribute.py

When I assign `sketch` to `skit`, I'm binding `sketch` to the same mutable function object as `skit`. When I then assign a new value to the function attribute `sketch.actor`, it is the same as assigning it to the function attribute `skit.actor`; it's an attribute on the same function object. If you're familiar with the troubles with mutable objects, such as lists passed as arguments, that behavior may not look surprising, especially packed into a dozen-line example. However, imagine this being scattered into a production code base of thousands of lines. This could be a horrible bug to attempt to locate and resolve.

As to my `multiplier()` function (Listing 15-21), if I really needed to be able to provide a `factor` in some manner other than as an argument, I'd write that function as a closure instead. That way, each callable would be, itself, stateless. (See Chapter 6 for more on that topic.)

If you do need to use function attributes, you should be careful to only modify them in ways that are clear, predictable, and easy to debug. One possible usage is to employ a decorator to provide a default value up front to a callable, and to never change that value at any point during the execution of the program. While a similar outcome can be achieved with a closure, using a decorator places the extension immediately before the definition of the function. This leaves the attribute open to inspection, something that is squarely impossible with a parameter in a closure.

Descriptors

Descriptors are objects with *binding behavior*, meaning that they control how the objects are used as attributes. You can think of a descriptor as a property, whose getter, setter, and deleter methods are encapsulated in a class with the data those methods work with.

For example, you could have a Book descriptor that contains a book's title, author, publisher, and publication year. When the descriptor is used as an attribute, all this information could be assigned directly via a string, and the descriptor could parse the information out of that string.

All methods, including static and class methods, as well as the super() function (discussed in Chapter 13), are actually descriptor objects. Properties are descriptors behind the scenes, too. Properties are only defined in the context of the class using them, while descriptors can be defined outside of the class and reused. This is similar to the difference between lambdas, which are defined where they're used, and functions, which are defined separately from their usage.

The Descriptor Protocol

An object is a descriptor if it implements at least one of the three special methods in the *descriptor protocol*: __get__(), __set__(), or __delete__(). If the object only implements __get__(), it is a *non-data descriptor*, which is typically used for methods behind the scenes. If it also implements __set__() and/or __delete__(), it's a *data descriptor*, which is what properties are an example of.

This matters to the *lookup chain* used by object.__getattribute__() and type.__getattribute__(). The lookup chain determines where Python searches for an attribute, and in what order. Data descriptors get first priority, followed by ordinary attributes stored on the object's __dict__, then non-data descriptors, and finally any attributes on the class and its base classes. This means that a data descriptor named foo will shadow, or even prevent the creation of, an attribute by the same name. Similarly, an attribute named update will shadow a method (non-data descriptor) named update().

A *read-only data descriptor* would still have __set__() defined, but that method would only raise an AttributeError. This is important for the descriptor to be considered a data descriptor in the lookup chain.

PEDANTIC NOTE   You could also write a valid descriptor with only __set__() and __delete__(), or even just one of those two methods. However, there are few, if any, practical uses for this.

Descriptors also have a __set_name__() method, which is called when the descriptor is bound to a name. I'll demonstrate this later in this section.

Writing a Descriptor Class (the Slightly Wrong Way)

While it is possible to write a descriptor class as a property on a class, you'd normally write a separate descriptor class to reduce code repetition. This can be useful if you want to use the descriptor in multiple unrelated classes, or if you want several instances of the same descriptor in the same instance.

As an example, I'll write a descriptor class that stores details about a book. I want to parse these details out of a string following the APA 7 citation format. Here's the first part of that descriptor class. Be advised, there is a logical error in this code, which I'll cover shortly:

```python
import re


class Book:
    pattern = re.compile(r'(.+)\(((\d+)\))\. (.+)\. (.+)\..*')

    def __set__(self, instance, value):
        matches = self.pattern.match(value)
        if not matches:
            raise ValueError("Book data must be specified in APA 7 format.")
        self.author = matches.group(1)
        self.year = matches.group(2)
        self.title = matches.group(3)
        self.publisher = matches.group(4)
```

Listing 15-23: book_club.py:1a

This class is a data descriptor (instead of a non-data descriptor) because it defines __set__(). (I'll define __get__() in Listing 15-24.) When the descriptor is an attribute of another class, a value can be assigned directly to that attribute, and the __set__() method is called. This method accepts exactly three arguments: self, the object to access on (instance), and the value being assigned to the descriptor (value).

Within __set__(), I use a regular expression that I precompiled and stored in the class attribute pattern to extract the author, title, year, and publisher from the string passed to the value parameter. These extracted values are stored in instance attributes. If value is not a string that matches the expectations of the regular expression, a ValueError is raised.

For this to be a descriptor, I must also provide a __get__() method in the Book descriptor class:

```python
    def __get__(self, instance, owner=None):
        try:
            return f"'{self.title}' by {self.author}"
        except AttributeError:
            return "nothing right now"
```

Listing 15-24: book_club.py:2a

When the descriptor is accessed as an attribute, this __get__() method is called, returning a new string containing the book's title and author. If the expected attributes haven't been defined, I return a string "nothing right now" instead of re-raising the AttributeError.

The __get__() method must accept the arguments self and instance, just like __set__() does, as well as the optional argument owner, which specifies which class the descriptor belongs to. When owner is set to the default value of None, the owning class is considered to be the same as type(instance).

You'll notice that the Book class has no __init__() method. Although a descriptor class *may* have an initializer if desired, you should not use it to initialize instance attributes as you would with an ordinary class. This is because only one instance of the descriptor is shared between all classes that use it, so all instance attributes will be shared, too. In fact, this unexpected behavior has already set me up for a problem in the example I'm crafting. Stay tuned.

Using a Descriptor

A descriptor only exhibits its binding behavior when used as an attribute in another class. To demonstrate this, I'll define a BookClub class, which will use the Book descriptor class to keep track of what book the club is currently reading:

```
class BookClub:
    reading = Book()

    def __init__(self, name):
        self.name = name
        self.members = []

    def new_member(self, member):
        self.members.append(member)
        print(
            "===== - - - - - - - - =====",
            f"Welcome to the {self.name} Book Club, {member}!",
            f"We are reading {self.reading}",
            "===== - - - - - - - - =====",
            sep='\n'
        )
```

Listing 15-25: book_club.py:3a

I put the Book descriptor to work by binding an instance of Book to the class attribute reading. I also defined a new_member() method for adding new members to the book club and welcoming them with information about the book the club is currently reading.

There's one important detail here: *the descriptor must be a class attribute!* Otherwise, all of the descriptor behavior will be ignored, and assignment will merely rebind the attribute to the value being assigned. This isn't too surprising if you think of where else descriptors show up: all methods and properties are declared at class scope, rather than as names on self (instance attributes).

Given that the descriptor is a class attribute with attributes of its own, a problem emerges when using the BookClub class. I'll demonstrate by creating two new book clubs: mystery_lovers and lattes_and_lit:

```
mystery_lovers = BookClub("Mystery Lovers")
lattes_and_lit = BookClub("Lattes and Lit")

mystery_lovers.reading = (
    "McDonald, J. C. (2019). "
    "Noah Clue, P.I. AJ Charleson Publishing."
```

```
)
lattes_and_lit.reading = (
    "Christie, A. (1926). "
    "The Murder of Roger Ackroyd. William Collins & Sons."
)

print(mystery_lovers.reading)  # prints "'The Murder of Roger Ackroyd...'"
print(lattes_and_lit.reading)  # prints "'The Murder of Roger Ackroyd...'"
```

Listing 15-26: book_club.py:4

The first club is reading a mystery novel from some weird programmer guy, so I assign a string containing the appropriately formatted book information to the reading attribute of mystery_lovers. This assignment is invoking the __set__() method on the Book data descriptor object bound to reading.

Meanwhile, the folks in the lattes_and_lit club are reading a classic Agatha Christie novel, so I assign the appropriate book information to lattes_and_lit.reading.

However, since reading is a class attribute, this second assignment changes what both clubs are reading, as you can see from the print() statements. How do I fix that?

Writing a Descriptor Class the Right Way

While the reading descriptor must be a class attribute on BookClub, I can modify the descriptor class by storing attributes on the class instance it exists on:

```
class Book:
    pattern = re.compile(r'(.+)\(((\d+)\)\. (.+)\. (.+)\..*')

    def __set__(self, instance, value):
        matches = self.pattern.match(value)
        if not matches:
            raise ValueError("Book data must be specified in APA 7 format.")
        instance.author = matches.group(1)
        instance.year = matches.group(2)
        instance.title = matches.group(3)
        instance.publisher = matches.group(4)
```

Listing 15-27: book_club.py:1b

Instead of having the Book descriptor store its own attributes, it should store them on the instance it is a member of, accessed via the instance argument.

Since I'm defining attributes on the instance, I provide a __delete__() method as well, so deleting the Book descriptor via the reading attribute on a BookClub instance will work appropriately:

```
    def __get__(self, instance, owner=None):
        try:
            return f"'{instance.title}' by {instance.author}"
        except AttributeError:
```

```
        return "nothing right now"

    def __delete__(self, instance):
        del instance.author
        del instance.year
        del instance.title
        del instance.publisher
```

Listing 15-28: book_club.py:2b

If I hadn't defined this, calling del on the reading attribute would have raised an exception.

With the descriptor's data safely stored on the appropriate owning instances, I find that the usage from earlier now works as expected:

```
mystery_lovers = BookClub("Mystery Lovers")
lattes_and_lit = BookClub("Lattes and Lit")

mystery_lovers.reading = (
    "McDonald, J. C. (2019). "
    "Noah Clue, P.I. AJ Charleson Publishing."
)
lattes_and_lit.reading = (
    "Christie, A. (1926). "
    "The Murder of Roger Ackroyd. William Collins & Sons."
)

print(mystery_lovers.reading)  # prints "'Noah Clue, P.I...."
print(lattes_and_lit.reading)  # prints "'The Murder of Roger Ackroyd..."
```

Listing 15-29: book_club.py:4

Here's a little more usage of this BookClub class, demonstrating calling del on the descriptor and adding a new member:

```
del lattes_and_lit.reading

lattes_and_lit.new_member("Jaime")

lattes_and_lit.reading = (
    "Hillerman, T. (1973). "
    "Dance Hall Of The Dead. Harper and Row."
)

lattes_and_lit.new_member("Danny")
```

Listing 15-30: book_club.py:5

I clear the current book so that the Lattes and Lit book club isn't reading anything right now. This calls the reading.__del__() method. Then, I add a new member, Jaime; the new_member() method will print out a welcome message announcing what the club is reading, which is currently nothing.

Next, I choose a book to be read by the club by assigning a string to the reading attribute; this calls reading.__set__().

Finally, I add one more member via new_member(), which once again prints out a welcome message and the current book.

Here's the complete output of that usage:

```
===== - - - - - - - - - =====
Welcome to the Lattes and Lit Book Club, Jaime!
We are reading nothing right now.
===== - - - - - - - - - =====
Welcome to the Lattes and Lit Book Club, Danny!
We are reading 'Dance Hall Of The Dead' by Hillerman, T.
```

Using Multiple Descriptors in the Same Class

There's one remaining problem with my design: the descriptor looks for the attributes title, author, and the like on the instance, so multiple Book descriptors on the same BookClub instance would mutate these same values repeatedly.

Consider if a book club wanted to track both their current selection and the book they're reading next:

```
class BookClub:
    reading = Book()
    reading_next = Book()

    # --snip--
```

Listing 15-31: book_club.py:3b

To demonstrate, I'll assign different books to the reading and reading_next descriptors. Logically, those two descriptors should behave separately, but that's not what happens:

```
mystery_lovers.reading = (
    "McDonald, J. C. (2019). "
    "Noah Clue, P.I. AJ Charleson Publishing."
)

mystery_lovers.reading_next = (
    "Chesterton, G.K. (1911). The Innocence of Father Brown. "
    "Cassell and Company, Ltd."
)
print(f"Now: {mystery_lovers.reading}")
print(f"Next: {mystery_lovers.reading_next}")
```

Listing 15-32: book_club.py:6

This code outputs the following:

```
Now: 'The Innocence of Father Brown' by Chesterton, G.K.
Next: 'The Innocence of Father Brown' by Chesterton, G.K.
```

That's wrong: the club is supposed to be reading *Noah Clue, P.I.* right now and *The Innocence of Father Brown* later. The trouble is, both the reading and reading_later descriptors are storing their data in the same instance attributes on mystery_lovers.

To get around that, I should instead store the desired attributes with the namespace of the descriptor it relates to, creating names like reading.author and reading_later.title. That requires a couple of additional methods on the descriptor, for a start:

```
import re

class Book:
    pattern = re.compile(r'(.+)\(((\d+)\))\. (.+)\. (.+)\..*')

    def __set_name__(self, owner, name):
        self.name = name

    def attr(self, attr):
        return f"{self.name}.{attr}"

    def __set__(self, instance, value):
        matches = self.pattern.match(value)
        if not matches:
            raise ValueError("Book data must be specified in APA 7 format.")
        setattr(instance, self.attr('author'), matches.group(1))
        setattr(instance, self.attr('year'), matches.group(2))
        setattr(instance, self.attr('title'), matches.group(3))
        setattr(instance, self.attr('publisher'), matches.group(4))
```

Listing 15-33: book_club.py:1c

The __set_name__() special method is called when the descriptor is first bound to a name on the owning class. In this case, I'm using it to store the name the descriptor is bound to.

I define another method that I've chosen to name attr(), where I attach the namespace of the descriptor's name to the beginning of the requested name. As a result, calling attr('title') on a descriptor bound to reading would return reading.title.

I implement this behavior throughout the __set__() method by using the setattr() function, to assign a value to the given attribute on instance.

I must similarly modify __get__() and __delete__():

```
    def __get__(self, instance, owner=None):
        try:
            title = getattr(instance, self.attr('title'))
            author = getattr(instance, self.attr('author'))
        except AttributeError:
            return "nothing right now"
        return f"{title} by {author}"

    def __delete__(self, instance):
        delattr(instance, self.attr('author'))
        delattr(instance, self.attr('year'))
```

```
delattr(instance, self.attr('title'))
delattr(instance, self.attr('publisher'))
```

Listing 15-34: book_club.py:2c

Here, I'm using getattr() and delattr() to respectively access and delete the given attributes, as composed by self.attr(), on instance.

Rerunning the usage in Listing 15-32, I get the following:

```
Now: 'Noah Clue, P.I.' by McDonald, J.C.
Next: 'The Innocence of Father Brown' by Chesterton, G.K.
```

The two descriptors are storing their attributes separately. This can be confirmed by printing out the names of all the attributes on the mystery_lovers object:

```
import pprint
pprint.pprint(dir(mystery_lovers))
```

Listing 15-35: book_club.py:7

This produces the following:

```
['__class__',
# --snip--
 'reading',
 'reading.author',
 'reading.publisher',
 'reading.title',
 'reading.year',
 'reading_next',
 'reading_next.author',
 'reading_next.publisher',
 'reading_next.title',
 'reading_next.year']
```

Slots

There's one downside to the fact that all attributes are stored and accessed on a dictionary: a dictionary collection has significant performance and memory overhead. Ordinarily, this is a reasonable tradeoff, given all the versatility that this approach makes possible.

If you need to improve performance of your class, you can use *slots* to predeclare the attributes you want. Accessing an attribute on a slot is faster than accessing one on a dictionary, and it reduces the memory taken up by the attributes.

Switching your class to use slots instead of an instance __dict__ is as simple as adding the __slots__ class attribute, which is a tuple of valid attribute names. This list should contain names of instance attributes, not methods or class attributes (which are stored on the class __dict__).

For example, here's a class for storing data about chemical elements:

```
class Element:
    __slots__ = (
        'name',
        'number',
        'symbol',
        'family',
        'iupac_num',
    )
```

Listing 15-36: element.py:1a

The __slots__ tuple contains five names. These will be the only valid instance attribute names on an Element instance, and working with these attributes will be faster than when using __dict__. Notice that none of the methods have to be listed in __slots__; only the instance attribute names do. What's more, the slots must never conflict with any names elsewhere on the class (with two exceptions, mentioned shortly).

Binding Attribute Names to Values

Although the attribute names are declared in __slots__, they don't have a value (not even None) until they're bound to values in the usual manner, such as within __init__():

```
    def __init__(self, symbol, number, name, family, numeration):
        self.symbol = symbol.title()
        self.number = number
        self.name = name.lower()
        self.family = family.lower()
        self.iupac_num = numeration

    def __str__(self):
        return f"{self.symbol} ({self.name}): {self.number}"
```

Listing 15-37: element.py:2

Here, I've added my initializer, as well as a function for converting the instance to a string.

From the outside, the class seems to behave the same as a typical class, although if I were to measure the performance, it would be improved:

```
oxygen = Element('O', 8, 'oxygen', 'non-metals', 16)
iron = Element('Fe', 26, 'iron', 'transition metal', 8)

print(oxygen)   # prints 'O (Oxygen): 8'
print(iron)     # prints 'Fe (Iron): 26'
```

Listing 15-38: element.py:3a

Using Arbitrary Attributes with Slots

The __slots__ attribute completely takes over attribute storage from the instance __dict__, preventing __dict__ from even being created for the instance, as you can see here:

```
iron.atomic_mass = 55.845  # raises AttributeError
```

Listing 15-39: element.py:4a

However, if I want the benefits of __slots__ for the primary attributes, while still allowing additional attributes to be defined later, I only need to add __dict__ to __slots__, like this:

```
class Element:
    __slots__ = (
        'name',
        'number',
        'symbol',
        'family',
        'iupac_num',
        '__dict__',
        '__weakref__',
    )
```

Listing 15-40: element.py:1b

The __dict__ special attribute is one of the two exceptions to the rule that slots must not conflict with class attribute names. The other exception is __weakref__, which you would add to __slots__ if you wanted your slotted class to support weak references or references to a value that don't increase the reference count or block garbage collection during their lifetime. I want both arbitrary attributes and weak references for Element instances, so I add the names to __slots__.

With this one change, the code in Listing 15-39 works correctly, instead of raising an AttributeError. This technique will diminish the space savings normally afforded by slots, but you will still have the performance gains on all slotted names.

Slots and Inheritance

Slots have some important effects on inheritance. First, you should only declare any given slot once in an inheritance tree. If I were to derive a class from Element, I should not redeclare any of the slots. Doing so would bloat the size of the derived class because all the slots are declared on each instance, even if some of the base class's slots are shadowed by the derived class's slots.

Second, you cannot inherit from multiple parents classes with non-empty slots. If you need to use slots in multiple inheritance scenarios, the best approach is to ensure that the base classes have only an empty tuple assigned to __slots__. That way, you can make the derived class use __dict__, __slots__, or both.

Immutable Classes

Technically, there's no formal mechanism for creating an immutable class. This fact can make it unfortunately tricky to implement a hashable class, since the __hash__() method must produce a hash value that never changes during the instance's lifetime, according to the documentation.

Although you cannot create a truly immutable class, you can get close enough that the fact it's technically mutable doesn't matter. Consider the core trait of an immutable object: once its attributes have been initially set, those attributes can never be modified by any means, nor can additional attributes be added. This is why all immutable objects are hashable. The most obvious way to emulate an immutable class (at least in my view), and the one that gives you the most control, is implemented using slots.

I want to make the Element class from earlier into an immutable class, and a hashable one at that. To accomplish that, I need to do the following:

- Implement all attributes as __slots__.

- Restrict adding further attributes by omitting __dict__ from __slots__.

- Allow the creation of weak references by including __weakref__ in __slots__ (not strictly necessary, but helpful enough in some use cases to be good practice).

- Implement __setattr__() and __delattr__() to prevent modifying or deleting existing attributes.

- Implement __hash__() to make instances hashable.

- Implement __eq__() and __gt__() to make instances comparable.

I'll start by defining the __slots__, as before:

```
class Element:
    __slots__ = (
        'name',
        'number',
        'symbol',
        '__weakref__',
    )

    def __init__(self, symbol, number, name):
        self.symbol = symbol.title()
        self.number = number
        self.name = name.lower()
```

Listing 15-41: element_immutable.py:1

If I wanted to store additional attributes about elements, I could use a dictionary to associate Element keys with instances of some other mutable object as values that contain the rest of the data. For brevity, I won't do that here.

I'll add the special methods for converting to string, for hashing, and for comparing between Element instances:

```
    def __repr__(self):
        return f"{self.symbol} ({self.name}): {self.number}"
```

```
def __str__(self):
    return self.symbol

def __hash__(self):
    return hash(self.symbol)

def __eq__(self, other):
    return self.symbol == other.symbol

def __lt__(self, other):
    return self.symbol < other.symbol

def __le__(self, other):
    return self.symbol <= other.symbol
```

Listing 15-42: element_immutable.py:2

In all these cases, I'm using `self.symbol` as the key attribute. Remember that `__eq__()`, `__lt__()`, and `__le__()` correspond to the equals (==), less-than (<), and less-than-or-equals (<=) operators, respectively. Not equals (!=), greater than (>), and greater than or equals (>=) are mirrors of these three, respectively, so I typically only need to implement one special method in each pair.

For objects of this class to be immutable, I have to prevent any modification of its attributes. However, I can't just make `__setattr__()` do nothing, as it's needed for initial assignment of values as well. Instead, I write this method to only allow assignment to uninitialized attributes:

```
def __setattr__(self, name, value):
    if hasattr(self, name):
        raise AttributeError(
            f"'{type(self)}' object attribute '{name}' is read-only"
        )
    object.__setattr__(self, name, value)
```

Listing 15-43: element_immutable.py:3

If the attribute already exists on the instance, I raise an `AttributeError`. The message here is designed to exactly match the one raised by modifying an attribute on any true immutable class.

Because I'm using slots, I don't need to worry about new attributes being added, so long as `__dict__` is not specified on `__slots__`.

If the attribute doesn't already exist, I use `object.__setattr__()` to assign the value to that attribute. I cannot just call the `setattr()` function, or I'll get infinite recursion.

I also must define `__delattr__()` to prevent deletion of an attribute:

```
def __delattr__(self, name):
    raise AttributeError(
        f"'{type(self)}' object attribute '{name}' is read-only"
    )
```

Listing 15-44: element_immutable.py:4

The __delattr__() method is simpler to implement, as I don't ever want to allow deleting an attribute from an immutable instance. Thus, any use of del on an attribute of this class raises an AttributeError.

This class now behaves as immutable, as you can see from the usage:

```
oxygen = Element('O', 8, 'oxygen')
iron = Element('Fe', 26, 'iron')

print(oxygen)                # prints O
print(f"{iron!r}")           # prints Fe (Iron): 26

iron.atomic_mass = 55.845  # raises AttributeError
iron.symbol = "Ir"          # raises AttributeError
del iron.symbol             # raises AttributeError
```

Listing 15-45: element_immutable.py:5

Some Python developers will happily point out that one can bypass the simulated immutability of the Element class by calling __setattr__() on the object directly:

```
object.__setattr__(iron, 'symbol', 'Ir')
```

While this indeed modifies the iron.symbol attribute, this nasty hack is a straw man argument against the pattern. No code outside of the class itself should ever call __setattr__(); Python and its standard library certainly never will.

Python does not pretend to be Java! While it's possible to bypass safety barriers—as is possible with most things in the Python language—if someone employs such an irrational and dirty hack, they deserve whatever bugs they've got coming to them. The hope of preventing such deliberate abuses does not justify the complexity and fragility of other immutability techniques, like inheriting from tuple, simulating objects with namedtuple, and so forth. If you want an immutable object, use __slots__ and __setattr__().

Alternatively, you can achieve something functionally similar with the @dataclasses.dataclass(frozen=True) class decorator, which is provided by the *dataclasses* module in the standard library. Dataclasses have some differences from normal classes, so if you want to use them, see the documentation at *https://docs.python.org/3/library/dataclasses.html*.

Single-Dispatch Generic Functions

By now, you're probably used to the idea of duck typing and its implications for function design. However, every now and then, you'll need a function to behave differently for parameters of different types. In Python, as in most languages, you can write *generic functions* to adapt to parameter types.

Generic functions in Python are made possible by two decorators from the *functools* standard library module: @singledispatch and @singledispatchmethod. Both of these decorators create a *single-dispatch generic function*, which can switch between multiple function implementations, based on the type of the first parameter (when using @singledispatch) or the first parameter that isn't self or cls (when using @singledispatchmethod). This is the only difference between the two decorators.

As an example, I'll expand on my Element class from earlier. I want to be able to compare Element instances to each other, as well as to a string containing an element symbol or an integer representing an element number. Instead of writing one big function with an if statement that checks the argument against isinstance(), I can use single-dispatch generic functions.

I'll begin by adding two import statements before the Element class definition to get the @singledispatchmethod and @overload decorators:

```
from functools import singledispatchmethod
from typing import overload

class Element:
  # --snip--
```

Listing 15-46: element_generic.py:1

There are three slightly different ways to write a single-dispatch generic function, which I'll cover in a moment. These techniques all work regardless of whether you're using @singledispatch or @singledispatchmethod, except that the second decorator allows you to have self or cls as the first argument, which is why I use it here.

Regardless of which technique is used, the __eq__() method must be declared first. This first version of the method should be the most type-dynamic version, since it'll be used as the fallback.

```
@singledispatchmethod
def __eq__(self, other):
    return self.symbol == other.symbol
```

Listing 15-47: element_generic.py:2

This method is declared with the @singledispatchmethod decorator, but it is otherwise the same as if it were an ordinary implementation of the __eq__() instance method.

The @singledispatchmethod decorator must be the outermost (first) decorator for it to work with other decorators, such as @classmethod. The @singledispatch decorator can typically exist anywhere in the stack of decorators, although you're best off ensuring it's first, to avoid surprises and because consistency is helpful.

Registering Single-Dispatch Functions with Type Hints

My single-dispatch __eq__() method above still accepts any type. I want to add versions based on the type of the first argument. One way to do that is by registering them with the automatically created @__eq__.register decorator. In this case, I'll create two more versions of the function: one that works with a string argument and another that works with either an integer or a floating-point number argument:

```
@__eq__.register
def _(self, other: str):
    return self.symbol == other

@overload
def _(self, other: float):
    ...
@__eq__.register
def _(self, other: int):
    return self.number == other
```

Listing 15-48: element_generic.py:3

The first of these methods accepts a string argument. The first parameter, the one being switched on, is annotated with a type hint for the expected type, which is a string (str) in this first case.

The second method here accepts either an integer or a float, and it is made possible with the @typing.overload decorator. When type hinting, you can mark one or more function headings with @overload, to indicate that they overload an upcoming function or method with the same name. The *Ellipsis* (...) is used in place of the suite of the overloaded method, so it can instead share the suite of the method below it. The function or method not decorated with @overload must come immediately after all the overloaded versions thereof.

Every single dispatch method conventionally has an underscore (_) as a name, to avoid undesired shadowing. The fact that they shadow each other won't matter, since they're being wrapped and registered, and thus, they won't need to be bound to names themselves.

When the __eq__() method is called, the type of the first parameter is checked. If it matches the type annotation for any of the registered methods, that method is used. Otherwise, the fallback method, the one marked with the @singledispatchmethod decorator, is called instead.

Registering Single-Dispatch Functions with Explicit Type

You can also achieve the same result without type annotations. In this case, instead of type hinting, I pass the expected type of the first non-self parameter to the register() decorator. I'll use this technique to define my __lt__() method:

```
@singledispatchmethod
def __lt__(self, other):
    return self.symbol < other.symbol

@__lt__.register(str)
def _(self, other):
```

```
        return self.symbol < other

@__lt__.register(int)
@__lt__.register(float)
def _(self, other):
    return self.number < other
```

Listing 15-49: element_generic.py:4

As before, the first version is the most dynamic, the second accepts a string, and the third accepts either an integer or a floating-point number.

Although it's not seen in this example, your single-dispatch function can accept as many arguments as you need and even different arguments on the different functions, but you can only switch method definitions on the data type of the first parameter.

Registering Single-Dispatch Functions with the register() Method

The third way to register to a single-dispatch function is to call register() as a method, rather than as a decorator, and directly pass any callable to it. I'll use this technique with the __le__() method.

```
@singledispatchmethod
def __le__(self, other):
    return self.symbol <= other.symbol

__le__.register(str, lambda self, other: self.symbol <= other)

__le__.register(int, lambda self, other: self.number <= other)
__le__.register(float, lambda self, other: self.number <= other)
```

Listing 15-50: element_generic.py:5

In this case, I define the generic single-dispatch method first, and then I directly register lambdas for handling strings, integers, and floating-point numbers. I could pass *any* callable in place of that lambda, whether it be a previously defined function, a callable, or anything else that accepts the appropriate argument.

Of these three techniques, I like the lambdas the best for these basic operator special methods, since they have less boilerplate. Otherwise, for more involved functions, I prefer to work with type annotations instead.

Using the Element Class

I've put a lot of work into this Element class, making it immutable and allowing the comparison of instances to strings and numbers. The benefits of all this work are apparent in the usage of the class, which I'll demonstrate by writing a Compound class to represent chemical compounds:

```
class Compound:

    def __init__(self, name):
```

```python
        self.name = name.title()
        self.components = {}

    def add_element(self, element, count):
        try:
            self.components[element] += count
        except KeyError:
            self.components[element] = count

    def __str__(self):
        s = ""
        formula = self.components.copy()
        # Hill system
        if 'C' in formula.keys():
            s += f"C{formula['C']}"
            del formula['C']
            if 1 in formula.keys():
                s += f"H{formula['H']}"
                del formula['H']
        for element, count in sorted(formula.items()):
            s += f"{element.symbol}{count if count > 1 else ''}"
        # substitute subscript digits for normal digits
        s = s.translate(str.maketrans("0123456789", "₀₁₂₃₄₅₆₇₈₉"))
        return s

    def __repr__(self):
        return f"{self.name}: {self}"
```

Listing 15-51: element_generic.py:6

I'll wager you could read through that code and understand everything going on. In short, this class allows me to instantiate a chemical compound with a name and add elements to the compound. Because `Element` is hashable and immutable, I can safely use `Element` instances as dictionary keys.

Because I can compare `Element` instances, either to strings representing element symbols or to integers representing element numbers, I can fairly easily implement the Hill system for outputting an empirical chemical formula for the compound.

Here's the `Compound` class in use:

```python
hydrogen = Element('H', 1, 'hydrogen')
carbon = Element('C', 6, 'carbon')
oxygen = Element('O', 8, 'oxygen')
iron = Element('Fe', 26, 'iron')

rust = Compound("iron oxide")
rust.add_element(oxygen, count=3)
rust.add_element(iron, count=2)
print(f"{rust!r}")      # prints 'Iron Oxide: Fe₂O₃'

aspirin = Compound("acetylsalicylic acid")
aspirin.add_element(hydrogen, 8)
aspirin.add_element(oxygen, 4)
aspirin.add_element(carbon, 9)
```

```
print(f"{aspirin!r}")  # prints 'Acetylsalicylic Acid: C₉H₈O₄'

water = Compound("water")
water.add_element(hydrogen, 2)
water.add_element(oxygen, 1)
print(f"{water!r}")    # prints 'Water: H₂O'
```

Listing 15-52: element_generic.py:7

I define four `Element` objects: hydrogen, carbon, oxygen, and iron. Then I use these to construct three `Compound` instances: rust, aspirin, and water. I print each `Compound` using the canonical string representation (from _repr_()) via the !r formatting flag.

As you can see, the `Compound` class and its usage are quite simple and clean, all because I designed `Element` with slots, __setattr__(), and single-dispatch generic functions.

Arbitrary Execution

Introspection also enables *arbitrary execution*, whereby strings can be directly executed as Python code. To this end, there are some built-in functions that you will encounter sooner or later and that may appeal to your inner hacker: eval(), compile(), and exec(). Yet hidden dangers lurk.

Here's a contrived little version of how this can go very wrong:

```
with open('input.dat', 'r') as file:
    nums = [value.strip() for value in file if value]

for num in nums:
    expression = f"{num} // 2 + 2"
    try:
        answer = eval(expression)
    except (NameError, ValueError, TypeError, SyntaxError) as e:
        print(e)
    finally:
        code = "print('The answer is', answer)"
        obj = compile(code, '<string>', mode='exec')
        exec(obj)
```

Listing 15-53: arbitrary.py

I read all the lines in from a file, *input.dat*, which I naively assume will contain only mathematical expressions.

For each line I read from *input.dat*, I compose a string containing a Python expression, which I bind to expression. Then I pass that string to the eval() built-in function, which evaluates it as a Python expression and converts it to a value that I bind to answer.

For the sake of demonstration, I compose a string containing a line of Python code, bound to code. I could execute it immediately as Python code by passing the string to the exec() built-in function. Instead, I compile it into a Python code object using compile(), and then I run that code object using exec(). This approach is slower for a single use but faster for code being called repeatedly. Again, I only have it here to demonstrate the technique.

The problem here is that arbitrary execution is a major security risk, especially as soon as it involves data provided from an external source, such as a file or user input. I'm expecting my *input.dat* to look something like this:

```
40
(30 + 7)
9 * 3
0xAA & 0xBB
80
```

Listing 15-54: input.dat:1a

These values produce some neat, safe-looking output:

```
The answer is 22
The answer is 20
The answer is 15
The answer is 10
The answer is 42
```

The danger here is a potential security threat. What would happen if an attacker somehow modified *input.dat* to look like this?

```
40
(30 + 7)
9 * 3
0xAA & 0xBB
80
exec('import os') or os.system('echo \"`whoami` is DOOMED\"') == 0 or 1
```

Listing 15-55: input.dat:1b

What would happen if I ran that code on a POSIX system, such as Linux?

```
The answer is 22
The answer is 20
The answer is 15
The answer is 10
The answer is 42
jason is DOOMED
The answer is True
```

That jason is DOOMED message should make your blood run cold, as that was *not* from a print statement; it was produced by a shell command executed directly on the operating system. This is known as a *code injection attack*, and it can lead to some pretty horrific security issues. (I'll revisit security in Chapter 19.)

There are many clever and esoteric ways to inject code into a string being passed to eval(), compile(), or exec(). As a result, although these functions may look like the key to some truly brilliant Python code, they're almost always best left alone. If you really, really need something like eval(), you should almost certainly use ast.literal_eval() instead, although it is unable to evaluate with operators (and thus, it cannot work with my *input.dat*). There are rare, advanced techniques that use eval(), compile(), or exec() safely, but that involve ensuring those functions can only ever receive *trusted* data, as opposed to external data, which is *untrusted.*

To learn more about how dangerous eval() (and exec(), by extension) is, check out Ned Batchelder's article, *Eval really is dangerous: https://nedbatchelder .com/blog/201206/eval_really_is_dangerous.html.* The discussion in the comments is also insightful.

Some of my cleverness-loving readers will have noticed os.system() can be used to execute shell commands. This, too, should seldom (if ever) be employed. Use the subprocess module instead: *https://docs.python.org/3/library/ subprocess.html.*

Wrapping Up

Classes and class instances store their attributes inside of special dictionaries, and this one detail empowers Python to know a lot about the internal composition of objects during runtime.

Descriptors—the magic behind properties, methods, and many other tricks—can be used to make your code easier to maintain. Slots unlock performance and enable you to write effectively immutable classes. Single-dispatch generic functions bring the versatility of overloaded functions to dynamic typing.

Python certainly looks magical at first blush, but it freely unlocks the backstage door and lets us in on all its illusions and secrets. By knowing how the tricks work, you, too, can write elegant classes and libraries that feel, well, dead simple to use.

16

ASYNCHRONY AND CONCURRENCY

You know the situation: you have to finish that TPS report for your boss, fix a bug that shipped to production, and figure out which of your co-workers borrowed your stapler (it's Jeff again, isn't it?), all before day's end. How will you get it all done? You can't make copies of yourself—and even if you could, the line for the copier is out the door—so you tackle these tasks with *concurrency*.

It's the same in Python. If your program needs to wait on user input, send data over a network, and crunch numbers, all while still updating the user interface, you can handle these tasks concurrently, thus improving your program's responsiveness.

There are two options for achieving concurrency in Python: either threading (see Chapter 17), wherein the operating system manages the multitasking, or asynchrony, where Python handles it. This chapter focuses on the latter.

THEORY RECAP: CONCURRENCY

Concurrency is the programming equivalent of multitasking: rapidly dividing a program's singular attention between multiple tasks. It is not the same as *parallelism*, wherein multiple tasks occur simultaneously (see Chapter 17). A program that uses concurrency is limited to one system process, and that process can only do one thing at a time in most implementations of Python.

Revisiting the busy-workday example, you can write the TPS report and shake down Jeff for your stapler, but not at the same time. Even if you called Jeff into your cubicle to talk to him while you filled out the TPS report, you would be dividing your attention between the two tasks, however short the periods of focus might be. While a casual observer might conclude you are doing two things at the same time, you are really just oscillating between the different tasks.

This has an important implication: *concurrency does not actually speed up execution time*. All told, you still need to spend 10 minutes filling out the TPS report and another five interrogating Jeff. The two tasks together will take 15 minutes, whether you finish your report before talking to Jeff or divide your attention between the two. In fact, because of the additional effort it takes to switch between tasks, it may take longer when employing concurrency. The same is true in programming. These tasks are effectively *CPU-bound*, because their speed is limited by your brain's abilities, which are analogous to the speed of the CPU. Concurrency is not helpful with CPU-bound tasks.

Concurrency is chiefly useful when dealing with *IO-bound* tasks, such as receiving a file over a network or waiting for a user to click a button. For example, imagine you have to laminate several copies of the meeting agenda for reasons known only to management. Each lamination job takes a couple of minutes, during which time, you're sitting and listening to the whine of the laminator. Your effort and attention are not required. Not a very good use of time, is it? This is an IO-bound task because your speed is limited primarily by waiting for the finished laminated page (the output). Now say you employ concurrency by starting a page in the laminator and then walking away and turning the office upside-down for your stapler. Every couple of minutes, you check the laminator, perhaps feed another page through, and then resume your search. By the time you've found your beloved stapler in Martha's desk drawer (sorry, Jeff!), you have also finished laminating the agendas for the meeting.

Concurrency is also useful for improving the *perceived responsiveness* of your program: even while the program performs a particularly long or heavy task, such as a complicated data analysis, it can respond to user input or update a progress bar. In reality, no single task is happening faster than before, but the program doesn't hang.

Lastly, concurrency is useful for performing a task at regular intervals, such as saving a temporary file every five minutes, regardless of what the rest of the program is doing.

Asynchrony in Python

As mentioned, there are two ways to achieve concurrency in Python. *Threading*, also known as *pre-emptive multitasking*, involves letting the operating system manage the multitasking by running each task in a single flow of execution called a *thread*. These multiple threads still share the same system *process*, which is an instance of a running computer program. If you open the system monitor on your computer, you can see a list of running processes on your machine. Any one of those processes can have multiple threads.

Traditional threading has a number of pitfalls, which is why I'll come back to it in Chapter 17. The alternative is *asynchrony*, also known as *cooperative multitasking*. It is the easiest way to achieve concurrency in Python—but that doesn't make it easy! The operating system only sees your code as running in a single process, with a single thread; it is Python itself that manages the multitasking, with some help from you, thereby sidestepping some of the issues that crop up with threading. Still, writing good asynchronous code in Python requires some forethought and planning.

It's important to keep in mind that asynchrony is not parallelism. In Python, a mechanism called the *Global Interpreter Lock (GIL)* ensures that any single Python process is constrained to a single CPU core, regardless of how many cores are available to the system. For this reason, parallelism cannot be achieved with either asynchrony or threading. This may sound like a design flaw, but efforts to eliminate the GIL from CPython have proven more technically challenging than imagined, and the results have had poorer performance thus far. As of this writing, progress has all but stalled on the most prominent of these efforts, Larry Hastings's Gilectomy. The GIL makes things run smoother in Python.

PEDANTIC NOTE There are a few other ways around the GIL, such as Python extensions, because they are written in C and executed in compiled machine code. Anytime your logic leaves the Python interpreter, it also goes beyond the jurisdiction of the GIL and becomes capable of running in parallel. I won't go into this further in this book, save mentioning a few extensions that do this in Chapter 21.

Asynchrony was originally possible in Python through third-party libraries, like Twisted. Later, Python 3.5 added syntax and functionality for natively achieving asynchrony. These features did not become stable until Python 3.7; as a result, many articles and online discussions about asynchrony are profoundly out-of-date. Your best source of information is always the official documentation. I've done my best to be up-to-date with Python 3.10.

Python makes asynchrony possible with two keywords borrowed from the C# language: async and await, as well as a special type of coroutine. (Many other languages implement similar syntax; these include JavaScript, Dart, and Scala.) Asynchronous execution is managed and run by an *event loop*, which is responsible for the multitasking. Python provides the *asyncio* module in the standard library for this purpose, and we'll use it in this chapter's examples.

It's worth noting that at the time of this writing, asyncio is dauntingly complicated beyond basic usage, even to some Python experts. For that reason, I'll stick to the essential concepts universal to asynchrony and avoid explaining or using asyncio any more than is absolutely unavoidable. Most of what you'll see are just plain asynchrony techniques; I'll call out the exceptions.

When you're ready to go further into this topic of asynchrony, pick up either the Trio or Curio library. Both are written to be user-friendly. They're well documented, with the beginner in mind, and they regularly provide design cues to asyncio's developers. Armed with the knowledge from this chapter, you should be able to learn either of those libraries from their documentation.

Curio was developed by David Beazley, an expert in Python and concurrency, with the goal of making asynchrony in Python more approachable. The official documentation can be found at *https://curio.readthedocs.io/*. That main page also has links to a number of excellent talks on Python asynchronous programming, including several talks that guide you through writing your *own* asynchrony module (although you likely won't ever need to do this).

Trio is based on Curio, and it furthers the library's goals of simplicity and usability. As of this writing, it's considered somewhat experimental, but it is still stable enough to use in production. Python developers most often recommend using Trio. Find the official documentation at *https:// trio.readthedocs.io/en/stable/*.

Earlier in this section, I mentioned the *Twisted* library, which added asynchronous behavior to Python some 20 years before asynchrony was added to the core language. It uses a number of dated patterns, rather than the modern asynchronous workflow model, but it's still an active and viable library with many use cases. A number of popular libraries use it under the hood. Learn more at *https://twistedmatrix.com/*.

The asyncio official documentation can be found at *https://docs.python .org/3/library/asyncio.html*. I recommend digging into asyncio in more detail only once you're comfortable with asynchronous programming via either Trio or Curio, as well as with the analogous concepts of threading (Chapter 17). Your grasp of the concepts and patterns of asynchrony and concurrency will help you make sense of the asyncio documentation.

In the midst of all this, remember that asynchrony is still in its relative infancy, both in Python and in the field of computer science as a whole. The asynchronous workflow model first appeared in the F# language in 2007, based on concepts introduced in Haskell around 1999 and several papers from the early 1990s. By contrast, the related concept of threading dates to the late 1960s. Many problems in asynchrony still don't have clear or established solutions. Who knows—you might be the first to solve one of them!

The Example Scenario: Collatz Game, Synchronous Version

To properly demonstrate how these concepts work, I'll create a small program that would benefit from concurrency. Because of the complexity of the issues at hand, I'll focus entirely on this one example for this chapter and the next, so you can get used to the working details.

I'll start with a *synchronous* working version, so you'll have a solid idea of what I'm doing. The complexity of this example will demonstrate some of the common issues involved in concurrency. Simplicity is the enemy of effectiveness for examples with these concepts.

For the example, I'll play with a strange phenomenon in math known as the *Collatz conjecture*, which works like this:

1. Start with any positive integer *n*.
2. If *n* is even, the next term in the sequence should be n / 2.
3. If *n* is odd, the next term in the sequence should be 3 * n + 1.
4. If *n* is 1, stop.

Even if you start with a fantastically large number, you'll always wind up at 1 after relatively few steps. Starting with 942,488,749,153,153, for example, the Collatz sequence arrives at 1 in only 1,863 steps.

There are all sorts of things you can do with the Collatz conjecture. For this example, I'll create a simple game that challenges the user to guess how many Collatz sequences have a particular length. I'll restrict the range of starting numbers to integers between 2 and 100,000 (which I can also represent as 10**5).

For example, exactly 782 starting numbers will yield Collatz sequences with a length of exactly 42 values. To play the game in the example, the user would enter 42 (the target length) and then guess how many starting numbers would produce Collatz sequences of the target length. If the user guessed 782, they'd win. (Okay, yes, it's a lousy game premise, but it works for demonstrating concurrency.)

At the top of my module, I'll define a constant, BOUND, for the maximum starting number. Counting zeros in constants is an invitation to error, so I'll define 100,000 as a power of 10 instead:

```
BOUND = 10**5
```

Listing 16-1: collatz_sync.py:1

Next is the function for finding the number of steps in a single Collatz sequence:

```
def collatz(n):
    steps = 0
    while n > 1:
        if n % 2:
            n = n * 3 + 1
        else:
            n = n / 2
```

```
        steps += 1
    return steps
```

Listing 16-2: collatz_sync.py:2

Nothing should surprise you here. This function follows the rules for calculating a Collatz sequence and returns the number of steps it took to reach 1.

I need another function for tracking how many times a target sequence length is met:

```
def length_counter(target):
    count = 0
    for i in range(2, BOUND):
        if collatz(i) == target:
            count += 1
    return count
```

Listing 16-3: collatz_sync.py:3

This function runs collatz() on every possible starting integer from 2 to BOUND and counts how many times a Collatz sequence had exactly target steps. It returns this count at the end.

Next, I create a function for getting a positive integer from the user, which I'll need to do a couple of times in the program run, first to get the desired Collatz target length, and second to get the user's guess of how many starting values produce Collatz sequences of the target length:

```
def get_input(prompt):
    while True:
        n = input(prompt)
        try:
            n = int(n)
        except ValueError:
            print("Value must be an integer.")
            continue
        if n <= 0:
            print("Value must be positive.")
        else:
            return n
```

Listing 16-4: collatz_sync.py:4

This function should also look pretty familiar by now. I get a string from the user with input(), attempt to convert it to an integer, and ensure that integer is not negative. If anything goes wrong, I display a message for the user and let them try again.

Tying it all together is the main function:

```
def main():
    print("Collatz Sequence Counter")

    target = get_input("Collatz sequence length to search for: ")
    print(f"Searching in range 1-{BOUND}...")
```

```
count = length_counter(target)
guess = get_input("How many times do you think it will appear? ")

if guess == count:
    print("Exactly right! I'm amazed.")
elif abs(guess - count) < 100:
    print(f"You're close! It was {count}.")
else:
    print(f"Nope. It was {count}.")
```

Listing 16-5: collatz_sync.py:5

I display the name of the program and ask the user to enter a target sequence length to search for. I perform the search for the sequence length with length_counter() and bind the result to count. Next, I get the user's guess, which I bind to guess, and compare it to count, giving the user some feedback on how close their guess was.

Lastly, I need to execute the main function:

```
if __name__ == "__main__":
    main()
```

Listing 16-6: collatz_sync.py:6

All in all, I've stuck with syntax and patterns you should be familiar with by now. But running this module shows why the program could do with some concurrency:

```
Collatz Sequence Counter
Collatz sequence length to search for: 42
Searching in range 1-100000...
```

At this point, the program hangs for several seconds, before continuing:

```
How many times do you think it will appear? 456
Nope. It was 782.
```

It works, but it doesn't feel particularly responsive. What's more, if I were to increase the value of BOUND by even one exponential value, to 10**6, the delay would increase dramatically; on my system, it went from 7 to 63 seconds!

Thankfully, there are a number of ways I could make this program feel more responsive. Over the next two chapters, I'll point these out to you and implement the changes.

Asynchrony

Let's see how asynchrony can help my Collatz program. First, notice that the several-second delay on running length_counter() is *CPU-bound*, as it relates to how long it takes the CPU to perform the math. That delay will remain until I apply parallelism in the next chapter.

But there's another source of delay in this program: the user. The program has to wait for an indefinite period of time until the user enters a valid number. This part of the program is *IO-bound*, because it is limited by the response time of something external, such as user input, a network response, or another program, rather than the working speed of the CPU.

I can improve the program's *perceived responsiveness*, how fast it seems to the user, by running the math concurrently with waiting for the user's guess. The calculations themselves won't actually happen any faster, but my users probably won't realize that: they'll be focusing on entering a guess while Python is running that heavy-duty math.

I'll use the built-in asyncio module to work with asynchrony in Python, so I import it at the start of my program:

```
import asyncio

BOUND = 10**5
```

Listing 16-7: collatz_async.py:1a

As in Listing 16-1, I'm defining my BOUND constant here. Now I can begin rewriting my code to be asynchronous.

Native Coroutines

In Chapter 10, I introduced simple coroutines, which are based on generators. Simple coroutines run until they hit a yield statement and then wait for data to be sent to the coroutine object with the send() method.

I'll make my game's code asynchronous by turning some of my program's functions into *native coroutines*. Also called *coroutine functions*, native coroutines build on the idea of simple coroutines: instead of waiting for data to be sent, they can be paused and resumed at specific places to achieve multitasking. In the rest of this chapter, I use the terms *coroutine function* and *native coroutine* somewhat interchangeably. Be advised that when most Python developers refer to coroutines, they almost always mean native coroutines, although it never hurts to clarify.

You declare a native coroutine by placing the async keyword in front of the definition, like this:

```
async def some_function():
    # ...
```

However, don't get the idea that to implement asynchrony, you only need to put the async keyword in front of all your function definitions. This is only the first of many steps toward making the code asynchronous.

When called, a coroutine function returns a native coroutine object, which is a special kind of object called an *awaitable*. These are callables that can pause and resume mid-execution. Awaitables must be called using the await keyword, which acts much like yield from. Here, I use the await keyword to call the awaitable coroutine function some_function():

```
await some_function()
```

There's another catch: the `await` keyword can only be used within an awaitable. When a native coroutine reaches an `await`, it pauses execution until the called awaitable is finished.

PEDANTIC NOTE   Although you won't see it in these examples, you can pass a native coroutine to a function to be called later, perhaps after some other task has been completed. When used this way, the native coroutine being passed is called a *callback*.

A function should only be turned into a coroutine function when it calls another awaitable, performs an IO-bound task, or is specifically intended to run concurrently with another awaitable. In the Collatz game, I'll need to make some decisions about which functions to turn into coroutine functions and which to leave as ordinary functions.

To begin with, consider the synchronous `collatz()` function:

```
def collatz(start):
    steps = 0
    n = start
    while n > 1:
        if n % 2:
            n = n * 3 + 1
        else:
            n = n / 2
        steps += 1
    return steps
```

Listing 16-8: collatz_async.py:2

This function will always return almost instantly, so it neither needs to call an awaitable nor run concurrently with another awaitable. It can remain as a normal function.

Meanwhile, `length_counter()` is labor intensive and CPU-bound. I want it to run concurrently with the code that waits for the user to input a guess, so it's a good candidate for a coroutine function. I'll rewrite the synchronous version from Listing 16-3:

```
async def length_counter(target):
    count = 0
    for i in range(2, BOUND):
        if collatz(i) == target:
            count += 1
        await asyncio.sleep(0)
    return count
```

Listing 16-9: collatz_async.py:3

I turn this function into a coroutine function with async and use await asyncio.sleep(0) to tell Python where the coroutine function can pause and let something else work. If I don't await something in the coroutine function, it will never be paused, which would defeat the purpose of making it a coroutine function in the first place. (Trio, Curio, and asyncio all offer a sleep() awaitable.)

I also want to turn the IO-bound get_input() function into a coroutine function, as the very nature of waiting for user input involves the ability to pause and resume. This first version of the coroutine function doesn't yet await anything else; I'll revisit that in a bit.

```
async def get_input(prompt):
    while True:
        n = input(prompt)
        try:
            n = int(n)
        except ValueError:
            print("Value must be an integer.")
            continue
        if n <= 0:
            print("Value must be positive.")
        else:
            return n
```

Listing 16-10: collatz_async.py:4a

There's one critical limitation to await: it can only be called from within an awaitable, such as a coroutine function. I want to call get_input() from main(), so main() must also be a coroutine function, as you'll see in Listing 16-11.

Behind the scenes, native coroutines are still used in a strikingly similar manner to simple coroutines. Because length_counter() is a coroutine function, I can force it to be executed manually (and synchronously) the same as I would a simple coroutine. This is just a side example that runs the coroutine function synchronously:

```
f = length_counter(100)
while True:
    try:
        f.send(None)
    except StopIteration as e:
        print(e)  # prints '255'
        break
```

I wouldn't ever use this approach in production, as coroutine functions need to be run in a special way to be useful.

Tasks

Now that get_input() and length_counter() are coroutine functions, I must call them using the await keyword. There are two different ways to invoke them, depending on how I want them to be run: by directly awaiting them or by scheduling them as *tasks*, which are special objects that run coroutine functions without blocking.

Both approaches require turning the Collatz example's main() function into a coroutine function, so I'll begin by doing that:

```python
async def main():
    print("Collatz Sequence Counter")

    target = await get_input("Collatz sequence length to search for: ")
    print(f"Searching in range 1-{BOUND}")

    length_counter_task = asyncio.create_task(length_counter(target))
    guess_task = asyncio.create_task(
        get_input("How many times do you think it will appear? ")
    )

    count = await length_counter_task
    guess = await guess_task

    if guess == count:
        print("Exactly right! I'm amazed.")
    elif abs(guess-count) < 100:
        print(f"You're close! It was {count}.")
    else:
        print(f"Nope. It was {count}.")
```

Listing 16-11: collatz_async.py:5a

Deciding how to call each awaitable requires some thought. First, before I can do anything else, I need to know what Collatz sequence length the user wants to search for. I call the get_input() coroutine function with the await keyword. Calling the coroutine function like this will block the program while literally awaiting the user input. This blocking is acceptable here, since we can't do any math calculations (or, really, anything else) without that initial user input.

Once I have the input, I can start the calculation in length_counter(), which I want to run concurrently with getting the user guess via another call to get_input(). To do this, I schedule the native coroutines as tasks. Always schedule a Task object rather than instantiating it directly. Here, I use asyncio .create_task() to schedule a task.

The two native coroutines are now scheduled to run as soon as there's an opening, that is, as soon as main() is awaiting something. I relinquish the main() coroutine function's control of execution by calling await on one of my tasks—at the moment, it doesn't matter which—thereby allowing another task to have a turn. Because both tasks are already scheduled, they'll take turns until length_counter_task returns the value returned by the length_counter() coroutine function. Then the program waits on the other task, guess_task, until it, too, returns a value. Depending on how quickly the user entered input, guess_task may have been waiting to return a value even while length_counter_task was still running.

The Trio and Curio libraries have tasks, just like asyncio does, although they're created a little differently. Consult the documentation for those libraries to learn more.

The Event Loop

At this point, it may seem like I've coded myself into a corner: coroutine functions and other awaitables must be called with await, but only coroutine functions can contain the await keyword. How can I start this program?

The *event loop* is the heart of asynchrony. It manages the multitasking between awaitables and provides the means of calling the first awaitable in the stack. Every asynchrony module provides an event loop mechanism. You can even write your own if you're feeling brave. In this example, I'll employ the default event loop provided by asyncio, like this:

```
if __name__ == "__main__":
    loop = ❶ asyncio.get_event_loop()
    ❷ loop.run_until_complete(main())
```

Listing 16-12: collatz_async.py:6a

I acquire an event loop ❶ and bind it to the name loop. An event loop object has a number of methods for controlling execution; in this case, I use loop.run_until_complete() to schedule and run the main() coroutine function ❷.

Since this is the most common way to start an event loop, it's not surprising that asyncio provides a shorter equivalent way to use the default event loop:

```
if __name__ == "__main__":
    asyncio.run(main())
```

Listing 16-13: collatz_async.py:6b

I can now run my module, and it works.

GOTCHA ALERT According to asyncio maintainer Andrew Svetlov, the development team is in the process of improving on asyncio's flawed design, including how event loops are used. If you're reading this book in the future, perhaps using Python 3.12 or later, there's a very good chance the above example code here is no longer the recommended approach. See the documentation!

Alternative asynchrony modules offer some important additional mechanisms for handling multiple tasks: Curio has TaskGroup, while Trio has (and requires use of) Nursery. See the documentation for those libraries to learn more. The asyncio module has no analogous structures yet, and implementing them is decidedly non-trivial.

If you run this code, you'll notice a remaining problem: *collatz_async.py* still hangs in the same place it did before! That's not very practical.

Making It (Actually) Asynchronous

The code isn't yet behaving concurrently because of this line from get_input()
in Listing 16-10, which I warned you about earlier:

```
n = input(prompt)
```

No matter how I write the rest of the program, input() is an IO-bound
blocking function, so it will hog the process until the user inputs something, such as their guess. It doesn't know how to take turns.

To get user input asynchronously, I must use a coroutine function
equivalent to input(). There's nothing of the sort in the standard library,
but the third-party library aioconsole provides an asynchronous equivalent
for input(), among a few other functions. I'll need to install this package to
my virtual environment.

GOTCHA ALERT   Getting input from the stdin stream asynchronously is a harder problem than
it appears, and it hasn't yet been fully solved. Creating a unified-streams API
is extraordinary difficult! If you're using a different asynchronous programming library, like Trio or Curio, you're in for quite a challenge. This is the only
reason I'm using asyncio for the example: aioconsole provides a limited but
effective workaround for the problem, but it's only compatible with asyncio.

Once it's installed, I import the ainput coroutine function I need:

```
import asyncio
from aioconsole import ainput

BOUND = 10**5
```

Listing 16-14: collatz_async.py:1b

The ainput coroutine function works exactly like the built-in function
input(), except that it's an awaitable, so it will periodically relinquish control
of the process, allowing other awaitables to run.

Conventionally, asynchronous equivalents to standard library functions
and modules are prepended with an a (for async). This is helpful to know
because there's not much in the way of documentation for aioconsole, as of
this writing. With any library of this sort, assume this naming convention
and identical usage to the standard library equivalent, unless otherwise
informed by documentation.

I adjust my get_input() coroutine function to use ainput:

```
async def get_input(prompt):
    while True:
        n = await ainput(prompt)
        try:
            n = int(n)
        except ValueError:
            print("Value must be an integer.")
            continue
```

```
        if n <= 0:
            print("Value must be positive.")
        else:
            return n
```

Listing 16-15: collatz_async.py:4b

Now, if I run the module, it works asynchronously. If I take more than a couple of seconds to input a valid guess, the results are printed immediately after I press ENTER. In contrast, if I input a valid guess immediately, the delay from the CPU-bound task can still be observed. As mentioned before, concurrency only improves the perceived responsiveness of the program, not the execution speed.

Scheduling and Asynchronous Execution Flow

When you're used to the execution flow of ordinary synchronous code, asynchrony can take more than a little bit of getting used to. To help reinforce the principles I've introduced, I'll break down the call stack of the complete *collatz_async.py* file.

At the outset of execution, I start the event loop:

```
asyncio.run(main())
```

This schedules the main() coroutine function as a task, which I'll refer to as main throughout this section. Because it's the only task scheduled, the event loop runs it immediately.

Next, the code needs some user input before it can logically do anything, so I await the return value of the coroutine function get_input():

```
target = await get_input("Collatz sequence length to search for: ")
```

The await statement causes the main task to relinquish control to the event loop so something else can run. The coroutine function get_input() is scheduled as an event in the background, it runs, and the value is returned and assigned to target. With that fulfilled, the main task proceeds.

Next, I schedule the get_input() coroutine function as a task to get the user's guess:

```
guess_task = asyncio.create_task(
    get_input("How many times do you think it will appear? ")
)
```

The task bound to guess_task is scheduled, but it does not immediately start. The main task still has control, and it hasn't relinquished it yet.

I also schedule the length_counter() coroutine function in the same manner:

```
length_counter_task = asyncio.create_task(length_counter(target))
```

Now, `length_counter_task` is scheduled to run at some point in the future. Next, this line is executed in the `main` task:

```
count = await length_counter_task
```

This code causes `main` to relinquish control to the event loop, in that it pauses and waits for `length_counter_task` to have a value for return. The event loop now has control.

The next scheduled task in the queue is `guess_task`, so that's started next. The `get_input()` coroutine function runs up to the following line:

```
n = await ainput(prompt)
```

Now, `get_input()` is waiting on another awaitable, `ainput()`, which is scheduled. Control is handed back to the event loop, which runs the next scheduled task, `length_counter_task`. The `length_counter()` coroutine function is started, and it runs up to its `await` command before returning control to the event loop.

Perhaps the user hasn't yet input anything—only a few milliseconds have passed, after all—so the event loop checks in with `main` and `guess_task`, which are both still waiting. The event loop again checks `length_counter_task`, which does some more work before pausing again. Then, the event loop checks back with `ainput` to see if the user has entered anything yet.

Execution continues in this manner until something finishes.

Bear in mind that `await` isn't a magical keyword that *itself* returns control to the event loop. Rather, some non-trivial logic under the hood determines which task is run next, but I won't go into that here, in the interests of time and sanity.

Once the `length_counter_task` has completed and is ready to return a value, the `await` in `main` is fulfilled, and that returned value is assigned to `count`. The next line in the `main()` coroutine function is run:

```
guess = await guess_task
```

For the purposes of this example, suppose the `guess_task` isn't done yet. The `main` task must wait some more, so it hands control back to the event loop, which now checks in on `guess_task`—still waiting—before checking on `ainput`. Notice it doesn't need to check on `length_counter_task` anymore, as that task is completed.

Once the user enters something, `ainput` has a value to return. The event loop checks in with the still-waiting `main` task and then allows `guess_task` to store the returned value from its await in `n` and continue its execution. There are no more `await` statements in the `get_input()` coroutine function, so aside from the event loop looking in on the napping `main` task, `guess_task` is able to return a value. With its `await` fulfilled and no other tasks in the queue, `main` is given priority again, and it finishes up.

There's an important rule here: the order in which concurrent tasks complete is never guaranteed! As you'll see in the next chapter, this can lead to some interesting problems.

Simplifying the Code

I can use the `asyncio.gather()` coroutine function instead of the prior method to run two tasks concurrently. This won't change the functionality of the program at all from what I'm already doing, but it will make the code cleaner:

```
async def main():
    print("Collatz Sequence Counter")

    target = await get_input("Collatz sequence length to search for: ")
    print(f"Searching in range 1-{BOUND}")

    (guess, count) = await asyncio.gather(
        get_input("How many times do you think it will appear? "),
        length_counter(target)
    )

    if guess == count:
        print("Exactly right! I'm amazed.")
    elif abs(guess-count) < 100:
        print(f"You're close! It was {count}.")
    else:
        print(f"Nope. It was {count}.")
```

Listing 16-16: collatz_async.py:5b

I pass the awaitables I want to run to `asyncio.gather()` in the order I want their values returned. While `asyncio.gather()` will create and schedule tasks for all native coroutines passed to it, remember not to depend on the order in which tasks will be started and run. The return values from the native coroutines are packed into a list, which is then returned from `asyncio.gather()`. In this case, I unpack the two values from the list into guess and count. The outcome is the same as that of Listing 16-11.

Asynchronous Iteration

Iterators work with asynchrony much the same as functions do: only iterators marked as async support the pause-and-resume behavior. By default, looping on an iterator is blocking, unless there's an explicit await somewhere in the suite. This particular feature of asynchrony has evolved quite a lot in the last several versions of Python and has only achieved some modicum of API stability in 3.7, so older code you may find will likely use outdated techniques.

To demonstrate this behavior, I'll rework my Collatz example to use an asynchronously iterable class, instead of a coroutine function. Understand that this technique is overpowered for this use case. In production code, I'd have stuck with the simpler native coroutine and saved the asynchronous iterator class for more complex logic.

All the new concepts below are part of the core Python language and not from asyncio. I start simply enough by creating a Collatz class, setting the bound and starting values as before:

```python
import asyncio
from aioconsole import ainput

BOUND = 10**5


class Collatz:

    def __init__(self):
        self.start = 2
```

Listing 16-17: collatz_aiter.py:1

Next, I'll write a new coroutine function that will contain all the logic for counting the steps in a single Collatz sequence. This really isn't much of a coroutine function, as it lacks a yield, but this approach will be convenient for the example:

```python
    async def count_steps(self, start_value):
        steps = 0
        n = start_value
        while n > 1:
            if n % 2:
                n = n * 3 + 1
            else:
                n = n // 2
            steps += 1
        return steps
```

Listing 16-18: collatz_aiter.py:2

For an object to be an ordinary, synchronous iterator, it needs to implement the special methods __iter__() and __next__(). Similarly, to be an *asynchronous iterator*, it must implement the special methods __aiter__() and __anext__(). You can define an *asynchronous iterable* in the same manner, by implementing __aiter__().

Here, I define the two special methods necessary to make Collatz an asynchronous iterator:

```python
    def __aiter__(self):
        return self

    async def __anext__(self):
        steps = await self.count_steps(self.start)
        self.start += 1
        if self.start == BOUND:
            raise StopAsyncIteration
        return steps
```

Listing 16-19: collatz_aiter.py:3

The __aiter__() method must return an asynchronous iterator object, which is just self in this case. You will notice that this method is not made awaitable with async. It must be directly callable.

The __anext__() special method has a couple of differences from __next__(). First and most importantly, it is marked async, making it awaitable. Otherwise, iterating over the iterator object would be blocking. Second, when there are no more values to iterate over, I raise StopAsyncIteration, instead of StopIteration, as with ordinary iterators.

In my __anext__() coroutine function, I also chose to include an await statement, which allows the coroutine function to pause if necessary and hand control back to the event loop. (Here, I really only do this to demonstrate that it's possible, especially since asynchronous iterators are particularly useful when a single iterative step is time consuming. However, since the execution time of the coroutine function is so brief in this example, I could have omitted it, as the mere usage of the asynchronous iterator involves an await under the hood.)

In my length_counter() coroutine function, I must use an async for to iterate over the asynchronous iterator:

```
async def length_counter(target):
    count = 0
    async for steps in ❶ Collatz():
        if steps == target:
            count += 1
    return count
```

Listing 16-20: collatz_aiter.py:4

The async for compound statement is specifically for iterating over an asynchronous iterator, which in this case is a Collatz instance ❶.

If you want to understand what's happening under the hood here, take a look at the equivalent logic for the async for loop in the context of this function:

```
async def length_counter(target):
    count = 0
    iter = Collatz().__aiter__()
    running = True
    while running:
        try:
            steps = await iter.__anext__()
        except StopAsyncIteration:
            running = False
        else:
            if steps == target:
                count += 1
    return count
```

Notice the use of the await keyword when calling __anext__() on the iterator. An async for loop will hand control back to the event loop on each iteration, but if a single iteration were to take a long time, I'd need the additional `await` statements in the `__anext__()` coroutine function to keep it from blocking.

As for the rest of this version of my code, I'm reusing Listings 16-16 and 16-13. The output and behavior are the same as before.

As I mentioned, asynchronous iterators are definitely overpowered for my Collatz example. Most of the time, asynchronous iterators are only useful if iteration is either IO-blocking or computationally heavy enough to justify some sort of progress indicator, or perhaps for concurrency with another IO-blocking task.

Asynchronous Context Managers

Context managers must also be written in a specific way to have them work with asynchrony. An asynchronous context manager has the special coroutine functions `__aenter__()` and `__aexit__()`, instead of the usual `__enter__()` and `__exit__()` special methods. Typically, you'd only write an asynchronous context manager if you needed to await something in `__aenter__()` or `__aexit__()`, such as a network connection.

An asynchronous context manager is used with `async with`, instead of `with`, but using it is otherwise the same as working with a regular context manager.

Asynchronous Generators

You can also create *asynchronous generators*, which are identical in all manners to ordinary generators (discussed in Chapter 10), except for being compatible with asynchrony. They were introduced in Python 3.6 via PEP 525.

You define an asynchronous generator with `async def` but use `yield` statements as with regular generators. As these generators are asynchronous, you can use `await`, `async for`, and `async with` in their suites as needed. When the asynchronous generator is called as normal (without `await`), it produces an *asynchronous generator iterator*, which can be used just as you would an asynchronous iterator.

Other Asynchrony Concepts

There are quite a number of other tools in your asynchrony toolkit: locks, pools, events, futures, and the like. Most of these concepts are borrowed from the older and considerably better-documented technique of threading, which I'll cover in Chapter 17. The main reason I've skipped over these concepts in this chapter is that the exact usage of each one varies between asynchrony modules. If you've done any amount of work in concurrency before, you've also noticed that I skipped some important problems, including race conditions and deadlocks. I'll introduce these issues in the next chapter as well.

One other advanced concept relating to asynchrony that you should be aware of is *context variables*, or contextvars. These allow you to store different values in variables depending on a context, meaning two different tasks can work with the same apparent variables but in fact retrieve entirely distinct values. If you want to learn more about context variables, see the official documentation at *https://docs.python.org/3/library/contextvars.html*. (The analogous threading concept is *thread-local storage*, which I won't cover in this book.)

Anyone considering a dive into asynchrony should push onward into the next chapter, as the same problems experienced in threading and traditional concurrency can creep into asynchronous programming. The exact solutions vary from one asynchrony library to the next and may even require a bit of trailblazing. If you want to excel at asynchrony, become comfortable with threading, even if you never plan on using threads in production.

Wrapping Up

The distinction between concurrency and asynchrony can be bewildering at first, so here's a quick recap. Concurrency improves your program's perceived responsiveness by allowing the code to do something else while waiting on an IO-bound process. It does not make your code faster, and it thus isn't useful for CPU-bound processes where the delays come from the code itself. Asynchrony is a relatively new way of achieving concurrency entirely within the code, without needing to resort to the more complex techniques.

In Python, asynchronous programming is achieved with the async/await model, which introduces two keywords. Roughly, async means, "This structure can be used asynchronously," and await means, "I'm waiting for a value, so you can do something else now, if you like." The await keyword can only be used inside of a native coroutine (also known as a coroutine function), which is a function declared with async def.

Asynchronous programming primarily consists of writing native coroutines and either awaiting them with await or scheduling them as tasks. The order in which current tasks will complete is never guaranteed.

Ultimately, asynchrony relies on an event loop to manage the execution of native coroutines and concurrent tasks. The Python standard library includes asyncio for this purpose, although this module is sometimes considered quite complex and obtuse. There are some much more intuitive alternatives, especially Trio. Alternatively, you could write your own custom event loop that's fit to your particular purpose, if you're feeling brave.

17

THREADING AND PARALLELISM

Before the advent of asynchrony in Python, you had two options to improve the responsiveness of your program: *threading* and *multiprocessing*. Although the two concepts are often seen as related, and even interchangeable in some languages, they couldn't be more different in Python.

Threading is a means of achieving concurrency, which is useful in working around IO-blocking tasks, wherein the code is limited by the speed of something external, like user input, the network, or another program. It is not useful by itself for working around CPU-blocking tasks, wherein the magnitude of processing is the cause of code slowdowns.

Parallelism is a technique used to deal with CPU-blocking tasks, by running different tasks at the same time on separate CPU cores. *Multiprocessing* is the way we accomplish parallelism in Python. It was introduced to the language in Python 2.6.

Concurrency and parallelism are often essential when programming user interfaces, scheduling events, working with networks, and performing labor-intensive tasks in code.

Unsurprisingly, there is a lot to threading and multiprocessing, far beyond the conceivable scope of this book. This chapter will anchor you in the core concepts of concurrency and parallelism in Python. From there, you can consult the official documentation: *https://docs.python.org/3/library/concurrency.html*. I'll assume you have already read Chapter 16, as I'll be reworking the Collatz example I introduced throughout that chapter.

Threading

A single sequence of instructions in a program is called a *thread of execution*, which is usually just referred to as a *thread*. Any Python program not written with concurrency or multiprocessing is contained within a single thread. *Multithreading*, typically just called *threading*, achieves concurrency by running multiple threads simultaneously in the same *process*, which is an instance of a running computer program.

In Python, only one thread can run at a time within a single process, so multiple threads have to take turns. Threading is also known as preemptive multitasking, because the operating system is *preempting*, or seizing control from, one running thread to give another thread a turn. This contrasts with asynchrony, also known as cooperative multitasking, wherein a particular task voluntarily gives up control.

While threading is mediated by the operating system, your code is responsible for starting the threads and managing the data they share. This is not a simple task, and a large portion of this chapter will focus on the difficulties of sharing data between threads.

Concurrency vs. Parallelism

Although they are often confused, concurrency and parallelism are not the same thing! According to Go co-creator Rob Pike, *concurrency* is the composition of multiple tasks, while *parallelism* involves running multiple tasks at the same time. Parallelism can be brought in as part of a concurrent solution, but you should first understand the concurrent design of your code before you invite multiprocessing to the party. (I highly recommend watching Pike's talk "Concurrency is not Parallelism" from the Heroku Waza conference: *https://blog.golang.org/waza-talk/*.)

In many programming languages, threading also achieves parallelism as a side effect of the language and system architecture. This is part of the reason why many confuse concurrency with parallelism. However, Python's Global Interpreter Lock prevents this implicit parallelism, since any Python process is constrained to run on a single CPU core.

Basic Threading

In Python, the `threading`, `concurrent.futures`, and `queue` modules provide all the classes, functions, and tools you'll need to work with threading. I'll use all three in this chapter.

PEDANTIC NOTE The threading module actually uses the _thread module, which provides the low-level primitives for threading. While you should nearly always stick with the threading and concurrent.futures modules, which are easier to use by far, _thread may be of use to you if you're doing something particularly advanced. See its documentation at *https://docs.python.org/3/library/_thread.html*.

To use threading effectively, first identify the IO-bound tasks in your code and isolate each such task behind a single function call. This design will make it easier to thread individual tasks later.

In the case of my Collatz example from Chapter 16, the function get_input() is IO-bound, since it waits on input from the user. The rest of the code is not IO-bound, so it can run synchronously. I want to run get_input() on a separate thread, so it can run concurrently with the rest of the program.

If you're coding along with me, open a fresh copy of *collatz_sync.py* (Listings 16-1 through 16-6) in your code editor. In Listing 17-1, I have the original synchronous version of the collatz() and length_counter() methods. I import the threading module at the top, as I'll be using functions from that module throughout this version of my program:

```
import threading

BOUND = 10**5


def collatz(n):
    steps = 0
    while n > 1:
        if n % 2:
            n = n * 3 + 1
        else:
            n = n // 2
        steps += 1
    return steps


def length_counter(target):
    count = 0
    for i in range(2, BOUND):
        if collatz(i) == target:
            count += 1
    return count
```

Listing 17-1: collatz_threaded.py:1

I need to iron out one little wrinkle in my prior design as I introduce threading: a function being run in a separate thread cannot return a value to the caller, but all my original functions return values. I therefore need a different solution for passing those values around.

The naive solution would be to create some sort of central location where the threaded function can store its data, and the most quick-and-dirty way to accomplish this is with a global name:

```
guess = None
```

```
def get_input(prompt):
    global guess
    while True:
        n = input(prompt)
        try:
            n = int(n)
        except ValueError:
            print("Value must be an integer.")
            continue
        if n <= 0:
            print("Value must be positive.")
        else:
            guess = n
            return n
```

Listing 17-2: collatz_threaded.py:2a

The get_input() function stores its return value in the new global name guess and then returns directly anyway.

Okay, yes, that design is repulsively non-Pythonic for this use case, and I'll build a cleaner solution a bit later, but it'll do for the moment. However, this version is analogous to a real-world pattern that *can* be Pythonic: you may need to allow threads to store data in a central, shared location, such as a database.

Now for the interesting part. I need to thread the function call—namely, get_input()—that I want to execute concurrently:

```
def main():
    print("Collatz Sequence Counter")

    target = get_input("Collatz sequence length to search for: ")
    print(f"Searching in range 1-{BOUND}...")

    t_guess = threading.Thread(
        target=get_input,
        args=("How many times do you think it will appear? ",)
    )
    t_guess.start()

    count = length_counter(target)

    t_guess.join()

    if guess == count:
        print("Exactly right! I'm amazed.")
    elif abs(guess - count) < 100:
```

```
        print(f"You're close! It was {count}.")
    else:
        print(f"Nope. It was {count}.")


if __name__ == "__main__":
    main()
```

Listing 17-3: collatz_threaded.py:3a

The program can't do anything until it gets the target value from the user, so I call get_input() the ordinary (synchronous) way the first time.

I want the *second* call to get_input(), wherein the user enters their guess, to run concurrently with the CPU-intensive Collatz calcuations. To run this concurrently, I create a thread with threading.Thread(). I pass the function to run in the thread to the target= keyword argument of Thread(). Any arguments that must be passed to the function being threaded have to be passed as a tuple to args=. (Note the trailing comma in the code above!) When the thread starts, it will call get_input() and pass it the arguments specified in args=. In this case, I am threading the call to get_input() and passing the input prompt message as a string.

I bind the thread object I created to t_guess and then start it in the background with t_guess.start(), so my code can continue as normal without waiting for the get_input() function to return.

Now I can start the CPU-intensive step of calling length_counter() synchronously. While I could thread this, too, there's no point, as my program can't really do anything else until length_counter() returns a value. Threads are quite a bit more expensive than asynchronous tasks, in terms of performance overhead for creating them. Therefore, you should only create threads when they provide a direct benefit to your program's performance or perceived responsiveness.

Once length_counter() has finished, the program really can't do anything more until the thread for get_input() is done working and has stored its return value in guess. I *join* the thread with t_guess.join(), meaning the code will wait for the thread to finish its work before continuing. If the thread is already done, the call to t_guess.join() it will immediately return.

From there, the program carries on as normal. If you run this complete program, you'll find it has the same behavior as the asynchronous version in Chapter 16: the calculations happen while the program waits on the user to input their guess.

Timeouts

Notice that the program hangs while waiting for a thread to finish up. For Listing 17-3, this is perfectly safe, as any delay in this scenario would come from the user being slow about entering a value. However, you would be justified in being a bit wary of this indefinite suspension. If your thread is IO-bound from using a network connection or another system process, an unexpected error might cause the thread to never return! Your program would hang indefinitely, without an explanation or error message, until the operating system reports to your bewildered user, The program has stopped responding.

To help mitigate this issue, you can introduce a *timeout*. This specifies the maximum time until the program gives up waiting on a thread to join, after which, it carries on with or without it.

To demonstrate this, I'll annoy my Collatz game user by making the program a bit impatient. (Yes, this is an absolutely terrible game design choice, but it's better than dragging you through a fresh example, right?)

```python
def main():
    # --snip--

    t_guess = threading.Thread(
        target=get_input,
        args=("How many times do you think it will appear? ",),
        daemon=True
    )
    t_guess.start()

    count = length_counter(target)

    t_guess.join(timeout=1.5)
    if t_guess.is_alive():
        print("\nYou took too long to respond!")
        return

    # --snip--

if __name__ == "__main__":
    main()
```

Listing 17-4: collatz_threaded.py:3b

I pass the timeout=1.5 keyword argument to join() to specify that, once the join() statement is reached, the program should only wait for one and a half seconds before continuing, regardless of whether the thread has finished. In effect, this means the user only has one and a half seconds to enter their answer.

Bear in mind, if the join() times out, it doesn't actually affect the thread at all. It's still running in the background. The main program just doesn't wait around for it anymore.

To determine whether a timeout has occurred, I check whether the thread is still alive. If it is, I complain to the user and quit the program.

Daemonic Threads

Another consideration is that exiting the main thread will *not* terminate the other threads. In Listing 17-4, if I timed out waiting for the t_guess thread, even when I reached the return statement, ending the main flow of execution, that t_guess thread would keep running in the background indefinitely. That's a problem, especially as the user would expect the program to have quit in its entirety.

Even so, Python deliberately supplies no obvious way of killing a thread, because doing so can result in some horrible effects, including utterly mangling your program state. However, without a way to abort the thread, it would hang forever after the complaint, and entering data would then do nothing. Once again, if the hanging thread were due to something like a network error, then either your program would go unresponsive, or the waiting thread would keep running in the background long after the main program was closed.

To mitigate this here, I make my thread *daemonic*, meaning I tie its lifespan to the lifespan of the process (the main program). When the main thread ends, all the associated daemonic threads are killed as well.

I define a thread as daemonic when I create it, by specifying the keyword argument daemon=True, as I did in Listing 17-4. Now, when I exit the main program, the thread is aborted too.

GOTCHA ALERT   You have to be *extremely careful* about daemonic threads! Because they abort abruptly when your program does, they don't finish their work or clean up after themselves. This can leave files and database connections open, changes partially written, and all manner of nasty things. Only make a thread daemonic if you are absolutely certain it's safe to suddenly abort it *anytime*.

Futures and Executors

That quick-and-dirty global-name technique for passing things around is less than ideal for this example, largely because global names are too easily shadowed or improperly mutated. On the other hand, I don't want to introduce side effects into my get_input() function by passing some mutable collection to store the data in instead. I need a more resilient way to return a value from the thread.

This is possible, thanks to *futures*, which are sometimes known as promises or delays in other languages. A future is an object that will contain a value at some point in the future but can be passed around like a normal object, even before it contains that value.

Carrying on with our current example, I import the concurrent.futures module that provides futures. Futures also provide a way to create threads directly, so I no longer need the threading module.

```
import concurrent.futures

BOUND = 10**5

def collatz(n):
    # --snip--
```

Listing 17-5: collatz_threaded.py:1b

In this version, I won't be needing the global name guess for storing the return value from get_input(), so I'll just remove the two lines that use it:

```
def get_input(prompt):
    while True:
        n = input(prompt)
        try:
            n = int(n)
        except ValueError:
            print("Value must be an integer.")
            continue
        if n <= 0:
            print("Value must be positive.")
        else:
            return n
```

Listing 17-6: collatz_threaded.py:2b

The function now looks like the synchronous version, although it will still work with threading via futures.

In my main method, I start the thread with a ThreadPoolExecutor object. This is a type of *executor*—an object that creates and manages threads:

```
def main():
    print("Collatz Sequence Counter")

    # --snip--

    executor = concurrent.futures.ThreadPoolExecutor()
    future_guess = executor.submit(
        get_input,
        "How many times do you think it will appear? "
    )

    count = length_counter(target)
    guess = future_guess.result()
    executor.shutdown()

    # --snip--

if __name__ == "__main__":
    main()
```

Listing 17-7: collatz_threaded.py:3c

I create a new ThreadPoolExecutor and bind it to the name executor. This name is conventional for thread pools and other executors. Then, I create a new thread in that pool with executor.submit(), passing the function to be threaded, as well as all its arguments. Unlike when I'm instantiating from a threading.Thread object, I do *not* need to wrap the arguments in a tuple.

The call to executor.submit() returns a future, which I bind to the name future_guess. The future object will eventually contain the value returned by get_input(), but at the moment, it's nothing more than a promise.

From here, I continue as normal, running those heavy calculations via length_counter().

Once that's done, I get the final value of the future with future_guess .result(). Like when joining a thread, this will hang until the thread returns a value.

After all the threads managed by the executor are done, I need to tell the executor to clean up after itself, which I accomplish with executor.shutdown(). This is safe to call, even before the threads are finished, as it will shut down the executor once all threads are finished. Once you've called shutdown() on an executor, attempting to start new threads with it will raise a RuntimeError.

A with statement can automatically shut down an executor in the same way it can automatically close files. This is useful, in case you forget to shut down your executor.

```
def main():
    print("Collatz Sequence Counter")

    # --snip--

    with concurrent.futures.ThreadPoolExecutor() as executor:
        future_guess = executor.submit(
            get_input,
            "How many times do you think it will appear? "
        )

        count = length_counter(target)

    guess = future_guess.result()

    # --snip--

if __name__ == "__main__":
    main()
```

Listing 17-8: collatz_threaded.py:3d

The call to executor.shutdown() occurs automatically at the end of the with statement. Any statements that should run concurrently with the thread(s) must be in the suite of the with, as it won't be possible for main control flow to leave the with statement until all the threads are finished.

In this case, I chose to retrieve the result of the future after the thread pool has been shut down, outside of the with statement. This order isn't strictly necessary, but it doesn't hurt, since the thread pool's preceding shutdown also implies the thread is done, so there will be no waiting to retrieve from the future.

Timeouts with Futures

The result() method on a future accepts a timeout= keyword argument, just as join() does on a Thread object. Unlike with Thread objects, you can determine if a timeout has occurred by catching the concurrent.futures.TimeoutError exception. However, this isn't as simple as it seems. While you can time out on waiting, there remains the problem of stopping the hanging thread.

Here's an example, although you probably shouldn't run this, as it will hang forever:

```
count = length_counter(target)
try:
    guess = future_guess.result(timeout=1.5)
except concurrent.futures.TimeoutError:
    print("\nYou took too long to respond!")
 ❶ executor.shutdown(wait=False, cancel_futures=True)
    return  # hangs forever!
else:
    executor.shutdown()
```

The trouble is, executors do not properly support daemonic threads and do not support them at all as of Python 3.9. Executors also do not offer any mechanism for canceling a thread that is already running. In handling the TimeoutError above, I cancel any threads that haven't started yet ❶, but once a thread has been started by an executor, it cannot be stopped externally without some horrible and inexcusable hackery.

If a thread started by an executor might need to abort under some circumstances, you would need to plan ahead and write custom code for the thread to handle its own timeout internally. This is easier said than done, and in the case of get_input(), it is non-trivial and even approaches impossible. To create a timeout for user input, I have to stick with the thread-based technique.

THEORY RECAP: THREAD SAFETY

According to developer Eiríkr Åsheim, "Some people, when confronted with a problem, think, 'I know, I'll use multithreading.' Nothhw tpe yawrve o oblems [*sic*]."

The joke here is that, in threading, you can never predict what order the threads will finish in. You have to be prepared for this. When your code is guaranteed to work correctly with threading, it is said to be *thread safe*. Thread-safe code is straightforward enough to write in a small, well-contained example like Collatz, but larger systems often contain some sneaky thread safety issues that are an utter nightmare to debug.

Asynchrony, which I introduced back in Chapter 16, is less prone to the issues I'll describe in this section, but it is not immune! Whether you're working with async/await, threads, or multiprocessing, be mindful of the issues that can arise with concurrency.

As you've seen so far, threads need to pass return values and other data between one another during execution. There are really only three ways to reliably move data around between threads: *shared state*, *futures*, or *passing messages*.

Passing messages is considered the safest technique of the three, but it requires careful planning and may involve some significant overhead. Futures, which I used earlier, are another reliable option in specific situations. There are some pitfalls with futures that I'll come back to.

Shared state, of which the global name in Listing 17-2 is an example, is the easiest-looking technique, and it has plenty of use cases. Shared state may consist of global names, mutable values, databases, streams, and files. Although it looks easy to implement, shared state is the most treacherous of the three options, because it is prone to *race conditions*. Race conditions can be particularly difficult to understand if you're new to threading, so here's a fairly robust real-world example.

Consider a shared data source in an office, such as a whiteboard list of supplies needed. Anyone can add new items to the list. To save the secretary time, the office has a tradition: if someone is going out for lunch, they can also pick up some of the items on the way back, using their company credit card. In an effort to ensure that items are not forgotten, there's one rule: you can't erase something from the board until you return with that item.

Jess is heading out for lunch at her favorite sushi place, which is right next to the office supply store, so she makes a note to herself to buy the five boxes of paperclips Peter needs for his quarterly report. A few minutes later, Vaidehi leaves to get a sandwich and decides to get something while she's out: the five boxes of paperclips. Meanwhile, Ben does the same thing while checking out the new food truck, and so does Lisa as she heads out for a coffee break. When everyone comes back from lunch, a confused Peter is greeted with 20 boxes of paperclips on his desk!

The problem is that Jess, Vaidehi, Ben, and Lisa were all operating concurrently (actually, in parallel), and because of the delay between reading and updating the data on the whiteboard, none of them could have known that someone else was getting the paperclips. What's worse, without a fair bit of detective work, it'll be hard to know why Peter is now making a kilometer-long paperclip chain and pondering how to better manage that pesky whiteboard.

Race conditions can crop up when you least expect them. In the analogy, the confusion arose because there were two indivisible steps that needed to take place in sequence: reading the board and updating the board.

There are two different locking strategies the team can employ to prevent a race condition. The first is *coarse-grained locking*: when Jess decides to get something, she writes her name along the side of the board, thereby *acquiring a lock* on the board. As long as her name is there, she is the only person who can edit the whiteboard, with no exceptions! Jess "owns" the whiteboard for the

(continued)

moment. When she returns from lunch, perhaps with a bottle of correction fluid that Jacob requested, she erases her name from the whiteboard, *releasing* it for anyone else to lock.

Coarse-grained locking often negatively impacts performance. Nobody else could get any of the items on the whiteboard during their lunch.

The alternative strategy is *fine-grained locking*: Jess writes her initials next to the "correction fluid" item on the whiteboard, meaning that particular item is locked. More items can still be added to the whiteboard, and other items can be claimed and locked, but only Jess can purchase the correction fluid or update that item. When she returns to the office, she erases the item and must also release the lock by erasing her name from the board.

Closely related to the topic of thread safety is *reentrancy*. A reentrant function can be paused mid-execution while being called again concurrently, without any odd effects. This can be violated if a function depends on a shared resource remaining unmodified for the entire operation.

Race Conditions

Race conditions are particularly hard to detect because a single line of code may hide many steps. For example, consider something as seemingly innocuous as incrementing an integer bound to a global name:

```
count = 0

def increment():
    global count
    count += 1
```

Listing 17-9: increment.py:1a

The augmented addition operator += is not *atomic*, meaning it consists of multiple instructions under the hood. You can see this by disassembling the increment() function with the dis module:

```
import dis

count = 0

def increment():
    global count
    count += 1

dis.dis(increment)
```

Listing 17-10: increment.py:1b

Running Listing 17-10 produces the following output:

```
7            0 LOAD_GLOBAL         0 (count)
             2 LOAD_CONST          1 (1)
             4 INPLACE_ADD
             6 STORE_GLOBAL        0 (count)
             8 LOAD_CONST          0 (None)
            10 RETURN_VALUE
```

The 7 in the leftmost column tells us that the bytecode here corresponds to the line 7 in the Python code, which is count += 1. All of these Python bytecode instructions, except the last two, take place on that one line of code! The value of count is read, the value 1 is added, and then the new value is stored. These three steps (across five instructions) must take place in uninterrupted succession. But consider what would happen if two threads both called increment() at the same time, as illustrated in Table 17-1.

Table 17-1: Model of Race Condition with Two Threads

	Thread A	count (global)	Thread B	
0	← Read	0	(Waiting)	
1	Increment	0	(Waiting)	
1	(Waiting)	0	Read →	0
1	Write →	1	(Waiting)	0
	(Done)	1	Increment	1
		1	← Write	1
		1	(Done)	

Although two separate threads are supposed to increment the global count value, Thread B has read the value 0 from the global count before Thread A has a chance to write its updated value.

The worst thing about a race condition is that there is no such thing as a RaceConditionError exception that can be raised. There's no error message and no linter error. Nothing is going to tell you that a race condition is happening—you can only determine it with some in-depth detective work. Since there's no way to predict when threads will pause and resume, a race condition can hide in plain sight for ages until the perfect conditions arise for it to manifest. This accounts for a terrifying number of "can't reproduce" bug reports.

A Race Condition Example

To demonstrate thread safety techniques, I'm going to rather uselessly thread the Collatz calculations. As mentioned before, concurrency will actually *slow down* CPU-bound tasks further. However, the threading pattern I'm about to apply would be useful if the functions involved had only been IO-bound. I'll also use this scenario to demonstrate multiple concurrency techniques, although some of them are ill-suited to the situation. Roll with it.

To reliably demonstrate a race condition, I will need to create a class to serve as a counter. I'll use this counter, instead of a normal integer, for storing global shared state between different threads working on the Collatz calculation. Again, this would be nonsense in real life, but it ensures I can reliably reproduce a race condition for demonstration purposes:

```python
import concurrent.futures
import functools
import time

BOUND = 10**5

class Counter:
    count = 0

    @classmethod
    def increment(cls):
        new = cls.count + 1
    ❶ time.sleep(0.1)   # forces the problem
        cls.count = new

    @classmethod
    def get(cls):
        return cls.count

    @classmethod
    def reset(cls):
        cls.count = 0
```

Listing 17-11: collatz_pool.py:1a

The likelihood of a race condition increases the more time there is between sequential steps in a process, like between reading and updating data. By slipping that time.sleep() call into the increment() class method ❶, I increase the time between calculating and storing the new count, and I thus practically guarantee the race condition will manifest.

Now, I'll thread my collatz() function for this example and have it accept a target number as an argument. Every time the Collatz sequence generated by the function has the target number of values, I increment the Counter instead of returning a value:

```python
def collatz(target, n):
    steps = 0
    while n > 1:
        if n % 2:
            n = n * 3 + 1
        else:
            n = n // 2
        steps += 1
```

```
    if steps == target:
        Counter.increment()
```

Listing 17-12: collatz_pool.py:2a

The situation is now prime for a race condition. Now, I only need to dispatch multiple threads—and my problem is aliiiiive! (Cue thunder and evil laughter.)

In the next section, I'll make some adjustments to the code, merely to create the race condition I'm trying to demonstrate. Understand that the problem isn't the threading technique itself. The code in the next section is valid. It's the code in Listings 17-11 and 17-12 that contains the real problem, and I'll come back around to fixing it in a little while.

Creating Multiple Threads with ThreadPoolExecutor

To demonstrate the race condition, I will first do away with the for loop in my original length_counter() method and replace it with a ThreadPoolExecutor. This will allow me to dispatch a new thread for each individual Collatz sequence calculation:

```
def length_counter(target):
  ❶ Counter.reset()
    with concurrent.futures.ThreadPoolExecutor(❷ max_workers=5) as executor:
        func = ❸ functools.partial(collatz, target)
      ❹ executor.map(func, range(2, BOUND))
    return Counter.get()
```

Listing 17-13: collatz_pool.py:3a

I start by resetting the Counter to 0 ❶. I define a ThreadPoolExecutor in a with statement, and I specify that it may run a maximum of five threads (also known as *workers*) at once ❷.

For this arbitrary example, I pulled this maximum of five workers out of thin air. The maximum number of workers you permit can have a significant impact on your program's performance: too few workers won't improve responsiveness enough, but too many can bloat overhead. When using threading, it's worth doing a bit of trial and error to find the sweet spot!

I need to pass two arguments to the function collatz(): the target number of steps (target) and the sequence's starting value (n). The target value never changes, but each value for n comes from an iterable, range(2, BOUND).

The executor.map() method can dispatch multiple threads iteratively. However, this method is only able to pass a single value, provided by an iterable, to the given function. Since I'm trying to dispatch my collatz() function, which accepts two arguments, I need another way to handle the first argument. To accomplish this, I generate a callable object with functools .partial(), with the target argument effectively passed in advance ❸. I bind this callable object to func.

The executor.map() method uses the range() iterable to provide the values for the remaining collatz() argument via func ❹. Each resulting function call will take place in a separate worker thread. The rest of this program is the same as in Listings 17-6 and 17-8.

If you run this code as is, you'll see that nasty race condition at work:

```
Collatz Sequence Counter
Collatz sequence length to search for: 123
Searching in range 1-100000...
How many times do you think it will appear? 210
Nope. It was 43.
```

My guess of 210 should be exactly right, but the race condition interfered so badly that the calculated result was wildly inaccurate. If you run this on your computer or update the time.sleep() duration, you might get a completely different number, maybe even coincidentally the right number at times. That unpredictability is why race conditions are so hard to debug.

Now that I've finished creating the problem, I can begin to fix it.

Locks

A *lock* can prevent race conditions by ensuring that only one thread can access a shared resource or perform an operation at a time. Any thread that wants to access a resource has to lock it first. If the resource already has a lock on it, the thread must wait until that lock is released.

I can resolve the race condition in the Collatz example by adding a lock to Counter.increment():

```
import concurrent.futures
import threading
import functools
import time

BOUND = 10**5


class Counter:
    count = 0
    _lock = ❶ threading.Lock()

    @classmethod
    def increment(cls):
        ❷ cls._lock.acquire()
        new = cls.count + 1
        time.sleep(0.1)
        cls.count = new
        ❸ cls._lock.release()

    # --snip--
```

Listing 17-14: collatz_pool.py:1b

I create a new Lock object, which in this case, I bind to a class attribute, _lock ❶. Every time Counter.increment() is called, the thread will try to *acquire* (take ownership of) the lock with the lock's `acquire()` method ❷. If another thread has ownership of the lock, any other call to `acquire()` will hang until that owning thread releases the lock. Once a thread acquires the lock, it can continue as before.

A thread must also *release* the lock, via the lock's `release()` method, as soon as possible after finishing work with the protected resource, so other threads can continue ❸. *Every lock that is acquired must be released.*

Because of this requirement, locks are also context managers. Instead of manually calling `acquire()` and `release()` on my `Lock`, I can handle both implicitly via a `with`, like this:

```
# --snip--

@classmethod
def increment(cls):
    with cls._lock:
        new = cls.count + 1
        time.sleep(0.1)
        cls.count = new

# --snip--
```

Listing 17-15: collatz_pool.py:1c

The `with` statement will acquire and release the lock automatically.

There's nothing inherently magical about a `Lock`; it's merely a glorified boolean value. Any thread can acquire an unowned `Lock`, and any thread can release a `Lock`, regardless of owner. You must ensure any code that would be prone to a race condition is hemmed in by the lock acquisition and release. Nothing prevents you from breaking the rules, but debugging such violations can be fraught with danger, or at least considerable annoyance.

Deadlock, Livelock, and Starvation

A *deadlock* situation occurs when the combined current status of your locks causes all your threads to wait, with no way forward. You can visualize a deadlock as two cars moving toward each other and blocking each other from crossing a one-lane bridge.

The similar *livelock* situation occurs when threads keep infinitely repeating the same interactions, instead of merely waiting, which also results in no real progress. Have you ever had a conversation with a significant other to the effect of "Where do you want to eat?" "I don't care, where do you want to eat?" If so, you have experienced a real-world example of livelock. Both threads perform work involved in waiting for or deferring to one another, but neither thread gets anywhere.

Deadlocks and livelocks will usually cause your program to go unresponsive, often without any messages or errors to suggest why. Whenever you're using locks, you must be extraordinarily careful to foresee and prevent deadlock and livelock scenarios.

To prevent deadlock and livelock, one must be mindful of potential circular wait conditions, in which two or more threads are all mutually waiting on one another to release resources. Because these are hard to depict believably in a code example, I'll illustrate a common circular wait condition in Figure 17-1.

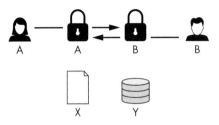

Figure 17-1: Deadlock between two processes

Threads A and B both require access to shared Resources X and Y at the same time. Thread A acquires a lock on Resource X, while Thread B concurrently acquires a lock on Resource Y. Now, Thread A is waiting on Lock B, and Thread B is waiting on Lock A. They're deadlocked.

The right way to resolve a deadlock or livelock will always depend on your particular situation, but you have a couple of tools at your disposal. First, you can specify a timeout= on the lock's acquire() method; if the call times out, it will return False. In the situation in Figure 17-1, if either thread encountered such a timeout, it could then release any locks it held, thereby allowing the other thread to proceed.

Second, any thread can release a lock, so you can forcibly break the deadlock if necessary. If Thread A recognizes a deadlock, it could release Thread B's lock on Resource Y and proceed anyway, thereby breaking the deadlock. The difficulty with this method is that you risk breaking a lock even if you're *not* in deadlock, which creates a race condition.

Locks are not the only culprits in a deadlock or livelock scenario. *Starvation* occurs when a thread is stuck waiting for a future or to join a thread, especially to acquire some data or resource it needs, but that thread or future never returns for some reason. This can even occur if two or more futures or threads wind up waiting for one another to complete.

A thread can even deadlock itself! If a single thread tries to acquire a Lock twice in a row without releasing it first, then it is stuck waiting for itself to release the lock it's waiting on! If there's any risk of this situation arising, you can use threading.RLock, instead of a threading.Lock. With an RLock, a single thread can acquire the same lock multiple times without deadlocking, and only the thread that acquired the lock may release it. While you still must release as many times as you acquire, a thread cannot directly deadlock itself with an RLock.

There is one catch: because an RLock may only be released by the owning thread, it's much harder to break a multithread deadlock with an RLock than with an ordinary Lock.

Passing Messages with Queue

You can sidestep the risk of race conditions and deadlocks by *passing messages*, at the cost of a bit more memory overhead. This is safer than using futures or a shared data source. Anytime futures don't work for your situation, your default strategy for exchanging and collating data with multiple threads should be to have those threads pass messages.

You would typically pass messages between threads with a queue. One or more threads can push data to the queue, and one or more other threads can pull data from the queue. This is analogous to a waiter passing written orders to a kitchen in a restaurant. Neither the sender nor the receiver needs to wait on the other, unless the message queue is full or empty.

Python's standard library includes the queue module, which provides collections that already implement thread safety and proper locking, thus negating the risk of deadlocks. Alternatively, you can use collections.deque in the same way for passing messages, because that collection has atomic operations like append() and popleft(), which make locking unnecessary.

PEDANTIC NOTE   Technically, a queue would still require a shared object, but it's considered different from other shared objects. The queue is a pipeline for passing pieces of data in *one* direction, as opposed to an object where all the threads update the same shared canonical data.

I'll update my *collatz_pool.py* example to pass results from worker threads back to the main thread via a queue, rather than using a shared object.

```
import concurrent.futures
import functools
import queue

BOUND = 10**5
```

Listing 17-16: collatz_pool.py:1d

I import the queue module and remove that pesky Counter.
Next, I'll adjust my collatz() function to push the results onto the queue:

```
def collatz(results, n):
    steps = 0
    while n > 1:
        if n % 2:
            n = n * 3 + 1
        else:
            n = n // 2
        steps += 1
    results.put(steps)
```

Listing 17-17: collatz_pool.py:2b

I accept a queue.Queue object on the results parameter, and I add an item to that collection via results.put().

My design decisions here are deliberate. Data should only flow in one direction via the queue, either input to the worker threads or output from the worker threads. Most design patterns involving queues react to the queue being empty, non-empty, or full, rather than to the contents of the data. If you try to create a queue for moving multiple types of data, it's all too easy to create a starvation or infinite loop situation.

In this case, the worker threads running collatz() will push their output data to the queue, and length_counter() will pull that data in from the queue. If I had needed two-way communication, I would have implemented a second queue to handle data flow in the other direction.

Each worker thread running collatz() must also have a dedicated queue for storing results, lest concurrent calls mix up their results. To do this, I pass the queue as an argument, instead of binding it to a global name. Although this technically violates the "no side effects" principle, it's acceptable because the queue is intended purely as a data transfer medium.

Here's my updated length_counter() method, using the queue:

```
def length_counter(target):
    results = queue.Queue()
    with concurrent.futures.ThreadPoolExecutor(max_workers=5) as executor:
        func = functools.partial(collatz, ❶ results)
        executor.map(func, range(2, BOUND))
    results = list(results.queue)
    return results.count(target)
```

Listing 17-18: collatz_pool.py:3b

I create the queue object and pass it to each of the workers ❶ in the same way I passed target in Listing 17-13. The workers will append the length of each generated Collatz sequence to the queue. Once they're all done, I convert the results queue to a list and return the number of times the target appears in that queue.

Futures with Multiple Workers

As I mentioned before, you can also solve deadlocks with futures. In fact, that's the best option for avoiding a deadlock in this multithreaded Collatz example. Futures have little risk of deadlocking, as long as you avoid having multiple threads waiting on futures from one another.

I'm revising my deadlock example further, to implement futures. I only need to import the concurrent.futures module to use this technique:

```
import concurrent.futures

BOUND = 10**5
```

Listing 17-19: collatz_pool.py:1e

I can also restore my `collatz()` method to its original form, where I am only returning a single value:

```
def collatz(n):
    steps = 0
    while n > 1:
        if n % 2:
            n = n * 3 + 1
        else:
            n = n // 2
        steps += 1
    return steps
```

Listing 17-20: collatz_pool.py:2c

The `executor.map()` method returns an iterable of futures, which I can use to collect the return values from the worker threads:

```
def length_counter(target):
    count = 0
    with concurrent.futures.ThreadPoolExecutor(max_workers=5) as executor:
        for result in executor.map(collatz, range(2, BOUND)):
            if result == target:
                count += 1
    return count
```

Listing 17-21: collatz_pool.py:3c

I iterate over each of the values returned by `executor.map()` and count how many of those values match the target. The `executor.map()` method is essentially a threaded drop-in replacement for the built-in `map()` function; while the input processing order is not guaranteed, the output order is. With most other techniques, you cannot rely on the order in which values are returned.

This is the cleanest approach of all, with minimal overhead.

THEORY RECAP: PARALLELISM

Parallelism is true multitasking, wherein multiple tasks are performed at the same time. It's heavily leveraged in the field of *high-performance computing (HPC)*, where extraordinarily processing-intensive tasks are broken down so that they may be completed in a reasonable span of time. In parallelism, when the primary process is busy, the task is moved to a separate process running on a separate CPU core, leaving the primary process and CPU core free to do other work. This only works when there are multiple CPU cores, as any one CPU core can only work on one task at a time.

To use an analogy borrowed from real life, say you need to make a dozen copies of a memo for distribution around the office. The copy machine (analogous to the CPU) is slow, so the line of employees (processes) waiting to use it is very long. You have other things to do, so you ask your co-worker Sangarshanan

(continued)

---

to handle it for you, since he's got some free time. The task (making copies) is moved to a separate process (Sangarshanan), leaving the primary process (you) free to do other work. When he's done with the copies, he leaves them in your cubicle for you to pick up at your leisure.

Parallelism is useful with a *CPU-bound* task, because it's primarily limited by how quickly the CPU can work. Just as the employees in line in the analogy are limited by the speed of the copy machine, CPU-bound tasks are limited by the speed of the CPU.

One important limitation of parallelism is that processes should not share resources! While there are techniques that allow you to bypass this limitation, they're fraught with peril. Instead, each resource is only accessed and used by one process at a time, and processes pass messages back and forth to communicate in their own timing. This way, it will not matter in what order the processes run or which ones are running concurrently, as both of those things are unpredictable in parallelism anyway.

Parallelism is a fairly involved technique, with a lot of hidden pitfalls that can be difficult to debug. As a result, it should be reserved for projects that have enough significant CPU-bound tasks to justify the added complexity. If it's a matter of preventing the user interface from freezing, concurrency (likely via asynchrony) is the better option.

Achieving Parallelism with Multiprocessing

Since Python 2.6, parallelism is possible via *multiprocessing*, wherein parallel tasks are handled by entirely separate system processes, each with its own dedicated instance of the Python interpreter. Multiprocessing bypasses the limitations imposed by Python's Global Interpreter Lock (GIL), since each process has its own Python interpreter, and thus its own GIL. This allows a single Python program to employ parallelism. A computer can run these multiple processes simultaneously by distributing them among different CPU cores, to be worked on at the same time. How processes are divided up among cores is the prerogative of the operating system.

Remember that multiprocessing has performance costs of its own, so merely adding it to your code will not automatically make everything faster. Improving performance requires dedicated thought and work. As with threading and asynchrony, you must carefully consider your code's design when implementing multiprocessing. You'll see these principles in action shortly.

Multiprocessing in Python follows a very similar structure to threading. Process objects are used exactly like Thread objects. The multiprocessing module also provides classes like Queue and Event, which are analogous to their threading-based cousins but specifically designed for multiprocessing. The concurrent.futures module provides ProcessPoolExecutor, which looks and acts much the same as ThreadPoolExecutor and makes it possible to use futures.

Multiprocessing seldom works in the interactive interpreter, because __main__ must be importable by subprocesses. You will need to run the code from a module or package instead.

Pickling Data

Some Python developers recoil at the thought of using multiprocessing for one reason: it uses pickle behind the scenes. If you recall from Chapter 12, pickle is extraordinarily slow and insecure as a data serialization format, so much so that Pythonistas avoid it like the plague, with good reason.

Even so, pickle does work reasonably well in the context of multiprocessing. First, we don't need to worry about pickle being insecure, because it is being used to transfer data directly between active processes started and managed by your code, so that data is considered trusted. Second, many of pickle's performance issues are offset by the tangible performance gains afforded by parallelism and the fact that the serialized data is never being written to a file, which is itself a CPU-intensive task.

Moreover, because pickle is used in multiprocessing, it is still actively maintained and improved; Python 3.8 saw the implementation of pickle protocol 5. You typically don't need to worry about pickle when using multiprocessing; it's merely an implementation detail most of the time.

It is important to remember that data must be *picklable*, meaning it can be serialized by the pickle protocol, for it to be passed between processes. According to the documentation, you can pickle the following data types:

None

True and False

Integers

Floating-point numbers

Complex numbers

Strings

Bytes-like objects

Tuples, lists, sets, and dictionaries only containing picklable objects

Functions (*but not lambdas*) at global scope

Classes at global scope, with additional requirements

For a class to be picklable, all of its instance attributes must be picklable and stored in the instance __dict__ attribute. When a class is pickled, methods and class attributes are omitted, along with anything else in the class __dict__ attribute. Alternatively, if a class uses slots or otherwise cannot fulfill this criteria, you can make it picklable by implementing the special instance method __getstate__(), which should return a picklable object. Typically, this would be a dictionary of picklable attributes. If the method returns False, it signals the class as unpicklable.

You can also implement the special instance method __setstate__(state), which accepts an unpickled object, which you would unpack into the instance attributes as appropriate. This is a more time-consuming approach, but it's a good way around the restrictions. If you don't define this method, one will be created automatically that accepts a dictionary and assigns it directly to the instance's __dict__ attribute.

If you're going to work a lot with picklable data, especially in the context of multithreading, it may be helpful to see the official documentation for the pickle module: *https://docs.python.org/3/library/pickle.html*.

Speed Considerations and ProcessPoolExecutor

Multiprocessing gets around the GIL, allowing the code to use multiple processes, so you might assume it will speed up that CPU-bound activity of calculating the Collatz sequences. Let's test out that idea.

Continuing from the previous example, I can make use of multiprocessing by swapping my ThreadPoolExecutor to a ProcessPoolExecutor. I can reuse Listings 17-19 and 17-20 (not shown below) and modify Listing 17-21 to look like this:

```
def length_counter(target):
    count = 0
    with concurrent.futures.ProcessPoolExecutor() as executor:
        for result in executor.map(collatz, range(2, BOUND)):
            if result == target:
                count += 1
    return count
```

Listing 17-22: collatz_multi.py:3a

All I needed to do was to replace ThreadPoolExecutor with ProcessPool Executor. Here, I didn't specify max_workers on the ProcessPoolExecutor, so it defaults to one worker per processor core on the machine. I happen to be on an 8-core machine, so when I run this code on my machine, the ProcessPoolExecutor will default to a max_workers value of 8. Your machine may be different.

I'm still using Listings 17-6 and 17-8 for the rest of the program, which threads the IO-bound task of getting user input. There's no sense in using multiprocessing to handle an IO-bound task.

If I run this program, however, it is actually the slowest version yet! My computer has an Intel i7 8-core processor, but it took a whopping *21 seconds* to get the results. The version with the ThreadPoolExecutor and futures (Listing 17-18) took 8 seconds, and the version that didn't thread the calculations at all (Listing 17-1) took less than 3 seconds.

Rest assured, the code is indeed creating multiple *subprocesses*—separate processes linked to the main process—and bypassing the GIL. The problem is, subprocesses themselves are extremely expensive to create and manage! The overhead of multiprocessing is outweighing any performance gains I might have.

Alternatively, I could drop the threading on the IO-bound task and instead move the CPU-bound task out to a single subprocess. However, that results in roughly the same performance as seen with threading alone, negating the point of multiprocessing here.

One cannot simply throw parallelism at a problem and expect the code to run faster. Effective multiprocessing requires planning. In order to take proper advantage of multiprocessing, I need to give each subprocess a reasonable amount of work to do. As you've seen, if I create too many subprocesses, the overhead of the multiprocessing nullifies any performance gains. If I create too few, there will be little to no difference from running it on a single subprocess.

I don't want to create a new subprocess for each call to collatz(), as I did before—a hundred thousand subprocesses is a huge strain on the system resources! Instead, I'll divide those among four separate subprocesses, each of which performs a quarter of the work. I can do this by *chunking*: defining how much of the work is given to a single subprocess:

```
def length_counter(target):
    count = 0
    with concurrent.futures.ProcessPoolExecutor() as executor:
        for result in executor.map(
            collatz,
            range(2, BOUND),
            chunksize=BOUND//4
        ):
            if result == target:
                count += 1
    return count
```

Listing 17-23: collatz_multi.py:3b

Within the executor.map() method, I use the keyword argument chunksize to specify that roughly one-quarter of the values being passed should go to each subprocess.

When I run the code, I find this version to be the fastest yet! With a BOUND = 10**5, it completes almost instantaneously. If I increase BOUND to 10**6, this version takes 5 seconds, versus 16 seconds for the final version of *collatz_threaded.py*. I can play with the chunking to find the ideal value, which is indeed 4; any higher value in this scenario won't make the program run faster than 5 seconds, and a value smaller than 4 is slower.

By carefully applying parallelism, I can bypass the GIL and speed up CPU-bound tasks.

The Producer/Consumer Problem

In parallelism and concurrency, one often classifies threads or processes as either *producers*, which provide data, or *consumers*, which intake that data and process it. It's possible for a thread or process to be both a producer and a consumer. The *producer/consumer problem* is a common situation in which one or more producers provide data, which is then processed by one or more consumers. The producers and consumers are working independently of one another, at potentially different speeds. The producer might produce values faster than the consumers can process them, or the consumers might process the data faster than it is produced. The challenge is preventing the queue of data being processed from getting too full, lest the consumers wait forever because they don't know whether the producer is slow or finished.

I'll model the producer/consumer problem with the Collatz example, merely so I don't need to build up a brand-new example. I'll have one producer provide the starting values of the Collatz sequences, and I'll have four consumers working in parallel to generate the sequences from those starting values and to determine how many have the target number of steps. (In practice, this pattern is overkill for something as simple as the Collatz example.)

At first blush, this program seems like it should be easy to write: create a queue, fill it with the starting values, and then start four subprocesses on the executor to take values out of that queue. In practice, there are a few problems that need to be solved.

First, I cannot wait until the producer has produced all the values before processing. If I tried to pack all the values into the queue at once, I'd have a whopping 3.8 MiB if I set my BOUND to 10**7; real-world examples of the producer-consumer problem can involve gigabytes or terabytes of data. Instead, the producer should provide more values only when there's space in the queue for them.

Second, the consumers need to know the difference between the queue being empty because the values are exhausted and the queue being empty because the producer is working on adding more. If something goes wrong to prevent values being added—or, conversely, if something prevents the consumers from processing values—then the code should be able to handle that error gracefully, rather than waiting forever for something to happen. Similarly, when the program is ready to end, each thread or subprocess should clean up after itself—closing files and streams, for example—rather than aborting abruptly.

Third, and perhaps hardest to implement, producers and consumers must be reentrant. In other words, if a consumer is paused mid-execution and another consumer is started before the first is resumed, the two consumers should not interfere with one another. Otherwise, they may be in danger of deadlocking (or livelocking) in subtle and unexpected ways.

Importing the Modules

I'm going to need quite a few modules to accomplish this program:

```
import concurrent.futures
import multiprocessing
import queue
import itertools
import signal
import time

BOUND = 10**5
```

Listing 17-24: collatz_producer_consumer.py:1

As before, the concurrent.futures module allows me to work with both threads and processes. The multiprocessing module provides the parallelism-specific versions of concurrency classes, including multiprocessing.Queue and multiprocessing.Event. The queue module provides the exceptions related to Queue. I'll also need repeat from itertools when dispatching consumers in my particular use case.

The signal module, which may be new to you, allows me to asynchronously monitor for and respond to process control signals coming from the operating system. This is important to ensuring that all my subprocesses shut down cleanly. I'll come back to this in a moment.

Monitoring the Queue

I need two shared objects from the multiprocessing module for the producer/consumer model to work. The Queue stores the data being passed from producer to consumer, and Event signals when no more data will be added to the Queue by the producer.

```
in_queue = multiprocessing.Queue(100)
exit_event = multiprocessing.Event()
```

Listing 17-25: collatz_producer_consumer.py:2

I'm using global names for these two objects because, unlike with threads, you cannot pass shared objects via arguments when dispatching subprocesses.

The producer subprocess will fill the queue with starting values, and the consumer subprocesses will read from it. The multiprocessing.Queue class has atomic put() and get() methods, like queue.Queue, so it isn't prone to race conditions. I pass the argument 100 to the Queue initializer here, which sets the queue to hold a maximum of 100 items. The maximum is somewhat arbitrary; you should experiment for your use cases.

The exit_event object is an *event*, a special flag that processes can monitor and react to. In this case, the event signals either that the producer will be adding no more values to the queue, or that the program itself has been aborted. The threading module provides an analogous Event object for concurrency.

You'll see both of these at work shortly.

Subprocess Cleanup

It is each subprocess's duty to clean up after itself and shut down properly. When the producer is finished producing data, the consumers need to process the remaining data in the queue and then clean themselves up. Similarly, if the main program is aborted, the subprocesses must all be informed so they can shut themselves down.

To handle both of these situations, I'll write my consumer and producer functions to monitor and respond to exit_event.

```
def exit_handler(signum, frame):
  ❶ exit_event.set()


signal.signal(❷ signal.SIGINT, exit_handler)
signal.signal(❸ signal.SIGTERM, exit_handler)
```

Listing 17-26: collatz_producer_consumer.py:3

I define an *event handler function*, exit_handler(), which is designed to respond to operating system events. The event handler function must accept two arguments: the *signal number* that corresponds to a particular system event and the current *stack frame*, which is roughly the current location and scope in the code. Both values will be provided automatically, so there's no need to worry about figuring out what they should be.

The exit_handler() function will set exit_event ❶. Later, I'll write my processes to clean up and shut down in response to exit_event.

I attach the handler to the two signals I want to monitor: signal.SIGTERM occurs when the main process terminates ❷, and signal.SIGINT occurs when it is interrupted, such as with CTRL-C on POSIX systems ❸.

Consumers

Here's my usual collatz() function, as well as my consumer function:

```
def collatz(n):
    steps = 0
    while n > 1:
        if n % 2:
            n = n * 3 + 1
        else:
            n = n // 2
        steps += 1
    return steps


def collatz_consumer(target):
    count = 0
    while True:
        if not in_queue.empty():
            try:
                n = in_queue.get(❶ timeout=1)
            except queue.Empty:
                return count

            if collatz(n) == target:
                count += 1

        if exit_event.is_set():
            return count
```

Listing 17-27: collatz_producer_consumer.py:4

The collatz_consumer() function accepts one argument: the target it is looking for. It loops infinitely, until explicitly exited with a return statement.

On each iteration, the consumer function checks whether the shared queue, in_queue, has anything in it. If it does, the function attempts to get the next item from the queue with in_queue.get(), which waits until there's an item in the queue. I provide a timeout of one second ❶, which is important to prevent deadlocks and to give the subprocess an opportunity to check and respond to events. One second is more than ample time for my producer process to put a new item into the queue. If in_queue.get() times out, the exception queue.Empty is raised, and I exit the subprocess immediately.

If the consumer is able to get a value from the queue, it runs the value through collatz(), checks the returned value against target, and updates count accordingly.

Finally, I check if exit_event is set; if it is, I return count, ending the subprocess cleanly.

Checking for an Empty Queue

If you look at the documentation for multiprocessing.Queue.empty() (queue.empty() in Listing 17-27) and similar methods, there's a rather ominous statement:

> Because of multithreading/multiprocessing semantics, this is not reliable.

This does not mean you cannot use the empty() method. The "unreliability" has to do with the dynamics I've already described at work in concurrency. By the time the subprocess determines that the queue is empty via the empty() method, it might *not* be empty anymore, since the producer is operating in parallel. This is okay, however. There's no harm in another iteration passing if the timing is off.

This dynamic really only becomes treacherous if you rely on empty() to ensure you can put() a new item in the queue. The queue might be filled up before the subprocess even reaches put(), even if it's the next statement. The same is true of checking full() before calling get(). That's why I invert the logic and check that the queue *is not* empty, while still wrapping the get() statement in a try clause.

Producers

Enough about the consumer. It's time to put some values in that queue with the producer. The producer function for the Collatz example pushes values to the queue when there's an empty spot to do so:

```
def range_producer():
    for n in range(2, BOUND):
      ❶ if exit_event.is_set():
            return
        try:
          ❷ in_queue.put(n, timeout=1)
```

```
        except queue.Full:
    ❸ exit_event.set()
          return

    while True:
        time.sleep(0.05)
        if in_queue.empty():
            exit_event.set()
            return
```

Listing 17-28: collatz_producer_consumer.py:5

In addition to pushing values to the queue when it isn't full, the producer function always checks if exit_event is set, so it can exit cleanly as soon as possible ❶.

I next try to put a value on the queue with put() ❷. In this particular example, if the operation takes more than a second, I want it to time out and thus indicate that the consumers have deadlocked or crashed in some way. If there's a timeout, the queue.Full exception is raised, and I set the exit_event ❸ and end the subprocess. Bear in mind, each situation will have its own ideal timeouts, which you'll have to figure out for yourself. It's better to have too long a timeout, rather than one that's too short.

If the loop reaches its end without a timeout, I don't want to set the exit_event right away, as that might cause the consumers to quit too early and not process some waiting items. Instead, I loop infinitely, checking whether the queue is empty. I can rely on the empty() method here to inform me when the consumers are finished processing the data, since this is the only producer adding values to the queue. On each iteration here, I also sleep for a few milliseconds, so the producer doesn't chew through processing power while it waits. Once the queue is empty, I set the exit_event. Then I exit the function, ending the subprocess.

Starting the Processes

Now that I have written my producers and consumers, it's time to dispatch them. I'll run the producer and all four consumers as subprocesses, which I start with a ProcessPoolExecutor:

```
def length_counter(target):
    with concurrent.futures.ProcessPoolExecutor() as executor:
        executor.submit(❶ range_producer)
        results = ❷ executor.map(
            collatz_consumer,
          ❸ itertools.repeat(target, 4)
        )

    return ❹ sum(results)
```

Listing 17-29: collatz_producer_consumer.py:6

I submit my producer function from Listing 17-28, range_producer(), to a single subprocess ❶.

I use executor.map() as a convenient way to dispatch multiple consumer subprocesses ❷, but I don't need to iteratively provide any data, which is the usual purpose of map(). Since that function requires an iterable as its second argument, I use itertools.repeat() to create an iterator providing exactly four copies of the value target ❸. The values in this iterable will be mapped to four separate subprocesses.

Finally, I collect and sum all the counts returned by the finished consumer subprocesses via results ❹. Because this statement is outside of the with statement's suite, it will only run once the producer subprocess and all four consumer subprocesses have exited.

I've designed my code architecture to work with a single producer. If I wanted more than one producer subprocess, I would need to refactor the code.

As before, I'm using Listings 17-6 and 17-8 for the rest of the program, which will still be threaded.

Performance Results

Running the code in Listing 17-29 is a bit slower than running the version in Listing 17-23—five seconds on my machine for a BOUND of 10**5, versus the nearly instant return of the previous version—but you can see that it works as expected:

```
Collatz Sequence Counter
Collatz sequence length to search for: 128
Searching in range 1-100000...
How many times do you think it will appear? 608
Exactly right! I'm amazed.
```

I chose 128 as my test target, as that's the length of the Collatz sequence starting with the value 10**5, which was the last value provided. This allowed me to confirm that the consumer subprocesses didn't exit before the queue was empty. There are 608 Collatz sequences that are 128 steps long, and that is what is reported after a few seconds.

Be aware that the design of this particular code isn't necessarily going to work for your producer/consumer scenario. You will need to carefully consider how messages and data are passed, how events are set and checked, and how subprocesses (or threads, for that matter) clean up after themselves. I highly recommend reading "Things I Wish They Told Me About Multiprocessing in Python" by Pamela McA'Nulty: *https://www.cloudcity.io/blog/2019/02/27/things-i-wish-they-told-me-about-multiprocessing-in-python/*.

Logging with Multiprocessing

There's one piece of multiprocessing that I've chosen to skip over. Normally, when working with multiple processes, you'd use a logging system that includes timestamps and unique identifiers for processes. This is extraordinarily helpful in debugging parallelized code, especially as most other debugging tools will not work across processes. Logging will allow you to see the status of different processes at any given moment in time, so you can tell which ones are working, which are waiting, and which have crashed. I'll cover logging in general in Chapter 19, and you can fit it to your purposes.

Wrapping Up

There are many helpful tools for threading and multiprocessing that I simply didn't have the opportunity to cover here. Now that you have a grasp of the fundamentals of concurrency and parallelism in Python, I highly recommend skimming through the official documentation for the modules I've been using, as well as two I've skipped:

`concurrent.futures`
> *https://docs.python.org/3/library/concurrent.futures.html*

`queue`
> *https://docs.python.org/3/library/queue.html*

`multiprocessing`
> *https://docs.python.org/3/library/multiprocessing.html*

`sched`
> *https://docs.python.org/3/library/sched.html*

`subprocess`
> *https://docs.python.org/3/library/subprocess.html*

`_thread`
> *https://docs.python.org/3/library/_thread.html*

`threading`
> *https://docs.python.org/3/library/threading.html*

Remember also that asynchrony libraries have analogous structures and patterns for nearly everything in threading, including locks, events, pools, and futures. Most of the time, if you can thread it, you can write it asynchronously.

In summary, there are three primary ways to multitask in Python: asynchrony (Chapter 16), threading, and multiprocessing. Asynchrony and threading are both for working with IO-bound tasks, while multiprocessing is for speeding up CPU-bound tasks.

Even so, remember that concurrency and parallelism are not magic bullets! They can improve your program's responsiveness and, at least in the case of multiprocessing, speed up execution times, but always at the cost of added complexity and the risk of some pretty snarly bugs. They demand careful planning and code architecture, and it's easy to get their usage wrong. I spent considerable time writing, testing, debugging, and fighting with the Collatz examples until I got them right—more so than with any other examples in this book! Even now, you may discover flaws in the design that I overlooked.

Concurrency and parallelism are essential when programming user interfaces, scheduling events, and performing labor-intensive tasks in code. Even so, there's often nothing wrong with old-fashioned synchronous code. If you don't need the extra power, then avoid the extra complexity.

For further understanding, you may want to look up other concurrency and parallelism patterns, such as the `subprocess` module, job queues like celery, and even external operating system utilities like `xargs -P` and `systemd`. There is far more to this than can fit into one chapter. Always carefully research the options for your particular situation.

PART V

BEYOND THE CODE

18

PACKAGING AND DISTRIBUTION

The best code in the world amounts to little if you never ship it. Once your project is functional, you should work out how you'll package and distribute it, before continuing development. The trouble is, packaging in Python sometimes feels like beating yourself with a wet trout.

Often, the difficulty doesn't come from packaging your own code—that's usually easy enough—but rather from handling your code's dependencies, especially its non-Python dependencies. Distribution can be a snarly issue for even experienced programmers, due in part to the diverse scenarios in which Python is used. Still, if you understand how things are supposed to work, you'll have a good foundation for pushing past the frustration and shipping working code.

In this chapter, I'll break down the essentials of packaging and distributing a Python project, first via the Python Package Index, and then as an installable binary. To do this, I'll walk you through packaging an actual application I wrote: Timecard. This project is well-suited as an example, because it has both Python and system dependencies, plus a few non-code resources, all of which need to be accounted for, somehow. The repository for this project is available on GitHub: *https://github.com/codemouse92/timecard/*. I've set up the `packaging_example` branch to contain only the project itself and none of the packaging files, so you can practice.

This chapter functions as an introduction to the packaging process in general, regardless of the tool you plan to use. However, to avoid getting lost in the weeds explaining the myriad packaging tools out there, I'll package Timecard using the popular setuptools package, from which we get the majority of modern packaging patterns.

Along the way, I'll touch on many other common tools, including a few popular third-party alternatives, but I won't go into detail on most of them. In case you want to learn more about these tools, I will link to their official documentation for your reference. Also, if you want to go deeper into packaging in general, one of the best resources is the community-maintained *Python Packaging User Guide* at *https://packaging.python.org/*, which covers a number of more advanced topics, such as packaging a CPython binary extension.

To make this whole idea of packaging feel less threatening to you, I'd also like to mention that the mascot of Python packaging is a happy, purple platypus: an odd little creature that seems to be made up of many disparate parts, is cute and generally friendly, and can lay eggs. (That last part is a pun you'll likely understand by the time this chapter is over.) If you're feeling intimidated by packaging right now, go to *https://monotreme.club/* and revel in the cuteness that is the Python Packaging mascot. They have stickers.

Planning Your Packaging

Before you begin packaging, you need a solid idea of what you're trying to accomplish, why, and how. Unfortunately, very few developers recognize this necessity and instead plunge headlong into writing their packaging scripts, with no real direction. These ad hoc packaging schemes can suffer from brittleness, unnecessary complexity, a lack of portability between systems, and poor or missing dependency installation.

The Dangers of Cargo Cult Programming

In an attempt to encourage the use of good packaging tools and practices, many well-meaning people will provide templates for the files *setup.py*, *setup.cfg*, or others used in packaging, with advice to copy and modify the templates. This practice, known as *cargo cult programming*, is widely employed in Python packaging, to the detriment of both project and ecosystem. Because configuration files are copied blind, errors, hacks, and anti-patterns propagate like plague-carrying rabbits.

A bug in packaging won't always manifest with a failed installation or a helpful error message. For example, a mistake in packaging a library may instead manifest when that library is used as a dependency. Distribution is especially pesky in this regard, as many related bugs are platform specific. Sometimes, you'll be able to install the package, but the program will fail in surprising ways! Issue trackers are rife with these sorts of tickets, many of which are unhelpfully closed with "Cannot reproduce," perhaps because the bug only occurs on that one version of Linux with a particular version of that one system library.

All that is to say, do not give in to the temptation of cargo cult programming! While it is reasonable to start from a proven template, aim to understand every single line of code therein. Read through the documentation. Be certain you haven't omitted a needed parameter the template may have overlooked, used some deprecated option, or even swapped the proper sequence of lines. (Yes, that last one is a thing.)

Thankfully, the *Python Packaging Authority* (*PyPA*) working group has done a lot to move the community away from this. The PyPA is a quasi-official group made up of Python community members who want to make Python packaging a better experience, and membership is open to anyone who maintains a project. They have extensively explained the whys and wherefores of each piece of their packaging templates and the Python Packaging User Guide they maintain.

A Note on Packaging Opinions

As you're about to discover, there are a plethora of ways to package and distribute Python projects. I'll focus primarily on the techniques advised by the PyPA, but there are plenty of alternatives.

Whatever packaging techniques you ultimately use, they must produce a reasonably portable, stable, "just works" package. Your end user should be able to run a predictable set of steps on any supported system and succeed at running your code. While it isn't uncommon for there to be variations in installation instructions from one platform to the next, you want to minimize the number of steps that your end user needs to follow. The more steps, the more chances for errors! Keep things simple and try to respect the recommended packaging and distribution practices for each platform. If your end users consistently report problems or confusion when installing your project, *fix the packaging*.

Determining Your Packaging Goals

Ultimately, the goal of any packaging tool is to create a single *artifact*, usually a file, that can be installed on an end user's environment, be it a personal computer, a server, a virtual machine, or another piece of hardware. There are a number of ways to package a project in Python for distribution. Selecting the right way all comes down to what your project is and who is going to be using it.

At the PyBay2017 conference, Mahmoud Hashemi presented a talk entitled "The Packaging Gradient" (*https://youtu.be/iLVNWfPWAC8*), in which he brought a lot of clarity to the Python packaging ecosystem. (I definitely recommend watching it.) In that talk, he introduced the concept of the *packaging gradient*, which visualizes the options for Python packaging and distribution like the layers of an onion.

Option 1: Python Modules

On the innermost layer of the packaging gradient is the *Python module*, which can be distributed by itself. If your entire project consists of a single Python module, such as some utility script, you may be able to simply distribute that. However, as you've probably noticed by now, this isn't practical whenever there is more than one module involved in the project.

Unfortunately, many Python developers chicken out at this point, zip up their whole project in a compressed file (perhaps with a README file), and leave the hapless end user to figure out how to run the package on their particular system. Don't do this to your users. It's not a great experience.

Option 2: Python Distribution Packages

So far in your Python journey, you've installed plenty of packages with pip. These are all provided by the *Python Package Index (PyPI)*, an online repository of Python packages. Each package in PyPI is in one or both of two formats: source distribution and built distribution.

The *source distribution*, or *sdist*, contains one or more Python packages bundled into a compressed archive, such as a *.tar.gz* file. This is fine as long as your project's code is solely in Python and only depends on Python packages. This is the second layer in the packaging gradient.

The third layer in the packaging gradient is the *built distribution*, or *bdist*, which contains precompiled Python bytecode, as well as binary files needed for the package to run. A built distribution is faster to install than a source distribution, and it can contain non-Python components.

A built distribution is packaged as a *wheel*, a standardized format defined in PEP 427. The name *wheel* refers to a wheel of cheese, which is a reference to the "cheese shop," the original code name for what is now PyPI. Prior to the 2012 adoption of the wheel standard, Python unofficially used another format called *eggs*, which had a number of technical limitations that wheel overcame.

The source distribution, and by extension, the associated built distribution, is known as a *distribution package* once it has been bundled together and versioned.

PyPI can distribute both wheels and sdists, so it's trivial (and thus recommended) to upload both. If you have to choose, favor sdists. If you were to upload only a *platform wheel*—a wheel built for a specific system—and omitted the sdist, users on other systems would not be able to install your package. Only publishing wheels also leaves out users in situations where auditing the source code is mandatory, such as in some corporations. Still, wheels are faster to install than sdists. Whenever you can, upload both.

Option 3: Application Distribution

There's just one problem so far: PyPI is intended for distributing to developers, not to end users. While it is possible to distribute an application on PyPI, it's not well-suited for deploying to end users or production environments; pip is too brittle to be that reliable!

This chapter's example project, Timecard, is certainly a good example of this. While providing a Python distribution package for my application doesn't hurt, many end users will be at a loss if I just tell them to install from pip. I will need an additional layer in my packaging later.

Determining the right distribution method for your application depends largely on your project dependencies, your target environments, and the needs of your end users. Later in this chapter, I'll cover several good options for distributing an application.

Project Structure: src or src-less

Before you start the process of packaging, you must decide whether to use a *src/* directory. Up to this point, all my examples in this book have used so-called *src-less* ("source-less") project structures, where the main project package sits directly in the repository. I chose this technique in prior chapters because of the ease of running the package via python3 -m *packagenamehere*, without the need for installation.

An alternative project structure involves placing all your project modules and scripts in a dedicated *src/* directory. Python developer Ionel Cristian Mărieș, one of the leading advocates of this approach, details several advantages of using a *src/* directory, which I can summarize:

- It simplifies maintenance of your packaging scripts.

- It keeps your packaging scripts and your project source code clearly separated.

- It prevents several common packaging mistakes.

- It prevents you from making assumptions about the current working directory.

- To test or run your package, you are forced to install your package, usually in a virtual environment.

That last item may seem like a peculiar benefit. Avoiding that situation is exactly why I didn't introduce this technique back in Chapter 2, since it would have been impossible to properly introduce *setup.cfg* and *setup.py* then.

In production-grade development, however, forcing yourself to install the package is highly beneficial. It immediately exposes flaws in packaging, assumptions about current working directories, and a number of related problems and anti-patterns. I didn't actually learn about this until researching this book, and I deeply wish I'd discovered it sooner, as it would have saved me many woes.

Another benefit of that approach is that it keeps you from putting off questions of packaging until the last step in a project. I can say from personal experience that there is little more frustrating than building an entire project, only to discover you cannot package anywhere but on your own machine! Figure out packaging as early in the development process as you can.

For the rest of this book, and in the Timecard project in particular, I'll use the *src/* directory approach. Even if you don't use a dedicated *src/* directory, you should install your package in a virtual environment when you want to test it. By the end of the next section, you'll have done exactly that.

Packaging a Distribution Package with setuptools

There are a lot of interesting packaging tools out there for Python, each with its own vocal proponents, so it can be easy to get overwhelmed. When in doubt, I recommend starting with *setuptools*, the de facto standard tool for Python packaging. Even if you decide to use another packaging tool later, many concepts from setuptools are borrowed by most of the other packaging tools.

The setuptools library is a fork of a Python standard library package called *distutils*. In its heyday, distutils was the official standard packaging tool (ergo, its inclusion), but as of Python 3.10, it is now deprecated in favor of setuptools.

To package Timecard as a distribution package, I will use the `setuptools` and `wheel` modules, the latter of which is not installed by default. It's good to ensure both are up-to-date in your environment, along with pip. You can do this with the following terminal command, *inside* your virtual environment:

```
pip install --upgrade pip setuptools wheel
```

Remember to run that inside of the virtual environment you're using, either by activating the virtual environment first or by directly invoking its captive pip binary (such as `venv/bin/pip`).

Project Files and Structure

Here's a quick overview of the files I'll create for this project:

- *README.md* is a Markdown file with project information.
- *LICENSE* contains the project license.
- *pyproject.toml* specifies the build backend and lists build requirements for the package.
- *setup.cfg* contains distribution package metadata, options, and dependencies.
- *setup.py* used to contain packaging instructions and dependencies; now it just ties things together in the source distribution package.
- *MANIFEST.in* lists all the non-code files that should be included in the distribution package.
- *requirements.txt* lists dependencies (which are used differently from *setup.cfg*; it's often useful to have both).

I'll cover each of these files in the sections to come.

The recommendations contained herein are based partly on the latest version of PyPA's sample project, which you can see at *https://github.com/pypa/sampleproject/*. The rest of the information comes from the PyCon 2021 talk "Packaging Python in 2021" by Jeremiah Paige. Bernát Gábor, a member of PyPA, generously reviewed this chapter to make sure it was up-to-date.

Where Metadata Belongs

These days, the Python packaging ecosystem is evolving quickly, and standards are stuck in an odd limbo between yesterday, today, and tomorrow.

Historically, all the metadata for your project—its title, description, and so forth—belonged in a file called *setup.py*. This file also contained other build instructions, such as dependencies to install. Even today, most Python projects still use this convention.

The current convention is to move all of this data into a file called *setup.cfg*, which is easier to maintain by merit of being *declarative*, meaning it focuses on data rather than implementation. This technique is the one I'm using herein. The *setup.py* file still has an occasional role to play, but it's mostly relegated to legacy builds.

In the near future, some packaging data, especially the metadata, will be moved to a third file: *pyproject.toml*. This will allow for a clear separation between the project metadata and options used by all packaging tools on the one hand, and the setuptools-specific configuration in *setup.cfg* on the other hand. As of the date of this writing, this new convention isn't yet implemented by some Python packaging tools, but it is expected to be very soon. In the meantime, *pyproject.toml* still plays the invaluable role of specifying what packaging tools are used.

The README.md and LICENSE Files

Every good project should have a *README* file, which describes the project, its authors, and its basic usage. Nowadays, these are typically written as Markdown files (*.md*), which are rendered with nice formatting by most version control platforms, such as GitHub, GitLab, Bitbucket, and Phorge.

It is a significant packaging mistake to skimp on your README! I like to put a bit of thought and time into mine, and I include (at minimum) the following:

- A project description, written to "sell" users on the project
- A list of authors and contributors
- Basic installation instructions
- Basic usage instructions, such as how to start the program
- The technology stack I used
- How to contribute code or report an issue

In addition, whether your code is open source or not, you should include a *LICENSE* file. In the case of free and open source software, this file should contain the complete text of the license. If you need help selecting an open source license for your project, check out *https://choose alicense.com/* and *https://tldrlegal.com/*. Otherwise, include the copyright information.

If you prefer, you can also include the *.txt* file extension (*LICENSE.txt*) or use Markdown (*LICENSE.md*).

On occasion, I may also include such files as *BUILDING.md* or *INSTALL.md*, to describe building (for development) or installing the project. Whether you use these is up to you.

The setup.cfg File

When creating a distribution package ultimately intended for production, one of the first files to create is *setup.cfg*, which is placed in the root of the repository. The *setup.cfg* file contains all the project metadata, dependencies, and options for setuptools, and it may be used by other packaging tools as well.

It may be tempting to grab a minimalist *setup.cfg* template, but I, like Mahmoud Hashemi, recommend you do not wait until the last phase of your project to start on packaging. Using a *src/* directory forces you to think about packaging early. This is one of those lessons I wish I'd learned years ago.

As soon as you start work on a project, create your *setup.cfg* file. I'll break down the one for Timecard in this section. This is the most important file in your packaging scripts, so I'll be spending a lot of time on this one file.

If you want to know about this file format, see the official documentation here: *https://setuptools.readthedocs.io/en/latest/userguide/declarative_config.html*.

Project Metadata

In writing the *setup.cfg* file for Timecard, I'll start with the basic metadata. The *setup.cfg* file is divided into *sections*, indicating the tool or set of options the parameters to follow belong to. Each section is marked out with the section name in square brackets. For example, all the metadata belongs under the [metadata] section:

```
[metadata]
name = timecard-app
```

Listing 18-1: setup.cfg:1

All the data in a *setup.cfg* file is in key-value pairs. The first key here is called name, and I pass the string value timecard-app. Notice that I didn't need to use quotes around the string value. (The documentation outlines the different types *setup.cfg* understands and what types it expects for each key.)

Although my program is called Timecard, I gave the distribution package the name "Timecard-App," to avoid confusion with the unrelated "Timecard" library published on PyPI. This is the name that will be used in the pip install command. PyPI further restricts this name: it must contain only ASCII letters and numbers, although you may include periods, underscores, and hyphens in the name, as long as they're not at the start or end.

The version must be a string following the format outlined in PEP 440, as demonstrated here:

```
version = 2.1.0
```

Listing 18-2: setup.cfg:2

In short, it must be made up of two or three integers, separated by dots: either in the format *major.minor* ('3.0') or *major.minor.micro* ('3.2.4'). I strongly recommend employing semantic versioning. In this case, the version of Timecard is major version 2, minor version 0, and micro (or "patch") version 5.

If you need to indicate something more in the version, such as a release candidate, beta version, postrelease, or development version, this is permitted using a suffix. For example, '3.1rc2' would mean "3.1, release candidate 2." See PEP 440 for more details on this convention.

Tools like *setuptools-scm* can handle version numbers for you, which can be helpful if you need to update them often: *https://pypi.org/project/setuptools-scm/*. I'll stick to the manual method for this book, however.

The `description` is a one-line description of the package, which I enter here explicitly:

```
description = Track time beautifully.
long_description = file: README.md
long_description_content_type = text/markdown; charset=UTF-8
```

Listing 18-3: setup.cfg:3

The `long_description` is a large multiline description, which I am deriving directly from the contents of the *README.md* file. The `file:` prefix indicates I'm reading from the file that follows. That file *must* exist in the same directory as *setup.cfg*, as paths are not supported here.

Since my README is a Markdown file, I also need to indicate that it needs to be processed as Markdown text with UTF-8 encoding, via the `long_description_content_type` keyword argument. If the README were instead written in reStructuredText (another markup language), I'd indicate that with the argument 'text/x-rst'. Otherwise, if this keyword argument is omitted, it defaults to 'text/plain'. If you view my project on PyPI (*https://pypi.org/project/Timecard-App/*), you'll see that the *README.md* is used as the body of the page.

I also include the license information. There are three ways to do that: explicitly via a string value on the `license` key, via a single file with `license_file`, or via multiple files with `license_files`. Since I only have one license for the whole project, and that is in a *LICENSE* file, I'll use the second option:

```
license_file = LICENSE
```

Listing 18-4: setup.cfg:4

Next, I'll include more information about the project authorship:

```
author = Jason C. McDonald
author_email = codemouse92@outlook.com
url = https://github.com/codemouse92/timecard
project_urls =
    Bug Reports = https://github.com/codemouse92/timecard/issues
    Funding = https://github.com/sponsors/CodeMouse92
    Source = https://github.com/codemouse92/timecard
```

Listing 18-5: setup.cfg:5

I indicate the author (myself) and the contact email for the author, author_email. In the case of this project, I'm also the project maintainer. If someone else were responsible for the packaging, their information would be included with the maintainer and maintainer_email keyword arguments.

I also include the url for more information about the project. Optionally, you can include any other links by passing a dictionary to the project_urls argument. The keys are all strings with the link names, as they will be displayed on the PyPI project page. The values are the actual URLs as strings.

To make finding my distribution package in PyPI easier, I include a space-delimited list of keywords:

```
keywords = time tracking office clock tool utility
```

Listing 18-6: setup.cfg:6

If you find yourself translating a *setup.py* file to a *setup.cfg*, be aware that *setup.py* uses a comma-separated list instead. Be sure to revise it when moving it to *setup.cfg*.

Classifiers

PyPI makes use of *classifiers*, standardized strings that facilitate organizing and searching for packages on the index. The complete list of classifiers can be found at *https://pypi.org/classifiers/*.

I include the relevant classifiers for Timecard in my *setup.cfg*, like this:

```
classifiers =
    Development Status :: 5 - Production/Stable
    Environment :: X11 Applications :: Qt
    Natural Language :: English
    Operating System :: OS Independent
    Intended Audience :: End Users/Desktop
    Topic :: Office/Business
    License :: OSI Approved :: BSD License
    Programming Language :: Python
    Programming Language :: Python :: 3
    Programming Language :: Python :: 3.6
    Programming Language :: Python :: 3.7
```

```
Programming Language :: Python :: 3.8
Programming Language :: Python :: 3 :: Only
Programming Language :: Python :: Implementation :: CPython
```

Listing 18-7: setup.cfg:7

I've included all of the relevant classifiers for my project above as a list of strings. Your project's classifier list will likely be different. Browse the complete classifier list from PyPI and find the ones relevant to your project. A good rule of thumb is to pick at least one for each of the categories—the part of each classifier before the first double colon—in the list above. (If this task feels overwhelming, you can skip this part until you're ready to distribute.)

Including Packages

Now I need to specify what files belong in my package. This is where the *src/* directory approach I used in structuring my repository really comes in handy. In a new section marked as [options], I include the following keys and values:

```
[options]
package_dir =
    = src
packages = ❶ find:
```

Listing 18-8: setup.cfg:8a

The package_dir key informs setuptools where to find all my packages. It accepts a *dict*, which in *setup.cfg* is denoted as an indented, comma-separated list of key-value pairs.

Because I'm using the *src/* directory approach, I only need to tell setuptools that all packages, denoted by the empty string as the key, are in the directory src. This is recursive, so any nested packages will also be found.

This key does not actually tell setuptools *what* packages it will find. For that part, I need the packages key. Instead of manually listing all my packages, I can tell setuptools to use its special find_packages() function by passing the value find: ❶ (note the trailing colon!). This technique is especially helpful when your project consists of multiple top-level packages.

The find: function can find all the packages in a given directory, but it has to know where to look first. I provide that information in a separate section:

```
[options.packages.find]
where = src
```

Listing 18-9: setup.cfg:9

On the key where, I provide the name of the directory to search for packages on, namely src.

Including Data

Not everything that ships in a package is code. I need to include some non-code files as well. Returning to my [options] section, I indicate that setuptools will be including some non-code files like this:

```
[options]
package_dir =
    = src
packages = find:
include_package_data = True
```

Listing 18-10: setup.cfg:8b

In *setup.cfg*, the values True and False are interpreted as boolean values, not as strings.

There are two ways to specify what non-code files to include. The approach I'm taking in this project is to use the *MANIFEST.in* file to list all non-code files I want included in the project. (I'll cover this file shortly.)

The second approach for including non-code files, which I'm not showing here, is to use the [options.package_data] section. This gives you finer-grained control over what is and isn't included, but it is likely overkill for your average project. The setuptools documentation has a good example with this approach: *https://setuptools.readthedocs.io/en/latest/userguide/declarative_config.html*.

Dependencies

Next, I'll define my project's dependencies in the [options] section:

```
[options]
package_dir =
    = src
packages = find:
include_package_data = True
python_requires = >=3.6, <4
```

Listing 18-11: setup.cfg:8c

I can specify the version of Python that the project requires, using python_requires in place of a package name. Notice the key and value are still separated by an equal sign, even though the value may also start with an equal, greater-than, or less-than sign. Something like python_requires = ==3.8 is completely valid, as the ==3.8 is a string.

I denote that Timecard requires Python 3.6 or later. I also assume it won't work with the theoretical Python 4, since major releases of Python aren't guaranteed to be backward compatible.

Next, I'll list the packages that my project depends on:

```
[options]
package_dir =
    = src
packages = find:
```

```
include_package_data = True
python_requires = >=3.6, <4
install_requires =
    PySide2>=5.15.0
    appdirs>=1.4.4
```

Listing 18-12: setup.cfg:8d

The install_requires key expects an indented list of values. Each value in the list specifies a Python package dependency. Timecard relies on the PySide2 library and uses features introduced in version 5.15.0 of that library. Technically, I could have omitted the version and merely listed PySide2, but that is often a bad idea. It's better to test the different versions and determine the oldest one your code will work with. You can always set this to the version you are currently using and change it later.

I could also require certain packages only for particular versions of Python. I don't need this behavior in this example, but here's what it might look like if I wanted to install PySide2 only for Python 3.7 and earlier:

```
install_requires =
    PySide2>=5.15.0; python_requires <= "3.7"
    appdirs>=1.4.4
```

After a semicolon at the end of the dependency I want to limit, I include python_requires, a comparison operator, and the version *in quotes.* The quotes are necessary, or you'll get a cryptic Expected stringEnd error.

In practice, it is seldom necessary to only install packages for certain versions of Python.

Optionally, I can use the [options.extras_require] section to specify additional packages used for certain optional features. For example, if I wanted to allow installing this distribution package with tests, I'd need the following:

```
[options.extras_require]
test =
    pytest
```

Listing 18-13: setup.cfg:10

When I install Timecard via pip install Timecard-App[test], it will install both the Timecard distribution package and everything I listed under test here. You can name the keys whatever you like, as long as you use alphanumeric characters and underscores. You can also include as many keys as you like.

Adding Entry Points

Lastly, I need to specify the *entry points,* the means by which a user starts the program. Instead of having to write custom executable Python scripts to serve as entry points, I can let setuptools do this for me. It will even create these scripts as *.exe* files on Windows.

Entry points are specified in the section [options.entry_points], like this:

```
[options.entry_points]
gui_scripts =
    Timecard-App = timecard.__main__:main
```

Listing 18-14: setup.cfg:11

There are two possible keys here: 'gui_scripts', for starting the program's GUI, and 'console_scripts', for starting the command-line version of the program. The value of each is a list of strings containing assignment statements, which assign a particular function to a name that will be the name of the executable file or script. In this case, Timecard needs a single GUI script named *Timecard-App*, which calls the main() function in the module *timecard/__main__.py*.

The setup.py File

Before *setup.cfg* became the convention, most projects used *setup.py* to store their project's metadata and build instructions. All the information now provided to *setup.cfg* was instead passed directly to the setuptools.setup() function as keyword arguments.

The *setup.py* file is a Python module like any other, so using it for packaging configuration is considered *imperative*—it focuses on how packaging takes place. This stands in contrast to the data-centric (and more error-proof) *declarative* approach with *setup.cfg*.

One difficulty with this approach was that folks tended to get clever about their setup configurations. All manner of unrelated functionality crept in: scraping versions from files, creating git tags, publishing to PyPI, and so on. This ran the risk of introducing confusing bugs into the packaging process, which is already particularly hard to debug and could utterly block someone else's packaging efforts. This has happened to me before!

Thankfully, in many modern projects, *setup.py* is no longer needed at all; *setup.cfg* can be used for all setuptools configurations instead.

However, if your project needs good backward compatibility, uses C-extensions, or requires tools that depend on *setup.py*, you will want to include the following minimal *setup.py* file:

```
from setuptools import setup
setup()
```

Listing 18-15: setup.py

That file merely imports the setup() function from the setuptools module and calls it. In the past, all the packaging data would have been passed to setup() as keyword arguments, but now, that all lives in *setup.cfg*.

No shebang line is necessary in this file; let the build tools find the interpreter they want to use.

The MANIFEST.in File

The *manifest template, MANIFEST.in,* provides a list of all the non-code files that should be included in the distribution package. These files can come from anywhere in your repository.

```
include LICENSE *.md
```

Listing 18-16: MANIFEST.in:1

Since my setup files are using the *README.md* and *LICENSE* files, I must include them here. I can list any number of files after an `include` directive, separating each with spaces. Manifest templates also support *glob patterns,* wherein I can use an asterisk (*) as a wildcard. For example, **.md* matches all Markdown files, so any markdown files in the root of my repository, including *README.md,* are automatically included.

I also want to include all the files in the directories *src/timecard/resources/* and *distribution_resources/*:

```
graft src/timecard/resources
graft distribution_resources
```

Listing 18-17: MANIFEST.in:2

The `graft` keyword includes all files that are in the specified directories and below. The *distribution_resources/* directory is where I keep OS-specific installation files for this particular project.

There are a few more important directives, which I'm not using for Timecard. Here's a more complex example with a different *MANIFEST.in* file (not belonging to my Timecard project):

```
recursive-include stuff *.ini
graft data
prune data/temp
recursive-exclude data/important *.scary
```

In this example, I add all files under the *stuff/* directory that have the *.ini* file extension. Next, I include the entire *data/* directory with the `graft` directive. The `prune` directive then goes back and excludes all files in the *data/temp/* subdirectory. I also exclude all files in *data/important/* that have the *.scary* file extension. None of the excluded files are deleted, but they are left out of the package.

The order of lines in the manifest template matters. Each subsequent directive adds to or removes from the list of files compiled by the prior lines. If you were to move the `prune` directive above the `graft` directive, the files in *data/temp/* would *not* be excluded!

Your manifest template will be used by setuptools to compile a *MANIFEST* file, which contains a complete list of all the non-code files being included in your distribution package. While you could theoretically write this *MANIFEST* file yourself, listing one file per line, this is strongly discouraged, as it's easier to mess up the *MANIFEST* file than the *MANIFEST.in* file. Trust setuptools to follow the directives you give it in the manifest template.

There are a few more directives and patterns that you can use in *MANIFEST.in*. Check out *https://packaging.python.org/guides/using-manifest-in/* for more information.

The requirements.txt File

You may remember this file from Chapter 2. The *requirements.txt* file contains a list of Python packages that your project depends on. This probably sounds like its duplicating install_requires from *setup.cfg*, but I usually recommend that you use both, for reasons I'll describe shortly.

Here's the *requirements.txt* for Timecard:

```
PySide2 >= 5.11.0
pytest
```

Listing 18-18: requirements.txt

You may wonder if there is a way to use the contents of *requirements.txt* in *setup.cfg*, but in fact, it's best if you keep the two separate. In practice, they serve slightly different purposes.

While the requirements listed in *setup.cfg* include everything you need to install your distribution package, the *requirements.txt* file is best thought of as a list of everything you need to re-create the complete development environment—all the optional packages and development tools needed to participate in developing your project, as opposed to merely using it.

Under some circumstances, you may omit *requirements.txt* if you list all your development dependencies as optional dependencies. The other benefit of using *requirements.txt*, however, is the ability to use a specific version of a library or tool—called *pinning*—for development, while enforcing looser version requirements for your users via *setup.cfg*. For example, your application might require click >= 7.0, but you're developing the new version to use click == 8.0.1 in particular. Pinning is mainly useful for application development. If you're developing a library, it's best to avoid pinning, since you can't really make good assumptions about the package versions that a user of your library will need.

Another major benefit of having a *requirements.txt* file is that, as mentioned in Chapter 2, you can quickly install everything needed for development in one step:

```
pip install -r requirements.txt
```

I still recommend you keep *requirements.txt* to the things that your project truly needs, especially when versions matter. You generally wouldn't include tools like black or flake8, which can be swapped out for other tools without breaking anything. Sometimes, I'll create a separate *dev-requirements.txt* file (or *requirements.dev.txt*, if you prefer) with all of my optional development tools. Then, to set up my complete environment in a virtual environment, I'll only need to run the following:

```
pip install -r requirements.txt -r dev-requirements.txt
```

If you have quite a number of packages installed in your working virtual environment, it can be a pain to try to turn this into a *requirements.txt* file. To aid you in this, you can use the command pip freeze to generate a complete list, with versions, of all packages installed in the environment. Then, you can redirect the contents into a file:

```
venv/bin/pip freeze > requirements.txt
```

That command works the same on Windows, macOS, and Linux, exporting the complete list of packages installed within *venv/*, dependencies and all, to the file *requirements.txt*. Be sure to inspect that file for errors and *remove your own package from it*—it wouldn't make sense for your package to rely on itself.

If you want both *requirements.txt* and *dev-requirements.txt*, you'll want to pip freeze on two separate virtual environments: one that runs your package, and the other that contains your complete development environment. In both cases, inspect the output file and remove your own package from it!

The pyproject.toml File

The *pyproject.toml* file serves a few purposes, but the most important is to specify the *build system* used to package your project, a standard introduced in PEP 517 and PEP 518.

```
[build-system]
requires = ["setuptools>=40.8.0", "wheel"]
build-backend = "setuptools.build_meta"
```

Listing 18-19: pyproject.toml

The [build-system] section contains information about what packages are needed for building the distribution package: in this case, setuptools and wheel. These requirements are specified by assigning a list of strings to requires, with each string following the same convention as install_requires in *setup.py*. You'll notice here that I can use any version of wheel, but I must use version 40.8.0 or later of setuptools. The latter is necessary since it is the first version of setuptools that supports PEP 517 and PEP 518.

The build-backend property specifies the scheme used for building the project, in this case, setuptools.build_meta. If you were using a different build tool, such as Poetry or Flit, you'd specify that here, according to the tool's documentation.

The *pyproject.toml* file is also one of the common files for storing Python tool configurations. Many of the major linters, autoformatters, and testing tools (albeit not all of them) support their configurations being stored in this file.

PEP 518 introduced the *pyproject.toml* file for project configuration, but it can increasingly be used to store tool configuration as well, thereby cutting down on the number of files in a project. There is heated debate about adding support for *pyproject.toml* to some prominent tools like Flake8. It's not as straightforward as it looks. If you really want Flake8 and *pyproject.toml* to play well together, check out *Flake9*, a fork of Flake8 that accomplishes just that.

Testing the Setup Configuration

If everything has been configured correctly, you'll be able to install your project in a virtual environment. I'll do that now, using the following command (assuming I have a fresh virtual environment called venv):

```
venv/bin/pip install .
```

I particularly recommend testing this out in a fresh virtual environment the first time. The trailing dot installs whatever package is detailed by the *setup.cfg* file in the current directory.

Watch the output when you install and correct any warnings or errors. Once your package is installed successfully, try to run your project using the entry point(s) you specified in the *setup.cfg*, which should be installed as executables in the *bin/* directory of the virtual environment. I'd run the following:

```
venv/bin/Timecard-App
```

If your project is a library, rather than an application, open the Python shell within the virtual environment (venv/bin/python) and import the library.

Troubleshooting

Take the time to test out your project now. Does everything work as expected? Most packaging and distribution tools depend on this instance working correctly! If you encounter any new bugs or errors, go back and fix them. A few common causes of problems appearing only in a virtual-environment installation of your project include the following:

- Missing dependencies that need to be added to *setup.cfg*
- Data files not being included correctly via the *MANIFEST.in* or *setup.cfg* files
- False assumptions in your code about the current working directory

Once you have your distribution package installed and working in a virtual environment, you're ready to move on to the next step!

Installing as Editable

In some circumstances, it can be useful to install your project in editable mode, so the virtual environment will directly use the source code files in *src/*. Any changes made to the code will immediately be reflected in the test installation.

To install in editable mode, supply the -e flag to pip, like this:

```
venv/bin/pip install -e .
```

Installing your package in editable mode makes testing and development a lot easier, as you don't have to reinstall the package each time. However, it's not without its drawbacks. Installing in editable mode can make it possible for the virtual environment to find external packages and modules that were not explicitly required in *setup.cfg*, thereby covering up packaging problems. Only use -e for testing your code, not your packaging.

Building Your Package

Once you've ensured that your *setup.cfg* and related files are configured correctly, it's time to build your source distribution and wheel artifacts. Run the following commands in your terminal, from the root of your project's repository.

```
python3 -m pip install --upgrade setuptools wheel build
python3 -m build
```

The installation command ensures that setuptools, wheel, and build are installed and up-to-date in the current environment.

The next command builds according to whatever build-backend is specified in *pyproject.toml*. In this case, the project will be built with setuptools, applying the configuration in the *setup.cfg* file in the current directory. This command builds a source distribution, or sdist, and a built distribution or wheel.

PEDANTIC NOTE   If you need to build your project for Python 2 or a very old Python 3—such that you're using either an old version of setuptools that doesn't support PEP 517 and PEP 518 or the deprecated distutils—you'll need to use the old-style *setup.py* and invoke that directly with python -m *setup.py* sdist bdist_wheel.

The two artifacts are saved in the newly created *dist/* directory: the *.tar.gz* is your source distribution, and the *.whl* is the build distribution wheel.

There are a few other commands available for build, which you will find in the documentation: *https://pypa-build.readthedocs.io/en/latest/*.

Alternatively, if you're only using the default invocation of build, you can just run pyproject-build.

Publishing on pip (Twine)

From here, you're ready to publish your distribution package! In this section, I'll do exactly that with Timecard.

Uploading to Test PyPI

Before you upload your project to the official PyPI index, test everything out one more time via Test PyPI, which is an altogether separate index specifically for testing out the tools. If you're experimenting, you're welcome to use Test PyPI. Packages and user accounts are periodically pruned, so don't worry if you leave a bit of a mess.

To upload to the index, you must first create an account at *https://test.pypi .org/account/register/*. If you had one a while back but it's not working now, don't worry; as part of the regular pruning, old accounts are deleted. You can safely make a new one.

Once you're logged in, go to **Account settings** and scroll down to **API tokens**. Select **Add API Token**. You can name this token whatever you like, but be certain you set Scope to **Entire account** if you're uploading a new project.

After creating the API token, you must save the entire token (including the leading `pypi-`) before leaving the page, as it will never be shown again. You'll need this token in the next step.

By the way, you can always delete tokens from the Account settings page. Do this any time you no longer remember the token or have no need of it anymore.

I'll upload my Timecard-App distribution package to Test PyPI. (You'll need to try uploading a package with a different name; Timecard-App will be taken by the time you read this.) For this step, I use a package called *twine*, which I install to my user environment:

```
python3 -m pip install --upgrade twine
```

I use twine to upload the artifacts from my project's *dist/* directory:

```
twine upload --repository testpypi dist/*
```

Notice I've explicitly specified that I'm uploading to the *testpypi* repository, which twine knows about by default.

When prompted, enter the username *__token__* and use your API key from earlier as the password:

```
Enter your username: __token__
Enter your password: (your API token here)
```

Watch the terminal output carefully for any errors or warnings. If you need to make any corrections to your project or its packaging files, be certain to delete the *dist/* directory and cleanly rebuild the *sdist* and *bdist_wheel* artifacts before trying to upload again.

If all goes well, you will be given a URL where you can see your distribution package on Test PyPI. Make sure everything on that page looks correct.

PEDANTIC NOTE   As you may have noticed, pip works with more than just the default PyPI. If you need to, you can run your *own* Python package repository using devpi (*https:// devpi.net/*) or your own PyPI mirror with Bandersnatch (*https://bandersnatch .readthedocs.io/*).

Installing Your Uploaded Package

Next, make sure you can install your distribution package from Test PyPI in a *fresh* virtual environment. I'll do that now with my Timecard-App distribution package.

For the next step to work, I'll need to manually install the dependencies for my package. This is one of the reasons I have a separate *requirements.txt* file:

```
venv/bin/pip install -r requirements.txt
```

Now, I can install the package itself. Because this is a particularly long command, I'm splitting it up UNIX-style, with the backslash character (\):

```
venv/bin/pip install \
    --index-url https://test.pypi.org/simple/ \
    --no-deps/ \
    Timecard-App
```

Because I'm testing the distribution package I uploaded to Test PyPI, rather than the regular PyPI, I have to explicitly tell pip to use that as the source repository, which I do with the `--index-url` argument. However, I don't want to install any of the package dependencies from *test.pypi.org*—they might be missing, broken, malicious copycats, or otherwise wrong—so I pass the `--no-deps` flag. Finally, I specify that I'm installing the distribution package `Timecard-App`.

GOTCHA ALERT   Don't get the idea that you can somehow get the dependency packages from the normal PyPI using the `--extra-index-url` argument you may have read about somewhere. If a package appears in both the main index and the extra index or indices you specify, Python isn't always predictable about which one it picks.

If all went well, I should be able to invoke Timecard-App within that virtual environment:

```
venv/bin/Timecard-App
```

I try it out as before, to make sure everything works as expected, and it does! At this point, I'd want to try it out on other machines to ensure it functions as expected. I can use the `pip install` command from a moment ago to install this distribution package on any machine that's connected to the internet.

Uploading to PyPI

Once I'm certain that Timecard-App is ready for prime time, I can repeat the entire upload process with PyPI at *https://pypi.org/*: create a user account (if necessary), log in, create an API key, and finally upload with this:

```
twine upload dist/*
```

The official PyPI is the default target, so once that upload completes, you'll be given a new URL: the one for your project on the PyPI. Congratulations! You can now share this link exuberantly. You've shipped software!

Alternative Packaging Tools

As you can see, pip, setuptools, wheel, and twine do a pretty good job these days, but there are a lot of steps and details to using them. There are a couple of alternative tools you may benefit from learning on your own.

Poetry

If you only learn one of these alternative tools, make it this one!

Instead of using four different tools, some Python developers prefer *Poetry*, which handles everything from dependency management to building and publishing your distribution package. Absolutely all of the packaging configuration, from dependencies to metadata, goes into *pyproject.toml*.

Learning how to use Poetry is easy because it has excellent, succinct documentation, which is especially clear if you're already somewhat familiar with setuptools. Information, installation instructions, and documentation can all be found at *https://python-poetry.org/*.

Flit

Flit is a tool that focuses on making the easy packaging scenarios easier—namely, by building and publishing pure Python distribution packages—and leaving the hard stuff for other, more complex tools to handle. It uses a few simple commands to handle building and publishing your distribution package. Many of the ideas from Flit have trickled into other tools and workflows.

The official documentation is the best place to find more information about Flit: *https://flit.readthedocs.io/en/latest/index.html*.

Distributing to End Users

There is still one leg of the journey to go before you reach your goal of being able to distribute software to end users. Installing via pip is not a good means of distributing your software to end users, for two reasons. First, most users don't know anything about pip. Second, pip was never intended to deploy software in that manner. There are too many things that could go wrong when installing from PyPI, all of which would require the intervention of a Python developer well-versed in the ways of pip. To ship software to non-developers, you need a more robust, user-oriented solution.

Mahmoud Hashemi describes layers of the packaging gradient for shipping to an end user. I've adapted them here:

1. **PEX:** Uses system-wide Python.
2. **Freezers:** Includes Python.
3. **Images and containers:** Includes most or all system dependencies.
4. **Virtual machines:** Includes *kernel*, the "heart" of the operating system.
5. **Hardware:** Includes . . . well, everything!

Let's look at each of these options in a little more depth and consider which would be appropriate for Timecard.

PEX

The lowest-level option for distributing a stand-alone artifact—one that doesn't need to be installed from pip—is a format called PEX (short for Python Executable). It allows you to package an entire virtual environment as a stand-alone file, which is essentially a neatly structured *.zip* file. This PEX file then relies on the Python interpreter provided by whatever system it's being run on. Once you have a PEX, you can distribute it to anyone on Mac or Linux who has Python installed.

PEX is far from intuitive, in terms of usage. It's easy enough to turn a virtual environment into a PEX, but actually specifying a script to run on execution takes a bit more work. What's more, PEX only works on Mac or Linux, so it's not a viable option if you need to distribute on Windows.

Since PEX is oriented toward developers, it's definitely not a good fit for distributing Timecard. If you want to learn more about PEX, read their documentation at *https://pex.readthedocs.io/*. Alex Leonhardt also has an excellent article about PEX (*https://medium.com/ovni/pex-python-executables-c0ea39cee7f1*) that is considerably easier to digest than the documentation.

Freezers

The most portable means by far of packaging and distributing a Python application is with a *freezer*, which bundles the compiled Python code, the Python interpreter, and all the package dependencies into a single artifact. With some freezers, system dependencies are included as well. The benefit of all this is that you wind up with a single executable file in the target system's preferred format, at the cost of an increased artifact size (usually by about 2–12 MB).

Far and away, this is one of the most common ways of distributing Python applications. It's used by such programs as Dropbox and Eve Online.

There are a number of freezers in existence, but the three most common at present are *PyInstaller, cx_Freeze,* and *py2app*. If you're building

GUI-based applications with the Qt 5 toolkit, *fman Build System* is another great option. Yet another option is *py2exe*, although it is presently unmaintained.

PyInstaller

My personal favorite freezer is PyInstaller. It has the particular advantage of working on all major operating systems. Although you will need to run PyInstaller separately on each of the targeted environments, you will seldom need to configure it more than once.

There is quite a bit to learn about PyInstaller. You'll find extensive guidance for its use, as well as how to handle various errors and tricky situations, in the official documentation: *https://pyinstaller.readthedocs.io/*.

PyOxidizer

One of the newer kids on the block is PyOxidizer. It's a promising-looking cross-platform tool for converting your project into a single executable file, bundled with the Python interpreter. The focus is on ensuring it remains easy to package, distribute, and install the end product.

Complete documentation, as well as a breakdown of what gives PyOxidizer an advantage over other tools, can be found at *https://pyoxidizer .readthedocs.io/en/stable/index.html*.

py2app

If you only want to package your project for macOS, *py2app* is a great option. It works off your project's *setup.py* file and freezes down into a single *.app* file.

To learn more about py2app, see the official documentation at *https:// py2app.readthedocs.io/en/latest/tutorial.html*.

cx_Freeze

Another option for freezing your project is *cx_Freeze*, a cross-platform tool for building on Windows, Mac, and Linux. It's quite a bit older than PyInstaller, but it still works well. If you're having trouble with PyInstaller or py2app, try this one.

Information and documentation can be found at *https://cx_freeze .readthedocs.org/*.

fman Build System

If you're building a GUI-based application using the Qt 5 library—Timecard is one such application—you can build and package your project once for all operating systems with *fman Build System*. Unlike other tools, it even creates an executable installer on Windows, a *.dmg* on macOS, a *.deb* package on Debian-based Linux, an *.rpm* on Fedora-based Linux, and a *.tar.xz* for everyone else.

The fman freezer requires you to set up your project in a particular manner, so if you want to use it, you'll have the best results if you use it from the start of your project. Otherwise, you'll need to restructure it according to what fman Build System needs (which is why Timecard doesn't use it).

You can find more information, a great tutorial, and the complete documentation at *https://build-system.fman.io/*.

Nuitka

I mentioned back in Chapter 1 that the *Nuitka* compiler allows you to transpile Python code to C and C++ and then assemble that down to machine code. Nuitka is practically a separate implementation, and the end-result executable is about two times faster than CPython.

As of the date of this writing, Nuitka has reached feature parity with Python 3.8. They're working on adding 3.9+ features and further optimization. In any case, this is an exciting project to watch.

If you want truly "compiled" Python code, this is the tool you're looking for. More information and documentation are available at *https://nuitka.net/pages/overview.html*.

Images and Containers

All the packaging options I've covered up to this point are limited by a common factor: what system libraries are installed on the user's machine. It's possible to bundle some of these libraries, such as is seen with PyInstaller, but those are still subject to their *own* dependencies, some of which cannot be bundled. When you start getting into more complex applications, this can become a tricky problem to solve.

This becomes particularly difficult when distributing on Linux. With so many Linux-based operating systems (each with multiple versions) and countless combinations of packages, building once for all can be a royal pain. The solution is found in *containers*, which are self-contained environments that bring all their own dependencies. Multiple applications can be installed on the system, each in its own container, and it won't matter if they have different or even conflicting dependencies.

Another advantage of using containers is *sandboxing*, which limits the containerized application's access to the system. This provides transparency and control to users: they know what privileges any given container has, and in many cases, they can control those privileges.

At present, there are four major containers: *Flatpak, Snapcraft, Appimage,* and *Docker*. Each one has unique advantages.

Flatpak

Flatpak allows you to package an application as a standalone unit that can be installed on virtually any Linux environment, as well as Chrome OS. It is highly forward compatible, meaning your package will continue to work even on as-yet unreleased versions of operating systems that support

Flatpak. It is not a container in the strictest sense, but it functions similarly. Even so, installed Flatpaks can share some dependencies they might have in common.

One of the reasons I particularly like Flatpak is that you can select or build each of the dependencies or components you need. I can know that if my Flatpak works on my machine, it will work on others. The extra degree of control and predictability it provides makes it easier to work with snarly packaging scenarios in Python.

Flatpak also has its own app store, *Flathub*, which makes it easy for end users to browse and install applications on their Linux machines. For more information about and complete documentation on Flatpak, see their official website: *https://flatpak.org/*.

You can see how I packaged Timecard with Flatpak here: *https://github .com/flathub/com.codemouse92.timecard*.

Snapcraft

The *Snapcraft* format, maintained by Canonical (the company behind the Ubuntu operating system), packages your application into a dedicated container with its own filesystem. It is sandboxed from the rest of the system, accessing and sharing as little as possible. Because of its structure, you can build snaps from any development environment, including Windows and macOS, although you cannot install snaps in those environments. Snapcraft also has its own associated app store, the *Snap Store.*

Unfortunately, the footprint of an installed snap can be quite large, as it brings everything *for each container*, excepting the kernel and a handful of core dependencies; it does not share dependencies between snaps. It also can be difficult to give a snap the correct permissions for many user applications to function. Due to these and other criticisms, some Linux environments have dropped their official support for Snapcraft.

Despite all this, Snapcraft is still a viable container format with a fairly loyal following. You can learn more about the format and find complete documentation at *https://snapcraft.io/*.

AppImage

The *AppImage* format provides self-contained executables that don't require anything, including themselves, to be installed. In many ways, an AppImage behaves like a macOS application. Unlike Flatpak and Snapcraft, AppImage requires no infrastructure on the target system, although the user may choose to use *appimaged* to automate registering AppImages with the system.

AppImage is intended to be decentralized, allowing you to provide your own download to the end user. You can even issue updates to your package by integrating *AppImageUpdate*. Technically, AppImage does have an app store of sorts, *AppImageHub*, where you can browse through many of the apps that are packaged in the format. New apps are added via a pull request against the store on GitHub.

The sole disadvantage of AppImage is that you need to test your package against every Linux distribution you plan to support. Your package *can* rely on existing system libraries, and in fact, it must do so for a few essentials like *libc* (the C language standard library, which is used by nearly everything). As a result, this can create a "works on my machine" scenario, where the AppImage may be implicitly relying on a system library and then may fail when run on another Linux system that lacks that library.

To achieve that same aim, it is recommended you build your AppImage on the oldest environment you want to support, as it collects and bundles libraries from the current environment itself. AppImages are pretty decently forward compatible, but they're not intended to be backward compatible.

Still, if you don't mind working with some extra environments, AppImage can be a fantastic way to distribute your software to any Linux machine, without any other infrastructure being required. More information about the format and complete documentation can be found at *https://appimage.org/*.

Docker

In modern software development parlance, *Docker* is usually the first thing that people think of when they hear "container." It allows you to define a custom environment, bringing everything except the kernel. This is the one format out of the four I'm covering that will work on Windows and macOS, in addition to Linux.

Docker is primarily geared toward deploying on servers, rather than for user applications, as it requires quite a bit of setup on the target machine. Once Docker is configured, it's relatively trivial to launch an image. This makes it ideal for distributing server applications.

Because a Docker image is a fully self-contained environment, it's easy to create one for your project. You start by defining a *Dockerfile*, which outlines the steps for building the image. You start with a base image, such as one for a particular operating system, and you install all the packages and dependencies you need. You can even install via pip in the context of the Dockerfile. Docker converts the Dockerfile into an image, which can be uploaded to a registry like *Docker Hub* and then downloaded onto the client machine.

Complete information and exhaustive documentation can be found at *https://www.docker.com/*.

A Note on Native Linux Packaging

Linux users will notice that I haven't touched native Debian or Fedora packaging at all. These packaging formats are still relevant, but decreasingly so as more portable formats like the preceding gain in adoption. Both Debian and Fedora packaging can be particularly difficult, while offering few, if any, advantages over portable formats.

In case this sounds faddish, I assure you that I have been among the slowest to consider Flatpak, Snapcraft, and Appimage as viable alternatives to my beloved Debian packages. The difference in end user experience is slightly improved in these newer portable formats, but more importantly, the *developer* experience is significantly better. All three leverage varying degrees of sandboxing, in a manner similar to virtual environments and in stark contrast to native packaging formats, where one must be concerned with the exact versions of dependencies on each end user machine. What's more, while portable packaging formats generally play well with virtual environments and PyPI, native packaging formats seldom do, especially when used in full compliance with the standards and policies of the distribution's package repositories.

If you want to package your Python project using Debian or Fedora packaging, you can certainly do so. Tools like *dh-virtualenv* can help! Still, be prepared for a battle if your project has any significant dependencies. Before you try to distribute your project in any native packaging format, be absolutely certain that portable packaging formats will not suffice. This is a decision only you can make.

Documentation

Every project needs documentation, and yes, that includes yours. The best code in the world means nothing if the end user doesn't know how to install and use it!

In the case of particularly small projects, a single *README.md* may be sufficient, so long as it is easily discoverable by users. For anything more robust, you need a better solution.

The historic answer to documentation in Python was the built-in module *pydoc*, but over the past several years, this has been utterly eclipsed by *Sphinx*. Nearly all documentation in the Python world, including the official documentation for Python itself, is built with Sphinx. In fact, while Sphinx was originally built for Python projects, its robust feature set and ease of use has led to its wide adoption across the entire programming industry.

Sphinx builds the documentation using a markup language called *reStructuredText*, abbreviated as *reST*. While a bit more complex and exacting than Markdown, reST is packed full of powerful features for even the most complicated technical writing. The end result can be exported to HTML, PDF, ePUB, Linux man pages, and many other formats.

Your project's documentation belongs in a separate directory, conventionally named *docs/*, in the project repository. If you have the sphinx package installed in your environment—usually, your development virtual environment—you can build the basic file structure and configuration by running the following command:

```
venv/bin/sphinx-quickstart
```

You will be guided through several questions. For most things, I recommend using the defaults, displayed in square brackets ([ ]) at each prompt, until you know better.

For most of your documentation, you will write your own reStructuredText (*.rst*) files by hand, saving them in this *docs/* directory. There is no replacement for handwritten documentation! Expecting a user to learn your software purely from API documentation is like teaching someone to use a toaster by explaining the electrical specifications of the heating element.

At the same time, in some projects, especially libraries, it is useful to pull in the docstrings from your code. This is possible with Sphinx as well, using its *autodoc* feature.

The best way to get started with Sphinx and reStructuredText, including the autodoc feature, is to read the official Quick Start Guide at *https://www.sphinx-doc.org/en/master/usage/quickstart.html*. That website also provides the rest of the Sphinx documentation.

When you're getting ready to release your project, you will almost certainly want to publish your documentation online. For open source projects, one of the easiest ways to do this is to sign up for a free account on Read the Docs. That service specifically works with Sphinx and reStructuredText, and it can automatically update your documentation from your repository. For more information and to sign up, visit *https://readthedocs.org/*.

Wrapping Up

When you're getting ready to start a project, consider how you want to handle packaging. There are a lot of options for packaging and distributing Python applications, so that leaves the question of which tools to use. As the developer of your own project, you're the only person who can ultimately determine the best packaging scheme for your situation. If you're completely lost, here's my own opinion.

First, I strongly recommend using a *src/* directory for your code. It makes everything else easier. Then, get your project set up so you can install it in a virtual environment with pip. Personally, I use setuptools, although both Poetry and Flit are excellent options; use whichever you like more.

If you're developing a library or command-line tool for other Python developers to use, plan to publish it to the PyPI. If your project is an end user application or command-line program, I recommend packaging it into a stand-alone artifact using a tool like PyInstaller. For Linux distribution, I also strongly recommend creating a Flatpak. If you're building a server application, on the other hand, I recommend packaging it into a Docker image.

The last level of the packaging gradient is to deploy your project embedded on hardware. There are countless ways to do this, but some of the more popular options include single-board computers like *Arduino* and *Raspberry Pi*. This is a deep enough topic that entire books are dedicated to it. In Chapter 21, I'll refer you to some resources for further study in this arena.

Once again, these are my opinions, based on my own adventures in Python packaging. Regardless, remember that all these tools exist for a reason, and something that works well for my projects may not be suitable for yours. As I said at the start of this chapter, whatever packaging techniques you ultimately use, they should produce a reasonably portable, stable, "just works" package.

19

DEBUGGING AND LOGGING

Mistakes in code are inevitable. The bugs you'll encounter can range from simple typos to malformed logic, from misunderstood usage to those strange errors that originate from deeper in the tech stack. As Lubarsky's Law of Cybernetic Entomology observes, "There is always one more bug." When things go horribly wrong in your code, you're going to need the tools to find and fix the problem. In this chapter, you'll learn all about those tools.

I'll begin by covering three features of the Python language that you can add to your code to help you debug it later: warnings, logging, and assertions. These are improvements over using print statements for debugging purposes, as you are likely to forget where your "debugging" print statements are or may be tempted to leave them in place in production.

Then, I'll guide you through the use of the Python debugger (pdb), which helps you step through the logic in your Python program, and faulthandler, which enables you to investigate undefined behavior in the C code behind Python. Finally, I'll discuss using Bandit to check for security problems in your code.

Warnings

You can use a *warning* to notify the user of a problem that the program worked around or alert a developer to an upcoming breaking change in a later version of your library. Unlike an exception, which we discussed in Chapter 8, a warning won't crash the program. This is preferable for problems that don't interfere with the program's normal function.

In addition, warnings are more convenient than print statements because they're output to the standard error stream by default. In a print statement like print("My warning message", file=sys.stderr), I must explicitly output to the standard error stream.

Python offers a warning module with a bevy of additional features and behaviors. To issue warnings, use the warnings.warn() function. For example, this rather theatrical (if silly) program aims to write some text to a file. If the value of thumbs is "pricking", I issue a warning that something evil is coming. After the warning, I open a file, *locks.txt*, and write some text to it:

```
import warnings

thumbs = "pricking"

if thumbs == "pricking":
    warnings.warn("Something wicked this way comes.")

with open('locks.txt', 'w') as file:
    file.write("Whoever knocks")
```

Listing 19-1: basic_warning.py:1a

Running that module outputs the following:

```
basic_warning.py:6: UserWarning: Something wicked this way comes.
  warnings.warn("Something wicked this way comes.")
```

The warning appears on the terminal via the standard error stream, but importantly, it does not crash the program. The file *locks.txt* is still created with the desired text:

```
Whoever knocks
```

Listing 19-2: locks.txt

Types of Warnings

Warnings come in different types, each of which can be treated differently, as you see fit. For example, you should probably let your user know if the program had to work around a missing file on their system, but you may not want to bother them with warnings about weird syntax in the code; such warnings are things only a developer would need to know. Warning categories allow you to handle these different situations in a manner appropriate to your project.

Table 19-1 lists the various types of warnings, all of which inherit from the `Warning` base class. Just as you can create a custom `Exception`, you can create your own types of warnings by inheriting from the `Warning` class of any of its subclasses in Table 19-1.

Table 19-1: Warning Categories

Class	Usage	Ignored by default
UserWarning	The default if no category is specified in warn()	
DeprecationWarning	Warnings about deprecated features, intended for developers	✓
PendingDeprecationWarning	Warnings about features that will be deprecated in the future	✓
FutureWarning	Warnings about deprecated features, intended for users (Prior to 3.7, this instead referred to a feature's behavior being changed.)	
SyntaxWarning	Warnings about potentially problematic syntax	
RuntimeWarning	Warnings about questionable runtime behavior	
ImportWarning	Warnings related to importing modules	✓
UnicodeWarning	Warnings related to Unicode	
BytesWarning	Warnings related to bytes-like objects	
ResourceWarning	Warnings related to hardware resource usage	✓

This table is up-to-date for Python 3.7 through at least Python 3.10. Earlier versions of Python ignore different warnings by default, meaning you'll have to explicitly enable those warnings to see them while running the program.

To issue a particular type of warning, pass the desired `Warning` class as the second argument of `warn()`. For irony's sake, I'll revise my earlier example to issue a `FutureWarning`:

```
import warnings

thumbs = "pricking"

if thumbs == "pricking":
    warnings.warn("Something wicked this way comes.", FutureWarning)

with open('locks.txt', 'w') as file:
    file.write("Whoever knocks")
```

Listing 19-3: basic_warning.py:1b

Running that code produces the following output on the terminal, in addition to creating the same *locks.txt* file as before:

```
basic_warning.py:6: FutureWarning: Something wicked this way comes.
  warnings.warn("Something wicked this way comes.", FutureWarning)
```

Filtering Warnings

The *warnings filter* controls how warnings are displayed, and it can be passed as an argument to the Python interpreter when you run a module or package. For example, you can display a warning once or multiple times, hide it altogether, or even cause it to crash a program. (I'll explain why you'd want to in the Converting Warnings to Exceptions section below.)

Warning filters are composed of five optional fields, separated by colons:

```
action:message:category:module:lineno
```

Table 19-2 explains what each of those fields does.

Table 19-2: Warning Filter Field

action	How the warning should be displayed. There are six options for this field: default, error, always, module, once, and ignore. (See Table 19-3.)
message	A regular expression that the warning message must match to be filtered.
category	The warning category to be filtered.
module	The module the warning must occur in to be filtered. (Not to be confused with the module option for the *action* field.)
lineno	The line number where the warning must occur to be filtered.

You can omit any field, but you'd still need to include the appropriate number of delimiting colons between fields. If you were to specify *action* and *category* but omit *message*, you'd still need the separating colons between them:

```
action::category
```

Notice, however, that I did not need any trailing colons for the omitted *module* and `lineno` fields, as those came after the last field I specified: *category*.

Using the *message* field, you can filter warnings that have a particular message. The *module* field can be used to filter warnings only in a particular module.

Hiding Duplicate Warnings

It isn't uncommon for a warning to be raised multiple times, such as if it appears in a function that is called more than once. The *action* field controls this. Table 19-3 shows the possible options you could pass to *action*.

Table 19-3: Warning Filter Action Options

`ignore`	Never show the warning.
`once`	Only show the warning once, for the whole program.
`module`	Only show the warning once per module.
`default`	Show the warning once per module and line number.
`always`	Always show the warning, no matter how often it occurs.
`error`	Convert the warning to an exception.

For example, if I only wanted to see the first instance of any particular warning in a module, I'd pass the string `module` to the *action* field, like this:

```
python3 -Wmodule basic_warning.py
```

I pass the warnings filter to the warning filter flag, -W, followed by the warning filter itself (with no space in between the flag and the filter.) This flag must come *before* the module to run, as it's an argument for Python itself. If it came at the end, it would be erroneously passed as an argument to the *basic_warning.py* module itself.

Likewise, you can alternatively print only the first occurrence of each warning in the entire program's run with -Wonce.

Ignoring Warnings

You can also use warning filters to hide an entire category of warnings from an end user by using the *ignore* action. Let's say you don't want the user to see all the deprecation warnings you plan to address in the next version of your program:

```
python3 -Wignore::DeprecationWarning basic_warning.py
```

The `ignore` action hides warnings, and `DeprecationWarning` in the *category* field causes only deprecation warnings to be hidden while the Python module is running.

Converting Warnings into Exceptions

Using the error action, you can convert warnings into fatal exceptions to crash the program. This is possible because the base class `Warning` inherits from the `Exception` class. The following example turns all warnings into errors when running a particular module:

```
python3 -Werror basic_warning.py
```

Since no other fields are provided in the filter, this error action will affect all warnings. This might be helpful in continuous integration systems where a pull request should automatically be rejected if there are warnings.

Another reason why you might raise warnings as exceptions is to ensure your program isn't using any deprecated code. You can turn all `DeprecationWarning` warnings into errors with `-Werror::DeprecationWarning` and then resolve them one by one, until your program runs.

However, turning errors into exceptions can have negative consequences because it also turns any warnings from within dependencies or the standard library into errors. To get around this, I need to limit the warning filter, like this:

```
python3 -Werror:::__main__ basic_warning.py
```

This warning filter will only convert warnings to errors in the module I'm directly executing, and it will handle any warnings from elsewhere according to the default rules.

To convert warnings to errors across an entire package, such as my `timecard` package, without getting warnings from dependencies and the standard library, I'd use the following filter:

```
python3 -Werror:::timecard[.*] basic_warning.py
```

The regular expression `timecard[.*]` matches any module contained in the `timecard` package or any subpackage thereof.

There is quite a bit more to warning filters that's outside the scope of this chapter. I recommend reading further at *https://docs.python.org/3/library/warnings.html*.

Logging

In Chapter 8, you learned how to log exceptions, rather than merely passing them to `print()`. This technique has a few advantages. It grants you control over whether messages are sent to the standard output or to a file, and it gives you the ability to filter messages based on their severity. The severity levels, in increasing order of severity, are as follows: DEBUG, INFO, WARNING, ERROR, and CRITICAL.

The patterns I used in Chapter 9 were sufficient to get you this far, but logging in a production-grade project requires a bit more thought. You must consider which messages should be visible under which circumstances and how different types of messages should be logged. A critical warning might need to be displayed on the terminal and stored in a file, while an informative message about a normal operation may be hidden, except when the user runs the program in a provided "verbose" mode.

To handle all things logging, Python provides the logging module, which defines four components: Logger, Handler, Filter, and Formatter. I'll break down each of these in turn.

Logger Objects

A Logger object handles your logging messages. It accepts messages to be logged as LogRecord objects and passes them on to one or more Handler objects, based on the reported severity. I'll come back to severity and Handler shortly.

A typical project has one Logger per module. Never instantiate these Logger objects yourself. Instead, you must acquire Logger objects with logger .getLogger(), instead of instantiating them. This ensures that more than one logger with the same name is never created:

```
import logging
logger = logging.getLogger(__name__)
```

The __name__ attribute is the name of the current module, as well as its parent packages (if any). If no Logger object yet exists by that name, it is created behind the scenes. In either case, the Logger object is bound to logger and becomes ready for use.

This pattern works in most situations. In the entry module for a package, however, you must explicitly declare the name of the logger, using the name of the package. Using the __name__ attribute here would be impractical, since it will always report the name of the entry module as __main__. This logger should have the package name, so it can serve as the primary logger for all the modules belonging to the package. All the other loggers will pass their messages up to this one.

To illustrate the use of Logger, I'll create a letter_counter package for determining the most commonly occurring letters in a given passage of text. The package will use logging to handle warnings and informative messages. Here is the beginning of my __main__.py module:

```
import pathlib
import argparse
import logging
```

```
from letter_counter.common import scrub_string
from letter_counter.letters import most_common_consonant, most_common_vowel

logger = ❶ logging.getLogger('letter_counter')
```

Listing 19-4: letter_counter/__main__.py:1

I acquire the `Logger` object by passing the name of the package explicitly
to the `logging.getLogger()` function ❶ and then binding that object to `logger`.

It's important that the name of this logger should match the package
name, so it can serve as the primary logger for the `letter_counter` package.

I must also acquire a `Logger` object for each module and subpackage
in this package that needs to perform logging. Here, the *letter.py* module
acquires a logger:

```
import logging
from collections import defaultdict

logger = logging.getLogger(__name__)
```

Listing 19-5: letter_counter/letters.py:1

Because this `__name__` expression resolves to `letter_counter.letters`, the
`letter_counter` logger created in Listing 19-4 automatically becomes the parent of this logger. As a result, all messages passed to the logger in *letters.py*
will be passed in turn to the `letter_counter` logger.

In the same way, I can add a logger to the other file in my package,
common.py:

```
import logging

logger = logging.getLogger(__name__)
```

Listing 19-6: letter_counter/common.py:1

Handler Objects

The `Handler` is responsible for sending the `LogRecord` objects to the right
place, whether that be the standard output, the standard error, a file, over
a network, or some other location. The logging module contains a number
of built-in `Handler` objects, all of which are thoroughly documented at *https://
docs.python.org/3/library/logging.handlers.html*. This chapter won't cover many
of these useful handlers, so the documentation is well worth a quick read.
In most situations, however, you'll wind up using one of the following:

- `StreamHandler` sends logging output to streams, especially the standard
  output and standard error streams. You may pass the desired output
  stream to the `logging.StreamHandler` class initializer; otherwise, `sys.stderr`
  is used by default. Although you can use this handler for logging to a
  file, `FileHandler` will give you better results for that use case.

- `FileHandler` sends logging output to files. You must pass the filename or `Path` to the target output file to the `logging.FileHandler` class initializer. (There are a number of further specialized `Handler` classes for dealing with rotating and system log files.)

- `SocketHandler` sends logging output to a network socket over TCP. You would pass the host and port as arguments to the `logging.handlers.SocketHandler` class initializer.

- `SMTPHandler` sends logging output to an email address via SMTP. The mail host, sender email address, recipient email address, subject, and login credentials all have to be passed to the `logging.handlers.SMTPHandler` class initializer.

- `NullHandler` sends logging output into the black hole at the heart of a captive dark star, never to be seen or heard from again. Nothing has to be passed to the `logging.NullHandler` class initializer.

GOTCHA ALERT   If your project is a library, use `NullHandler` as its only logging handler, so as to not clutter or confuse any logging systems employed by end developers. This will explicitly suppress all logging from the library. An end developer can attach a different handler to the library's logger, if desired.

I'll continue my `letter_counter` package example by printing all the `LogRecord` objects in the `letter_counter` package to the terminal with `logging.StreamHandler()`, which sends logs to the standard-output or standard-error streams. I add this handler to my top-level `Logger` object like this:

```
stream_handler = logging.StreamHandler()
logger.addHandler(stream_handler)
```

Listing 19-7: letter_counter/__main__.py:2

Because I did not specify a stream with the `StreamHandler()` constructor, `stream_handler` will pass messages to the `sys.stderr` stream.

Notice that I only need to add the `Handler` to the `letter_counter` logger. Since the loggers for `letter_counter.letters` and `letter_counter.common` are children, they will pass all their `LogRecord` objects up to their parent.

You may attach as many handlers as you like, to any of the loggers. Child loggers will still relay their `LogRecord` objects to their parents in addition to employing their own handlers, unless you set the `propagate` attribute of a child logger to `False`:

```
logger.propagate = False
```

In my example, I don't need to add any handlers to the child loggers. I can let the loggers pass their `LogRecord` objects back up to the parent logger, which has the one `StreamHandler` attached.

Logging with Levels

My logging example is still incomplete because it doesn't include the *severity level* of each message, which indicates the message's relative importance.

Logging with levels allows you to configure a logging system to display only messages that are at or above a given severity level. For example, you may want to see all DEBUG messages while developing, but end users should only see WARNING messages and above.

There are six built-in severity levels, as outlined in Table 19-4.

Table 19-4: Logging Severity Levels

Level	Numeric value	Use
CRITICAL	50	Messages related to horrible, terrible, no good, very bad, everything-is-broken situations
ERROR	40	Messages related to an error that can probably be recovered from (meaning at least all is not lost)
WARNING	30	Messages related to problems that are not (yet) errors but may require attention
INFO	20	Informative and useful messages that are not related to actual problems
DEBUG	10	Messages that are only of interest to developers, particularly when hunting for bugs
NOTSET	0	Only used to specify that all messages should be displayed (never used as a message severity level)

To assign a level to a message when logging it, use the Logger instance method corresponding to the level for the message, as I do in this function from *letter_counter/common.py*:

```
def scrub_string(string):
    string = string.lower()
    string = ''.join(filter(str.isalpha, string))
    logger.debug(f"{len(string)} letters detected.")
    return string
```

Listing 19-8: letter_counter/common.py:2

This function converts a string to all lowercase and filters it down to contain only letters. The important part of this example is the logger .debug() method call, which passes a LogRecord to this module's logger object (Listing 19-6) with level DEBUG.

Meanwhile, over in *letter_counter/letters.py*, I have some INFO level messages I need to output under certain circumstances:

```
consonants = 'bcdfghjklmnpqrstvwxyz'
vowels = 'aeiou'


def count_letters(string, letter_set):
```

```
        counts = defaultdict(lambda: 0)
        for ch in string:
            if ch in letter_set:
                counts[ch] += 1
        return counts


    def most_common_consonant(string):
        if not len(string):
          ❶ logger.info("No consonants in empty string.")
            return ""
        counts = count_letters(string, consonants)
        return max(counts, key=counts.get).upper()


    def most_common_vowel(string):
        if not len(string):
          ❷ logger.info("No vowels in empty string.")
            return ""
        counts = count_letters(string, vowels)
        return max(counts, key=counts.get).upper()
```

Listing 19-9: letter_counter/letters.py:1

These functions count up the number of vowels and consonants in a given string, and they return the vowel or consonant that appears most frequently. The important parts here are the two calls to logger.info() ❶ ❷. Notice that these messages are logged only if an empty string is passed to most_common_consonant() or most_common_vowel().

Controlling the Log Level

Any given Logger object can be set to pick up LogRecord objects with a particular level or higher, using the setLevel() method. As with adding Handler objects, you only need to set the level on the top-level logger. While you *can* set it on child loggers if you see fit to do so, they will no longer delegate their LogRecord objects to their parents. By default, a Logger has a level of NOTSET, causing it to delegate its LogRecord objects up the hierarchy. As soon as a Logger with a level other than NOTSET is encountered in that hierarchy, the chain of delegation stops.

In my example, I set the logging level on the top-level logger to WARNING by default, but I allow users to pass a -v argument on the invocation of my package to instead set the level to INFO. I'm using the built-in argparse module to handle command-line arguments:

```
parser = argparse.ArgumentParser(description="Find which letters appear most.")
parser.add_argument("-v", help="Show all messages.", action="store_true") ❶
parser.add_argument("raw_path", metavar="P", type=str, help="The file to read.") ❷

def main():
    args = parser.parse_args()
```

```
    if args.v:
 ❸     logger.setLevel(logging.INFO)
    else:
        logger.setLevel(logging.WARNING)
```

Listing 19-10: letter_counter/__main__.py:3

I won't go into the usage of argparse in much detail here, as it's largely off-topic and the official argparse tutorial does a decent job of introducing it: *https://docs.python.org/3/howto/argparse.html.* Suffice to say that I define two arguments: a -v flag for toggling verbose mode ❶ and the path to the file the program should read from ❷. That flag is the important part in this situation. If it was passed in the package invocation, I set the level of logger to logging.INFO ❸. Otherwise, I use logging.WARNING, thereby ignoring all messages logged with logger.info().

Here's the rest of my __main__.py module, which reads the file, calls the functions to count letters, and displays the output:

```
    path = pathlib.Path(args.raw_path).resolve()
 ❶ logger.info(f"Opening {path}")

    if not path.exists():
 ❷     logger.warning("File does not exist.")
        return

    with path.open('r') as file:
        string = scrub_string(file.read())
        print(f"Most common vowel: {most_common_vowel(string)}")
        print(f"Most common consonant: {most_common_consonant(string)}")


if __name__ == "__main__":
    main()
```

Listing 19-11: letter_counter/__main__.py:4

Nothing much to see here in relation to logging, except for a couple more logged messages: one at INFO level ❶ and one at WARNING level ❷.

Running the Example

To demonstrate the logging system at work, I'll invoke my package from the command line, passing it a path to a text file containing The Zen of Python:

```
python3 -m letter_counter zen.txt
```

Because I omitted the -v flag, the logging level is WARNING, meaning only messages at level WARNING, ERROR, or CRITICAL will be logged. Since *zen.txt* is a valid path, I see the following output:

```
Most common vowel: E
Most common consonant: T
```

Now, I'll add that -v flag to my invocation, which should change the logger level according to the logic in Listing 19-10:

```
python3 -m letter_counter -v zen.txt
```

This causes the output to change a bit:

```
Opening /home/jason/Documents/DeadSimplePython/Code/ch19/zen.txt
Most common vowel: E
Most common consonant: T
```

I now see the INFO level message from *letter_counter/__main__.py*. However, since the file exists and isn't empty, I don't see any of the INFO messages from the other modules. To see those, I'll pass a path to an empty file instead:

```
python3 -m letter_counter -v empty.txt
```

The output now contains additional messages:

```
Opening /home/jason/Documents/DeadSimplePython/Code/ch19/empty.txt
No vowels in empty string.
Most common vowel:
No consonants in empty string.
Most common consonant:
```

You'll notice one other message that is absent: the letter count message from *letter_counter/common.py* (Listing 19-8). As it was logged at level DEBUG, it is still being ignored with the logger set to level INFO. I would have to modify my code to see it.

For one last test, I'll drop the -v flag, thereby using the WARNING level on the logger, and I will pass an invalid file name in the invocation:

```
python3 -m letter_counter invalid.txt
```

This time, I see the following output:

```
File does not exist.
```

That output would be the same in this scenario whether I passed the -v flag to my program or not, as WARNING is higher priority than INFO.

Filter, Formatter, and Configuration

There are two more components you can add to a logging system: a *Filter* and a *Formatter*.

A Filter object further defines where to pick up LogRecord objects, and it can be applied to a Logger or Handler using the addFilter() method. You can also use any callable object as a filter.

A Formatter object is responsible for converting a LogRecord object to a string. These are usually defined by passing a special format string to the logging.`Formatter()` function. You can also add a single `Formatter` to a `Handler` object with the `setFormatter()` method.

It is also possible to configure a logger using a specialized configuration file.

For additional information on logging, I recommend reading the official *Logging HOWTO* tutorial by Vinay Sajip at *https://docs.python.org/3/howto/logging.html*, followed by the official documentation at *https://docs.python.org/3/library/logging.html*.

Alternatively, you could use a third-party logging library like *eliot* (*https://eliot.readthedocs.io/*) or *loguru* (*https://github.com/Delgan/loguru*). These libraries have their own patterns and techniques, so you'll want to see their documentation to learn more.

Assert Statements

While coding, you may sometimes become aware of conditions that would render your logic nonsensical. You can check for these conditions using an assert statement, which will raise an `AssertionError` exception if an expression fails.

However, while these checks are useful during development or debugging, they're often extraneous during normal operation by the end user. If you pass the `-O` flag (for *optimize*) to the Python interpreter when invoking your package or module, all assert statements are removed from the code by the Python interpreter.

For this reason, only use assert statements to check for mistakes *you* made! Never use them for data validation, nor in response to user mistakes, as users should never be able to disable data and input validation. Use exceptions and warnings for those scenarios.

Instead, use assertions to aid you in debugging particularly *brittle* areas of your code: places where a minor or seemingly unrelated change to the code could have unintended side effects. The following simple example will demonstrate where assert is and is not useful.

Proper Use of assert

In this example program, I want to calculate how many vinyl records I can store on any given bookshelf. There's one key constant in the program: the thickness of a single vinyl record in its jacket:

```
THICKNESS = 0.125   # must be a positive number
```

Listing 19-12: vinyl_collector.py:1a

Using a constant for this value is helpful for making the code maintainable. If I need to update this thickness later—perhaps because I do some complicated statistics to find a more precise average—I need to make sure the value I'm using is still valid. I know in advance that I'll need to use this constant as the divisor in some later math, which means the constant absolutely cannot be zero. It should also be a positive number, as vinyl records can't have a negative thickness. Thus, the comment is somewhat helpful here . . . but then again, it won't do anything to stop me from assigning a nonsense value to the constant!

Since a wrong value will cause major problems in the code itself, and since the value is not externally sourced data or user input, I can make an assertion. Under the hood, an assert statement looks like this:

```
THICKNESS = 0.125
if __debug__:
    if not THICKNESS > 0:
        raise AssertionError("Vinyl must have a positive thickness!")
```

Listing 19-13: vinyl_collector.py:1b

The __debug__ constant is defined by the interpreter and set to True by default. If the -O flag is passed to the interpreter, it is set to False. It is not possible to assign a value to __debug__ directly, so as long as -O was not passed to the interpreter, the assertion condition is evaluated. In this case, if THICKNESS is not greater than 0, I raise an AssertionError.

The assert statement wraps all this logic into one line:

```
THICKNESS = 0.125
assert THICKNESS > 0, "Vinyl must have a positive thickness!"
```

Listing 19-14: vinyl_collector.py:1c

Note the lack of parentheses involved here, as assert is a keyword, not a function. The condition THICKNESS > 0 is checked, and if it fails, an AssertionError is raised, with the string after the comma used as the error's message.

The reason for placing the assert here becomes clearer given the next part of the code, which performs some operations using THICKNESS:

```
def fit_records(width, shelves):
    records_per_shelf = width / THICKNESS
    records = records_per_shelf * shelves
    return int(records)
```

Listing 19-15: vinyl_collector.py:2

If THICKNESS were ever 0, the division in this function would raise a ZeroDivisionError. That error could point me in the right direction while debugging, but there are three issues. First, the actual problem is where I define THICKNESS, which could (theoretically) be some distance away from this function. Second, the error would only surface once this function is called, meaning that if I don't happen to invoke this function during my testing, I could miss the bug entirely. Third, a negative value in THICKNESS would produce nonsense output, but the math would still be valid, so the bug might slip past.

The purpose of placing the assertion right next to the definition of the constant is to alert me to a bug at its source, as early in the execution flow as possible.

Wrong Use of assert

As I mentioned earlier, assert should not be used for data or input validation. Regular exceptions and conditions should be used for those instead.

For example, this function prompts the user to input a value and then attempts to convert it to an integer. This first version improperly uses assert to ensure that the number is positive:

```
def get_number(prompt):
    while True:
        value = input(prompt)
        try:
            assert value.isnumeric(), "You must enter a whole number"
            value = int(value)
            assert value > 0, "You must enter a positive number."
        except AssertionError as e:
            print(e)
            continue
        value = int(value)
        return value
```

Listing 19-16: vinyl_collector.py:3a

You may be able to see where this is going, but I'll finish up with the rest of the program so we can see the problem in action:

```
def main():
    width = get_number("What is the bookcase shelf width (in inches)? ")
    print("How many shelves are...")
    shelves_lp = get_number("    12+ inches high? ")
    shelves_78 = get_number("    10-11.5 inches high? ")
    shelves_single = get_number("    7-9.5 inches high? ")

    records_lp = fit_records(width, shelves_lp)
    records_single = fit_records(width, shelves_single)
    records_78 = fit_records(width, shelves_78)

    print(f"You can fit {records_lp} LPs, "
          f"{records_single} singles, and "
          f"{records_78} 78s.")


if __name__ == "__main__":
    main()
```

Listing 19-17: vinyl_collector.py:4

If I run the program normally, this seems to work pretty well. However, if I pass the -O flag to the interpreter, I find that my input validation has vanished:

```
$ python3 -O vinyl_collector.py
What is the bookcase shelf width (in inches)? -4
How many shelves are...
```

```
12+ inches high? 0
10-11.5 inches high? 4
7-9.5 inches high? -4
You can fit 0 LPs, 128 singles, and -128 78s.
```

Input validation isn't very useful if it can be turned off. This is why assert should never be used for validating external data or user input. Instead, I use other techniques and leave assert out of it:

```
def get_number(prompt):
    while True:
        value = input(prompt)
        try:
            value = int(value)
        except ValueError:
            print("You must enter a whole number.")
            continue

        if value <= 0:
            print("You must enter a positive number.")
            continue

        return value
```

Listing 19-18: vinyl_collector.py:3b

Now, even if I run the program with the -0 flag, data validation will work as expected.

Seeing assert in Action

The final program only uses assert to catch a nonsense value being assigned to the THICKNESS constant in code, and nothing else. For the sake of example, I'll change THICKNESS to a negative value, to get on the bad side of the assert statement:

```
THICKNESS = -0.125   # HACK: this value is now wrong, for test purposes
assert THICKNESS > 0, "Vinyl must have a positive thickness!"
```

Listing 19-19: vinyl_collector.py:1d

I invoke the program in the ordinary way:

```
python3 vinyl_collector.py
```

That outputs the expected AssertionError, since the value of THICKNESS is negative:

```
Traceback (most recent call last):
  File "./vinyl_collector.py", line 2, in <module>
    assert THICKNESS > 0, "Vinyl must have a positive thickness!"
AssertionError: Vinyl must have a positive thickness!
```

I can jump right to line 2, which is immediately next to the source of the problem. I can fix the problem, although I won't do that yet, for the sake of example.

If I instead pass -O to the interpreter, that will turn on optimizations and thereby suppress the assertion:

```
python3 -O vinyl_collector.py
```

Even though the value of THICKNESS is wrong, the program will try to work with it anyway, as if the assert statement weren't even there:

```
What is the bookcase shelf width (in inches)? 1
How many shelves are at least...
    12 inches high? 1
    10 inches high? 2
    7 inches high? 3
You can fit -8 LPs, -24 singles, or -16 78s.
```

Nonsense output, sure, but I was expecting problems since I ran the program with -O, without fixing the assertion errors. In reality, you'll only want to invoke with -O once you're reasonably certain there are no assertion errors in your program; it's a flag you'll only ever use in *production*, not in development.

The inspect Module

One more useful tool in your debugging toolbox is the inspect module, which provides a number of functions to return data about objects and modules in Python, as well as code and traceback information. This data can be used to log more insightful debug messages.

As a fun little aside, outside of debugging, one of my favorite tricks I've ever done with inspect is to send the source of a Python function over a network to a remote machine. This allowed me to perform automated testing on those machines, without first having to install anything special.

The documentation is sufficient to introduce the functionality of this module: *https://docs.python.org/3/library/inspect.html*.

Using pdb

Warnings, logging, and assert statements make it possible to perform quite a bit of manual debugging, without the use of external tools. While this is useful for many scenarios, there are a number of other tools that can help you quickly home in on a problem in your code. These are primarily helpful when there's a possibility that the source of the error is some distance from its manifestation or when there are multiple components involved in the problem.

The *Python Debugger* (pdb) is a full-featured debugger for Python. Its workflow is similar to other command-line debuggers like gdb (for C++) and jdb (for Java). You use it by setting *breakpoints*, places in the program where control is turned over to the debugger, allowing you to step through the code line by line to observe what's going on.

If you're using an IDE, it may include features that integrate with pdb or else offer its own alternative debugger. While you should familiarize yourself with your IDE's debugging tools, it is also helpful to know how to use pdb on the command line, especially for those cases where you don't have access to your development environment of choice.

A Debugging Example

The best way to learn how to use the debugger is to try it out. Listing 19-20 is a complete module with a fairly pesky bug. If you take the time to read it, you'll probably figure out the problem yourself, but production code is rarely this linear. So, even if you think you've identified the problem, enter this code into a file as is. I'll work with this code quite a lot through the rest of the chapter.

```python
from datetime import time


def get_timetable(train):
    # Pretend this gets data from a server.
    return [
        {"station": "target_field", "arrives": time(hour=16, minute=27)},
        {"station": "fridley", "arrives": time(hour=16, minute=41)},
        {"station": "coon_rapids_fridley", "arrives": time(hour=16, minute=50)},
        {"station": "anoka", "arrives": time(hour=16, minute=54)},
        {"station": "ramsey", "arrives": time(hour=16, minute=59)},
        {"station": "elk_river", "arrives": time(hour=17, minute=4)},
        {"station": "big_lake", "arrives": time(hour=17, minute=17)},
    ]


def next_station(now, timetable):
    """Return the name of the next station."""
    station = None
    for stop in timetable:
        if stop['arrives'] > now:
            station = stop
            break
    station['station'] = station['station'].replace('_', ' ').title()
    return station


def arrives_at(station, timetable):
    for stop in timetable:
        if station == stop['station']:
            return stop


timetable = get_timetable('nstar_northbound')
```

```
station = next_station(time(hour=16, minute=43), timetable)
print(f"Next station is {station['station']}.")

stop = arrives_at('coon_rapids_fridley', timetable)
print(f"Arrives at {stop['arrives']}.")
```

Listing 19-20: train_timetable.py

This module simulates grabbing live data about a particular train, perhaps from API transit data. It then processes that data to find particular information. (A more realistic example might work with data in the widely used *General Transit Feed Specification (GTFS)* format; this imaginary API merely serves up a list of dictionaries.)

If you run this code, it crashes with an exception that may seem indicative of a simple mistake in my code:

```
Traceback (most recent call last):
  File "./train_timetable.py", line 40, in <module>
    stop = arrives_at('coon_rapids_fridley', timetable)
TypeError: 'NoneType' object is not subscriptable
```

"Oh, sure," I might say to myself. "I must have forgotten my return statement." But when I check the arrives_at() function, the logic makes sense. Besides, the station ID 'coon_rapids_fridley' is *right there* in the test data! Something spooky is going on here.

Enter debugger, stage left.

Starting the Debugger

You'll usually want to run the debugger directly on your code. One way is to invoke pdb from the command line when you run your program. For example, if I wanted to invoke the debugger on my *train_timetable.py* module, I could do this:

```
python3 -m pdb train_timetable.py
```

Since Python 3.7, the pdb module can also run a package with -m in the same manner as the interpreter. If I wanted to run my timecard package within the debugger, I'd do this:

```
python3 -m pdb -m timecard
```

Either way, the module or package is started in the pdb shell. The debugger immediately stops the program, awaiting a command.

```
> ./train_timetable.py(1)<module>()
-> from datetime import time
(Pdb)
```

At the (Pdb) prompt, I can enter debugger shell commands. I'll come back to the usage of this debugger shell in a moment.

Another way of starting the debugger is by setting a breakpoint directly in your code. When you run the code normally, it will hit this breakpoint and hand off control to pdb.

From Python 3.7 onward, you can set a breakpoint anywhere in your code with the following built-in function:

```
breakpoint()
```

Prior to 3.7, you could do the same with the following:

```
import pdb; pdb.set_trace()
```

Breakpoints will save you considerable time if you have an idea where the bug might originate from, or at least where the problematic execution stack begins. If you have a breakpoint set in your code, you only need to execute the program normally:

```
python3 the_module_being_debugged.py
```

This command starts the program normally, but as soon as it hits the breakpoint, the Python interpreter hands off execution control to pdb.

Debugger Shell Commands

The pdb tool has quite a few commands you can enter at the (Pdb) prompt to control and monitor the execution of the code.

In Appendix B, I document the most important pdb commands. These commands are also exhaustively documented at *https://docs.python.org/3/library/pdb.html*, although that page can be a bit hard to navigate when you're looking for something in particular.

While I won't be able to demonstrate many of the pdb commands, I'll walk you through debugging this particular example from Listing 19-20.

Stepping Through the Code

For this example, I'll start debugging at the top of my code by invoking pdb directly, like this:

```
python3 -m pdb train_timetable.py
```

I'll use the debugger as shown below. I strongly encourage you to follow along.

The pdb session starts at the top of the module, but the problem is farther down. I use the **next** (or **n**) command to move down to the beginning of the usage section of my module.

```
> ./train_timetable.py(1)<module>()
-> from datetime import time
(Pdb) next
> ./train_timetable.py(4)<module>()
-> def get_timetable(train):
```

```
(Pdb) n
> ./train_timetable.py(17)<module>()
-> def next_station(now, timetable):
(Pdb) n
> ./train_timetable.py(28)<module>()
-> def arrives_at(station, timetable):
(Pdb) n
> ./train_timetable.py(34)<module>()
❶ -> timetable = get_timetable('nstar_northbound')
(Pdb) list
 29            for stop in timetable:
 30                if station == stop['station']:
 31                    return stop
 32
 33
 34  -> timetable = get_timetable('nstar_northbound')
 35
 36      station = next_station(time(hour=16, minute=43), timetable)
 37      print(f"Next station is {station['station']}.")
 38
 39      stop = arrives_at('coon_rapids_fridley', timetable)
```

When I reach the first function call ❶, I use the **list** (or **l**) command to see the nearby code. I'm currently stopped on line 34, as indicated by the -> in the code.

Setting a Breakpoint and Stepping into a Function

I know I'm having a problem around line 39, so I'll set a breakpoint there:

```
(Pdb) break 39
Breakpoint 1 at ./train_timetable.py:39
(Pdb) continue
Next station is Coon Rapids Fridley.
> ./train_timetable.py(39)<module>()
-> stop = arrives_at('coon_rapids_fridley', timetable)
```

The command **break 39** sets a breakpoint on line 39. I then use the **continue** command to proceed to that breakpoint, since it is later in the execution flow than the present position.

Next, I use the **step** (or **s**) command to step into the arrives_at() function. Then, before checking that code, I use the **args** command to see what values were passed to the function:

```
(Pdb) step
--Call--
> ./train_timetable.py(28)arrives_at()
-> def arrives_at(station, timetable):
(Pdb) s
> ./train_timetable.py(29)arrives_at()
-> for stop in timetable:
(Pdb) args
❶ station = 'coon_rapids_fridley'
```

```
timetable = (
    {'station': 'target_field', 'arrives': datetime.time(16, 27)},
    {'station': 'fridley', 'arrives': datetime.time(16, 41)},
❷   {'station': 'Coon Rapids Fridley', 'arrives': datetime.time(16, 50)},
    {'station': 'anoka', 'arrives': datetime.time(16, 54)},
    {'station': 'ramsey', 'arrives': datetime.time(16, 59)},
    {'station': 'elk_river', 'arrives': datetime.time(17, 4)},
    {'station': 'big_lake', 'arrives': datetime.time(17, 17)}
)
```

The station ID for Coon Rapids Fridley looks odd ❷, and it certainly doesn't match the station ID I'm looking for ❶. The data in timetable is getting mutated somewhere, and this is probably part of the reason why my code is returning None. Still, I need to confirm my theory.

Moving Through the Execution Stack

Since I didn't change the station ID in this part of the code, the problem must exist in an earlier part of the code. I *could* start over with a fresh debugging session, so I could stop earlier in the execution stack, but when debugging in a large, real-world program, that could be a royal pain. Thankfully, pdb provides an alternative.

First, I need to know where I am in the execution stack. The **where** command shows me the current stack trace, which is composed of four frames:

```
(Pdb) where
  /usr/local/lib/python3.9/bdb.py(580)run()
-> exec(cmd, globals, locals)
  <string>(1)<module>()
  ./train_timetable.py(39)<module>()
-> stop = arrives_at('coon_rapids_fridley', timetable)
❶ > ./train_timetable.py(29)arrives_at()
-> for stop in timetable:
(Pdb) up
> ./train_timetable.py(39)<module>()
-> stop = arrives_at('coon_rapids_fridley', timetable)
```

I'm currently at the bottommost frame, as indicated by the > character ❶. I can move up one frame with the up command, which changes my focus to this line:

```
stop = arrives_at('coon_rapids_fridley', timetable)
```

Next, I'll inspect the nearby code:

```
(Pdb) l
 34       timetable = get_timetable('nstar_northbound')
 35
 36       station = next_station(time(hour=16, minute=43), timetable)
 37       print(f"Next station is {station['station']}.")
 38
 39 B->   stop = arrives_at('coon_rapids_fridley', timetable)
 40       print(f"Arrives at {stop['arrives']}.")
```

```
[EOF]
(Pdb) b 36
Breakpoint 2 at ./train_timetable.py:36
```

I use the l command (an alias for list) to see the surrounding code. You can see that line 39 has a breakpoint, indicated by the B. The -> also indicates that this is my current position.

I know from earlier that timetable is getting mutated somewhere unexpected. The first suspect is that next_station() function call on line 36, so I set a breakpoint there with **b 36** (the same as break 36).

I must move backward in the execution stack, which is one of the cool features of pdb. There are two ways to do this: either I could use the restart command from this point and then continue to the new breakpoint, or I could use jump. Because the latter is a bit trickier, I'll show how to accomplish it here.

The difficulty with using jump comes from the fact that I cannot jump from any position other than the newest frame, and I'm one level removed from that. There are a few ways around this. I could set a breakpoint at a later line on the outer scope and then continue to it. My present situation is simple enough, so I can use the next command from this point to step out of the current function call:

```
(Pdb) next
> ./train_timetable.py(40)<module>()
-> print(f"Arrives at {stop['arrives']}.")
```

I'm now in a position to jump. However, an important distinction between restart and jump is that while the former starts afresh, the latter executes with the current state staying as it is. This means that if I want to get an accurate picture of what's happening, I need to get a fresh value for timetable without changing anything else. The easiest way to do that in this code is to jump to line 34:

```
(Pdb) jump 34
> ./train_timetable.py(36)<module>()
-> timetable = get_timetable('nstar_northbound')
(Pdb) n
> ./train_timetable.py(36)<module>()
-> station = next_station(time(hour=16, minute=43), timetable)
(Pdb) pp timetable
({'arrives': datetime.time(16, 27), 'station': 'target_field'},
 {'arrives': datetime.time(16, 41), 'station': 'fridley'},
 {'arrives': datetime.time(16, 50), 'station': 'coon_rapids_fridley'},
 {'arrives': datetime.time(16, 54), 'station': 'anoka'},
 {'arrives': datetime.time(16, 59), 'station': 'ramsey'},
 {'arrives': datetime.time(17, 4), 'station': 'elk_river'},
 {'arrives': datetime.time(17, 17), 'station': 'big_lake'})
```

Immediately after making the jump, pdb stays paused, awaiting further instructions. I run this line with n and then confirm that timetable is back to what it should be by pretty-printing it with pp timetable.

Inspecting the Source

Now, I'll see how `timetable` is getting messed up. I don't need to continue at this point, as I'm already sitting on line 36, where I'd wanted to check next. I know that the data in `timetable` is being mutated, so I inspect the code of `next_station()` with the **source next_station** command:

```
(Pdb) source next_station
 17     def next_station(now, timetable):
 18         """Return the name of the next station."""
 19         station = None
 20         for stop in timetable:
 21             if stop['arrives'] > now:
 22                 station = stop
 23                 break
 24         station['station'] = station['station'].replace('_', ' ').title()
 25         return station
(Pdb) b 24
Breakpoint 2 at ./train_timetable.py:24
(Pdb) c
> ./train_timetable.py(22)next_station()
-> station = stop
```

Hmm . . . line 24 is intriguing, isn't it? That's the logic for changing from so-called *lower_snake_case* to *Title Case*. I don't want to waste time stepping through that for loop, so I set a breakpoint on the suspect line with **b 24** and then continue execution with **c**.

Now I can check the before-and-after state of `station`:

```
(Pdb) p station
{'station': 'coon_rapids_fridley', 'arrives': datetime.time(16, 50)}
(Pdb) n
> ./ch19/train_timetable.py(25)next_station()
-> return station
(Pdb) p station
{'station': 'Coon Rapids Fridley', 'arrives': datetime.time(16, 50)}
(Pdb) pp timetable
({'arrives': datetime.time(16, 27), 'station': 'target_field'},
 {'arrives': datetime.time(16, 41), 'station': 'fridley'},
 {'arrives': datetime.time(16, 50), 'station': 'Coon Rapids Fridley'},
 {'arrives': datetime.time(16, 54), 'station': 'anoka'},
 {'arrives': datetime.time(16, 59), 'station': 'ramsey'},
 {'arrives': datetime.time(17, 4), 'station': 'elk_river'},
 {'arrives': datetime.time(17, 17), 'station': 'big_lake'})
```

Aha! The first time I check station with **p station**, it has the correct station ID. After running that suspect line with **n**, I check the value again and find it has changed. That's not so bad in itself, but if I look at the value `timetable` with **pp timetable**, I find the change was made there.

Although a tuple itself is immutable, this isn't necessary true of its items, and a dictionary is most certainly mutable. By binding an item from the tuple to `station` and then mutating it, that change is visible in the tuple.

The next_station() function has side effects. The arrives_at() function couldn't find the station with the expected ID because the ID had been changed.

Checking a Solution

Once I have found the problem, I can quit the debugger and fix it. However, if I'm wrong, I have to start all over, and that could be a pain! Since I'm already located at the point of error, I'll try changing the dictionary back to what it should be.

I can execute a Python statement at the current position, effectively before the line I'm stopped on, using the ! command:

```
(Pdb) !station['station'] = 'coon_rapids_fridley'
(Pdb) pp timetable
({'arrives': datetime.time(16, 27), 'station': 'target_field'},
 {'arrives': datetime.time(16, 41), 'station': 'fridley'},
 {'arrives': datetime.time(16, 50), 'station': 'coon_rapids_fridley'},
 {'arrives': datetime.time(16, 54), 'station': 'anoka'},
 {'arrives': datetime.time(16, 59), 'station': 'ramsey'},
 {'arrives': datetime.time(17, 4), 'station': 'elk_river'},
 {'arrives': datetime.time(17, 17), 'station': 'big_lake'})
(Pdb) n
--Return--
> ./train_timetable.py(25)next_station()->{'arrives': datetime.time(16, 50),
'station': 'coon_rapids_fridley'}
-> return station
```

After running the statement that fixes the value of station, I confirm that the fix worked with pp timetable. Sure enough, the 'coon_rapids_fridley' entry changed to what it should be. Then, I move forward to the next line of code with the n command.

Just because I fixed a problem in the code doesn't mean I fixed the only problem. I need to let the program finish running to be absolutely certain the problem is resolved. I list all the breakpoints with b (or break) without arguments. For this example, I'll clear breakpoints 1 and 2, as those are the ones that will get in the way when I continue:

```
(Pdb) b
Num Type          Disp Enb   Where
1   breakpoint    keep yes    at ./train_timetable.py:39
        breakpoint already hit 1 time
2   breakpoint    keep yes    at ./train_timetable.py:36
        breakpoint already hit 1 time
3   breakpoint    keep yes    at ./train_timetable.py:24
        breakpoint already hit 1 time
(Pdb) clear 1 2
Deleted breakpoint 1 at ./train_timetable.py:39
Deleted breakpoint 2 at ./train_timetable.py:36
```

Now, I have removed the breakpoints I don't need anymore. (I could also have cleared all breakpoints using clear.)

I continue from here using the `continue` command:

```
(Pdb) continue
Next station is coon_rapids_fridley.
Arrives at 16:50:00.
The program finished and will be restarted
> ./train_timetable.py(1)<module>()
-> from datetime import time
(Pdb) q
```

While the output for "Next station is . . . " isn't what I want—I'll have to work out a solution for that—the rest of the code functions without crashing. I've solved it! Finally, I can exit the pdb shell with q and then change my code based on what I discovered.

Postmortem Debugging

So far, you've seen that you can run a debugger from the top of a program or from a preset breakpoint. A third way to run a debugger is *postmortem*, meaning after a fatal crash has taken place. This is best thought of as a snapshot of the moment of the crash. You cannot move about in the code, set breakpoints, step into function calls, or jump around. However, you *can* inspect anything you want from the point of the crash.

There are a couple of ways to start postmortem debugging. The easiest way is to start the module in the interactive Python shell and allow it to crash, then invoke the postmortem debugger with `import pdb; pdb.pm()`:

```
$ python3 -i train_timetable.py
Next station is Coon Rapids Fridley.
Traceback (most recent call last):
  File "/home/jason/IBP Nextcloud/Documents/NoStarchPress/DeadSimplePython/
Code/ch19/train_timetable.py", line 40, in <module>
    print(f"Arrives at {stop['arrives']}.")
TypeError: 'NoneType' object is not subscriptable
> import pdb; pdb.pm()
> /home/jason/IBP Nextcloud/Documents/NoStarchPress/DeadSimplePython/Code/
ch19/train_timetable.py(40)<module>()
-> print(f"Arrives at {stop['arrives']}.")
(Pdb)
```

There's not much I can do here apart from inspection, which means this technique isn't terribly helpful in this particular scenario. That said, I could still check the value bound to the names timetable and station, which might grant me some initial insight:

```
(Pdb) pp timetable
({'arrives': datetime.time(16, 27), 'station': 'target_field'},
 {'arrives': datetime.time(16, 41), 'station': 'fridley'},
 {'arrives': datetime.time(16, 50), 'station': 'Coon Rapids Fridley'},
 {'arrives': datetime.time(16, 54), 'station': 'anoka'},
 {'arrives': datetime.time(16, 59), 'station': 'ramsey'},
 {'arrives': datetime.time(17, 4), 'station': 'elk_river'},
```

```
{'arrives': datetime.time(17, 17), 'station': 'big_lake'})
(Pdb) p station
{'station': 'Coon Rapids Fridley', 'arrives': datetime.time(16, 50)}
```

This is quite similar to print statement debugging, at least from the point of failure. From this, I could ascertain that the timetable itself might have been mutated unexpectedly, which is a useful insight. From here, I could start the module over in regular debugging mode and follow up that idea, as you saw me do earlier.

Using faulthandler

If you've ever worked with C or C++, you may be familiar with the concept of *undefined behavior*, or a situation in code with no formal definition for how it should be handled. Code with undefined behavior may do anything: it might appear to work, fail with an error, or even do something weird.

You may hear many Python developers say, "Python doesn't have undefined behavior!" This is only partly true. Nothing in Python's own language specification is marked as "undefined behavior." Everything should either work in a defined fashion or fail with a specific error.

True as that may be, CPython (the default interpreter) and many common Python extensions and libraries are still built with C, and undefined behavior is a possibility in C. If you search for the term *undefined* in the Python documentation, you'll find a few advanced situations where undefined behavior is possible.

When you believe you're up against undefined behavior, particularly *segmentation faults*—fatal system errors resulting from a program trying to access computer memory it doesn't have permission to access—the faulthandler module is one of the most helpful tools in your toolbox.

To demonstrate this tool's use, consider the following brief segment of Python code with undefined behavior:

```
import ctypes

ctypes.memset(0, 254, 1)
```

Listing 19-21: segfault.py:1a

The undefined behavior here comes from the underlying C code: I attempt to set the memory at address 0, the *null pointer*, to the value 254. The behavior of accessing or modifying memory at the null pointer is undefined. While anything could happen, this particular action almost always results in a segmentation fault:

```
Segmentation fault (core dumped)
```

It's easy to spot this problem in a simple, two-line program, but imagine if this error occurred in a vast project with hundreds of lines.

This is where `faulthandler` comes in handy. It allows you to quickly locate the line in your code that contains the undefined behavior. There are two ways to run this tool for a project. The first way is to invoke it with `-X faulthandler` when you run the interpreter:

```
python3 -X faulthandler segfault.py
```

Alternatively, you can enable `faulthandler` directly in your code:

```
import ctypes

import faulthandler; faulthandler.enable()

ctypes.memset(0, 254, 1)
```

Listing 19-22: segfault.py:1b

Because the line enabling `faulthandler` is intended to be removed once the problem has been found, it's acceptable to cram the import statement onto the same line as the call to `enable()`.

Regardless of how you enable `faulthandler`, the output is essentially the same. As soon as a segmentation fault or similar fatal error is encountered, you'll see a complete stack trace:

```
Fatal Python error: Segmentation fault

Current thread 0x00007f7af346a280 (most recent call first):
  File "/home/jason/DeadSimplePython/segfault.py", line 5 in <module>
Segmentation fault (core dumped)
```

Based on this traceback, you can see that the problem is on line 5 of *segfault.py* (from Listing 19-22), which contains the invalid call to `ctypes .memset`.

Evaluating Your Program's Security with Bandit

As I've alluded to throughout this book, your choices about what modules and libraries you use and how you use them may introduce risks of a number of security concerns into your code. While you should try to stay informed about vulnerabilities, it's not practical to memorize every single possible issue. Thankfully, you can employ a tool to help monitor your code's security.

Bandit is a security-focused static analyzer. It checks your code for security issues by building and testing it as an *abstract syntax tree (AST)*, which is a tree data structure that represents the overall structure of the code. You can install the `bandit` package from pip and use it in the manner of most other static analyzers.

Consider the following very small program, which contains a significant security issue:

```
equation = input("Enter an equation: ")
result = eval(equation)
print(f"{equation} = {result}")
```

Listing 19-23: magic_calculator.py:1a

Rather than point out the security problem here myself, I'll run this program through Bandit to see what issues it finds:

```
python3 -m bandit magic_calculator.py
```

Here's the output:

```
[main]  INFO    profile include tests: None
[main]  INFO    profile exclude tests: None
[main]  INFO    cli include tests: None
[main]  INFO    cli exclude tests: None
[main]  INFO    running on Python 3.9.0
[node_visitor]  INFO    Unable to find qualified name for module: super_calculator.py
Run started:2022-05-29 22:25:37.497963

Test results:
Issue: [B322:blacklist] The input method in Python 2 will read from standard input, evaluate,
and run the resulting string as python source code. This is similar to, though in many ways
worse than, using eval. On Python 2, use raw_input instead. Input is safe in Python 3. ❶
   Severity: High    Confidence: High
   Location: super_calculator.py:1
   More Info: https://bandit.readthedocs.io/en/latest/blacklists/blacklist_calls.html#b322-
input
1       equation = input("Enter an equation: ")
2       result = eval(equation)
3       print(f"{equation} = {result}")

--------------------------------------------------
Issue: [B307:blacklist] Use of possibly insecure function - consider using safer ast.literal_
eval. ❷
   Severity: Medium   Confidence: High
   Location: super_calculator.py:2
   More Info: https://bandit.readthedocs.io/en/latest/blacklists/blacklist_calls.html#b307-eval
1       equation = input("Enter an equation: ")
2       result = eval(equation)
3       print(f"{equation} = {result}")

--------------------------------------------------

Code scanned:
        Total lines of code: 3
        Total lines skipped (#nosec): 0

Run metrics:
```

```
Total issues (by severity):
        Undefined: 0.0
        Low: 0.0
        Medium: 1.0
        High: 1.0
Total issues (by confidence):
        Undefined: 0.0
        Low: 0.0
        Medium: 0.0
        High: 2.0
Files skipped (0):
```

The first warning ❶ complains about the input() built-in function being insecure in Python 2. In looking at that warning, a developer might be tempted to say, "Oh, Bandit must be wrong. It's complaining about Python 2, and I'm using Python 3!" In fact, it's not wrong here. I am assuming that the code will be run in Python 3, but it might accidentally get executed by Python 2, where input() actually *is* insecure.

To fix this, I need to add a shebang to the top of my module, to ensure that the code will be executed by Python 3:

```python
#!/usr/bin/env python3

equation = input("Enter an equation: ")
result = eval(equation)
print(f"{equation} = {result}")
```

Listing 19-24: magic_calculator.py:1b

Bandit's second issue ❷ comes with a suggestion: switch to ast.literal _eval() instead of eval(), as the latter is vulnerable to code injection attacks. I'll revise accordingly:

```python
#!/bin/env/python3
import ast

equation = input("Enter an equation: ")
result = ast.literal_eval(equation)
print(f"{equation} = {result}")
```

Listing 19-25: magic_calculator.py:1c

Rerunning Bandit on this revised code shows no more issues. You can find the tool's full documentation at *https://bandit.readthedocs.io/en/latest/*.

The topic of security may feel irrelevant to your project, but you must remember that it doesn't necessarily have anything to do with the data your program works with! Many security issues are related to an attacker using your code as a vector or tool in an oft-unrelated attack. Security flaws are like a screen door on a bank vault. It doesn't matter how it got there, who is meant to use it, or how helpful it is to the authorized users. Sooner or later, someone is going to abuse it for illicit or unauthorized purposes.

All claims about your program's security are myths until they're tested. A clean analysis report from Bandit is not a guarantee your code is secure. Stay up-to-date on the latest security vulnerabilities, including those of any third-party dependencies or their dependencies. When your code even remotely involves system or data security, be prepared to do some fairly rigorous testing.

Reporting Bugs to Python

Sometimes, the problem in your code isn't your fault! Python, like all code, has bugs that crop up now and then. Once you're quite certain the bug isn't coming from your own code or a third-party module or package, you are strongly encouraged to report the bug to the Python developers.

Your first step should be to check whether the bug has already been reported. In any issue tracker, this can be tricky, so be patient with this step. All issues for Python are tracked at *https://bugs.python.org/*, so it's worthwhile to have an account there. Try searching the site for different words, focusing on the parts of the language you're using and any keywords in error messages you've received. Make sure to omit any words that are unique to your code, as they probably won't appear in other bug reports. Also, don't count out previously closed bugs as candidates. Regressions happen. If you find an existing bug that matches your situation, leave a comment with the information you have.

If you can't find a matching issue, open a new bug report. Be prepared to put some time and effort into it. Since you're the one facing the bug, you're in a better position than anyone to pin it down. Provide as much information as possible to help the Python developers reproduce it. Be prepared to respond to further questions, as you'll likely need to try some things out to prove your code isn't the real issue.

The Python documentation has a helpful guide explaining how to report bugs effectively. Before reporting an issue, please read that guide at *https://docs.python.org/3/bugs.html*.

Security issues should be handled separately from normal bugs, as they need to be treated with confidentiality to minimize the risks to existing code. If you come across a security flaw in Python, please report it via email to *security@python.org*, following the instructions at *https://www.python.org/dev/security/*.

Wrapping Up

When it comes to combating bugs, the best defense is a good offense. Writing your code to make good use of exceptions, warnings, assertions, and logging will save you debugging work later.

When bugs do happen, don't limit yourself to cramming print() statements into every part of your code. Logging and assert statements are helpful for manual debugging and catching problems while developing.

Meanwhile, the Python debugger (pdb) is one of the most useful tools in your toolbox, and it is well worth learning to use, no matter how fancy the debugger in your IDE is.

Python's default implementation, CPython, and many extensions besides, are built in C. This means that undefined behavior and other C-related bugs can creep into your Python code. When this happens, faulthandler is your best friend.

Finally, be prepared to check for and address security flaws in your code before anyone can take advantage of them. Bandit helps you get started with this, though true security testing will go beyond the scope of that tool.

Bugs may be inevitable, but the Python ecosystem provides excellent tools for catching, examining, and fixing them!

20

TESTING AND PROFILING

There are two important rules about code: untested code is broken code, and all claims of performance are mythical until proven otherwise. Thankfully, the Python ecosystem offers a wide variety of tools to test and profile your code.

Testing is one component of *quality assurance (QA)*, which in software development aims to improve the overall stability and maintainability of code. While many companies have dedicated QA teams, testing should be the shared responsibility of *every single developer* on a project. Similarly, *profiling* is a critical part of confirming that a project meets its performance goals. Even if some design pattern or algorithm looks faster on paper, profiling ensures that your implementation is meaningfully better performing than some alternative. In this chapter, I'll cover the essentials of testing and profiling in Python, primarily with the pytest testing framework and with an eye toward production code.

Most experienced developers find it most effective to test their programs as part of the coding process, rather than testing the entire finished program after the fact. This approach allows developers the flexibility of catching and correcting issues early, when identifying and performing fixes is easier. I follow this process in this chapter. I'll walk through the development of a complete (if small) multifile project, writing and expanding tests for each section before continuing with development. You'll learn how to run basic unit tests, conditionally run tests, and correct flaky tests. You'll additionally learn how to use fixtures, mocks, and parametrization. I'll also touch on measuring test coverage, automating testing, benchmarking code, and profiling.

What About TDD?

The practice of testing should not be confused with the specific methodology of *test-driven development (TDD)*, wherein you write tests before writing the code and then write the code to make the tests pass. TDD is not mandatory, as you can just as effectively write the tests just after writing your code.

If you're already a practitioner of TDD, I encourage you to continue applying it throughout this chapter, by writing your tests first. If you're like me and prefer writing the code before the tests, you can stick with that. The important thing is to write tests, and the sooner, the better.

Test Frameworks

There are several frameworks for running tests in Python, many with unique features and use cases. The most popular testing framework for Python is *pytest*, a streamlined alternative to unittest-based frameworks with minimal boilerplate code. If you don't know which framework to use, this is the one to pick up. You can find out more from the official documentation at *https://docs.pytest.org/*, and you can install the pytest package from PyPI via pip.

This chapter also uses *tox*, which ensures that your packaging works across different Python environments and automatically runs your test suites in each of those environments. You can find the official tox documentation at *https://tox.readthedocs.io/*, and you can install the tox package from PyPI via pip.

Before I dive into testing, I want to touch on a few of the other testing frameworks in regular use in Python projects.

Python's standard library includes unittest, which has a long history of use. Python 2 had both unittest and unittest2, and the latter became just unittest in Python 3 (*https://docs.python.org/3/library/unittest.html*). The standard library also includes doctest, which allows you to write simple tests in docstrings (*https://docs.python.org/3/library/doctest.html*). Both of these can be useful when you need to write tests without installing any packages.

The unittest module was further extended and improved by the now discontinued nose framework, which added support for plug-ins. This was in turn replaced by nose2. However, nose2 is largely considered outdated, so it's usually best to rewrite nose2 tests to pytest or another modern framework when possible. The pytest documentation has a guide to this at *https://docs.pytest.org/en/stable/nose.html*.

There are newer testing libraries, many of which apply innovative ideas and offer simpler interfaces. One such example is *Hypothesis*, which automatically finds edge cases you may have overlooked simply by writing assertions describing what the code *should* do. More information is available in the documentation at *https://hypothesis.readthedocs.io/*.

My personal favorite testing library is *Ward*, which features improved test organization and clearer output. It also works with Hypothesis, and it is fully compatible with asynchrony. You can learn more at *https://wardpy.com/*.

Finally, *RobotFramework* is a test automation framework that integrates with many other tools. It is better suited to large and complex systems that are harder to test, rather than small and compact stand-alone projects. You can learn more about RobotFramework at *https://robotframework.org/*.

The Example Project

To demonstrate real-world Python testing, I'll build a complete (but small) command-line program that performs a proofread check on a plaintext file. The program will accept a file path as input, and then it will check the contents of that file for spelling and grammar errors, using a free API. It will then prompt the user to correct the errors by allowing them to choose between suggested revisions. The corrected text will then be written out to another file.

The complete source code for this project can be found on my GitHub, at *https://github.com/codemouse92/textproof*. However, I'll be demonstrating good testing habits in this chapter by testing the program as I write it. I encourage you to follow along. The example_starter branch on that repository contains the initial folder structure and packaging scripts for this example.

To implement the actual spelling and grammar checking, I'll use the free web API for *LanguageTool*, an open-source proofreading tool and service (*https://languagetool.org/*).

With the exception of the third-party modules requests and click and the LanguageTool API, this example only uses features and techniques you've already learned elsewhere in this book.

To use the LanguageTool API, you make a POST request with requests, to which you pass a plaintext string and some other necessary information packed in dictionaries that will be converted behind the scenes to JSON. The LanguageTool service will reply with a very large JSON object containing, among other things, all detected grammar and spelling errors and their suggested corrections. The requests module will return this as a Python dictionary. From there, my code will need to pick out whatever information it needs.

You can find more information about the API, as well as a web interface for trying it out, at *https://languagetool.org/http-api/swagger-ui/#!/default/post_check*.

The click module provides a more intuitive way to design a command-line interface than argparse, which I used in Chapter 19. I'll use only the decorators @click.command(), @click.argument(), and @click.option().

You can install the `requests` and `click` modules in your virtual environment via pip. The official documentation for `requests` can be found at *https://requests.readthedocs.io/*, although I'll only use the `requests.post()` method and the `requests.Response` object it returns. The `click` module is documented at *https://click.palletsprojects.com/*.

If the LanguageTool API is offline, or if you're otherwise unable to access it, rest assured that nearly all my tests run *without* access to the API. Thus, even without an internet connection, you should be able to work through most of the examples and ultimately prove that the code works correctly. This is the beauty of testing.

Testing and Project Structure

Before you start testing, it's critical to get the project structure right. Back in Chapter 18, I introduced the recommended layout for a Python project, including the all-important *setup.cfg* file. I'll expand on a similar structure for this example:

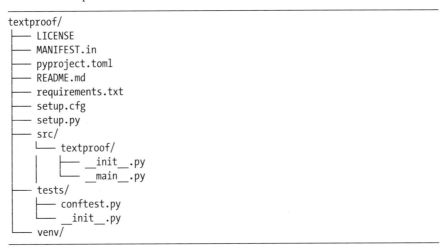

```
textproof/
├── LICENSE
├── MANIFEST.in
├── pyproject.toml
├── README.md
├── requirements.txt
├── setup.cfg
├── setup.py
├── src/
│   └── textproof/
│       ├── __init__.py
│       └── __main__.py
├── tests/
│   ├── conftest.py
│   └── __init__.py
└── venv/
```

Listing 20-1: Project directory tree for textproof/

The source code for the textproof package belongs in *src/textproof/*. As I mentioned back in Chapter 18, use of a *src/* directory is optional but strongly recommended. Not only does it make packaging easier, but it also simplifies configuration of testing tools. What's more, it forces you to install your package directly before testing, exposing packaging flaws and any wrong assumptions about the current working directory in your code.

In this structure, the tests themselves will go in the *tests/* directory. This is known as *out-of-place testing*.

I'll briefly review the setup-related files here, focusing primarily on their effect on the testing configuration. See Chapter 18 for a full explanation of each.

LICENSE and *README.md* are fairly self-explanatory, so I won't reproduce those here. Similarly, *setup.py* is the same as in Chapter 18, so it's omitted here.

The *setup.cfg* file is largely the same as the one for the Timecard project in Chapter 18, except for the metadata and the dependencies. I've omitted the metadata to save space:

```
[options]
package_dir =
    = src
packages = find:
include_package_data = True
install_requires =
    requests
    click
python_version = >=3.6, <4

[options.packages.find]
where = src
exclude = tests

[options.extras_require]
test =
    pytest

[options.entry_points]
console_scripts =
    textproof = textproof.__main__:main

[flake8]
max-line-length = 120
```

Listing 20-2: setup.cfg:1a

I'm using two libraries in this project: *requests*, for working with the API, and *click*, for creating the command-line interface. I'm also using pytest for testing; I'll add some tools here later.

I don't have any non-code data to include in the package this time, so my *MANIFEST.in* is pretty sparse:

```
include LICENSE *.md
```

Listing 20-3: MANIFEST.in

The most interesting setup-related file for this example is going to be *pyproject.toml*, which will ultimately store settings for some testing tools I'm using. For the moment, it looks like the one in Chapter 18:

```
[build-system]
requires = ["setuptools>40.8.0", "wheel"]
build-backend = "setuptools.build_meta"
```

Listing 20-4: pyproject.toml:1a

Under the project structure in Listing 20-1, my source code belongs in *src/textproof/*, and my tests belong in *tests/*.

Testing Basics

In this first part, I'll write some initial code and a few basic tests, which I'll be able to run even before the full program can be executed.

Starting the Example

The first thing my code needs to do is become able to load a text file and save it back out again. I'll make that happen in my project with a FileIO class, which I'll use for storing the file contents while I'm working with them:

```python
import pathlib


class FileIO:

    def __init__(self, in_file, out_file=None):
        self.in_file = pathlib.Path(in_file)

        if out_file is None:
            out_file = in_file
        self.out_file = pathlib.Path(out_file)
        self.out_file_tmp = pathlib.Path(out_file + '.tmp')

        self.data = None

    def load(self):
        if not self.data:
            with self.in_file.open('r') as file:
                self.data = file.read()

        return self.data

    def save(self):
        if not self.data:
            raise RuntimeError("Nothing to save.")

        with self.out_file_tmp.open('w') as file:
            file.write(self.data)
        self.out_file_tmp.rename(self.out_file)
```

Listing 20-5: src/textproof/fileio.py:1a

The FileIO class's initializer accepts a path to a file to read and optionally a path for writing back out; if no out_file path is specified, it will write to the same file it reads. The load() instance method reads the specified file into a data instance attribute, and the save() instance method writes data out to a file.

Unit Testing

I test individual behaviors of my code so far with *unit tests*, so named because each one tests a single *unit*, such as a function, or in this case, a particular conditional path through a function.

Before I write any more code, I want to test the behaviors of this class so far. In my *tests/* directory, I create *test_fileio.py*. By default in pytest, all test modules must start with test_ to be detected by the framework. If I named the file *tests/fileio.py*, none of these tests would run.

Each test is written as a function containing one or more assert statements:

```python
import pathlib
import pytest
from textproof.fileio import FileIO

class TestFileIO:

    def test_in_path(self):
        file = FileIO('tests/to_be.txt')
        assert file.in_file == pathlib.Path('tests/to_be.txt')

    def test_out_path(self):
        file = FileIO('tests/to_be.txt', 'tests/out.txt')
        assert file.out_file == pathlib.Path('tests/out.txt')

    def test_no_out_path(self):
        file = FileIO('tests/to_be.txt')
        assert file.in_file == file.out_file
```

Listing 20-6: tests/test_fileio.py:1a

Because all these tests relate to the same part of the code base, it is useful for organizational purposes to group them together in a class.

The first two tests check that the path string passed to the FileIO initializer is turned into a pathlib.Path object bound to the in_file and out_file attributes, respectively. The third test checks that, if only one path string is provided, that path will be used for both in_file and out_file.

Although these may seem like needlessly obvious things to check, these unit tests become invaluable as the code becomes more complex. If any change to the code causes the code to no longer behave in the manner these tests expect, I will be alerted by the failing tests, rather than by some sort of unexpected behavior that must be debugged.

Good testing practice demands that each unit test check only one behavior, which is why I wrote three individual tests, instead of one that checks all three things. This helps me zero in on a particular behavior that isn't working, instead of having to pick through multiple assertions to find what's broken.

I also didn't create constants to hold the string literals I keep repeating. While this is contrary to the coding practice of DRY, it is often considered good practice in Python testing, so your tests never run the risk of false positives if a function under testing rebinds, mutates, or otherwise interacts with a variable in an odd way. Avoid using the same variable for both the input and the output.

Lastly, notice that pytest requires test functions to start with test_, and requires test classes to start with Test, in the same way the module must start with test_. If I named that first test only *in_path()*, it would not be run as a test. You can change this behavior in the settings for pytest: *https://docs .pytest.org/en/latest/example/pythoncollection.html*. Some other testing frameworks, like Ward, do not have this default convention.

Executing the Tests with pytest

To run these tests, I must first install my package in a virtual environment. In the example below, I already created a virtual environment, *venv/*. I will now install the package, along with its optional testing dependencies, by running the following in the command line from the root of the project:

```
venv/bin/pip install -e '.[test]'
```

This installs the local package according to *setup.cfg*, including any packages needed for testing—namely pytest—which were specified in the [options.extras_require] section (see Listing 20-2). You'll notice that I wrap the .[test] in single quotes, to keep the command line from misinterpreting those square brackets as a glob pattern.

I'm also installing my package in *editable* mode via the -e argument, meaning the installation is directly using the files in *src/textproof/*, rather than copying them into the virtual environment. This is extremely useful if I need to run the code through a debugger!

To run my project's tests with pytest, I issue the following command:

```
venv/bin/pytest
```

This automatically scans the entire current directory for any modules starting with *test_*, any classes starting with *Test*, and any functions starting with *test_*. When pytest finds these test functions, it runs them, outputting the results onto the terminal in colorful, insightful detail, like this (sans color here in the book, unfortunately):

```
======================= test session starts =======================
platform linux --
rootdir: /home/jason/Code/Repositories/textproof
collected 3 items

tests/test_fileio.py ...                                    [100%]

======================= 3 passed in 0.02s =======================
```

All's green and passing! The pytest tool found three tests in the module *tests/test_fileio.py*, and all three passed, as represented by the three dots after the module name.

Testing for Exceptions

One significant danger when testing is receiving false positives, wherein a test passes only due to a bug or logic error in the code. For example, have you noticed something odd about those passing tests? They all refer to a file called *tests/to_be.txt*, but that file does not exist in the project. If FileIO is passed a path to a file that doesn't exist, it should raise a FileNotFoundError instead of proceeding quietly.

I'll put that expectation into the form of a test:

```
def test_invalid_in_path(self):
    with pytest.raises(FileNotFoundError):
        FileIO('tests/idonotexist.txt')
```

Listing 20-7: tests/test_fileio.py:2a

To test that an exception is raised, I use the context manager pytest .raises() instead of an ordinary assert statement. In the suite of the with statement, I run the code that should raise the expected exception.

Re-running pytest shows the test is failing:

```
===================== test session starts =====================
platform linux --
rootdir: /home/jason/Code/Repositories/textproof
collected 4 items

tests/test_fileio.py ... ❶ F                              [100%]

=========================== FAILURES ===========================
_____ TestFileIO.test_invalid_in_path _____

self = <tests.test_fileio.TestFileIO object at 0x7f9945d29580>

    def test_invalid_in_path(self):
        with pytest.raises(FileNotFoundError):
>           FileIO('tests/idonotexist.txt')
E       ❷   Failed: DID NOT RAISE <class 'FileNotFoundError'>

tests/test_fileio.py:21: Failed
==================== short test summary info ====================
FAILED tests/test_fileio.py::TestFileIO::test_invalid_in_path
================== 1 failed, 3 passed in 0.03s ==================
```

The F after the module name indicates a failed test ❶. More details follow the FAILURES header, indicating that the expected exception was not raised ❷.

Remember that, in this case, failure is a good thing! It means the test has detected a mismatch between the expectations of the test and the behavior of the code.

Now I set about making the test pass, which, in this case, is as simple as adding some logic to the initializer of the `FileIO` object:

```python
import pathlib


class FileIO:

    def __init__(self, in_file, out_file=None):
        self.in_file = pathlib.Path(in_file)
        if not self.in_file.exists():
            raise FileNotFoundError(f"Invalid input file: {self.in_file}")

        if out_file is None:
            out_file = in_file
        # --snip--
```

Listing 20-8: src/textproof/fileio.py:1b

Because I installed my local package as editable, I do not have to reinstall before running pytest again—the virtual environment directly uses the source code, so my changes are visible in that context immediately.

Running the tests now shows the first three tests failing and the fourth passing. Readers familiar with the practice of testing will recognize that this is a step forward, not backward: it reveals that the first three tests were originally passing erroneously!

Test Fixtures

Those tests failed not because of a flaw in the code, but due to their own logic. All three wrongly assumed the presence of a particular file, *tests/to_be.txt*. I could create that file myself, but it would be better to use the test framework to ensure that file is always there in advance. I can do so by creating a *software test fixture*, usually known as a *test fixture* or a *fixture*, which is a function or method that sets up anything a test might need, especially things that are shared by multiple tests. Fixtures can also perform *teardown*—tasks like closing a stream or database connection or deleting temporary files. By using a fixture, you cut down on errors in writing your tests and save time besides.

I'll add a fixture to my `TestFileIO` test class, to create that demo file my tests are expecting.

```python
import pytest
import pathlib
from textproof.fileio import FileIO


class TestFileIO:

    demo_data = "To be, or not to be, that is the question!"

    @pytest.fixture
```

```
def demo_in_file(self, tmp_path):
    test_in_file = pathlib.Path(tmp_path) / 'to_be.txt'
    with test_in_file.open('w') as file:
        file.write(self.demo_data)
    return str(test_in_file)

@pytest.fixture
def demo_out_file(self, tmp_path):
    test_out_file = pathlib.Path(tmp_path) / 'out.txt'
    return str(test_out_file)

# --snip--
```

Listing 20-9: tests/test_fileio.py:1c

I define the contents of the demo file in the class attribute demo_data. This is acceptable for populating a fixture with example data, so long as I don't also use the attribute in the test itself as part of an assertion.

The demo_in_file() and demo_out_file() functions are turned into fixtures via the @pytest.fixture decorator. Both fixtures have two important parameters. The tmp_path parameter is actually a fixture that is automatically provided by pytest via *dependency injection*, wherein an object receives the other objects it needs when it is created or called. In this case, merely *naming* the parameter tmp_path "magically" causes pytest to provide the tmp_path fixture object to this fixture. The tmp_path fixture will create a temporary directory on the filesystem, and it will automatically delete that directory and its contents when the fixture is torn down.

The demo_in_file() fixture itself writes demo_data to the file, and then it returns the path to that file. Whatever is returned by the fixture is provided directly to any test using said fixture. You can use yield in place of return in a fixture if you need to add teardown logic after that statement, such as closing a database connection.

The demo_out_file() fixture returns a path to an *out.txt* file (which doesn't yet exist) in the temporary directory provided by tmp_path.

I use the fixtures in my tests like this:

```
# --snip--
def test_in_path(self, demo_in_file):
    file = FileIO(demo_in_file)
    assert file.in_file == pathlib.Path(demo_in_file)

def test_out_path(self, demo_in_file, demo_out_file):
    file = FileIO(demo_in_file, demo_out_file)
    assert file.out_file == pathlib.Path(demo_out_file)

def test_no_out_path(self, demo_in_file):
    file = FileIO(demo_in_file)
    assert file.in_file == file.out_file
```

Listing 20-10: tests/test_fileio.py:1c (continued)

Like before, fixtures are added to tests via dependency injection. I need only add a parameter with the fixture's name (demo_in_file), and pytest will inject the fixture. In the context of the test, demo_in_file will then refer to whatever value was returned or yielded by the fixture; in this case, that's a string representation of the path to the demo file the fixture created.

I run pytest again and find that all four tests are passing.

Here are a few more unit tests, checking the read-write logic of my FileIO class:

```
def test_load(self, demo_in_file):
    file = FileIO(demo_in_file)
    file.load()
    assert file.data == self.demo_data

def test_save(self, demo_in_file, demo_out_file):
    file = FileIO(demo_in_file, demo_out_file)
    file.data = self.demo_data
    file.save()
    with pathlib.Path(demo_out_file).open('r') as check_file:
        assert check_file.read() == self.demo_data

def test_save__no_load(self, demo_in_file, demo_out_file):
    file = FileIO(demo_in_file, demo_out_file)
    with pytest.raises(RuntimeError):
        file.save()
```

Listing 20-11: tests/test_fileio.py:3

There's not much to explain here. I test loading a file, saving a file, and ensuring that saving before loading raises a RuntimeError. These also pass on the first try.

The one thing worth noting is the name test_save__no_load. Some developers like using the naming convention test_*subject*__*scenario*, using the double-underscore to separate the subject of the test from the description of the scenario under which the subject is being tested.

Continuing the Example: Using the API

Now that I have the basic file-reading and file-writing functionality built, I can add the next piece: communicating with the LanguageTool API. Here's how I do that in my program:

```
import requests


def api_query(text):
    lang = "en-US"
    response = requests.post(
        "https://languagetool.org/api/v2/check",
        headers={"Content-Type": "application/json"},
        data={"text": text, "language": lang},
    )
```

```
    if response.status_code != 200:
        raise RuntimeError(f"API error: [{response}] {response.text}")

    software = response.json()["software"]
    print(f"{software['name']} v{software['version']}")
    print(response.json()['language']['name'])
    return response.json()["matches"]
```

Listing 20-12: src/textproof/api.py

I use the requests module to send a POST request to the public API end-point at *https://languagetool.org/api/v2/check*. The API will respond with JSON data, which requests will automatically convert to a Python dictionary and return from requests.post(); I bind this dictionary to response.

I check the status code of the POST request; if it's not 200, that indicates a problem communicating with or using the API, and I'd want to raise a RuntimeError with the details.

Otherwise, for a successful response, I print out the name and version of the API on the console for reference, as well as the language I'm checking against. Finally, I return the list of errors detected by LanguageTool. (I know about the keys and structure of the dictionary from trying it out at *https://languagetool.org/http-api/swagger-ui/#!/default/post_check*.)

This either works or doesn't work, so I won't test this function directly—although some may see testing it as justifiable. I *will* test the assumptions it makes about the API response later.

Sharing Data Between Test Modules

I need most of my tests to work without internet, for two reasons. First, I want them to work even if I'm disconnected or the API I'm using is tempo-rarily unavailable. Second, I don't want to send unnecessary API requests just to test my code. Instead, I want to use predetermined local data for most of my tests. This means I'll need all my tests to have access to this data.

I also need to ensure my assumptions about the API, which are what my code and tests are based on, are correct. This looks like a job for testing!

In my *tests/* directory, I create a special *conftest.py* module. This module, *with this exact name*, is used by pytest to perform initial setup and share fix-tures and the like between test modules. Here, I define the data I want my tests to use:

```
import pytest

example_text = "He and me went too the stor."

example_output = "He and I went to the store."

example_api_response = [
    {
        'context': {
            'length': 2,
            'offset': 7,
```

```
                         'text': 'He and me went too the stor.'
                },
                'length': 2,
                'message': 'Did you mean "I"?',
                'offset': 7,
                'replacements': [{'value': 'I'}],
        },
        {
                'context': {
                        'length': 7,
                        'offset': 15,
                        'text': 'He and me went too the stor.'
                },
                'length': 7,
                'message': 'Did you mean "to the"?',
                'offset': 15,
                'replacements': [{'value': 'to the'}],
        },
        {
                'context': {
                    'length': 4,
                    'offset': 23,
                    'text': 'He and me went too the stor.'
                },
                'length': 4,
                'message': 'Possible spelling mistake found.',
                'offset': 23,
                'replacements': [{'value': 'story'},
                                 {'value': 'stop'},
                                 {'value': 'store'},
                                 {'value': 'storm'}]
        }
]


def pytest_configure(config):
    pytest.example_text = example_text
    pytest.example_output = example_output
    pytest.example_api_response = example_api_response
```

Listing 20-13: tests/conftest.py:1a

The value bound to example_api_response is adapted directly from the
['matches'] value of the LanguageTool API server response for example_text,
but I've removed all the fields I don't use in my code. I'll use this data for
many other tests later. The string literal bound to example_output is the
grammatically correct form of example_text, after applying the corrections
suggested by LanguageTool.

To make these names available to all test modules in the *tests/* directory,
I override the pytest_configure() function and add them as attributes of the
pytest namespace. I can access them in any test module in the *tests/* directory as attributes on pytest.

Flaky Tests and Conditionally Skipping Tests

Sometimes, there are conditions under which you might want to skip a test, rather than have it fail. The pytest framework offers a function for doing exactly that.

For example, my API test is the only test dependent on having a working internet connection and the LanguageTool API's availability. If I'm not careful how I write it, it could easily become a *flaky test*, which is a test that may fail unexpectedly or periodically for reasons other than a flaw in the code it's testing. Deal with flaky tests as soon as you find them, lest you condition yourself to ignore false negatives. The pytest documentation has an entire section on flaky tests and how to mitigate them at *https://docs.pytest.org/en/stable/flaky.html*.

In this case, I need to skip my API layout test when the public API server is unavailable or having other problems. In the following code, I do this with the pytest.skip() function:

```python
import pytest
import requests


def test_api_layout():
    response = requests.post(
        "https://languagetool.org/api/v2/check",
        headers={"Content-Type": "application/json"},
        data={"text": pytest.example_text, "language": "en-US"},
    )
    if response.status_code != 200:
        pytest.skip("Server unavailable")

    matches = response.json()["matches"]
    for from_api, expected in zip(matches, pytest.example_api_response):
        from_api = set(from_api.keys())
        expected = set(expected.keys())
        assert expected.issubset(from_api)
```

Listing 20-14: tests/test_api.py

The first part of the test is almost identical to my textproof.api.api_query() function, as I'm sending a POST request with the example_text and storing the response.

Next, I want to skip the test if response.status_code is any value other than 200, thereby indicating some sort of problem with the API itself.

I skip a test with pytest.skip(). The pytest results will show that this test was skipped, rather than indicate a failure.

If the API request was successful, then I iterate over the values in the list bound to the ["matches"] key in the dictionary representing the API response, and I iterate over the same in pytest.example_api_response as defined in *tests/conftest.py*. I create a set from each of those lists, and then I ensure that all the expected keys, as outlined in pytest.example_api_response, are also found in the API response.

It is okay to write tests that call an API or access another external resource your program depends on, but you should do this in as few tests as possible. The point is to avoid accidentally hammering the API or resource with too many requests. Making one or two requests in the whole suite of tests is reasonable.

Advanced Fixtures: Mocking and Parametrizing

One of the more challenging components of testing is replicating external inputs, such as user inputs or network responses. *Mocking* enables you to temporarily replace parts of the code with versions that will simulate inputs or other scenarios during testing.

Parametrizing expands a single test out into multiple tests, each one with the same logic but different data. This is especially helpful for testing how your code handles different input data.

Continuing the Example: Representing a Typo

Mocking and parametrizing are particularly useful for testing how code handles different user input. In the case of textproof, I'll be using these concepts to test the command-line user interface, but I have to build that interface first.

In my textproof program, I want to represent a single error found by LanguageTool as an object:

```
class Typo:
    def __init__(self, typo):
        context = typo["context"]
        self.text = context["text"]
        self.hint_offset = int(context["offset"])
        self.offset = int(typo["offset"])
        self.length = int(typo["length"])
        self.message = typo["message"]
        self.suggestions = typo["replacements"]

    def __str__(self):
        underline = "".join((" " * self.hint_offset, "^" * self.length))
        return "\n".join((self.text, underline, self.message))
```

Listing 20-15: src/textproof/typo.py:1

In the initializer, I populate the instance attributes with data from the API response. In the __str__() special instance method, I convert the typo to a string representation by showing the original sentence, underlining the typo with caret symbols (^), and then describing the typo on the next line. The result would look something like this:

```
He and me went too the stor.
      ^^
Did you mean "I"?
```

Displaying a typo is one thing, but it won't do much good unless the user can change it somehow. LanguageTool provides some suggestions, and I want to allow a user to choose between them.

Here's the instance method for getting the user's choice, where each suggested correction from LanguageTool is numbered from one onward, and where 0 is "skip":

```python
def get_choice(self):
    while True:
        raw = input("Select an option: ")
        try:
            choice = int(raw)
        except ValueError:
            print("Please enter a valid integer.")
            continue

        if choice < 0 or choice > len(self.suggestions):
            print("Invalid choice.")
            continue

        return choice
```

Listing 20-16: src/textproof/typo.py:2

Finally, here's the instance method for displaying all the suggestions, which will also call get_choice() and act on the user's choice:

```python
def select_fix(self):
    print('')
    print(self)

    for num, suggestion in enumerate(self.suggestions, 1):
        if "shortDescription" in suggestion:
            print(
                f"{num}: {suggestion['value']} "
                f"({suggestion['shortDescription']})"
            )
        else:
            print(f"{num}: {suggestion['value']}")
    print("0: (Skip)")

    choice = self.get_choice()
    if choice > 0:
        suggestion = self.suggestions[choice - 1]["value"]
        length_change = len(suggestion) - self.length
        return (suggestion, self.offset, self.length, length_change)
    else:
        return (None, 0, 0, 0)
```

Listing 20-17: src/textproof/typo.py:3

With that code in place, I move onward to tests!

Parametrizing

The first thing I want to test is that the Typo initializer is storing values where and how I expect them. It's all too easy to mess up dictionary access, after all! I want to test on multiple scenarios, namely the three typos I have the example data for in my *conftest.py* module.

Parametrization allows you to generate multiple scenarios from the same test function. This is preferred over hardcoding all the scenarios in one test, so you can isolate which specific scenarios are failing. In pytest, this is accomplished with the @pytest.mark.parametrize() decorator:

```
import pytest
from textproof.typo import Typo


class TestTypo:

    @pytest.mark.parametrize("index", range(3))
    def test_create_typo(self, index):
        example_response = pytest.example_api_response[index]
        example_typo = Typo(example_response)
        assert example_typo.offset == example_response['offset']
        assert example_typo.length == example_response['length']
        assert example_typo.message == example_response['message']
        assert example_typo.suggestions == example_response['replacements']
```

Listing 20-18: tests/test_typo.py:1a

In this case, I want to run test_create_typo() three times: once for each of the three valid indices on pytest.example_api_response (defined in Listing 20-14).

The @pytest.mark.parametrize decorator accepts two arguments. The first is the string representation of the name of the parameter to pass values to, which is "index" in this case. The second decorator argument is an iterable of values to pass to the named parameter.

The test itself must have a parameter of the same name, index here, which will receive the values from parametrization. I use that herein to access a particular item in the list pytest.example_api_response.

If I run this with pytest, I see the following:

```
======================= test session starts =======================
platform linux -- Python 3.8.10, pytest-7.1.2, pluggy-1.0.0
rootdir: /home/jason/Code/Repositories/textproof
collected 11 items

tests/test_api.py .                                          [  9%]
tests/test_fileio.py .......                                 [ 72%]
tests/test_typo.py ...                                       [100%]

======================= 11 passed in 0.58s =======================
```

You'll notice three dots next to *tests/test_typo.py*, indicating three tests were run. These were the three scenarios for test_create_typo(), as generated by parametrization.

If one were to fail, you'd see the value passed to the parameter, like this:

```
FAILED tests/test_typo.py::TestTypo::test_create_typo[1] - ...
```

The [1] after the test name indicates the parametrized value, from which you'd know that the problem occurred with the scenario where index was 1.

Indirect Parametrization of Fixtures

Thinking forward to some other tests I'll write later, I don't want to have to directly access items in the pytest.example_api_response list every time, as this is going to be repetitive. Instead, I want to provide a fixture that returns part of the example API response. I want this fixture to be available to all tests, not just those defined in the *tests/test_typo.py* module, so it belongs in *conftest.py*.

For this new fixture to work, I will need it to work with parametrization of tests. This is possible via *indirect parametrization*, where parametrized values are relayed to the fixture.

PEDANTIC NOTE   My editors astutely point out that there are less-brittle ways to write many of the following tests. That said, I chose these techniques so I could demonstrate some of the more difficult corners of pytest. These are finely tuned examples, not bastions of best practice. It will be up to you to decide how to best structure your tests and fixtures, based on your situation.

Here's my new fixture:

```
@pytest.fixture
def example_response(request):
    return example_api_response[request.param]
```

Listing 20-19: tests/conftest.py:2a

To work with parametrization, this fixture *must* have a parameter named request, which correlates with pytest's request fixture. Don't confuse this with the requests module I've been using to work with the API. (Can you tell yet that pytest is extraordinarily picky about names?) This will be used to receive the indirect parametrization value; I access that value via request.param.

I'll also add a similar fixture for generating a Typo object:

```
@pytest.fixture
def example_typo(request):
    from textproof.typo import Typo
    return Typo(example_api_response[request.param])
```

Listing 20-20: tests/conftest.py:3a

Tests and fixtures are among the rare exceptions to the rule of placing import statements at the top of the module. I want to perform the import when the fixture is used and only make the imported names available in the context of the fixture. That way, these imports won't leak into other fixtures, which is especially helpful if I need to import conflicting names from elsewhere in a different fixture.

Now I rewrite my test to use these fixtures:

```python
import pytest
from textproof.typo import Typo


class TestTypo:

    @pytest.mark.parametrize(
        ("example_typo", "example_response"),
        [(0, 0), (1, 1), (2, 2)],
        indirect=("example_typo", "example_response")
    )
    def test_create_typo(self, example_typo, example_response):
        assert example_typo.offset == example_response['offset']
        assert example_typo.length == example_response['length']
        assert example_typo.message == example_response['message']
        assert example_typo.suggestions == example_response['replacements']
```

Listing 20-21: tests/test_typo.py:1b

The test itself doesn't need to change much, since I was already using the names example_typo and example_response in the suite of the test function. (It's almost like I planned this!) I add the new fixtures example_typo and example_response to the parameter list of the test function—these are provided by the special *conftest.py* module—and those names are locally bound to the values returned by those fixtures.

I need to parametrize on the fixtures, so I once again use the @pytest .mark.parametrize decorator. The first argument is a tuple of names (as strings) I'm parametrizing on. The second is an iterable of tuples, with each tuple representing the values passed to each name. The third argument, the indirect= keyword argument, is a tuple (or other iterable) of names that actually refer to fixtures that will receive the values. In this case, both names are fixtures, although that does not necessarily have to be the case.

Running pytest again shows three tests in *test_typo.py* as passing, indicating that the parametrization is working!

GOTCHA ALERT I should say, the parametrization *appears* to work! Once you get the test passing, it's good to be in the habit of veryfing your assumptions by temporarily printing some of your values and running pytest with the -s flag, to allow print statements through to the standard output. (More on that in a later section.) In an early attempt to write this test, I was inadvertently running the same scenario three times and skipping the other two scenarios completely.

Mocking Inputs with Monkeypatch

The way to know that the `Typo.get_choice()` method is working is to give it some user input. Instead of bribing my four-year-old niece to hammer in some input on the keyboard every time I need to run the test—even though she would work for snacks—I'll create a *mock* to temporarily replace Python's built-in `input()` method and provide some inputs for the test. In pytest, mocking is performed by a tool called `monkeypatch`.

I'll add a fixture to *conftest.py* for monkeypatching `input()`:

```python
@pytest.fixture
def fake_inputs(request, monkeypatch):
    def fake():
        value = iter(request.param)

        def input(_):
            return next(value)

        return input

    monkeypatch.setattr('builtins.input', fake())
```

Listing 20-22: tests/conftest.py:4

This fixture uses two other fixtures: `request` and `monkeypatch`. I intend to have this fixture receive an iterable via parametrization. I'll use a closure, provided by `fake()`, to return each value in that iterable with each subsequent call to the closure.

I then temporarily replace the built-in `input()` method with this closure via `monkeypatch.setattr()`. Note that I am actually calling `fake()` here, as I want to monkeypatch the closure itself in place of `input()`.

Note that I return nothing from this fixture! Its sole purpose is to mock `input()` for the lifespan of the test using the fixture. The `monkeypatch` fixture will automatically undo itself during teardown.

Here's the first version of my test for the `Typo.get_choice()` unit:

```python
@pytest.mark.parametrize(
    "fake_inputs",
    [('-1', '20', '3'), ('3',), ('fish', '1.1', '3')],
    indirect=True
)
def test_choice(self, fake_inputs):
    example_response = pytest.example_api_response[2]
    example_typo = Typo(example_response)
    assert example_typo.get_choice() == 3
```

Listing 20-23: tests/test_typo.py:2a

I parametrize on `fake_inputs`, creating three separate scenarios. The first scenario should act as the user inputting -1, 20, and 3; the first two inputs would prompt the user to try again. The second scenario would act as if the user had input 3 on the first try. Finally, the third scenario, my favorite, would involve two nonsense inputs: `fish` and 1.1, followed by the valid input 3. The `indirect=True` parameter indicates that the other parameters should be passed on to the `fake_inputs` fixture.

I've designed these inputs to be used only with the scenario presented in the third typo scenario; ergo, my explicitly fetching `pytest.example_api_response[2]`.

Marking

I want to be able to use my `example_typo` fixture, instead of manually accessing the `pytest.example_api_response` list in this test, but it's rather overkill to parametrize the same value each time to the `example_response` fixture. Instead, I can pass a single parameter with *marking*, which is the application of metadata to tests and fixtures. (Parametrization is a type of marking.)

I'll use my own custom mark called `typo_id` to specify a scenario number. I want this same mark to work on `example_response` and `example_typo`. Here's the adjusted `example_response` fixture:

```
@pytest.fixture
def example_response(request):
    marker = request.node.get_closest_marker("typo_id")
    if marker:
        index = marker.args[0]
    else:
        index = request.param
    return example_api_response[index]
```

Listing 20-24: tests/conftest:2b

In short, I try to get the value passed to the `typo_id` mark, but if it's not provided, I default to using the value provided by parametrization. If a value is not provided to the fixture by either means, an `AttributeError` will be raised from trying to access the then-undefined `request.param`.

While I'm here, I'll modify the `example_typo` fixture in the same way:

```
@pytest.fixture
def example_typo(request):
    marker = request.node.get_closest_marker("typo_id")
    if marker:
        index = marker.args[0]
    else:
        index = request.param

    from textproof.typo import Typo
    return Typo(example_api_response[index])
```

Listing 20-25: tests/conftest:3b

I can now rewrite my `test_choice` test to use the `example_typo` fixture with marking:

```
@pytest.mark.typo_id(2)
@pytest.mark.parametrize(
    "fake_inputs",
```

```
                [('-1', '20', '3'), '3', ('fish', '1.1', '3')],
        indirect=True
    )
    def test_choice(self, example_typo, fake_inputs):
        assert example_typo.get_choice() == 3
```

Listing 20-26: tests/test_typo.py:2b

I use the `@pytest.mark.typo_id` decorator to pass a value to the `typo_id` mark, and that is used by the `example_typo` fixture.

Running pytest again shows this is successful, with one small hiccup:

```
===================== test session starts ======================
platform linux --
rootdir: /home/jason/Code/Repositories/textproof
collected 14 items

tests/test_api.py .                                    [  7%]
tests/test_fileio.py .......                           [ 57%]
tests/test_typo.py ......                              [100%]


======================= warnings summary =======================
tests/test_typo.py:38
  /home/jason/Code/Repositories/textproof/tests/test_typo.py:38:
PytestUnknownMarkWarning: Unknown pytest.mark.typo_id - is this a typo?  You
can register custom marks to avoid this warning - for details, see https://
docs.pytest.org/en/stable/mark.html
    @pytest.mark.typo_id(2)

-- Docs: https://docs.pytest.org/en/stable/warnings.html
================ 14 passed, 1 warning in 0.89s =================
```

There is now a warning about using an unknown mark. To fix this, I need to register the mark with pytest. There are two primary ways I can do this. The first way is to use a configuration file named *pytest.ini*; the second is to add the setting (using slightly different syntax) to *pyproject.toml*. Of the two, the latter is preferred, as it allows you to collect nearly all the configuration settings for various Python tools into one *pyproject.toml* file. I'll use that approach in this example:

```
[build-system]
requires = ["setuptools>40.8.0", "wheel"]
build-backend = "setuptools.build_meta"

[tool.pytest.ini_options]
markers = [
    "typo_id: the example scenario number"
]
```

Listing 20-27: pyproject.toml:1b

Below the section [tool.pytest.ini_options], I assign to `markers` a list of all custom mark names as strings. The part of the string after the colon is the mark's optional description, not part of the mark name.

Alternatively, I could register the mark from the pytest_configure() function in *conftest.py*, like this:

```
def pytest_configure(config):
    pytest.example_text = example_text
    pytest.example_output = example_output
    pytest.example_api_response = example_api_response

    config.addinivalue_line(
        "markers", "typo_id: the example scenario number"
    )
```

However, I'll stick with the *pyproject.toml* approach in Listing 20-27 instead.

Whichever way you register the mark, running pytest again shows that the warning is resolved.

Capturing from Standard Streams

If I want to test Typo.select_fix(), I need to not only be able to provide input, but also verify the output. By default, pytest captures everything sent to the standard output and standard error streams, including everything sent from print statements. This is why you cannot use print() directly in a test and see the output during the run, unless you invoke pytest with the -s argument to shut off standard output and standard error capture. Because pytest captures output, that output can be accessed directly using the capsys fixture.

Before continuing, I must add the expected outputs to *conftest.py*:

```
# --snip--

example_prompts = [
"""

He and me went too the stor.
      ^^

Did you mean "I"?
1: I
0: (Skip)
""",
"""

He and me went too the stor.
             ^^^^^^

Did you mean "to the"?
1: to the
0: (Skip)
""",
"""

He and me went too the stor.
                 ^^^^

Possible spelling mistake found.
1: story
2: stop
3: store
4: storm
0: (Skip)
```

```
    """
]

def pytest_configure(config):
    pytest.example_text = example_text
    pytest.example_output = example_output
    pytest.example_api_response = example_api_response
    pytest.example_prompts = example_prompts
```

Listing 20-28: tests/conftest.py:1b

I'll also add a fixture for accessing these prompts using parametrization or the typo_id mark:

```
@pytest.fixture
def example_prompt(request):
    marker = request.node.get_closest_marker("typo_id")
    if marker:
        index = marker.args[0]
    else:
        index = request.param

    return example_prompts[index]
```

Listing 20-29: tests/conftest.py:5

Here's the test for Typo.select_fix():

```
@pytest.mark.parametrize(
    ("example_typo, example_prompt"),
    [(n, n) for n in range(3)],
    indirect=["example_typo", "example_prompt"]
)
def test_prompt(self, example_typo, example_prompt, capsys, monkeypatch):
    monkeypatch.setattr('builtins.input', lambda _: '0')
    example_typo.select_fix()
    captured = capsys.readouterr()
    assert captured.out == example_prompt
```

Listing 20-30: tests/test_typo.py:3

I indirectly parametrize on the fixtures example_typo and example_prompt. I monkeypatch input() to always simulate the user entering 0 at choice prompts. *After* running the example_typo.select_fix() method, I retrieve the captured output and ensure it matches the expected output as defined in example_prompts from *conftest.py.*

GUI Testing

Mocking input() and capturing from the standard output stream is all well and good for command-line applications, but what about GUI-based and web-based applications? Although testing a user interface is considerably more complicated, there are a number of libraries that make this easier.

PyAutoGUI is one such tool, allowing you to control the mouse and keyboard from Python. It's compatible with any Python test framework, and it works on Windows, macOS, and Linux (but not on mobile). More information is available in the official documentation: *https://pyautogui.readthedocs.io/*.

If you're using the Qt GUI framework (PyQt5, PyQt6, PySide2, or PySide6), consider *pytest-qt*, which is designed specifically for testing Qt 5 applications. As the name suggests, this is a plug-in for the pytest framework. Check out their official documentation at *https://pytest-qt.readthedocs.io/*.

If you work with web development, you may already be familiar with *Selenium*, a browser automation tool for testing web applications. Selenium has official Python bindings, which are available on pip simply as selenium. You can learn more about Selenium at *https://www.selenium.dev/* or by reading the unofficial documentation, *Selenium with Python* by Baiju Muthukadan, at *https://selenium-python.readthedocs.io/*.

For mobile development, *Appium* is one of the leading test automation frameworks. It borrows some concepts and specifications from Selenium, as the name implies. *Appium-Python-Client* is the official Appium client for Python, and it is available through pip. For more information about Appium, see *https://appium.io/* and *https://github.com/appium/python-client*.

Continuing the Example: Connecting the API to Typo

In my program, I now need to connect the API request logic and the Typo class. I'll create a CheckedText class to store the text being edited, alongside the typos detected in it.

```python
from textproof.typo import Typo
from textproof.api import api_query


class CheckedText:
    def __init__(self, text):
        self.text = text
        self.revised = text
        self.length_change = 0
        self.typos = [Typo(typo) for typo in api_query(text)]

    def __str__(self):
        return self.revised

    def fix_typos(self):
        for typo in self.typos:
            suggestion, offset, length, change = typo.select_fix()
            if not suggestion:
                continue
            offset += self.length_change
            self.revised = "".join(
                (
                    self.revised[:offset],
                    suggestion,
```

```
                    self.revised[offset + length:]
            )
        )
        self.length_change += change
```

Listing 20-31: src/textproof/checked_text.py

I'll let you read through the logic yourself, using what you know. In short, the initializer creates a CheckedText object by running a provided string of plaintext through the API and then initializing Typo objects for each typo reported by the API.

The fix_typos() instance method will iterate over each Typo, prompting the user to select what to do about each via the Typo.select_fix() instance method. Then, the method will make the selected correction directly in a copy of the text, bound to self.revised. In this logic, I had to work out how to deal with a correction having a different length from the original text being replaced, then factor that into future edits. One of the upcoming tests will confirm this logic worked.

Autouse Fixtures

All my tests up to this point, except one, have been able to sidestep use of the API. I need to start tying together all the logic in my textproof program, so my upcoming tests will need to monkeypatch the API call. In tests, I *always* want a call to textproof.api.api_query() to return example_api_response, rather than send a request to the public API. I don't want to leave it to my (infamously bad) memory to include the fixture on each test that might have such a call. To get around this, I'll make an *autouse fixture*, which is automatically applied to all tests.

I add the following fixture to *conftest.py*:

```
@pytest.fixture(autouse=True)
def fake_api_query(monkeypatch):
    def mock_api_query(_):
        print("FAKING IT")
        return example_api_response

    monkeypatch.setattr('textproof.api.api_query', mock_api_query)
```

Listing 20-32: tests/conftest.py:6a

The autouse=True argument passed to the @pytest.fixture decorator causes this fixture to be used by *all* tests.

In this fixture, I have a callable that can be called in the same way as textproof.api.api_query, accepting one argument, which I ignore. The callable returns example_api_response. I also print "FAKING IT" to the screen, instead of the public API information that textproof.api.api_query() prints. This is ordinarily invisible, since pytest captures all output, but if I invoke the test with pytest -s, I can confirm that the monkeypatched function is being used instead of the real thing.

There's one surprising problem with this fixture: it won't actually monkey-patch the api_query() function in the context of the *src/textproof/checked_text.py* module. This is because of this import line:

```
from textproof.api import api_query
```

Monkeypatching occurs *after* the modules have performed all their imports, so replacing textproof.api.api_query doesn't shadow the function that was already imported into this module as api_query. In other words, the import statement bound the function in question to a second fully qualified name: textproof.checked_text.api_query.

Instead, I need to monkeypatch each fully qualified name that the function may be bound to:

```
@pytest.fixture(autouse=True)
def fake_api_query(monkeypatch):
    def mock_api_query(_):
        print("FAKING IT")
        return example_api_response

    monkeypatch.setattr('textproof.api.api_query', mock_api_query)
    monkeypatch.setattr('textproof.checked_text.api_query', mock_api_query)
```

Listing 20-33: tests/conftest.py:6b

If I import api_query elsewhere in my program, I'll need to add any other fully qualified names to this fixture.

Once this fixture is in place, there's nothing else I need to do to use it. Because it's an autouse fixture, all the tests in this project will automatically use it. I can now safely proceed with testing *src/textproof/checked_text.py*, knowing that no actual API requests will take place in the process:

```
import pytest
from textproof.checked_text import CheckedText


class TestCheckedText:

    @pytest.fixture
    def example_checked(self, monkeypatch):
        return CheckedText(pytest.example_text)

    def test_checked_text__init(self, example_checked):
        assert example_checked.text == pytest.example_text
        assert len(example_checked.typos) == 3
```

Listing 20-34: tests/test_checked_text.py:1

That new fixture and test employ the concepts I've already introduced, so I won't rehash them.

Monkeypatch cannot be used to provide a function, class, or module that just doesn't exist. If you need pytest to work despite a missing module, you can write your own module with the same interface as the one that's missing. Then, in *conftest.py*, you can add that module to the environment with the dictionary sys.modules, with the key being the name of the module you're missing.

Mixed Parametrization

It is possible to mix direct and indirect parametrization in the same test. For example, to test different outcomes with the CheckedText object, I will need to use the fake_inputs fixture while directly providing the expected outcome. I can do that like so:

```
@pytest.mark.parametrize(
    ("fake_inputs", "expected"),
    [
        ((0, 0, 0), pytest.example_text),
        ((1, 1, 3), pytest.example_output)
    ],
    indirect=["fake_inputs"]
)
def test_fix_typo(self, example_checked, fake_inputs, expected):
    example_checked.fix_typos()
    assert example_checked.revised == expected
```

Listing 20-35: tests/test_checked_text.py:2

The trick here is that, although I've specified two arguments to parametrize, I've only made one of them—fake_inputs—indirect. I can then run the example_checked.fix_typos() method, which will use the monkeypatched input() function provided by the fake_inputs fixture, and then compare example_checked.revised to the expected result parametrized on expected.

I should point out that although this test corresponds to a unit, CheckedText.fix_typos(), it is also an *integration test*, because it demonstrates several other units working together correctly. Integration tests are just as important as unit tests, as it's perfectly possible to have multiple working units that simply don't interact correctly.

Fuzzing

In the program I built in this chapter, I provided explicit input values for all my tests. However, passing tests may conceal many bugs, because it's all too easy to overlook edge cases. *Fuzzing* is a technique that can help catch these edge cases, generating random inputs in tests to find ones that fail in unexpected ways.

The *pythonfuzz* tool, currently maintained by GitLab, is designed to conduct fuzz testing on Python. It works independently of any other testing framework. To learn more about pythonfuzz, check out the README and examples in the official repository: *https://gitlab.com/gitlab-org/security -products/analyzers/fuzzers/pythonfuzz*.

Wrapping Up the Example

Have you noticed that I haven't even run the textproof package directly yet? It isn't a complete or valid program, but even now, I know that all the pieces will work as expected. This is the beauty of testing while coding. I can confirm my work on each part as I go, even if the whole is not complete.

Still, this example would feel wrong if it didn't result in a complete program, so here's the last needed module: *src/textproof/__main__.py*:

```python
#!/usr/bin/env python3

import click
from textproof.fileio import FileIO
from textproof.checked_text import CheckedText

@click.command()
@click.argument('path')
@click.option('--output', default=None, help="the path to write to")
def main(path, output):
    file = FileIO(path, output)
    try:
        file.load()
    except FileNotFoundError:
        print(f"Could not open file {path}")
        return

    check = CheckedText(file.data)
    check.fix_typos()
    file.data = str(check)

    file.save()


if __name__ == "__main__":
    main()
```

Listing 20-36: src/textproof/__main__.py:1a

This module defines my program's command-line interface, using the popular click package, which is easier to use than the similar built-in argparse module. On the command line, I accept one required parameter, *path*, where I want to read the text from. The optional --output flag accepts a path depicting where I want to write the revised text to.

I define the FileIO object with these paths, read in the text, and instantiate a CheckedText object from that text. As you will remember, in the process of instantiating the CheckedText object, a request is sent to the LanguageTool public API, and the suggested revisions are sent back.

The call to check.fix_typos() will walk the user through each suggestion, prompting them to select a fix, which will be immediately applied. The revised text is given back to the FileIO object file and saved to the file.

That's it! Now I can try this out. First, I'll create a file containing text to revise, which for this example, I'll just save in the root of the *textproof/* project directory, next to *setup.cfg*:

```
He and me went too the stor.
We gott three bags of chips for the prty.
the cola was too much so we gott lemon lime insted.
```

Listing 20-37: fixme.txt

Finally, I'll invoke my textproof program in the virtual environment, like this:

```
venv/bin/textproof fixme.txt --output fixmeout.txt
```

Assuming I have an internet connection with access to the LanguageTool public API, the program will display the first error and prompt me to select a fix. I'll omit the full output here, since it's quite long, but I encourage you to try out the program yourself if you've been building along with me.

Code Coverage

When you start talking to developers about testing, you'll likely hear the term *code coverage* a lot. Code coverage refers to the percentage of lines of code in your project that your tests execute, or *cover*. Good code coverage is important because any uncovered code is likewise not tested and could be harboring bugs or other undesirable behavior.

Python offers two built-in modules that track which statements are executed: trace and ctrace. Instead of using these directly, most Python developers use the third-party tool *coverage.py* (coverage in pip), which employs trace and ctrace behind the scenes to generate code coverage reports.

I'll test my code coverage now. If you're using pytest specifically, you can use *pytest-cov*, a plug-in that allows you to invoke coverage.py from pytest. I won't use that plug-in here, to keep this example as framework agnostic as possible. Instead, I've adapted and expanded a technique from developer Will Price (*https://www.willprice.dev/2019/01/03/python-code-coverage.html*).

First, I want to add the coverage package to my testing dependencies in *setup.cfg*, like this:

```
# --snip--
[options.extras_require]
test =
    pytest
    coverage
# --snip--
```

Listing 20-38: setup.cfg:1b

Next, I'll ensure that the package is installed in the virtual environment by issuing the following in the command line:

```
venv/bin/pip install -e '.[test]'
```

Code coverage will be assessed the same, whether you install your package as editable (with -e) or not.

I also need to tell coverage.py what files to scan and tell it about any replication of those files. This is especially important with an src-based project configuration, where tests may be running code installed in a virtual environment. To inform coverage.py what to scan, I add two new sections to the *pyproject.toml* file:

```
[tool.coverage.run]
source = [
    "textproof",
]

[tool.coverage.paths]
source = [
    "src/textproof",
    "**/site-packages/textproof"
]
```

Listing 20-39: pyproject.toml:2

In the first section, [tool.coverage.run], I specify a list of packages I am testing. In the second section, [tool.coverage.paths], I indicate the path to the original source code and where the source code can be found inside a virtual environment. These paths will be considered equivalent, as far as coverage.py is concerned; the tool will recognize *src/textproof/api.py* and *venv/lib64/python3.9/site-packages/textproof/api.py* as the same module, in terms of results.

Finally, I can invoke coverage.py from the command line, like this:

```
venv/bin/coverage run -m pytest
venv/bin/coverage combine
venv/bin/coverage report
```

The first command invokes pytest in the context of coverage.py. Although I don't pass any arguments to pytest here, you can. If you're using a different test suite, you can invoke that instead of pytest here.

PEDANTIC NOTE   You can also invoke coverage.py on your program itself to help find potentially "dead" code—code that is never used by the program—during manual testing. Be careful about the conclusions you draw, however, as a lot of code exists to handle edge and corner cases that might not normally come up.

Next, I combine reports for the same files in different locations, following the guidance I provided in the [tool.coverage.paths] section of *pyproject.toml*. Depending on your circumstances, this command may not have anything to combine, but it never hurts to check.

Finally, I display the coverage report:

Name	Stmts	Miss	Cover
venv/lib/python3.10/site-packages/textproof/__init__.py	0	0	100%
venv/lib/python3.10/site-packages/textproof/__main__.py	19	19	0%
venv/lib/python3.10/site-packages/textproof/api.py	10	8	20%
venv/lib/python3.10/site-packages/textproof/checked_text.py	17	1	94%
venv/lib/python3.10/site-packages/textproof/fileio.py	22	0	100%
venv/lib/python3.10/site-packages/textproof/typo.py	37	1	97%
TOTAL	105	29	72%

Seventy-two percent isn't too bad for a first attempt! I could go back and add more tests if I wished, pushing this number ever closer to 100 percent.

Code coverage is a useful metric to have, so long as you remember that it is part of a larger picture. In his article, "Flaws in coverage measurement" (*https://nedbatchelder.com/blog/200710/flaws_in_coverage_measurement.html*), coverage.py developer Ned Batchelder points out that 100 percent coverage can create a false sense of security:

> There are dozens of ways your code or your tests could still [be] broken, but now you aren't getting any directions. The measurement coverage.py provides is more accurately called statement coverage, because it tells you which statements were executed. Statement coverage testing has taken you to the end of its road, and the bad news is, you aren't at your destination, but you've run out of road.

Similarly, in a 2000 paper entitled "How to Misuse Code Coverage," Brian Marick makes this observation:

> If a part of your test suite is weak in a way that coverage can detect, it's likely also weak in a way coverage can't detect.

That 72-percent code coverage I achieved tells me that *at least* 28 percent of the code is not being tested, but the true percentage of untested code is almost certainly more. Code coverage can point out areas where additional testing will be helpful, but it cannot issue any guarantees that additional testing isn't needed elsewhere.

You can learn more about coverage.py from the official documentation: *https://coverage.readthedocs.io/*.

Automating Testing with tox

Up to this point, I've been testing on one virtual environment, which in my case is running Python 3.9. I also like to believe that said virtual environment only contains the packages demanded explicitly by *setup.cfg*, but I may have forgotten about something I manually installed or something I'd previously specified as a requirement that I've since dropped but forgotten to uninstall.

The *tox* tool is a fairly essential part of a testing system, because it automates installing and testing your package in fresh virtual environments for multiple versions of Python. In this section, I'll demonstrate this tool's use within my Timecard project.

I should first add tox to my *setup.cfg*:

```
# --snip--
[options.extras_require]
test =
    pytest
    coverage
    tox
# --snip--
```

Listing 20-40: setup.cfg:1c

Traditionally, all of the configuration for tox belongs in a *tox.ini* file. More recently, the trend is shifting toward use of *pyproject.toml* instead, for as much as possible. As I write, however, native support for *pyproject.toml* syntax is still forthcoming. You'll need to embed the *tox.ini* file contents directly in *pyproject.toml*, like this:

```
[tool.tox]
legacy_tox_ini = """
[tox]
isolated_build = True
envlist = py38, py39, py310

[testenv]
deps = pytest
commands = pytest
"""
```

Listing 20-41: pyproject.toml:3

Whatever I would have saved in *tox.ini* now belongs in the multiline string assigned to legacy_tox_ini, under the [tool.tox] section.

Within the *tox.ini*-style data itself, I have two sections. Under [tox], I use isolated_build to specify that tox should create fresh, isolated virtual environments for its tests. The field envlist is a comma-separated list of Python environments I want to test against. The tox tool supports Python 2.7 (py27), Python 3.4 (py34) through the latest release (py310, at the moment), Pypy's latest releases (pypy27 and pypy35), and Jython (jython). (See Chapter 21 to learn more about Pypy and Jython.)

The tox tool is not magic. You will need to have each Python interpreter you want to test with installed on your base system.

Under the [testenv] section, I list the testing dependencies with deps. You'll notice I omitted coverage here, since there's no need to run coverage in all these different environments. I set commands to the command I use to invoke tests: in this case, that's just pytest. This command will be run directly in each virtual environment, so I don't need to worry about the venv/bin/ prefix, which would be wrong anyway.

I ensure tox is installed in my primary virtual environment via the following, as usual:

```
venv/bin/pip install '.[test]'
```

Finally, I can invoke tox:

```
venv/bin/tox
```

It may take several minutes to run. As it does, you'll notice the textproof package and its dependencies (but not the optional [test] dependencies) being installed in each virtual environment and the tests being run.

After everything has run, you'll see a summary report:

```
_____ summary _____
  py38: commands succeeded
  py39: commands succeeded
  py310: commands succeeded
  congratulations :)
```

I know that my package installs and my tests work on Python 3.8, Python 3.9, and Python 3.10, so I'm also reasonably confident textproof could run in any of those environments on other machines.

You can learn more about tox from the official documentation: *https://tox.readthedocs.io/*.

Benchmarking and Profiling

As programmers, we're often very interested in making our code run faster. You will likely make many decisions about your code, based primarily on the notion that one technique will run faster than another. As I mentioned at the top of the chapter, all claims of performance are mythical until proven otherwise.

Benchmarking is how you establish that one piece of code is faster than another. The closely related technique of *profiling* is how you find areas where existing code can be optimized, by locating performance bottlenecks and common inefficiencies.

Python offers four built-in tools that are useful for these tasks: timeit, cProfile, profile, and tracemalloc. I'll cover each briefly.

Benchmarking with timeit

When you need to quickly verify that one chunk of code is faster than another, timeit is an excellent tool. For example, you may encounter a claim online that multiple assignment in Python is faster than the ordinary single assignment I've used throughout the book. You can verify that claim using timeit, like this:

```
from timeit import timeit

count = 10_000_000

def multiple_assign():
    x, y, z = 'foo', 'bar', 'baz'

time_multiple_assign = timeit(multiple_assign)

def single_assign():
    x = 'foo'
    y = 'bar'
    z = 'baz'

time_single_assign = timeit(single_assign)

print("Multiple assignment:", time_multiple_assign, sep='\t')
print("Individual assignment:", time_single_assign, sep='\t')
```

Listing 20-42: profiling_with_timeit.py

Each statement I'm measuring should be in a function or other callable object. I also must determine how many times to evaluate and run each statement. This needs to be a large number of times for the results to be meaningful, and the larger the number is, the more accurate the results will be. I bound this value, 10_000_000 (10 million), to count and passed it to the optional number= keyword argument of timeit, rather than risk entering different numbers on the two function calls, which would skew the results.

The number of seconds that elapsed while running the statement repeatedly is returned by timeit. I bind the results to time_multiple_assign and time_single_assign. Finally, I print out the results. I use a tab separator in the print statement to line up the two numbers.

Running the code, here are the results:

```
Multiple assignment:     0.21586943799957226
Individual assignment:   0.18725779700071143
```

You'll get different results each time because your computer manages processes via pre-emptive multitasking (recall Chapter 16), meaning the Python process may get suspended at any time to allow another process to work for a few milliseconds. One profiling result is not conclusive; instead, look for trends among a large sample of results.

There's not a profound difference between the two, but it's fairly clear that multiple assignment is *not* faster; it is rather slightly slower, at least on Python 3.10 on my environment.

Alternatively, I could pass a string literal containing the code to be timed. In this case, that code must be able to run by itself and not depend on anything else in the module. If I needed to perform some setup, I could pass any amount of code as a string to the `setup=` keyword argument of `timeit`.

The `timeit` module also can be used from the command line. Here, I'll benchmark the exact same code as in Listing 20-42, but in a UNIX terminal. The responses are inline:

```
$ python3 -m timeit -n 10000000 'x, y, z = "foo", "bar", "baz"'
10000000 loops, best of 5: 20.8 nsec per loop
$ python3 -m timeit -n 10000000 'x = "foo"; y = "bar"; z = "baz"'
10000000 loops, best of 5: 19.1 nsec per loop
```

The `-n` argument is where I specify how many times the code is executed. The last argument is the required one: the Python code to run, as a string. (If you're using Bash, remember to wrap the string in single quotes, rather than double quotes, to prevent Bash from trying to interpret anything in the Python code.)

Profiling with cProfile or profile

While benchmarking produces a single measurement for each code snippet measured, profiling generates a table of measurements, allowing you to see what parts of the code take the most time to run.

Python offers two tools for conducting in-depth code profiling: `cProfile` and `profile`. These both have exactly the same interface, but while `cProfile` is written as a C extension, thereby minimizing overhead and bypassing the GIL, the `profile` module is written purely in Python and has considerably more overhead as a result. For this reason, I use `cProfile` whenever possible and only use `profile` when `cProfile` is not available, such as when I'm using an alternative Python implementation.

Unlike `timeit`, the `cProfile` and `profile` modules are aware of their own surroundings and can call any functions or methods available in the current namespace.

You *can* perform benchmarks with `cProfile` or `profile`, merely by running the two competing statements or function calls in separate calls to `run()`. However, `timeit` is usually better suited for this purpose. I'm instead going to use `cProfile` for the purpose it's best suited to: identifying possible performance bottlenecks.

I'll call `cProfile` on the `main()` function from the textproof package's default entry point, like this:

```
# --snip--

if __name__ == "__main__":
    # main()
    import cProfile
    cProfile.run('main()')
```

Listing 20-43: src/textproof/__main__.py:1b

Since this is temporary code, I import cProfile right here, instead of at the top of the file. Both cProfile and profile provide identical methods, including run(). If you use profile instead of cProfile, everything else in my examples is the same.

I pass a string containing the Python statement to profile. In this case, I want to profile the entire program by calling the main() function.

Now I can install and invoke my program. I must not use the usual entry point provided by textproof, as that will bypass this whole if __name__ clause. Instead, I need to execute the package directly:

```
venv/bin/pip install -e .
venv/bin/python3 -m textproof fixme.txt --output fixmeout.txt
```

The program will start as normal, and I can interact with it.

PEDANTIC NOTE   This is why I still like having a default package entry point via if __name__ == "__main__". It provides me with a place to make temporary changes to how the program runs, for experimentation, debugging, and testing purposes, without affecting the primary entry point(s) provided by *setup.cfg*.

After I finish using the program and it exits, cProfile displays a report on the terminal. However, this report is huge, difficult to navigate, and unhelpfully sorted by name. I need to sort on something more useful, such as, say, the number of calls.

The class cProfile.Profile() provides a bit more control. Ordinarily, I can use it like this, although there's one critical problem particular to my code that I'll come back to:

```
if __name__ == "__main__":
    # main()
    import cProfile, pstats
    pr = cProfile.Profile()
    pr.enable()
    main()
    pr.disable()
    stats = pstats.Stats(pr)
    stats.strip_dirs()
    stats.sort_stats(pstats.SortKey.CUMULATIVE)
    stats.print_stats(10)
```

Listing 20-44: src/textproof/__main__.py:1c

I create a new cProfile.Profile object and bind it to the name pr. I enable it with pr.enable(), after which I have the code I want to profile. When I'm done, I disable the profiler in the same manner, with pr.disable().

To sort the profiling results, I create a pstats.Stats() object. I strip out the path information with strip_dirs(), so I see only module names. Then I sort by the *cumulative runtime* of each function with sort_stats(), meaning the total time the program spent running that function.

Finally, I print out the stats with print_stats(), specifying that I only want to see the first 10 lines of output, instead of the hundreds that would be displayed. I could also pass a floating-point number here, representing a percentage of lines to display.

As of Python 3.8, cProfile.Profile is also a context manager, so I can use this syntax instead of manually enabling and disabling:

```python
if __name__ == "__main__":
    # main()
    import cProfile, pstats
    with cProfile.Profile() as pr:
        main()
    stats = pstats.Stats(pr)
    stats.strip_dirs()
    stats.sort_stats(pstats.SortKey.CUMULATIVE)
    stats.print_stats(10)
```

Listing 20-45: src/textproof/__main__.py:1d

If you try to run the code from either Listing 20-44 or Listing 20-45, you'll notice that *there is no output.* I spent about half an hour scratching my head over this one. I finally realized that, because I decorated main() with @click.command(), Click causes the program to exit immediately at the end of main(), instead of returning here to finish up. This sort of problem isn't exclusive to Click. In real-world applications, there are many situations that will cause the program to terminate without returning from main() or another function normally. Perhaps the user closes a window or clicks the Quit button.

In this case, I can get the best results by moving the logic right into my main() function:

```python
#!/usr/bin/env python3

import click
from textproof.fileio import FileIO
from textproof.checked_text import CheckedText

@click.command()
@click.argument('path')
@click.option('--output', default=None, help="the path to write to")
def main(path, output):
    import cProfile, pstats
    with cProfile.Profile() as pr:
        file = FileIO(path, output)
        # --snip--

        file.save()
    stats = pstats.Stats(pr)
    stats.strip_dirs()
    stats.sort_stats(pstats.SortKey.CUMULATIVE)
    stats.print_stats(10)
```

```
if __name__ == "__main__":
    main()
```

Listing 20-46: src/textproof/__main__.py:1e

Executing that will *finally* give me some useful output:

```
7146 function calls (7110 primitive calls) in 3.521 seconds

Ordered by: cumulative time
List reduced from 652 to 10 due to restriction <10>

ncalls  tottime  percall  cumtime  percall filename:lineno(function)
     1    0.000    0.000    2.693    2.693 checked_text.py:15(fix_typos)
     9    0.000    0.000    2.693    0.299 typo.py:30(select_fix)
     9    0.000    0.000    2.692    0.299 typo.py:15(get_choice)
     9    2.691    0.299    2.691    0.299 {built-in method builtins.input}
     1    0.000    0.000    0.827    0.827 checked_text.py:6(__init__)
     1    0.000    0.000    0.827    0.827 api.py:4(api_query)
     1    0.000    0.000    0.825    0.825 api.py:107(post)
     1    0.000    0.000    0.825    0.825 api.py:16(request)
     1    0.000    0.000    0.824    0.824 sessions.py:463(request)
     1    0.000    0.000    0.820    0.820 sessions.py:614(send)
```

The columns here are the number of calls (ncalls), the total time spent in the function itself (tottime), the average time spent in the function (percall), the total time spent in the function and anything it calls (cumtime), and the average thereof (percall). The most insightful of these is cumtime, which I sorted on.

I might have expected the API call to take the longest, but in fact, it's sixth on this list, with a cumulative runtime of 0.827 seconds. The method fix_typos() from *checked_text.py* is the winner, at 2.693 seconds, but on closer examination, I can see that virtually all this time was spent in the input() function. The program's runtime is IO-bound, but since it feels perfectly responsive, it needs no further attention.

I could increase the number of results displayed and continue to work my way through it, looking for possible bottlenecks, but you get the idea.

You can also invoke cProfile or profile from the command line. By itself, this does not provide a means of showing only a segment of results, which makes seeing the results decidedly non-trivial. Instead, you can view the results graphically with the tool *SnakeViz*, installable from pip as snakeviz. Then, I use it like this:

```
venv/bin/python3 -m cProfile ❶ -o profile_out venv/bin/textproof fixme.txt --output fixmeout.
txt
venv/bin/snakeviz profile_out
```

I invoke cProfile directly on the command line, specifying that the profiling results will be saved in the file *profile_out* ❶. Then, I open *profile_out* with snakeviz, which will open an interactive graph of the results in your default web browser.

You can learn more about SnakeViz at *https://jiffyclub.github.io/snakeviz/*. There's quite a lot more to profiling on Python. The official documentation does an excellent job of demonstrating how to perform effective profiling and the various considerations that go into it: *https://docs.python.org/3/library/profile.html*.

tracemalloc

If cProfile or profile gives you a picture of time complexity in your code, what about space complexity? If you're using CPython, you can use *tracemalloc* to examine how memory is allocated on the system and see what parts of your code are using the most memory.

Bearing in mind the logistical issues I mentioned with cProfile, the documentation is more than sufficient to demonstrate how this works: *https://docs.python.org/3/library/tracemalloc.html*.

Wrapping Up

Testing is a critical component of any production-grade project. The Python ecosystem offers many tools for testing code, as well as tools for checking code coverage and automating testing in different environments. In practice, it takes a bit of work to get all these components to work together seamlessly, although using an src-based project structure helps. Once your test system is working smoothly, it becomes easier to continually verify that each change you make to the code is a step in the right direction.

The project structure I've demonstrated also works well with *continuous integration* tools, like GitHub Actions, Travis CI, CircleCI, and Jenkins, which automatically run tests on repository commits or pull requests.

In addition to this, you can gain insights on the performance of your code by benchmarking with timeit, profiling with cProfile or profile, and checking memory allocation with tracemalloc.

I've also got some incredible news for you: if you've been following me since Chapter 1, you've now seen, learned, and practiced nearly every essential component of the core language, a good chunk of the standard library, and much of the Python ecosystem as a whole. We now have just one more stop to go on our tour.

21

THE PARTING OF THE WAYS

You've reached an important milestone on your programming journey: you now know Python! You've become familiar with the syntax and patterns, and you've learned how to structure, design, and ship production-quality software in the Python language. Equipped with this foundational knowledge, you'll be able to understand the official documentation and even participate in the pedantic discussions so common among Python developers.

However, there is a profound difference between knowing a language and mastering it. Only by writing real-world code can you truly *think* in Python. If you've been working on an actual project while reading this book, you may already have reached this milestone. Otherwise, your next step is quite simple and yet incredibly complicated: go build something!

"Yes, but what?" you might say. "I know how Python works now, but what can I really make with it?"

You're at a crossroads. From here, you can go in many directions. In this chapter, I'll point out several of the best-traveled roads and suggest further resources for the next leg of your journey, whatever that may be. Finally, I'll show you how to get plugged into the Python community as a whole.

About the Future

Python is under perpetual development. Each version brings new features, and each new feature typically starts life as a PEP, which can stem from conversations anywhere in the community. From there, the PEP may be debated, adjusted, reworked, and ultimately either accepted or rejected.

Due to the nature of software development, not all changes to the language are smooth. When a package is under consideration for addition to the standard library, it may be marked as a *provisional package* or *provisional API*, meaning it may change at any time, without regard to backward compatibility. The documentation will warn you of provisional packages, according to the rules outlined in PEP 411.

On occasion, when a feature is slated to be released in a later version of Python but the core developers want to allow users of the language to test a preview version in live code in advance, the feature will be added to a special module called __future__. The upcoming feature can be imported from that module and used as if it had already been made part of the language. As of the date of this writing, there's only one upcoming feature in __future__: postponed evaluation of annotations (PEP 563), which is a feature of Python 3.10.

If you want an insider's view of possible new features and the future of the language, sign up for the official forums at *https://discuss.python.org/* and subscribe to the python-dev mailing list at *https://mail.python.org/mailman3/lists/python-dev.python.org/*.

Where Do You Go from Here?

Python's versatility is a key reason it remains one of the most popular programming languages. Yet it's essential to remember: you cannot learn everything, nor should you attempt it! Programming is not like riding a bike. Knowledge, once gained, must be regularly practiced or it will be lost.

The better route is to find a problem that you care about solving and build a solution for it. The purpose of this section is to give you a sampling of the sorts of problems Python is commonly used to solve.

The future is in your hands. What will you build?

Application Development in Python

I personally enjoy building GUI-based user applications in Python. Whether you're developing for the desktop or mobile, Python is a great language for application development because of its intuitive syntax and wide selection of frameworks.

Even in this internet age, desktop and mobile applications still have a firm place in the market. Services like Spotify and Dropbox provide client applications (both written in Python!) with additional device integration. Desktop applications are still reliable workhorses in many fields and work-flows, from graphics design to data visualization. They are also in a position to fully utilize system resources and hardware in ways that may be more challenging in the browser.

There are a number of GUI frameworks available for Python, including *Tkinter*, the Python binding for the Tk framework. It's one of the easiest GUI frameworks to pick up, but its default graphics style is noticeably outdated. Tkinter is included in the Python standard library, although some Linux distributions distribute it as a separate package.

GOTCHA ALERT If you want to use Tkinter on macOS 10.6 through at least 10.14, you'll need to install a newer version of Python than the one that ships with the operating system. There are serious bugs in the version of Tkinter that ships with the Apple-provided Python distribution.

One of the most prominent GUI frameworks is Qt (officially pronounced "cute"), which provides everything you need to build clean, modern applications across a spectacular array of environments and devices. There are two Python bindings for the Qt framework: *PySide2* (Qt 5) and *PySide6* (Qt 6), the official bindings maintained by The Qt Company; and *PyQt5* or *PyQt6*, which are maintained by Riverbank Computing.

Another popular GUI framework is *GTK*, a mature and robust framework that is particularly prominent on Linux. *PyGObject* is the Python binding for GTK3 and GTK4.

Kivy is a GUI toolkit that works across major desktop and mobile operating systems. It's especially geared toward touch screen devices (although it supports keyboard and mouse) and is particularly well-suited for game development. As of this writing, it's particularly difficult (and not fully supported) to package a Kivy application for Linux. Some improvements made in Kivy 2.0 are promising on this front, but I still strongly recommend that you figure out your packaging *before* you start building.

There are quite a few more GUI frameworks, such as *wxPython* and *Flexx*, but there are far too many to enumerate here. You can find a fairly up-to-date list here: *https://wiki.python.org/moin/GuiProgramming*.

If you don't know where to start with GUI applications, I recommend you start with Qt. If you prefer a guided approach, check out *Create GUI*

Applications with Python & Qt5 by Martin Fitzpatrick. He has editions of the book for both PySide2 and PyQt5. Visit his website at *https://www.learnpyqt .com/* for more information, plus tutorials and examples.

Game Development in Python

Although it's not as robust as many game engines, Python lends itself to fairly streamlined game development. Prominent games like *Civilization IV, EVE Online, Frets on Fire*, and *Toontown Online* were all built with Python. Depending on the game, you may be able to get by with one of the general-purpose GUI frameworks, but for best results, you'll often want to pick up a dedicated game development library.

PyGame is one of the oldest and most frequently cited Python game development libraries. It's primarily a wrapper around the *Simple DirectMedia Layer (SDL2)*, which provides cross-platform access to the hardware for working with graphics, sound, and devices. It also interfaces with other graphics APIs, like *OpenGL, Direct3D*, and *Vulkan*.

There are more options beyond PyGame, depending on the sort of game you want to build. *Wasabi2D* and *pyglet* both work with OpenGL, which is the underpinning of most major game engines. *Panda3D* and *Ogre* are two popular options for creating real-time 3D games. There are many other libraries besides.

Whichever game development framework you want to use, its documentation is the best place to start. Alternatively, if you'd prefer a shallow learning curve with plenty of guided examples, check out Al Sweigart's *Invent Your Own Computer Games with Python,* 4th Edition (No Starch Press, 2016), which will get you acclimated to PyGame and, more importantly, the different concepts associated with game development.

Web Development in Python

Python excels as a server-side language, especially for rapidly developing web applications and APIs. There are three libraries in the spotlight at present for this: *Django, Flask*, and *FastAPI*.

Django is the batteries-included option. It employs a Model View Template (MVT) architecture, and it includes database integration, an object-relational mapper (ORM), and just about everything you could need to build a web application or API in Python. Django is used by BitBucket, Instagram, the Public Broadcasting Service (PBS), and the *Washington Times*, among others. To get started with Django, visit their website at *https://www .djangoproject.com/*. Django Girls also has a particularly excellent tutorial at *https://tutorial.djangogirls.org/*.

Flask, by contrast, is the minimalist option. It's lightweight, providing the bare-minimum framework and leaving it to the developer to choose what tools and components to use. The Flask community provides a wide variety of extensions for adding functionality on par with Django, all of which are selected and installed separately. Flask emphasizes leaving as much control in the hands of the developer as possible. Websites like Pinterest and LinkedIn are built in Flask. If you want to learn Flask, their documentation will guide you through the entire process of setting up, getting started, and working with every part of the framework: *https://flask.palletsprojects.com/*.

FastAPI is a framework aimed at web API design specifically. It is designed for performance and stability, and it is fully compliant with the OpenAPI (Swagger) and JSON Schema. See the documentation at *https://fastapi.tiangolo.com/*.

Client-Side Python

You may wonder if it is possible to run Python in the browser, client-side. At present, there are a few implementations of Python attempting exactly that. Here are just a few.

Brython, which is short for *Browser Python*, is the more mature of the two options. It works by transpiling Python to JavaScript. Brython is designed to work with the W3C Document Object Model (DOM). More information and full documentation are available at *https://www.brython.info/* and on the project's GitHub at *https://github.com/brython-dev/brython*.

Skulpt is a newer solution; it's intended to be a complete implementation of the Python language in JavaScript, as opposed to a transpiler. As of this writing, Skulpt is still missing a lot of core language features. More information is at *https://skulpt.org/*.

Pyodide is a third option. It's a port of CPython to WebAssembly and Emscripten, and has support for many C extensions. More information and documentation can be found at *https://pyodide.org/en/stable/*.

Data Science in Python

Python is one of the leading languages in the field of *data science*, which focuses on gaining insights and extracting information by aggregating and analyzing data. Data science is considered applied statistics and related to but distinct from computer science. The task of distilling information out of a data set is sometimes referred to as *data mining*. The term *big data* refers to work with particularly large data sets.

There is a vast ecosystem geared especially toward data science, although many of these tools are also useful in software development.

The Data Science Environment

Jupyter Notebook is perhaps the single most important tool in the data science ecosystem. It is a complete interactive-development environment and is particularly well-suited to data science and scientific computing, as it combines executable Python code with Markdown-formatted text, mathematics equations, live charts and graphs, and other rich media. A *notebook document* is a single Jupyter Notebook file, ending in the file extension *.ipynb* (for IPython Notebook, the former name of Jupyter Notebook). In addition to supporting Python, Jupyter works with the other two most popular languages in data science, namely *Julia* and *R*. You can learn more about Jupyter Notebook and its related projects at *https://jupyter.org/*.

Anaconda is a distinct Python distribution geared specifically toward data science and scientific computing. It ships with over 250 of the most common data science libraries and tools preinstalled, including Jupyter Notebook. It also comes with its own integrated development environment, *Anaconda Navigator*, and a dedicated package manager, *conda*. In addition to all this, Anaconda offers a data science–oriented cloud service with both free and paid plans. More information can be found at *https://anaconda.org/*.

Data Science Packages

There are hundreds of packages for data science in Python, but there are a handful of particularly notable ones, many of which consistently lead the pack:

Pandas is considered essential for processing data. It supplies *dataframes*, which allow you to select, merge, reshape, and process data from databases, spreadsheets, tables, CSV files, and more, similar to the R language. Learn more at *https://pandas.pydata.org/*.

NumPy is the leading package for handling numeric computing, everything from mathematics to statistical analysis, and even performing advanced processing of lists and arrays. Learn more at *https://numpy.org/about/*.

SciPy (the library) expands on NumPy, offering additional numeric routines for scientific computing, including linear algebra and numerical optimization. It is part of the *SciPy ecosystem*, along with NumPy, pandas, and several other tenants of this list. Learn more at *https://scipy.org/*.

Matplotlib is one of the most popular libraries for generating plots, charts, graphs, and other data visualizations. Learn more at *https://matplotlib.org/*.

Seaborn expands on Matplotlib and is integrated with pandas, to provide more advanced data visualization tools (with all the pretty colors!) Learn more at *https://seaborn.pydata.org/*.

Bokeh is another popular visualization library, independent of Matplotlib, that allows you to create interactive data visualizations that can be embedded in web pages and Jupyter notebooks. Learn more at *https://bokeh.org/*.

Dask is a Python parallelism library that is built specifically for working with major packages in data science and related fields. It allows you to speed up the execution time, especially when working with large data sets or CPU-intensive analysis. Learn more at *https://dask.org/*.

Kedro is relatively new to the party, but it fulfills an important role in data science: the need for a framework to keep data pipelines scalable, easily maintainable, and production ready. Learn more at *https://kedro.readthedocs.io/*.

There are plenty of subtopics in the realm of data science, including *geographic information systems (GIS)* and the many branches of *scientific computing*. These fields often have their own common libraries and tools.

Also worth a mention is *Numba*, a just-in-time (JIT) compiler for Python and NumPy, which allows you to compile specific, selected parts of your Python program to machine code.

One way to learn more about the Anaconda ecosystem, including many of the libraries listed here, is to read *Doing Science with Python* by Lee Vaughan (No Starch Press, 2022).

Machine Learning in Python

Another popular topic in Python is *machine learning*, which is at the heart of artificial intelligence. Machine learning is the process by which an algorithm can be made to improve automatically over time, based on data and feedback provided to it. This is a process known as *training*. For example, your smartphone uses machine learning to improve its autocompletion suggestions while you type. The more you use your smartphone, the better that algorithm gets at suggesting the word you're typing.

Machine learning works using *neural networks*, which are data structures that replicate the structure and behavior of biological neural networks, such as the brain you are using right now. When you layer neural networks together, you get into the topic of *deep learning*.

The structure of a neural network isn't particularly difficult to comprehend, but there is a fair bit of advanced mathematics involved, including linear algebra, multivariate calculus, and probability. If you're interested in machine learning, invest some time in understanding this math well. Don't worry about doing the math on paper; focus on mastering the concepts and let the computer do the number crunching for you.

Machine learning is often closely associated with data science. (The data used to train the neural network has to come from somewhere!) Therefore, you'll find many of the same packages used across both specialties.

Here are the five most popular machine learning packages:

TensorFlow is a C++ and Python symbolic math library behind some of today's larger machine learning projects, including artificial intelligence work at Google, where it got its start. It's harder to learn than many of the other options, but it's widely used, especially due to its speed. Learn more at *https://www.tensorflow.org/*.

Keras is a deep-learning API that expands on TensorFlow, and it is generally considered easier to use besides. If you're looking for a place to start, this is an excellent option. Learn more at *https://keras.io/*.

Scikit-learn is a simpler machine learning library built atop NumPy. It is particularly useful for predictive data analysis and other data science applications. Learn more at *https://scikit-learn.org/*.

PyTorch is based on Facebook's Torch framework. It independently brings the same functionality you'd get out of NumPy, SciPy, and Scikit-learn. PyTorch offers acceleration via the GPU, and it can work with deep neural networks. Learn more at *https://pytorch.org/*.

Aesera is a Python-only machine learning library that tightly integrates with NumPy and focuses primarily on some of the mathematics involved.

Although it can be used by itself, it's most often employed alongside other options, like Keras. Aesera is a continuation of the *Theano* library. Learn more at *https://aesara.readthedocs.io/en/latest/*.

Within the arena of machine learning are a number of other specialties, including natural language processing and computer vision. Once you understand the basics of machine learning, you can branch out into whatever subtopics you find interesting.

If you're interested in this field, two books to get you started are *Deep Learning: A Visual Approach* by Andrew Glassner (No Starch Press, 2021) and *Practical Deep Learning* by Ronald T. Kneusel (No Starch Press, 2021). If you prefer to learn as you go, start with Keras or Scikit-learn.

Security

Python is increasingly popular in the field of *information security*, or *infosec*, which focuses on ensuring data, software, and computer systems are safe and secure.

A word of caution is prudent here. The techniques used to find flaws in security that need to be shored up are the same techniques used to exploit those flaws. The entire field of infosec operates on a fine legal and ethical line, which separates ethical ("white hat") hackers from criminal ("black hat") hackers. Both sides know how to construct and deploy malware, reverse engineer software, and hack into systems: the difference is that the ethical hackers use these techniques to find and report or close security holes before criminal hackers can exploit them. For example, the infamous Heartbleed and Spectre bugs were discovered and reported by ethical hackers before they could be exploited.

Two of the best books about Python and infosec are *Black Hat Python*, 2nd Edition, by Justin Seitz and Tim Arnold (No Starch Press, 2021) and *Gray Hat Python*, also by Justin Seitz (No Starch Press, 2009). (The titles are deliberately ironic.) If you're interested in this field, those books provide the best place to start.

But once again, let me remind you: it is your responsibility to use your powers for good. Using computers to commit crimes or cause trouble is *never* okay, and doing so will earn you the derision of the entire Python community. Keep your hacking ethical.

Embedded Development in Python

If maker culture is more your speed, you'll be pleased to know that Python is currently the fastest-growing language in *embedded development*, wherein code is shipped directly on the hardware it controls. This means you can use Python for robotics, Internet-of-Things devices, and many other hardware projects.

Python works with Raspberry Pi, which comes with the *Thonny* Python IDE preinstalled. More information can be found at *https://www.raspberrypi .com/documentation/computers/os.html*.

Python can be used to program the *Arduino* microcontroller via *pyserial*: *https://pythonhosted.org/pyserial/*.

MicroPython is a separate implementation of Python that is geared specifically toward embedded development. It works best with the *pyboard* microcontroller. You can learn more about MicroPython and pyboard at *https://micropython.org/*.

CircuitPython is another Python implementation. It is based on MicroPython but geared primarily toward *Adafruit* microcontrollers. It can also be used on a number of Raspberry Pi and Ardunio microcontrollers, as well as hardware from many other brands. Device-specific downloads and links to documentation, tutorials, and guides can be found at *https://circuitpython.org/*.

Scripting

With all these vast and impressive uses of Python, it's easy to forget that one of the reasons this language exists is to facilitate automation and scripting. Countless libraries exist to allow Python to interact with all sorts of software, operating systems, and hardware. If you have a repetitive task that needs a clean solution, there's a good chance that Python can help with that.

Two excellent books for learning how to automate with Python are *Real-World Python* by Lee Vaughan (No Starch Press, 2020) and *Automate the Boring Stuff with Python*, 2nd Edition, by Al Sweigart (No Starch Press, 2019).

Python Flavors

As you've probably gathered, the default implementation of Python, known formally as *CPython*, isn't the only implementation out there. Quite a few others exist, most of them with special uses.

I have to start by mentioning a highly specialized implementation, *RPython*, which is geared toward building interpreted languages. It's a restricted subset of the Python language with a *just-in-time (JIT) compiler*, meaning the language is built to machine code immediately before execution, instead of being interpreted during execution by an interpreter. RPython is extensively documented at *https://rpython.readthedocs.io/*.

PyPy is another implementation, and it is notable for being quite a bit faster than CPython. It is implemented on RPython, instead of C. It owes its speed to the fact that it is JIT compiled, instead of interpreted, allowing it to reach performance comparable to C++ or Java. PyPy is always several versions behind CPython—as of this writing, it is up to Python 3.6—but for projects where performance matters, this is an acceptable compromise. Additionally, because PyPy does not rely on C, it typically doesn't work with binary extensions, except for some built to that purpose in CFFI.

Stackless Python is another peculiar implementation of Python that offers some unique tools for improved concurrency and code structure. Stackless is its own beast in many ways, and it must be learned as such. The best place to start is with its wiki, which has links to further reading and resources: *https://github.com/stackless-dev/stackless/wiki*.

Earlier, I mentioned *Brython* (*https://www.brython.info/*), *Skulpt* (*https://skulpt.org/*), and *Pyodide* (*https://pyodide.org/en/stable/*), which are in-browser implementations of Python geared toward web development. I also mentioned *MicroPython* (*https://micropython.org/*) and *CircuitPython* (*https://circuitpython.org/*), which are implementations for embedded development.

Besides these, there are a handful of implementations of the Python interpreter built in different languages. The four most notable of these are RustPython, implemented in Rust; IronPython and *Python.NET*, both of which integrate tightly with the .NET framework; and *Jython*, which is written in Java for integration with the *Java Virtual Machine (JVM)*. As of this writing, RustPython supports up to Python 3.9, and Python.NET supports up to Python 3.8, while IronPython is only on Python 3.4, and Jython is still in line with Python 2.7. You can learn more about RustPython at *https://rustpython.github.io/*, IronPython at *https://ironpython.net/*, Python.NET at *https://pythonnet.github.io/*, and Jython at *https://www.jython.org/*.

No matter what implementation you use, remember that the official implementation, CPython, serves as the baseline for all of them. Even if you plan to spend most of your time in another implementation, it's important to know how to use CPython well.

Developing for Python

The Python ecosystem itself is maintained by thousands of developers around the world. Some write libraries to answer specific needs, while others extend and improve the Python language in all its different implementations.

If you'd like to become involved in the development of Python, it would be helpful for you to have some experience or interest in other branches of development, so you'll understand what needs exist and how to best address them. Very few developers set out to work on Python; rather, they drift into it after recognizing an area of need in their own work. Even so, when you're able to contribute to the Python ecosystem, it's a great feeling indeed.

Developing Python Packages and Tools

The techniques you've learned in this book have fully prepared you to build and ship production-quality packages, libraries, and development tools. Maybe you have some ideas already, or maybe you're still pondering what you could build.

In either case, I strongly recommend learning more about the existing tools and packages you use on a regular basis. A large majority of projects are maintained by a handful of volunteers, often thanklessly, and issues sometimes come in faster than the volunteers can resolve them. Before you set out to build a brand-new thing, consider if you could instead improve an existing solution. Contributing to open source projects is an incredible way to build your skills and make new professional connections. Your contributions don't even have to be massive. Whether you're performing code reviews on backlogged pull requests, fixing minor bugs, doing small "housekeeping" tasks, tidying up the documentation, or polishing the packaging, it all helps!

There are also a number of projects that are abandoned or otherwise unmaintained and are in need of a new maintainer to step up and take over.

When you adopt an abandoned project, you get the benefits of a working code base (for some definitions of "working") and an existing user base. Often, projects are abandoned because they need to be ported to Python 3. Also, working with legacy code can be a very rewarding experience.

Nearly all packages on the Python Package Index (PyPI) have links to the official website, source code, and issue tracker. Other packages list an email address for the present maintainer. When you find a package that you use regularly, you should seriously consider getting involved in its development and maintenance.

As for new projects, if you find yourself building a tool or library for solving a problem you're having in your development efforts, consider publishing it for the rest of the world to use!

Developing Python Extensions

Binary extension modules, often just called *extension modules* or *extensions*, add new functionality atop the CPython interpreter and allow you to integrate CPython with C and C++ code.

Wrapper modules expose C libraries to Python. PyGObject is an example of this, as it wraps the GTK C library and several others besides, and it makes them available to Python. Extensions can also wrap C++ and FORTRAN libraries, among others.

Another common use case for extensions is to provide low-level access to the operating system, hardware, or the CPython runtime.

Accelerator modules offer equivalent behavior to a pure Python module, but they are actually written in C. One particular advantage of accelerator modules is that they can be written to bypass the Global Interpreter Lock, since they run as compiled machine code. These modules should provide a pure Python fallback module for situations where the extension may not work.

There are quite a few ways to develop extensions. Traditionally, you can include the *Python.h* header file in your C code and build from there. Details and documentation about this can be found at *https://docs.python .org/3/extending/index.html*.

However, working directly with *Python.h* is no longer considered the best approach. Aside from this technique being quite clunky and error-prone, extensions built this way often have significant difficulty working with PyPy and other implementations of Python. Instead, there are a number of third-party tools for building extensions, which are far simpler and more obvious in their usage.

The *C Foreign Function Interface* (*CFFI*) is one of the more popular options. Unlike some other tools, CFFI doesn't require you to learn an additional specialty language. Instead, it uses purely C and Python. It works with both CPython and PyPy. You can learn more about CFFI from its extensive official documentation: *https://cffi.readthedocs.io/*.

CFFI does not work with C++, so if you need C++ and Python interoperability, check out *cppyy*. Official documentation lives at *https://cppyy .readthedocs.io/*.

Cython is a separate programming language that is a superset of Python and provides direct access to C and C++. You compile your Cython code up front, as you would with C. More information and official documentation can be found at *https://cython.org/*.

Simplified Wrapper and Interface Generator (SWIG) is a tool for interoperability between over a dozen programming languages, including Python, C, C++, Java, C#, Perl, JavaScript, and Ruby. It can be used to create Python binary extensions. Information, documentation, and tutorials can be found on its official website at *http://www.swig.org/*.

Development of Python binary extensions is a particularly deep topic, especially as it involves the C language. The Python Packaging Authority has an excellent guide that explores binary extension development, particularly from a packaging standpoint: *https://packaging.python.org/guides/packaging-binary-extensions/*.

Contributing to Python

Python is an open source project with a rich community and a well-maintained development pipeline. If you're passionate about Python, the language itself always welcomes new contributors! Your contributions could include fixing bugs, testing patches, implementing new features, and updating documentation. Even if you don't have incredible C-coding skills, there's plenty for you to do. If you want to get started contributing to Python, read through the official Python Developer's Guide at *https://devguide.python.org/*.

If Java or .NET is more your speed, or if you're fascinated with RPython, you can instead contribute to Jython, RustPython, Python.NET, IronPython, or PyPy. These are all considered important implementations in the Python ecosystem, and there's always more to do.

Changing the Language

Because Python is built by the community, you can propose changes to the Python language or its standard library. This will involve a considerable amount of work on your part, along with quite a bit of discussion, diplomacy, debate, and testing. Somewhere along the way, you will need to create a PEP outlining your proposed changes and all the discussion that's gone into it so far.

Don't embark on this process lightly! Even if your idea seems obvious to you, you are likely underestimating the depth or merit of other viewpoints. We all want Python to be the best it can be, and that means factoring in the wildly divergent needs and perspectives of our diverse user base. That's why proposing a PEP is a significant time investment.

If you're certain you're up for the challenge, see the official guides: *https://devguide.python.org/langchanges/* for language changes and *https://devguide.python.org/stdlibchanges/* for standard library changes.

Becoming a Core Developer

Once you've been making quality contributions to CPython for some time, you can apply to become a *core developer*, which brings with it additional authority and responsibility. Core developers are involved in leading Python development, and their opinions regarding language direction and proposed changes bear much weight.

If you want to become a Python core developer, start by contributing *patches*, which consist of code fixing a bug or implementing an approved feature, to CPython. Keep at this until a core developer offers you commit privileges. They'll keep an eye on your work after that and help mentor you in the Python development process. Eventually, if you do this well, you may be offered an official opportunity to become a core developer.

The entire process and all the responsibilities and steps involved are outlined in the guide at *https://devguide.python.org/coredev/*, which itself is based on the Python Language Governance policies outlined in PEP 13.

Getting Involved with Python

Wherever you go from here, I strongly recommend getting involved in the Python community! You will learn a lot from your fellow Python developers, and you can greatly benefit from helping and mentoring others. There are a number of official and unofficial communities around the internet, including the following:

- The DEV Community: *https://dev.to/t/python*
- Discord: *https://pythondiscord.com/*
- Forums (Official): *https://www.python.org/community/forums/*
- Libera.Chat IRC (Official): *https://www.python.org/community/irc/*
- Mailing Lists/Newsgroups (Official): *https://www.python.org/community/lists/*
- Reddit: *https://www.reddit.com/r/learnpython/*
- Slack: *https://pyslackers.com/web*

Of the ones on this list, my personal favorites are DEV, where this book got its start, and Libera.Chat IRC, where I met most of my technical editors.

Asking Questions

The primary reason developers first join a community is to ask questions. This can feel intimidating at first, no matter what platform you're on! Here are a few principles for asking questions and getting help in the Python community. These guidelines are true across most programming communities, but especially in Python!

First, do some research and experimentation yourself. *Read the documentation.* Try out some possible solutions and take note of what doesn't work. We in the Python community are happy to help you, but we want to see you bring your own efforts to the table, too.

Second, be specific. The more information you can provide, the better we can help you. When possible, give us code we can inspect and run, the exact text of error messages or wrong output, details about your environment (operating system, Python version, and library versions), and insight into the outcomes of your own experimentation. When providing all this information, be careful to follow community rules regarding large pastes. Many platforms, including Libera.Chat IRC, ask that you use a paste-sharing tool like *bpaste.net*, instead of dumping pastes into chat, where they will clog up the backlog. Never paste multiple lines of code or output directly into chat!

Third, be prepared for unexpected threads of feedback. If a bug is precipitating from poor design, incorrect assumptions, or nonidiomatic practice, we'd much rather help you fix the design than the bug. We aren't interested in *working* code, so much as *idiomatic* code. You will likely be asked things like "What is your goal, why are you doing it this way, and is there a reason you aren't doing X?" Stay calm and work with us.

GOTCHA ALERT Expect us to challenge your implementation and goals! We are not making comments about you or your skills, only about your your code. Getting combative is the surest way to burn bridges and minimize your chances of getting help, now or later. We're challenging you because we believe you to be smart and capable enough to handle it; we expect to be treated the same by our peers.

Fourth, be polite and patient. All the online communities I've mentioned are staffed by volunteers who give freely of their time and effort to help others. It may take time to get an answer. Just ask your question outright in the public space—never "ask to ask" or inquire after an expert in such and such, as it only wastes people's time—and then wait for someone to respond. In the case of IRC, *stay logged in* or you'll miss our response! In any chat-based medium, if your message gets completely buried in backlog (I'm talking three or more desktop screen pages), calmly repost it. On forum-like platforms, resist the temptation to "bump" the thread.

When you get a response, read it thoroughly and answer thoughtfully. We will probably have many more questions for you as we try to home in on the solution.

Answering Questions

Having made it through *Dead Simple Python*, you now know quite a lot about Python! As a result, you will encounter questions from other community members that you may be able to answer. This is a great way to give back to the community and build relationships with other developers. You'll learn quite a bit in the process, too. Even so, when you're getting started, it can feel intimidating. Here are a few tips.

First, don't be afraid of making mistakes. If you feel like you can answer a question, give it your best shot. This is a benefit of answering questions in the community: if you get something wrong, someone else will often be there to correct you. Python developers love pedantic correctness! (Seriously; you should see some comments I've gotten from my technical editors.) In the worst-case scenario, you'll walk away from the encounter having learned something. No one worthwhile will think less of you for it, I promise.

Second, more than half of the process of answering a question is *asking more questions*. Like The Zen of Python says, "In the face of ambiguity, refuse the temptation to guess." Ultimately, your goal should be to guide the asker toward the most Pythonic solution to the problem they're trying to solve.

Third, it's important to be kind. The only things up for critique are *code* and *practice*, never people. Resist the temptation to deploy put-downs or shutdowns, no matter how clever or "funny" they may be.

On that note, be careful of issuing "read the documentation" admonishments. Documentation can be infamously obtuse and difficult to parse, especially for a beginner. It's okay to share a link to the relevant page or section, or to any other helpful resource, but you should *never* shame anyone for not having previously read or understood the documentation or other material. The same goes for web search results—it can sometimes take real skill to determine which keywords are the best or which results are relevant. In any case, be prepared in case they say that the link doesn't solve their problem; you may need to ask more questions to better understand what issue they're stuck on.

User Groups

Online communities are excellent resources, but nothing beats in-person networking and collaboration! There are over 1,600 Python user groups worldwide, providing opportunities for developers of all backgrounds and skill levels to exchange knowledge, especially through events like social meetings, speaking presentations, hack sessions, and even local conferences.

A complete list of Python user groups is maintained on the official Python wiki: *https://wiki.python.org/moin/LocalUserGroups*. Consider connecting with one in your area. If you don't have a nearby user group, you may consider starting one yourself! The wiki has a guide for that, too: *https://wiki.python.org/moin/StartingYourUsersGroup*.

PyLadies

Of particular note is *PyLadies*, a group organized by the Python Software Foundation, which focuses on supporting and mentoring female developers in the Python community.

PyLadies organizes meetups and other events, and it provides resources. In addition to the international online community, there are a number of local PyLadies groups all over the world. If there isn't one near you, perhaps you could organize one. More information about PyLadies is available at *https://pyladies.com/*. The official list of PyLadies groups is maintained here: *https://pyladies.com/locations/*.

Conferences

Attending conferences is an incredible way to learn and grow as a developer, while connecting with the larger Python community. There are a number of fantastic conferences in the Python world, including PyCon US (the official conference), Pyjamas, SciPy, Python Pizza, and PyData. There are also versions of PyCon in many countries.

The first thing that comes to mind when you think of a conference is probably all the lectures. Talks are certainly among the highlights, especially keynote presentations from important people in the Python community, but they're not the only thing going on. *Workshops* present opportunities to get hands-on with a new topic. *Lightning talk* sessions are a lot of fun, too: they let anyone present a 5- or 10-minute talk, sometimes improvised right on the spot. Some presentations are amazingly insightful, and others are downright hilarious. Many conferences also have *sprints*, collaborative coding sessions (think "hackathon") where attendees can freely join teams to build or improve code.

While attending a conference can be a lot of fun, getting involved can be even more exciting! If you want to present a talk at a conference, be on the lookout for the *Call for Proposals (CFP)*, when you can submit a proposal for a talk or workshop. If you're brand-new to speaking, you may consider presenting to your local Python User Group or giving a lightning talk. You could also submit a project for a sprint, which can be an excellent way to get new contributors and users while improving your code.

Most conferences rely pretty heavily on volunteers, so consider contacting any conference you're thinking about attending, and then see how you can help out. You'll get to meet a lot of great people that way, and volunteering is really fun.

If you want to attend a conference but can't afford to go, you can check if there are scholarships or other financial aid available, especially if you're a volunteer. If you're employed as a programmer, your employer may also be willing to help with some of your conference expenses. After all, when you get smarter, they benefit!

A list of Python conferences is maintained on the Python wiki: *https://www.python.org/community/workshops/.*

Joining the Python Software Foundation

The *Python Software Foundation (PSF)* is the nonprofit organization that officially manages the Python language. They're responsible for all the major decisions, and they help to grow the community worldwide.

The Python Software Foundation is an open-membership organization, meaning anyone can join for free. Basic members need only sign up and agree to the PSF Code of Conduct, which is the set of guidelines that the entire Python community operates on. Members are subscribed to the Python Software Foundation newsletter.

There are three special types of members, all of whom get to vote in the PSF Board of Directors elections. *Supporting members* donate to the PSF annually. *Managing members* volunteer at least five hours a month in the

Python community, including helping to organize events and user groups or volunteering on Python Software Foundation projects. *Contributing members* volunteer at least five hours a month on free, publicly available open source projects that advance the mission of the PSF. You can learn more about PSF membership at *https://www.python.org/psf/membership/*.

And the Road Goes Ever On . . .

This, dear reader, is where I leave you. The direction you take from here is up to you! I am certain there are many adventures ahead of you. I send you forward into the brave frontier beyond with three final pieces of advice. If you've been coding for a while, you may already know these things, but they are always worth hearing again.

First, *it is dangerous to go alone.* Shiny new solutions call to you from the shadows, tempting you to stray from time-tested development paths. Clever solutions lure you away as they steal time and sanity from your future self and your colleagues. Bugs lurk in the dark recesses of your code, waiting for midnight on a Friday to leap out at you with bared teeth and inexplicable log files. The comradeship of your fellow Python developers is the surest defense against these and many more dangers! There is safety in numbers. I could never have written *Dead Simple Python* without the all the support, insight, debate, and encouragement from the Python community. We need each other to thrive.

Second, *embrace the adventure of making mistakes!* You will always learn more from solving a bug, working through a difficult problem, or making a mistake, than you will ever learn from writing or reading the best code in the world. I love how my colleague Wilfrantz Dede puts it whenever he embarks on a new task: "I'm going to go write some bugs." Mistakes are an inevitable part of the learning process. Learn to expect them, embrace them, conquer them, and laugh at them! Share your coding mistakes with your colleagues. I promise you that most will think more of you for it, not less, and anyone who *would* look down on you is merely covering up their own egregious errors.

Third and finally, *you are a real programmer.* Never again question that! No matter how long you're in this industry, you will always have more to learn. There are even expert developers who have been programming for decades but still feel the call of knowledge not yet gained.

The journey is never really over. There is always one more crest of the hill, one more bend in the road, and one more vast plain stretching ahead! Embrace every step of the adventure. It never gets old.

A

SPECIAL ATTRIBUTES AND METHODS

This appendix is a categorized list of all the special attributes and methods in the Python language. If you're looking for a particular special method by name, see the index instead.

Complete documentation can be found at *https://docs.python.org/3/reference/datamodel.html*.

Special Methods

These methods are declared on a class to add support for various Python operators, built-in functions, and compound statements. These are all typically declared as instance methods, unless otherwise indicated.

Table A-1: Conversion and Coercion

Method	Typical purpose	Invocation
obj.__bool__(self)	Returns a boolean: True or False.	bool(obj) if obj: pass
obj.__int__(self)	Returns an integer.	int(obj)
obj.__trunc__(self)	Returns an integer by truncating the decimal part.	trunc(obj)
obj.__floor__(self)	Returns an integer by rounding down.	floor(obj)
obj.__ceil__(self)	Returns an integer by rounding up.	ceil(obj)
obj.__index__(self)	Returns an integer, converted losslessly (without omitting part of the data). *Indicates obj is the integer type.*	operator.index(obj)
obj.__float__(self)	Returns a floating-point number.	float(obj)
obj.__complex__(self)	Returns a complex number.	complex(obj)
obj.__round__(self, ndigits=None)	Returns a floating-point number, rounded to ndigits precision. Returns an integer by rounding if ndigits is None.	float(obj) float(obj, *ndigits*)
obj.__bytes__(self)	Returns a bytes object.	bytes(obj)
obj.__repr__(self)	Returns a canonical representation as a string.	repr(obj) f"{obj!r}"
obj.__str__(self)	Returns a string.	str(obj)
obj.__format__(self, format_spec="")	Returns a string, formatted according to format_spec.	format(obj, *format_spec*)

Table A-2: Capabilities and Traits

Method	Typical purpose	Invocation
obj.__index__(self)	Returns an integer, created losslessly. Indicates an object is an integer.	operator.index(obj)
obj.__call__(self)	Implementing makes obj callable.	obj()
obj.__iter__(self)	Returns an iterator corresponding to obj.	iter(obj)
obj.__next__(self)	Returns the next value, according to the iterator obj.	next(obj)
obj.__enter__(self)	Enters the runtime context related to the context manager obj.	with obj: pass
obj.__exit__(self)	Exits the runtime context related to the context manager obj.	with obj: pass

Method	Typical purpose	Invocation
obj.__len__(self)	Returns the length of obj, such as the number of items in a collection.	len(obj)
obj.__length_hint__ (self)	Returns the estimated length for obj as a non-negative integer. Optional.	operator. length_hint(obj)
obj.__getitem__(self, key)	Returns an item in obj at *key*. Ideally, it should be valid to pass a slice to *key*.	obj[*key*]
obj.__setitem__(self, key, value)	Sets the value in obj of *key* to *value*.	obj[*key*] = *value*
obj.__delitem__(self, key)	Deletes the value in obj of *key*.	del obj[*key*]
obj.__missing__(self)	Called by __getitem__() method of dict subclasses when *key* is not in the dictionary.	
obj.__reversed__(self)	Returns a new iterator object that iterates over objects in the container, in reverse order. Should only be provided if implementation is faster than using __len__() and __getitem__() to iterate in reverse.	reversed(obj)
obj.__contains__(self, item)	Checks if *item* is contained in obj, then returns a boolean.	*item* in obj
obj.__hash__(self)	Returns hash of obj.	hash(obj)
obj.__get__(self, instance)	Getter for a descriptor.	
obj.__set__(self, instance, value)	Setter for a descriptor.	
obj.__delete__(self, instance)	Deleter for a descriptor.	
obj.__set_name__(self, owner, name)	Initializer for a descriptor. Called when the owning class owner is created.	
obj.__await__(self)	Makes obj awaitable. Returns an iterator.	await obj
obj.__aiter__(self)	Returns an asynchronous iterator object.	async for i in obj: pass
obj.__anext__(self)	Returns an awaitable that yields the next value of the asynchronous iterator.	async for i in obj: pass
obj.__aenter__(self)	Same as __enter__() but returns an awaitable.	async with obj: pass
obj.__aexit__(self)	Same as __exit__() but returns an awaitable.	async with obj: pass

Table A-3: Comparison Operations

Method	Typical purpose	Invocation
obj.__lt__(self, other)	Returns True if self < other; or else, returns False.	self < other
obj.__le__(self, other)	Returns True if self <= other; or else, returns False.	self <= other
obj.__eq__(self, other)	Returns True if self == other; or else, returns False.	self == other
obj.__ne__(self, other)	Returns True if self != other; or else, returns False.	self != other
obj.__gt__(self, other)	Returns True if self > other; or else, returns False.	self > other
obj.__ge__(self, other)	Returns True if self >= other; or else, returns False.	self >= other

Table A-4: Arithmetic Operations

Method	Typical purpose	Invocation
obj.__add__(self, other)	Returns the sum of obj and *other* or concatenates obj and *other*.	obj + other operator.add(obj, other)
obj.__sub__(self, other)	Returns the difference of obj and *other*.	obj - other operator.sub(obj, other)
obj.__mul__(self, other)	Returns the product of obj and *other*.	obj * other operator.mul(obj, other)
obj.__matmul__(self, other)	Performs matrix multiplication of obj and *other*.	obj @ other operator.matmul(obj, other)
obj.__truediv__(self, other)	Performs true division of obj and *other*.	obj / other operator.truediv(obj, other)

obj.__floordiv__(self, other)	Performs floor division (integer division) of obj and *other*.	obj // other
		operator.floordiv(obj, other)

obj.__mod__(self, other)	Returns the remainder of division of obj and *other*.	obj % other operator.mod(obj, other)
obj.__divmod__(self, other)	Performs both floor division and modulo, then returns results in a tuple. Same as (obj // *other*, obj % *other*).	divmod(obj, other)
obj.__pow__(self, other, mod=None)	Raises obj to the power *other*. If a mod is provided, the result is the same as pow(obj, *other*) % *mod*, but calculated more efficiently.	obj ** other pow(obj, other) pow(obj, other, *mod*) operator.pow(obj, other)

Method	Typical purpose	Invocation
`obj.__neg__(self)`	Negation.	`-obj` `operator.neg(obj)`
`obj.__pos__(self)`	Ordinarily, just returns self.	`+obj` `operator.pos(obj, other)`
`obj.__abs__(self, other)`	Absolute value.	`abs(obj)` `operator.abs(obj, other)`
`obj.__radd__(self, other)`	Returns the sum of *other* and obj. Reflected operators are only called if *other* does not support the operation.	`other + obj` `operator.pos(other, obj)`
`obj.__rsub__(self, other)`	Returns the difference of *other* and obj. (Reflected)	`other - obj` `operator.sub(other, obj)`
`obj.__rmul__(self, other)`	Returns the product of *other* and obj. (Reflected)	`other * obj` `operator.mul(other, obj)`
`obj.__rmatmul__(self, other)`	Returns the result of matrix multiplication of *other* and obj. (Reflected)	`other @ obj` `operator.matmul(other, obj)`
`obj.__rtruediv__(self, other)`	Returns the quotient of true division of *other* and obj. (Reflected)	`other / obj` `operator.truediv(other, obj)`
`obj.__rfloordiv__(self, other)`	Returns the quotient of floor division (integer division) of *other* and obj. (Reflected)	`other // obj` `operator.floordiv(other, obj)`
`obj.__rmod__(self, other)`	Returns the remainder of division of *other* and obj. (Reflected)	`other % obj` `operator.mod(other, obj)`
`obj.__rdivmod__(self, other)`	Performs both floor division and modulo, then returns results in a tuple. Same as (*other* // obj, *other* % obj). (Reflected)	`divmod(other, obj)`

`obj.__rpow__(self, other, mod=None)`	Raises *other* to the power obj.
	If a mod is provided, the result is the same as pow(*other*, obj) % *mod*, but calculated more efficiently.
		`other ** obj`
		`pow(other, obj)`
		`pow(other, obj, mod)`
		`operator.pow(other, obj)`

`obj.__iadd__(self, other)`	Stores the sum of obj and *other* in obj.	`obj += other`
`obj.__isub__(self, other)`	Stores the difference of obj and *other* in obj.	`obj -= other`
`obj.__imul__(self, other)`	Stores the product of obj and *other* in obj.	`obj *= other`

(continued)

Table A-4: Arithmetic Operations *(continued)*

Method	Typical purpose	Invocation
obj.__imatmul__(self, other)	Stores the result of matrix multiplication of obj and *other* in obj.	obj @= other
obj.__itruediv__(self, other)	Stores the quotient of true division of obj and *other* in obj.	obj /= other
obj.__ifloordiv__(self, other)	Stores the quotient of floor division (integer division) of obj and *other* in obj.	obj //= other
obj.__imod__(self, other)	Stores the remainder of division of obj and *other* in obj.	obj %= other
obj.__ipow__(self, other)	Stores the result of obj, raised to the power *other* in obj.	obj **= other

Table A-5: Bitwise Operations

Method	Typical purpose	Invocation
obj.__invert__(self)	Returns the bitwise inversion of obj.	~obj operator.invert(obj)
obj.__and__(self, other)	Returns the bitwise AND of obj and *other*.	obj & other operator.and(obj, other)
obj.__or__(self, other)	Returns the bitwise OR of obj and *other*.	obj | other operator.or(obj, other)
obj.__xor__(self, other)	Returns the bitwise XOR of obj and *other*.	obj ^ other operator.xor(obj, other)
obj.__lshift__(self, other)	Returns the bitwise left shift of obj and *other*.	obj << other operator.lshift(obj, other)
obj.__rshift__(self, other)	Returns the bitwise right shift of obj and *other*.	obj >> other operator.rshift(obj, other)
obj.__rand__(self, other)	Returns the bitwise AND of *other* and obj. Reflected operators are only called if *other* does not support the operation.	other & obj operator.and(other, obj)
obj.__ror__(self, other)	Returns the bitwise OR of *other* and obj. (Reflected)	other | obj operator.or(other, obj)
obj.__rxor__(self, other)	Returns the bitwise XOR of *other* and obj. (Reflected)	other ^ obj operator.xor(other, obj)
obj.__rlshift__(self, other)	Returns the bitwise left shift of *other* and obj. (Reflected)	other <<= obj operator.lshift(other, obj)

Method	Typical purpose	Invocation
obj.__rrshift__(self, other)	Returns the bitwise right shift of *other* and obj. (Reflected)	other >> obj operator.rshift(other, obj)
obj.__iand__(self, other)	Stores the result of the bitwise AND of obj and *other* in obj.	obj &= other
obj.__ior__(self, other)	Stores the result of the bitwise OR of obj and *other* in obj.	obj |= other
obj.__ixor__(self, other)	Stores the result of the bitwise XOR of obj and *other* in obj.	obj ^= other
obj.__ilshift__(self, other)	Stores the result of the bitwise left shift of obj and *other* in obj.	obj <<= other
obj.__irshift__(self, other)	Stores the result of the bitwise right shift of obj and *other* in obj.	obj >>= other

Table A-6: Objects, Classes, and Metaclasses

Method	Typical purpose	Invocation
obj.__new__(cls, ...)	Returns a new instance of cls.	obj = cls()
obj.__init__(self, ...)	Initializer for the object obj.	obj = cls()
obj.__del__(self)	Finalizer for the object obj.	del obj # indirect only
obj.__import__(self, ...)	DO NOT IMPLEMENT!	
obj.__getattr__(self, name)	Returns an attribute *name* on obj.	obj.name
obj.__setattr__(self, name, value)	Assigns a value *value* to an attribute *name* on obj.	obj.name = value
obj.__delattr__(self, name)	Deletes an attribute *name* on obj.	del obj.name
obj.__dir__(self)	Returns a list of valid attributes on obj.	dir(obj)
@classmethod obj.__init_subclass__(cls)	Called when cls is subclassed. Returns nothing.	
cls.__instancecheck__(self, instance)	Returns True if instance is an instance of cls or an instance of one of its subclasses; or else, returns False.	isinstance(instance, cls)

(continued)

Table A-6: Objects, Classes, and Metaclasses *(continued)*

Method	Typical purpose	Invocation
cls.__subclasscheck__ (self, subclass)	Returns True if subclass is a subclass of cls or one of its subclasses; or else, returns False.	issubclass(instance, subclass)
@classmethod obj.__subclasshook__ (cls, subclass)	Returns True if subclass should be considered a subclass of cls; or else, returns False.	issubclass(instance, subclass)
@classmethod obj.__class_getitem__ (cls, key)	Returns an object that is the specialization of a generic class cls. Mainly used with generic types. See PEP 484 and PEP 560.	
meta.__new__(self, name, bases, namespace)	Returns a new class instantiated from the metaclass meta.	cls = meta()
@classmethod meta.__prepare__(cls, name, bases, ...)	Creates and returns the dictionary storing all the methods and class attributes for the class being created.	

Special Attributes

Some special attributes that are only interesting or useful to the language's internals are omitted here.

Table A-7: Special Attributes on Modules

Method	Typical purpose
__doc__	The docstring on the module. If no docstring is defined, this has the value None.
__name__	The name of the module.
__loader__	The loader that loaded the module. Used by the import system.
__package__	The package containing the module. If the module is a package, this is the same as __name__. Used by the import system.
__file__	The path to the module file. May be None in some cases. Used by the import system.
__path__	The path to the package. Only defined on packages. Used by the import system.
__cached__	The path to the compiled Python bytecode representation of the module.

Method	Typical purpose
__spec__	The module's corresponding ModuleSpec object. This is a technical detail used by the import system. The object contains much of the same data as the other special attributes on the module.
__builtins__	The module containing all of Python's built-in functions, objects, and attributes (everything you never have to import).

Table A-8: Special Attributes on Functions

Method	Typical purpose
func.__annotations__	A dictionary of type annotations for parameters. The key 'return' is associated with the type annotation for the return value.
func.__closure__	A read-only tuple of *cells*, special objects containing bindings to values in memory, for all closure variables.
func.__code__	A string representation of the function's compiled code. (If you want the string representation of the function's code instead, use inspect.getsource().)
func.__defaults__	A tuple containing default arguments. The value is simply None if there are no default arguments.
func.__dict__	A dictionary containing all function attributes.
func.__doc__	The docstring on the function. If no docstring is defined, this has the value None.
func.__globals__	A read-only reference to the dictionary of global variables.
func.__kwdefaults__	A dictionary of default arguments for keyword-only parameters.
func.__module__	The name of the module where the function was defined, or None if not applicable.
func.__name__	The name of the module, callable, object, or class.
func.__qualname__	The fully qualified name of the object.

Table A-9: Special Attributes on Instances (Objects)

Method	Typical purpose
obj.__class__	The instance's class.
obj.__dict__	The dictionary of instance attributes.
obj.__doc__	The instance's docstring.
obj.__module__	The name of the module where the instance was defined, or None if not applicable.

Table A-10: Special Attributes on Classes

Method	Typical purpose
cls.__bases__	The tuple of base classes for the class, in the order specified in the inheritance list when the class was defined.
cls.__dict__	The dictionary containing the class attributes and instance methods.
cls.__doc__	The docstring on the module. If no docstring is defined, this has the value None.
cls.__module__	The name of the module where the class was defined, or None if not applicable.
cls.__mro__	The method resolution order of the class, represented as a tuple of classes.
cls.__name__	The name of the class.
cls.__qualname__	The fully qualified name of the class.
cls.__slots__	A sequence of variable names as strings that should be reserved. When defined, this prevents the automatic creation of the __dict__ and __weakref__ attributes, unless these names are specified in __slots__.
cls.__weakref__	An object that references all weak references to the current object. You should never have to work with this attribute directly, but it's good to be aware of its purpose when working with cls.__slots__ (see that entry).

B

PYTHON DEBUGGER (PDB) COMMANDS

The Python DeBugger (pdb) tool has quite a few commands you can enter at the (Pdb) prompt to control and monitor the execution of the code. In this appendix, I outline the most important pdb commands in an easy-to-use table.

If you need even more information, you will find all pdb commands exhaustively documented at *https://docs.python.org/3/library/pdb.html.*

Command(s)	Purpose
h *command* help *command*	Shows help for a command. If a command is omitted, this lists all available commands.
q quit	Quits the current pdb session.

Moving around

Command(s)	Purpose
w where	Prints the stack trace for the current position.
u *count* up *count*	Moves the focus higher up the current stack trace, by *count* levels, or one level by default.
d *count* down *count*	Moves the focus further down the current stack trace, by *count* levels, or one level by default.
s step	Executes and steps into the current line.
n next	Executes and steps over the current line.
r return	Executes the rest of the current function.
c cont continue	Continues execution until another breakpoint is hit.
unt *lineno* until *lineno*	Continues execution until *lineno*, or until any line number greater than the current one.
j *lineno* jump *lineno*	After the current line, executes the line of code at *lineno*. You can only do this on the bottommost frame, and you cannot do this in certain situations. One use for this is if you want to temporarily skip some code you think might be causing a problem.
run restart	Restarts debugging from the beginning of the program, while retaining options, breakpoints, and history. This only works when you've invoked pdb directly.

Inspecting things

Command(s)	Purpose
p *expression*	Runs print(*expression*).
pp *expression*	Runs pprint(*expression*) (pretty-print with pprint module).
whatis *expression*	Prints type(*expression*).
a args	Prints the argument list for the current function.
retval	Prints the last returned value for the current function.
display *expression*	Watches the value of *expression*, printing it each time the debugger stops in the current frame.
undisplay *expression*	Stops watching *expression*. If *expression* is omitted, this stops watching all expressions.
l *lineno* list *lineno*	Displays the 11 lines of source code around line *lineno*, or around the current line if *lineno* is omitted.
l *from to* list *from to*	Displays the source code from line number *from* to line number *to*.

Command(s)	Purpose
source *name*	Displays the source code for the given code object *object*, such as a function, method, class, or module.
Interacting with things	
! *statement*	Executes the given one-line statement in the current context, as if it were the next line of code.
interact	Switches to an interactive Python shell at the current context, so you can run additional code.
debug *code*	Starts another pdb session for debugging the statement *code*. When you quit that session, you'll return to the session you ran this command in.
Managing breakpoints	
b break	Lists all breakpoints in the file, including how many times each one has been hit.
b *lineno* break *lineno* b *file:lineno* break *file:lineno*	Sets a breakpoint at line number *lineno* in the current file or at line number *lineno* in the file with filename *file*.
b *function* break *function*	Sets a breakpoint at the top of the function *function*.
tbreak *where*	Sets a temporary breakpoint at the location *where* (following the same syntax as the break command). The first time the temporary breakpoint is hit, it is removed.
cl clear	Clears all breakpoints. Confirms before clearing everything.
cl *file:lineno* clear *file:lineno*	Clears the breakpoint on line *lineno* in the file with filename *file*.
cl *number* clear *number*	Clears the breakpoint *number*. You can specify multiple numbers, separated by spaces, to clear multiple breakpoints.

GLOSSARY

A

abstract base class (ABC)
A class that specifies an interface that must be implemented by any derived class. An ABC cannot itself be instantiated. (See also *virtual subclassing*.)

abstract syntax tree (AST)
A tree data structure that represents the overall structure of the code. Used by some static analyzers, such as Bandit.

accelerator module
A binary extension module that offers behavior equivalent to that of a pure Python module but that is written in C, making it faster and able to bypass the GIL. (See also *wrapper module*.)

alias (v.)
To bind a mutable value to more than one name. Mutations performed on a value bound to one name will be visible on all names bound to that mutable value.

and

A logical operator where both operand expressions must evaluate to True for this operator to evaluate as True itself. (See also *not, or.*)

annotation

A piece of valid language syntax that is ignored by the language itself but that provides additional information to the programmer or to a static analyzer. (See also *type hint.*)

anonymous

Describes any callable that is defined without a name; anonymous callables can still be bound to names. (See also *generator expression; lambda.*)

arbitrary argument list

See *argument, variadic.*

arbitrary execution

A technique whereby strings can be directly executed as Python code. (See also *code injection attack.*)

argument

A value passed to a parameter of a callable. (See also *argument, keyword; argument, positional.*)

argument, keyword

An argument that is mapped to a parameter based on direct assignment to a parameter name within the argument list. (See also *argument, positional.*)

argument, positional

An argument that is mapped to a parameter based on its sequential position in the argument list. (See also *argument, keyword.*)

argument, variadic

An argument that is passed to a variadic parameter. (See also *argument, variadic keyword; parameter, variadic positional.*)

argument, variadic keyword

An argument that is passed to a variadic keyword parameter. (See also *argument, variadic; parameter, variadic keyword.*)

artifact

A by-product or end product of software development, especially one that can be installed on an end user's environment to run the finished program.

assembling

The act of compiling to native machine code.

assert

A keyword to declare an assert statement, the expression of which must return `True` or the program will abort with an `AssertionError`. Assert statements may be optimized out by the interpreter under some circumstances, so they should not be used for data or input validation.

assignment

The act of binding a value to a name. Assignment never copies data.

assignment expression

An expression that allows you to assign a value to a name and use that value in another expression at the same time. The special operator in an assignment expression (`:=`) is known as the *walrus operator.*

assignment operator (=)

The operator that assigns a value to a name.

async

A keyword to declare a native coroutine or asynchronous generator (`async def`), a `for` loop over an asynchronous iterator (`async for`), or a `with` statement using an asynchronous context manager (`async with`).

asynchronous

Describes anything that is compatible with asynchrony. There are asynchronous iterators, iterables, generators, and coroutines (which are typically called native coroutines; see *coroutine, native*).

asynchrony

A form of concurrency in which Python manages the multitasking within a single thread.

atomic

Describes an operation or function that consists of a single, indivisible CPU instruction under the hood. Nonatomic operations are at risk of causing race conditions when used in concurrency.

attribute

A variable that is a member of a class or instance.

attribute, class

An attribute that belongs to a class; its value is accessible, both on the class itself and on any instance of the class.

attribute, instance

An attribute that belongs to a single instance of a class (an object) and is not accessible from any other instance or from the class itself.

attribute, special

An attribute that is utilized by a core Python language feature. The name of a special attribute always starts and ends with two underscores (__).

augmented assignment operator

An operator that performs an operation with the left and right operands and assigns the result to the left operand.

autouse fixture

See *fixture, autouse.*

await

A keyword that calls an awaitable.

awaitable

A callable that can pause and resume midexecution.

B

base class

A class that is inherited by one or more other classes. (See also *derived class.*)

bdist

See *built distribution (bdist).*

benchmarking

The technique by which you establish that one piece of code is faster than another. (See also *profiling.*)

big-endian

See *byte order.*

binary

A base-2 number system consisting of only the digits *0* and *1*, which correspond to the closed and open positions of gates on circuit boards. In Python, binary literal (integers) are prefixed with 0b. (See also *hexadecimal; octal.*)

binary extension module

An importable extension written in C that adds new functionality atop the CPython interpreter. (See also *accelerator module; wrapper module.*)

bind

To create a reference between a name and a value.

binding behavior

Behavior wherein an object controls how it is used as an attribute; its getter, setter, and deleter methods are encapsulated.

bit

A single binary digit; the smallest unit of digital information.

bitmask

A binary value used in a bitwise operation to filter out unwanted bits in the other operand.

bitwise operation

A low-level binary operation that works on individual bits in the operands.

break

A statement that exits the containing loop immediately. (See also *continue*; *for*; *while*.)

breakpoint

A place in the program where control is turned over to the debugger.

bubble up

To reraise an exception that has been caught.

buffer

A queue-like structure that data is pushed into and where data waits until it is retrieved.

buffer protocol

A set of methods that provide and govern access to an underlying memory array.

built distribution (bdist)

An artifact containing precompiled Python bytecode and any binary files needed for the package to run.

byte

A unit of digital information that typically consists of eight bits.

bytearray

An immutable bytes-like object. (See also *bytes (object)*.)

bytecode

Compact codes representing instructions for the Python interpreter to execute. Python source code is compiled to bytecode.

byte order

The sequence in which bytes composing a larger value appear. The sequence can be either *big-endian*, with the largest part of the composite value represented first (on the left), or *little-endian*, with the smallest part of the composite value represented first.

bytes (object)

An immutable bytes-like object. (See also *bytearray*.)

bytes-like object

An object that stores binary data with a fixed size and a specified byte order.

bytes literal

A literal representation of a binary value. It looks like a string literal prepended with b.

C

C3 method resolution order (C3 MRO)

See *method resolution order*.

C3 superclass linearization

See *superclass linearization*.

call (n.)

The execution of a callable.

callable

Any object that can be executed, typically by entering its name followed by parentheses; zero or more values can be passed to the callable as arguments by listing them in the parentheses.

callback

A native coroutine passed to a function to be called later.

call stack

The sequence of calls leading to the currently executing statement. (See also *traceback*.)

camel case

A naming convention wherein the first letter of each word is uppercase and the rest of the letters are lowercase (e.g., FishAndChips). If the first letter is capitalized, the naming convention is upper camel case; otherwise, it's lower camel case. Upper camel case is used for class names, according to PEP 8. (See also *screaming snake case*; *snake case*.)

canonical string representation

A human-readable representation of a value or an object, generally containing all the information needed to re-create the value or object. Returned by repr().

cargo cult programming

An antipattern in which one imitates actions or structures in programming without understanding them, in hopes of achieving a related outcome. Especially prevalent in packaging.

chunking

The act of defining how much of a larger set of work is given to a single thread or subprocess.

class

A compound statement that contains attributes (variables) and methods (functions), and from which an instance (object) may be created. (See also *attribute*; *instance*; *method*; *object*.)

class, static

A class that contains only class attributes and class or static methods but that is not intended to be instantiated. This technique is preferred over singletons.

classifier

In packaging, a standardized string that facilitates organizing and searching for packages on a package index, especially PyPI.

clause

A single part of a compound statement; it consists of a header and a suite.

closure

A callable that returns another callable that "closes over" one or more nonlocal names.

closure, stateful

A closure that retains a little bit of state between calls.

cls

The name conventionally given to the first parameter of a class method, which is intended to be bound to the class itself.

code coverage

The percentage of lines of code in a project that are executed, or covered, by tests.

code injection attack

An attack in which your code can be used to execute code written by a third party on an end user's machine, typically for malicious purposes. (See also *arbitrary execution.*)

coercion

Implicitly casting a value from one type to another.

collection

An object that stores multiple values in an organized fashion; this is Python's name for a "data structure." (See also *dictionary; list; set; tuple.*)

complex number

A number type that can store an imaginary part. (See also `Decimal`; *floating-point number*; `Fraction`; *integer.*)

composition

The relationship between two classes A and B, such that class B contains one or more instances of class A as attributes. Also known as a "has-a" relationship. (See also *inheritance.*)

compound assignment operator

See *augmented assignment operator* or *assignment expression.*

comprehension

A form of a generator expression that directly evaluates to a collection. (See also *generator expression.*)

comprehension, dictionary

A form of a generator expression that produces a dictionary. Enclosed in braces ({ }) and defines both the key and the value in the first part of the generator expression, with a colon (:) separating the key and the value.

comprehension, list

A form of a generator expression that produces a list. Enclosed in square brackets ([ ]).

comprehension, set

A form of a generator expression that produces a set. Enclosed in braces ({ }).

concatenate

To combine two or more strings into one.

concurrency

A technique in which a single thread of execution switches between multiple tasks, thereby increasing the perceived responsiveness of the code. Only one task is ever worked at a time. (See also *asynchrony, parallelism, threading.*)

constructor

The special class method __new__(), which creates and returns a new instance from the class. The initializer is called immediately afterward. (See also *finalizer*; *initializer*.)

consumer

A thread or process that intakes data and processes it. (See also *producer*.)

context management protocol

A protocol that specifies that an object must implement __enter__() and __exit__() to be compatible with a with statement.

context manager

An object that is compatible with a with statement and that can handle its own setup and/or cleanup tasks.

context variables

Variables that can store different values, depending on which asynchronous task accesses them. Also known as contextvars.

contextvars

See *context variables*.

continue

A statement that immediately skips the current iteration of the containing loop. (See also *break*; *for*; *while*.)

conversion

The act of explicitly casting a value from one type to another.

cooperative multitasking

See *asynchrony*.

copy (v.)

To create a new value in memory from the same data as another value.

core developers

Developers who are involved in leading Python development. Their opinions regarding language direction and proposed changes bear much weight.

coroutine, native

An awaitable coroutine that is based on a simple coroutine but that is capable of being paused and resumed for use with asynchrony.

coroutine, simple

A generator that consumes data on demand, instead of (or in addition to) producing data.

Counter

A variant of the dictionary designed for counting hashable objects. (See also *defaultdict*; *OrderedDict*.)

coverage

See *code coverage*.

CPU-bound

Describes any code execution whose speed is limited by the speed of the CPU. (See also *IO-bound*.)

CPython

The default implementation of Python, written in C.

current working directory

The directory the user (or system) is running commands from.

D

daemonic

Describes a thread that is tied to the lifespan of the process; when the main thread ends, all associated daemonic threads are killed as well.

data

Information stored in a value. You may have copies of such data stored in other values.

deadlock

An erroneous situation that occurs when the combined current status of two or more locks causes all involved threads to wait, with no way to proceed. (See also *livelock*; *starvation*.)

Decimal

An object that stores fixed-point decimal numbers, rather than floating-point numbers, thereby representing an exact numeric value with a decimal part. (See also *complex number*; *floating-point number*; *Fraction*; *integer*.)

decorator

A special type of callable that "wraps" another callable or a class, modifying its behavior without actually changing the callable's suite. Usually implemented as a closure.

deep-copy (v.)

To both copy an object to a new value *and* copy all the data from values referenced within that object to new values.

default argument value

The value assigned to a parameter if no argument is passed. Defining this in the parameter list makes the parameter optional. (See *parameter, optional.*)

defaultdict

A variant of the dictionary in which a default value is provided when accessing on undefined keys. (See also *Counter*; *OrderedDict*.)

delay

See *future.*

deque

A mutable, sequential (array-like) collection optimized for accessing the first and last items. Deque literals are created by passing a list literal to the deque() initializer. (See also *dictionary*; *list*; *set*; *tuple*.)

derived class

A class that inherits, or *derives*, from another class. (See also *base class.*)

descriptor

An object with binding behavior.

descriptor, data

A descriptor that implements __get__(), as well as __set__() and/or __delete__().

descriptor, non-data

A descriptor that only implements __get__().

descriptor, read-only data

A descriptor that implements both __get__() and __set__() but raises an AttributeError from the latter.

descriptor protocol

A protocol that states that for an object to be a descriptor, it must implement at least one of __get__(), __set__(), and __delete__().

deserialization

The process of converting stored data to Python values. (See also *serialization.*)

destructor

See *finalizer.*

dict

The type name for a *dictionary* collection.

dict comprehension

See *comprehension, dictionary.*

dictionary

A mutable, unordered collection of key-value pairs. Keys must be hashable. Dictionary literals are comma delimited (with colons separating the key and value in each pair) and enclosed in braces ({ }). (See also *deque; set; tuple.*)

distribution package

An artifact that bundles and versions the source distribution and the associated built distribution (if any).

docstring

A string literal that appears at the top (just below the header, if any) of a function, class, or module and contains documentation.

duck typing

Working with objects based on their functionality, rather than their data type.

dunder method

See *method, special.*

E

eager evaluation

Behavior wherein each item in an iterable is evaluated when the iterable is defined or initialized. (See also *lazy evaluation.*)

Easier to Ask Forgiveness than Permission (EAFP)

A coding philosophy wherein you catch and utilize exceptions to control normal execution flow. (See also *Look Before You Leap (LBYL).*)

eggs

See *wheel.*

elif

A clause in an if statement that is executed only if the conditions in all preceding headers fail and the condition in its own header succeeds. (See also *else; if.*)

Ellipsis

A seldom-used built-in value consisting of three dots (...). Used in varying ways by various libraries and modules, but not by the core language.

else

A clause that is (1) in an if statement that is executed only if all the conditions in the headers of the other clauses fail, or (2) in a try statement that is executed only if no exceptions are raised within the try suite, or (3) in a while or for compound statement that is executed only once the condition in the while or for clause header fails. (See also *elif*; *else*; *finally*; *if*; *try*.)

encapsulation
The intended purpose of classes: to associate data (attributes) with the functions (methods) written to interpret or mutate that data.

endianness
See *byte order*.

entry point
The code that is run first when importing or executing a project.

error
An exception representing a program state caused by unexpected and improper behavior. (See also *exceptional state*.)

event loop
The loop in asynchrony that manages multitasking between awaitables and provides the means of calling the first awaitable in the stack.

except
A clause in a try statement whose suite is executed if any exceptions indicated in the header are raised within the try suite. (See also *else*; *finally*; *try*.)

exception
An object that represents an exceptional program state and stores information associated with that state. When unhandled, exceptions are fatal. (See also *error*; *exceptional state*; *warning*.)

exceptional state
A program state wherein, in most cases, data must be changed or program flow must be redirected to allow valid continued execution. (See also *exception*; *happy path*.)

exception chaining
The act of associating an exception with one or more preceding exceptions in the call stack.

executor
An object that creates and manages threads in threading.

expression
A section of code that evaluates to a single value.

extension module
See *binary extension module*.

F

falsey
See *truthiness.*

field
See *attribute.*

file-like object
See *stream.*

file object
See *stream.*

finalizer
The special instance method __del__(), which is called when the instance is deleted either with the del operator or by the garbage collector. (See also *constructor; initializer.*)

finally
A clause in a try statement that is always run after the other clauses, even if the suite in another clause raises an exception or returns. (See also *else*; *except*; *try*.)

finder
An object that locates the module being imported.

finder, meta path
A finder that uses a particular strategy to find a module.

finder, path-based
A type of meta path finder that searches the filesystem for a module. Calls one or more path entry finders.

finder, path entry
A finder that searches the filesystem for a module in a particular manner, such as searching compressed files.

first-class citizen
A designation that indicates something can be treated as an object. Functions are examples of first-class citizens in Python.

fixture
A function or method that sets up anything a test might need, especially things that are shared by multiple tests. Can also perform *teardown.*

fixture, autouse
A fixture that is automatically applied to all tests.

flaky test
A test that may fail unexpectedly or periodically, for reasons other than a flaw in the code that it's testing.

float
See *floating-point number*.

floating-point number
A number with a decimal part that is stored internally according to the IEEE 754 standard. In Python, these are always stored with double precision. Floating-point numbers are infamous for being unable to store exact values. (See also *complex number*; Decimal; Fraction; *integer*.)

flush (v.)
To force the retrieval of all data in a buffer; usually refers to printing all data in the standard output stream or standard error stream.

for
A compound statement that defines a loop, iterates over the iterable(s) in the header, and executes the suite on each iteration, unless explicitly exited. (See also while.)

format specification
A mini-language of various flags that control how a value is formatted in a *formatted string*.

formatted string
A type of string literal that allows you to insert and format expressions and their resulting values directly in the string value. Denoted by an f before the opening quote. (See also *raw string*; *string*; *string literal*.)

Fraction
An object that stores an exact fraction, rather than floating-point numbers, thereby representing an exact fractional numeric value. (See also *complex number*; Decimal; *floating-point number*; *integer*.)

freeze (v.)
To execute the process of compiling Python source code to frozen code.

freezer
A tool that bundles the compiled Python code, the Python interpreter, and all the package dependencies into a single artifact.

frozen code

C arrays of Python bytecode that is assembled into machine code. Frozen code must still be executed by the Python interpreter.

frozenset

An immutable variant of a set.

f-string

See *formatted string*.

fully qualified name

The name of an object, such as a function, as the import system sees it; includes the names of the packages and the module the object is contained within. (See also *qualified name*.)

function

A callable with a name that contains a suite of statements and can optionally accept one or more arguments. (See also *callable*.)

function, member

See *method*.

function, pure

A function or callable that (a) has no side effects, (b) does not affect the behavior of other functions, and (c) is repeatable and stateless, such that input X will always yield output Y.

functional programming

A programming paradigm that organizes around pure, stateless functions. (See also *object-oriented programming*; *procedural programming*).

function annotation

Type hints applied to a function.

future

An object that will contain a value at some point in the future but can be passed around like a normal object, even before it contains that value. Often used in threading and multiprocessing. Known as a "promise" or "delay" in other languages.

fuzzing

The act of generating random inputs in tests to find inputs that cause the code to fail in unexpected ways.

G

garbage collection
The process of removing unneeded objects from memory.

garbage collector, generational
A garbage collector that handles all the odd situations a reference-counting garbage collector cannot. (See also *garbage collector, reference-counting.*)

garbage collector, reference-counting
A garbage collector that removes values when their reference count reaches zero. (See also *garbage collector, generational.*)

generator
See *generator function* or *generator object.*

generator expression
An anonymous generator that is defined by a single expression and that evaluates to a generator object. A generator expression is to a generator as a lambda is to a function. (See also *comprehension.*)

generator function
A function containing one or more yield statements. When called directly, it produces a *generator object.*

generator object
An iterable object that produces values on demand. (See also *comprehension.*)

generic function
See *single-dispatch generic function.*

generic type
A type hint, usually referring to a collection, where the type of items in the collection is passed as a parameter.

Global Interpreter Lock (GIL)
A mechanism in CPython that ensures any single Python process is constrained to a single CPU core, regardless of how many cores are available to the system.

god class
An antipattern; a class that violates the single-responsibility principle by having too many purposes or functionalities. Prone to bugs and difficult to maintain.

H

happy path
A program execution flow wherein all data and conditions are logically correct and valid, such that no errors can occur. (See also *exceptional state.*)

hashable
Describes an object for which a hash value can be created and for which the hash value never changes during the object's lifetime. Must implement the special method __hash__(). All immutable values are hashable, while many mutable types are not.

hash value
A unique, immutable value, typically an integer, that is generated by processing an object in some way. Two objects that have the same hash value are usually guaranteed to be equivalent. Hash values are used by some collections and algorithms because it's faster to compare hash values than most other values.

header
The first line of a clause, always terminated with a colon (:).

hexadecimal
A base-16 number system consisting of the digits *0* through *9*, as well as the digits *A* through *F* (which represent decimal values *10* through *15*). In Python, hexadecimal literals are prefixed with 0x. (See also *binary; octal.*)

hook, meta
A meta path finder stored in sys.meta_path.

hook, path entry
A path entry finder stored in sys.path_hooks.

I

identity
A reference to a particular value in memory. When two names share an identity, they are bound to the same value in memory.

identity operator
See *is.*

if
A compound statement that executes a suite based on the condition of one or more clause headers. If the if header condition fails, each subsequent elif header in the compound statement is evaluated; if all conditions fail, the else clause executes, if one is present. (See also *elif; else.*)

immutable

Describes a value that CANNOT be modified in place. Attempting to mutate on a name referencing an immutable value will instead rebind the name to a new value. (See also *mutable*.)

import, absolute

An import statement that uses the fully qualified name of the module, starting from the top-level package.

import, relative

An import statement that uses the qualified name of a module relative to the current package.

importer

An object that serves as both a finder and a loader.

importer, built-in

An importer that finds and loads built-in modules.

importer, frozen

An importer that finds and loads frozen modules.

in

An operator that is used to check whether a particular value is contained in any collection or other object that implements the special method __contains__().

indirect parametrization

See *parametrization, indirect*.

infinite iterator

An iterator that will continue to yield values until explicitly stopped.

infinite loop

A loop with no means of exiting; see *loop, infinite*.

inheritance

The relationship between two classes A and B, such that class B has one or more attributes or methods defined in class A, in addition to one or more attributes or methods first defined and/or redefined in class B. Also known as an "is-a" relationship. (See also *composition*.)

initializer

The special instance method __init__(), which is called immediately after a new instance is created from a class by the constructor. (See also *constructor*; *finalizer*.)

instance
An organized collection of attributes (variables) and methods (functions) created according to a class and existing in memory as a single value. (See also *class*; *object*.)

integer
A whole number.

interactive session
A console in which you enter and run code through the interpreter in real time and see the outcomes.

interface
The set of public methods that are used to interact with the class or object.

interpreted language
A language in which the source code or the bytecode created from the source code is interpreted and executed at runtime, on the client's machine, by the language's *interpreter*.

interpreter
A program that interprets and executes source code or bytecode.

interpreter shutdown
A special phase of the interpreter, wherein all allocated resources are gradually freed.

intra-package reference
See *import, relative*.

introspection
The ability of code to access information about itself at runtime.

is
An operator comparing the identity of two operands. Typically only used when comparing an operand with the value True, False, or None.

iterable
An object that can be traversed by an iterator; must supply an iterator object via the special method __iter__(). All *collections* are iterables. (See also *iteration*; *iterative*; *iterator*.)

iteration
The process of acting on each individual value in a group of one or more values, which are either contained within a collection or provided one by one, on demand, by a statement. (See also *iterable*; *iterative*; *iterator*.)

iterative

Describes something employing iteration.

iterator

An object that can traverse an iterable object; must implement the special method __next__() and return itself from __iter__(). (See also *iterable*; *iteration*; *iterative*.)

K

key function

A callable that returns the part of a collection or object that should be used for sorting.

L

lambda

An anonymous function made up of a single expression, the value of which is implicitly returned.

lazy evaluation

Behavior wherein each item in an iterable is evaluated on demand, instead of up front. (See also *eager evaluation*.)

LEGB

See *scope resolution order*.

linter

A static analyzer that checks source code for common mistakes, potential errors, and style inconsistencies.

list

A mutable, sequential (array-like) collection. List literals are comma delimited and enclosed in square brackets ([ ]). (See also *deque*; *dictionary*; *set*; *tuple*.)

list comprehension

See *comprehension, list*.

literal

An expression that explicitly defines a value in place.

little-endian

See *byte order*.

livelock

An erroneous situation similar to *deadlock*, except that threads keep infinitely repeating the same interactions, instead of merely waiting on one other. (See also *starvation*.)

loader

An object that loads a module using its module spec.

lock

An object that ensures only one task, thread, or process can access a shared resource at once, to help prevent race conditions. (See also *deadlock, livelock, starvation*.)

Look Before You Leap (LBYL)

A coding philosophy wherein you prevent errors by testing a value before using it. (See also *Easier to Ask Forgiveness than Permission (EAFP)*.)

lookup chain

The rules that determine where Python searches for an attribute and in what order. The order is as follows: data descriptors, object attributes, non-data descriptors, and finally class attributes according to the superclass linearization.

loop, infinite

A loop with no means of exiting. (See *infinite loop*.)

loose coupling

A pattern in which two or more components interact solely via their public interfaces, without regard to their implementation.

M

magic method

See *method, special*.

marking

The application of metadata to tests and fixtures. (See also *parametrization*.)

`memoryview`

An object that provides access to the raw memory of any object implementing the buffer protocol.

metaclass

The object from which a class is instantiated.

meta hook

See *hook, meta.*

meta path finder

See *finder, meta path.*

method

A function that is a member of a class or instance.

method, class

A method that belongs to the class itself and can be called on the class or on any instance of the class. Can access class attributes but cannot access instance attributes. (See also *method, instance; method, static.*)

method, dunder

See *method, special.*

method, instance

A method that belongs to the instance and can access the attributes of the particular instance. (See also *method, class; method, static.*)

method, magic

See *method, special.*

method, special

A method that implements a core Python language feature on a class or instance; for example, any instance that supports the addition operator (+) implements the special method __add__(). The name of a special method always starts and ends with two underscores (__).

method, static

A method that belongs to the class but cannot access either the class attributes or the instance attributes. (See also *method, class; method, instance.*)

method resolution order

The rules that determine the order in which the classes in an inheritance relationship are checked for a method or attribute. (See also *superclass linearization.*)

mixin

A class that exists purely to contain methods and attributes that you may want to compose into other classes. It may be incomplete or even invalid by itself, as it is not intended to be instantiated directly.

mocking

The act of temporarily replacing parts of the code with versions that will simulate inputs or other scenarios during testing.

module

An object of organization in Python. Usually executable and often implemented as a Python file (*.py*). (See also *package*.)

module search path

The directory that defines where Python looks for packages and modules and what order it searches in.

module spec

An object containing all the information about how to load a module.

multiprocessing

A technique for achieving parallelism in Python by running tasks on different independent Python processes. (See also *concurrency*; *parallelism*; *threading*.)

mutable

Describes a value that can be modified in place.

mutate

To change a value in place.

N

name

A token composed of letters, numbers, and underscores, which is always bound to a value. Commonly thought of as a "variable" in Python. Names have scope but not type.

namedtuple

A tuple with named fields.

name mangling

A behavior of Python wherein a name belonging to a class is renamed, usually to prevent naming conflicts or to provide a weak form of data hiding. Any name belonging to a class that is preceded by two underscores (__) will be name mangled. (See also *non-public*; *public*.)

namespace

An explicitly defined path to something, such as a function.

None

A dedicated value universally representing a lack of a value, rather than a value equivalent to False or 0.

NoneType

The data type of the None value.

non-public

An attribute or method that is *not* intended to be called or mutated outside of the containing class, although such access is still possible. Non-public names always begin with an underscore (_). (See also *name mangling*; *public*.)

not

A logical operator that reverses the boolean result of an expression. When paired with the is operator (is not), it checks that two values do not have the same identity. (See also *and*; *or*.)

number system

A system whereby numeric values are represented with sequences of digits. For example, the decimal, or base-10, number system consists of the digits *0* through *9*. (See also *binary*; *hexadecimal*; *octal*.)

O

object

An instance of a class. In Python, the maxim is "Everything is an object."

object-oriented programming

A programming paradigm that is organized around classes and objects by coupling data and its related logic. (See also *functional programming*.)

obvious

How any idiomatic Python solution should feel, once you know it.

octal

A base-8 number system consisting of the digits *0* through *7*. In Python, octal literals are prefixed with 0o. (See also *binary*; *hexadecimal*.)

operator

A token, usually a symbol, which together with one or two operands (values) forms an expression. All operators in Python call a special method behind the scenes.

operator, binary

An operator that accepts two operands.

operator, unary

An operator that accepts one operand.

or

A logical operator where one or both operand expressions must evaluate to True for the operator to return True. (See also *and*; *not*.)

OrderedDict

A variant of the dictionary with extra functionality for tracking and managing the order of key-value pairs. (See also *Counter*; *defaultdict*.)

P

package

A term that usually refers to a regular package. (See *package, regular.*)

package, namespace

A specialized type of package, lacking an *__init__.py* module, which allows you to distribute a package in multiple portions. Should not be confused with a *package, regular.*

package, regular

A special type of module containing other modules or packages. Usually exists as a directory containing an *__init__.py* module.

parallelism

A technique in which multiple tasks are executed simultaneously on different CPU cores. (See also *concurrency*; *multiprocessing.*)

parameter

A name defined in the header of a function to which a value can be passed (assigned) when the function is called. (See also *argument.*)

parameter, keyword-only

A parameter that only accepts a keyword argument. (See also *parameter, positional-only.*)

parameter, optional

A parameter for which an argument may be omitted in the call. A parameter is made optional by defining a *default argument value* in the parameter list. (See also *parameter, required.*)

parameter, positional-only

A parameter that only accepts a positional argument. (See also *parameter, keyword-only.*)

parameter, required

A parameter for which an argument must be provided in the call. (See also *parameter, optional.*)

parameter, variadic
See *parameter, variadic positional.*

parameter, variadic keyword
A parameter that can accept an arbitrary number of keyword arguments and that packs them into a dictionary. The variadic keyword parameter name is preceded by two asterisks (**). Conventionally named kwargs. (See also *argument, variadic keyword*; *parameter, variadic.*)

parameter, variadic positional
A parameter that can accept an arbitrary number of positional arguments, packing them into a tuple. The variadic parameter name is preceded by a single asterisk (*). Conventionally named args. (See also *argument, variadic*; *parameter, variadic keyword.*)

parametrization
The expansion of a single test out into multiple tests, each with the same logic but different data. Accomplished via marking.

parametrization, indirect
The act of relaying parametrized values to a fixture.

pass
A keyword that has no effect. Usually used as a placeholder for a suite.

path, absolute
A path that starts from the root of the filesystem.

path, concrete
A path-like object that provides methods for interacting with the filesystem.

path, pure
A path-like object that does not access the underlying filesystem.

path, relative
A path that starts from some nonroot location on the filesystem.

path-like object
An object that represents a filesystem path. Inherits from the abstract class os.Pathlike.

pdb
See *Python Debugger (pdb).*

PEP
See *Python Enhancement Proposal.*

PEP 8
The Python style guide.

picklable
Describes any value that can be serialized by the pickle protocol.

pickle
A serialization format that is extraordinarily slow and insecure in most use cases, but which remains useful in multiprocessing.

pin (v.)
To set a dependency in packaging to use a specific version of the dependency.

platform wheel
See *wheel, platform.*

polymorphism
A pattern wherein multiple classes, with different behaviors and features, offer a common interface.

portion
Part of a larger package distributed with namespace packages.

postmortem (v.)
To run a debugger after a fatal crash has taken place.

pre-emptive multitasking
See *threading.*

priming
The act of making an initial call to a simple coroutine, advancing it to its first yield statement so it can receive a value via send(). Performed either by calling send(None) on the simple coroutine or by passing the simple coroutine to next().

procedural programming
A programming paradigm that organizes around control blocks and focuses on control flow. (See also *functional programming; object-oriented programming.*)

process (n.)
An instance of a running computer program on a system. (See also *multiprocessing; subprocess; thread.*)

producer
A thread or process that provides data. (See also *consumer.*)

profiling

The technique by which you identify performance bottlenecks and common inefficiencies in existing code, thus finding where that code can be optimized. (See also *benchmarking*.)

promise

See *future*.

provisional

A term applied to a package or API that may change at any time, without regard to backward compatibility.

property

A name belonging to a class instance. Behaves externally like an attribute but is internally implemented as one to three instance methods: a getter, a setter, and a deleter.

public

An attribute or method that is intended to be called or mutated outside of the containing class. (See also *non-public*.)

pure function

See *function, pure*.

PyPA

See *Python Packaging Authority (PyPA)*.

PyPI

See *Python Package Index (PyPI)*.

Python Debugger (pdb)

A debugger for Python, with a workflow similar to other command line debuggers.

Python Enhancement Proposal (PEP)

A document formally proposing an addition or modification to an official policy, standard, or specification related to the Python programming language.

Pythonic

Describes idiomatic Python code, which is code that makes good use of Python's syntax and behavior.

Python Package Index (PyPI)

An online repository of Python packages.

Python Packaging Authority (PyPA)

A quasi-official working group made up of Python community members who maintain projects and who want to make Python packaging a better experience.

Python Software Foundation (PSF)

The nonprofit organization that officially manages the Python language.

Q

qualified name

The name of an object, such as a function, preceded by its complete namespace within one of its modules and packages, if any. (See also *fully qualified name*.)

R

race condition

A bug-causing situation in concurrency or parallelism where an outcome is dependent on the order in which various tasks, threads, or processes start, pause, resume, and/or finish. (This order is always unpredictable.) Race conditions can be infamously hard to detect and debug. (See also *lock*.)

raw string

A type of string literal wherein the backslash is always treated as a literal character, rather than an escape character. Denoted by an r before the opening quote. (See also *formatted string*; *string*; *string literal*.)

rebind

To bind an existing name to a different value.

recursion

A callable calling itself; can be used as a form of looping. (See also *recursion*.)

recursion depth

The number of open (not yet returned) recursive calls to a callable from itself.

recursion limit

The maximum recursion depth before Python raises an error; can be set via sys.setrecursionlimit().

reentrant (adj.)

Describes something that can be paused mid-execution while being called again concurrently, without any odd effects. This is an important concept in *concurrency* and *parallelism*.

reference

The association between a name and a value.

reference count

A count of how many references exist for a given value.

repr

See *canonical string representation*.

return

A statement that immediately exits a function, optionally passing back to the function caller the value that follows the keyword.

S

scope

The enclosing code structure within which a name is accessible. (See also *scope, global; scope, local; scope, nonlocal*.)

scope, global

The scope shared by the entire program; any name defined in the top level of a module is in global scope.

scope, local

The scope that is defined by a function, lambda, or comprehension; any name defined within local scope is only accessible within that scope.

scope, nonlocal

The scope that is local to the enclosing scope, rather than the present scope. Seen in nested functions, where function A contains function B; A is the nonlocal scope of B.

scope resolution order

The order in which scopes are searched for a given name. Best remembered via the acronym *LEGB*, for *local, enclosing-function local* (aka nonlocal), *global,* and *built-in*.

screaming snake case

A naming convention using all-caps letters (screaming) and underscores (snakes); for example, INTEREST_RATE. Normally used for variables intended to be used as constants, according to PEP 8. (See also *camel case; snake case*.)

sdist
See *source distribution (sdist)*.

segmentation fault
A fatal system error resulting from a program trying to access computer memory it doesn't have permission to access. This is a common possible outcome of undefined behavior.

self
The name conventionally given to the first parameter of an instance method, which is intended to be bound to the instance itself.

sequence
An array-like collection.

serialization
The process of converting data to a format that can be stored. (See also *deserialization*.)

set
A mutable, unordered collection where all items are guaranteed to be unique. Set literals are comma delimited and enclosed in braces ({ }). (See also *deque*; *dictionary*; *frozenset*; *tuple*.)

set comprehension
See *comprehension, set*.

severity level
The relative importance of a message sent to a logger.

shadow (v.)
To obscure a name with another name; especially, to obscure a built-in or global name with a local name or to obscure a class attribute with an instance attribute.

shallow copy
See *copy*.

shebang
A special comment at the top of a Python file by which you can make the file directly executable. Short for "haSH-BANG" (#!), which appears at the beginning of the comment.

side effects
Any changes made to state outside of the local scope of a function.

simple coroutine
See *coroutine, simple.*

single-dispatch generic function
A function that behaves differently for parameters of different types.

single-responsibility principle
A principle stating that a function, class, or module should have one clear and distinct responsibility.

singleton
A design pattern in which a class only allows one version of itself to be instantiated at any one time. Generally discouraged in Python; static classes are preferred. (See *class, static.*)

slice notation
A form of subscripting by which you can iterate over multiple values in a specified range or pattern. Slice notation is enclosed in square brackets ([ ]) and consists of three integer parts: [start: stop: step]. Any of these three parts may be omitted.

slots
A tuple of predefined attributes on an object, declared with the __slots__ special class attribute. Using slots is faster than the default behavior, wherein attributes are stored in a dictionary.

snake case
A naming convention, typically using all lowercase letters, with underscores (snakes) in place of spaces (e.g., interest_rate). Normally used for variable and function names in Python, according to PEP 8. (See also *camel case*; *screaming snake case.*)

software test fixture
See *fixture.*

source distribution (sdist)
One or more Python packages bundled into a compressed archive.

special attribute
See *attribute, special.*

special method
See *method, special.*

starred expression
A name that is preceded by an asterisk (*) and into which multiple values may be unpacked.

starvation
An erroneous situation in which a thread is permanently stuck, waiting for a future or waiting to join a thread, especially to acquire some data or resource it needs. (See also *deadlock*; *livelock*.)

state
Data stored between executions of a callable that typically affect the callable's behavior.

statement
A single executable unit of code in Python; analogous to a sentence in English. (See also *expression*; *statement, compound*.)

statement, compound
A structure that organizes additional statements into one or more clauses and affects the execution of those statements in some manner. Python has seven types of compound statements: if, while, for, try, with, def, and class.

statement, simple
Typically, a single line of code. (See also *statement*.)

static analyzer
A tool that checks source code for potential problems or deviations from standards. (See also *linter*.)

stream
A buffer object that offers methods for reading from or writing to a file or other input/output source.

stream, standard error
A stream provided by the operating system. Serves as a buffer that prints to the terminal but marks the messages as related to errors, instead of normal output.

stream, standard input
A stream provided by the operating system. Serves as a buffer that contains data typed into the terminal.

stream, standard output
A stream provided by the operating system. Serves as a buffer that prints to the terminal.

string

A value consisting of one or more Unicode or ASCII characters. (See also *formatted string; raw string; string literal.*)

string literal

A literal representation of a string. It is wrapped in a matching pair of single quotes ('...'), double quotes ("..."), or triple quotes ("""...""").

struct

A module for converting between Python values and binary data, including for interoperability with C values.

stub class

A class that contains little to no data.

subprocess

A separate process that is linked to the main process. (See also *multiprocessing.*)

subscript

A reference to an individual value within a collection or other object created by specifying an index integer in square brackets ([ ]).

subscriptable

Describes any collection or object that allows you to access, modify, or delete individual items by specifying an index integer in square brackets ([ ]). For an object to be subscriptable, it must implement one or more of the following special methods, as appropriate: __getitem__(), __setitem__(), __delitem__(). (See also *slice notation.*)

suite

A "block" of code; one or more statements that belong to (are the "body" of) a clause and thus belong to a compound statement, which controls their execution.

super()

A function that accesses the next class in the *superclass linearization* for the current class.

superclass linearization

The list of base classes a class inherits from, in the order they are to be searched for the method being called. (See also *method resolution order.*)

T

task

A special object that runs native coroutines without blocking.

teardown

Cleanup tasks like closing streams or database connections or deleting temporary files. (See also *fixture.*)

ternary expression

A compact conditional expression that produces a value. Follows the form *a* if `expression` else *b*, where the ternary expression evaluates to *a* if `expression` evaluates to `True`, or to *b* otherwise.

test fixture

See *fixture.*

test-driven development (TDD)

The practice of writing tests before writing the code and then writing the code to make the tests pass.

thread

A single flow of execution within a process. A single process may have multiple threads.

threading

A form of concurrency in which the operating system manages multitasking by running each task in a thread. (See also *asynchrony, parallelism.*)

thread safety

Techniques to avoid concurrency-related bugs, especially race conditions.

timeout

In concurrency and parallelism, the maximum time until the program gives up waiting on a thread or process to join.

traceback

The complete call stack leading to an exception, along with any information about the exception itself.

truthiness

The implied boolean value of any expression or value; it is *truthy* if evaluating to `True` and *falsey* if evaluating to `False`. Values equivalent to `False`, `0`, or `None` are falsey; all others are truthy.

truthy

See *truthiness.*

try

A compound statement that catches any exceptions raised within the initial clause and handles them according to the subsequent except, else, and finally clauses. (See also *else*; *except*; *finally*.)

tuple

An immutable, sequential (array-like) collection. Tuple literals are comma delimited and normally enclosed in parentheses (( )). (See also *deque*; *dictionary*; *list*; *namedtuple*; *set*.)

Turing-complete

Describes a quality of a language whereby you could implement any other programming language in it and execute any program written in that language.

type

The metaclass from which nearly all classes are instantiated.

type alias

A name bound to a type hint, especially a parameterized generic type, for easier reuse.

type annotations

See *type hint*.

type hint

An annotation that describes the expected data type associated with a name, parameter, or function return. Only used by certain static analyzers; entirely ignored by the Python language itself.

U

undefined behavior

A situation in code with no formal definition for how it should be handled. (See also *segmentation fault*.)

unit test

A test that verifies the behavior of a single unit, such as a function or a conditional path through a function.

unpack

To assign each of the values in a collection or other iterable to multiple names.

V

value
A unique copy of data in memory. There must be a reference to the value, or else it is deleted. Values have type but not scope.

variable
A term referring to a name and its value together.

variable, member
See *attribute.*

version control system
Software that tracks revisions to source code and other files. Git is a major example.

virtual environment
A sandboxed environment containing separate installations of desired packages.

virtual subclassing
A technique wherein an ABC reports certain classes as being derived, even if they aren't.

W

walrus operator
See *assignment expression.*

warning
A message about a problem that has been worked around or another piece of important information. Warnings are nonfatal by default. (See also *exception.*)

warnings filter
An argument passed to the Python interpreter that controls which warnings are displayed and how.

weakref
A reference that doesn't increase the reference count on the value.

wheel
A standardized format for Python built distributions, defined in PEP 237. Superseded *eggs*, a more limited format with similar goals.

wheel, platform
A wheel built for a specific system.

while
A compound statement that defines a loop; as long as the condition in the header is true, the suite is executed, unless explicitly exited. (See also *for*.)

wrapper module
A binary extension module that exposes a C library to Python. (See also *accelerator module*.)

Y

yield
A keyword used in generators and simple coroutines. Either (a) returns the value of the expression following the operator to the caller of the generator's __next__() method or (b) passes to the assignment operator preceding this operator the value sent to the coroutine via its send() method. (See also *generator*; *yield from*.)

yield from
A statement that passes execution control flow from the current generator to the iterable following this operator. (See also *generator*; *yield*.)

Z

Zen of Python, The
A poem by Tim Peters that expresses the philosophy of the Python language.

INDEX

BufferError, 209
buffers, 291–292, 655
build system (*pyproject.toml*), 529–530
built distribution (bdist), 516, 531
built-in importer, 90
__builtins__, 645
bullet journal example, 385–388
bytearray objects, 348, 363
bytecode, 6, 91
byteorder attribute, 349
bytes
    defined, 338
    order, 342–343, 349–350, 352, 656
bytes() method, 348–349
__bytes__() method, 171, 638
bytes-like objects
    about, 347
    bitwise operations on, 357–361
    bytes vs. bytearray, 348
    creating, 348–349
    and integer conversions, 349–351
    and memory consumption,
        361–363
    sequence operations, 351
    and struct module, 352
bytes literals, 346–347
BytesWarning, 545

C

C Foreign Function Interface
        (CFFI), 629
C3 Method Resolution Order (C3
        MRO), 389–392, 395
__cached__ attribute, 644
cached bytecode, 91
Call for Proposals (CFPs), 634
__call__() method, 175–176, 638
call stacks, 186–187
callable instances, 175–176
callable objects (callables),
        131–132, 656
callbacks, 465
camel case, 656
canonical string representation, 61,
        168–169
capture patterns, 69–70
cargo cult programming, 514, 657

carriage return (\r), 294, 307
CBOR (Concise Binary Object
        Representation) serialization
        format, 376
__ceil__() method, 171, 638
chain() (itertools module)
        function, 252
chr() function, 161
chunking, 501
CircuitPython, 627
__class__ attribute, 645
class attributes, 105–106, 646
__class_getitem__() method, 644
class methods, 158–159
classes. *See also* abstract base classes
        (ABCs); inheritance;
        metaclasses; virtual subclasses
    about, 150
    base vs. derived, 384
    and bitwise operations, 346
    decisions about using, 181–182
    declaring, 151–154
    as immutable, 447–449
    and SOLID principles, 382–384
    syntax, 63–64
classifiers (PyPI), 522–523
@classmethod decorator, 159
clauses, 657
click module, 579–580, 615
close() method, 265, 296, 297
closing generators, 264–266
__closure__ attribute, 645
closures, 135–138
coarse-grained locking, 487–488
code
    autoformatting, 33–34
    boilerplate, 151
    brittle, 247, 556
    "dead", 608
    editors, 34–36
    frozen, 666
    security evaluation, 571–574
    style, 27–29, 31
    testing frameworks, 34
    and thread safety, 486–488
    tightly coupled, 120
__code__ attribute, 645

D

daemonic threads, 482–483, 660

Dask, 624

data

    defined, 117

    as packaged files, 524

    picklable, 499

data descriptors, 437

data hiding, 157

data science, 623–625

data types

    in binary data conversions, 353

    mutable and immutable, 106–107

    treatment in Python, 44, 98–100

data validation vs. assertion, 558–559

dataclasses, 449

dataframes, 624

deactivate command, 20

deadlocks, 493–494

debugging. *See also* logging; Python
        Debugger (pdb)

    and assertions, 556–560

    example, 561–562

    loops vs. generator expressions,
        281–282

    and packaging, 514–515

    tools, 560–561

    undefined behavior, 570–571

    and warnings, 544–548

Decimal number type, 45–46

declarative programming, 120

decode() method, 368

decorators

    about, 660

    class, 176–177

    defining properties with, 164–166

    on functions, 142–145, 436

deep copy (deepcopy()), 113–114, 117

def keyword, 63

default argument values, 126–128, 146

defaultdict, 224

__defaults__ attribute, 645

__del__() method, 154, 643

del operator, 154, 223

delattr() method, 433

__delattr__() method, 433, 643

__delete__() method, 437, 639

deleters, 162–163

__delitem__() method, 231, 235, 639

dependencies, 15–16, 22–23, 524–525,
    537–539

dependency injections, 587

Dependency Inversion Principle,
    383–384

DeprecationWarning, 545

deques (deque), 219–220, 495

descriptors

    about, 436–437, 661

    using multiple, 442–444

    writing, 437–442

deserialization. *See* serialization

design patterns, 373, 407–408

development environments. *See also*
        IDEs (integrated development
        environments)

    and *requirements.txt* file, 528–529

dialects, 332

diamond inheritance problem, 389

diaper anti-pattern, 190–192

dice roll program example

    basic function, 122–123

    closures, 135–138

    with default arguments, 125–128

    with keyword arguments, 128–134

    with recursion, 124–125, 134–135

    with type hints, 145–146

__dict__ attribute

    about, 426–428, 645, 646

    listing, 428–429

    vs. slots, 444–445

dict type, 222

dictionaries

    about, 222–224

    unpacking, 227–228

    variants, 224–225

dictionary comprehensions, 279

difference (-) set operator, 221

dir() function, 429

__dir__() method, 429, 643

directories. *See also* paths

    dist/, 531

    and project structure, 74–77

    src/, 517–518, 580

    virtual environment, 19, 23–24

discard() method, 221

dist/ directory, 531

@overload decorator, 451
overloaded functions, 129–130
overwrite (\r), 294, 307

P

pack() (struct module) method, 352, 353–355
__package__ attribute, 644
package manager. *See* pip
packages. *See also* imports; uploads
    about, 18–19, 74–75
    contributing to, 628–629
    editable, 531
    entry points, 86–87
    finding, 23
    including files and additional, 523–524, 525
    installing, 21–22, 531, 533
    naming conventions, 75
    provisional, 620
    removing, 22–23
    upgrading, 22
    virtual environment access, 20, 21
packaging
    artifacts build, 531
    distribution options, 515–517
    for end user distribution, 534–540
    files and structure, 518–530
    planning, 514–515, 517–518
    publishing on pip, 532–534
    and relative paths, 323–325
    resources on, 514
packaging gradient, 516, 535
packaging tools, 534. *See also* setuptools library
padding, 354–355, 360–361
Paige, Jeremiah, 519
Pandas, 624
parallelism
    about, 477, 497–498
    vs. asynchrony, 459
    vs. concurrency, 478
    with multiprocessing, 498–501
parameters
    about, 123, 676–677
    and assignment, 107–109
    optional vs. required, 126

positional and keyword, 132–134
    type hints, 146–147
parametrization, 592, 594–596, 605
parent directory (..), 84, 318, 322
parentheses () operator, 46, 217
parents (path module) property, 317
partial() (functools module) function, 491
parts() (PurePath module) method, 317
Pascal strings, 354
pass keyword, 42
passing functions, 140–141
passing messages technique, 487, 495–496
patches, 631
__path__ attribute, 74, 91, 644
path-based finder, 90
path entry finders (path entries), 90–91
pathlib module
    about, 315
    classes, 315–316
    operations, 320–323, 325–328
    and path parts, 316–320
paths
    about, 314
    absolute, 316–320
    modules, 315
    objects, 315–316
    relative, 322–325
patterns. *See also* anti-patterns
    glob, 527
    singleton, 407–408
    structural matching, 68–71, 177–180, 228–230
    virtual machine design, 373
pdb. *See* Python Debugger (pdb)
PendingDeprecationWarning, 545
PEP 8 (style guide), 27–29, 33–34, 75
PEP 20 (The Zen of Python), 8–9
PEPs (Python Enhancement Proposals), 9, 630
performance
    benchmarking, 611, 612–613
    and concurrency, 458
    exception handling, 187–189, 223–224
    perceived responsiveness, 463–464

performance *(continued)*
    profiling, 577, 613–617
    program factors, 4–5
    and programming paradigms, 121
permutations() (itertools module)
        function, 252
Peters, Tim, 8, 10, 404, 407
PEX (Python Executable), 535
pi constant, 47
pickle module, 374–375, 499–500
Pike, Rob, 478
pinning, 528
pip
    about, 21
    pip freeze command, 529
    pip install command, 21–22, 23,
        528–529
    pip uninstall command, 22
pip-tools, 27
Pipenv tool, 27
Pirnat, Mike, 190
pkg_resources module, 325
place values, 339
plaintext files. *See* files
platform wheels, 516
.plist (property list) serialization
        format, 375
Poetry, 27, 534
polymorphism, 384
pop() method, 218, 221
popleft() method, 219–220
__pos__() method, 175, 641
positional arguments, 128–129
positional-only parameters, 133–134
POSIX file paths, 314, 319–320
PosixPath initializer, 320
__pow__() method, 174, 640
PowerShell, 19
pprint (pretty print) module, 427
precision flag, 58
__prepare__() method, 406, 644
Preston-Werner, Tom, 334
Price, Will, 607
priming, 678
print() function, 40, 290–294,
        306–307
procedural programming, 120
process objects, 498

ProcessPoolExecutor, 498, 500
producer/consumer problem
    about, 501–502
    Collatz program implementation,
        502–507
product() (itertools module) function,
        248, 252
profile module, 613–617
profiling, 577, 611
program entry points, 88–89
programming
    fields of study, 620–627
    motivation, 11, 456, 635
    paradigms, 120–122, 149
projects. *See also* packaging
    licensing, 519–520, 521
    metadata, 519, 522
    naming, 520–521
    setup, 74, 77
    versions, 521
    virtual environments for, 19
    working with, 6
prompt keyword, 294–295
properties
    about, 160, 679
    application of, 166–167
    defining with decorators, 164–166
    instance methods, 161–164
property() function, 163, 164–165, 166
property list (*.plist*) serialization
        format, 375
Protocol Buffers (Google), 377
provisional packages, 620
prune directive, 527
.pth file extension, 89
public attributes, 156
pure paths, 315–316
PurePath objects, 316
PureWindowsPath initializer, 320
.py files, 18
py2app, 536
py2exe tool, 5
PyAutoGUI, 602
.pyc files, 6, 91
PyCharm, 35, 145
pycodestyle, 31
PyDev plug-in, 36
pydoc, 540

RESOURCES

Visit https://nostarch.com/dead-simple-python/ for errata and more information.